TRANSITIONAL JUSTICE, CULTURE, AND SOCIETY

This volume is the sixth in the *Advancing Transitional Justice Series*, a joint project of the International Center for Transitional Justice and the Social Science Research Council. Other volumes include:

Roger Duthie, ed., *Transitional Justice and Displacement*

Alexander Mayer-Rieckh and Pablo de Greiff, eds., *Justice as Prevention: Vetting Public Employees in Transitional Societies*

Ruth Rubio-Marín, ed., *What Happened to the Women? Gender and Reparations for Human Rights Violations*

Pablo de Greiff and Roger Duthie, eds., *Transitional Justice and Development: Making Connections*

Ana Cutter Patel, Pablo de Greiff, and Lars Waldorf, eds., *Disarming the Past: Transitional Justice and Ex-combatants*

ADVANCING TRANSITIONAL JUSTICE SERIES

TRANSITIONAL JUSTICE, CULTURE, AND SOCIETY: BEYOND OUTREACH

EDITED BY CLARA RAMÍREZ-BARAT
INTERNATIONAL CENTER FOR TRANSITIONAL JUSTICE

SOCIAL SCIENCE RESEARCH COUNCIL • NEW YORK • 2014

INTERNATIONAL CENTER FOR TRANSITIONAL JUSTICE

The International Center for Transitional Justice (ICTJ) helps societies in transition address legacies of massive human rights violations and build civic trust in state institutions as protectors of human rights. In the aftermath of mass atrocity and repression, ICTJ assists institutions and civil society groups in considering measures to provide truth, accountability, and redress for past abuses. Committed to the vindication of victims' rights and the promotion of gender justice, ICTJ provides expert technical advice and knowledge of relevant comparative experiences in transitional justice efforts from across the globe, including criminal prosecutions, reparations initiatives, truth seeking, memorialization efforts, and institutional reform. Learn more about ICTJ at www.ictj.org.

SOCIAL SCIENCE RESEARCH COUNCIL

The Social Science Research Council (SSRC) is an independent, international, nonprofit organization founded in 1923. It fosters innovative research, nurtures new generations of social scientists, deepens how inquiry is practiced within and across disciplines, and mobilizes necessary knowledge on important public issues. Learn more about the work of the Council at www.ssrc.org.

The views expressed by the contributors to this volume are their own, and do not necessarily reflect the views of the International Center for Transitional Justice.

Published by the Social Science Research Council
Printed in the United States of America

Series design by Julie Fry
Cover and typesetting by Debra Yoo
Cover photograph by Iñigo Royo: *Desaparecidos* (Disappeared), Gervasio Sánchez photography exhibition, 10th Human Rights Film Festival, San Sebastian, Spain, April 2012.

Library of Congress Cataloging-in-Publication Data

Transitional justice, culture, and society : beyond outreach / edited by Clara Ramirez-Barat, International Center For Transitional Justice.
pages cm. — (Advancing transitional justice series ; 6)
Includes bibliographical references.
ISBN 978-0-911400-02-1 (pbk. : alk. paper)
1. Transitional justice—Case studies. 2. Human rights—Case studies.
I. Ramirez-Barat, Clara.

JC571.T69935 2013
320.01'1—dc23 2013036247

Contents

PART II: CONFLICT, MEDIA, AND JUSTICE

PART III: ART, CULTURE, AND TRANSITIONAL JUSTICE

PREFACE

On Making the Invisible Visible: The Role of Cultural Interventions in Transitional Justice Processes

Pablo de Greiff

Sociologists are fond of distinguishing three different levels of analysis and corresponding spheres of intervention: the cultural, social, and personal.[1] Significant debates persist about the definition and precise boundaries of each of these terms, particularly about the correct way of understanding their interrelationships. For my purposes, however, the distinction between the three spheres and the fact that they relate to one another in complex ways are sufficient to locate transitional justice measures in a broader context—and, more specifically, to highlight the distinctiveness of this volume.

Most transitional justice work, academic and practical, concentrates on social institutions. Obviously, this preface is not the place to present even a stylized position on the proper way to conceptualize the relationship between cultural, social, and individual transformations—an issue that remains unsettled in sociology, philosophy, and political science. However, no sophisticated conception of that relationship is necessary to see that the sort of broad transformations to which transitional justice seeks to contribute will ultimately succeed only if changes in culture and individual outlooks accompany institutional changes. Because transitional justice has integrated so little of these debates, reviewing some ideas that might promote more thinking about the role of transitional justice in this constellation of spheres would be useful.

Not surprisingly, the effort to establish relations between culture, society, and individuals originally took the shape of hierarchies, with different professional academic disciplines emerging in the eighteenth and, particularly, the nineteenth centuries that tended to claim primacy for their own spheres;[2] hence, moral theory and psychology have generally considered individual decisions and outlooks as the fulcrum on which all changes hinge, including those in social institutions and the culture overall. One need not endorse this hierarchical ordering, which prioritizes the role of individuals, to acknowledge that transitional justice is so far from having an adequate understanding of individuals' and personality structures' roles in transitional processes that more work on this issue would be beneficial. Independently of whether changes at the level of the individual are the condition on which institutional and cultural changes depend, a successful transition ultimately will have to manifest itself in changes at the level of individual outlooks, including relevant principles, dispositions, and attitudes.[3]

The priority of culture has also had its defenders. Anthropologists, primarily but not exclusively, have emphasized the centrality of culture in understanding society and individuals.[4] Because culture is much less open to direct intervention than personality structures and institutional frameworks, the claims of culture are usually made in a diagnostic or explanatory rather than instrumentalist vein. One strain of the liberal-communitarian debate in political theory, for example, concentrates on whether liberalism, understood primarily as an institutional theory, is capable of fostering the cultural conditions and personal dispositions that, according to communitarianism, liberal institutions themselves need.[5] Again, one need not agree with the claim about the priority of culture over institutions or individuals, even at the explanatory level, to accept that transitional justice has generally and systematically ignored claims of culture.

Finally, and perhaps more predictably, the idea that institutions are the primary variable in resolving the problem of stability in the social order—and that, indeed, changes at this level trigger changes in the spheres of culture and the individual—has such a long and cross-disciplinary history that it hardly needs mentioning. The list of such approaches to social order that express this idea is long and diverse, including the project of liberal constitutionalism with its aspiration to establish institutions that would function well regardless of the virtues of the people who run them.[6] Such a list also includes the otherwise seemingly disparate Marxian account of the reducibility of the cultural "suprastructure" to the productive "infrastructure" or "base"; at the level of individual outlooks, the Marxian account of alienation—which, although not fixed, as is the liberal tradition, on the *political* framework—prioritizes one segment of the social sphere, namely, the *economic*, productive framework.[7] More concretely and closer to our interests, this institutionalist concentration is also shared by Douglas North's "new institutionalism"—for so many reasons nowadays an influential approach to economics,[8] political science,[9] and even the study of conflict.[10] Despite the fact that North defines "institutions" broadly, including references to practices that are legally formalized and those that are not (and, hence, it would not be inconsistent with his definition of the term to talk both about voting and courting as "institutions"[11]), the fact is that his work focuses almost exclusively on formal institutions and virtually not at all on the cultural and the individual dimensions of life within institutions.

Transitional justice, in the literature and in practice, reflects this institutionalist bias. While cultural and individual dimensions are clearly and detrimentally left out of transitional justice, some good reasons exist for this approach:

- Transitional justice measures are implemented after great havoc. The brutality of the past not only highlights the insufficiency of predecessor institutions to guarantee basic rights but makes plain the need for new or reformed institutions to prevent the repetition of so much abuse. Indeed, the foregoing understates the case, for it is framed in terms of institutional *insufficiency*. The origins of transitional justice in postauthoritarian settings in which state institutions were not merely ineffective in protecting the rights of citizens but were in fact responsible for the overwhelming majority of the abuses surely help to explain the field's institutional focus. The history of state terror—the alignment and coordination of state institutions for abusive purposes—is inscribed in the history of the field.[12]
- Transitional periods are deeply political ones in the life of nations, periods during which at least some of the terms of the social contract seem to be up for renegotiation. The bulk of political activity is geared toward institutional transformation. Unofficial extra-institutional action is not unimportant in times of transition—quite the contrary. Although a few transitions have taken place through regime collapse, in most transitions, social activism and even mobilization are important indeed. But because social mobilization is not enough to guarantee the stability or the enduring transformative effects of transitions, activism focuses mainly on achieving institutional transformations.

Still deeper reasons underlie this concentration on the institutional level; although our knowledge of institutional transformation processes is deficient, it still outstrips our ability to effect changes in culture or personality.[13] Again, this is not the result of mere chance. Culture and personality structures, by their nature liable to even deliberate change—as the history of art or "virtue" shows—are resistant to direct interventions.[14]

Transitional justice practitioners' and researchers' almost exclusive concentration on institutions, however, obscures the ways in which successful institutional change relates to cultural and individual transformations. To the extent that concentrating exclusively on institutional change ignores the connection between those changes and changes in culture and individuals, it also obscures the ways in which institutional change can effect changes in the other two spheres. Setting aside relations of dependence and priority, however, paying no attention to the cultural and individual dimensions of transitional processes limits the tools available to those of us interested in broad social change.

The writings in this innovative collection represent an effort to shed some light on the contributions that cultural interventions can make to the cause of transitional justice.[15] That such interventions have received so little attention should be surprising, because cultural interventions of various sorts have become increasingly important in transitional processes. To begin with the most obvious, transitional justice measures have become more aware of the importance of engaging not just policymakers or their direct users but the public at large—hence the incipient but growing awareness of the importance of outreach efforts framed in terms that go beyond the vocabulary of policymakers.[16]

Another way to see the need for closely examining dimensions of transitional justice processes aside from the activities of participants in formal policy mechanisms is to attend to the important role of other actors and the media that they characteristically use. While in all transitions, civil society organizations have tended to occupy a central and still insufficiently recognized role, the most recent transitions—those in the Middle East and northern Africa—would hardly have occurred without massive social mobilization in which new social media were essential tools. As mentioned before, much social activism aims at achieving institutional change and having its claims reflected in institutional responses. But ignoring the significance of cultural shifts in these transitions—including those facilitated by demographics (a bulge not just in youth but educated youth) and new technologies, whose role would be underestimated if conceived solely as enabling tools—would be a mistake. Technology did not merely allow people to coordinate meetings and demonstrations; it also played a role in shaping people's aspirations. In this sense, the line between shifts in technology and shifts in culture is porous.[17]

In thinking about the motivations for examining cultural interventions in transitional processes in more detail, we should keep in mind two other phenomena. First, a number of truth commissions have sponsored photography exhibits and other forms of artistic events. The Peruvian Truth and Reconciliation Commission's *Yuyanapaq* photo exhibit is a particularly compelling instance but not the only one.[18] Second and more broadly, transitional processes are accompanied by a wealth of cultural manifestations. Some are institutionalized in museums and memorials, and some—such as movies, plays, books, and documentaries—do not require the support of formal structures. These products are not formally linked in any way with official transitional justice institutions but are instead typically spontaneous and nonorganized interventions in the public sphere. Some such interventions have become influential in shaping views about different aspects of the transitions; consider Primo Levi's work on the Holocaust and Ariel Dorfman's play *Death and the Maiden*, as well as the latter's subsequent movie adaptation.[19] With the prevailing institutionalist biases of the field, the frequency, magnitude, and significance of this large constellation of work has not been properly integrated into transitional justice processes.

In the remainder of this preface I do not attempt to replicate nor summarize the work of the book's contributors. Instead, I would like to articulate explicitly some reasons why cultural interventions should be taken more seriously in transitional processes. Two caveats are in order, however. First, in trying to engage seriously the contributions that various cultural and artistic manifestations can make to transitional processes, I am not arguing on behalf of the primacy of culture over social or individual change. Indeed, anyone who has even a remote familiarity with the literature or has reflected on the matter would know that thinking about the relationship between culture, society, and individuals in terms of relations of primacy and dependence perniciously distorts and oversimplifies the issue. In a sort of blissful parochialism, most members of the established disciplines who continue to proceed in their everyday work do not give enough thought to this relationship. Participants in particular disciplines tend to take the object of study of their own field as if it either exhausted the potential universe of concern or as if changes within its sphere of reference were largely independent of changes in the others—interdisciplinarity and the emergence of hybrid studies notwithstanding.

As an illustration of an influential line of thinking that takes a distinctly nonhierarchical view of the relationship between culture, society, and individuals, consider work that takes its cue from systems theory.[20] On this account, the three spheres are analogous to organized and enclosed systems that aim at preservation and reproduction. Systems are enclosed in the sense that each has its own code and rules of transformation. But obviously no successful self-reproducing (autopoietic) system is hermetically closed; each operates in an environment precisely constituted by other systems and their own transformations and adaptations to their environment. The system-environment relationship is not to be understood *mechanically*, in terms of one-to-one causal relationships, but rather *biologically*, in terms of the ways in which each system, in accordance with the characteristics of its own code, accommodates changes in its environment and perpetually tries to reproduce itself. This approach leads to a decentered, nonhierarchical view of the relationship between culture, society, and individuals.[21]

The second caveat is that in concentrating on the contributions that cultural products can make to transitional justice, I do not mean to offer a reductionistic or functionalist account of such products and activities. I do not argue that the primary role of art or media is to raise awareness, promote a particular cause, or achieve any given end. This is true even if the author (using the term broadly) intended his or her work in this way. I take it that after the decline of representational art and discussions about the autonomy not only of readers but of texts themselves and generally of the plurality of meaning, only reactionary defenders of original intent (whose theory of interpretation suspiciously aligns with their political agendas) remain attached to such reductionistic perspectives. Here I emphasize the contribution that cultural events and products can make to justice without suggesting that such contribution is their only function or source of value.

But enough caveats. The following are some of the ways in which interventions in the cultural sphere can be understood to contribute to the cause of transitional justice.

As mentioned earlier, political theory, in its normative and descriptive variants, is better at articulating end states than capturing or offering guidance about processes of transformation. The same can also be said of moral theory. This characteristic of moral and political theory has opened up normative theorizing to the charge that it starts too late, worrying mainly about extending to new constituencies forms of moral and political *consideration*. The criticism is that this mode of doing things already presupposes grounds and motivations, which are different factors, for such forms of consideration. In other words, the criticism is that moral theory, in concentrating on situations of choice—and political theory, on institutional designs—leaves out a prior, essential issue. In the case of moral theory, left out is the issue of construing a particular situation of choice as one that calls for a *moral* response; in the case of political theory, what is taken as given is the idea that the basic problem of institutional design consists of finding ways to include others previously unprotected by the preferred institutions. In summary, moral and political theory both presuppose that the antecedent fundamental issue relating to perception of the situation is one in which others appear as raising a claim to moral and political consideration.[22]

The charge is not an empty one. Putting aside disciplinary debates, the fact is that a good number of struggles for recognition that ultimately take the shape of struggles for rights go through a stage in which the claimants' very humanity seems to be in need of affirmation. Consider the struggles to abolish slavery and extend the franchise to women as well as current debates about gay rights. In a different but relevant domain, conflict is often seen as a threat to national interests or the established order—or even the interests of elites, as if conflict were "victimless." To take one example, elites for decades represented the conflict in Colombia as a problem of "public order" that threatened mainly the productive infrastructure of the country. Victims were largely invisible.

Interventions in the media, literature, film, and other forms of art can make a significant contribution to generating the forms of sensibility that can then receive institutional expression in the enshrinement of rights. Lynn Hunt argues that the rise of epistolary novels in France and England in the 1740s played a crucial role in the development of the idea of *human* (that is, universal) rights by fostering a broad type of empathy—a necessary disposition for the eventual institutionalization of generalized rights. Epistolary novels allowed the reader to peer into the inner life of their characters and to experience almost firsthand what the characters were feeling. Obviously, people had experienced empathy before the 1740s but generally toward a circumscribed circle—mostly their social equals. Because characters in these novels were ordinary (and mostly female), these works "enabled readers to empathize across class, sex, and national lines." The basic message that the novels gave was that "all people are fundamentally similar because of their inner feelings."[23] From these novels, two crucial processes were set in motion. First, the choice of characters (not illustrious but ordinary) and their reactions to their own experiences triggered identification, such that readers could see themselves reacting in the same way. The second, related process was the sort of ideal role taking that moral psychologists would much later argue is critical to the emergence of the attitude of the "impartial spectator," part and parcel of the development of universalistic morality.[24] The novels afforded the opportunity to step into someone else's shoes and enlarge one's perspective by relativizing one's immediate responses and culturally determined preferences, as well as opening up space for the sort of impartiality that is crucial to modern, egalitarian, principle-based approaches to morality. While this last point may seem to emphasize a question of judgment, more important is developing *conditions* for the exercise of judgment—namely, new forms of solidarity and empathy across social distinctions that were previously considered to be moral watersheds. The suffering of slaves, serfs, and servants, for example, was at one point not taken to be *real* suffering, or at least not of the sort that called for moral concern, which, of course, is relevant to the existence of these categories. At some point that changed—a process that needs to be accounted for and to which cultural interventions can make a crucial contribution.

Regardless of the historical accuracy of Hunt's position, the contribution that cultural interventions can make to transitional justice processes that I would like to stress is that of making victims visible. In a world in which, despite forms of rapid communication that include visual media, it is still possible to live one's entire life in increasingly unequal enclaves of comfort—solidly walled off from the intrusions of other people's suffering—making victims appear for the first time is no small achievement. Cultural interventions do much more than give visibility to victims generically; indeed, some of the artistic and cultural forms addressed in this volume can have this effect precisely because they are adept at focusing on concrete others.[25] My main point here is not that focusing on particular individuals and their stories is typically a more effective way of generating empathy and solidarity—which is true, but part of my earlier point—but that some of the cultural products and activities discussed in this volume can raise awareness of the depth, breadth, and effects of rights violations in a way that other forms of communication can hardly aspire to, including not only cold statistical data but also official truth commission reports. Different cultural interventions can avail themselves of media that are appropriate to their diverse aims and therefore more effective at representing pain, suffering, indignation, and rage, as well as determination, endurance, and dignity—in sum, the complex of affective reactions that can accompany human rights violations. Some of these reactions are not captured, of course, by merely describing the facts surrounding the violations, no matter how thorough the description. Similarly, cultural interventions can provide a richer account of the manifold effects of violations across the various spheres of victims' lives; severe human rights violations are usually no mere temporary incidents or momentary interruptions that leave behind unhappy but otherwise fleeting and inconsequential memories. Violations often shift the course of entire lives, frequently with devastating effects, whether because of the interruption of education or employment, severe changes in family circumstances, or resulting disabilities and traumas, among other factors. A proper understanding (particularly but not exclusively a proper *public* understanding) of the multifarious effects that violations have on victims calls for a variety of resources, some of which fall precisely in the domain of cultural products and activities.

These last two points can be framed in terms of the contributions that cultural interventions can make to increasing the depth and the scope of our understanding of the effects of human rights violations on the lives of victims—and, as a consequence, to the reactions we might have to them, including via the implementation of transitional justice measures. Two further related contributions in the same vein are worth highlighting. Human rights violations have consequences that ripple from victims to others, across space and time. As the effects of violations spread, the causal links become more complex and less direct—although not necessarily less real or severe. Forensic discourse, which—for reasons mainly related to its justified interest in clarifying issues about attributing responsibility—emphasizes clear and direct causal links, needs to be complemented with interventions that are less constrained and more adept at capturing the complexity and indirection of the social and intergenerational effects of massive human rights violations. These effects include, for example, the impact on political discourse, patterns of socialization relating to the proper ways of exercising authority even at the level of family structure, and the subsequent replication of such patterns generation after generation.[26] Cultural interventions are particularly adept at uncovering those expanding, rippling effects. Think, for instance, of works such as Gunther Grass's *Tin Drum,* Peter Esterhazy's *Celestial Harmonies,* Peter Nádas's *A Book of Memories,* and Javier Cercas's *Soldiers of Salamis,* to name only a few of the most obvious European novels that accomplish such ends.[27]

I have concentrated thus far on the effects that cultural interventions can have on their audience. Of course, changing societal attitudes toward victimization and rights, among other things, is a crucial variable in determining the fate of a transition, particularly in the long run. In accounting for the contributions that cultural interventions can make to transitional justice processes, however, we should also recognize their capacity to affect victims themselves. Some of the activities, media, and forms that the authors in this volume address afford victims spaces in which their experiences can be articulated safely, sometimes for the first time.

The significance of this enabling role is underestimated if the relevant cultural activities and products are conceived simply in terms of *staging*—providing a safe space for enacting already processed experiences that people merely have kept silent about—or even of *magnifying*—providing a megaphone of sorts and securing a public to hear these experiences. If institutionalizing new rights regimes is going to be sufficiently meaningful to achieve the fundamental aim behind that project—creating conditions under which no one need be a supplicant before others, especially those who run state institutions—then adopting the identity of a rights bearer, someone entitled to raise claims, is an essential part of this process. While a crucial institutional dimension exists to processes of identity formation—it is no mere accident, of course, that the identity of citizens *as citizens* is particularly weak where institutions are weak—such processes also do not take place by legal fiat alone, emphasizing yet again the importance of thinking about relationships between individuals, culture, and institutions. Cultural interventions can contribute to transitional processes precisely by enabling spaces where identities can be tried out, including the identity of a rights claimant. The observation that under certain institutional contexts individuals can appear reluctant to consider themselves as citizens, to see themselves as entitled to raise claims and demands, is not new. The question is how to overcome this reluctance; part of the answer offered in this book is that cultural interventions provide some of the tools to catalyze these transformations.

Cultural interventions can make yet another contribution to transitional processes. Up to this point, I have concentrated on the many roles such interventions can play in *presencing*—in making present people who were previously not just neglected but abused but also seemingly and contradictorily absent or invisible. Thus, I have referred to giving a richer, thicker sense of victims' experiences and reactions; the ways in which cultural interventions enrich our understanding of the legacies that human rights violations leave in their wake; and how such interactions may enable victims and others to set forth on what may be a long and tortuous process of adopting the identity of citizenship. This is all positive, but no one should be fooled. Art and culture cannot, of course, undo anything.

Indeed, I would like to close this brief intervention of my own by highlighting an unparalleled potential of cultural interventions. In articulating *absences*, interventions can help make visible the permanent remnants of debts to those who perished, debts that can never be totally redeemed. Germano Gustavo's photographs of missing siblings as reviewed by Eduardo González Cueva and Florencia Librizzi in their chapter for this collection—pairings of an early picture of say, two sisters, and a later picture, in the same spot, of the sole surviving one—speak more loudly than any forensic report ever could of those who can never be brought back and of the world that could have been but never will be. Of course, those absences, as well as their various specific portrayals, may generate many reactions, including the commitment to do our best so that such things never happen again. Transitional justice attempts such a contribution. Moreover, cultural interventions have always played—and if this book succeeds in its mission, should increasingly play—a role in such transformations.

NOTES

1 Cf., e.g., Max Weber, *Protestantism and the Spirit of Capitalism* (London: Unwin and Hyman, 1930); Talcott Parsons, *The Social System* (London: Routledge and Kegan Paul, 1951); Jürgen Habermas, *The Theory of Communicative Action*, vol. 1, *Reason and the Rationalization of Society*, and vol. 2, *Lifeworld and System: A Critique of Functionalist Reason*, trans. Thomas McCarthy (Boston: Beacon Press, 1985).

2 For an illuminating account of the organization of disciplines, see Peter Burke, *A Social History of Knowledge*, vol. 1, *From Guttenberg to Diderot* (Cambridge: Polity Press, 2000), esp. chap. 5.

3 The indifference of the transitional justice literature to the question of the complicated relationship between culture, society, and individuals can be seen in its selectivity, and not just in its overwhelming focus on issues of institutional change (abstracting from considerations about culture and personality structures). The literature on reconciliation and healing, for example, has wavered. On the one hand, certain strands concentrate on individuals to the exclusion of cultural and institutional factors, with the result that reconciliation emerges as something akin to a "conversion," a turning that happens within individuals, ignoring social and cultural conditions—often including the fulfillment of the claims to justice. On the other hand, some of the literature engages in a sort of reification of culture, assuming that practices of healing and reconciliation will be effective provided that they are "culturally authentic." Saying that this literature has *prioritized* analyses of individuals or of culture would be incorrect; rather, the literature has concentrated on a particular level of analysis to the exclusion of the others. The literature on the role of individuals in transitional processes is scant. See Tzvetan Todorov, *Facing the Extreme: Moral Life in the Concentration Camps* (New York: Holt Paperbacks, 1997), and Leigh Payne, *Unsettling Accounts: Neither Truth nor Reconciliation in Confessions of State Violence* (Durham, NC: Duke University Press, 2008).

4 See, e.g., Clifford Geertz's classic *The Interpretation of Cultures* (New York: Basic Books, 1973).

5 Cf., e.g., Michael Sandel, *Liberalism and the Limits of Justice* (Cambridge: Cambridge University Press, 1982); Charles Taylor, *The Malaise of Modernity* (Toronto: House of Anansi Press, 1991); Steve Macedo, *Liberal Virtues: Citizenship, Virtue, and Community in Liberal Constitutionalism* (New York: Oxford University Press, 1990); and Peter Berkowitz, *Virtue and the Making of Modern Liberalism* (Princeton, NJ: Princeton University Press, 2000).

6 Such aspiration is frequently illustrated by reference to Kant's formulation in his essay *On Perpetual Peace*. After expressing the common doubt as to whether a republican form of government ("the only one compatible with the rights of men") requires angels as citizens for it to be established and maintained, Kant states, "As hard as it may sound, the problem of organizing a nation is solvable even for a people comprised of devils (if only they possess understanding)" (Immanuel Kant, *Perpetual Peace and Other Essays*, trans. Ted Humphrey [Indianapolis: Hackett, 1983], 124 [Ak. 8:366]).

7 Cf. Karl Marx, "Introduction," *A Contribution to the Critique of Political Economy* (1859; Moscow: Progress Publishers, 1977); and Raymond Williams, "Base and Superstructure in Marxist Cultural Theory," *New Left Review* 82 (November/December 1973): 2–16.

8 Douglas North, John J. Wallis, and Barry R. Weingast, *Violence and Social Orders: A Conceptual Framework for Interpreting Recorded Human History* (Cambridge: Cambridge University Press, 2009); Daron Acemoglu and James Robinson, *Why Nations Fail: The Origins of Power, Prosperity, and Poverty* (New York: Crown Publishers, 2012).

9 Cf., e.g., Peter A. Hall, "Political Science and the Three New Institutionalisms," *Political Studies* 44, no. 5 (December 1996): 936–57 and Hall, "Historical Institutionalism in Rationalist and Sociological Perspective," in *Explaining Institutional Change: Ambiguity, Agency, and Power*, ed. James Mahoney and Kathleen Thelen (Cambridge: Cambridge University Press, 2009).

10 Arguably, North's new institutionalism played an important role in the articulation of the World Bank's *World Development Report 2011: Conflict, Security, and Development* (Washington, DC: World Bank, 2011).

11 Douglas North, "Institutions," *Journal of Economic Perspectives* 5, no. 1 (1991): 97–112.

12 Cf., e.g., Carlos Nino, *Radical Evil on Trial* (New Haven, CT: Yale University Press, 1996).

13 This judgment does not rest on an exalted conception of politics as a science in the mechanical seventeenth-century sense. The judgment rests on the sense that political knowledge lacks understanding of dynamics more than mechanics. Political theory, such as it is, has much more to say about end states (either desirable ones—the subject matter of normative politics—or current ones—the subject matter of descriptive political science) than about the processes that lead from here to there. Our understanding of the processes of political change and transformation is quite primitive.

14 On changes in culture, cf. Wittgenstein's insightful remark that no one can invent a style of art on his own: "For is even our style of painting arbitrary? Can we choose one at pleasure?" (Ludwig Wittgenstein, *Philosophical Investigations*, trans. G. E. M. Anscombe [New York: Macmillan, 1968], 230). On the openness of character to voluntary change,

see the still-relevant account of the education of virtue in books 3, 4, and 6 of Aristotle's *Nicomachean Ethics.*

15 I am using the expression "cultural interventions" as shorthand for a broad class of activities and products that come into being outside institutions that are formally responsible for policymaking, despite the fact that some of these activities and products, such as op-ed pieces, may aim at influencing debates and outcomes in such institutions. These activities and products include interventions in the press and other media and presentations such as novels, movies, plays, and exhibits. They are interventions in the public sphere relating to transitional justice themes.

16 Clara Ramírez-Barat, *Making an Impact: Guidelines on Designing and Implementing Outreach Programs for Transitional Justice* (New York: International Center for Transitional Justice, 2011).

17 The role of new social media in transitions in the Middle East and northern Africa has been remarked upon often; the chapters by Camille Crittenden and others in part 2 of the present volume address this topic. In a way, social media's role is not entirely new; authoritarian governments have a long history of trying to control new media. The complete story would have to include efforts on the part of former Communist regimes to restrict access to radio broadcasts, the role that access to West German TV played in modeling East German aspirations, and the ongoing efforts of the Chinese and North Korean governments to restrict access to the World Wide Web. See Marshall T. Poe, *History of Communications: Media and Society from the Evolution of Speech to the Internet* (Cambridge: Cambridge University Press, 2011).

18 For discussion of the *Yuyanapaq* exhibit, see the chapter on photography by Eduardo González Cueva and M. Florencia Librizzi in this volume. Other examples include the Poster Exhibition by the CAVR in Timor-Leste (see http://www.cavr-timorleste.org/Posters/CAVR_poster.htm) and the National Vision for Sierra Leone project by the Truth and Reconciliation Commission of Sierra Leone (see http://www.sierraleonetrc.org/index.php/national-vision-for-sl).

19 Primo Levi, *If This Is a Man* [or *Survival in Auschwitz*] (1947; New York: Orion Press, 1959); Ariel Dorfman, *Death and the Maiden* (New York: Penguin Books, 1991). On the latter, see David Luban, "On Dorfman's *Death and the Maiden*," *Yale Journal of Law and the Humanities* 10, no. 1 (1998): 115–34.

20 Cf., e.g., Niklas Luhmann's *Introduction to Systems Theory* (Cambridge: Polity, 2012), *Law as a Social System* (Oxford: Oxford University Press, 2008), and *Art as a Social System* (Palo Alto, CA: Stanford University Press, 2000).

21 I am, of course, eliding all complications to offer an impression of a more appropriately complex account of these relationships and to reinforce the point that taking an interest in the cultural dimensions of transitional justice need not be seen as part of an effort to prioritize this sphere. In addition to Luhmann's work, see also the work of Jürgen

Habermas, who adopts part of this account in order to offer a two-track model in which steering media such as money and power play part of the role of accounting for social order and change, but a role that needs to be complemented by language and reason, which cut across the different systems. See Habermas, *Theory of Communicative Action*, esp. vol. 2.

22 Martha Nussbaum, *Love's Knowledge: Essays on Philosophy and Literature* (New York: Oxford University Press, 1992), esp. "The Discernment of Perception"; and Arne Johann Vetlesen, *Perception, Empathy, and Judgment: An Inquiry into the Preconditions of Moral Performance* (University Park: Pennsylvania State University Press, 1994), esp. chaps. 1, 4, and 5.

23 Lynn Hunt, *Inventing Human Rights: A History* (New York: W. W. Norton and Company, 1998), chap. 1; quotations from 38 and 39.

24 See Lawrence Kohlberg, "Justice as Reversibility: The Claim to Moral Adequacy of a Highest Stage of Moral Judgment," in *Essays on Moral Development*, vol. 1, *The Philosophy of Moral Development* (San Francisco: Harper and Row, 1981), 194ff.; George Herbert Mead, "Fragments on Ethics," in *Mind, Self, and Society: From the Standpoint of a Social Behaviorist* (Chicago: University of Chicago Press, 1934); Habermas, *Lifeworld and System*, esp. 92ff.

25 See Seyla Benhabib, "The Generalized and the Concrete Other: The Kohlberg-Gilligan Controversy and Feminist Theory," *Praxis International* 5, no. 4 (1986): esp. 410ff.

26 See, e.g., Gesine Schwan, *Politics and Guilt: The Destructive Power of Silence* (Lincoln: University of Nebraska Press, 2001), which traces the psychological and cultural effects of Nazism in Germany.

27 Grass, *The Tin Drum* (1959; New York: Houghton Mifflin Harcourt, 2010); Esterhazy, *Celestial Harmonies* (New York: Ecco, 2004); Nádas, *A Book of Memories* (1986; New York: Picador, 2008); and Cercas, *Soldiers of Salamis* (New York: Bloomsbury, 2004). Daniel Mendelson's *The Lost: A Search for Six of Six Million* (New York: Harper Perennial, 2007), a work that is not fictional but that in many ways crosses genres, provides a compelling example of how a focus on particular individuals can lead to insightful reflections about atrocities' social and intergenerational effects.

INTRODUCTION

Transitional Justice and the Public Sphere

Clara Ramírez-Barat

> Story-telling embodies the sharing of power. Stories create culture and society.
>
> —Jessica Senehi and Sean Byrne (quoted in *Troublemakers or Peacemakers? Youth and Post-accord Peace Building*)

The establishment of transitional justice measures opens a political process with a fundamental public dimension.[1] Understood as justice interventions that aim to help societies with the daunting task of dealing with legacies of political repression and mass atrocity—and, as such, importantly justified through backward-looking considerations—transitional justice measures are also future-oriented projects to the extent that redressing past violations is precisely understood as a way of contributing to the construction of a democratic and peaceful future. In this respect, transitional justice measures play a key symbolic role: figuratively establishing a sort of break with the past by (re)affirming that certain norms and the values that support them matter. As such, from an institutional perspective, the success of transitional justice measures mainly depends on two factors. First, such measures should properly accomplish their most immediate functions—that is, truth commissions should finish their investigations on time and publish credible reports, reparations programs should provide acceptable measures of redress to the relevant universe of beneficiaries, and tribunals should deliver at least a minimum number of fair trials. Second, the measures themselves need political credibility; they should demonstrate clearly the political will to make changes. However, moving beyond this institutional perspective, and to the extent that transitional justice measures ultimately aim to catalyze a transformation of a previous culture of impunity and conflict into one of respect for the democratic rule of law and human rights, the attitudes and involvement of the public in such processes play a major role in their ultimate impact. Indeed, in countries where the society at large has been more engaged in transitional justice processes and where, accordingly, such processes have been perceived to be more legitimate, transitional justice measures have arguably been able to construct more concrete and durable legacies.[2]

For example, in Argentina, after thirty years of civil society activism, the former regime's amnesty laws were finally revoked in 2005. However, a high level of public interest was already present in 1983 when the paperback edition of the truth commission's report became a bestseller immediately after its publication. Similarly, in Peru, after the truth and reconciliation commission closed its doors, the engagement of a number of civil society and victims' groups that pressed for the implementation of the commission's recommendations was of major importance for the subsequent establishment of the country's reparations program, although the program had significant shortcomings. In contrast, processes perceived as primarily internationally driven or imposed from above, or in which the population at large does not believe, struggle to gain social legitimacy and may yield poor results if they are unsuccessful. The perceptions of the International Criminal Tribunal for the former Yugoslavia in the countries of the region have often been used as an example of this type of problem, although this context may not be the only one in which the failure of transitional justice measures to gain social support has had considerable negative effects.

BACKGROUND TO THE PROJECT

Despite the importance that social engagement plays in transitional justice processes, the public's understanding and support of transitional justice measures cannot be taken for granted. In some cases, transitional justice processes have to face generalized social indifference or distrust, if not direct and targeted political criticism and denial. In other cases, their establishment alone may quickly give rise to unrealistically high expectations that, when unfulfilled, will likely lead to disappointment. Transitional justice processes involve novel institutions with complex mandates, rules, and procedures that can be technical and difficult to understand. It should not be assumed that they will function in public discourse in the same way as consolidated institutions with which populations are already familiar through everyday channels of socialization. Moreover, the legacies of previous conflicts or regimes—including deep social divisions and poor traditions of transparency, accountability, and democratic interaction, with a subsequent general lack of civic trust in public institutions—may also pose severe challenges for transitional justice measures that seek to gain popular acceptance and support. Finally, many contexts in which transitional justice measures are established suffer from severe economic deficits, and every choice in their implementation is therefore accompanied by competing demands in terms of financial investment. In situations of institutional weakness and general scarcity, the role, importance, and relevance of transitional justice processes are not immediately apparent to many.

With the precise aim of bridging the gap between justice processes and the societies in which they take place, many transitional justice measures—including truth commissions, criminal prosecutions, and reparations programs—have established some sort of public education program or, as they have unfortunately been called, "outreach programs."[3] In a practical sense, for our purposes, this type of programming can be defined as a set of tools and strategies that transitional justice measures intentionally put in place in order to build direct channels of communication with the societies in which they operate. Such channels of communication can include dissemination of information, promotion of an open dialogue, establishment of consultation channels with different stakeholders, and, ideally, the opening of avenues for local participation. Devised to raise awareness and promote understanding about the goals and functioning of transitional justice measures, outreach programs ultimately aim to contribute to the legitimacy of transitional justice initiatives and engage the social body according to the values of the normative democratic shift they seek to promote.

Despite its importance for transitional justice initiatives, practitioners and policymakers in the field have not always recognized the role of outreach. As a result, activities are often underfunded, understaffed, and loosely strategized. Taking this observation as a starting point, in late 2009 the Research Unit of the International Center for Transitional Justice (ICTJ) began a project that sought to examine the outreach programs of different transitional justice measures, with the primary aim of providing practical guidance and useful tools for practitioners to aid in crafting programs more sensitive to the challenges of current transitional justice processes. More broadly, the project also intended to reflect on and better understand the general function of outreach as a component of transitional justice initiatives. While the first of these aims led to the publication of a practically oriented document in early 2011 titled *Making an Impact: Guidelines on Designing and Implementing Outreach Programs for Transitional Justice*,[4] the development of the research raised further questions about the nature and importance of outreach in such contexts. Along with other factors, such as their performance and credibility, the impact of transitional justice measures is significantly related to the relationship they establish with the societies in which they operate. This relationship can be understood in at least three different ways: in regard to their day-to-day functioning, legitimacy, and legitimation and impact.

First, on a practical level, for members of affected communities to be able to participate in and contribute to the justice process (whether as witnesses, testimony givers, or beneficiaries), they need to be properly informed and to understand the work of transitional justice measures, along with knowing their options and especially their rights for participation. For example, developing such a relationship has proved to be key for many truth commissions that, at the early stages of their proceedings, have struggled to raise awareness and gain legitimacy among victims so that they might collect statements and information from the population. The same could also be said about reparations programs, which need to make sure that potential beneficiaries are informed of their rights to receive reparations—or about tribunals, which must seek out witnesses to gather evidence and participate in their proceedings. Hence, transitional justice measures have to take proactive steps to build direct communication with different stakeholders and to reach remote areas when necessary, while making complex information accessible to the general population and to specific groups.

Second, to build trust within the society and enhance their legitimacy, transitional justice measures must be as transparent, inclusive, and participatory as possible. For starters, outreach cannot be approached as a public relations strategy—as it sometimes has been—but rather as an exercise of transparency and public answerability that seeks to clarify misperceptions and promote understanding. Moreover, given their aim of promoting democratic change, transitional justice measures should be as inclusive and participatory as possible. In this respect, the more that the community and especially key stakeholders are able to have a voice in crafting their development—for example, by contributing to the drafting of a truth commission's mandate, giving recommendations on the benefits of a reparations program, and even providing input on prosecutorial strategies regarding whom they perceived to be the "most responsible"—the more capacity such measures will arguably have to reflect the real demands and expectations of the affected populations, thus enhancing their relevance and potential impact in the longer run.

Finally, if one considers the goals of transitional justice measures, outreach activities are important with regard to the legitimation and potential legacy of such institutions. In the most immediate sense, to the extent that the message of acknowledging past abuses and recognizing victims needs to be delivered, it is essential to explain and broadly publicize the aims and results of the process.

Justice must not only be done, it must also be seen to be done. Thus, beyond what happens inside a court chamber, reparations process, or testimony-gathering exercise, practitioners need to consider the way in which these actions resonate or are acknowledged at the societal level. Because transitional justice measures aim to promote a broader social transformation—relating to other goals such as supporting peace, strengthening the democratic rule of law, or fostering reconciliation—the normative shift of values they embody must take hold within the population. If transitional justice measures are to have lasting legacies, they should strive to promote public engagement and ownership of the process, as society as a whole has the responsibility to keep pushing for the reforms and changes that such measures can only begin to advance.[5] In this sense, the role that outreach performs is also substantively linked to the aims of transitional justice measures. An initiative that no one is even aware of can hardly achieve any broader social changes. Moreover, beyond the formal achievement of mandates and the political changes they are supposed to reflect, the success of transitional justice initiatives also depends on their capacity to catalyze change in a country's political culture, toward greater respect for human rights norms and the democratic rule of law.

BEYOND OUTREACH: CULTURE AND SOCIETY

Articulating such a rich notion of outreach—one linked to the understanding of the legitimacy and legitimation of transitional justice measures in democratic terms—has consequences that extend beyond the notion of outreach itself.[6] Emphasizing the key role that the public's access to information, discussion, and participation plays in the potential longer-term impact of transitional justice measures implies paying attention not only to the social repercussions of initiatives promoted at the institutional or official level but also to the possibility of the democratic regeneration of the social web itself, which conflict and its enduring legacies have also affected. Outreach programs ideally aim to generate this sort of informed public discussion around transitional justice measures and the abuses to which they are responding, to the extent that they are conducted by institutions or bodies established within the political and juridical spheres. However, other paths within the social realm—such as mass media, cultural practices, and educational frameworks—offer a place through which messages can be more naturally transmitted and promoted, but they may also be silenced or undermined. Transitional justice processes do not happen in a vacuum; they operate in social and historical contexts that extend far beyond the operational life and reach of their constituent measures.[7] Accordingly, the ways in which mass media, educational institutions, intellectuals, and artists portray new narratives—and how the larger social body subsequently appropriates them—become relevant components for understanding the social resonance of transitional justice processes as well as for making normative changes actually happen in a country's public culture.

Political processes have clear manifestations in a society's public life and culture. Societies have historically interpreted, configured, and portrayed past events using different means of expression and codes—including formal methods such as academic research or journalistic chronicles and also more informal and spontaneous forms of artistic work, popular culture, and day-to-day communicative interactions. While different forms of cultural expression may be able to capture and represent—at least in partial or fractured ways—the universe of beliefs and values that a given society shares, they also contribute to articulating and shaping those beliefs and values, producing new sources of knowledge and triggering further reflection and discussion. In this respect, among the many types of historical experiences that tend to be culturally appropriated, transitional justice processes and the periods of abuse and distress that precede them are especially noteworthy. They have a profound impact not only on the images that societies build of their history and themselves but also on the political and moral interpretations that societies give to those images, and therefore on the consequences that these images have for the future. Experience indicates that transitional justice processes are usually accompanied by an eruption of creative activities of this sort.[8]

When trying to understand the role of these manifestations in the public space of a society with regard to the legacies of mass abuse, a variety of exercises are possible. For example, one might provide a descriptive or interpretative analysis of such phenomena or consider their roles as vehicles for learning and socialization. However, from a more specific perspective, directly related to the normative shift that transitional justice measures seek to advance, one can approach the different forms of cultural expression as communicative practices with political intention. From this point of view, analyzing such processes in transitional contexts becomes relevant in regard to their potential roles in (re)constructing a democratic public sphere.

On first consideration, the concept of the public sphere aims at capturing the realm of communicative interactions that take place within a society—as opposed to within the state apparatus—in which particular citizens engage in discussions about matters of public concern or "issues raised by the administration of the state."[9] The public sphere is the space in which citizens are conceived not as mere recipients of the state's actions nor in terms of their private relations as individuals, but rather as political agents with a say in the processes that affect them. In this respect, the notion of the public sphere captures the role of individuals as citizens who can organize themselves according to common interests to be defended in the public arena, thus signaling the role that communicative interactions play as vehicles for political participation. Indeed, as Craig Calhoun has emphasized, "The importance of the public sphere lies in its potential as a mode of societal integration. Public discourse (and communicative action) is a possible mode of coordination of human life, as are state power and market economies."[10]

Now, the concept of the public sphere is useful because it makes visible the relationship between social communicative interactions and the exercise of citizenship. The concept of the public sphere also has a normative importance within democratic societies—not only because the weakness or total absence of a public sphere is normally characteristic of repressive regimes and conflictive environments, but also because, while stressing the importance of political participation, the concept of the public sphere establishes a set of considerations for properly playing its role. As different scholars have argued, the public sphere has to be inclusive, egalitarian, and guided by issues that revolve around the common good rather than the promotion of particular interests.[11] The democratic strength of a country's public space is directly proportional to considerations such as the population's capacity to access accurate information, decent levels of education, and platforms to exercise freedom of expression and association under conditions of equality and inclusiveness.

Theoretical considerations aside, the concept of the public sphere in a practical sense can refer to the variety of communicative interactions that take place within a given society that directly interrelate with and reinforce institutional practices. More specifically, the concept of the public sphere can also be used to understand the role that culture, media, and other communicative endeavors can play in societies overcoming mass abuse. Such endeavors are not mere informational practices, aesthetic forms of expression, or vehicles of socialization but more concretely consider their potential contributions to nurturing forms of social participation and engagement and promote a culture of democratic citizenship. Indeed, the notion of the public sphere can be especially valuable for understanding the fundamental role that civil society—and more important, the general public—plays in countries that are engaging in transitional justice processes. The notion of the public sphere is also useful for identifying the communicative and social conditions that must be in place to ensure that discussions among citizens about transitional justice in contexts that political conflict have socially disrupted can help to foster a culture of democratic debate. This argument has two different components. First, by using the notion of the public sphere in reflections about transitional justice, we are able to adopt a wider perspective on the overall justice process, because it leads us to recognize the role that communicative interactions might play in strengthening or weakening the adequate functioning and social impact of official transitional justice initiatives. Second, the notion of the public sphere is also useful in raising awareness of the fact that such communicative interactions have to meet certain standards if they are going to contribute positively to creating a space for public reflection around the legacies of mass abuse and therefore strengthen, rather than undermine, democratic practices. From this perspective, the space of social communicative interactions itself acquires a unique role in transitional societies, as the space in which the public culture of a country can actually articulate the shift of norms and values that transitional justice measures promote. As one author has eloquently put it, the longer-term effects of transitional justice processes depend on their "ability to delegitimize the conflict-era discourse and create an opening for a new, and newly legitimated, discourse that is negotiated by equal competitors in the public arena."[12]

The concept of the public sphere provides a valuable notion through which to articulate methods for individuals or civil society participating in or engaging with transitional justice processes. Together with their institutional apparatuses, democratic forms of governance require an actively involved and vigilant citizenry. As Pablo de Greiff has argued, one of the ways in which transitional justice measures can be understood to contribute to strengthening the democratic rule of law in transitional societies is through their capacity to catalyze the (re)articulation of civil society organizations.[13] In this respect, the role of civil society can be understood in terms of the contributions that, for example, human rights organizations or victims' groups can make by directly supporting institutional processes or conducting justice-related projects on their own.[14] Another way to look at this phenomenon is to consider the broader contributions that communicative practices play in the formation of a nascent public sphere, understood as a space for the exchange of information, articulation of rights-based claims, and development of debate within a society. Making use of the notion of the public sphere in transitional contexts allows us to make visible the space in which citizens, as distinct from the state, can exercise an important role in the functioning of official mechanisms themselves. Citizens can use the variety of communicative means of expression available to them, thus emphasizing that rather than merely being subject to its actions, citizens have an important role to play in supervising the actions of the state. The notion of the public sphere in transitional societies thus highlights the capacity of the public to effectively monitor and criticize their government's actions to redress the past, advance proposals on how to improve these policies, or advocate for pending tasks that need to be included in the transitional agenda. Indeed, to the extent that transitional justice measures aim to strengthen the democratic rule of law, the sufficient reconstruction of the social body to enable it to adequately play such a supervisory role can be understood as an essential component of that same transformative agenda.

Moreover, focusing attention on the public sphere as the fundamental space for developing a country's political culture of democratic citizenship in transitional justice contexts also reveals the importance of reconstructing the society's communicative web in itself. To be sure, damages from political oppression and conflict affect not only the relationship between the state and its citizens but also relationships among citizens themselves. Past repressive practices can be deeply entrenched in a country's political culture; conflict and abuse, in addition, deeply undermine the levels of civic trust among citizens within a given community—in both cases precisely at the expense of a free, inclusive, vibrant, and respectful public space.[15] To the extent that well-crafted outreach programs can contribute to laying some of the conditions necessary to catalyze civic trust between citizens and official institutions, the myriad communicative interactions that take place in the social realm can in turn help to establish conditions for catalyzing trust among citizens themselves, while contributing to the societal articulation of new cultural values and norms. Making use of discursive and emotional means—through film, performing arts, educative projects, or reliable media coverage—the public sphere in a transitional society can be a powerful space for amplifying and deepening the messages that transitional justice measures can only advance and even help to compensate for some of their limitations. For example, cultural projects can create a space for public mourning and the symbolic recognition of victims; in this way, such projects can foster public awareness and reflection about the legacies of mass abuse, making them a matter of shared social concern. Moreover, by undertaking projects that challenge earlier narratives of abuse and repression, the public sphere can become a space in which those previously silenced voices are given public credibility and visibility, helping catalyze new social dynamics of solidarity and inclusion. Thus, beyond the official role of transitional justice measures, the public sphere of a country can become a fundamental platform for advancing deeper social and political transformation—signaling not the state's but society's public recognition of its commitment to the new normative discourse that transitional justice seeks to promote.

Turning to the second component of the argument, the public sphere as an analytical tool for interpreting the role and different ways of social engagement in a transitional society is also important for reflecting upon the necessary conditions for the adequate articulation of such a space. A country's public space can contribute to undermining transitional justice issues, if not being completely silent about them.[16] In this respect, trying to employ the notion of the public sphere to interpret the role of public forms of expression and communication in transitional societies—which conflict and mass abuse characteristically shatter and which carry legacies of profound power imbalances (typically represented in a clear division between victims and perpetrators)—raises questions as real and urgent as they are difficult to answer. Some of these questions might be as follows: What are the rules that make conversation possible in a nascent democratic public sphere? Where does the difference lie between imposing a univocal interpretation of a conflicted past and offering a moral reading of it? How should societies in which many victims of such atrocities still live and important imbalances in power still persist balance the protection of rights such as freedom of speech in the face of narratives of denial? What degree of social consensus is necessary and desirable for making sense of a shared historical past? What aspects of that history should be taught in schools, and how should they be taught? To what extent is it necessary to intervene to guarantee the existence of a pluralistic media system that provides necessary information rather than serving particular interests? How can the public sphere advance new and more informal possibilities for social and political transformation beyond the initiatives implemented at the official level? How can the media or artistic forms of expression be used creatively to promote awareness and engage society in discussions around justice issues? These are only some of the questions among many that might be asked, and answering them all in one volume would be impossible. As I explain in the next section, though, this compilation of essays and the motivation underlying them represent an attempt to draw attention to and take seriously the sort of problems to which these questions point.

THE STRUCTURE OF THE BOOK

Looking into the broader role that society and culture play in transitional justice contexts, this book primarily focuses on the ways in which different types of communicative practices contribute to raising social awareness and promoting public reflection about the legacies of mass abuse. The most immediate means through which such awareness is triggered is the creation of strong outreach approaches, which transitional justice measures establish to provide information directly to the public with the aim of fostering discussion and engagement. Other avenues may be initiated by media networks, social actors, or individual citizens, which can share very similar goals. Incorporating these other avenues into the scope of this book first became relevant when considering how cultural practices and media approaches could contribute to making outreach initiatives more effective. On a second look, however, attributing this kind of effect to such approaches raised a more interesting and complex question about the role and importance of cultural and media projects in societies embarked on transitional justice processes. The goal of this volume is thus to help develop a more ambitious—though still tentative—reflection on the ways in which the effects of transitional justice measures spill over beyond the institutional domain in which they operate, through cultural and media initiatives, into the public sphere of societies working to construct new forms of citizenship. With this goal in mind, we identified a set of issues to be covered under three different sections: (1) outreach programs for transitional justice measures, which would include a series of case studies on this topic; (2) media and conflict, with chapters that would approach the relationships between these subjects and transitional justice; and (3) cultural and artistic projects, which would analyze how different means of expression open a broader perspective for understanding the social significance of transitional justice processes. The book should be read as a preliminary discussion of the roles that the media and different forms of cultural and artistic expression can play in transitional justice processes as well as some of the challenges raised.

The first part of the book compiles three case studies on outreach programs for transitional justice measures. In chapter 1 Maya Karwande analyzes the outreach efforts of the Special Court of Sierra Leone as the first war crimes tribunal to adopt a so-called engagement model of outreach, which, in contrast to programs conducted by earlier courts, made important efforts to establish a two-way communication process. Stephanie Barbour examines in chapter 2 the outreach program of the domestic war crime chambers of Bosnia and Herzegovina (WCC), which have operated in parallel to the International Tribunal for the former Yugoslavia, and also considers the roles of the country's cantonal and district courts. The chapter analyzes the successes and failures of outreach efforts in Bosnia and Herzegovina that have sought to ensure the intended social impact of domestic war crimes trials. Patrick Burgess and Galuh Wandita, authors of chapter 3, focus their attention on the challenges that the Commission for Reception, Truth and Reconciliation of East Timor

(Comissão de Acolhimento, Verdade e Reconciliação, CAVR) faced in reaching out to the population of a country severely shattered after decades of war. Putting special emphasis on the strategies developed by the commission to reach out to victims and communities at the local level—implemented as part of its mandate to conduct a community reconciliation process—the chapter also provides some valuable lessons learned from that particular experience. In chapter 4 Virginie Ladisch and I consider the importance of involving children and youth in transitional justice processes through outreach programming; also important is providing a framework for doing so in a meaningful and safe manner, acknowledging the tension that such efforts must address between the principles of protection and participation.

The second part of the book deals with the role that the media play in conflict and post-conflict contexts in relation to transitional justice measures, by looking into the experiences of particular countries, and more generally by analyzing some of the ways in which the media have been used creatively to promote public engagement around transitional justice processes. Once identified as the fourth estate of political power, the role of the mass media in contemporary democratic societies is of fundamental importance. Because of their pervasive reach, mass media are the most important means that societies have for accessing information. To be sure, media do more than simply provide information; they also offer analysis and contribute to the shaping of public opinion through the selection of the issues they cover as well as through the ways in which they depict them. When such work is not performed according to adequate standards—and here the concept of the public sphere could be used as a useful measure of reference—the media can play a distortive role with far-reaching consequences in transitional justice contexts. Some of these possible deviations and the problems that may result from a deficient media landscape in societies emerging from conflict are analyzed in the case of Serbia in chapter 5, authored by Nidžara Ahmetašević and Tanja Matić, and in Rwanda in chapter 6, authored by Timothy Longman. Despite the evident differences between the two contexts, both chapters analyze the media's evolution from their problematic role before the conflict—which in Rwanda was in some cases one of direct instigation—and the difficulties this history creates for a post-conflict setting in which the media system itself is part of a legacy of abuse. Such situations provide insight into the role of the media in relation to justice processes and raise important questions about the necessity of including the media system among the institutions requiring reform in transitional societies.

The role of the media is not always negative. Because of their reach, media actors or outlets can become powerful tools for spreading knowledge and promoting debate among the population. From this perspective, the remaining chapters of part 2 explore a variety of methods through which different media can be used in creative and positive ways for advancing social discussions on justice. In chapter 7, after pointing out the limitations of traditional reporting in societies that are devastated by war and that lack a strong media culture and a properly functioning rule of law system, Wanda Hall explores innovative ways in which radio can be used to create open spaces for discussion among citizens about rule of law, human rights, and transitional justice topics; her example is the Interactive Radio Justice Project, which she led for several years. Charlotte Cole and June Lee in chapter 8 describe the experiences of Sesame Workshop's international programs. In these cases, child-oriented TV programs help foster mutual understanding among children in post-conflict contexts. Their specific focus is on Sesame Workshop's program in Kosovo, considering the process and methods that the workshop has employed, as well as analyzing some evidence of the program's impact. In the final chapter of part 2, Camille Crittenden analyzes some of the early uses of new media by international criminal justice tribunals to evaluate the possibilities and dangers of employing such tools to promote engagement around justice processes.

The final part of the book contains chapters that discuss the different means through which cultural and artistic projects—including theater, literature, music, photography, film, and memorials—can engage individuals and societies in the (new) moral narratives that transitional justice measures seek to construct. While the media's relevance lies in their capacity to provide information on a massive scale, projects of a cultural nature are especially interesting. Although they may reach a lower number of people, their ability to communicate the experiences of harm and abuse across different expressive languages allows them to use emotional approaches to promote public engagement. In this respect, one of their key qualities is the ability to not only represent past abuses by stating truths that can be factually verified but also, and more importantly, to construct and re-create the meanings that individuals and communities ascribe to those facts. Inhabiting a space more open to experimentation, artistic and cultural projects display many means of interpreting and making sense of particular realities. By using symbols, metaphors, or parables—or by linking individual and personal experiences to collective narratives—artistic projects can become powerful means for capturing the attention of the public as well as triggering empathy and feelings of solidarity; fostering social recognition and discussion in the public sphere is also an outcome. Cultural endeavors can thus provide new sources of knowledge using discursive and emotional means, and they can link the two types of discourses by treating the receptor as both moral agent and citizen. Finally, because of their more flexible and informal nature, cultural activities are often especially well-suited to dealing with transitional justice topics; without having to renounce the power of critique, they can create intimate spaces that, free of institutional constraints, provide a sense of safety for discussions about human rights abuses. Cultural activities can also potentially be more democratic, in terms of the capacity of individuals to initiate new projects as well as their ability to participate in projects promoted by others.

Following these lines, in chapter 10 Nadia Siddiqui and Hjalmar Joffre-Eichhorn analyze how human rights groups have used participatory theater techniques in Afghanistan to open spaces for communities, and especially victims, to share their stories and construct collective meanings. Given the constraints of the context, these methods have been used in the absence of transitional justice measures; the authors explore the impacts that such exercises have for those who are invited to participate as well as the role that these projects can play in raising awareness at the community level about transitional justice topics. Testimony, as an utterance that carries with it a truth claim, is the vehicle that Catherine Cole chooses in chapter 11 to analyze how different media and artistic projects have appropriated and reinterpreted the truth and reconciliation commission process in South Africa. In a series of successive reverberations—from spoken word to transcript, from statement to television reportage, and from nonfiction to fiction—Cole traces how the particular experience of Father Michel Lapsley has been portrayed in the public domain of South Africa and raises questions about the moral dilemmas that arise when third parties use real stories for purposes that go beyond an original truth-telling exercise. In chapter 12 Eduardo González Cueva and Florencia Librizzi analyze the use of photography in transitional justice measures. After explaining the risks of considering photography as a mere technical tool with the capacity to capture reality, the authors present photography as a discursive practice that requires decodification and interpretation. From that perspective, through a series of four snapshots, they examine some of the possibilities and challenges that its use presents in transitional justice contexts. Carolyn Patty Blum offers an account in chapter 13 of how films, through their capacity to re-create situations and stories, are especially well-suited to provoking a variety of responses in spectators, as moral individuals and as citizens. Using six different productions to guide the discussion, Blum explores different issues that films have raised in transitional justice contexts, including those that portray the reality of abuses and the potential justice responses—among them, institutional reform, reparations, criminal justice, and truth-seeking initiatives. Louis Bickford's chapter 14 analyzes how public memorials—museums, interpretive sites, sites of conscience, and monuments built in the aftermath of mass atrocity with commemorative purposes—can be understood to work in transitional justice contexts, focusing on their capacity to promote a type of learning related to the notion of prevention. Finally, in chapter 15 Carlos Thiebaut Luis-André seeks to capture the different ways in which literary texts can depict the experiences of harm embodied in mass atrocities and human rights abuse. Articulating a relationship between the private act of reading and the public demands that some literary texts make—connecting the moral individual to the citizen—Thiebaut identifies three temporal moments from which such experiences of harm can be conceptualized: as warning, before the harm has occurred; when it is occurring, in relation to the capacity to name such harm as harm; and regarding the elaboration, in terms of justice and memory, that comes after the harm has been inflicted.

Partly because this book was originally conceived as a continuation of a previous research project on outreach and as a supplementary effort to provide a broader account of some of the questions that emerged as its result, the work advanced here should be read as a proposal and an invitation. The volume constitutes a serious attempt to conduct a preliminary exploration into the relations between transitional justice and the cultural and social spheres, an area of research that, despite the remarkable growth of the field of transitional justice during the last thirty years, remains largely unexplored. As an invitation, precisely because of the scarcity of the literature and the importance of the topic, my hope is that this book contributes to raising awareness about why considerations of the role of the public sphere—whether through media, cultural activities, or education—should be included in the transitional justice research agenda. The authors of the essays collected here provide interesting and lucid answers to some initial questions while calling attention to new challenges and dilemmas. As a whole, the book represents an honest attempt to recognize the communicative richness of the social contexts in which transitional justice processes unfold and offers a valuable account of the intersections between transitional justice, culture, and society.

ACKNOWLEDGMENTS

Numerous persons made this project possible. First, I wish to express my obvious gratitude to the chapters' authors, who persisted through several delays in the process, including numerous rounds of comments and editorial suggestions. This appreciation also goes out to those who were involved in different ways and at different stages of the project, including Mychelle Balthazard, Naima Benwakrim, Julie Guillerot, Pierre Hazan, Iris Jave Pinedo, Habib Nassar, and Jonathan VanAntwerpen, as well as to the participants at the two meetings that the International Center of Transitional Justice organized in Cambodia in the late winter of 2010. Many ideas articulated through the project came from countless conversations about outreach, art, culture, media, and transitional justice at these and other venues, with too many people involved to name them all here.

During the time it took to develop and finish this volume, the number of interns who contributed in different manners to the project kept increasing: Rachel LaForgia, Kaitlin McNally-Murphy, Juan Diego Prieto, Laura Ann Reed, and very especially Juan Menchero. My most sincere thanks to all of them, as well as to Cecilia Naddeo, who was an ICTJ fellow during the summer of 2012. Likewise I would like to thank, for their generous permission to print their work, photographers Marina García Burgos, Gustavo Germano, Oscar Medrano, and Iñigo Royo. At the SSRC, special thanks go to Michael Simon for his great patience and professionalism during the book production process.

Three institutions merit recognition: first, for financial support, the International Development Research Center (IDRC) of Canada. Second, publication of this research would not have been possible without the support of the Institute of Public Knowledge (IPK) at New York University, which hosted me as visiting scholar during the period when I was developing this project. I am especially thankful to Craig Calhoun, Samuel Carter, and Jessica Coffey. Third, my gratitude goes to ICTJ as a whole. In particular I want to thank my colleagues Roger Duthie, Julie Guillerot, Mohamed Suma, and Anthony Triolo. Most especially I would also like to acknowledge the sustained support of Shaina Wright, who provided more than extensive assistance to make this book possible, and Refik Hodzic, for fine-tuning my thinking on outreach from the time that we met in 2010. Finally, my sincere appreciation goes to Pablo de Greiff, who, combining respectful supervision and invaluable intellectual support, has been a constant source of encouragement for many years now.

New York
December 2012

NOTES

1 Broadly speaking, transitional justice refers to the set of judicial and nonjudicial measures—most notably truth seeking, reparations programs, institutional reform, and criminal justice processes—that governments implement in order to redress the legacies of massive human rights abuses and serious crimes under international law in the aftermath of conflict or authoritarian repression as a means of (re)constructing democracy and peace.

2 Needless to say, the society's interest in, advocacy for, and endorsement of justice measures before the process even starts, along with other contextual variables—including the level of development and institutional capacity—are also important components in explaining its impact and follow-up.

3 The problem with the term "outreach" needs some explanation. To begin with, the English noun "outreach" is difficult to translate to many other languages. This practical and even anecdotal challenge is less significant than the fact that the term is often interpreted to represent merely technical and even supplementary activity, rather than as a core element to enhance the legitimacy of transitional justice measures, as I argue here.

4 Clara Ramírez-Barat, *Making an Impact: Guidelines on Designing and Implementing Outreach Programs for Transitional Justice* (New York: International Center for Transitional Justice, 2011).

5 For this reason, from a practical and normative perspective, transitional justice processes should be conceived in democratic terms, in relation to both their present legitimacy and further legitimation or social validation. Under democratic norm making, the legitimation of the outcomes converges with the legitimacy of the process itself; in theory, people who participate in the formulation of laws ultimately have to accept them as well.

6 While the notion of society doesn't need to be explained here, the concept of culture would benefit from some clarification. We can talk about culture in two different although related senses. The first one takes an anthropological perspective, referring to a set of values, rules, and practices that a given society or social group shares. In the second one, adopting a sociological approach, culture can be understood as the sphere of expression and communication in a given society that differentiates itself from social systems and political institutions (e.g., through art, literature, music, comics, etc.). While, understood in the first sense, culture does play an important role in transitional justice processes (hence the numerous debates in the field about multiculturalism and the meaning that different societies ascribe to notions such as justice and reconciliation), in the second sense—the one used in this book—the importance of culture to transitional justice resides in its being the space in which citizens reflect on, discuss, and construct meaning about a shared past.

7 Taking this sort of contextuality seriously also brings in a note of caution when thinking about outreach programs, as doing so recognizes that despite their important role

and beyond the practical obstacles that these programs face—especially given the immensity of their tasks—outreach programs themselves have important limitations. No matter how well crafted, no outreach program can change beliefs and values within a given society in the short run, nor can an outreach program take the place of socialization processes through which beliefs and values are naturally reproduced.

8 A beautiful collection of such artistic works can be found in Ksenija Bilbija, Jo Ellen Fair, Cynthia E. Milton, and Leigh A. Payne, eds., *The Art of Truth-Telling about Authoritarian Rule* (Madison: University of Wisconsin Press, 2005).

9 Craig Calhoun, "Introduction: Habermas and the Public Sphere," in *Habermas and the Public Sphere*, ed. Craig Calhoun (Cambridge: MIT Press, 1992), 8.

10 Ibid., 6.

11 In this respect, the concept of the public sphere is normative in nature. As originally articulated by the German philosopher Jürgen Habermas, its significance does not lie exclusively in the fact that it stresses the importance of social participation in politics but also in the idea that such participation is to be regulated according to the "public use of reason"—according to the rules of procedural rationality following which judgments are to be based only on reasons, rather than in private interests or according to status. See ibid., 2–4; and Jürgen Habermas, *The Structural Transformation of the Public Sphere: An Inquiry into a Category of Bourgeois Society* (Cambridge: MIT Press, 1991), 1–3.

12 Julie M. Mazzei, "Finding Shame in Truth: The Importance of Public Engagement in Truth Commissions," *Human Rights Quarterly* 3, no. 2 (May 2011): 433.

13 Pablo de Greiff, "Transitional Justice, Security and Development," World Development Report 2011, background paper, World Bank, October 2010, 17–19.

14 For examples, see David A. Crocker, "Transitional Justice and International Civil Society: Toward a Normative Framework," *Constellation* 5, no. 4 (1998): 492–517; and Roger Duthie, "Building Trust and Capacity: Civil Society and Transitional Justice from a Development Perspective," International Center for Transitional Justice, New York, November 2009.

15 Interestingly enough, repressive regimes have proved to be experts in political propaganda precisely at the expense of suppressing the public sphere, as quintessentially represented by the Nazi Ministry of Public Enlightenment and Propaganda headed by Joseph Goebbels. Strongly investing in diverse socialization techniques, including education, media, art, and monument building, authoritarian governments powerfully impose a unique narrative that shapes political spaces, leaving no place for dissent or portraying victims' stories.

16 Spain is an interesting example in this respect. When, after forty years of repression that followed a terrible civil war, the society at large decided to institutionally put the past behind it, the civil war became one of the most studied topics for the historians of the time. Around 2000, and with justice still a pending issue, the number of studies, novels,

and films that remembered, analyzed, and vindicated the silenced memories of the civil war experienced more than a notable growth. Most of these projects, which appeared at the same time as a more articulated civil society movement, were vindicating the rights of the victims, which at that time were still almost absent from the official political agenda.

PART 1

Outreach in Transitional Justice

CHAPTER 1

Implementing an Engagement Model: Outreach at the Special Court for Sierra Leone

Maya Karwande

International courts have struggled to make their trials relevant and accessible to the public in the countries in which they operate. As perhaps the most prominent examples, the efforts of the ad hoc tribunals in the former Yugoslavia and Rwanda were plagued by the disconnect between their goals, which included contributing to peace in the affected regions, and the lack of local knowledge of and support for their work. In response, both courts established outreach units to help make the tribunals and trials better known among the affected populations. The goals of these first "outreach" programs were relatively modest: the units focused simply on ensuring basic transparency and disseminating accurate information about the trials. The conception of the role of outreach has since evolved, and academics and practitioners now broadly accept that outreach programs should go beyond merely providing information to serve the greater aim of creating a dialogue between the court and the general public. This *engagement* model of outreach, as it has been called, supports the development of two-way communication between the court and civil society, the public, and specific target groups.[1] On a conceptual level, the engagement model is premised on the recognition that fostering public involvement with, participation in, and, ideally, acceptance of a tribunal is in fact part of a court's core mandate. The engagement model often generates correspondingly high expectations for the long-term impact that the tribunal will have on the local justice system. Thus, on a more technical or practical level, outreach programs that have adopted the engagement model require a different array of methods in order to achieve these more ambitious goals.

The Special Court for Sierra Leone (SCSL, or Special Court) was the first international court to adopt an engagement model of outreach from its initial planning stages. Senior Special Court officials recognized from the start that outreach would be a vital component in achieving the tribunal's aims and maximizing the benefits of its hybrid structure. Unlike the ad hoc tribunals, whose efforts to connect with their constituencies were hampered by geographic and cultural distance, the Special Court is located within Sierra Leone and is composed of a mixture of international and national officials and judges. However, the Special Court understood that in order to translate these structural advantages into a more profound and lasting impact, a robust outreach program was required. This realization was a welcome development and has resulted in the strongest outreach program of any war crimes tribunal to date.

The pioneering outreach efforts of the Special Court offer important insights into the difficulties of actually implementing and achieving the grand ideals of public participation. The structure of the court has both promoted and limited these goals, as have a variety of factors beyond the court's control that the technical elements of outreach programming cannot easily address. The Special Court's hybrid structure was supposed to facilitate a broader goal of engagement through its mixture of international and national staff, its accessible domestic location, and the intended quick pace of its proceedings. However, the court's selective mandate, the absence of key defendants, and the move of the Charles Taylor trial to The Hague presented issues that affected the public's discourse and opinions about the court. Outreach programming to address these issues could have been more robust, but practical factors also unavoidably limited such efforts.

The experience of the Special Court has substantially influenced the international courts and tribunals that have followed it, serving as a particularly important case study for the International Criminal Court. In this chapter I analyze the implementation of outreach at the Special Court and identify accomplishments and challenges that it faced. Following a brief background on the conflict and the court's establishment, I discuss the structure and activities of its outreach program, as well as the key challenges that the outreach section faced in implementing the engagement model. I conclude by identifying lessons learned from the experience of the SCSL and considerations that it raises for future outreach programs at other international courts and transitional justice measures more generally.

HISTORY OF THE CONFLICT

The violence in Sierra Leone began in March 1991, when the Revolutionary United Front (RUF), a Sierra Leonean group based in Liberia, crossed the border into Sierra Leone and began a rebellion against the government. This incursion initiated a brutal conflict that would terrorize the country for the next eleven years. The war progressed through different phases of fighting between multiple actors in the region, including multiple coups and changes in government leadership and an international intervention by Economic Community of West African States Monitoring Group (ECOMOG) forces. A few of the key moments in the hostilities included the military coup in 1992 that installed the National Provisional Ruling Council (NPRC); the 1996 elections that brought the Sierra Leone People's Party (SLPP), led by Ahmad Tejan Kabbah, to power; President Kabbah's 1996 consolidation of pro-government militias into the Civil Defense Forces (CDF); the 1997 military coup that installed Major Johnny Paul Koroma as the leader of the Armed Forces Revolutionary Council (AFRC); and the 1998 military intervention by ECOMOG forces that put President Kabbah back into power.[2]

After eight years of violence, the Lomé Peace Agreement was signed on July 7, 1999. The agreement was meant to end the conflict through a two-pronged approach: military resolution through disarmament and political resolution through a power-sharing agreement. The Lomé accords also provided an amnesty to all parties to the agreement for any crimes committed before its signing (although the United Nations did not endorse this provision) and led to the establishment of the UN Mission in Sierra Leone (UNAMSIL) to oversee the peace process. While the agreement marked the beginning of the peace process, the violence continued for some time as neither side fully complied with its terms. In a particularly flagrant violation of the agreement, RUF and AFRC forces captured and held hostage five hundred UN peacekeepers in May 2000. Demobilization efforts continued until January 2002, when the war was officially declared over with a weapon-burning ceremony. In March 2002, peaceful elections were held, and President Kabbah was reelected with 70 percent of the vote.[3]

NATURE OF THE CONFLICT

All sides of the conflict specifically targeted civilians, and the most common violations committed were forced displacement, abductions, arbitrary detentions, and killings. The war was "characterized by indiscriminate violence. It broke longstanding rules, defiled cherished traditions, sullied human respect, and tore apart the very fabric of society."[4] The RUF was responsible for the greatest number of human rights violations during the conflict. Led by Foday Sankoh, the RUF was also supported by Charles Taylor, who at the time was president of Liberia and leader of the National Patriotic Front of Liberia (NPFL), a Liberian rebel group. Taylor provided material support to the RUF, and the NPFL and RUF often coordinated their attacks. In the early stages of the war, Taylor and Sankoh agreed on a common military strategy that included targeting civilian settlements.[5] RUF fighters were often drugged, which may have contributed to crazed and particularly brutal acts of violence.[6] Hand and arm amputations, particularly around the 1996 elections, were another common RUF tactic intended to instill fear and discourage voting.[7]

On the government side, the CDF and AFRC also committed significant atrocities. The Kamajor group of the CDF was responsible for the majority of CDF violations after 1996. In particular, the Kamajors targeted several ethnic groups in the northern part of the country and have been linked to acts of forced cannibalism.[8] The AFRC was responsible for large-scale atrocities in the northern region and in Kono District, committing a large number of amputations.[9]

In addition, the various factions in the conflict often specifically targeted women and girls, who suffered abduction, rape, sexual slavery, and other acts of sexual violence. Even though the violence has ended, many victims are still stigmatized as a result of their experiences. Many women who have borne children as a result of rape are shunned for giving birth to "rebel" children.[10] Children were also targeted, and all armed factions in the conflict practiced forced recruitment[11]—in particular the RUF, which pioneered this strategy.[12] An estimated fifteen thousand children were separated from their families during the conflict;[13] of these, Amnesty International estimates that more than ten thousand were associated with a fighting faction.[14] Child combatants were often forced to perform brutal acts of violence, such as amputations, rape, and torture. After the conflict, many child combatants were rejected by their families because of their former affiliations.[15]

SIERRA LEONE TODAY

Although the conflict has ended in Sierra Leone, the effects of the war continue to present challenges. The militias at the time systematically plundered Sierra Leone, one of the poorest countries in the world before the war.[16] The warring factions demolished a significant amount of the country's infrastructure, including large parts of Freetown, the capital city, and villages around the country. Economically, Sierra Leone was devastated, and the nation faces rising unemployment.[17] Since the end of the conflict, Sierra Leone has consistently been ranked near the bottom of the UN Human Development Index, which measures life expectancy, literacy, access to education, and standard of living.[18] Only 40 percent of the population over fifteen years old is literate, and the population, particularly women, has limited access to social services such as health and education.[19] With regard to governance, however, Sierra Leone has made some improvements in its democratic institutions. In 2007 Sierra Leone held parliamentary and presidential elections—its second elections since the conflict's end—which resulted in a peaceful, democratic change in power.[20]

TRANSITIONAL JUSTICE IN SIERRA LEONE

After the conflict ended, the government of Sierra Leone implemented a variety of processes to provide accountability for the atrocities committed during the war. The Lomé Peace Agreement provided for the creation of a truth and reconciliation commission (TRC) to address the human rights violations that had occurred in Sierra Leone since 1991. The commission was meant to provide a forum for victims and perpetrators, establish a clear record of the past, and make recommendations for future rehabilitation measures.[21] In addition, in 2000 President Kabbah requested UN assistance in setting up a mixed national and international court in Sierra Leone to bring "credible" justice to members of the RUF for their crimes against the people of Sierra Leone and taking UN peacekeepers hostage. Although the Lomé accords had provided for an amnesty to all parties to the agreement, the Sierra Leone government stated that the RUF's subsequent breaches of the agreement afforded sufficient justification for the government's request for assistance in prosecuting the alleged crimes that the RUF committed.[22] Furthermore, the international community had not recognized the amnesty provision even at the signing of the Lomé Peace Agreement; the special representative of the secretary-general had attached a reservation to it, stating that the United Nations would not recognize amnesty for genocide, crimes against humanity, war crimes, and other serious violations of international law.[23]

The United Nations acceded to President Kabbah's request and sent a planning mission to Sierra Leone to gather information for the development of the court's statute.[24] The mission consulted with the government, human rights nongovernmental organizations (NGOs), prison and police authorities, members of the local bar association, representatives of the RUF and CDF, local chiefs, and traditional leaders about the planned structure and operations of the Special Court.[25] After the planning mission report was completed, negotiations took place between the secretary-general and the Security Council about the Special Court's structure,[26] followed by seventeen months of negotiations between the United Nations and the government of Sierra Leone. Finally, on January 16, 2002, the United Nations and Sierra Leone signed an agreement creating the Special Court for Sierra Leone.[27] Despite the initial round of local consultations, this process raised concerns among many national groups in Sierra Leone. While they had supported the creation of a tribunal, many local human rights organizations felt they had been neglected during the negotiations, which were perceived to have taken place almost entirely in New York.[28] In particular, many resented that more Sierra Leoneans had not been invited to an expert group meeting about the relationship between the TRC and the Special Court, which took place before the statute was signed.[29]

The Special Court was established in Sierra Leone, and as such was the first ad hoc tribunal to be located in the country in which the crimes under prosecution had occurred, as well as the first hybrid international and national court.[30] The court is a temporary institution, mandated to prosecute "those bearing the greatest responsibility" for serious violations of international humanitarian law and Sierra Leonean law that took place in Sierra Leone, beginning on November 30, 1996. The court's limited temporal mandate and focus on those most responsible was intended to facilitate quick delivery of justice, and the trials were initially expected to be completed in three years.[31] The limited mandate was controversial, however, raising a number of challenges in terms of managing the population's expectations for the trials. International involvement was seen as necessary because Sierra Leone lacked the requisite judicial infrastructure, resources, and expertise in international criminal law to implement the prosecutions on its own.[32] However, the court was designed to be a hybrid institution: the government of Sierra Leone had the authority to appoint one-third of its judges, and a large number of its staff were Sierra Leoneans (although, especially at the beginning, they primarily filled administrative positions). The international community and other interested parties hoped that this hybrid structure would not only increase the court's accessibility to the affected populations but also foster a positive impact on the capacity of the national judiciary.[33] Finally, unlike the previous ad hoc tribunals, the Special Court was established via a treaty between the government of Sierra Leone and the United Nations. As a result, the court is not steadily funded by the United Nations but rather is supported by voluntary contributions from interested states with oversight from the management committee, a body with representatives from donor states and other interested parties.[34]

Since its establishment, the Special Court has issued a total of thirteen indictments for leaders of the RUF, CDF, and AFRC, as well as the former president of Liberia, Charles Taylor. Of the thirteen indictees, the court obtained custody over ten. Two of the RUF leaders who were indicted, Sam Bockarie and Foday Sankoh, died before the trial, and another indictee, Johnny Paul Koroma, remains at large as of May 2013. Nine of the cases were consolidated into three trials based on the affiliations of the accused. The court held one trial for the RUF leaders, a second trial for the AFRC leaders, and a third trial for the CDF leaders. These trials have all been completed and reached final judgments. One of the accused, CDF leader Sam Hinga Norman, died while awaiting the trial judgment, and the charges against him were dropped. Charles Taylor remained at large until March 2006 and was then tried separately. Due to concerns about the impact that a trial might have on security in the region, Taylor was transferred to The Hague to stand trial.[35] The proceedings began in June 2007, and in April 2012 Taylor was found guilty on all eleven counts charged, including aiding, abetting, and planning the commission of war crimes and crimes against humanity,[36] making him the first former head of state since Nuremberg to be so convicted. In May 2012 Taylor was sentenced to fifty years of imprisonment, although the judgment and sentence have been appealed.[37]

OUTREACH AT THE SPECIAL COURT

Unlike at previous tribunals, those who planned and implemented the Special Court recognized from the early stages of its establishment that some kind of public education campaign would be necessary in order to help Sierra Leoneans understand the court's role in ending impunity and developing the rule of law, although a few months passed before the Special Court's formal outreach program began its activities.[38] In particular, those who were active in establishing the court identified two key issues specific to the Sierra Leonean context as requiring explanation: (1) the relationship between the Special Court and the TRC and (2) the tribunal's limited mandate.[39]

EARLY OUTREACH EFFORTS BY NGOS (2001–3)

As early as 2001 the international human rights NGO No Peace without Justice (NPWJ)[40] established an outreach program in Sierra Leone to reduce confusion between the Special Court and the TRC and increase public knowledge of the mandate and operations of the Special Court, as well as of human rights and humanitarian law more broadly.[41] In addition to administering this general outreach program, NPWJ also collaborated with the Special Court Working Group (SCWG),[42] a coalition of Sierra Leonean civil society groups, to organize trainings around the country that explained the Special Court's principles, aims, and limitations.[43] In addition, NPWJ's Legal Profession Program worked in partnership with the Sierra Leone Bar Association to promote knowledge of international criminal law, human rights, and humanitarian law among legal professionals in Sierra Leone and facilitate their participation in the Special Court.[44] In 2002 the Post-conflict Reintegration Initiative for Development and Empowerment (PRIDE) also conducted a series of outreach events specifically targeting ex-combatants.[45] Such efforts were particularly critical as combatants were perceived to be a potentially destabilizing segment of society and were concerned themselves about prosecution by the Special Court. The potential for backlash against the court by ex-combatants was a real fear in the region; many civil society groups as a result were hesitant to engage in initial outreach efforts because of the fear that advocating for the tribunal would generate animosity or retaliation.[46] In 2003 the court's official outreach program was established, and NPWJ therefore concluded its own outreach work and efforts to support the SCWG. In the last stages of its program, though, NPWJ conducted joint training sessions aimed at selected target groups with the newly established outreach section in the court; over eighty seminars were held with about two thousand people attending. As a whole, these early outreach activities by NPWJ, the SCWG, and PRIDE created a strong foundation of information about the basic structure of the Special Court on which the court's official outreach program could build, and the SCWG in particular established a structure for cooperating with civil society on outreach issues.[47]

OUTREACH BY THE SPECIAL COURT

At the court, early outreach efforts were organized within the Office of the Prosecutor (OTP) and carried out by only three staff. In September 2002 the OTP took the unprecedented step of organizing a series of town hall meetings throughout the country, conducted by Chief Prosecutor David Crane (at times accompanied by Registrar Robin Vincent). The town hall structure was chosen because it was already a well-established, community-based format of communication in Sierra Leone. Held in each of the fourteen districts of Sierra Leone, typically with audiences of approximately 350 people, the meetings took place before any indictments had been issued. Their goal was to allow the prosecutor to meet his "clients," explain the purpose and limited mandate of the court, and answer questions.[48]

A Sierra Leonean activist working as an outreach coordinator for the OTP organized the meetings, beginning the process by contacting local traditional and religious leaders and asking them to participate in the outreach program, in the belief that their presence would increase public participation and trust in the events and, subsequently, in the court. To help them tailor the meeting for the specific population, the coordinator would also prepare the prosecutor and registrar by providing information about the demographics and war experiences of the district.[49] In some cases, representatives from the OTP would travel to the communities in advance and hold smaller meetings with specific groups, such as Sierra Leonean soldiers,[50] to allow members of these constituencies to voice their concerns and ask questions that reflected their needs.

This initial series of town hall meetings signaled the importance that the Special Court accorded to outreach and public communication; it was the first international or hybrid court to directly engage with the population at such an early stage in the process. Furthermore, the personal participation of the chief prosecutor and registrar, who is responsible for the overall management of the court, demonstrated that high-level officials at the court believed that outreach should be a priority. The interactive structure of the town hall meetings also set the tone for an engagement model of outreach. Unlike the initial outreach efforts of the International Criminal Tribunals for the former Yugoslavia and Rwanda, which were focused simply on disseminating information, the town hall meetings involved two-way communication between high-level court officials and meeting participants.

As the first attempt at town hall meetings by an international or hybrid tribunal, the Special Court's initial program offers a positive example of early, interactive outreach events. However, the meetings resulted in a few unanticipated consequences that future outreach programs should consider. First, the meetings emphasized the role of the prosecutor, with the possible effect of conflating the Special Court with the prosecutor, rather than conveying an image of the court as an independent institution.[51] Perhaps compounding this problem, no representatives of the Defense Office were available to participate in these early meetings, as the Defense Office had not yet been established.[52] Second, although the meetings were interactive in structure, some researchers have argued that the meetings still only offered, in practice, a one-way flow of information. To some analysts, the prosecutor appeared "aloof," and the court seemed like it failed to "come down to the ground."[53] Finally, although David Crane seemed generally well-liked by Sierra Leoneans, some people believe that his attitude and his perceptions of the conflict may have negatively affected the court's credibility. The chief prosecutor seemed to view the conflict differently from many Sierra Leoneans, leading to concerns that the court was a part of a wider US foreign policy agenda.[54] In addition, the chief prosecutor was often very passionate and emotional in these meetings and in his presentations in the courtroom about the impact that the court would have in bringing peace to the region and justice to individuals who suffered. This tone may have had the unintended consequence of raising unrealistic expectations for what the court could achieve.[55] While these issues may have somewhat negatively affected the town hall meetings, they were partly a product of factors outside the control of the outreach section; on the whole, the meetings were still very effective in making the court and its officials visible throughout the country in the early stages of the process.[56]

ESTABLISHMENT OF THE OUTREACH SECTION: MARCH 2003

After these initial efforts, and nearly six months after the court had begun operations, the official outreach section was established in the registry in March 2003. The section's formation is largely attributable to then registrar of the court, Robin Vincent, who made outreach a priority. At the time, the management committee was not convinced that outreach should be part of the court's core budget, and Vincent had to seek outside funding from the European Union in order to make the unit functional. She also appointed Binta Mansaray, a prominent and capable leader in Sierra Leonean civil society, to lead the outreach section. This appointment and Robin Vincent's commitment were crucial to the section's establishment and success.

The outreach section, which is still active at the time of this writing, defines its mission as "fostering an environment of two-way communication between Sierra Leoneans and the Special Court."[57] The section distinguishes two different levels of interaction within this overall directive. The first is to provide comprehensive factual information about the actions of and basis for the Special Court. Its second stated "core aim" is to "serve as a catalyst for informed and reasoned dialogue about the Special Court and transitional justice."[58] The section emphasizes engaging in dialogue with and receiving feedback from Sierra Leonean communities. This approach indicates that the outreach section has adopted an engagement strategy that aims to do more than simply disseminate information about the court and proactively seeks to establish a dialogue between the court and Sierra Leoneans.

The structure of the outreach section facilitates its goal of developing a dialogue with the different communities of Sierra Leone. Perhaps most notably, the outreach section has been staffed exclusively by Sierra Leoneans, all of whom speak the local language and are familiar with the context and culture.[59] The section is headquartered in Freetown, and at its inception five additional district outreach officers (DOOs) were situated in different districts of the country. Establishing a field presence early on helped the section avoid the common misstep of neglecting areas outside the capital, but the initial number of DOOs was still relatively limited considering that there were twelve districts in Sierra Leone at the time. Since 2003 the number of DOOs has increased to seventeen with an average of two per district, making the section's regional outreach programs the most well-staffed of any international court or tribunal. Throughout the programs' operations, every DOO has been from the particular region and is therefore fluent in the local language,[60] a considerable asset in enabling the DOOs to build relationships of trust with their communities and facilitate the distribution of information in local languages.[61] In order to complement and support their own activities as representatives of the court's outreach section, the DOOs also work with civil society organizations and "community animators."[62] These partnerships allow the DOOs to reach more people within their districts, especially those who would otherwise be difficult to access, as collaboration with respected locals can help foster trust in the court.

The outreach section also works with the court's press and public affairs office. The public affairs office defines its mission as striving "to ensure maximum transparency, so people see that justice is being done."[63] Former registrar Robin Vincent emphasized the distinction between outreach and press and public affairs, pushing for the functions to be carried out by separate offices. The press and public affairs office was intended to be the court's mouthpiece, while the outreach section was meant to objectively disseminate information and foster a dialogue about the court.[64] Established in 2002, before the outreach section had begun its operations, the press and public affairs office coordinates the court's media strategy and provides information to the local and international media.[65] As such, the office's main responsibility is developing an internal media policy to ensure consistency in the messages of the different organs of the court. In addition, the office organizes workshops for journalists, issues press releases, and produces audio and video summaries of trials, which the outreach section then uses in its programming. Other press section activities include coordinating interviews, organizing press conferences, and maintaining the court website.

The press and public affairs section and the outreach section seem to have worked together well, and eventually did develop a strategy to coordinate their activities to address public communication more holistically. However, future outreach efforts should note that the late establishment of the outreach unit delayed the development of this integrated public relations strategy. As mentioned above, the outreach section was not officially established until March

2003—several weeks after the OTP publicly issued the first five arrest warrants. As a result, no plan was in place for the sections to respond to this important and unexpected event at the court. If it had been established as an independent unit within the registry earlier, the outreach section would have had more time to develop a strategy and been better prepared to respond to key developments at the court.

As trial activity at the court decreased, the public affairs and outreach units were consolidated into one section in April 2008.[66] According to the head of the new combined section, this merger has not affected the work of outreach or public affairs. The tasks of the two former units are still divided within the new unit; one designated staff member is in charge of outreach and another is in charge of public affairs.[67]

OUTREACH STRATEGY OF THE SPECIAL COURT: IMPLEMENTING AN ENGAGEMENT MODEL

In order to achieve the goal of fostering a two-way communication process with the affected population, the outreach section has undertaken a wide range of activities. Among other efforts, it has organized public town hall meetings with representatives from the outreach section or different offices of the court (including the prosecutor, the defense, and the registry). The section has also provided radio programs covering the court's activities, including expert interviews and panel discussions, and produced and distributed a variety of materials including video summaries of the trials (along with televisions to screen the videos), printed booklets, leaflets, and posters. In addition, the section has organized visits to the court, conferences, and training-the-trainer programs. All of these activities have been carefully designed to respond to the specific context of Sierra Leone, where the population is largely illiterate and speaks and understands English, Krio, or other local languages.[68] The section's activities target the general population as well as specific groups, including "the military, the police, students at all levels, the judiciary, prison officers, religious leaders, civil society, and national and international NGOs."[69]

Another key element of the outreach section's mandate is facilitating the participation of the court's other organs in outreach activities—in particular, town hall meetings, school meetings, seminars, trainings, and radio panel discussions. Participation by representatives and principals of the prosecution, defense, and registry allows for direct lines of communication between the court and the public, helping to establish a genuine dialogue. The Special

Court does not have public information positions in different sections of the court, such as the OTP or witness support service; instead, all outreach-related activities are organized through the outreach and the press sections. However, although outreach has not been structurally integrated into each organ of the court, it seems that all of the court's organs are willing to participate in outreach activities; as a whole the court has demonstrated its institutional commitment to these efforts. Each organ of the court has demonstrated that it considers outreach activities to be a part of its mandate and prioritizes participation in the activities.[70] For example, all sections of the court report on the outreach activities they conduct as part of their annual reports.[71]

Finally, the court's outreach strategy also incorporated a focus on the legacy of the court.[72] Officials in the court recognized the importance of fulfilling the institution's potential to leave a lasting impact on Sierra Leone. The court created a legacy working group, established in May 2005, to conceive of and implement a range of projects that would contribute to this goal.[73]

Legacy programming has been guided by the themes of promoting rule of law, promoting human rights, developing the local legal profession, and building legal capacity among civil society organizations in Sierra Leone.[74] These themes have considerable overlap with the goals of the outreach section, and legacy programming was seemingly intended in part to be an extension of outreach programming.[75] The two sections have also collaborated on specific initiatives, such as training programs and a project to create a justice-themed radio station. Similarly, the outreach section has labeled some of its programs as "outreach legacy projects," because they explicitly reflect the goals of the legacy working group. For example, town hall meetings and outreach to schoolchildren are also labeled as legacy activities because they are intended to promote the rule of law and accountability.[76] The outreach section's consideration of the long-term impacts of its work, beyond the completion of the trial phase and the Special Court's existence, is a notable and important feature of its strategy. However, the implementation of projects proposed by the legacy working group—and correspondingly the outreach section—has been hindered by a lack of both funding and clarity about the scope and goals of the legacy programs.[77] These obstacles have led to a disparity between the very ambitious promises and high expectations regarding the court's legacy and the actual resources allocated to fulfill these goals.

CHANNELS OF COMMUNICATION

PRINTED MATERIALS

The outreach unit produces posters and printed materials for public distribution in order to fulfill a variety of functions. Some of them emphasize particular concepts for a wide audience;[78] for example, the section produced illustrated posters with text in English that were used as talking points during community meetings. However, according to some field research, the posters were difficult for many people to understand; moreover, they have not been commonly viewed around the country. Instead, they were mainly hung in the offices of NGOs and in universities and colleges in Freetown.[79] In 2004 the outreach section produced an illustrated booklet *Wetin na di Spɛshal Kot?* (The Special Court made simple), intended to explain the creation and mandate of the court to groups with limited educational backgrounds.[80] A second booklet, *Wetin na intanashɔnal umaniterian lɔ?* (International law made simple),[81] was produced in 2006 and aimed to increase knowledge of the basic principles of international humanitarian law, explaining that "even in wartime, soldiers and civilians have rights and obligations."[82] Both of these booklets try to explain these concepts with illustrations by a local artist, accompanied by minimal text.[83] The section also distributes materials generated by other sections of the court.[84]

The section has stated that its printed materials are an "integral" part of the court's outreach efforts and has taken steps accordingly to ensure that a wide range of audiences understand the materials.[85] However, the section has struggled to ensure that the materials were actually distributed to citizens in remote provinces. To meet this challenge, the section carried out some distribution through schools, the DOOs, and civil society partners.[86] The section also did some initial distribution through paramount chiefs,[87] but the chiefs sometimes did not distribute materials if they did not support the court. In addition, the status of and trust in the paramount chiefs varied depending on the community. As a result, the section decided to develop independent networks of distribution instead of relying on existing government structures.[88] While this decision may have been important to maintain the court's neutrality as an independent institution, a slower distribution process may also have resulted.

TOWN HALL MEETINGS

As discussed above, town hall meetings have been a distinguishing feature of the Special Court's outreach approach. Following the initial series of meetings organized by the prosecutor and registrar, the outreach section has continued to hold public meetings throughout the operation of the court. These meetings are usually led by a DOO, often with participation from representatives of the prosecution, defense, and registry. These joint presentations are important for demonstrating the neutrality of the institution and the due process rights of the defense. Presentations are usually ten to twenty minutes long and may include information about international humanitarian law, the court's rules of procedure, and updates on the trials. After the presentations, members of the public are invited to ask questions. In the early stages of the court's operation, these questions focused on the mandate of the court, Sam Hinga Norman's indictment, and whether the court was necessary.[89] After the trials began, the nature and complexity of the questions changed, including inquiries and concerns about specific aspects of the trials, fairness, and sentencing.[90] The evolving nature of the questions indicates a developing relationship between the court and the community and, despite some criticisms, demonstrates that the town hall meetings have effectively communicated some information about the court.

RADIO

Radio has been recognized as a core component of the section's outreach efforts because it is a common means of communication in Sierra Leone, partly due to the low literacy rate and poor infrastructure that limits physical access to many parts of the country.[91] The section considered producing live radio broadcasts of the trials, which raised concerns about witness protection, and redacting recorded testimonies before broadcast was deemed to be too expensive.[92] Instead, the outreach section elected to broadcast ten- to fifteen-minute audio summaries produced by the public affairs section. The summaries are recorded in English and Krio and were initially broadcast weekly in collaboration with eight local radio stations around the country.[93] The outreach staff worked to increase radio coverage and succeeded in reaching two new stations in 2005.[94] The next year, additional radio stations were added through collaboration with radio stations Cotton Tree News and Search for Common Ground.[95] The production of these audio and video summaries of the trials is a notable point of collaboration between the outreach section and the press and public affairs section. The Special Court has had an in-house audio and video production unit since November 2003,[96] giving the court the unique capacity to produce its own audiovisual materials, including radio programs, introductory videos, and summaries of the trials. Other programming has included panel discussions and call-ins from the public.[97]

The outreach section also hoped to increase coverage of the Special Court through an independent radio station. The proposed Radio Justice station would have broadcast the proceedings of the Special Court and also offered programming on broader justice issues. Planners envisioned that, after the Special Court was closed, the station might continue under the management of an editorial board of NGOs.[98] Although the outreach section was unfortunately unable to secure funding for this initiative and the idea for an independent radio station was never realized, the variety and quantity of relevant radio programming on existing stations has increased since 2005. In September 2005 a new monthly program titled *Focus on the Special Court* was broadcast on Radio UNAMSIL, providing a summary of the latest news about the trials and other developments at the court.[99] The outreach section also began broadcasting interviews with experts, joint interviews with the chief prosecutor and principal defense counsel, and panel discussions.[100] In addition, the Special Court has made a notable effort to improve access to timely and accurate information for radio stations around the country through remote communications systems. For example, a phone line has been set up with recorded news releases to which interested radio stations can call and retrieve information in a timely manner without needing access to the Internet. In addition, text messaging is being used to reach radio stations in the northern reaches of the country that have a limited communication infrastructure.[101]

The outreach section's efforts to reach communities through radio have been laudable. However, the section did encounter some problems that future outreach programs should seek to address—particularly, difficulty in reaching the more remote communities in Sierra Leone that lacked radio access. Unfortunately, some of these communities would have benefited most from early information about the court, as they were often in areas in which massive atrocities had taken place or the population had strong views about the conflict and the trials. For example, Kenema is a community that was the center of support for Chief Sam Hinga Norman, one of the defendants in the CDF trial. Unfortunately, Kenema did not have radio access until 2008, five years after the court was established. As a result, this community had little direct access to impartial information about Hinga Norman's trial. The section did constantly seek to expand access to radio broadcasts; however, its efforts might have been more effective targeting communities with a particular need for information. Moreover, even when the broadcasts were available in a region in general, they still failed to reach those people without access to a radio and who could not afford to buy one.[102]

In addition, some challenges for conducting outreach through radio may be difficult to avoid but should be noted nonetheless. For example, the timeliness of the summaries is limited by the time required to produce them, resulting in an inevitable lag between when the events occur and when information about them is broadcast to the public. The Special Court was able to minimize this delay through an in-house production unit, but producing and distributing the programs still take time. The limited frequency of the shows also required advance planning by community members who wished to listen to them. Many complained that they missed the radio programs because they had difficulty figuring out when the program would be broadcast.[103] In the future, efforts should be made to ensure that the schedules of radio programs are made clear. If possible, rebroadcasting shows at different times of day throughout the week would also be helpful.

VIDEO SUMMARIES

Produced by the press and public affairs section, video summaries are another important component of the court's outreach program. They aim to give the vast majority of Sierra Leoneans who cannot attend the trials in person a sense of how the proceedings actually operate.[104] The summaries are produced in English, Krio, and, for the Taylor trial, also in Liberian English.[105] Trial summaries are produced every one to two weeks, with additional summaries for closing arguments and sentencing decisions.[106] Varying in length, the summaries are broadcast on television and are also utilized by district outreach officers in public screenings in remote regions of the country, displaying either a television or a larger screen depending on the size of the audience.[107] In addition to the trial summaries, the public affairs section worked with the ABC station in Freetown to produce a weekly show titled *Eye on Sierra Leone*, which included videos from the public affairs section and interviews with court officials. These shows are also screened by DOOs in the field and act as important complements to the trial summaries. Through the TV show, communities in remote villages can become familiar with the court officials as well as the trials. The screenings are generally well received, but some people have complained about the timing of the events and the inability to see the screen.[108] In particular, the events often take place during the day, and many people are unable to leave work to attend them.

COURT VISITS

One of the benefits of the court's domestic location is that it, at least theoretically, allows Sierra Leoneans to attend the trials and see for themselves what is happening.[109] Although Sierra Leoneans have generally expressed an interest in visiting the court, the number of people actually able to make it to the public gallery has varied.[110] Several factors account for this inconsistent attendance. According to Jessica Lincoln, some people perceived the court's building to be physically inaccessible to visitors because of its intimidating physical structure and high security.[111] Also, the legalese and unfamiliar procedures made the actual proceedings obscure to many Sierra Leoneans. Interest in the trials has also fluctuated depending on whether the events in the courtroom were of particular interest. Finally, despite its domestic location, it was still prohibitively expensive for many Sierra Leoneans to travel to the court. Even for those who lived in Freetown, visiting the court would require taking time off work.[112] Furthermore, the court frequently and unpredictably went into closed sessions, which meant that even getting to the court did not guarantee that a visitor would see a trial. Perhaps for these reasons, the outreach section did not engage in large-scale efforts to bring people to the court, instead opting to focus on bringing the court to the people through the use of radio programs, video summaries, town hall meetings, and printed materials.[113]

EFFORTS TO REACH SPECIFIC GROUPS

In addition to efforts designed to inform the general population, the outreach section understood that targeted outreach activities would be essential to reach specific groups. These initiatives allow for information to be adapted to the particular constituency and are also usually conducted on a smaller scale than the three-hundred- to four-hundred-person gatherings for the general public. More people can ask questions and express their views in such an environment, where other individuals are likely to have similar concerns. The outreach section, together with the press and public affairs section, has specifically designed initiatives to reach three main categories of people: socially disempowered groups (women, victims, children, and the disabled), potentially destabilizing groups (ex-combatants, military, and youth), and law enforcement agencies and civil society leaders (the judiciary, religious leaders, the police, prison officers, and traditional leaders). Specifically targeting socially disempowered groups is important because these individuals are less likely to have access to mass communications and may also have difficulty relating to content in regular communication formats, especially those in written form.[114] Efforts to reach potentially destabilizing groups focused on calming fears about the Special Court and emphasizing the importance of the rule of law. Finally, efforts to reach influential society and justice sector leaders were aimed at making these leaders more effective in advocating for broader justice goals and ensuring that they understood the structure and importance of the Special Court and could share this information with others. Different groups within these broad categories have even more specific needs, which the outreach section tries to address through its programming.

VICTIMS AND SOCIALLY DISEMPOWERED GROUPS

Victims often have specific questions and expectations regarding how the Special Court can or should address their needs. In addition, the outreach section has found that because of their experiences, victims may feel more comfortable talking about the court in the company of other victims instead of in a mixed audience.[115] For victims, the court's limited mandate and inability to provide reparations or social services is a frequent source of frustration and concern,[116] and outreach efforts to victims have focused on clarifying expectations about what exactly the court can and cannot do for them.[117] Between 2004 and 2005 the Special Court organized a series of Victim Commemoration Conferences that culminated in a national conference held in Freetown in March 2005.[118] The aim of the conferences was to bring together representatives from the government, justice, and reform sectors at the village, national, and international levels to discuss the legacy of the court and identify services that victims need as well as key institutions mandated to address those needs. By identifying other sources that should provide victims with support, the conferences were meant to address the concerns of civil society leaders about the court's limited mandate. Delegates at the final Freetown conference developed an action plan focused on initiatives for reparation and rehabilitation for victims, which included efforts to encourage communities and civil society groups to participate in projects for victims, as well as lobbying the government of Sierra Leone to establish a trust fund for victims. Conference participants gave the outreach section positive feedback on its efforts to engage with the victim population, but the majority of participants continued to be concerned about both the court's limited mandate and the indictees who remained at large.[119]

Women were disproportionately targeted during the war, and many suffered gender-based crimes and sexual assault. As a result, the Special Court's work is particularly relevant to women, but they often have a harder time accessing information about it because they are more likely to be illiterate and are often socially and economically disadvantaged. The outreach section specifically encourages the participation of women in all outreach events and has made additional efforts to engage women through targeted training programs.[120] In 2006 the section collaborated with the Sierra Leone Market Women's Association, a community-based organization that works to protect and promote the rights and interests of women, to organize "Transitional Justice and the Special Court" training seminars. These countrywide regional seminars targeted approximately five thousand market women—typically poor, urban-dwelling women who work and trade in local produce markets.[121] Outreach efforts that seek to reach out to women have also complemented the court's broader institutional actions to be sensitive to the impact of its work on women in Sierra Leone. For example, the Office of the Prosecutor conducted consultations with women's groups about forced marriages before filing amendments with the court to add the crime to the indictments.[122] However, despite these specifically tailored efforts, the court has had difficulty reaching rural areas in the eastern part of the country, where many women were victims of sexual violence and continue to suffer the aftermath of these violations. These women have often been rejected from their communities and have had limited access to rehabilitation and justice initiatives. These areas are very difficult to access due to the lack of physical infrastructure, and the women have remained isolated as a result, without opportunities to attend outreach events and learn about commemoration events and efforts to establish a reparations program.[123]

As another disempowered group, children of all ages were particularly vulnerable to abuses during the war; many children were victims of forced recruitment and abduction during the conflict. Specific efforts must be made to provide outreach materials for children, who may not be able to understand information targeted to adults. In this regard, the court arranges for groups of students to visit the court every Wednesday.[124] This program has been in place since 2003, complemented by a robust program of visits by outreach officials and court principals to schools, peaking at a total of 1,322 school visits in 2009,[125] as well as an annual gathering of hundreds of schoolchildren at the court on the Day of the African Child.[126] In addition, the court frequently arranges for high-level officials to visit schools for question-and-answer sessions. Youth can also participate in *Kids Talking to Kids* radio programs, quiz competitions, and debates at schools around the country.[127]

Given the prevalence of forced recruitment and child combatants during the war, children and youth need to be informed of the Special Court's approach to these issues.[128] As child combatants, many children were sexually abused, physically mistreated, and often forced to commit attacks on others; many children thus have the dual status of victim and perpetrator. The Special Court has jurisdiction over crimes committed by minors ages fifteen to eighteen,[129] and many people feared that the court would prosecute reintegrated former child combatants. The first chief prosecutor of the court, David Crane, addressed this issue early on, stating unequivocally at town hall meetings that he was "not interested in prosecuting children" because they could not bear the "greatest responsibility."[130] The court has taken the position that, although many children were combatants, they should be viewed primarily as victims of the conflict. Although this approach might have facilitated engagement between the court and former child combatants, it also generated debates within communities, as many saw these children as perpetrators and believed they should be punished. The court did recognize the need to explain to the population in general its approach to child combatants, and these efforts may have had a positive impact. According to delegates at the National Victims Commemoration Conference, the court has contributed to restoring the dignity of children.[131]

The outreach section has also worked to ensure that disabled people have access to outreach materials. Specifically, key court documents were translated into Braille, and the court has conducted outreach meetings specifically for groups of disabled people.[132]

POTENTIALLY DESTABILIZING GROUPS

Ex-combatants constitute an unstable portion of society and may have particular concerns about what impact the Special Court will have on them. In order to prevent destabilization and open a dialogue about what happened during the war, ex-combatants need accurate information about the court as well as a space in which to voice their opinions. Outreach to ex-combatants initially focused on the relationship between the Special Court and the TRC, which was a specific source of concern for many.[133] Later outreach events focused on increasing awareness about international humanitarian laws and the limits of acceptable behavior in times of war.[134]

The outreach section identified university-level youths as another potentially destabilizing group because of their history of involvement in past violent protests.[135] On the other hand, proponents of outreach also hoped that these youths might act as a stabilizing force by working toward the development of rule of law in Sierra Leone. To reach this demographic, the outreach section established innovative Accountability Now Clubs (ANCs) at eight universities in Sierra Leone.[136] The main goal of these clubs was to promote understanding of the Special Court among university-level students and their peers and to engage students in discussions of broader justice issues, such as transitional justice and human rights. In addition to the content of their activities, the clubs are also structurally designed to demonstrate the efficient and transparent management of organizations,[137] and they are intended to be permanent institutions at the universities. While the short-term goal of the ANCs is to promote participation in the Special Court process, their long-term goal is to promote student involvement in broader legal and social transformations.[138] Participants in the ANCs are chosen selectively, generally from respected members of their communities. The clubs then implement independent outreach events that primarily target university- and secondary-level students.[139]

The ANCs became independent in 2005 but still received instruction and training from the outreach section. Unfortunately, many ANC members expected that their organizations would receive funding from the court, expressing disappointment when this proved not to be the case. Future initiatives should clearly inform participants of the financial relationship between the court and the project. In addition, the impact of the ANCs has been somewhat limited because of the low literacy level among the population and the concentration of universities in Freetown. However, given these unavoidable constraints, the ANCs have still been highly "successful in generating significant interest and debate on judicial issues, both domestic and international."[140]

Finally, the outreach section also targeted the Sierra Leone military and civil defense forces. Outreach to these groups is important because of the history of military coups in Sierra Leone and the military's concerns about potential indictments before the Special Court. Outreach meetings typically took place at military barracks, focusing on discussions of the Special Court's mandate, as well as general rule-of-law concepts.[141]

INFLUENTIAL SOCIAL AND JUSTICE SECTOR LEADERS

The outreach section, through targeted training sessions, has specifically engaged influential social figures such as teachers, people who enforce local customary law, and religious and other traditional leaders.[142] The section has also conducted targeted trainings for the justice sector—including police and law enforcement agencies, prison officers, and the national judiciary—in conjunction with its legacy program. However, the court's relationship with the Sierra Leone judiciary has been rocky, despite its recognition that this sector constitutes a key audience for outreach efforts. Although expectations for the positive impact that a hybrid institution would have on the national judiciary were initially high, a cooperative relationship between the court and the national bar association has failed to emerge. In the early stages of its operations, the court deliberately kept itself isolated from the national judiciary for political reasons.[143] The court has since attempted to mend its relationship with the judiciary, which has proven difficult. For example, when the Special Court invited national judges to court proceedings or trainings for Special Court staff, the judges declined. The court also held training sessions on the Special Court and on international criminal law and humanitarian law; however, they were generally not well received. Some criticized the trainings as condescending and felt that the international issues covered were of little relevance to the national bar. Some bitterness toward the Special Court also exists within the national judiciary, as the latter has witnessed resources being poured into the court while the national judicial system suffers from a severe lack of funding.[144] In 2005 Human Rights Watch advised the court to try to hold monthly discussions with national justice system judges and staff. This initiative was not implemented, and in 2006 the Sierra Leone Bar Association explicitly disavowed any relationship with the court.[145]

WORKING WITH CIVIL SOCIETY

The outreach section's relationship with civil society is one of the program's strongest achievements. Early outreach activities conducted by No Peace without Justice created a solid foundation for collaboration with civil society organizations through the Special Court Working Group. Once the official outreach section was established, the court continued to consult with civil society groups.[146] Starting in July 2002 the outreach section began facilitating regular interactions between the registrar and civil society through monthly meetings of the Special Court Interaction Forum.[147] At these events, the registrar meets with a variety of Sierra Leonean activists to discuss their concerns and expectations regarding the court's work;[148] there have been some indications that the registrar and outreach section are indeed responsive to the ideas and issues raised in these discussions. For example, the section initiated outreach efforts that targeted religious leaders in Sierra Leone after that suggestion was made in one of the forums.[149] According to Human Rights Watch, these dialogues have been quite successful, and many civil society leaders who were previously skeptical of the court are now more supportive; in one meeting, a representative of civil society stated, "We believe that the SCSL is helping change the views and perceptions of justice in Sierra Leone society in a good, healthy way."[150]

The outreach section has also worked directly with civil society groups to organize trainings through the Partnership Project. The section claims that its greatest success has been its collaboration through this project with partner organizations across the country, allowing outreach efforts to reach a wider audience. However, according to Lincoln, some members of civil society have been less positive about the relationship. Common complaints are the lack of two-way communication and that outreach often ignores civil society's recommendations. In response, the outreach section explains that they do not ignore the recommendations; they simply do not have the resources to implement the suggestions. As a result, however, although the majority of organizations remain willing to work with the court, some are disillusioned with the court or skeptical of its overall outreach strategy.[151]

A NEW CHALLENGE: OUTREACH FOR THE CHARLES TAYLOR TRIAL

The arrest of Charles Taylor was a crucial moment for the Special Court. After it had appeared for years that Taylor would escape his indictment, his arrest and trial demonstrated that even a former head of state could be held to account for his actions. Among the people in Sierra Leone, Taylor was perceived to be one of the leaders most responsible for the war in the region. Especially considering that of the three others widely considered most responsible for the atrocities, Foday Sankoh and Sam Bockerie died before their trials and Johnny Paul Koroma remains at large, Taylor's trial was particularly important.[152]

The Taylor trial began when the court's other trials were winding down. The timing allowed the outreach section the opportunity to develop a robust and focused approach specifically for Taylor's prosecution. However, the decision to transfer the proceedings to The Hague generated many of the obstacles that the hybrid structure of the Special Court had been explicitly designed to avoid. Perhaps most importantly, the distance of the tribunal presented obvious barriers to accessibility for citizens and local media. In addition, the regional relevance of the trial required that efforts be made to reach Liberia as well as Sierra Leone. As Taylor still has a significant amount of support in

Liberia, in the absence of accurate information from the Special Court, Taylor's proponents could still have manipulated coverage of the trial.[153] Many members of civil society criticized the decision to relocate the trial as based more on politics than on immediate security issues, voicing concern that the transfer defeated the purpose of the hybrid structure.[154] The UN Security Council noted the importance of maintaining accessibility, and the resolution authorizing the transfer included an explicit request for the court to ensure that the trial proceedings were "accessible to the people of the sub region."[155]

In order to facilitate this accessibility, the Special Court tried to overcome the challenges through a variety of initiatives, including establishment of a suboffice in The Hague in May 2007. A collaboration between the outreach section and the press and public affairs section, the suboffice has one permanent staff member and two national interns whom the European Union funds to serve two six-month terms.[156] This small staff worked to facilitate coverage of the Taylor trial within Sierra Leone, and to assist with visits and viewing of the trial by civil society, traditional leaders, foreign judiciaries, diplomats, journalists, and university students.[157] Facilitating journalists' reporting on the proceedings was another key component of the outreach strategy for the Taylor trial. As the proceedings were located in The Hague, it was generally prohibitively expensive for local reporters to travel to the court.[158] The BBC World Service Trust program sent two reporters from the region to The Hague and helped them produce reports throughout the trial, which were disseminated to radio stations in Sierra Leone and Liberia. However, considering the importance of the trial and the high level of local interest in the proceedings, this number is still very limited. As a consequence, most of the local media in Sierra Leone and Liberia had to rely on the information provided by the Hague suboffice for reporting. A blog hosted by the Open Society Justice Initiative (OSJI) called *Charles Taylor Trial* has also been a useful source of information.[159] This popular site was updated daily during the trial, with summaries of the proceedings written by a Sierra Leonean attorney. The summaries were usually relatively neutral, providing comprehensive digests of the trial in an easy-to-understand format. In addition, the blog served as an interactive forum with many comments on court updates that represented a variety of opinions. OSJI also facilitated interviews with high-level court officials based on readers' questions.[160]

Efforts to ensure that reporters have access to accurate information are important, but they cannot fully compensate for the lack of firsthand reporting on and experience of the trial. The reliance on secondhand sources may also make it difficult to sustain local interest in the trial, as the international media and the court may not necessarily highlight the aspects of the trial of greatest concern to people in the subregion.[161] To this end, the Special Court has made efforts to facilitate visits to the court by journalists and civil society leaders from Sierra Leone and Liberia. In 2009, for example, the court helped to enable visits by sixty-two civil society and traditional leaders whom civil society organizations chose to observe the trial.[162]

Video streaming of the trial was meant to be a core component of the outreach strategy for the Taylor trial.[163] The outreach section planned to set up public centers in Freetown and Monrovia to allow citizens to watch the trial. However, the bandwidth available in these public centers could not handle live video streaming, and the initiative was cancelled after several failed attempts to show the proceedings.[164] Video streaming was set up in one of the trial chambers of the Special Court; however, few people actually travelled there to watch the trial. On a more positive note, though, the DOOs continued to show video summaries of the trial in their districts in Sierra Leone.[165]

Access to video streaming is even more difficult in Liberia, where viewing the proceedings was almost impossible. Although live streaming was theoretically available on the Special Court's website, finding Internet access with enough bandwidth to support it was difficult. The outreach center in Monrovia screened a few of the trial summaries produced by the Special Court, but, according to Thierry Cruvellier, they were not well received by the audience, which accused court officials of "doctoring" the clips.[166] As a result, the office stopped showing the summaries in Liberia. The town hall meetings that accompanied the screenings were also cancelled, mainly due to lack of funding.[167] The outreach section continued to coordinate with civil society groups in Liberia, but these efforts, although important, have had limited success. In 2006 an association of civil society groups established the Outreach Secretariat of Liberia as an organization independent from the court. The outreach section worked with these civil society groups to assist them in organizing radio panels and screenings of the Taylor trial video summaries.[168] However, Cruvellier reports that the civil society groups in the secretariat were often not informed of opportunities to view the trial online through the court's website, and even those who were aware of the streaming had difficulty accessing it. As a result, most people in Liberia followed the Taylor trial through the radio programs produced by the court and by the journalists supported by the BBC World Service Trust.[169]

The Special Court also utilized Twitter beginning in 2010 to provide real-time updates about what was happening at the court and during the Taylor trial, as well as access to photos, documents, and video summaries.[170] The information on Twitter was updated frequently, with multiple posts daily about the trial schedule, key witnesses, outreach, and public events. The information was much more up to date than on the official Special Court website, which does not provide access to many of the key documents on Twitter, such as a summary of the Charles Taylor judgment or link to a video summary of the judgment. Although the use of Twitter is helpful in making the information more accessible, it could be improved it if were merged with the official website, or if the official website directed visitors to Twitter.

All these factors and methods came into play as Charles Taylor became the first head of state since the Nuremberg trials convicted for war crimes and crimes against humanity, a flash point for national and international news. The verdict was broadcast on national television and radio stations in the region, which provided broad coverage of the outcome without any specific efforts by the outreach section to encourage it. The public gallery at the trial chamber seated eighty people and was filled with "NGO representatives, civil society groups, including victims of the conflict from Sierra Leone and Liberia, former SCSL staff, diplomats, journalists, and members of Taylor's own family."[171] In Freetown, civil society and victims' groups were specifically invited to watch a live broadcast of the proceedings on the premises of the court, and the outreach program reported that over twelve hundred Sierra Leoneans attended.[172] The audience included most of the paramount chiefs, who, ideally, could share information about the judgment with their communities. In addition, the court posted links to a live video feed of the judgment on Twitter and the official website, and a video and audio summary of the judgment and the sentencing judgment and a short summary of the twenty-five-hundred-page judgment were also shared on Twitter. After the judgment was released, the prosecutor traveled to Sierra Leone and Liberia to conduct town hall meetings about the conviction and sentencing judgment in areas that had been most affected by the conflict.[173] The main questions of the Sierra Leonean public seemed to be whether Taylor was found guilty and how long his sentence would be.[174] Other issues of interest included where Taylor would serve his sentence, how the appeals process would function and how long it would take, and what was being done for the victims.[175]

LESSONS LEARNED

The outreach section of the SCSL has defined success as "meeting its aim of stimulating discussion and debate about the court as opposed to simply arguing on its behalf."[176] This standard demonstrates the court's commitment to a participatory conception of outreach that goes beyond the basic distribution of information. With regard to evaluating its success in meeting this ideal, the outreach section has acknowledged the need for some kind of monitoring, but believes it is too late to implement such a program.[177] However, the outreach section did commission a study by an external consultant on public perceptions of the court. The findings were extremely favorable to the court and the outreach section. For example, 91 percent of those surveyed stated that the Special Court has contributed to peacebuilding in Sierra Leone.[178] While the report's close association with the court raises some doubts about its findings' independence and credibility,[179] independent studies have also found that the court's outreach efforts achieved a high level of awareness about the Special Court's existence and mandate.[180] Considering the resources and staffing allocated to the outreach unit, this level of understanding is a significant achievement. On the other hand, the depth of knowledge and degree of genuine participation in the process is less clear. According to a survey by the BBC World Service Trust, of those who were aware of the court, only 7 percent reported that they knew a lot about the proceedings, while 93 percent said they knew a little.[181] Jessica Lincoln's field research also supports the conclusion that significant gaps existed in the popular understanding.[182]

Despite these limitations, when compared to other international courts, the outreach efforts at the Special Court have been exemplary. The highest officials of the Special Court prioritized outreach from the outset, setting a strong standard of participation for the rest of the institution. Qualified personnel worked to understand the specific audiences within Sierra Leone and design strategies to address their concerns. The Special Court was able to work effectively with civil society but did not rely on civil society to conduct outreach work on the court's behalf. Given its level of success, several important lessons can be gleaned from the experience of the Special Court; they may also apply to the International Criminal Court and to future transitional justice processes.[183]

THE IMPORTANCE OF STARTING EARLY

Early efforts by the NPWJ helped create a network of civil society organizations (CSOs) for the outreach section to work with, and these efforts were also important in addressing the difference between the mandates of the Special Court and the TRC. Initial outreach exercises conducted by the prosecutor and registrar, although not without fault, were crucial demonstrations of the court principals' commitment to engaging with and informing the public. The early introduction of the court's mandate also allowed for the development of a basic level of awareness and understanding about the court in advance of what would turn out to be controversial indictment decisions.

ENGAGING COURT PRINCIPALS TO DEVELOP AN INSTITUTIONAL OUTREACH APPROACH

The principals of the Special Court, including the registrar, prosecutor, principal defender, and president, have been consistently willing to participate in outreach activities. Furthermore, these activities have been included in the annual reports of the court's various sections as components of their specific mandates. Support for outreach may have been particularly strong within the Special Court as a result of the institution's emphasis on the legacy that it would leave in Sierra Leone, the need to justify the limits of its mandate and the cost of the trials, and the pressure to respond to previous criticisms of purely international forms of justice. However, for any outreach program to succeed, the court or the institution's most senior officials need to recognize the importance of engaging with the populations they are meant to serve and to be willing to personally participate in outreach activities.

THE NEED TO EXPLAIN UNIQUE FEATURES OF THE COURT

The Special Court is a unique institution, differing in important ways from previously existing justice institutions in Sierra Leone. Many aspects of the court's operation and existence needed to be explained to the public, including questions about why the cost of the court was so high and why scarce resources were being devoted to the Special Court instead of to social services such as roads, schools, and hospitals. Other concerns arose about the need for a defense office within the court and the rights of the defendant generally. Such questions are asked of most international courts, raising issues about the fundamental legitimacy of the process. Although outreach programs should be prepared to respond to these questions accurately, they will be limited by external events as well as events in the proceedings at the court.

One particularly difficult issue that the outreach section of the Special Court confronted was a selective prosecutorial strategy. The court's limited mandate was hailed as an approach that would ensure accountability for those with the greatest responsibility without dragging on for years or costing too much money. However, while a selective prosecution approach can advance the goals of sustaining peace and restoring the rule of law, choosing the appropriate selection criteria and justifying such decisions to the public is challenging.[184] At the Special Court, for example, it was determined that extending the court's jurisdiction back to the beginning of the conflict in 1991 would overburden the court, delay the trials, and contradict the principle of quick and efficient justice. Several alternative start dates for the mandate were considered, and the secretary-general ultimately recommended November 30, 1996, the date of the Abidjan Peace Agreement. This date was chosen because it was thought to establish the period within which all parties and armed groups committed the most serious crimes.[185] However, this date still excluded several years in which atrocities were committed, the majority of which occurred in rural areas. Many Sierra Leoneans perceive this start date as arbitrary, supporting a perception that the court is biased toward those in Freetown and international interests—and especially skewed toward prosecuting those people who took the UN peacekeepers hostage.[186] According to Alison Smith, the court might have gained more support and relevance with the Sierra Leonean public if it had extended its jurisdiction to include crimes committed since 1991.[187]

The court's mandate was further limited to "those bearing the greatest responsibility."[188] The first chief prosecutor of the Special Court, David Crane, interpreted "greatest responsibility" as meaning that the accused would have to be in high-ranking or command positions. The process through which indictments were determined is not widely known but did involve consultations to discern who was considered most responsible in the public discourse. When asked who was most responsible, the public's responses were relatively consistent.[189] However, many in Sierra Leone were surprised and offended by the indictment of Chief Sam Hinga Norman, the former leader of the CDF, who was serving as the minister of the interior for the Kabbah government at the time of his arrest.[190] The public in Sierra Leone generally considers Hinga Norman and the CDF to be the restorers of peace and democracy in Sierra Leone and that they should not be put on trial. For many, it was unclear why Hinga Norman was indicted when other high-profile people in the government were not,[191] and for some, the perceived arbitrariness of the indictments led to a perception that the court was politically motivated. More generally, it created a perception that the chief prosecutor did not fully understand the conflict and was indicting the wrong people.[192] The Hinga Norman indictment and trial presented the most challenging issue for the outreach section. Many people refused to listen to the reasons that he was indicted, and members of the public also criticized the outreach section for failing to explain the indictment process sufficiently.[193]

In addition, human rights organizations criticized the limited total number of indictments as an overly narrow interpretation of the court's mandate that excludes many notorious mid-level commanders.[194] These exclusions have also been difficult to justify to the public and were a substantial source of questioning and debate in early outreach sessions. Some think that the mid-level commanders who have testified—and have often received substantial witness protection benefits—bear responsibility and should be put on trial. Many victims believe that the people who hurt them directly should be brought to justice.[195] In addition, many people criticized the idea that such a small mandate would be adequate to ensure the peace, reasoning that it would not be enough to deter low-level commanders from future crimes. After voicing these concerns in outreach meetings, many members of the public became frustrated when the mandate remained unchanged. Even though the outreach section explained that it had no power to change the court's mandate and structure, many people felt that the outreach personnel were not really listening or did not have the power to adequately represent the public's views to the court.[196]

This lesson has particular applicability for the International Criminal Court (ICC), which also pursues a strategy of selective prosecution. Transparency surrounding the indictment process and awareness of how indictments are likely to be perceived are crucial to promoting the ICC's credibility. Although public perceptions should not dictate the indictment process, the ICC needs to prepare for the public's reaction and develop a strategy to respond to the criticisms that its decisions may provoke.

REALISTIC EXPECTATIONS FOR IMPACT

The high expectations for the impact that the court and specifically its outreach efforts would have on promoting the rule of law and a positive legacy in general were unrealistic, especially considering the limited funding afforded to these activities. However, from the perspective of most Sierra Leoneans, the court is a very wealthy institution.[197] The high cost of the Special Court has been an issue of public contention, with many criticizing the use of funds and suggesting that they would be better spent on other sectors in Sierra Leone, such as the domestic judicial system or development programs.[198] Others had high expectations regarding what the court might contribute toward socioeconomic development and were disappointed by the court's limited mandate. Unlike the ICC, the Special Court does not have the financial support to set up a compensation fund for victims.[199] The outreach section has attempted to counter these expectations by emphasizing that the court will not provide direct assistance but will instead contribute to the country by supporting the development of a lasting peace.

FUNDING

Despite the recognized importance and success of outreach within the Special Court, the outreach section was allocated only limited funding within the court's official budget. When the section was first established, the registrar had to solicit outside funds from the European Union to support it, as outreach was not considered one of the court's primary functions by those in charge of its funding. This mismatch between the level of conceptual and financial commitment to outreach has been typical of all tribunals, but the Special Court's unique voluntary contribution system has added complexity to the funding process. Despite early rhetoric endorsing the importance of ensuring the court's legacy, there was pressure from some members of the management committee to focus on the court's "primary" mandate.[200] The issue of funding has thus revealed a critical disparity between officials' stated commitment to the goals of the engagement model and the material support that they are willing to provide in order to implement outreach programs capable of fulfilling those goals. Although in principle the engagement model elevates public participation to a core mandate of a court, a corresponding level of funding for the programs to achieve this mandate does not always follow. Furthermore, limiting a program because of a lack of funding is often difficult to justify to the public, which perceives the tribunal to be a wealthy institution.

Despite these financial difficulties, the court was able to implement a robust outreach program and demonstrate the importance of funding outreach as an essential part of an international court's operations. The experience of the Special Court informed the ICC's decision to include some funding for outreach as part of the institution's core budget. This inclusion reflects the growing recognition of the importance of outreach, which is, at least in part, a result of the Special Court's efforts. However, a significant disparity still typically exists between the rhetoric regarding the importance of outreach and the level of funds channeled to the programs tasked with carrying it out.

LIMITS OF OUTREACH WITH REGARD TO DEVELOPING LOCAL OWNERSHIP

The hybrid structure and domestic location of the Special Court were intended to avoid the perception that the initiative was purely international. However, when the court was first established, it did not include any Sierra Leoneans in high-level positions, and only a few were appointed as judges. This staffing imbalance created the impression that the court was simply "an international tribunal incorporating nationals,"[201] rather than a genuinely hybrid institution. Additionally, differences between the Special Court and national jurisprudence with regard to punishment and standards of detention may have reinforced public perceptions that the court was essentially an international institution.[202] According to Jessica Lincoln, many people in Sierra Leone perceive the court to be an institution of "white man's law." This term is often used by people who are not aware of many details about the court but simply think of it as an international, not Sierra Leonean, court.[203]

Furthermore, many of the factors that affect public perceptions and may impede a sense of local ownership of the court are beyond the outreach section's control. The selection of who to indict, the progress of the trials, the limited mandate of the court, delays in the proceedings, and procedural issues all affect how the Special Court is perceived, often regardless of outreach attempts to explain the process or rationale behind these decisions. This reality can present a tension between the goals of the outreach section and the means available to achieve them.

CONCLUSION

The outreach section of the Special Court for Sierra Leone has set a strong example for implementing the approach that, in technical terms, has been called the engagement model of outreach. The court's hybrid structure brought with it great expectations; it was intended to be less expensive than previous tribunals, yet have a greater impact. As part of this latter goal, high-level court officials recognized that effective outreach would be an essential part of ensuring the Special Court's positive effects on the development of rule of law in Sierra Leone. However, the experience of the outreach section also highlights the difficulties in achieving the goals of an engagement model, and the limitations of common programmatic activities—such as town hall meetings, court visits, and radio broadcasts—in achieving these goals on their own. Although these methods can facilitate genuine dialogue, their ability to garner public engagement with and support for an institution are inevitably constrained by the course of that institution's actual operations.

The ultimate impact of the Special Court's outreach efforts is unknown, but its outreach section is commonly viewed as a model for other international courts. In this regard, the court's implementation of early outreach efforts, its adoption of an engagement model of outreach, its engagement with civil society, and the participation of court principals should be especially emphasized as positive initiatives worthy of emulation. However, the problems posed by the program's funding and its struggle to explain the court's choice of indictments should also be heeded as lessons for future outreach programs. Also, when evaluating the success of the court's outreach as a whole, one must acknowledge that outreach efforts surrounding the Taylor trial proved to be disappointing, to some extent mitigating the positive record developed from the successful outreach work around the first three trials.

In addition, only limited discussion has taken place on the role of outreach and the importance of continuing the work of the outreach section in relation to planned legacy projects. Legacy projects include a peace museum, a national witness protection program, an archives development program, and a professional development program.[204] Outreach for these efforts was intended to be part of the strategic plan to implement the engagement model; if proper funding can be secured for these activities, the Special Court has the potential to set an important precedent regarding the enduring importance of outreach even once the trials have been completed. Outreach will also have a role once the planned Residual Special Court, which will address issues related to the Special Court that arise in the future, is established. The Residual Special Court may deal with the possible trial of fugitive Johnny Paul Koroma, contempt proceedings, consideration of any requests for review of judgments, protection of witnesses, supervision of the enforcement of sentences, assistance to national authorities, and management of the archives.[205] It will be important for Sierra Leoneans to be informed of these potential developments, as well as the basic fact of the Residual Special Court's existence.

The Special Court's outreach section has set a new standard for outreach, having the potential to continue to develop innovative approaches with regard to outreach even after the court is closed. In the future, hopefully the bar set by the Special Court's outreach will not be considered extraordinary but rather viewed as standard procedure for a transitional justice measure.

NOTES

I would like to thank Clara Ramírez-Barat for her insightful comments on several drafts of this chapter and help throughout the writing process. I am also very appreciative of Anthony Triolo's comments and feedback. The views expressed in this chapter are my own and do not necessarily reflect the views of the International Center for Transitional Justice.

1 For a discussion of these contrasting models of outreach, the transparency and engagement models, see Victor Peskin, "Courting Rwanda: The Promises and Pitfalls of the ICTR Outreach Program," *Journal of International Criminal Justice* 3, no. 4 (September 2005): 950–61. See also Clara Ramírez-Barat, *Making an Impact: Guidelines on Designing and Implementing Outreach Programs for Transitional Justice* (New York: International Center for Transitional Justice, 2011).

2 Sierra Leone Truth and Reconciliation Commission (TRC), *Witness to Truth: Report of the Sierra Leone Truth and Reconciliation Commission*, vol. 2 (Accra: Graphic Packaging, 2004), 3–22.

3 "President of Sierra Leone Wins Re-election by a Wide Margin," *New York Times*, May 20, 2002, http://www.nytimes.com/2002/05/20/world/president-of-sierra-leone-wins-re-election-by-a-wide-margin.html?ref=ahmadtejankabbah.

4 TRC, *Witness to Truth*, 27.

5 Ibid., 40–47.

6 Ibid., 11.

7 Ibid., 44.

8 Ibid., 11, 76–80.

9 Ibid., 11, 59–62.

10 Ibid., 11–15.

11 Ibid., 96.

12 Ibid., 43.

13 Ibid., 15 (citing the estimate of the Ministry of Social Welfare, Gender, and Children Affairs).

14 Amnesty International, *Sierra Leone: Childhood—A Casualty of Conflict*, August 30, 2000, http://www.amnesty.org/en/library/info/AFR51/069/2000/en.

15 TRC, *Witness to Truth*, 16.

16 Ibid., 36.

17 UN Development Programme (UNDP), *Sierra Leone Human Development Report 2007: Empowering Local Government for Sustainable Development and Poverty Reduction*, 2007, http://www.3adi.org/tl_files/3ADIDocuments/Country%20information/Sierra%20Leone/Human_development_report_SierraLeone_2007_en.pdf, 6.

18 UN Development Programme (UNDP), *Sierra Leone: As Seen through Economic and Social Indicators*, 2009, http://www.sl.undp.org/1_doc/indicators_sl.pdf, 2–3. In 2009 Sierra

Leone was ranked 180 out of 182 countries; UNDP, *Human Development Report 2009: Overcoming Barriers—Human Mobility and Development*, 2009, http://hdr.undp.org/en/reports/global/hdr2009/chapters/, 146.

19 UNICEF, "At a Glance: Sierra Leone—Statistics," accessed June 5, 2011, http://www.unicef.org/infobycountry/sierraleone_statistics.html.

20 UNDP, *Sierra Leone: As Seen*, 4.

21 Peace Agreement between the Government of Sierra Leone and the Revolutionary United Front of Sierra Leone (Lomé Peace Agreement), July 7, 1999, art. XXVI.

22 UN Security Council, *Letter Dated 9 August 2000 from the Permanent Representative of Sierra Leone to the United Nations Addressed to the President of the Security Council (Annex: Letter from the President of Sierra Leone)*, UN Doc. S/2000/786, August 10, 2000, http://www.undemocracy.com/S-2000-786.pdf.

23 UN Secretary-General, *Seventh Report of the Secretary-General on the United Nations Observer Mission in Sierra Leone*, UN Doc. S/1999/836, July 30, 1999, para. 7. The United Nations was not an official party to the agreement, but signed it as a moral guarantor that both parties would implement the agreement with integrity and in good faith. See Lomé Peace Agreement, art. XXXIV.

24 See UN Security Council, Resolution 1315, UN Doc. S/RES/1315 (2000), August 14, 2000; UN Security Council, *Letter Dated 6 March 2002 from the Secretary-General Addressed to the President of the Security Council*, UN Doc. S/2002/246, March 8, 2002.

25 UN Security Council, *Letter Dated 6 March 2002 from the Secretary-General Addressed to the President of the Security Council—Annex: Report of the Planning Mission on the Establishment of the Special Court for Sierra Leone*, UN Doc. S/2002/246, March 8, 2002, para. 5.

26 Beth Dougherty, "Right-Sizing International Criminal Justice: The Hybrid Experiment at the Special Court for Sierra Leone," *International Affairs* 80, no. 2 (March 2004): 319. The secretariat advocated for a mandate to prosecute "those most responsible" and called for the court to be funded through assessed contributions from member states. See UN Secretary-General, *Report of the Secretary-General on the Establishment of a Special Court for Sierra Leone*, UN Doc. S/2000/915, October 4, 2000, paras. 29–31, 71.

27 *Agreement between the United Nations and the Government of Sierra Leone on the Establishment of a Special Court for Sierra Leone*, January 16, 2002, http://www.sc-sl.org/LinkClick.aspx?fileticket=CLk1rMQtCHg%3D&tabid=176 (hereafter, Special Court Agreement).

28 Sigal Horovitz, "Transitional Criminal Justice in Sierra Leone," in *Transitional Justice in the Twenty-First Century: Beyond Truth versus Justice*, ed. Naomi Roht-Arriaza and Javier Mariezcurrena (Cambridge: Cambridge University Press, 2006), 49.

29 Tom Perriello and Marieke Wierda, "The Special Court for Sierra Leone under Scrutiny" (Prosecutions Case Study Series, International Center for Transitional Justice, March 2006), 13–14.

30 Special Court Agreement, arts. 2–4.

31 Ibid., art. 1; see also UN Security Council, *Letter Dated 12 January 2001 from the Secretary-General Addressed to the President of the Security Council*, UN Doc. S/2001/40, January 12, 2001, para. 12: "three years, which in my view is the minimum time required for the investigation, prosecution, and trial of a very limited number of accused."

32 UN Security Council, *Letter from the President of Sierra Leone.*

33 See Geoffrey Robertson (president of the Special Court), Foreword to Special Court for Sierra Leone, *First Annual Report of the President of the Special Court for Sierra Leone: For the Period 2 December 2002–1 December 2003* (Freetown: Special Court for Sierra Leone, 2003), 3; Stephen Rapp, "The Compact Model in International Criminal Justice: The Special Court for Sierra Leone," *Drake Law Review* 57, no. 1 (Fall 2008): 11–49; Thierry Cruvellier, "From the Taylor Trial to a Lasting Legacy: Putting the Special Court Model to the Test" (Prosecutions Case Studies Series, International Center for Transitional Justice and Sierra Leone Court Monitoring Program, 2009), 4.

34 Special Court Agreement, arts. 6–7: "The management committee shall be composed of important contributors to the Special Court" and "assist . . . in obtaining adequate funding, and provide advice and policy direction on all non-judicial aspects of the operation of the Court." The management committee comprises Canada, Lesotho, the Netherlands, Nigeria, Sierra Leone, the United Kingdom, the United States, and the sections of the UN Secretariat; see Special Court for Sierra Leone, *First Annual Report*, Annex V.

35 See Rapp, "Compact Model," 28; "Taylor Trial 'May Move to Hague,'" *BBC News*, March 30, 2006, http://news.bbc.co.uk/2/hi/africa/4860976.stm.

36 Special Court for Sierra Leone, Judgment, *Prosecutor v. Charles Taylor* (SCSL-03-01-T), Trial Chamber II, May 18, 2012.

37 Special Court for Sierra Leone, Sentencing Judgment, *Prosecutor v. Charles Taylor* (SCSL-03-01-T), Trial Chamber II, May 30, 2012.

38 For a discussion of the desirability of giving outreach a statutory basis, see Patrick Kuebart, "Engaging with the People: Outreach at the Special Court for Sierra Leone," *Journal of International Law of Peace and Armed Conflict* 19, no. 3 (2006): 236.

39 See UN Secretary-General, *Report of the Secretary General on the Establishment of a Special Court*, para. 7, highlighting the need to explain why the court will not have a death penalty and why the court will treat child combatants as victims first; UN Security Council, *Letter Dated 6 March 2002—Annex: Report of the Planning Mission*, para. 11: "A dynamic strategy of dissemination of information and education should be developed by the Special Court for the general public. This outreach campaign would explain the nature of Special Court, its territorial, temporal, and personal scope of jurisdiction and the relationship between the Special Court and the Truth and Reconciliation Commission."

40 The NPWJ is an international nonprofit organization that works for the protection and promotion of human rights, democracy, the rule of law, and international justice. See http://www.npwj.org/.

41 No Peace without Justice, "Sierra Leone Program," accessed June 11, 2011, http://www.npwj.org/ICC/Sierra-Leone-Program.html.

42 The SCWG was established in 2001, emerging from the Freetown Conference on Accountability Mechanisms for Violations of International Humanitarian Law in Sierra Leone. See Jessica Lincoln, *Transitional Justice, Peace, and Accountability: Outreach and the Role of International Courts after Conflict* (New York: Routledge, 2011), 87n3.

43 Lincoln, *Transitional Justice*, 87–88. There were initially thirty-nine training seminars with an estimated total of six hundred participants.

44 No Peace without Justice, "Sierra Leone Program."

45 See PRIDE, "Ex-Combatant Views of the Truth and Reconciliation Commission and the Special Court in Sierra Leone" (in partnership with the International Center for Transitional Justice, Freetown, September 12, 2002).

46 Perriello and Wierda, "Special Court for Sierra Leone under Scrutiny," 35.

47 Lincoln, *Transitional Justice*, 89–90.

48 For a personal account of the outreach meetings, see David Crane, "Dancing with the Devil: Prosecuting West Africa's Warlords: Building Initial Prosecutorial Strategy for an International Tribunal after Third-World Armed Conflicts," *Case Western Reserve Journal of International Law* 37, no. 1 (2005): 6: "In town hall meetings throughout Sierra Leone, I listened to citizens from all walks of life tell me what happened. I began to feel, taste, touch, smell, and see what took place. In turn, the people of Sierra Leone got to see their prosecutor and to understand my strong belief in being completely independent from outside influence."

49 Mohamed Suma, executive director of the Center for Accountability and Rule of Law, interview with author, February 11, 2010.

50 Special Court for Sierra Leone, "Prosecutor Visits Makeni," news release, October 16, 2002, http://www.sc-sl.org/LinkClick.aspx?fileticket=JuyIvRNNhQA%3d&tabid=115.

51 Perriello and Wierda, "Special Court for Sierra Leone under Scrutiny," 37; Lincoln, *Transitional Justice*, 90–91.

52 Vincent Nmehielle and Charles Chernor Jalloh, "The Legacy of the Special Court for Sierra Leone," *Fletcher Forum of World Affairs* 30, no. 2 (Summer 2006): 108.

53 Lansana Gberie, "Briefing: The Special Court of Sierra Leone," *African Affairs* 102, no. 409 (October 2003): 647; see also Rachel Kerr and Jessica Lincoln, "The Special Court for Sierra Leone: Outreach, Legacy, and Impact" (Final Report, War Crimes Research Group, Department of War Studies, Kings College, London, February 9, 2008), 21.

54 Lincoln, *Transitional Justice*, 80; International Crisis Group (ICG), "The Special Court for Sierra Leone: Promises and Pitfalls of a 'New Model'" (Africa Briefing no. 16, Freetown/Brussels, August 4, 2003), 14–15.

55 Lincoln, *Transitional Justice*, 90–91.

56 According to the International Crisis Group, in a poll conducted in November 2002 and January 2003 by the NGO Campaign for Good Governance, 67 percent of the population had heard of the Special Court (ICG, "Special Court for Sierra Leone," 17).

57 Special Court for Sierra Leone, *First Annual Report*, 26; Special Court for Sierra Leone, *Special Court Outreach Report 2003–2005*, 2007, 12.

58 Special Court for Sierra Leone, *Special Court Outreach Report 2003–2005*, 12.

59 Perriello and Wierda, "Special Court for Sierra Leone under Scrutiny," 36.

60 In Sierra Leone, most members of the educated class understand English, and the majority of the population speaks Krio. Two other widely used languages in the provinces are Mende and Temne; see Lincoln, *Transitional Justice*, 7.

61 Ibid., 101.

62 According to an interview by Lincoln, community animators "complement the work of the outreach officers. They live in the headquarter towns of the chiefdoms. Do not know, but are kept up to date by Outreach officers with literature, etc. Go to villages, also monitor but do not penetrate. Process has worked well, it has helped prepare people's minds before or after" (Lincoln, *Transitional Justice*, 162n38).

63 Special Court for Sierra Leone, *Third Annual Report of the President of the Special Court for Sierra Leone: January 2005–January 2006* (Freetown: Special Court for Sierra Leone, 2006), 38.

64 See also Robin Vincent, *An Administrative Practices Manual for Internationally Assisted Criminal Justice Institutions* (New York: International Center for Transitional Justice, 2007), 86.

65 Special Court for Sierra Leone, *First Annual Report*, 27.

66 Special Court for Sierra Leone, *Fifth Annual Report of the President of the Special Court for Sierra Leone: June 2007 to May 2008* (Freetown: Special Court for Sierra Leone, 2008), 53.

67 Peter Andersen, head of the public affairs and outreach section, interview with author, February 1, 2010. In 2010 the unit was staffed by Peter Andersen, the chief of outreach and public affairs; Patrick Fatoma, the outreach coordinator; several outreach officers and interns; a video producer; a radio producer; a translator; a staffer tasked with logging the trial; and seventeen outreach field officers.

68 See Special Court for Sierra Leone, *Special Court Outreach Report 2003–2005*, 15; UNICEF, "At a Glance."

69 Special Court for Sierra Leone, "Outreach and Public Affairs," accessed April 2010, http://www.sc-sl.org/ABOUT/CourtOrganization/TheRegistry/OutreachandPublicAffairs/tabid/83/Default.aspx.

70 There are limits to how far this commitment should extend; the primary responsibility of high-level officials is not to act as spokespersons for the court. See Varda Hussain, "Sustaining Judicial Rescues: The Role of Outreach and Capacity-Building Efforts in War Crimes Tribunals," *Virginia Journal of International Law* 45, no. 2 (Winter 2005), quoting Chief Prosecutor Crane in 2004: "Am I here to prosecute or to talk to people?" (578).

71 See, for example, Special Court for Sierra Leone, *Third Annual Report*, 20–21.

72 Special Court for Sierra Leone, *Special Court Outreach Report* 2003–2005, 19–20.

73 UN Secretary-General, *Identical Letters Dated 26 May 2005 from the Secretary-General Addressed to the President of the General Assembly and the President of the Security Council: Annex: Special Court for Sierra Leone Completion Strategy* (18 May 2005), UN Doc. A/59/816–S/2005/350, May 27, 2005.

74 Nmehielle and Jalloh, "Legacy of the Special Court for Sierra Leone," 13; Special Court for Sierra Leone, *Special Court Outreach Report* 2003–2005, 24.

75 Special Court for Sierra Leone, *Special Court Outreach Report* 2003–2005, 24.

76 Ibid.

77 Lincoln, *Transitional Justice*, 123–26.

78 Special Court for Sierra Leone, *Special Court Outreach Report* 2003–2005, 16.

79 Lincoln, *Transitional Justice*, 136.

80 Special Court for Sierra Leone, *Special Court Outreach Report* 2003–2005, 16; Patrick Kuebart, "Engaging with the People," 238.

81 Initially, one thousand copies were produced, with an anticipated one hundred thousand copies to eventually be distributed. Special Court for Sierra Leone, "Special Court Launches International Humanitarian Law Booklet," news release, February 17, 2006, http://www.sc-sl.org/LinkClick.aspx?fileticket=j8EQMSdGq8w%3D&tabid=111.

82 Ibid.

83 Kuebart, "Engaging with the People," 238.

84 Special Court for Sierra Leone, *Special Court Outreach Report* 2003–2005, 16.

85 Ibid. Printed materials were presumably used because they are a common and inexpensive way to communicate information.

86 Special Court for Sierra Leone, "Special Court Launches International Humanitarian Law Booklet." According to Kuebart, reading materials are sought after in Sierra Leone, and their free distribution is uncommon. These booklets are seen as a valuable resource ("Engaging with the People," 238).

87 Paramount chiefs are leaders in a traditional system of chiefdoms that was altered and codified under British rule; in modern Sierra Leone, the population of each district outside of Freetown elects one paramount chief to head the district's chiefdoms and hold a seat as a nonpartisan Member of Parliament ("Background on Sierra Leone," *Advocates for Human Rights*, accessed November 2012, http://www.theadvocatesforhumanrights.org/Background_on_Sierra_Leone.html).

88 Hussain, "Sustaining Judicial Rescues," 576.

89 Special Court for Sierra Leone, *Special Court Outreach Report* 2003–2005, 15; Kuebart, "Engaging with the People," 237.

90 See, for example, a question asked at an outreach event with the Sierra Leone Amputee Football Association: "People are saying that General Issa Sesay is a man who has done

bad things, but they say in another way, he brought peace. So he did a bad thing first, but then he brought peace. So there are two scales here. How will the Court balance?" (*War Don Don*, documentary, directed by Rebecca Richman Cohen [Naked Edge Films and Racing Horse Productions, USA, 2010]).

91 Special Court for Sierra Leone, *Special Court Outreach Report 2003–2005*, 16.

92 Horovitz, "Transitional Criminal Justice," 58.

93 UNDP, *Sierra Leone Human Development Report 2007*, 8; Human Rights Watch, *Justice in Motion: The Trial Phase of the Special Court for Sierra Leone*, 2005, http://www.hrw.org/sites/default/files/reports/sierraleone1105wcover.pdf, 31.

94 Special Court for Sierra Leone, *Third Annual Report*, 38.

95 Special Court for Sierra Leone, *Fourth Annual Report of the President of the Special Court for Sierra Leone: January 2006 to May 2007* (Freetown: Special Court for Sierra Leone, 2007), 54.

96 Special Court for Sierra Leone, *First Annual Report*, 12.

97 Special Court for Sierra Leone, *Special Court Outreach Report 2003–2005*, 16.

98 Special Court for Sierra Leone, *Second Annual Report of the President of the Special Court for Sierra Leone: 1 January 2004–17 January 2005* (Freetown: Special Court for Sierra Leone, 2005), 35.

99 See the chapter by Wanda Hall in this volume on the limits of this kind of traditional radio outreach approach and the potential to use radio as a tool for interactive communication. The Special Court did make use of some call-in radio programs, but the focus of its radio outreach strategy seems to be dissemination.

100 Special Court for Sierra Leone, *Third Annual Report*, 38.

101 Special Court for Sierra Leone, *Fifth Annual Report*, 53.

102 Lincoln, *Transitional Justice*, 107–8: "Kailuhun, Bo, and Pujehun [Provinces] in the south and east had the lowest listenership of radio and the lowest levels of literacy overall."

103 Ibid., 108.

104 Special Court of Sierra Leone, *Special Court Outreach Report 2003–2005*, 16.

105 The outreach section considered translating all of the video summaries into additional local languages, but decided against it because it would have meant a greater time lag before they would be ready (Andersen, interview with author, February 1, 2010).

106 The video summaries are also available for download on the Special Court's website, http://www.sc-sl.org/PRESSROOM/VideoSummaries/tabid/122/Default.aspx.

107 The screenings occur frequently; for example, in 2009, 535 video screenings were conducted in the provinces, 225 in Freetown and surrounding communities, and 329 in Liberia; see Special Court for Sierra Leone, *Seventh Annual Report of the President of the Special Court for Sierra Leone: June 2009 to May 2010* (Freetown: Special Court for Sierra Leone, 2010), 43.

108 Kerr and Lincoln, "Special Court for Sierra Leone," 19.

109 See Rapp, "Compact Model," 21.

110 Lincoln, *Transitional Justice*, 70, 99.

111 Ibid., 99; see also Horovitz, "Transitional Criminal Justice," describing "the intimidating number of armed security guards and barbed wire surrounding the Court's site, which from the outside resembles a high security prison" (57).

112 Lincoln, *Transitional Justice*, 70, 99.

113 See an explanation from an outreach officer in a session in Tombodu: "Most of you can't visit the Court, so we have the outreach section. That is, it sends people into communities. For those that can't come to Freetown to see the Court, we bring the Court to you" (from *War Don Don*, dir. Cohen). This approach contrasts with the strategy of the outreach program of the Extraordinary Chambers in the Courts of Cambodia, which chartered buses for thousands of people throughout that nation to attend the trials or simply visit the court when the trials were not in session.

114 Special Court for Sierra Leone, *Special Court Outreach Report* 2003–2005, 17.

115 Ibid., 18.

116 Sara Kendall and Michelle Staggs, "From Mandate to Legacy: The Special Court for Sierra Leone as a Model for 'Hybrid Justice'" (War Crimes Study Center, University of California, Berkeley, April 2005), 33; Lincoln, *Transitional Justice*.

117 Special Court for Sierra Leone, *Special Court Outreach Report* 2003–2005, 18.

118 These conferences were organized in conjunction with the Inter-Religious Council, the Forum for African Women Educationalists, and the International Center for Transitional Justice.

119 Kendall and Staggs, "From Mandate to Legacy," 33.

120 The outreach unit's attention to women's needs may be partly attributable to the leadership of Registrar Binta Mansaray, a woman with extensive experience advocating for victims of sexual violence; see Special Court for Sierra Leone, "Pressroom—Court Principals," accessed February 2010, http://www.sc-sl.org/PRESSROOM/CourtPrincipals/tabid/98/Default.aspx. See also Kuebart, "Engaging with the People," 239.

121 Special Court of Sierra Leone, *Fourth Annual Report*, 38; Peacebuilding Portal, "Sierra Leone Market Women Association," accessed April 5, 2012, http://www.peacebuildingportal.org/index.asp?pgid=9&org=3677.

122 Perriello and Wierda, "Special Court for Sierra Leone under Scrutiny," 27. Some gender advocates still criticized the decision to add the charge of forced marriage. They feared it would contribute to the stigmatization of victims and, furthermore, could already be addressed under the charges of enslavement and rape. The OTP argued that the decision was taken after consultation with women's groups and was made in an effort to be sensitive to the particularities of the cultural context.

123 See Amnesty International, *Sierra Leone: Getting Reparations Right for Survivors of Sexual Violence*, AFR 51/005/2007, November 1, 2007, http://www.amnesty.org/en/library/asset/

AFR51/005/2007/en/4cda5d8e-d370-11dd-a329-2f46302a8cc6/afr510052007en.pdf; Lincoln, *Transitional Justice*, 100.

124 Lincoln, *Transitional Justice*, 99. These visits were also well-received by court officials.

125 Special Court for Sierra Leone, *Sixth Annual Report of the President of the Special Court for Sierra Leone: June 2008 to May 2009* (Freetown: Special Court for Sierra Leone, 2009), 41.

126 Special Court for Sierra Leone, *Eighth Annual Report of the President of the Special Court for Sierra Leone: June 2010 to May 2011* (Freetown: Special Court for Sierra Leone, 2011), 44.

127 Special Court for Sierra Leone, *Second Annual Report*, 34.

128 Special Court for Sierra Leone, *Special Court Outreach Report 2003–2005*, 18.

129 Statute of the Special Court for Sierra Leone, January 16, 2002, art. 7.

130 Special Court for Sierra Leone, "Special Court Prosecutor Says He Will Not Prosecute Children," news release, November 2, 2002, http://www.sc-sl.org/PRESSROOM/OTPPressReleases/tabid/196/Default.aspx: "The children of Sierra Leone have suffered enough both as victims and perpetrators. I am not interested in prosecuting children. I want to prosecute the people who forced thousands of people to commit unspeakable crimes."

131 Perriello and Wierda, "Special Court for Sierra Leone under Scrutiny," 38.

132 Special Court for Sierra Leone, *Special Court Outreach Report 2003–2005*, 18.

133 See PRIDE, "Ex-Combatant Views," and the previous discussion in this chapter of early outreach efforts by NGOs and issues arising from the simultaneous operation of the TRC.

134 Kuebart, "Engaging with the People," 239.

135 Special Court for Sierra Leone, *Special Court Outreach Report 2003–2005*, 20.

136 Special Court for Sierra Leone, *Second Annual Report*, 34.

137 Special Court for Sierra Leone, *Third Annual Report*, 38.

138 Horovitz, "Transitional Criminal Justice," 59.

139 Mohamed Suma, "Accountability Now Clubs (ANCs)" (presentation at "State of the Field: Children and Transitional Justice," International Center for Transitional Justice, New York, March 23–24, 2011).

140 Lincoln, *Transitional Justice*, 94.

141 Special Court for Sierra Leone, *Special Court Outreach Report 2003–2005*, 20.

142 Ibid., 21.

143 Perriello and Wierda, "Special Court for Sierra Leone under Scrutiny," 27; Cruvellier, "From the Taylor Trial to a Lasting Legacy," quoting Binta Mansaray: "At the beginning, there was a deliberate effort to keep away from the national judiciary, for political reasons, in order to remain independent from it. There was a time when the national judiciary felt alienated from the process. That was a time when the court should have made contact" (32).

144 Lincoln, *Transitional Justice*, 101–2.

145 See Yada Williams, "Welcome Address by Yada Williams (Acting President of the Sierra Leone Bar Association)," *Awareness Times*, July 16, 2007, http://news.sl/drwebsite/exec/view.cgi?archive=4&num=6014. At the address, the bar association president stated, "It is wrong and misleading for the two gentlemen [the interim registrar and head of the legacy program at the Special Court] to say the Bar has being [*sic*] working with the Special Court to train lawyers and judges. The Bar Association has not done any business with the Special Court for the last twelve months."

146 Andersen, interview with author, February 1, 2010. Also, many of the outreach section staff were recruited from civil society organizations.

147 The Special Court Interaction Forum was established when the outreach section was still located in the Office of the Prosecutor.

148 Human Rights Watch, *Bringing Justice: The Special Court for Sierra Leone: Accomplishments, Shortcomings, and Needed Support* (New York: Human Rights Watch, 2004), 33n146.

149 Human Rights Watch, *Justice in Motion*, 30.

150 Human Rights Watch, *Bringing Justice*, 37.

151 Lincoln, *Transitional Justice*, 112–13.

152 Gberie, "Briefing," 646.

153 Cruvellier, "From the Taylor Trial to a Lasting Legacy," 19. The public's perception of the International Criminal Tribunal for the former Yugoslavia (ICTY) trials was plagued by manipulation and false information, eventually prompting creation of the ICTY's outreach program.

154 Cruvellier, "From the Taylor Trial to a Lasting Legacy," 14; see also Padraig McAuliffe, "Transitional Justice in Transit: Why Transferring a Special Court for Sierra Leone Trial to The Hague Defeats the Purposes of Hybrid Tribunals," *Netherlands International Law Review* 55, no. 3 (2008): 365–93.

155 UN Security Council Resolution 1688, UN Doc. S/Res/1688 (2006), June 16, 2006, para. 6.

156 Special Court for Sierra Leone, *Sixth Annual Report*, 42.

157 Ibid.

158 See Rapp, "Compact Model," 21.

159 At www.charlestaylortrial.org. See Cruvellier, "From the Taylor Trial to a Lasting Legacy," 18; Suma, interview with author.

160 See, for example, "Charles Taylor's Defense Counsel, Courtenay Griffiths, Answers Your Questions," *Charles Taylor Trial*, March 19, 2010, http://www.charlestaylortrial.org/2010/03/19/charles-taylors-defense-counsel-courtenay-griffiths-answers-your-questions-part-ii/.

161 Cruvellier, "From the Taylor Trial to a Lasting Legacy," 15–16. According to a senior Sierra Leonean who has worked with the OTP, "News-wise, we are suffering a lot with Taylor being tried in the Hague. We only have secondhand information" (ibid., 16).

162 Special Court for Sierra Leone, *Sixth Annual Report*, 42.

163 See UN Security Council Resolution 1688, para. 6, explicitly mentioning that efforts should include "video-link."

164 Andersen, interview with author, February 1, 2010.

165 Cruvellier, "From the Taylor Trial to a Lasting Legacy," 15; Andersen, interview with author, February 1, 2010.

166 Cruvellier, "From the Taylor Trial to a Lasting Legacy," 17.

167 Ibid.

168 The idea for the secretariat emerged from an experience-sharing seminar with civil society groups from Liberia and Sierra Leone; see Special Court for Sierra Leone, "Outreach and Public Affairs," accessed April 2010, http://www.sc-sl.org/ABOUT/CourtOrganization/TheRegistry/OutreachandPublicAffairs/tabid/83/Default.aspx.

169 Cruvellier, "From the Taylor Trial to a Lasting Legacy," 15–18.

170 Solomon Moriba, outreach and press officer in The Hague, interview with author, July 24, 2012. See http://twitter.com/#!/SpecialCourt.

171 Taegin Stevenson, "Charles Taylor Judgment: From the Public Gallery," *Charles Taylor Trial*, April 30, 2012, http://www.charlestaylortrial.org/2012/04/30/charles-taylor-judgment-from-the-public-gallery/.

172 Special Court for Sierra Leone, "Prosecutor Hollis Applauds the People of Sierra Leone Following Charles Taylor's Conviction," press release, May 14, 2012, http://www.sc-sl.org/LinkClick.aspx?fileticket=80DmKZPdPwQ%3d&tabid=196; Moriba, interview with author, July 24, 2012.

173 See Special Court for Sierra Leone, "Pros. Brenda Hollis held town hall meetings throughout Northern Province last week to discuss the Taylor sentencing judgment," Twitter posting, June 11, 2012; Special Court for Sierra Leone, "Prosecutor Hollis Applauds the People."

174 Moriba, interview with author, July 24, 2012; Ibrahim Tommy, director of the Center for Accountability and Rule of Law, interview with author, July 17, 2012.

175 Moriba, interview with author, July 24, 2012.

176 Special Court for Sierra Leone, *Special Court Outreach Report 2003–2005*, 13.

177 Lincoln, *Transitional Justice*, 111. In 2007 the outreach unit commissioned a survey that produced results that were very favorable to the court and the outreach unit. This survey has been widely criticized as poorly designed and potentially biased. See Perriello and Wierda, "Special Court for Sierra Leone under Scrutiny," 41 (see n. 26).

178 Memunatu Baby Pratt, "Nation-wide Survey Report on Public Perceptions of the Special Court for Sierra Leone," Outreach Section of the Special Court for Sierra Leone, March 2007, 23.

179 Cruvellier, "From the Taylor Trial to a Lasting Legacy," 30.

180 BBC World Service Trust and Search for Common Ground, "Building a Better Tomorrow: A Survey of Knowledge and Attitudes toward Transitional Justice in Sierra Leone," August 2008, 20.

181 Ibid., 19–20.

182 Lincoln, *Transitional Justice*, 111.

183 See also Vincent, *Administrative Practices Manual*, 91–92.

184 Horovitz, "Transitional Criminal Justice," 48.

185 *Report of the Secretary General on the Establishment of a Special Court*, paras. 26–27. Other start dates considered included May 25, 1997, the date of the AFRC coup d'état, and January 6, 1999, when the AFRC/RUF invaded Freetown (Dougherty, "Right-Sizing International Criminal Justice," 321).

186 Lincoln, *Transitional Justice*, 58–59.

187 Alison Smith, "Sierra Leone: Law, Policy, and Practice," in *Internationalized Criminal Courts and Tribunals: Sierra Leone, East Timor, Kosovo, and Cambodia*, ed. Cesare Romano, Andre Nollkaemper, and Jann K. Kleffner (Oxford: Oxford University Press, 2004), 131.

188 The secretary-general had suggested that jurisdiction should be changed to "persons most responsible," which could include mid-level commanders responsible for particularly severe or massive crimes; see *Report of the Secretary-General on the Establishment of a Special Court*, para. 30.

189 Perriello and Wierda, "Special Court for Sierra Leone under Scrutiny," 19, 27.

190 See Special Court for Sierra Leone, *First Annual Report*, 14; Lincoln, *Transitional Justice*, 68–69, 81.

191 Lincoln, *Transitional Justice*, 81.

192 See ICG, "Special Court for Sierra Leone," 13–17. This perception was compounded by the prosecutor's emphasis on the role of diamonds and external actors in the conflict. For example: "This is the most black-and-white, good-versus-evil situation that I have ever seen in 30 years of public service. They didn't start this conflict for ethnic, political, cultural or religious reasons—not that this excuses anything.... The bottom line is, it boils down to the diamonds in eastern Sierra Leone." Eric Pape, "A New Breed of Tribunal" (interview with David Crane), *Newsweek*, March 4, 2003, http://www.newsweek.com/2003/03/03/a-new-breed-of-tribunal.html.

193 Lincoln, *Transitional Justice*, 97, 118.

194 Human Rights Watch, *Bringing Justice*, 5.

195 See Horovitz, "Transitional Criminal Justice," 48; Lincoln, *Transitional Justice*, 50.

196 Lincoln, *Transitional Justice*, 95.

197 Ibid., 119.

198 Cruvellier, "From the Taylor Trial to a Lasting Legacy," 23; Lincoln, *Transitional Justice*, 99.

199 Lincoln, *Transitional Justice*, 42.

200 Human Rights Watch, *Justice in Motion*, 38; Perriello and Wierda, "Special Court for Sierra Leone under Scrutiny," 39.

201 Cruvellier, "From the Taylor Trial to a Lasting Legacy," 31.

202 Horovitz, "Transitional Criminal Justice," 60, citing Peter Penfold, "Will Justice Help Peace in Sierra Leone?" *The Guardian*, October 20, 2002, http://www.guardian.co.uk/world/2002/oct/20/sierraleone.theworldtodayessays.

203 Lincoln, *Transitional Justice*, 57.

204 See Special Court for Sierra Leone, "Legacy," accessed September 2012, http://www.sc-sl.org/LEGACY/tabid/224/Default.aspx.

205 Open Society Justice Initiative, *Legacy: Completing the Work of the Special Court for Sierra Leone*, 2011, http://www.opensocietyfoundations.org/reports/legacy-completing-work-special-court-sierra-leone, 7.

CHAPTER 2

Making Justice Visible: Bosnia and Herzegovina's Domestic War Crimes Trials Outreach

Stephanie A. Barbour

In Bosnia and Herzegovina (BiH), criminal prosecution was and remains the most significant state-sponsored transitional justice initiative employed to redress the serious violations of human rights that occurred during the 1992–95 war in its territory.[1] Efforts to hold accountable the perpetrators of war crimes, crimes against humanity, and genocide began before the end of the conflict and continue to this day. In fact, three models of criminal justice—international, hybrid, and local—have addressed the legacy of war crimes in BiH. Since the International Criminal Tribunal for the former Yugoslavia (ICTY) was asked to wrap up its work,[2] an increasing emphasis has been placed on the importance of the countries of the region dealing with the war crimes caseload themselves,[3] not least because it was felt that local efforts could have a more direct impact on the recovery of BiH—and its neighboring states—from the conflict.

In this chapter I examine the outreach program of the domestic War Crime Chamber within the court and the Prosecutor's Office of BiH—as a central part of the efforts that have been made to ensure that domestic war crimes trials have their intended impact on society—and analyze the extent of its success or failure. After a brief section that offers general background on the establishment and general function of the domestic criminal justice institutions, I then look at the outreach work of the Court of BiH and the BiH Prosecutor's Office, the two state-level criminal justice institutions established in 2000 and given jurisdiction over the most serious forms of crime, including war crimes, throughout the territory of BiH.[4] Then I address the functioning of outreach programs and their core activities, providing a close examination of efforts to reinvigorate outreach following aborted early initiatives. I consider the challenges of conducting outreach for war crimes trials taking place before the cantonal and district courts in BiH, and then I discuss the differing needs of audiences and target groups in relation to war crimes processing, as well as the role of external actors in supporting justice outreach. Finally, I reflect on the core challenges of politicization and passivity and offer a prognosis for building a sense of ownership over BiH's efforts to combat impunity in the future.

BACKGROUND

WAR CRIMES PROCESSING IN BIH

The ICTY is vested with primacy over war crimes cases in the former Yugoslavia from 1991 onward. However, its jurisdiction is also concurrent, meaning that the countries in the region—primarily BiH, Croatia, Serbia, Montenegro, Kosovo, and Macedonia—may process those cases over which the ICTY declines to exercise jurisdiction or refers to a national prosecution authority. As a result of this arrangement, many low- to mid-level perpetrators have been dealt with in the courts of the region rather than by the ICTY, as the latter has mainly focused on the top echelons of political and military leadership. In 1996 a mechanism known as the "Rules of the Road" procedure was established in order to allow the ICTY to review prosecutions undertaken by national authorities, thereby providing coordination among the domestic prosecution initiatives and lowering the risk of arbitrary or politically motivated arrests.[5] Later on, however, it became evident that BiH—the territory within which a large majority of the crimes had taken place—faced severe problems in domestic war crimes processing. Naturally, these problems were partly due to the consequences of the conflict itself. The domestic courts and prosecutors' offices were underresourced and nonspecialized in war crimes matters and struggled to deal with the caseload of present-day crimes in addition to past war crimes. Moreover, the legal and institutional framework applicable to war crimes processing was—and remains—complex. Owing to the postwar structure of the BiH state, no fewer than sixteen courts/prosecutors' offices were capable of exercising jurisdiction over war crimes cases.

The Dayton Peace Agreement divided BiH into two territorial "entities"—the Federation of BiH, with 51 percent of the land area, and the Republika Srpska (RS), with 49 percent—and the internationally administered area of Brčko District. The Federation of BiH's criminal jurisdiction is divided territorially among ten cantonal courts with appeals to the Federation Supreme Court, while the RS has five district courts with appeals to the RS Supreme Court. Brčko District Basic Court and its appellate section also have jurisdiction over war crimes committed in the area. The high degree of fragmentation in BiH's criminal justice system resulted in numerous problems for war crimes processing, among them a high risk that crimes were reported to authorities that did *not* have territorial competence over the offenses in question.[6] This could—and did—easily occur when victims fled the site of a war crime and only reported what had happened when they reached friendly territory. By the early 2000s, there was also a considerable feeling that war crimes prosecutions before BiH's domestic courts were susceptible to selectivity on political and ethnic grounds.[7]

The situation described above was neither conducive to the ICTY having sufficient confidence to transfer cases back to BiH courts nor to assuring the public that justice would be served in domestic war crimes proceedings. As a direct result, in 2003 the ICTY requested that a war crimes chamber be established in BiH.[8] The creation of the Court of BiH and the BiH Prosecutor's Office in 2000 was part of a package of sweeping rule of law reforms driven largely by the international community, which has been a strong presence in BiH since the end of the conflict. Accordingly, Section I for War Crimes was established within the Court of BiH, and the Special Department for War Crimes was established within the BiH Prosecutor's Office in 2004.[9]

The Court of BiH and the BiH Prosecutor's Office were devised to operate as hybrid institutions comprising international and national personnel. They are, however, fully based on domestic law and are permanent institutions in the BiH criminal justice system.[10] Notwithstanding the primacy of the ICTY over war crimes cases, the Court of BiH and the BiH Prosecutor's Office are responsible for investigating, prosecuting, and adjudicating war crimes cases within the territory of BiH—and for reviewing and referring cases to the local-level justice system it does not plan to pursue.[11] Cantonal and district courts and prosecutors' offices around BiH retain limited competencies to handle war crimes cases (discussed later). Although not within the scope of this chapter, the court and the Prosecutor's Office also exercise jurisdiction over other serious crimes, including organized crime, terrorism, and human trafficking.

PERCEPTIONS OF WAR CRIMES TRIALS IN BIH

When the first war crimes proceedings began at the Court of BiH and the BiH Prosecutor's Office in March 2005, it was understood as the beginning of a serious effort to investigate, prosecute, and adjudicate the large backlog of war crimes cases at the national level so as to speed up the justice process. By mid-2012 the ICTY had concluded proceedings against 126 accused persons in approximately 80 cases in the seventeen years since its establishment.[12] Section I of the Court of BiH and the Special Department for War Crimes of the BiH Prosecutor's Office, which became fully functional on March 9, 2005, concluded an impressive 79 cases against 108 accused in that relatively short space of time—with a further 68 cases ongoing at the end of May 2012.[13] The role that local-level courts in BiH have played is perhaps less well known.

Between 2004 and 2012, for example, the courts of the two entities within BiH and Brčko District completed a total of 105 cases concerning 178 accused, all while continuing to process "ordinary" crime.[14] Yet in comparison to the magnitude of the crimes committed,[15] the justice dispensed is demonstrably meager: of an estimated 8,000 perpetrators, only some 412 have been prosecuted in a trial that has reached a final verdict.[16] Considering that a number of these processed cases ended in acquittal, light sentencing, or early release of those who did face justice, that there has been marked dissatisfaction among the affected populations is not surprising.[17] A lack of efforts to explain to the constituencies of each of these judicial institutions how the process of criminal accountability works in the whole territory, its achievements, and its constraints has compounded a feeling—particularly acute among victims—that justice is selective, weak, or even biased.[18] At the same time, the appetite for criminal justice remains high in BiH,[19] prompting the need to ensure that the public is well informed about war crimes processing and can access avenues of communication with the Court of BiH, BiH Prosecutor's Office, and cantonal and district authorities dealing with war crimes cases. Even the best endeavors to inform and engage key audiences have been limited in their ability to offset disappointment. However, outreach measures can help to set limits on towering expectations and establish more realistic ones, based on an informed understanding of the legal and practical obstacles to ending impunity.

Outreach was the solution that the ICTY devised to make its work more visible and thus combat the risk that negative public perceptions would prevent the tribunal from holding perpetrators accountable, deterring future atrocities, and establishing a historical record of the crimes. Arguably, the Court of BiH and the BiH Prosecutor's Office have even more compelling grounds to embrace outreach. Since they are permanent domestic institutions with jurisdiction over all forms of serious crime, establishing their legitimacy is paramount not only for dealing with war crimes but for ensuring the public's trust in the criminal justice system as a whole.[20] War crimes processing has unfolded amid the complex process of judicial reform in BiH, which included vetting the judiciary, reorganizing the entire criminal justice system, and establishing state-level institutions.[21] Thus, the judiciary faces the task of building trust in fledgling institutions while taking over full responsibility for dealing with the legacy of war crimes. Moreover, BiH has yet to emerge from the post-conflict political maelstrom plagued by continued division between leaders of the three main ethnonationalist groups: Bosnian Serbs, Croats, and Muslims (Bosniaks). In that landscape, the sensitive topics of judicial reform and war crimes processing are ripe targets for manipulation to serve political ends. As the Court of BiH and the BiH Prosecutor's Office are both symbols of a unitary state that is not universally supported in the country, and they are entrusted with handling sensitive state affairs (processing war crimes and organized crime), these institutions are frequently the target of negative propaganda.[22] This situation heightens the need for robust efforts to strengthen the reputation of the Court of BiH and the BiH Prosecutor's Office, as well as the local courts, in the eyes of the public and to create a sense of ownership over domestic war crimes processing.

ESTABLISHING A PUBLIC INFORMATION AND OUTREACH APPARATUS IN THE COURT OF BIH AND THE BIH PROSECUTOR'S OFFICE

Owing to the fierce criticism that the ICTY faced for the lack of controlled messages about its work in the region, the need for outreach was well understood from the inception of the Court of BiH and the BiH Prosecutor's Office. The ICTY developed public information and outreach apparatuses in the region in 1997, having recognized that its work faced a severe risk of being undermined by a misinformation campaign underway in the countries of the former Yugoslavia.[23] By 2005, therefore, it was axiomatic that the hybrid institution established in BiH to share the burden of war crimes processing would be constituted in a similar fashion as the ICTY—including in-house departments for criminal defense, witness support, and outreach.

Unlike "the Hague Tribunal," as it is known in the region, the Court of BiH and the BiH Prosecutor's Office were not established at arm's length from their constituencies. The physical proximity of the court and the Prosecutor's Office, as well as the domestic legal nature of the institutions, gave rise to hope that they would not face the negative perceptions that the ICTY had suffered. Nonetheless, three considerations highlighted a degree of risk that the institutions would not necessarily garner natural support. First, the Court of BiH and the BiH Prosecutor's Office both represent part of the delicate process of statebuilding taking place in BiH; as such, they were not automatically assured of being viewed as legitimate institutions. Second, by virtue of the powers of the BiH Prosecutor's Office to indict persons accused of involvement in present-day corruption, organized crime, and other serious economic crimes, the institution was sure to generate enemies once it began to tackle the country's key criminal structures. Third, the hybrid nature of the state institutions also became a matter of controversy, with opponents of the Court of BiH and the BiH Prosecutor's Office voicing concerns that domestic justice institutions were under the control of the "international community," given the presence of foreign judges and prosecutors. In such a climate, ensuring that the institutions were equipped with means of conveying to the public messages about their legitimacy, professionalism, and impartiality was of the utmost importance.

ESTABLISHMENT OF THE PUBLIC INFORMATION AND OUTREACH UNITS

The court and the Prosecutor's Office are two distinct institutions under BiH law, although they are located in the same building in the Sarajevo suburbs. Thus, the task of outreach is performed by separate offices attached to each of the respective institutions. The Public Information and Outreach Section (PIOS) was established under the wing of the court's Registry. This office, initially headed by a former ICTY spokesperson,[24] began operating in 2005. PIOS was, in fact, one of the first units to become fully functional, organizing the opening ceremony of the court in March 2005. In the Prosecutor's Office, the Public Relations Department was created and has also operated since the early days of the institution. The tasks of public information and outreach are treated as complementary and are married into a single program of activities in both the Court of BiH and the BiH Prosecutor's Office. Even though combining these tasks in a single program differs from the practice at the ICTY and other international tribunals, the creation of a full-time, professional, and dedicated staff for such functions is still quite significant, as it is an exception rather than the rule in BiH.[25]

In contrast to the hybrid nature of the Court of BiH and the BiH Prosecutor's Office overall, outreach functions are managed and carried out entirely by national personnel. This appears less by design than as a result of the fact that the international presence in the Court of BiH and the BiH Prosecutor's Office was originally envisaged as including only judges, prosecutors, a registrar, advisors to defense counsel, and a small legal support contingent for those officials. Nonetheless, placing public information and outreach in the hands of nationals who speak the country's official languages and understand the political and cultural context in which the outreach programs operate is believed to benefit the task of reaching the institution's constituencies.

In considering the significance of the divide between the court and the Prosecutor's Office in performing outreach activities, it is important to note that the distinction goes beyond having separate offices for the two legally distinct institutions. First, the court and the Prosecutor's Office may wish to address differing messages to the public on the same issue—for instance, on a particular case.[26] Second, they owe different duties of transparency to the public; the court must uphold the right to a public trial, while the Prosecutor's Office is required to protect the integrity of its investigations until the correct moment in the legal process to release certain information. Third and most important, while both institutions must be prepared to weather political attacks and send a message that they work on behalf of all citizens equally to uphold the rule of law, the purpose of public information and outreach fundamentally differ between the two institutions. The most urgent task for the Court of BiH, as a new and prominent judicial institution, is to assure all citizens of its independence, impartiality, and competence. In contrast, the Prosecutor's Office needs to do the aforementioned tasks while building public trust in order to ensure cooperation with its investigations and prosecutions.

DEFINING THE CONCEPT OF OUTREACH IN BIH

The difficulty in translating the word *outreach* into the local languages of BiH[27] is perhaps illustrative of the broader challenge in designing and building outreach programs suited to the region. Unlike the outreach section at the ICTY, whose main goal is to make the tribunal's work accessible to its target audiences in the region, the task of outreach at the Court of BiH and the BiH Prosecutor's Office is to display that the new BiH judicial institutions are transparent, independent, and effective.[28] This order is tall indeed, since citizens are inured to such messages, as they have experienced exactly the opposite from their criminal justice system in the past. According to public polling on levels of trust in the domestic system to handle war crimes cases, only about a third of citizens have total trust in this, while almost two-thirds state that they have none whatsoever. The Organization for Security and Cooperation in Europe (OSCE) Mission to Bosnia and Herzegovina published the following findings from three consecutive years of polling a representative sample of citizens:

> On average, nearly 60% of all respondents did not have any faith in the Court of BiH to try the war crimes and produce a fair and just result. The Serb respondents expressed particularly low confidence in the Court of BiH, with only 25% of respondents indicating they had "some trust" in its impartiality. Respondents across all ethnic groups had slightly higher confidence in the entity courts, but the trends were still disappointingly low.[29]

The operational definitions of *outreach* at the ICTY and at the Court of BiH and the BiH Prosecutor's Office differ. In the case of the ICTY's outreach program, outreach operates separately from press relations. The ICTY outreach section primarily deals with arranging access to the tribunal for visitors, providing points of contact in the region (e.g., liaison officers based in Belgrade and Sarajevo), and, from time to time, organizing presentations of the tribunal's work in the region—for example, a series of Bridging the Gap events held in BiH in 2005.[30] By 2012 the ICTY was also considering the establishment of several information centers in the region of the former Yugoslavia to serve as outreach hubs and focal points for the tribunal's legacy. At the same time, outreach at the ICTY also includes a significant focus on creating links with judicial communities in the region, in an effort to contribute to capacity building.[31] For example, study visits by BiH judges to The Hague are deemed part of the tribunal's outreach program rather than part of its transition process (although gradually this has shifted to being considered a part of the tribunal's "legacy-building" initiatives).[32] Thus, activities that stimulate improved judicial cooperation with the region but that have little to do with promoting transparency and building public trust are accommodated within the outreach program of the ICTY. While this exercise is important for ensuring knowledge sharing between the tribunal and its regional counterparts, the exercise also demonstrates one of the core differences between the definitions of *outreach* at the ICTY and in BiH.

Overall, aside from the recognition that outreach was necessary at the Court of BiH and the BiH Prosecutor's Office, discerning any significant process of lesson learning from the ICTY's journey in developing outreach is difficult. Starting with a blank slate—in contrast to the ICTY's latecomer outreach program—the goal of public information and outreach activities at the Court of BiH and the BiH Prosecutor's Office was to ensure that citizens felt they had ownership over the institutions and thus over efforts to combat impunity. The concept of *serving a constituency of BiH citizens* was integral to how the outreach programs were designed and implemented. At the same time, the court and the Prosecutor's Office also understood that they needed to convey the impartiality and professionalism of the reformed criminal justice system by sending the message that guilt for war crimes is individual and not group-based.

DEVELOPING AN APPROACH TO OUTREACH IN THE BIH CONTEXT

From 2005 to 2006 the outreach programs of the Court of BiH and the BiH Prosecutor's Office had three main prongs. The first was to enlist the support of local communities to create opportunities for engagement with the court and the Prosecutor's Office. The underlying idea was that creating a sense of social solidarity around the act of testifying would cement citizens' support for domestic war crimes processing. Second, judges and prosecutors would be sent into the field to explain to the people the institutions and how they worked. Third, key stakeholders such as victims' groups were invited to visit the court and meet with its principal actors even before trials were underway. In addition to these outreach components, public information activities were initiated, including publishing pamphlets and planning a website.

THE COURT SUPPORT NETWORK (2006–7)

The invitation that PIOS extended to victims' groups to visit the Court of BiH in the early phase of its operations proved to be important for bringing around particularly hostile constituencies. For example, the Republika Srpska Association of Camp Inmates had declared its intent not to cooperate with the "Sarajevo Court" precisely because of its location in the postwar Muslim-dominated capital city, amid fears it would be biased against non-Muslim victims. However, after their meeting with the president of the Court of BiH, representatives of the association told press members waiting at the gate that the court would have their support. Public information and outreach were off to a promising start at the Court of BiH and the BiH Prosecutor's Office.

The next PIOS outreach activity was establishing the Court Support Network (CSN), which formally came into existence on October 31, 2006. The network was conceived as a way of enlisting the help of local nongovernmental organizations (NGOs) to distribute information around the country about the court's work, taking advantage of NGOs' existing footholds in small communities. The thinking was that if community; organizations of any description—such as a football club—could be used to disseminate information about the Court of BiH and the BiH Prosecutor's Office, it would help to promote acceptance of and build solidarity behind individuals who cooperated with prosecutions.

The network consisted of an inner and an outer ring of NGOs. The inner ring of NGOs was to work directly with the court, while the outer ring would receive information and strategic direction from the inner ring and accordingly plan field-based activities. Five prominent domestic NGOs formed the inner ring. These included the Mostar-based office of the Center for Civic Initiatives, an organization with a mandate to ensure transparency and democratic participation in BiH institutions; Žene Ženema,[33] one of the leading women's advocacy NGOs in BiH, based in Sarajevo; the RS Helsinki

Committee for Human Rights, one of the foremost human rights NGOs in the country, and based in the Republika Srpska town of Bijeljina; and Izvor,[34] the Association of Women from Prijedor, one of the most active victims' advocacy groups, which operates in the northwestern region of BiH.[35] Through these five NGOs, the entire territory of BiH was theoretically covered,[36] but in reality the level of success depended on each of the inner-ring NGOs enlisting further members in the second ring.[37] It is notable that civil society organizations are a relatively young sector in BiH, and they are still beset with a number of challenges in ensuring professionalism, neutrality, and sustainability, as I discuss later in the chapter.

Some of the network's activities were to include establishing outreach centers in towns around BiH and the creation of a hotline that members of the public could call for information on everything from how to arrange a visit to the court to how to contact the Prosecutor's Office (or the Criminal Defense Section [Odsjek Krivične Odbrane, OKO]) to provide evidence regarding a specific incident. While this hotline was staffed with the NGO members, they could refer individuals to PIOS. Officials of the court or the Prosecutor's Office were usually available to represent the institutions at public meetings organized by network members. However, the Court Support Network was not long-lived and became defunct less than a year after its establishment, although some of the NGOs remained active in independent outreach and witness support activities.[38] The CSN partners attributed the network's downfall to a lack of sufficient PIOS coordination efforts. Sparse communication took place between the five main partners of the network. Moreover, PIOS funding was only available during the network's initial six-month period. Thereafter, the lack of institutional support or independent sources of funding made it difficult for the NGOs to continue their involvement. More tellingly, all sides can acknowledge that the differing mandates and modus operandi of the NGOs did not bode well for their ability to unite in a common endeavor unless they were given continued tangible support while cementing their connections.

The network did have some positive impact, even during its short existence. During the network's heyday, the hotline served as an important tool for relaying the views of the court and the Prosecutor's Office constituencies back to actors within the institutions.[39] In hindsight, some NGO leaders recall the network's purpose as a means of contacting potential witnesses and delivering witness support services rather than having the goal of outreach. However, the lack of common understanding regarding the core purpose of the CSN made both of these functions difficult to sustain.

A SHIFT IN DIRECTION

Unfortunately, in 2006, only a little over a year after the establishment of the Court of BiH and the BiH Prosecutor's Office, the outreach program radically altered course. Strong disagreements about the vision for outreach emerged between PIOS—which was leading the early efforts to build public support for the court—and the Registry. PIOS wished to continue its efforts to create a sense of local ownership among citizens, while the Registry grew increasingly impatient with the lack of visible results and pushed for the use of more spin and propaganda about the court's work in the media. This disagreement led to the departure of key staff from PIOS, followed by the cancellation of grants to CSN partners and a significant retreat from proactive outreach activities by the institutions at the end of 2006.

In light of this, since 2007, both PIOS and the PR department identify their primary mandate as ensuring transparency in the work of the Court of BiH and the BiH Prosecutor's Office. This translates, in turn, to a strong emphasis on activities that fall into the category of public information rather than outreach per se.[40] Thus, from that time on, public information and outreach activities in the court and the Prosecutor's Office were largely curtailed to issuing press releases, answering press inquiries,[41] granting interviews,[42] and organizing visits.[43] According to the PR department, its "active" public information effort consists of releasing interesting information to the media. Indeed, issuing legalistic press releases in Bosnian, Serbian, and Croatian, as well as in English, is the most visible activity of both PIOS and the PR department.[44] All significant milestones in cases are publicized on the court's or the Prosecutor's Office's website.[45] Comments from the Prosecutor's Office spokesperson can regularly be found in national newspapers, although the principal public faces of the Court of BiH and the BiH Prosecutor's Office are the court president and chief prosecutor, who both regularly accept public speaking engagements.[46]

"PASSIVE" PUBLIC INFORMATION AND OUTREACH

From 2007 to 2010 PIOS did not organize external events to publicize and explain the structure and nature of the court's work to the broader public. This was a symptom of the lack of a strategic plan to engage with victims, perpetrator communities, politicians, or religious and community leaders to build popular support for the court's efforts to combat impunity. Somewhat predictably, concerned citizens, civil society organizations, and groups representing victims continue to express frustration at the lack of opportunities to address judges and prosecutors, to know how the caseload is managed, and to find out how to be a witness.[47]

On the other hand, during this period, both PIOS and the PR department facilitated the participation of officials from the court and the Prosecutor's Office in activities organized by external interlocutors. In 2009 the PR department facilitated the participation of the Prosecutor's Office in ten such outreach events.[48] While laudable, the quality of such events was liable to vary. The RS Helsinki Committee for Human Rights, one of the original members of the Court Support Network, continued to organize outreach events, including three public roundtables in 2009 in the towns of Mostar, Višegrad, and Jajce. Both PIOS and the PR department eagerly cooperated with organizing these events, which are generally recognized as being of good quality and based on the simple and effective idea of presenting the outcomes of final and binding cases affecting that particular locality.[49] However, not all outreach events achieved positive outcomes. For example, at a roundtable held in Višegrad in December 2009, the audience reacted negatively to the presentation of a case's outcome. Given the potential for this reaction to recur in many communities, outsourcing the process of engaging with the public, and particularly affected communities, should be viewed with caution.

AN OUTREACH EXPERIMENT BY THE BIH PROSECUTOR'S OFFICE (2008)

One notable exception to the lack of proactive outreach by the Prosecutor's Office occurred in the summer of 2008. The BiH Prosecutor's Office tried to win over the public, victims' groups, and strongholds of opposition within the Serb-dominated entity of the Republika Srpska by traveling around BiH to publicize its new strategy for prioritizing and selecting cases for prosecution.[50] Through a series of town hall–style meetings, the Prosecutor's Office sought to respond to public curiosity about the development of a national strategy for war crimes processing, which was happening behind closed doors, and to explain the approach to investigations and building cases.[51]

Unfortunately, these events were not well executed.[52] A pamphlet distributed to audiences noted the numbers of victims falling into different ethnic categories—and neglected to mention Bosnian Muslims as a category at all.[53] This (accidental) omission alone was enough to spark outrage, but the overall message that "ethnicity was not a criterion in choosing suspects" was lost amid the explanation that, under the "new approach," cases concerning the gravest incidents with the largest numbers of victims would be prioritized for prosecution. To Serbs and Croats, this explanation sounded as though the Prosecutor's Office was not going to get around to investigating crimes against their peoples in view of the fact that these groups had not suffered as many large massacres during the conflict, in comparison to Bosniaks. In contrast, mass killings—understood mainly to have been perpetrated by Serb forces—seemed the top priority for prosecution, and hence Serbs seemed singled out for justice. The additional connotation that forced displacement, rape, and torture were also not priorities of the Prosecutor's Office displeased almost everyone. Reportedly, many members of the audiences reacted fiercely or stormed out. From that point on, the head of the Special Department for War Crimes limited his public remarks in the company of victims' groups to explaining that his strategy was based on a study of the worst times and places in the war, but he avoided stating further specifics of the prosecution policy. Overall, the series was a mixed success and resulted in a retreat from outreach. However, the initiative can also be viewed as a laudable effort to engage the public and build support for the work of the war crimes prosecutions, given that it followed two years of almost no activities of this kind led by the institution.

During this period, the court also struggled to accommodate the requests of media and civil society for access to information about the war crimes trials, despite the strong support of the president of the Court of BiH, a firm advocate of transparency. By law, no electronic recording is permitted in courtrooms without the explicit permission of the president. In 2009 this policy presented a challenge for the nonprofit specialized reporting agency BIRN (the Balkan Investigative Reporting Network), which was preparing to launch a regular program called *TV Justice*. BIRN spent more than twelve months negotiating the release of audiovisual records. Initially, PIOS declined the request, explaining that it would be technically impossible to release any recordings from trial days where the session was closed to the public for a period of time—even if the court was in closed session for only two minutes. This answer was highly problematic for the *TV Justice* team, which was aware that witnesses and victims had given highly compelling testimony on days when the trial had been in closed session very briefly. For example, a short time in closed session during the trial day in the 2009 *Koričanske Stijene No. 1* case would prevent the wider public from ever learning of the shocking revelations made in the courtroom about the massacre of 180 men on Mount Vlasić by ten members of the Prijedor Police Intervention Squad, and the dumping of the victims' bodies over a precipice.[54]

Later in the negotiations, however, PIOS determined that providing the material was possible, but vetting the closed sessions was too time consuming for the technicians. BIRN offered to provide the resources to carry this out, continuing to press the argument of strong public interest in releasing the material from open sessions. Eventually, PIOS agreed to release the material with a delay of about a week from when it was collected. This agreement, reached in December 2009, allowed the first episode of *TV Justice* to air on schedule on January 4, 2010. PIOS retains the right to withhold any material that a judge objects to releasing; some judges have expressed concerns that the media are "abusive" of any footage related to the court.[55] Indeed, there are numerous documented instances of media actors releasing the names of protected witnesses and anonymous victims.[56] On the other hand, the potential for such disclosure does not justify withholding materials of public record from the media. Rather, the court needs to be more vigilant about what information is spoken in open court by the parties to the proceedings and to sanction journalists and media outlets that break the law with regard to protected information.

The fact that the Court of BiH eventually recognized the advantage of allowing BIRN access to the materials appears to pave the way for a more flexible access policy for all media organizations in the future, despite the remaining restrictions. However, the lack of photographs from inside courtrooms and dearth of current images of defendants remains a longstanding problem for news directors, who complain of having to publish the same photo of a defendant repeatedly.[57]

A NEW STRATEGIC APPROACH TO PUBLIC INFORMATION AND OUTREACH STRATEGY (2008)

The passivity of the outreach activities at the Court of BiH and the BiH Prosecutor's Office is not the only major obstacle faced in bringing its work closer to the people. A notable trade-off results from placing the responsibility for outreach in the hands of units that are separate from the organs carrying out the core work of the institutions—that is, the judges, prosecutors, and legal support staff. In the Prosecutor's Office, for example, it was a long and hard process to convince prosecutors that they needed to inform the PR department whenever a formal legal step was taken in a case (e.g., ordering an arrest or raising an indictment), so that the information could be released publicly. Indeed, in the early days of the Prosecutor's Office, the PR department would occasionally learn of a development in a case from the press rather than the Prosecutor's Office because prosecutors were bypassing the spokesperson and his team and communicating directly with journalists.

The staff of PIOS and the PR department must rely on the interpretation of the duties of transparency, disclosure, and the public interest given to them by the judicial officials in the institutions. Unfortunately, a discernible reluctance exists among the judiciary to engage in outreach-oriented activities. The judicial culture in the former Yugoslavia was not one that embraced public relations activities, but rather one in which belief in the dignity, integrity, and good faith of the judiciary was expected as a matter of course. The benefits of outreach, therefore, are not readily accepted. Similarly, international judges and prosecutors, who most often come from the Western European or North American legal culture, fail to appreciate the overwhelming apathy and lack of trust felt by the public toward war crimes processing in BiH that necessitates a campaign of confidence building and engagement. Moreover, for most of the prosecutors and judges—with some notable exceptions—the public perception of the Court of BiH and the BiH Prosecutor's Office is an ancillary matter to their day-to-day work of prosecuting and adjudicating cases. All of the factors mentioned above indicate a disconnect between the outreach program and the core work of the institutions.

The issue of a passive, disconnected, and failing outreach apparatus was one of the chief motivating factors behind the formation of the Outreach Working Group in 2007. This working group decided first to carry out public opinion research on attitudes toward the court and the Prosecutor's Office.[58] While the results of that research were for internal use only, people privy to their contents admit that the polling indicated that the institutions were experiencing a public relations catastrophe.[59] Not only was the public poorly informed about the work of the new state-level institutions to combat the legacies of war crimes, but a majority held deep misconceptions about both the court and the Prosecutor's Office—for example, that they are ethnically biased against Serbs. These beliefs appeared to stem from political propaganda and distorted media reports.[60]

On the basis of this research, the court and the Prosecutor's Office requested that the donors engage an expert to develop new strategic approaches to outreach for their institutions. New strategies were adopted in 2008, accompanied by promises from the donors who sponsored their development to support the implementation phase, and from the heads of institutions to pave the way for such support. The strategies sought to establish a new overarching goal for the outreach programs—namely, creating a sense of ownership in BiH citizens over the process of dealing with the legacy of crimes committed during the war.[61] The strategies noted that this fact must be clear to the public and to the judges and prosecutors—the implication being that the latter group too often feels that they are only under an obligation to act transparently rather than to build trust in the institutions.[62]

As a precondition to reconceptualizing outreach at the Court of BiH and the BiH Prosecutor's Office, the strategies called for a team of professionals in public information and outreach to create an annual plan of activities, including development of a media strategy as a chief priority. The strategies specified the staffing changes that would be necessary in PIOS and the PR department, respectively.[63] A clear set of short-term[64] and long-term[65] goals were suggested. In addition, each strategy contained a set of recommendations, which might serve well as a roadmap to step-by-step implementation of the suggested recipe for success.[66] The measures proposed to improve society's sense of ownership over domestic war crimes processing took into consideration the unique challenges that each of the institutions faced. Taking note of the fact that the Prosecutor's Office needs citizens to "provide support to its efforts to gather evidence in cases of organised crime and war crimes,"[67] the strategy envisioned tackling the perceptions of ethnoreligious bias as a priority. For example, a more forceful approach to countering misinformation and negative propaganda as it emerges was recommended.[68] The court's strategy also emphasized a more genuine approach to ensuring transparency by providing unimpeded access to the courtrooms through a variety of channels.[69] The importance of allowing radio and television access was stressed, as well as the need to ensure no logistical or procedural barriers to such an initiative.[70]

Both strategies had the development of a new media plan as a central pillar. The Prosecutor's Office was to adopt a more transparent approach to the media (without jeopardizing investigations).[71] The court, for its part, was to set up a regular means of communication with PIOS in order to transform its approach to news coverage from a passive and reactionary style into a proactive and premeditated one. In essence, this meant meeting the oft-repeated requests of journalists for weekly press briefings, instead of relying on press releases and occasional statements. The Prosecutor's Office was similarly advised to organize such briefings, including one hosted by the chief prosecutor every six months.[72] A proactive effort to capture the interest of media based outside of Sarajevo was also outlined in both strategies.

Additionally, a renewed emphasis was placed on outreach toward local communities—particularly toward victims' groups. The court was told it should devise "a detailed plan of conventional community outreach activities" that aimed to stress the fairness of the procedures of the court, as well as present the facts from final and binding verdicts.[73] The Prosecutor's Office was also advised to organize community events, focusing on sending a message of fairness and professionalism, as well as on providing avenues of receiving possible evidence. The intention was that these events should work to place the micro-events of cases into a larger context, so that they could be correctly understood by the public at large. The public information and outreach staff needed to be able to place the history of cases into this context, too, meaning that they needed to be sufficiently close to the key staff in their institutions to be knowledgeable about the caseload.[74]

Reviving the concept of a network of civil society organizations was also central to the strategies' goal of improving outreach—they suggested that the court and the Prosecutor's Office together should recruit justice-sector-oriented NGOs to be partners in disseminating information about war crimes processing in local communities. The strategies contained few suggestions for preventing problems like those experienced the first time, aside from expressing a strong and public commitment to supporting the NGOs. This absence perhaps reflects a belief that lack of coordination from the institutions was the downfall of the first incarnation of the Court Support Network. However, the suggestion seems to be that these NGOs would operate more loosely as a coalition for justice (similar to the Coalition for the International Criminal Court) that would also focus broadly on rule of law issues in BiH and capitalize on several burgeoning civil society networks and initiatives.[75] Finally, the strategies called for the program of visits to the institutions themselves to be refocused to serve the main outreach goals—for example, proactively organizing visits for citizens of BiH, including victims' groups, students, NGOs, members of political parties, and others—instead of only responding to requests for visits, which frequently arose from visiting international groups.[76] In short, if fully implemented, the strategy offered great potential for improving the quantity and quality of public information and outreach work from the Court of BiH and the BiH Prosecutor's Office.

However, the proposed changes to the configuration of the public information and outreach teams were met with negative reactions on the part of institutions. Consequently, the initial endorsements of the strategies by the Court of BiH president and the Prosecutor's Office did not translate into immediate implementation, according to observers of strategic planning and management at the Court of BiH and the BiH Prosecutor's Office. Another pressing question was where to find the funds to strengthen the PIOS teams and sponsor the new range of activities. Indeed, these difficulties presented a formidable obstacle to making outreach more effective, since both strategies were premised on putting in place professional teams that ideally could work closely with the judges and prosecutors to reduce the gap between the institutions and their mouthpieces.

Throughout 2010 the Court of BiH continued to debate the content of the strategies, and thus they were not implemented.[77] Even more troubling were suggestions from the institutions leading outreach initiatives that it had "all been done before," and moreover it would be too costly and time-consuming to attempt. Judges often cited the prohibition on commenting on cases in which the final judgment has not yet been reached, while prosecutors noted that they are barred from revealing sensitive information during investigations. Consequently, by 2011, both institutions were increasingly embracing outreach activities organized by external actors. For example, the Prosecutor's Office was participating in outreach organized by Izvor, the RS Helsinki Committee for Human Rights, and the OSCE Mission to BiH but was not planning to spearhead its own initiatives. This approach can be problematic for a number of reasons, but, importantly, it hampers the ability of the institutions to conduct a consistent and effective outreach program that follows the goal of building cross-community ownership over the court and the Prosecutor's Office.

In 2010, even the laudable efforts of the court and the Prosecutor's Office to be transparent through the posting of indictments, judgments, and other public court documents on their respective websites took a blow. The BiH Agency for the Protection of Private Data, in response to a complaint from an individual convicted by the court, ordered the institutions to redact the defendants' names and other personal data about them.[78] While prompted by a non-war-crimes-related case, the edict applied to all court documents available to the public. This situation presented a serious challenge to the institutions, neither of which had the means to redact judgments and indictments to comply with the ruling; the court and the Prosecutor's Office were forced to remove all names and related data from the websites.[79] The result is the somewhat absurd situation that the names of defendants can be found in the media—and many previous judgments are available from other online sources—but are not accessible on the websites of the institutions with the responsibility to disseminate information about its work tackling war crimes cases. Despite attempts to negotiate a balance between the privacy rights of accused persons and both the right to truth and the public interest in knowing who is alleged to be or found responsible for war crimes, crimes against humanity, and genocide—and other serious crimes under the jurisdiction of the court and the Prosecutor's Office—this unfortunate situation persists as of May 2013.

PUBLIC INFORMATION AND OUTREACH IN LOCAL-LEVEL WAR CRIMES TRIALS

Under the National Strategy for War Crimes Processing, adopted at the end of 2008, "less complex" cases should be dealt with at the entity level, leaving "more complex" cases to be handled at the Court of BiH and the BiH Prosecutor's Office.[80] Unfortunately, a widespread perception exists within BiH society that the entity-level judiciary is untrustworthy and ethnically and politically biased when it comes to war crimes cases. While little or no evidence has been produced to corroborate this perception, courts and prosecutors' offices still fail to correct the public's misconceptions about the role of the entity courts and their handling of war crimes cases. To be sure, entity courts lack specialization and adequate resources, and they experience serious problems in protecting witnesses and conducting effective and efficient trials.[81] Still, the contribution of the entity justice systems to bringing about justice for wartime atrocities is not even widely known, despite the fact that they collectively resolved 105 cases between 2004 and June 2012.[82] As a result of this lack of public acknowledgment, the potential for war crimes prosecutions in the entity courts to contribute to a sense of achieving justice and reestablishing the rule of law at the local level is imperiled.

In the cantonal and district courts and prosecutors' offices, no formal structures for public information and outreach exist. Public information functions are assigned to a focal point in order to conform with the Law on Free Access to Information, but this often does not meet the deeper need for external engagement. Whether this focal point is an official spokesperson, court president, war crimes prosecutor, court secretary, or office clerk simply depends on what practice has developed over time in each institution.[83] Very few courts and prosecutors' offices have the resources to create a post for a spokesperson—still fewer for an outreach officer. Thus, under the prevailing conditions, an organized outreach program exists only at the state level, contrary to the hopes of NGO actors that these courts and prosecutors' offices would undertake outreach efforts at the entity level. In the absence of full-time, professional outreach staff, little impetus exists to carry out outreach activities at all. Generally speaking, there is an even greater lack of recognition of the need for outreach in the cantonal and district courts and prosecutors' offices than at the state level. According to a study carried out by the OSCE Mission to Bosnia and Herzegovina,[84] "Members of the judiciary at the entity level generally speaking do not recognize the need for such services, especially Outreach, in their institutions."[85] The study notes, "In this atmosphere, and without empirical knowledge and concrete experiences of the potential benefits, it is difficult for [the entity judiciary] to consider the development of PI and Outreach services to be an urgent priority."[86] Naturally, there are exceptions. For example, the Banja Luka district prosecutor, Branko Mitrović, has actively reached out to victims' groups for their cooperation—an endeavor that has helped the Banja Luka DPO to pursue vigorously an impressive number of war crimes cases.[87]

The reality of small and close-knit communities in BiH means that many members of the judiciary do not see a problem with sharing even confidential information with journalists.[88] Draft model guidelines developed by the OSCE Mission to Bosnia and Herzegovina highlight these issues and propose ways of overcoming them.[89] The guidelines also recommend four steps for implementing outreach activities in cantonal and district courts and prosecutors' offices, including (1) initial assessment of specific situations and local needs of each jurisdiction, (2) defining SMART goals,[90] (3) defining the scope of outreach (including target groups), and (4) setting up regular monitoring and assessment.[91]

The OSCE Mission to Bosnia and Herzegovina has a program on promoting outreach that focuses on a range of activities designed to encourage improved public information and outreach activities by the cantonal and district courts and prosecutors' offices. The overall goal of the OSCE program is to enable two-way communication between the institutions, on one hand, and the media and public, on the other. In theory, the two-way nature of this communication should mean that reliable and objective information is shared, and that the main stakeholders in war crimes processing can raise questions and concerns and provide input.[92] Since 2004, the OSCE Mission has also engaged in a program of extensive monitoring of the criminal justice system at the state level, focused on judicial and legal reform, domestic war crimes processing, and vulnerable persons in contact with the justice system—especially victims of war crimes, trafficking, hate crimes, and domestic violence; child victims; and juvenile perpetrators. Findings from this trial monitoring program have indicated that, despite the thorough vetting of judicial institutions and reorganization of the court system, the public and key stakeholders lacked confidence in the judicial system's fairness and efficiency. The OSCE subsequently established advocacy initiatives, such as the production of a documentary, *Justice Requires Outreach*. Aimed at judges and prosecutors, the film profiled the efforts of two local prosecutors to reach out to victims and obtain their cooperation with war crimes prosecutions—a highly novel approach in the setting of BiH. Other OSCE activities include the sponsoring of public meetings for victims' groups and local NGOs to meet with judges and prosecutors; the organization of radio shows to which listeners can call in to speak with prosecutors; the publication of a leaflet, *Approaches to Outreach,* aimed at the judiciary; and the provision of small grants to NGOs to serve as bridges between the judiciary and communities, in a way akin to a smaller-scale version of the Court Support Network.

TAKING AIM: AUDIENCES OR TARGET GROUPS?

The Court of BiH and the BiH Prosecutor's Office have been highly successful in bringing in, informing, and engaging with audiences that are prepared to seek this interaction out by applying to visit the court or subscribing to *Justice Report.* For example, NGOs, academics, and particularly concerned citizens all are part of this core audience already paying attention to the progress of war crimes trials in the country, and they may actively seek out opportunities to learn more. In stark contrast, the Court of BiH and the BiH Prosecutor's Office have both lacked initiatives to engage target groups that may be apathetic, hostile, or simply unaware. Cantonal and district courts and prosecutors' offices have had even greater difficulty in identifying target groups and devising ways of connecting with them.

REACHING THE PUBLIC

Despite the consistent press work carried out by PIOS and the PR department, the Court of BiH and the BiH Prosecutor's Office's most obvious target group—the public at large—appears to be not well informed about the nature of the institutions.[93] The daily news from war crimes trials is seldom put into context for ordinary citizens. On any given day, at least the main wire services and large daily newspapers are likely to carry stories about an arrest, conviction, or extradition related to war crimes. Yet larger issues about fairness, efficiency, the facts established during trials, the problems faced in building cases, and so on are not conveyed in a consistent or programmatic manner, and improvement has been marginal and halting in this area. Suggesting that a regular stream of information from the media to the broader public can accomplish the goal of building a sense of ownership over the process among citizens is insufficient. Rather, achieving that sense of ownership requires careful thought and planning of a multipronged strategy that utilizes not only media but other means of engaging targets as well.

Most information released by the public information and outreach apparatuses at the Court of BiH and the BiH Prosecutor's Office is published on both institutions' websites. The press information page of the Prosecutor's Office, in particular, provides detailed information about what kind of queries it can deal with through the PR department and the limits of the Prosecutor's Office disclosure policy, an FAQ describing in lay terms how the criminal process works, and e-forms for requesting interviews or access to other information.[94] While laudable, the service is likely only to be useful for media and elite audiences.

VICTIMS, WITNESSES, AND PERPETRATORS

As noted, the views of victims in BiH are strongly influenced by whether they have appeared as witnesses and had access to objective and detailed information about trials, or whether they have been excluded from the process.[95] Few victims get to be witnesses, owing to the need for prosecutors to build cases based on strong and, if possible, eyewitness testimony. Victims not selected to be witnesses are unlikely to receive detailed information about the progress of cases. In the absence of any efforts to address this group as a special audience, they have grown increasingly marginalized from and critical of the justice-seeking process.[96] Many victims' associations obviously feel excluded from the process of seeking justice.

However, in BiH, the reality is that many of the most hostile pockets of resistance to war crimes processing are in fact "perpetrator communities." In such places, popular opinion supports those who, in the eyes of the community, defended their people and towns rather than engaged in criminal offenses that amounted to gross human rights violations. These communities are thus against any attempts to target war crimes suspects, as this action is perceived to be unfair and politically motivated. In these places, assertively presenting an image of the justice system as fair, impartial, and independent is important. The basic message that *guilt is individual and not group-based* is also essential if opponents are to be converted. Outreach efforts to date, however, have shied away from tackling this challenging target group.

POLITICAL, COMMUNITY, AND RELIGIOUS LEADERS

The political sphere comprises an elite group in BiH with the power to shape the views of their ethnonationalist constituencies. Religious leaders are also an elite group with such power. No discernible effort was made to bring these groups into outreach efforts in the past. The judiciary has stated their reluctance in this regard, as they need to be insulated from political considerations in order to preserve the independence of their institutions. Moreover, some of the chief attacks and misinformation have originated from these groups, which makes targeting outreach toward them extremely challenging. Nonetheless, doing so is critical, which further illustrates the need for a professional PIOS staff that can enlist this support without judges and prosecutors needing to become direct interlocutors with political actors.

THE ROLE OF CIVIL SOCIETY AND OTHER EXTERNAL ACTORS IN OUTREACH IN BIH'S WAR CRIMES TRIALS

THE ROLE OF NGOS

In the lifetime of the Court of BiH and the BiH Prosecutor's Office, various NGOs have been involved in organizing visits to the court. However, most of these NGOs do not consider outreach or court support to be part of their core activities. A limited number of organizations have been willing to undertake activities in the witness support vein. In the absence of a strong range of outreach activities by the court and the Prosecutor's Office, outreach done by NGOs has tended to target victims and witnesses of war crimes more than the general public. Contrary to the view of PIOS, most NGOs believe that the main responsibility for outreach must lie with the court, as well as with the Prosecutor's Office. In addition, many NGOs perceive that there would be a lack of political support if they were to increase their focus on promoting war crimes prosecution.

NGOs in BiH exist on a broad spectrum of professionalism. At one end of this spectrum lie developed organizations with a mandate for human rights or justice issues, such as the Balkan Investigative Reporting Network, while at the other end are large numbers of associations of victims, families of missing persons, families of fallen soldiers, and war veterans that tend to lack even minimal structure and cohesion among their members. Many NGOs concerned with war crimes and accountability fall somewhere along the middle of this spectrum—that is, while they might have organized enough to engage in some activities or lobbying, overall they lack clear focus, funding, and the requisite expertise to pursue their goals successfully. This situation makes engaging NGOs in partnerships a particularly daunting task for domestic institutions and international organizations alike. At the same time, one of the chief problems with engaging NGOs as outreach or witness support partners is that they may be viewed as aligned with particular (ethnic) constituencies, and thus unable to reach the other constituencies in a local community. Experience indicates that events organized by neutral institutions, such as the ICTY or other international organizations—the OSCE, UNDP—tend to attract a broader cross-section of communities.[97]

Similarly, the international donor community has been reluctant to fund NGOs that fail to demonstrate that they are ethnically inclusive in their outreach efforts.[98] There is particular concern that victims' associations may operate with bias if engaged as formal partners, since they are often organized along ethnic lines. Some municipalities in BiH have multiple associations of victims or families of missing persons in the same place because they serve different ethnic communities. The number of associations that have aspired, and managed, to rise above ethnic or religious distinctions and embrace all victims has been regrettably very few.[99] Naturally, associations fill a fundamental role in providing a conduit for victims' voices to be raised and heard. Unfortunately, some of these associations also spend their energies on criticizing one another in public rather than working together for their mutual interests, such as justice and discovering the location of missing persons. Almost all associations lack the minimum level of leadership, structure, and professionalism necessary to operate as human rights organizations or other kinds of lobby group. They do, however, remain a good way of accessing important constituencies for war crimes processing and serve intrinsic purposes such as demonstrating solidarity among victims and bearing witness for relatives who did not survive massacres, detention camps, and other atrocities during the war.

JUSTICE REPORT, RADIO JUSTICE, AND *JUSTICE TV*

Despite the lack of successful outreach by the institutions themselves, the nongovernmental sector has presented considerable opportunities for improving public confidence in war crimes processing. The most significant contribution to raising the profile of domestic war crimes processing has been made by a specialized nonprofit reporting agency, the Balkan Investigative Reporting Network. Since early 2006, BIRN's journalists have monitored trials taking place at the Court of BiH and published daily reports about them in their free online publication, *Justice Report,* which are then often recycled in mainstream media outlets. These reports are concise, use plain language, and have the benefit of being on the whole accurate, objective, and impartial.[100] *Justice Report* has a wide circulation, and the website receives hits from within BiH and from

Serbia, the United States, Canada, Croatia, Norway, and Scandinavia, which indicates a high level of interest among nationals of the region and countries with large Bosnian diaspora communities.

In 2007 BIRN decided to work through another medium in light of the low level of Internet penetration in BiH.[101] Shortened versions of the reports are now available on audio recordings and provided free of charge to local, national, and diaspora radio stations. These *Radio Justice* segments reach hundreds of thousands more people, especially in BiH's rural communities, where even newspapers have low circulation.[102] In 2010 *TV Justice*, a monthly program about the work of the Court of BiH and the BiH Prosecutor's Office and current issues in transitional justice, was launched. The OSCE Mission to Bosnia and Herzegovina and others have also released reports from time to time analyzing the progress and obstacles in domestic war crimes proceedings.[103]

THE ASSOCIATION OF COURT REPORTERS OF THE COURT OF BIH

The Association of Court Reporters (AIS) was established through a BIRN initiative to organize the journalists who required better information and transparency from the Court of BiH and the BiH Prosecutor's Office. In addition to their lobbying efforts, the AIS developed a code of ethical practice for reporting on court cases.[104] The code is of great importance, considering that many members of the BiH judiciary have been hesitant to cooperate with the media, criticizing the sometimes unprofessional and biased nature of reporting. Journalists have regularly released the names of protected witnesses and victims, for example.[105] Therefore, the AIS also provides continuing education to the press about some of the most important aspects of the press code. Ensuring that journalists understand their obligation to abide by provisions relating to the protection of witnesses is a fundamental component of establishing good relations with the judiciary, and thereby to ensuring access to court proceedings, interviews, and so on.[106] The association has also lobbied for improved transparency—for example, urging that press briefings be instituted by the court and the Prosecutor's Office. Under its "transparency of courts and responsibility of media" portfolio, AIS and BIRN have promoted better cooperation, higher standards, and the fundamental rationales behind keeping citizens well-informed about domestic war crimes processing.

INTERNATIONAL COMMUNITY

A small number of the donor countries that support the Court of BiH and the Prosecutor's Office are also interested in supporting outreach activities.

Support from the United Kingdom, Norway, and Switzerland has been crucial in this regard. These donors are coordinated in their approach to supporting outreach and the justice system more generally. Thus, they have asked for clear commitments and indicators of success and overall progress. Without these, donors are more easily persuaded to give funding to promising civil society projects rather than to the stalling outreach program at the Court of BiH and the BiH Prosecutor's Office.

In 2009 an international donor project funded by the US Agency for International Development (USAID) began a series of capacity-building initiatives designed, inter alia, to enhance public confidence in the judiciary. The Justice Sector Development Project (JSDP) began an initiative to establish the Justice Sector Network (JSN), a group of NGOs that would coordinate work on rule-of-law issues in BiH and serve as a foundation for partnerships on a variety of issues, from juvenile justice to the establishment of a Supreme Court. The assembly of NGOs and the well-thought-out process that brought them together under the JSN banner could serve well as a model, or indeed as an aid, to revisiting the idea of a Coalition for Justice around the war crimes processing institutions. In addition, the JSDP project has given BIRN a grant to recruit and train a cadre of thirty journalists who work in smaller communities around BiH where cantonal and district courts are processing war crimes cases. The hope is to awaken journalists to the important cases being transferred to the local courts and to equip them to report on the cases in a reliable and unbiased fashion.[107] The above-mentioned OSCE initiatives to support the development of an institutional framework for public information and outreach at the entity level are also important, as little international support has been directed to this neglected area.

THE CORE CHALLENGES: POLITICIZATION AND PASSIVITY

The chief challenge that the ICTY faced in ensuring that adequate and unbiased information reaches the region—the physical distance of the seat of the trials from their main audiences—is not an issue for the domestic judicial institutions in BiH that deal with war crimes cases. In the several years of the existence of the Court of BiH and the BiH Prosecutor's Office, however, it has become clear that it nonetheless faces some daunting hurdles. The politicization of all matters related to war crimes processing, as well as the rising opposition in some quarters toward anything perceived as a "project" of the international community, have proved to be powerful forces against the comparably mild efforts to trumpet the work of the Court of BiH and the BiH Prosecutor's Office and other courts dealing with the war crimes caseload around the country.

Detractors of the institutions have openly and vociferously criticized and condemned the work of the Sarajevo court as biased and unfair.[108] Naturally, the court and the Prosecutor's Office are both well aware of the negative attacks in the media and attribute this in part to the reality that political and social elites still include many persons responsible for serious criminal activity, both past and present. Indeed, a large portion of the hostility toward the institutions seems to stem from their role in combating organized crime rather than their jurisdiction over war crimes cases. Overall, however, this situation raises a dilemma for the institutions as to whether to view such attacks as occasions to carry out their obligation to combat misinformation, or as times to avoid being baited into engaging in a highly politicized and fraught public debate. Usually, they have chosen not to refute such attacks, which has arguably been a contributing factor in the poor public opinion regarding the court and the Prosecutor's Office.

The current political climate discourages the institutions from conducting outreach. As a result, PIOS, supported by many if not all of the judges, believes that outreach is best conducted by the NGO community and that the court should focus instead on simply ensuring its transparency. That said, a notable exception to the general policy of not fending off undue criticism was the publication of an open letter to the citizens of BiH by the chief prosecutor in November 2009, refuting several spurious allegations and efforts to misrepresent an investigation into financial wrongdoing by Milorad Dodik, the then prime minister of the Republika Srpska and one of the highest-ranking officials in the country. The open letter was significant because it also asserted an important message about the integrity of the institution:

> BiH Prosecutor's Office has no personal feelings about any of the institutions or entities in BiH. We work on behalf of disempowered citizens, for their protection and protection of the entire state and social community from criminal offense perpetrators in the aim of fairness, protection of justice and compliance with laws passed by the Parliament and Assemblies of Bosnia and Herzegovina and its Entities.[109]

In contrast to earlier efforts to ensure robust public information and outreach activities, there now appears to be a lack of support within the Court of BiH and the BiH Prosecutor's Office for taking a more hands-on approach to engaging with key audiences. While the heads of both institutions use opportunities that arise to assert the independence and impartiality of the institutions, little systematic effort takes place to highlight the importance of the Court of BiH and the BiH Prosecutor's Office to the people as a mechanism of removing perpetrators from society and bringing about a more just social reality. That not a single NGO or civil society actor publicly defended the court and the Prosecutor's Office during a period of vigorous and sustained attacks against the integrity of judges, prosecutors, and war crimes processing in general from 2009 and 2011 is highly telling for the results of the outreach program.[110] Given the mandate of the Court of BiH and the BiH Prosecutor's Office to bring justice in the wake of genocide, crimes against humanity, and war crimes, and at the same time demonstrate the effectiveness of the rule of law in post-conflict BiH, this lack of support is regrettable.

CONCLUSION

Many lessons can be taken from the experience of the outreach conducted in relation to BiH's domestic war crimes trials, which may serve equally well for future initiatives in BiH as well as those in other contexts. The lessons are also critical for the Court of BiH and the BiH Prosecutor's Office as they move past their first five years and seek to mature into symbols of positive values—such as justice, fairness, and the rule of law—that may become entrenched in BiH society and culture.

A dichotomy has emerged between an informative model and an engagement model of outreach as practiced in BiH. This dichotomy is in view in the case of the Court of BiH and the BiH Prosecutor's Office in the extent to which their turning away from efforts to partner with civil society and reach target groups has had a measurable effect, in terms of both failing to increase public trust in domestic war crimes processing over time and the withering away of civil society support for the institutions. Concentrating public information activities in a single medium—press releases—has left the institutions even less visible than the distant ICTY. The very language used in those statements is also a lesson learned regarding the importance of explaining legal issues to nonlawyers—and especially explaining sensitive issues to victims and witnesses—in a way that captures the interest of media and the broader public. Lack of support in the early stages coupled with enormous pressure to accomplish things virtually overnight meant that PIOS, in particular, became an embattled team that was unable to advance its agenda and eventually became handicapped in its efforts. Outreach staff need support from and integration into the institutions, but simply adding outreach to the duties of judges and prosecutors, as happens at the entity level in BiH, does not suffice.

Five years into serious efforts to process war crimes cases in the domestic criminal justice system of BiH, few judges and prosecutors acknowledge that their contribution to building trust in the institutions is important, and many of them continue to suggest that "letting the case speak for itself" in the courtroom is sufficient. Finally, the institutions' failure to implement quality public information and outreach activities has, in turn, somewhat diminished the interest of the donor community in supporting the programs. For example, from 2008 onward, donors to the Court of BiH have instead funneled donations to civil society organizations that are contributing to transparency of war crimes processing—such as *Justice Report* and its offshoots. A lack of initiative to secure funding from the state budget has compounded the resource problems in the area of public information and outreach.

Thus, public information and outreach apparatuses are still struggling to meet the goal of building a sense of local ownership over war crimes processing and trust in the domestic judicial institutions. At the entity level, an even more acute problem exists in this regard owing to the lack of institutional capacity to perform outreach at all. This realization should come as a deeply troubling one, especially to those who have participated in bringing more than two hundred domestic trials to a close in this short time span. Supporters of war crimes trials and broader rule of law–building efforts in BiH should be equally troubled by the increasingly hostile political environment in which war crimes trials take place, with both the institutions and the main actors subject to attack, particularly from strongholds of Serb opposition. This climate, in turn, has had a chilling effect on outreach activities and the willingness of the judiciary to implement them. While I do not have enough space here to explore the long-term consequences of linking post-conflict justice with rule-of-law reforms in the transitional justice setting and the potential cross-fertilization of risks between the two, such processes are self-evidently delicate, and failure to pay careful attention to building confidence works to the detriment of both projects.

In BiH, the prevailing negative opinion and narratives about domestic war crimes trials and the institutions responsible for them clearly threaten to undermine the sense that justice is being done. This is truly a pity, especially when considered in light of the fact that BiH society has received a greater quantity and quality of justice in comparison to many post-conflict or transitional societies around the globe. Without a strong commitment to outreach, the risk will grow that the Court of BiH, the BiH Prosecutor's Office, and the entity courts and prosecutors' offices will become as distant from their audiences as the ICTY. This development would be an immense and possibly irreversible shame, as one of the central rationales behind establishing domestic war crimes trials was to ensure that efforts to combat impunity would receive buy-in and have legitimacy in the eyes of the people. As stated earlier, even the most finely tuned outreach program cannot counteract the results of disappointing outcomes in war crimes trials and the sentiments of groups fundamentally opposed to pursuing justice. Outreach, however, could still play a valuable role in setting and limiting expectations and building trust among key audiences. This situation has yet to be achieved in BiH, although the efforts of a dedicated community of legal professionals, journalists, human rights activists, and victims' representatives continue. Without such efforts, and in the absence of visible growth in confidence in domestic war crimes trials, the final result can only be that society will eventually call into question one of the few transitional justice measures vigorously pursued in BiH: individual criminal accountability.

NOTES

The author is grateful to the Court of BiH Public Information and Outreach Section and the BiH Prosecutor's Office Public Relations Department for their cooperation with research for this piece. The author would like to thank Manuela Hodzić (Court of BiH), Boris Grubešić (BiH Prosecutor's Office), Refik Hodzić (formerly ICTY), Dalida Dzidić (British Embassy in Sarajevo), Anisa Sučeska Vekić (Balkan Investigative Reporting Network BiH), and Elmerina Ahmetaj Hrelja (Justice Sector Development Project II) for sharing their views and experiences on outreach with the author. The facts and analysis in this chapter draw on interviews with these individuals; the views expressed by participants in the Regional Conference on Transparency of Courts and Responsibility of Media held in Sarajevo in September 2009; and the author's experiences and exchanges with members of the NGO community, international community, and criminal justice system working on transitional justice and outreach issues in BiH between 2008 and 2011 as legal advisor on war crimes and transitional justice in the Organization for Security and Cooperation in Europe (OSCE) Mission to Bosnia and Herzegovina. All views expressed in this report are the author's alone and are not necessarily shared or endorsed by the OSCE, the OSCE Mission to Bosnia and Herzegovina or any of their employees or partners, or by ICTJ. The author is also grateful to James Rodehaver, Clara Ramírez-Barat, and Eoin Ansbro for helpful comments provided on earlier drafts of this work. Any errors or omissions remain the author's.

1 However, another transitional justice measure that has achieved considerable success in BiH is the location of the remains of missing persons. See "Number of DNA-Assisted Identifications of Persons Missing: Countries/Regions of Southeastern Europe Affected by the Conflicts of the 1990s," International Commission of Missing Persons, 2008, http://www.ic-mp.org/icmp-worldwide/southeast-europe/.

2 See ICTY Completion Strategy, http://www.icty.org/sid/10016; see also UN Security Council Resolution 1534, UN Doc. S/RES/1534 (2004), March 26, 2004, http://www.icty.org/x/file/Legal%20Library/Statute/statute_1534_2004_en.pdf.

3 In BiH, the term "war crimes" is commonly used to refer to all international crimes committed during the 1992–95 conflict—namely, genocide, crimes against humanity, and violations of the laws and customs of war.

4 The Law on the Court of BiH and the Law on the State BiH Prosecutor's Office were promulgated by Decision of the High Representative of BiH on November 12, 2000, and August 6, 2002. Thereafter, the laws were repeatedly amended before the institutions became functional between 2003 and 2005. See Office of the High Representative/European Union Special Representative, "Decisions in the Field of Judicial Reform," accessed August 23, 2012, http://www.ohr.int/decisions/judicialrdec/archive.asp.

5 See the Rome Statement, reflecting the work of the Joint Civilian Commission Sarajevo Compliance Conference, signed on February 18, 1996 (English version: http://www.nato.int/ifor/general/d960218a.htm).

6 See OSCE Mission to BiH, *Delivering Justice in BiH: An Overview of War Crimes Processing from 2005 to 2010*, May 2011, http://www.oscebih.org/documents/osce_bih_doc_2011051909500706eng.pdf.

7 OSCE Mission Report, *War Crimes Trials before the Courts of Bosnia and Herzegovina: Progress and Obstacles*, March 2005, http://www.oscebih.org/documents/1407-eng.pdf.

8 ICTY, "OHR-ICTY Working Group on Development of BiH Capacity for War Crimes Trial Successfully Completed," press release, OHR/P.I.S./731e, February 21, 2003, noting that creation of a "war crimes chamber" within the Court of BiH is an "essential part of the establishment of the rule of law and fundamental to the reconciliation process, creating necessary conditions to secure a lasting peace in BiH."

9 Ibid. Although the term *war crimes chamber* is often used to describe the institution(s) handling war crimes cases at the state level in BiH, the correct terms are, in fact, the Court of BiH and the BiH Prosecutor's Office.

10 The Court of BiH and the BiH Prosecutor's Office fall closer to domestic institutions on the spectrum of hybridity; international personnel are intended to be fully phased out. See the Registry Agreement of 2006 ("Agreement between the High Representative for BiH on the Registry for Section I for War Crimes and Section II for Organized Crime, Economic Crime, and Corruption of the Criminal and Appellate Division of the Court of BiH and for the Special Department for War Crimes and the Special Department for Organized Crime, Economic Crime, and Corruption of the BiH Prosecutor's Office").

11 See *National Strategy for War Crimes Processing of BiH* (2008), http://www.geneva-academy.ch/RULAC/pdf_state/War-Crimes-Strategy-f-18-12-08.pdf. See also Article 27(a) of the BiH Criminal Procedure Code, which deals with transfer of jurisdiction for criminal offenses referred to in Chapter XVII of the BiH Criminal Code (i.e., war crimes, crimes against humanity, and genocide).

12 See ICTY, "Key Figures of ICTY Cases," May 20, 2012, http://www.icty.org/x/file/Cases/keyfigures/key_figures_en.pdf. Note, however, that thirty-six persons had their indictments withdrawn or are deceased (twenty-two cases). The figure cited above does not include the seven cases involving thirteen accused that were transferred to national jurisdictions under the Rule 11*bis* procedure after the ICTY had confirmed the indictment in the case, six of which were transferred to BiH and are therefore included in the figures for BiH.

13 OSCE Mission to Bosnia and Herzegovina Trial Monitoring Programme, *War Crimes Proceedings Statistics* (unpublished figures correct as of May 31, 2012; copy on file with author).

14 Ibid. The first-instance (cantonal) courts of the Federation of BiH had completed sixty-nine cases with thirty-one more ongoing at various phases of the proceedings in June 2012, while the first-instance (district) courts of the Republika Srpska had completed thirty-two cases (thirty-two ongoing), and Brčko District Basic Court had completed four cases (nine ongoing).

15 According to the Human Losses in BiH: 1992–1995 Project carried out by the Sarajevo-based Research and Documentation Center, some 97,000 persons lost their lives as a direct result of the war. See http://www.idc.org.ba/index.php?option=com_content&view=section&id=35&Itemid=126&lang=bs. This staggering figure does not take into account the tens of thousands of instances of torture, rape, unlawful detention, forced displacement, destruction of cultural and religious objects, and other international core crimes. See also ICTY, "War Demographics: Victims of the War in Bosnia and Herzegovina (BiH), 1992–1995, Estimated Complete Death Toll," March 2011, putting the estimate of the war dead at 104,732 (figures also available at ICTY, "New War Demographics Feature on the ICTY Website," press release, March 29, 2011, http://www.icty.org/sid/10622).

16 However, proceedings are ongoing against dozens more defendants. The figure of 8,000 suspects was reported by the BiH Prosecutor's Office to the Supervisory Body of the National Strategy for War Crimes Processing at its tenth session on April 13, 2010. According to a caseload inventory completed on March 22, 2010, there then were some 1,381 cases in which the charges were classified as war crimes, concerning some 8,249 suspects. The figure of proceedings concluded against 412 accused does not take into consideration cases prosecuted by third states or pending proceedings. See OSCE Mission to BiH, *Delivering Justice in BiH*.

17 See ICTY, "Key Figures of ICTY Cases," 2006. See also OSCE, *War Crimes Trials before the Domestic Courts of BiH*, May 2011; Human Rights Watch, *Looking for Justice: The War Crimes*

Chamber in Bosnia and Herzegovina (New York: HRW, 2006); and ICTJ, *The War Crimes Chamber in Bosnia and Herzegovina: From Hybrid to Domestic Court*, Prosecutions Case Studies Series (New York: ICTJ, 2008).

18 Refik Hodzić, "Living the Legacy of Mass Atrocities: Victims' Perspectives in War Crimes Trials," *Journal of International Criminal Justice* 8, no. 1 (March 2010): 113–36, discussing the results of a survey of victims in the Prijedor region of BiH on their feelings about justice for wartime atrocities.

19 Of citizens surveyed in 2008, 40.7 percent said that criminal prosecutions are the most important way to deal with the legacy of war crimes (OSCE, *Delivering Justice in BiH*, part 7).

20 Note that Sections II and III of the Criminal Division of the Court of BiH and the BiH Prosecutor's Office also deal with economic crime, corruption, and organized crimes, such as terrorism and human trafficking, as well as general crime. See Court of Bosnia and Herzegovina, "Common Secretariat: Jurisdiction, Organization, and Structure of the Court of Bosnia and Herzegovina," accessed August 24, 2012, http://www.sudbih.gov.ba/?opcija=sadrzaj&kat=3&id=3&jezik=e.

21 The state institutions include the Court of BiH, the State BiH Prosecutor's Office, and the High Judicial and Prosecutorial Council of BiH (the body entrusted with safeguarding the independence and integrity of the judiciary). For further details about judicial reform in BiH past and future, see Bosnia and Herzegovina Ministry of Justice, *Bosnia and Herzegovina Justice Sector Reform Strategy: 2008–2012*, http://issat.dcaf.ch/Home/Community-of-Practice/Resource-Library/Policy-and-Research-Papers/Bosnia-and-Herzegovina-Justice-Sector-Reform-Strategy-2008-2012.

22 See OSCE Mission to BiH, *Spot Report on Independence of the Judiciary: Undue Pressure on BiH Judicial Institutions*, December 2009, http://www.oscebih.org/documents/osce_bih_doc_2010122314120729eng.pdf, describing clear political interference with the judicial process through statements that, due to their harsh content, unsubstantiated nature, and frequency, overstep the limits of acceptable criticism and constitute undue pressure on these independent institutions.

23 The catalyst for the establishment of the ICTY outreach program was the rejectionist reaction of Bosnian Serbs to the tribunal's first verdict and conviction—in the case of Duško Tadić for crimes committed in the Prijedor region; *Prosecutor v. Tadić* IT-94-1-T (1997). See Hodzić, "Living the Legacy of Mass Atrocities," nn. 6, 65, citing an interview with the then president of the ICTY, Gabrielle Kirk McDonald.

24 Refik Hodzić, a former journalist, a filmmaker, and an outreach professional, is currently the director of communications at the International Center for Transitional Justice. Following his production of the documentary *Justice Unseen* (Sarajevo: XY Films, 2004), Hodzić filled public information and outreach posts in both the ICTY and the Court of BiH and the BiH Prosecutor's Office.

25 Under domestic law, BiH institutions are merely required to appoint a focal point for public requests for information. See Law on Free Access to Information (Official Gazette of BiH no. 28/2000), art. 14.

26 However, instances of the court and the Prosecutor's Office adopting conflicting public stances have been few.

27 There is no literal translation for "outreach" in Bosnian/Croatian/Serbian. Initially, OSCE and others used the word *iskorak*, which means "a step forward." Eventually, however, the practice of simply using the English word and adding a definition in the local language emerged, while PIOS uses "Ured Za Odnose s Javnošću" (Office of Public Relations) as its local language moniker.

28 E.g., OSCE, "Justice Must Not Only Be Done, It Must Be Seen to Be Done," press release, September 1, 2009, http://www.oscebih.org/News.aspx?newsid=226&lang=EN, calling on the judiciary and media to "inform citizens about how the justice system functions, what challenges it faces, and how these challenges can be overcome."

29 OSCE Mission to Bosnia and Herzegovina, *Delivering Justice in BiH,* 90.

30 The ICTY's Bridging the Gap initiative consisted of a series of five conferences that took place in 2004 and 2005 in BiH towns that had experienced crimes dealt with by the tribunals (Foća, Srebrenica, Prijedor, Brčko, and Konjic). The aim of the series was to provide local audiences with presentations from tribunal officials that would describe "the context in which they worked, the manner that evidence was collected, and what, ultimately, was established in relevant cases and judgments." See "Bridging the Gap with Local Communities," ICTY Outreach Program, accessed March 25, 2011, http://www.icty.org/sections/Outreach/BridgingtheGapwithlocalcommunities.

31 See "Capacity Building," ICTY Outreach Program, accessed February 2010, http://www.icty.org/sections/Outreach/CapacityBuilding: "Between 2002 and 2004, the UN Security Council repeatedly called on the international community and donors to assist the national judiciaries to ensure the success of war crimes trials in the region and asked the Tribunal to contribute to such capacity building efforts through its Outreach Programme."

32 For the tribunal's program of legacy-building initiatives, see http://www.icty.org/sections/Outreach/CapacityBuilding.

33 In English, *Women to Women.*

34 In English, *Source.*

35 Another NGO, Forum Građana Tuzle, joined the network in July 2007 to replace an NGO that had bowed out of the network due to funding problems.

36 The network was structured loosely to conform with the organization of the Prosecutor's Office, which has five teams covering the BiH regions (with an additional team for the Srebrenica situation).

37 For instance, the Center for Civic Initiatives was highly successful in building the second ring of the network in the Herzegovina region, enlisting over one hundred organizations of all descriptions.

38 After the demise of the Court Support Network, some of the main partners fell away while others continued to work on outreach-oriented activities. Izvor has continued to undertake outreach projects targeting both the Court of BiH and the two local courts near the Prijedor region (Banja Luka District Court and Bihać Cantonal Court) and also to provide important witness support services to victim-witnesses. The RS Helsinki Committee has continued to promote war crimes processing—organizing local roundtables and inviting representatives from the Court of BiH and the BiH Prosecutor's Office to address communities. The Center for Civic Initiatives also continued to do policy-oriented work on justice and outreach issues for a time, but by 2010 was no longer focused on this area.

39 A PIOS officer collected all comments received through the hotline and prepared summaries of the views of victims and members of the public about the direction of the court and the Prosecutor's Office. This avenue of communication proved to be important for addressing certain problems, such as complaints that victims were not being offered so much as a glass of water when they were interviewed at the Prosecutor's Office. Many small but important issues were resolved in such a manner.

40 For a helpful elaboration of activities defined as *outreach* in the context of post-conflict justice, see OSCE Office for Democratic Institutions and Human Rights, International Center for Transitional Justice, and UN Interregional Crime and Justice Research Institute, *Supporting the Transition Process: Lessons Learned and Best Practices in Knowledge Transfer: Final Report,* Annex 7, "Collected Best Practices in Outreach," September 2009, http://www.icty.org/x/file/About/Reports%20and%20Publications/report_supporting_transition_en.pdf, 91.

41 The PR department of the Prosecutor's Office receives, on average, five to ten media inquiries per day, with that number rising on days when there is a story of major interest. Although by law the Prosecutor's Office is only compelled to comply with such requests within fifteen days, the general policy is to respond within twenty-four hours.

42 In 2009 the Prosecutor's Office granted approximately thirty interviews to media, the majority of these with the chief prosecutor or deputy chief prosecutor and with the head of the Special Department for War Crimes. See *Annual Report of the BiH Prosecutor's Office* (Sarajevo: Registry of the Court and Prosecutor's Office of BiH, 2009).

43 In 2009, 1,223 people visited the courthouse (where the Prosecutor's Office is also located) and met with judges, prosecutors, and key staff and observed trials. See *Annual Report of the Registry* (2009), http://www.registrarbih.gov.ba/files/docs/ANNUAL_REPORT_2009.pdf), 1.6.2. However, observers note that most of these visitors were from foreign delegations, and not enough citizens actually take advantage of the right to enter the court.

44 According to the unpublished *Report of the Court of BiH* (2009, copy on file with author), 327 press releases were issued in 2009. According to the *Report of the BiH Prosecutor's Office* (Sarajevo: Registry of the Court and Prosecutor's Office of BiH, 2009), around 250

press releases were issued in 2009, about one or two per working day. The stated policy of both sections is to automatically release all information that can be public.

45 See www.sudbih.gov.ba and www.tuzilastvobih.gov.ba.

46 See, for example, interviews given in January 2010 by President Kreso and then chief prosecutor Barašin to *Justice TV*, accessed February 20, 2010, http://www.balkaninsight.com/en/main/video/?tpid=414.

47 See Hodzić, "Living the Legacy of Mass Atrocities."

48 *Annual Report of the BiH Prosecutor's Office* (2009).

49 The general practice at these events is for the PIOS staff to present general information about the institutions, while staff members who worked on the cases comment on the factual and legal findings

50 Given that the size and nature of the caseload of outstanding war crimes in BiH was unknown, the manner of selecting and prioritizing cases for prosecution was hitherto a largely invisible process, which gave rise to major misconceptions about the basis for initiating proceedings against an individual—a state of affairs easily susceptible to manipulation for political ends. For example, in 2009 Milorad Dodik, who was then prime minister of the Republika Srpska and leader of the SNSD (Union of Independent Social Democrats), repeatedly suggested that the court and the Prosecutor's Office were biased against the Republika Srpska, declaring to the press on one occasion that "it is unacceptable for the RS to be judged by Muslim judges" (Media Intelligence Agency, "Morning Media Brief," December 11, 2008). Dodik reiterated his distrust toward judges and prosecutors of Bosniak ethnicity during the TV program *Aktuelni intervju*, aired by RTRS on June 12, 2009.

51 The National Strategy for War Crimes Processing deals with a diverse range of issues affecting the capacity of the domestic justice system to handle war crimes cases—including matters such as witness protection and support, regional cooperation, and financial planning—and was the product of efforts by leaders of the entire justice sector. The internal prosecution policy of the Prosecutor's Office, however, is a distinct policy based on the discretion of the chief prosecutor and the head of the Special Department for War Crimes and has never been disseminated.

52 As the new outreach strategy developed soon after noted, "The fierce reactions from some victim groups to the new approach by the War Crimes Section have demonstrated the need for public information professionals' involvement in the planning and implementation of similar outreach exercises" (*Public Information and Outreach Strategy* [*Prosecutor's Office*], 3 [unpublished, copy on file with author]).

53 BiH Prosecutor's Office, "New Way, A New Beginning," brochure, 2008.

54 See, for example, Denis Dzidic, "Analysis: Witnesses Recall Massacre at Koricanske Stijene," Bosnian Investigative Reporting Network, December 2, 2009, http://www.bim.ba/en/195/10/24129/.

55 See BIRN BiH, *Report on the Regional Conference on Transparency of Courts and Responsibility of Media* (BIRN: Sarajevo, 2009); see also http://birn.eu.com/en/1/20/21735/?tpl=30.

56 See OSCE, *Witness Protection and Support in BiH Domestic War Crimes Trials: Obstacles and Recommendations a Year after Adoption of the National Strategy for War Crimes Processing,* May 2010, http://www.oscebih.org/documents/osce_bih_doc_2010122314375593eng.pdf.

57 A factor in this grievance is that media outlets prefer images that relate to the season, so photographs of someone clad for a Balkan winter in papers being printed in August are problematic. See Association of Court Reporters from the Court of Bosnia and Herzegovina, "Public Outreach Section Letter," October 28, 2009, http://www.bim.ba/en/1/40/23238/. Under the rules of the Criminal Procedure Code, the Prosecutor's Office cannot take such photos and release them, in accordance with the rights of the defendant. PIOS, on the other hand, has the power to release current images from the courtroom.

58 A public opinion survey and focus group research were carried out by Prism Research on behalf of the Registry of the Court of BiH and the BiH Prosecutor's Office in July 2003.

59 For a hint at the poor results of the public opinion research, see *Public Information and Outreach Strategy (Prosecutor's Office)*, 4, which notes, "The majority of those polled have deeply rooted misperceptions about the institution, its attitude towards different ethnic groups and the degree of politicisation of its work."

60 Ibid.

61 *Public Information and Outreach Strategy for the Court of BiH,* 2008 (unpublished, copy on file with author; hereafter, *PIO Strategy* [*Court*]), 7. "[The] BiH Prosecutor's Office and Court of BiH do not own the process of prosecuting and trying the worst perpetrators of organised crime and war crimes. Nor can they hope for success by solely relying on the complex legislative framework and the powers given to them by the law. It is the Bosnian society, its citizens, who own the process and have the most interest in seeing PO BiH and Court of BiH succeed in implementing their mandates" (3, emphasis in original).

62 Ibid., 5.

63 The court's team was to comprise the head of public information and outreach, a court spokesperson, an outreach officer, and a single public information assistant (*PIO Strategy* [*Court*]). The Prosecutor's Office team would comprise a head of public information and outreach, the spokesperson, a public information officer, and a public information assistant (*Public Information and Outreach Strategy for the BiH Prosecutor's Office,* 2008 [unpublished, copy on file with author; hereafter, *PIO Strategy* (*PO*)], 9).

64 For the Prosecutor's Office, the short-term goals include the following: "[i] Identify the main misperceptions affecting the image of PO BiH; [ii] Identify the different target audiences in BiH and the messages to be delivered; [iii] Address various audiences in BiH through media and directly, through community outreach, on regular basis; [iv] Initiate

creation of support network in the BiH civil society and abroad; [v] Disseminate information to media and others on regular basis; [vi] Have a strong and constantly present voice in public debate on PO BiH" (*PIO Strategy* [PO], 5). For the court, the short-term goals include the following: "[i] Identify and address the specific misperceptions about the Court of BiH; [ii] Identify the main messages and address various audiences through most effective channels of communication; [iii] Establish regular presence in the media across the country; [iv] Ensure direct TV and radio coverage of trials; [v] Achieve creation of support network in the BiH civil society and abroad; [vi] Have a strong and constantly present voice in public debate on war crimes and organized crime" (*PIO Strategy* [PO], 6). For quotations in this note and the next, bracketed numbers replace bullet points in the original.

65 The Prosecutor's Office long-term goals are defined as "[i] Public well-informed about PO BiH and its strategy in dealing with organized crime and war crimes; [ii] Expectations of the PO BiH realistic and in line with the role and capacity of PO BiH; [iii] Public taking an active interest in ongoing cases and supportive of PO BiH efforts; [iv] Public assisting PO BiH in various ways; [v] Work of PO BiH transparent within its legal framework" (*PIO Strategy* [PO], 5). For the court, the long-term goals include the following: "[i] Public able to closely follow the cases conducted before the Court of BiH; [ii] Media and partner organisations able to effectively relay the proceedings to the wider public; [iii] Information and court documents (including judgements) accessible to public and actively disseminated; [iv] Public able to engage with the Court of BiH (including registry) on various levels; [v] Public taking an active interest in ongoing cases and supportive of Court of BiH; [vi] Achievements of the Court of BiH known to BiH public and abroad; [vii] Court of BiH enjoys a perception of an open and fair court working on behalf of all citizens" (*PIO Strategy* [PO], 6).

66 *PIO Strategy* (*Court*), 11–13; *PIO Strategy* (*PO*), 9–12.

67 *PIO Strategy* (*PO*), 5.

68 "Unfounded criticism and politically motivated attacks on the PO BiH must be responded to by PIO team and senior officials where required—the record must be set straight on all important issues as the failure to do so results in myths and misperceptions becoming cemented" (ibid., 7).

69 *PIO Strategy* (*Court*), 5.

70 Ibid., 8. The emergence of *TV Justice*, described above, has made imperative the strategy's exhortation for the Court to ensure "timely access to the courtroom footage and relevant documents, and provide other assistance as required" (8).

71 *PIO Strategy* (*PO*), 7.

72 Ibid.

73 *PIO Strategy* (*Court*), 10.

74 OSCE Mission to BiH, *Developing Public Information and Outreach for War Crimes Proceedings in Bosnia and Herzegovina: Guidance for Courts and Prosecutor's Offices at the Entity Level,*

2010 (unpublished, copy on file with author; hereafter, *Draft Model Guidelines*), 10.

75 E.g., "Witness support NGOs gathered into an informal network by the ICTY Victims and Witnesses Section, UNDP's network of NGOs engaged in the transitional justice consultation process, the network of NGOs involved in the initiative to form a regional truth-telling body, the loose network of victim groups gathered around ICMP, etc." (*PIO Strategy* [*Court*], 10).

76 Ibid., 8.

77 A committee comprising two international judges, two national judges, and the PIOS head was formed at the end of 2009 to review the strategies and make recommendations to the Collegium of Judges about which aspects to implement and, apparently, to abandon.

78 BIRN BiH, "NGOs Say Privacy Law Jeopardizes Struggle for Justice," July 16, 2010, http://www.bim.ba/en/227/10/29515/.

79 See OSCE Mission to BiH, *Delivering Justice in BiH*, 88.

80 See *National Strategy for War Crimes Processing of BiH.*

81 See OSCE Mission Report, *War Crimes Trials before the Courts of Bosnia and Herzegovina;* OSCE, *Delivering Justice.*

82 Figures updated as of July 2012. OSCE Mission to Bosnia and Herzegovina Trial Monitoring Program, *War Crimes Proceedings Statistics* (unpublished, copy on file with author).

83 OSCE Trial Monitoring Program, "Findings," December 2009 (unpublished, copy on file with author).

84 The OSCE is the largest regional security organization in the world, with fifty-six participating states. Among its field operations is the OSCE Mission to BiH, which is mandated, inter alia, to monitor the human rights situation in the country under Annex VI of the Dayton Peace Agreement. Today, the OSCE is the only international organization with an extensive presence on the ground in BiH. See www.osce.org and www.oscebih.org.

85 *Draft Model Guidelines*, 3–4.

86 Ibid., 3.

87 According to trial monitoring data collected by the OSCE Mission to BiH, Banja Luka completed twenty-five war crimes cases (involving fifty-two Serbs, two Bosniaks, and three Croats) between 2004 and 2010 (OSCE Mission to Bosnia and Herzegovina Trial Monitoring Program, *War Crimes Proceedings Statistics*; figures updated as of February 4, 2011). The proactive efforts of prosecutors such as Mitrović seem to have resulted in a greater willingness of victims to endure the frequent indignities that come with trials conducted at the entity level—which may include having to sit beside the perpetrator in cramped courtrooms and spend recesses in the same hallways. See Hodzić, "Living the Legacy of Mass Atrocities," nn. 34, 35. See also OSCE Mission to BiH and XY Films, *Justice Requires Outreach*, 2007 (see "Justice Requires Outreach / Pravda treba iskorak," June 2, 2010, http://www.youtube.com/watch?v=uGgScpIPI5Q, parts 1–4).

88 For example, a judge in Travnik was reported to have told a journalist that an indictment against a local man had been confirmed even before the court had officially accepted the indictment proposed by the prosecutor.

89 *Draft Model Guidelines*, 71.

90 *SMART* stands for "specific, measurable, attainable, realistic, and time-based."

91 *Draft Model Guidelines*, 5.

92 Ibid., 11. "All listed messages need to be carefully shaped in each community on the basis of assessed prejudices, prevailing opinions, persistent propaganda and other relevant factors" (ibid.). Simple messages like "members of judiciary do not have hidden agendas" need to be delivered in some places, in recognition of the prevailing prejudices, while in others it simply needs to be asserted that "local courts are taking up the battle against impunity for war crimes."

93 See the public opinion survey and focus group research carried out on behalf of the Registry of the Court of BiH and BiH Prosecutor's Office in Prism Research, *Public Perceptions of the Work of the Court and Prosecutor's Office of B&H: Final Report*, July 2008 (unpublished).

94 See www.tuzilastvobih.gov.ba.

95 Hodzić, "Living the Legacy of Mass Atrocities," part 4.

96 Victims repudiate trial outcomes and sentences with alarmingly increasing frequency. See, for example, Dalio Sijah, "Sarajevo Embittered by Courts' Silence over Market Massacre," Balkan Investigative Reporting Network, February 4, 2010, http://www.bim.ba/en/204/10/25541/.

97 For instance, the Bridging the Gap series organized by the ICTY in five towns in BiH in 2005 was assessed as more effective than NGO-led events (Hodzić, "Living the Legacy of Mass Atrocities," 126–27). A roundtable meeting about local war crimes processing in Canton 6 (Central Bosnia Canton [Srednjobosanksi kanton]) organized by the OSCE Mission in 2009 succeeded in gathering representatives of Bosnian Muslim and Bosnian Croat associations of victims, missing persons, and fallen soldiers in the same room for the first time to meet with the cantonal prosecutor.

98 See OSCE, *Call for Proposals on Strengthening Outreach in War Crimes Cases* (Sarajevo: OSCE, 2009), requesting applicants that could demonstrate, inter alia, nondiscriminatory internal practices.

99 Izvor is a positive example of an association that works with victims and potential witnesses from all ethnic backgrounds. The BiH Association of Camp Inmates is a state-level umbrella organization that is inclusive of all local, entity, and regional associations of former camp inmates regardless of ethnic background.

100 For example, many academic institutions rely on BIRN's reports. At Duke University in the United States, BIRN materials are assigned as mandatory reading in some undergraduate courses.

101 According to the BiH Regulatory Agency for Communications, *Annual Survey on the Provision of Permits for Internet Services in BiH* (Sarajevo: BiH Regulatory Agency for Communications, 2008), 4–6, BiH had 336,163 Internet subscribers in 2008 with an estimated 1,307,585 users overall. With an estimated population of 4.2 million persons (no official postwar census data are available for BiH), the rate of Internet usage is around 34 percent. However, the figures for 2008 represent a significant increase in user rates from previous years. According to the Commission of the European Communities, *Bosnia and Herzegovina 2009 Progress Report: Enlargement Strategy and Main Challenges 2009–2010*, Doc. No. SEC (2009) 1338, Brussels, October 14, 2009, only 6.6 percent of BiH citizens had home Internet access in 2006 (65).

102 For example, the weekly magazine edition of *Radio Justice* is carried by 180 stations in BiH and enjoys very high listenership. The daily edition is aired twice a day on 152 radio stations, some 136 of which broadcast within BiH itself.

103 See, for example, OSCE, *Delivering Justice*; OSCE, *War Crimes Trials before the Domestic Courts of BiH;* and OSCE, *Witness Protection and Support in BiH Domestic War Crimes Trials.*

104 "Press Code of Bosnia and Herzegovina," adopted by the Press Council in Bosnia-Herzegovina, Association "BH Journalists," the BH Journalist Union, Association of Croat Journalists in B&H, and Association of Journalists in Republika Srpska in 2006, http://ethicnet.uta.fi/bosnia_and_herzegovina/press_code_of_bosnia_and_herzegovina.

105 For example, on March 28, 2001, the BiH Prosecutor's Office announced the prosecution of two journalists who had allegedly released the name of a victim-witness of multiple wartime rapes and sexual abuse. See "Podignuta optužnika protiv novinara i urednika 'Buma'" [Indictment filed against journalists and editors "Buma"], *Sarajevo-x.com*, March 28, 2011, http://www.sarajevo-x.com/bih/clanak/110328026.

106 "Press Code of Bosnia and Herzegovina," Article 10a: Protection of Witnesses, states, "Newspapers and periodicals shall take the utmost care when reporting on witnesses in war crime process[es], respecting rules and regulations in terms of [not] identifying the protected witnesses. Newspapers and periodicals shall generally avoid identifying witnesses in court trials for war crimes, as well as identifying their relatives and friends, unless their identification is necessary for complete, fair, and accurate reporting on [a] court trial, and if such identifying does not cause misinterpretation of [the] truth or [the] trial process."

107 Under the National Strategy for War Crimes Processing of 2008, and following prescribed amendments to the Criminal Procedure Code of BiH in 2009 (see working version of the BiH Criminal Procedure Code, *BiH Official Gazette* no. 3/03 with Corrections and Amendments of the BiH Criminal Procedure Code, as published in the *BiH Official Gazette* no. 93/09), an increased number of less complex war crimes cases were to be transferred from the state level to cantonal and district courts and prosecutors' offices beginning in 2010.

108 For example, see OSCE Mission to BiH, *Spot Report on Independence of the Judiciary.*

109 Prosecutor's Office of BiH, "Open Letter," Ref. No. A-814/09, Sarajevo, November 11, 2009, http://www.tuzilastvobih.gov.ba/files/docs/Otvoreno_pismoENG.pdf.

110 See OSCE Mission to BiH, *Spot Report on Independence of the Judiciary.*

CHAPTER 3

Reaching Out to Victims and Communities: The CAVR's Experiences in Timor-Leste

Patrick Burgess and Galuh Wandita

The island of Timor was divided during its colonial history, the western half being controlled by the Dutch, the eastern by Portugal. In 1945, following the end of World War II, the nationalist independence movement was victorious in its struggle against the Dutch, resulting in the birth of the state of Indonesia, which included the western half of Timor island. The eastern half of the island, known as Portuguese Timor, continued to be administered by Portugal. In 1974 the bloodless "Carnation Revolution" in Lisbon led to a decision by the Portuguese government to release all colonial holdings, including East Timor, which led to the rapid formation of local political parties and deep divisions between those who wanted Timor to become an independent nation immediately and others who favored integration with Indonesia. A short but bloody civil war ended with the victorious Fretilin party unilaterally declaring the independence of the Democratic Republic of Timor-Leste on November 28, 1975.[1]

In the polarized context of the Cold War, Western powers such as the United States and Australia viewed the left-leaning Fretilin party's control of East Timor as a threat. In addition, the new nation was strategically situated between the Indonesian archipelago and Australia and had significant resources, particularly natural gas and oil reserves. On December 6, 1975, US president Gerald Ford met with the Indonesian dictator General Suharto and informed him that no objection would be raised if Indonesia annexed the territory.[2] Immediately after, on December 10, 1975, Indonesia launched a massive military invasion of East Timor with support from Timorese minority factions that the Fretilin party had defeated in the civil war and that favored integration with Indonesia.

During the invasion and subsequent twenty-four-year military occupation of East Timor, Indonesian security forces, together with groups of Timorese allies, were involved in serious human rights violations on a massive scale. With a population estimated at fewer than 700,000, the violations were dramatic; they resulted in at least 102,800 deaths, and the actual count may have been significantly higher.[3] The resistance movement that fought for Timorese self-determination continued its operations throughout the period, and a large proportion of the human rights violations systematically targeted supporters of the independence movement. As in many similar contexts, the state's toleration of atrocities committed allegedly for the sake of maintaining security created a cloak of impunity under which killing, rape, and torture were committed with a complete lack of accountability. In 1998 the fall of Suharto's military regime in Indonesia brought an opportunity for the international community to press the issue of East Timor's right to determine its own status. A UN-sponsored ballot on August 30, 1999, resulted in 78.5 percent of the population voting in favor of independence in defiance of acts of intimidation by Indonesian security forces and the Timorese militia they had created and armed.[4] These acts of terror, which began in 1998 and became widespread during the months leading up to the ballot, were intended to pressure the population to vote for integration with Indonesia.[5] The announcement of the results in early September 1999 triggered a scorched-earth response by the security forces and militia, which killed an estimated 1,200 to 1,500 people, burned thousands of houses, and displaced 550,000 people during a one-month period that ended with their retreat over the border into Indonesia following the October 1999 deployment of an international peacekeeping force.[6]

In October 1999 the UN Security Council established the United Nations Transitional Administration for East Timor (UNTAET), providing it the unprecedented mandate to administer all aspects of governance in East Timor, including the administration of justice, and to prepare the country for independence, which it eventually achieved in May 2002.[7] A UN staff member was appointed as deputy-general prosecutor for serious crimes, and the Special Panels of the Dili District Court were created as a hybrid court involving panels of international and national judges, tasked with investigating crimes committed during the 1999 violence.[8] In early 2000 the National Council of Timorese Resistance (Conselho Nacional da Resistência Timorense, CNRT), an alliance of Timorese political groups that had supported independence, conducted a national congress that unanimously passed a resolution to establish a truth and reconciliation commission (TRC). At this point in time, there had still been little progress on the UN-administered process to prosecute serious crimes, amid "concerns for the potential for violence to reignite, especially in the context of the virtually complete impunity enjoyed by perpetrators of crimes," many of whom were returning to East Timor.[9] At the CNRT's request, the head of UNTAET directed the mission's human rights section to provide assistance for the establishment of such a commission.

This chapter describes the efforts of the East Timor Commission for Reception, Truth and Reconciliation (Comissão de Acolhimento, Verdade e

Reconciliação, CAVR) to reach out to local communities, key actors, and the general public. After providing a short background on the history of violence in East Timor, we discuss the process leading up to the CAVR's creation and its early relations with civil society organizations. Following an explanation of the body's mandate and core work, we describe the CAVR's activities and strategies for reaching out to victims, civil society organizations, and communities at the local level, with a special focus on local reconciliation activities (the Community Reconciliation Process, CRP) and efforts to reach out to specific sectors of society. We then discuss the production and dissemination of the commission's final report and the creation of the Post-CAVR Technical Secretariat, designed to follow up on the CAVR's work after the end of its mandate. We conclude by highlighting some of the most important challenges for outreach faced in East Timor as well as a number of key lessons to learn from that country's experience.

THE CAVR'S ORIGINS AND EARLY OUTREACH EFFORTS

Although the CAVR was formally established in July 2001, substantial preparations were required before operations eventually began in early 2002. From these very first steps—recruiting staff, setting up offices, establishing administrative systems, planning programs, and drafting procedures—it was accepted that key principles in the success of any commission would be ownership by and involvement of the whole East Timorese community, assisted by appropriate international technical expertise.[10] Several defining factors of the Timor context meant that the CAVR's ability to ensure the participation of Timorese communities would be critical for its success.

For example, hundreds of thousands of Timorese were displaced over the border to Indonesia during the violence in late 1999. Although many had not been involved in the conflict and had fled in terror or been forced onto trucks and boats, thousands of young men had participated in the militia groups responsible for the violence. Many had been coerced into joining these groups and had reluctantly complied; others had been involved in low-level violence, such as beatings and looting; still others had been directly involved in killings, rape, and the widespread burning of houses. One goal of the commission was to promote reconciliation between those who had favored independence and those who had been involved in the struggle on the pro-Indonesia side, including the safe reintegration into their communities of people who had been displaced. These goals called for substantial engagement on the part of the CAVR with local communities.

Another essential reason for community involvement was the dearth of public records available to help the commission piece together the picture of what had taken place and, therefore, to learn lessons from the conflict. Journalists and foreign visitors were prohibited from entering East Timor during most of the occupation, and the scorched-earth policy of the retreating forces had resulted in most records being destroyed. Some human rights workers and members of the international peacekeeping force tried to salvage documents from the ruins of strategic buildings, such as the military headquarters, but most archives had been destroyed in the inferno.[11] The truth about the past would clearly not be made available through written records, increasing the importance of oral testimony from the thousands of victims and witnesses whose experiences of human rights violations had never been documented.

COMMUNITY INVOLVEMENT IN ESTABLISHING THE CAVR MANDATE

In 2000 a steering committee was established comprising representatives of eight Timorese political and civil society groups and three UN representatives.[12] Shortly after its appointment, and with the aim of adopting an inclusive approach, the Steering Committee began to formulate a model of the proposed commission; consultations included meetings with local communities in each of the territory's thirteen districts and at refugee camps in West Timor (Indonesia). In some areas the interaction was with the district leaders and representatives. In others it was at the subdistrict level, while still other meetings were held in villages. In this way, feedback came from horizontal as well as vertical community structures and representatives across the territory.

During these consultations, the following points came up repeatedly. The commission later included these points in its mandate, thus helping to shape the way it conducted its work:[13]

- There was a widespread belief that those responsible for the most serious crimes must face a formal trial and imprisonment if found guilty. [Sections 22.2, 27.5, 27.6]
- Communities wanted to deal with the thousands who had been involved in less serious crimes; the communities felt that traditional justice mechanisms should have a place. However, traditional mechanisms were felt to be not strong enough to deal with the scale and nature of the crimes, and people in the communities said they wanted the formal justice system to be involved. [Sections 22–33 on Community Reconciliation Process and Community Reconciliation Agreements]

- Local communities wanted to hear directly from local perpetrators and victims. [Sections 22–33 on Community Reconciliation Process and Community Reconciliation Agreements]
- Many communities reported stories reflecting how they were dramatically affected by the conflict, but that the effects had never been officially documented. [The CAVR's community mapping/profile process.]
- Enforced famine had been a significant characteristic of the conflict during the early 1980s, causing tens of thousands of deaths. This major aspect of the conflict needed to be included. [The CAVR established a special research unit on famine and displacement and dedicates an entire section to it (chapter 7.3).]
- Sexual abuse was a common practice among members of the Indonesian security forces, although it had not been widely reported due to victims' reluctance to speak about their experiences. [Section 13.2(a)]
- Violations of social, economic, and cultural rights contributed to people's suffering, including manipulation and monopolization of the coffee crop, sandalwood trees, and so on. [See definition of "victim" in the mandate, Section 1(n), and *Chega!*, chapter 7.9, on social and economic rights.]

Following these consultations, and significantly informed by them,[14] the Steering Committee drafted the law that included the CAVR's mandate, obligations, and powers. The UNTAET Human Rights Section and the International Center for Transitional Justice (ICTJ) assisted members of the Steering Committee in the task's technical aspects.[15] Establishment of the CAVR was formalized by the passage of UNTAET Regulation No. 2001/10, which was adopted as a law of the new nation of Timor-Leste upon independence on May 20, 2002. The mandate obliged the CAVR to undertake three broad categories of activities: (1) conduct inquiries in order to ascertain the truth in relation to the human rights violations that had occurred and write a report including its findings and recommendations, (2) promote reconciliation, and (3) assist victims.[16]

COMMUNITY PARTICIPATION IN THE SELECTION OF COMMISSIONERS

As UNTAET Regulation No. 2001/10 required, a selection panel was formed in 2001 to facilitate the nomination process for national and regional commissioners.[17] Newspapers, radio, television, posters, and local networks combined to inform the public of the commission's role. Following a call for nominations from the people of East Timor, the selection panel compiled a list of 60 names for national commissioners and 160 names for regional commissioners as official candidates, solicited during community meetings or through written submissions. The regulation establishing the commission provided a set of criteria for nominating candidates,[18] and the panel was required to give special consideration to representing a diversity of experiences and views, and regional and fair gender representation.[19] The regulation also mandated the appointment of one national commissioner whose political views represented Timorese who had supported integration of East Timor as part of Indonesia. After conducting a number of public meetings in West Timor, the selection panel then interviewed a short list of candidates for national commissioners and made recommendations to the UN special representative of the secretary-general (SRSG).[20]

The broad consultations and transparent manner of selection were fundamental in creating a sense of ownership and connection between ordinary people and the commission. However, in a country where much of the population lives in remote villages, creating and maintaining these links would inevitably continue to be a major challenge. In order to nominate individuals as potential commissioners, the communities had to understand what the commission would be doing, but at the beginning of this process, the population had little understanding or experience of the role of truth and reconciliation commissions (TRCs). The selection process became an extensive outreach program that stimulated public debate around issues of truth, justice, and reconciliation even before the commission had been formally established.[21] Most significantly, a genuine effort took place to engage pro-Indonesia elements in West Timor in the process.

EARLY CHALLENGES IN RELATIONS WITH CIVIL SOCIETY

One problem that emerged during these early steps and continued to affect the commission throughout the period of its mandate was that some human rights civil society organizations (CSOs) in Timor regarded the commission with skepticism. The leaders of the main national human rights nongovernmental organizations (NGOs) were members of the Steering Committee and, therefore, involved in the initial decisionmaking processes. Despite this arrangement, repeated public criticisms arose that the commission was not consulting enough with members of these organizations and the community. Although such criticism also indicated communication problems within these organizations themselves, it nevertheless fed a growing rift between Timorese civil society actors and initiatives thought to be connected to the UN mission and large international presence.

The divisions between the international community and Timor-based civil society groups, which persisted and grew in the intervening years, were exacerbated by the influx of thousands of UN staff with little or no knowledge of Timor and its history, no local language skills, and a dubious ability to impart skills through capacity-building programs. Many CSOs had been deeply involved in defending the rights of the population and victims, as well as carrying out small-scale reconciliation programs, at significant cost and risk to themselves during the occupation and the violence surrounding the ballot. Additionally, the fact that some donors channeled the resources available for human rights issues to the CAVR may have made it difficult for national organizations to rebuild and recover after the violence, thus worsening the tensions between them and the CAVR. From the beginning, the Steering Committee tried to mitigate these tensions and issues by organizing additional meetings with civil society representatives. Also, the person eventually appointed as chair of the CAVR was the former head of the HAK Foundation, the most significant human rights NGO in the country.[22] However, these efforts did not fully resolve the problem, and the commission arguably could have done more to recognize or lessen these tensions.

Another source of tension was that some CSOs suspected that the CAVR would not strongly support prosecuting perpetrators. Such a perception of TRCs is common in transitional settings, largely due to the overwhelming international profile of the South African TRC, which offered amnesty to perpetrators who had fulfilled certain conditions. However, these same CSOs have welcomed the CAVR's *Final Report*, which included strong recommendations on prosecuting perpetrators, and which also continues to be used as an important resource to advocate for accountability for gross human rights violations committed during the conflict.

Despite these tensions, some CSOs worked closely with the CAVR on various issues. For example, Fokupers (East Timor Women's Forum), one of the leading Timorese organizations that worked on women's rights, became a significant partner of the commission, conducting research on violations committed against women and helping to deliver the CAVR's urgent reparations program. Together with other local organizations, Fokupers also became involved in the Community Reconciliation Programs.[23] However, the lack of understanding and support from some national NGOs continued throughout the life of the commission's work, a situation that might have been averted had the commission engaged with these organizations' broad networks to conduct public information and outreach activities. Such coalitions might also have assisted with these NGOs' financial recovery and reduced discord and tension.[24]

THE CAVR'S CORE WORK

> The most fundamental lesson around how to do effective outreach was getting the principles of the institution established by the leadership of the institution—the commission—and then having that well-understood by the staff as they came, at whatever level.
>
> —Kieran Dwyer, CAVR advisor (interview with author, February 12, 2010)

By the time the CAVR began its operations in early 2002, the vast majority of the displaced population had gradually returned home, leaving thirty-five thousand still in West Timor—most of whom were former members of militia groups, or Timorese who had worked as Indonesian civil servants, and their family members. Many people who had returned to East Timor were unable to go back to their villages for fear of violent retribution stemming from their involvement in the 1999 violence. Others still in West Timor held the same fears. The CAVR saw itself as a way to break the cycle of violence by uncovering the causes of the conflict and opening a process of reconciliation. The commission anticipated "payback violence" against returning refugees, and described and included among its own goals "developing and implementing a strategy to prevent the expected violence through concrete programs focused on the peaceful reception of refugees, reconciliation between factions, and promoting national unity through establishing the truth of the history of the conflict, allowing past wounds to be cleaned and healed."[25] The CAVR articulated its priorities as follows:

- Assist the reconciliation of past differences.
- Assist national healing by allowing victims to publicly or privately recount their suffering and compile these testimonies and other materials into a national report.
- Deal with a significant proportion of the thousands of minor crimes committed between 1974 and 1999 in a faster, less expensive, less formal way than the formal legal system and with a community-based mechanism. Such a mechanism gives a voice to victims, perpetrators, and community members who negotiate a solution acceptable to all parties. This agreement is then checked and formalized by an Order of the District Court.
- Provide a formal mechanism that the returnees from West Timor can utilize to assist their reintegration into their communities in East Timor.[26]

Programmatically, this strategy led to establishing three divisions responsible for carrying out the three main pillars of truth, reconciliation, and victim support. Extensive needs for outreach related to each of these pillars, and the scale and type of this work depended on the program developed for each pillar.

TRUTH SEEKING

The division responsible for truth seeking took statements, coded and entered these statements into a database for analysis, conducted research, facilitated submissions from individuals and institutions based on key themes prioritized by the CAVR, and organized public hearings. As described below, the public hearings were critical to spreading the word about the CAVR's work. At the end of its mandate, the CAVR had taken 7,824 statements from victims and witnesses from the thirteen districts, documenting violations that took place during the period stipulated by the CAVR's mandate: 1974–99.[27] The CAVR research unit also conducted targeted interviews with experts, key figures, and more than one thousand persons, covering ten main topics of inquiry:

- Famine and forced displacement
- Structure, policies, and practices of the Indonesian military and police
- Structure, policies, and practices of the resistance
- Political imprisonment, torture, and forced disappearances
- Killings, including massacres
- Death toll (including a graveyard census and retrospective mortality survey)
- Children and youth
- Women and conflict
- Political party conflict and civil war
- The role of international actors in relation to Timor's right to self-determination

The CAVR district teams conducted a consultation meeting in each subdistrict to develop these truth-seeking priorities. In order to gather information available in Indonesia, the research team also collaborated with ELSAM (Lembaga Studi dan Advokasi Masyarakat), a Jakarta-based NGO that collected documents and identified some witnesses who could help the commission.

COMMUNITY RECONCILIATION

The community reconciliation division was responsible for aiding in community-based mediation. The goal of this program was to facilitate the return of those who had been involved in "harmful acts" during the conflict and their acceptance by their victims.[28] This goal was of major importance; the conflict was characterized by divisions among those living in the same villages, and sometimes among members of the same families. The political nature of the divisions, either pro-independence or pro-integration with Indonesia, had led to much animosity, but also could be seen as less enduring and more able to be healed than other conflicts based on ethnic, national, or religious differences. During the Community Reconciliation Process hearings conducted in the villages in which the divided parties lived, perpetrators were given the opportunity to speak publicly about their offenses and ask for forgiveness. Victims and community members were then asked to respond. A reconciliation panel comprising a regional commissioner and local community leaders mediated the hearings. If an agreement was reached and the act of reconciliation completed (usually in the form of a public apology or community work), then the act was registered at the local court, thereby creating a permanent stay of prosecution for the acts included in the perpetrator's statement. (The CRP and the specific challenges it posed for outreach are discussed in greater depth in a later section.)

RECEPTION AND VICTIM SUPPORT

The division for reception and victim support was established to accompany victims throughout all the CAVR processes and to help victims move forward in their healing process. Staff members in this division were tasked to

- organize public meetings in the communities about the CAVR as part of the socialization process;
- support the survivors/victims of human rights violations who participated in the CAVR processes (e.g., those who gave statements, testified at public hearings, and participated in community reconciliation processes);
- facilitate group discussions at the village level on the impact of human rights violations upon the communities;
- assist survivors by referral to appropriate agencies; and
- identify recommendations for the final report that relate to support for victims of human rights violations and the provision of reparations.

In 2003 the CAVR established a working group comprising church members, NGO representatives, and the CAVR staff to assist the most vulnerable victims through an urgent reparations program supported by the World Bank and the Community Empowerment Project. At the end of its mandate, the CAVR had helped more than seven hundred victims—about 10 percent of the total number of people who testified to the CAVR. Although the total number assisted was relatively small, it was quite significant considering that the CAVR had no funds to develop a reparations scheme. The program was important both at a symbolic level and as a model of how a full-fledged, government-run reparations program could function. The CAVR also invited survivors of human rights violations to attend a three-day participatory healing workshop. During these workshops, survivors had the opportunity to share their stories, using art and music, as well as to express their hopes for the future. At the end of the workshop, survivors received a small grant of two hundred US dollars for their urgent needs.[29]

BRINGING THE CAVR TO THE VILLAGES

> I found that messaging is very important for people's participation in any program because the message can change people's minds. ... The message we used was: "CAVR, the road to peace." Why is it the road to peace? Because we are looking back at our history through the truth-seeking process, and at the same time we heal our wounds and the statements given are part of building peace, of healing ourselves ... [and] we can heal ourselves by telling the truth.
>
> —Jose Caetano Guterres, CAVR coordinator for community outreach and public information (interview with author, February 15, 2010)

As mentioned above, the CAVR had three programmatic divisions responsible for carrying out the substantive mandates of truth seeking, community reconciliation, and victim support, respectively. In addition to the administrative and finance divisions, a separate section housed various functions that supported the CAVR's programs. This division, called Program Support, included community outreach / public information, media relations, institutional development, and training. A Timorese coordinator with a team of five to six persons and one international advisor led the division. The bulk of the funding for the division was integrated into the institution-wide budget (approximately US$5 million) with some small outreach projects directly supported by donors. Community outreach was defined as

> developing a working relationship with all the main community organizations and community leaders. At the National Office level this meant liaising with civil society organizations, church groups and other religious organizations. In the district and regional teams this meant building a cooperative relationship with the grassroots extensions of such organizations, in particular women's organizations, church representatives, youth groups and local leaders.[30]

Again, the CAVR was highly aware of the need to build partnerships in order to effectively convey its messages to the people.

Part of the work of the Program Support Division was increasing awareness among the public and key stakeholders about the CAVR and its work through an education and media campaign. The commission developed its own radio team to report on the commission's progress. The resulting program, *Dalan ba dame* (Road to peace), began weekly broadcasts at the end of 2002 on Timor's national radio network and a private station owned by the Catholic Church, as well as airing rebroadcasts on community radio outlets in the districts. A senior Timorese female radio journalist led the radio team, with a staff of two people. They worked closely with the international advisor in the Program Support Division. This division also was in charge of producing different types of information and branding materials such as pamphlets, brochures, posters, T-shirts, and short reports on the CAVR's public hearings. In addition, the Program Support Division ensured television and radio coverage of a number of community reconciliation hearings and all the national public hearings held at the CAVR office, the former Balide prison. Radio coverage was particularly effective in a country where many communities are isolated and its general population has a low level of literacy. As one senior advisor observed,

> We had the radio program on before with a young woman from Suai telling her story. And people from Oecussi had probably never been to Suai … [yet] they were all telling the story of this one woman, and how brave she was to speak about her rape, and how she was stolen and taken [to West Timor], and how she escaped and got back with her baby to Timor. And everyone in this village [Oecussi] was talking about this story. And so that was the power of the radio.[31]

Soon after the CAVR began its work, it became clear that accessing victims in Timor-Leste's remote interior regions must be included as a priority in all plans and activities. Community outreach, therefore, needed to be integrated into all of the commission's work, and not rest as the sole responsibility of an outreach unit. This realization led to the development of a strategic plan. According to this plan, the CAVR's approach was not to service the regions with separate aspects of the commission's work through occasional visits of different thematic teams, but rather to create district teams, each with the capacity to take statements, provide support for victims, and facilitate community reconciliation. A district team would spend three months in each of the sixty-five subdistricts in East Timor. Before commencing its three-month stay in the field, each team visited that region to explain the CAVR's mission, and to solicit information on priority incidents that should be investigated and priority villages to be targeted for the Community Reconciliation Processes.

Thus, CAVR district teams delivered outreach systematically to every subdistrict because the population needed to understand before any of the activities began what the commission was and what it planned to do. By combining the outreach program with other core activities, a single team could make contact with a community, provide education on the work of the CAVR, and answer questions; then the same team could take statements and conduct CRPs and other programs. This organization also made sense in terms of the geography of Timor-Leste, where many areas are inaccessible or only accessible by foot during the rainy season. A single team could logistically and more effectively set up its base in a remote subdistrict for three months rather than trying to organize repeated visits by various teams. The local population also became accustomed to the presence of the CAVR team during the intense three-month program, which would have been different had the work taken place through short-term, irregular visits. The disadvantage of this system was that, following the three-month period, subdistricts had only limited direct contact with the CAVR. One CAVR advisor reflected,

> [The participatory approach] stemmed from the fundamental decision to say, we want this Commission to be meaningful to people in their lives as it is going on, not just in the Final Report. We believe that that meaning will come from the ability to relate to the Commission, that it's their Commission and that it can be with them in their communities.[32]

The same advisor believed that the presence in the communities of regional commissioners and staff who spoke the local language and understood the context was critical to the CAVR's success:

> The first, most effective strategy was recruiting the teams in the district, with regional representation—not just staff, but regional commissioners. That made people feel that the commission was in the community ... and people told us that often. If it was just staff, they wouldn't feel that they were being honored with the commissioners' presence. So, in effect, everybody was an outreach officer.[33]

A consortium of international donors funded the CAVR. In addition, the conflict itself had been international in nature, with Indonesia, Portugal, the United States, and Australia as well as the United Nations having played significant roles. The CAVR's deep research into the historical context and its focus on reconciliation meant that the international community was closely monitoring its work. A number of steps were taken to ensure that information on the CAVR's activities was available not only to the Timorese population but also to those in other countries who were monitoring its performance progress. The CAVR produced many of its outreach products in Tetum (the lingua franca in East Timor), Indonesian, Portuguese, and English. Producing materials and the final report in multiple languages brought a major challenge to the CAVR staff, particularly as many of the words and terms used in one language did not have exact translations in the other relevant languages.

In addition to tools to facilitate internal communication and organization—such as summaries of the CAVR's mandate, procedures, and other functional issues—the commission also produced a range of products designed to disseminate accurate information about its work.

Regular updates in English and Bahasa Indonesian included a summary about program implementation, CAVR activities, and future plans. These bimonthly updates were printed and distributed to civil society groups, donors, and UN agencies. Electronic versions also went out by email and were available on the CAVR website. The CAVR's radio program also broadcast a summary of these updates.

Public hearing summaries included compilations of press clippings and testimonies from the public hearings. Printed booklets were produced in English, Tetum, and Indonesian for three of the public hearings: *Women and the Conflict, Forced Displacement and Famine,* and *Massacres*. Publication of similar booklets planned for the remaining public hearings had not been implemented at the time of this writing.

Production of the film Dalan ba dame provided a visual history of the conflict in Timor, including interviews and historical footage that the CAVR obtained. The documentary is approximately two and a half hours long and was produced in Tetum with subtitles in English, Portuguese, and Indonesian. DVDs of this film were available throughout Timor-Leste. In addition, a CD was produced in Tetum only and distributed within Timor.

A *book of photographs by well-known Indonesian photographer Poriaman Sitanggang* documented victims who shared their stories with the CAVR and included short statements from the victims about their hopes for the country's future. The book, titled *Hear Our Voices*, was produced in Tetum and English.

A *booklet on the history of the Comarca Balide Prison* traced its use as the former colonial prison in Dili and a torture center during the Indonesian occupation, and the CAVR's rehabilitation of the prison in 2002 for use as its national headquarters.

A *book of posters*, The History of Timor-Leste in Posters, compiled reproductions of twenty posters produced for the CAVR, each documenting a different period of Timor's history from Portuguese times to 1999.[34]

COMMUNITY RECONCILIATION PROCESS: A CHALLENGE FOR OUTREACH

As discussed above, the CRP sought—through dialogue and restorative processes at the local level—to facilitate the return to their communities of people who had been involved in lesser offenses during the conflict. Although the program was a new mechanism, it included aspects of traditional ceremonial dispute resolution practices. In particular, the practice of *Biti Bo'ot* (big mat) was widely used as part of the CRP. In this traditional process a large woven mat would be unfurled, and parties to a dispute would sit on it, together with community leaders, with no one allowed to leave until a solution had been found. Other traditional practices were also included in the hearings, depending on the local context.

In 2002 the step-by-step implementation of the CRP hearings was formulated, teams were trained, and a pilot program was carried out with high expectations that the program would quickly involve entire communities and increase the potential for reconciliation. However, the staff involved in the process found that alleged perpetrators were unwilling to participate, particularly as there was little understanding among these groups of the value of this process. As one commissioner reflected,

> For East Timorese ... in our culture, to really say that you have done something wrong publicly, it's a shame to you and to your family. Somehow, to them, it's a relief, as well, to get that out into the open. But to say, in 1999, "I did this," it's a big thing for the family, it's a shame not only for yourself but for your family or community.[35]

The CAVR had to find a way to tackle these barriers to participation in the CRP program. National political and church leaders agreed to encourage individuals who had been involved in violent acts to come forward and participate. The president, Xanana Gusmao, publicly supported the program, and many Catholic priests encouraged those at Sunday Mass to "confess" their crimes to the CAVR. As a result of these additional outreach strategies, participation in the CRP's activities increased. The early hearings produced very positive results, leading to a significant number of cases in which perpetrators of crimes such as house burning, beating, and looting admitted the harmful acts they had committed, asked for forgiveness, offered to carry out some community service or provide modest or symbolic compensation to victims, and so were accepted back into their communities. Word of these results quickly spread through local information grapevines until more requests for hearings came than the CAVR could accommodate. At the time this program closed, over thirteen hundred individual perpetrators of lesser crimes had completed this reconciliation process, while several thousand others were estimated to be ready and willing to participate in the program.[36]

The CRP hearings became a flagship program of the CAVR. Although the legislation included provisions for a process involving perpetrators of particular "harmful acts," in practice, each event became a much broader symbol for what the CAVR was trying to achieve. CRP hearings in many places represented not only a means of dealing with these particular acts, but a means of recalling and symbolically closing the experience of the community during the entire period of the conflict. The hearings also made a major contribution to reducing the large outstanding caseload confronting the newly established judiciary and legal systems, thus providing a form of closure for perpetrators, victims, and community members where otherwise no solution would have been possible.

As one CAVR senior staff member observed,

> [During a] community reconciliation meeting in Liquica, one of the perpetrators stood up and confessed everything he did.... And at the end, the victims came to him and said, "Okay, you

> are telling the truth. We are family, come and support me, I am building my house. Come and support me, and we will build my house together; we are a family." It was a small thing, only involving one person, but … they understood the global picture, the national level, and wanted to contribute to that.[37]

REACHING OUT TO SPECIAL GROUPS

> And the outreach side of that is just … to reach out to the people who are least likely to be allowed to be involved in these things. That's the fundamental point of it. … Unless you have a really strong outreach program, those who are most marginalized will remain the most marginalized and actually become more marginalized by not being part of this process.
>
> —Kieran Dwyer, CAVR advisor (interview with author, February 12, 2010)

Due to the nature of the conflict, at least two specific groups needed special attention to ensure their participation in the CAVR's processes: women and refugees in West Timor. Prior to the start of the CAVR's work, women's groups, human rights NGOs, and various UN bodies had already issued reports on gender-based violations. The CAVR was compelled to document the stories of women victims and the gendered impact of the conflict. Another key consideration for the implementation of the commission's reconciliation mandate was the displacement of tens of thousands of refugees who had fled or were forcibly transported to West Timor, Indonesia. Among those refugees were leaders and members of militia groups.

WOMEN

The CAVR made two key decisions that had a significant effect on how the commission dealt with gender issues. One was to ensure that women constituted 50 percent of its field-based staff engaged in the key functions of the commission (statement taking, community outreach, victim support). Staff positions were advertised as gender-specific; for example, each district team advertised for two male and two female statement takers, and one male and one female for outreach/victim support. The second key decision was to engage Fokupers—a leading women's NGO with a track record of working with women victims and documenting their testimonies—to conduct a special research project on women and conflict.

In terms of statement taking, the CAVR set a target of getting 30 percent of its testimonies from women, and eventually achieved approximately 20 percent, reflecting the real difficulties in reaching women. Although equal numbers of women and men should theoretically have been involved, women faced social and cultural expectations of their public roles that in reality placed competing demands on their time and made this ideal goal difficult to achieve. According to their traditional roles, women were busy at home caring for children, working in their fields, fetching water, and so on. In addition, the cultural barriers that prevented women from speaking in public about matters considered political were significant. Too, women had less access to information. Without the CAVR's special efforts to reach women, the number of statements from women would undoubtedly have been even lower.

The work of the designated women's team within the research unit provided another way for the CAVR to increase the gender balance in its programs. Using the expertise and contacts of the women's NGOs, and assisted by an experienced international researcher, the women's team collected more than two hundred interviews. It also provided substantive input on the public hearing that focused on women's experience during the conflict as well as the names of women to testify at the hearing. Broadcast via television and radio across the nation, this hearing inspired more women to come forward to tell their stories. Together with a range of other initiatives, the CAVR was able to increase women's participation in its programs.[38]

WEST TIMOR

The CAVR developed a special program to disseminate information about its mandate while also taking a limited number of statements from refugees in West Timor who wanted to give evidence to the commission. The CAVR worked with a group of eighteen staff members who were drawn from a network of NGOs from West Timor (Indonesia). This team worked for six months in the refugee camps to facilitate discussions and conduct an information campaign, using videos and other public information materials. This outreach program was based on a loose agreement between the government of Indonesia and the transitional administration of Timor-Leste. More than 120 meetings were organized with the participation of about five thousand male and one thousand female refugees. The team also organized and broadcast a series of radio programs for the West Timor context. This programming included radio broadcasts on the mandate and work of the CAVR that had already been produced for use inside East Timor, as well as a number of new interactive radio programs in which commissioners and senior staff provided information and answered questions from refugees. Commissioners and senior staff also visited West Timor and participated in some of the public meetings there. These meetings often included emotional expressions of feelings by refugees who had been separated from their homeland by the conflict and for whom the future remained quite uncertain.

THE FINAL REPORT AND THE CREATION OF THE POST-CAVR TECHNICAL SECRETARIAT

Because East Timor had been closed to journalists, researchers, and historians for most of Indonesia's twenty-four-year occupation, the CAVR's research and final report provided the most likely opportunity for the new country to produce an account of this crucial period of its history. As a result, the scope of the research and resulting report was broad, covering such areas as the colonial context in which the conflict arose; the resistance movements; the role of the United Nations, other governments, and international civil society; women and the conflict; children and the conflict; and social and economic rights, such as the Indonesian military's takeover of the coffee crop. The final report was more than two thousand pages long. Because people working on the report included international advisors as well as East Timorese staff, drafts of the report were produced simultaneously in English and Indonesian, with a translation into Portuguese.

The process of editing and translating in multiple languages was a massive undertaking and required far more work and resources than had been anticipated. During the writing of the final report, a large number of translators were required to complete the work within the time constraints. Despite coordination, the resulting different-language versions, which had to deal with hundreds of particular context-specific terms, showed significant inconsistency. Editing, copyediting, and proofreading of the final report continued for several years, even after the content had been approved by the commissioners, before an Indonesian-language version was finally printed in 2010.

One mistake often made by TRCs is that plans for funding and operations provide support to a commission only until the final report is completed and officially presented to the stipulated governmental body (either the president or Parliament, depending on the legislative requirements of each particular commission). However, although representing the closing of one major chapter in the work of a TRC, delivery of the report also marks the beginning of a new chapter in which the information gathered and recommendations made should be put to work in helping to make the necessary reforms in education, policymaking, and maintaining peace. All of this work depends on carrying out different methods of outreach to share the findings and recommendations of the commission with a broader audience.

The CAVR also suffered from a lack of adequate preparation and planning for post-commission work, although senior staff and advisors recognized these needs during the latter stages of the commission's mandate. The CAVR was initially mandated to work for two years, but several extensions required the national Parliament to amend the CAVR legislation. Drafts of the last of these amendments included a provision for a body that would implement the recommendations of the CAVR's final report, but Parliament did not approve this provision. Then completion of the final report demanded so much attention that it was difficult for staff and advisors to adequately focus on the next steps of the process, although they did recognize that producing the report was merely a preparatory step for giving life to that body of work—through disseminating the information, findings, and recommendations to the population of Timor-Leste, Indonesia, and the rest of the world.

However, after some last-minute lobbying with government representatives and donors during the latter stages of the CAVR's mandate, the president agreed to establish the Post-CAVR Technical Secretariat on December 20, 2005, the same day the commission was formally dissolved. The secretariat, which is still active, is a technical body that reports to the Office of the President. Its mandate includes the following:

- Completing a number of the CAVR's technical tasks—including finalizing the CAVR's accounts for a final government audit and formatting the CAVR's final report—and several publications, including *Chega!* (the final report in book form), remaining public hearing booklets, and a popular illustrated version of *Chega!*
- Disseminating *Chega!* and related products, particularly throughout Timor-Leste, down to the subdistrict level
- Managing and maintaining the former Balide Comarca heritage complex
- Managing the security and organization of the CAVR archives[39]

Renewed conflict in Timor in 2006 disrupted the dissemination of the final report and other CAVR products. Following this, post-CAVR teams disseminated copies of *Chega!*, the published version of the CAVR final report;

screened the *Dalan ba dame* film; broadcast weekly radio programs; and conducted workshops and seminars in each of the thirteen district capitals.

An important example of post-TRC outreach was the publication of an illustrated comic-book version of the CAVR's final report, produced by ICTJ and the Post-CAVR Technical Secretariat.[40] This project was more complex than expected and required considerable time and resources. The cartoonists had to draw each page in a culturally appropriate manner while producing an accurate representation of the information and findings of the two-thousand-plus-page report, including relationships between the conflicting parties; the artists themselves had to understand the report well. Ensuring that the short text in comic-book form included an accurate summary of the much longer report was also a significant challenge. However, the end result was an extremely valuable tool. The majority of the Timorese population will probably never read any of the formal report, although some may read the executive summary. However, seven thousand copies of the comic book have now been printed and are being distributed. This short, easy-to-read version can be used in schools to teach children about their history and thus reach a far greater proportion of the population than the formal report. ICTJ is working with civil society groups and the Ministry of Education to develop a simple manual for teachers, to provide guidance on how to use the illustrated report in the classroom.

CHALLENGES

Despite its emphasis on consultation and public outreach, the CAVR also faced some challenges, including its relationship with some human rights groups as discussed above, the difficulties experienced when working with the victims involved in the Community Reconciliation Process, and the failure to anticipate the need to do more advanced briefing with civil society on the content of the final report before its launch.

INSUFFICIENT CONSULTATION WITH VICTIMS ABOUT THE CRPS

A significant proportion of victims who participated in various ways in the CRP process were probably less than satisfied with the results. Many victims reported that they felt significantly better after the perpetrators had admitted their crimes, apologized to them in front of their communities, and provided some token reparations. However, other research indicates that some victims felt that the process was too focused on providing a solution for the perpetrator and the community, without enough attention to victims' particular needs. The CAVR did not sufficiently consult with victims during the CRP program to assess their feelings and factor such information into the way that the program was conducted.

This issue is complicated because indicators to identify and quantify victims' satisfaction are not universal. For example, researchers from developed countries tend to use an individual rights framework to assess the satisfaction of people involved in a process. However, the issue of identity may involve individual and community aspects that are extremely important to East Timorese but alien to foreign observers. The CRP process was often viewed as important for communities to resolve their experience of the conflict and find a way to reintegrate perpetrators of crimes and other harmful acts. However, the hearings may have been disappointing on a personal level for some victims. A victim whose identity, values, and priorities include both individual and communal aspects may, therefore, have a satisfactory community experience while feeling disappointed on a personal level. This level of insight was not sufficiently taken into account in the planning and implementation of the CAVR's outreach or implementation of the CRP process. Thus, while victims were quite broadly consulted, the views of community leaders rather than those of victims probably dominated the design and implementation of hearings, resulting in some disappointment for victims at the personal level.

FINAL REPORT ISSUES

Because the commission was granted several extensions, and most of its support ended with the publication of the final report, the commission's consultation with local communities about its findings was a slow process that diminished the report's potential effectiveness. This result might have been avoided had the commissioners, staff, and advisors sufficiently recognized that the end of the writing process should not be the end of the work but rather a transition to a major outreach program. Donors also did not adequately understand this issue, which made securing funding for the post-CAVR work difficult.

Another challenge to maximizing the report's impact was the long delay before the Parliament finally, in December 2009, produced a resolution on the CAVR and the Commission for Truth and Friendship reports.[41] The CAVR report recommended that those people responsible for mass crimes should be brought to justice, which may include the need for international mechanisms such as a UN-backed tribunal. Political party platforms and the views of the political leadership have been far less clear, in many cases tending toward a conciliatory relationship with Indonesia at the cost of bringing to justice Indonesian military commanders responsible for the mass crimes. The December 2009 resolution authorized a committee within the Parliament to propose concrete steps to implement the two commissions' recommendations. The committee produced two draft bills on the establishment of an institute of memory that would continue disseminating the results of the CAVR's work and a national reparations program. However, debate on the draft bills, which remains emotionally charged, has been consistently delayed at the national Parliament of Timor-Leste.[42]

LESSONS LEARNED

Many of the techniques and programs aimed at reaching out to the population of East Timor were designed through painful trial and error by the CAVR staff. In this process, staff and advisors learned a great deal. Some of the most important lessons from the CAVR process on outreach and consultations are as follows:

1. *Broad consultation and mapping of the conflict need to be undertaken as soon as possible following the end of hostilities.* In that way, the context—the big picture—can inform the design and mandates of transitional justice mechanisms such as truth commissions while encouraging local actors' confidence in those mechanisms.
2. *When reaching women particularly, sensitive and strategic consultations on the issue of sexual crimes should take place at an early stage in order to inform the design of outreach programs.* Cooperation with local organizations that work specifically on the issue of sexual violence against women is a valuable way to overcome potential resistance through the provision of support, confidentiality, and sharing of appropriate information.
3. *Good relationships with local counterparts must be given appropriate priority and resources and must not be considered marginal.* This point is particularly important as it relates to national-level human rights organizations, which should be included in the work of a truth commission, if possible. Extra efforts are often necessary to ensure that NGOs understand what a TRC is doing. Civil society support is essential to ensuring a sustainable approach to the long-term work of rebuilding peace.
4. *Much can be learned from the experiences of other TRCs. However, the complexities of each context should not be underestimated.* Only broad and deep

consultation with civil society prior to the drafting of the mandate will reveal issues of possibly significant impact. Care needs to be taken not to simply transplant lessons learned from other contexts that may be inappropriate.

5. *Commissioners are crucial to the success of any TRC.* If the public feels it was not consulted in the selection of commissioners, the community is more likely to be alienated from all that the commission later achieves and less likely to cooperate and support it. To achieve the necessary level of public confidence, the selection of commissioners must involve a nomination process based on broad participation. In that way, the public feels some level of responsibility and connection to the appointed commissioners. The selection process can also serve as an early means of introducing a TRC to the community, even before the TRC is established.
6. *Any TRC must conduct regular consultations and reviews of its progress with its stakeholders in order to address difficulties in a timely manner.* If particular groups appear not to be supporting the work of a TRC, further consultations must take place quickly to avoid the negative impact of prolonged polarization. Care needs to be taken not to avoid this often unpleasant work, and excuses are always available, such as having too much else to do.
7. *Ensuring that the various perspectives of stakeholders are adequately recognized during outreach programs is important.* For example, the complex role of victims—as individuals who have suffered as a result of crimes and as members of communities that may desire reconciliation for past crimes in order to foster inclusiveness and harmony—needs to be recognized and considered.
8. *The design of TRCs should include provisions for the dissemination of and consultation on the final report soon after its publication.* The TRC's work is not complete when the final report appears. On the contrary, the final report represents the beginning of a new phase of its work. Plans for a follow-up institution to continue the outreach and dissemination should be made during the life of the TRC.

The challenges in developing and implementing a truth and reconciliation commission in a context saturated by anger, division, poverty, and severe trauma will always appear almost insuperable. In Timor, weight was added by the fact that most of the country's infrastructure had been destroyed, and there was little relevant experience to draw upon for guidance. However, one of the advantageous conditions of the Timor context was that the status quo had shifted: most of those responsible for the human rights violations had fled the territory on the arrival of international peacekeepers.

These conditions made it possible for a largely inexperienced but highly motivated staff to achieve some remarkable results, adapting from others' experiences and creating new ways to reach out to the communities and bring them into the work of the CAVR. The key to success in creating a truth and reconciliation commission is that the people feel that it is "our commission," not "theirs."

The Timor commission was unable to achieve a number of its aims but in other areas achieved extraordinary success. Perhaps most important were the efforts made to draw into the process ordinary people and leaders from all social, economic, and political backgrounds, to make them feel that the CAVR was "our commission." Hopefully some of the struggles and lessons from the commission's experience will provide guidance for those seeking to design a process to assist them in dealing with their own unique challenges in search of justice, truth, and reconciliation.

NOTES

The views presented in this chapter are from the authors alone and do not necessarily represent those of the International Center for Transitional Justice.

1 For more on the history of East Timor, see "Annex: A Brief History of East Timor," in *Ukun Rasik A'an, The Way Ahead: East Timor Human Development Report* (Dili: UNDP, 2002), 70–72; Michele Turner, *Telling—East Timor: Personal Testimonies, 1942–1992* (Kensington: New South Wales University Press, 1992); and John G. Taylor, *Indonesia's Forgotten War: The Hidden History of East Timor* (London: Zed Books, 1991). On the civil war, see Ben Kiernan, "War, Genocide, and Resistance in East Timor, 1975–1999: Comparative Reflections on Cambodia," in *War and State Terror: The United States, Japan, and the Asia-Pacific in the Long Twentieth Century*, ed. Mark Selden and Alvin Y. So (Lanham, MD: Routledge, 2003), 199–233, and Peter Carey and G. Carter Bentley, eds., *East Timor at the Crossroads: The Forging of a Nation* (Honolulu: University of Hawaii Press, 1995).

2 William Burr and Michael L. Evans, eds., *East Timor Revisited: Ford, Kissinger, and the Indonesian Invasion, 1975–76*, National Security Archive Electronic Briefing Book no. 62, December 6, 2001, http://www.gwu.edu/~nsarchiv/NSAEBB/NSAEBB62; Memorandum of Conversation between Presidents Ford and Suharto, July 5, 1975, Gerald R. Ford Library, http://www.gwu.edu/~nsarchiv/NSAEBB/NSAEBB62/index2.html#docs; see also John Pilger, "Our Model Dictator," *The Guardian*, January 28, 2008, http://www.guardian.co.uk/commentisfree/2008/jan/28/indonesia.world. This was not the first time that the United States supported Indonesia for a military offensive. Indeed, from 1958 to 1965, the United States trained, funded, and supplied Indonesia's army as part of its Cold War strategy against the expansion of Communism. In 1965 the Indonesian army launched a massive purge of perceived Communist and Socialist sympathizers, resulting in the killing of up to a million people and the forced detention of hundreds of thousands of others, including poets, writers, musicians, members of the women's rights movement, and those aligned with cooperatives and unions. See John Roosa, *Pretext for Mass Murder: The September 30th Movement and Suharto's Coup d'État in Indonesia* (Madison: University of Wisconsin Press, 2006).

3 *Chega! The Report of the Commission for Reception, Truth and Reconciliation (CAVR)* (Dili: CAVR, 2005), chapter 6, "Key Findings," 6.1.1, http://www.cavr-timorleste.org/en/chegaReport.htm.

4 Referendum results as announced by the UN secretary-general on September 3, 1999 (see UN Security Council, Letter S/1999/944, September 3, 1999, http://www.un.org/peace/etimor99/N9925500.pdf).

5 Condemnation of the violence before and after the ballot was expressed in United Nations, "Security Council Welcomes Successful Popular Consultation in East Timor,

Condemns Violence before and after Ballot," press release SC/6723, September 3, 1999, http://www.un.org/News/Press/docs/1999/19990903.sc6723.html; see also Richard Tanter, Gerry van Klinken, and Desmond Ball, *Masters of Terror: Indonesia's Military and Violence in East Timor* (Lanham, MD: Rowman and Littlefield Publishers, 2006).

6 For statistics related to postelection violence, see *Chega!*, chapter 3, "Indonesia Departs: Scorched Earth," 3.21; James Dunn, "Crimes against Humanity in East Timor, January to October 1999, Their Nature and Causes," East Timor and Indonesia Action Network, Dili, 2001, http://www.etan.org/etanpdf/pdf1/dunn.pdf; and Geoffrey Robinson, "People's War: Militias in East Timor and Indonesia," *South East Asia Research* 9, no. 3 (2001): 271–318.

7 UN Security Council Resolution 1272, S/RES/1972 (1999), October 25, 1999.

8 UNTAET Regulation No. 2000/15, "On the Establishment of Panels with Exclusive Jurisdiction over Serious Criminal Offenses," June 6, 2000. At the time of its closure in 2005, this process had resulted in the conviction of eighty-four perpetrators. However, all of these were East Timorese who could be considered relatively minor offenders. The people responsible for planning, organizing, and orchestrating the violence, including senior members of the Indonesian security forces, as well as civilian officials, continued to enjoy impunity in Indonesia. See Megan Hirst and Howard Varney, "Justice Abandoned? An Assessment of the Serious Crimes Process in East Timor" (ICTJ Occasional Paper Series, International Center for Transitional Justice, New York, June 2005) and David Cohen, "Intended to Fail: The Trials before the Ad Hoc Human Rights Court in Jakarta" (ICTJ Occasional Paper Series, International Center for Transitional Justice, New York, August 2003).

9 *Chega!*, chap. 1, "Introduction," para. 5.

10 Jacinto Alves, former CAVR commissioner and member of the CAVR Steering Committee, interview with author, Dili, August 2006.

11 Sidney Jones, "Human Rights and Peacekeeping in East Timor," April 2001 (draft paper prepared for the Aspen Institute [copy on file with the authors]).

12 On the work of the Steering Committee and formation of the CAVR, see *Chega!*, chap. 1, "Introduction," paras. 36–42.

13 "On the Establishment of a Commission for Reception, Truth and Reconciliation in East Timor," UNTAET Regulation No. 2001/10, http://www.un.org/en/peacekeeping/missions/past/etimor/untaetR/Reg10e.pdf.

14 See UNTAET, "Update on the Establishment of the Commission for Reception, Truth and Reconciliation in East Timor," Steering Committee for the Commission and Human Rights Unit, March 12, 2001, Dili, East Timor. The results of the Steering Committee consultations are also listed in *Chega!*, chap. 1, "Introduction."

15 ICTJ was established in 2001 to help local stakeholders look at options to promote accountability for the past as a basis for building a more democratic and just future. See www.ictj.org. In East Timor, the United Nations engaged ICTJ cofounders Priscilla

Hayner and Paul van Zyl as consultants to present options at the CNRT conference in 2000, and later to work with the Steering Committee.

16 The CAVR's tasks are spelled out in "Objectives and Functions of the Commission," UNTAET Regulation No. 2001/10, July 13, 2001, sec. 3.

17 The selection panel comprised individuals appointed by major political parties, civil society organizations, and the United Nations (UNTAET Regulation No. 2001/20, secs. 4.2, 4.3).

18 Candidates were to be individuals with "high moral character, impartiality, and integrity who are competent to deal with the issues under the present Regulation and shall not have a high political profile, and have a demonstrated commitment to human rights principles" (UNTAET Regulation No. 2001/10, sec. 4).

19 In East Timor, this step necessitated meetings organized by the United Nations in each district, as well as with local nongovernmental organizations (NGOs). In West Timor, Indonesia, the selection panel relied on Indonesian humanitarian NGOs working with refugees and organizations affiliated with churches to organize the consultation meetings. For more on the selection process, see UNTAET Regulation No. 2001/10, sec. 4, "Composition of the Commission and Selection Procedure," and sec. 11, "Regional Commissioners."

20 One of the first tasks of the national commissioners was to interview and select regional commissioners from the short list that the selection panel provided. By May 2002, twenty-nine regional commissioners were appointed to conduct the CAVR's work in the districts (*Chega!*, chap. 1, "Introduction," paras. 56–59).

21 See CAVR, "Progress Report Selection Panel Consultations," November 14, 2001, Dili, East Timor.

22 *Hak* means "rights" in Bahasa Indonesian.

23 As described below, these programs sought to address violations such as assault, arson, and theft at the local level, using public and participatory mechanisms with some traditional elements.

24 This strategy was in fact used in the CAVR's outreach in West Timor, Indonesia, where NGOs were contracted to conduct the CAVR's outreach, as well as deliver the CAVR's collective urgent reparations for communities that suffered a severe impact as a result of the conflict. Three NGOs—Fokupers, HAK, and ETWAVE (East Timorese Women Against Violence and Support Child Care)—were subcontracted to facilitate community development projects as collective reparations.

25 CAVR Generic Proposal, 2004 (unpublished, copy on file with authors).

26 Ibid.

27 *Chega!*, chap. 1, "Introduction," para. 82.

28 The community reconciliation process was available to those who committed lesser crimes—i.e., those who looted or committed arson or assault—but not to those who

murdered, committed rape, or organized large-scale violence. People who committed these more serious crimes fell under the jurisdiction of the serious crimes process. This distinction was a key outreach message of the CAVR.

29 According to the commission's final report, "The cash grant component of the Urgent Reparations Scheme was distributed between September 2003 and March 2004. In this period, 516 men (73% of the recipients) and 196 women (27%) each received US$200 for a total of $142,400 to 712 survivors of human rights abuses. All 156 participants in the healing workshops at the national headquarters of the Commission received the Urgent Reparations grant" (*Chega!*, chap. 10, "*Acolhimento* and Victim Support," paras. 181, 182a). See also Galuh Wandita, Karen Campbell-Nelson, and Manuela Leong Pereira, "Learning to Engender Reparations in Timor-Leste: Reaching Out to Female Victims," in *What Happened to the Women? Gender and Reparations for Human Rights Violations*, ed. Ruth Rubio-Marín (New York: ICTJ–Social Science Research Council, 2006).

30 CAVR Generic Proposal, 2004.

31 Kieran Dwyer, CAVR advisor, interview with author, February 12, 2010.

32 Ibid.

33 Ibid.

34 For information on CAVR products, see http://www.cavr-timorleste.org/en/Other_CAVR_products.htm.

35 Isabel Guterres, CAVR commissioner, interview with author, February 23, 2010.

36 In its final report, completed in 2005, the CAVR made comprehensive recommendations for continuing its mandate for reconciliation. However, the Parliament only began to discuss implementation of CAVR recommendations in December 2009. Between 2006 and 2008 Timor-Leste experienced a resurgence of violence triggered by tensions within its security forces. See IFP Security Cluster, "Country Case Study: Security Sector Reform in Timor-Leste," Initiative for Peacebuilding and International Center for Transitional Justice, New York, June 2009, http://ictj.org/publication/security-sector-reform-timor-leste.

37 Jose Caetano Guterres, CAVR coordinator for community outreach and public information, interview with author, February 15, 2010.

38 See "Update on the Establishment of the Commission for Reception, Truth and Reconciliation in East Timor."

39 See the STP/Post-CAVR Technical Secretariat website, http://www.cavr-timorleste.org/en/STP-CAVR.htm.

40 The illustrated version of *Chega!* was designed by the International Center for Transitional Justice (ICTJ), the Post-CAVR Technical Secretariat, and INSIST Press, and publicly released on August 30, 2010. It is written in Tetum, while the original report was published in English, Indonesian, and Portuguese. See http://es.ictj.org/en/news/press/release/4030.html.

41 The Commission for Truth and Friendship of Indonesia and Timor-Leste was established by the governments of both countries in August 2005 with a mandate to investigate violations that Indonesia committed during the occupation. Its final report, titled *From Remembering Comes Hope*, was presented in 2008. See Megan Hirst, "Too Much Friendship, Too Little Truth: Monitoring Report on the Commission of Truth and Friendship in Indonesia and Timor-Leste" (ICTJ Occasional Paper Series, International Center for Transitional Justice, New York, January 2008).

42 See ICTJ, "Timor-Leste: Parliament Denies Justice for Victims Again," press release, February 16, 2011, http://www.ictj.org/news/timor-leste-parliament-denies-victims-justice-again.

CHAPTER 4

Between Protection and Participation: Involving Children and Youth in Transitional Justice Processes

Virginie Ladisch and Clara Ramírez-Barat

A person comes, tells us their story, we listen and transfer their testimony to their file. But the fact of listening to them also implies a process for me. It helps me grow as a person.

—Patricia Figueroa, PROVER youth truth commission volunteer, Peru

Only very recently have outreach programs for transitional justice (TJ) measures begun to specifically include children and youth in their design and programming. As a result, there is little knowledge yet about how to design programs in a safe and meaningful manner. Furthermore, in contexts of scarce resources and numerous demands, outreach to children and youth may not be considered a priority by those leading the transitional justice process. Developing outreach programs specifically geared to children and youth should not be seen as a burden or drain on resources but rather an essential part of the transitional justice process that can in fact enhance its effectiveness.

Our aim in this chapter is to advance current debates on outreach programs for transitional justice measures by focusing on how to conduct outreach activities tailored for youth and children. After providing an account of the concept of outreach, emphasizing the importance that public engagement plays in transitional justice processes, in the following section we make the case for why focusing on children and youth when establishing this sort of program is important. As we argue here, child- and youth-sensitive outreach is important for children and youth themselves, to help strengthen the TJ measure, and to enhance the potential benefit to society as a whole. Then we consider four different methods for including children and youth in outreach programming, looking into how best to promote their participation. Adapting to the nuances of the context, we turn our discussion to the specific measures that should be taken into account when including children and youth in outreach strategies, considering both the international protection framework and children's right to participation.

According to the Convention on the Rights of the Child (CRC), children are defined as those under the age of eighteen unless majority is attained earlier.[1] In contrast to the clear international legal definition of a child, *youth* is an ambiguous category with definitions ranging from ages fifteen to thirty or even forty.[2] At times the category of youth is demarcated according to age limits, but in other cases according to biological markers such as the period between puberty and parenthood.[3] For the purposes of transitional justice programming, initiatives targeting younger generations should not be limited strictly to those under eighteen. By the time a transitional justice measure is established and becomes operational, many of those who were affected as children will be over eighteen, but they may still require specific and targeted attention. In the context of this chapter, and of transitional justice initiatives in general, we are advocating for a more nuanced and inclusive approach to outreach that looks at adolescents and youth. We therefore use the terms *children* and *youth* throughout this chapter, referring to those in the age range of twelve to twenty-five years old, with an emphasis on the fact that the important element is to target those affected/victimized as children.

In considering the age spectrum, from a programmatic perspective it is important to avoid generalized perceptions that could negatively impact or bias efforts to involve children and youth in transitional justice. On the one hand, when speaking of children, a sometimes overly protective discourse presents children primarily as passive beneficiaries of protection. Work in the area of child protection tends to emphasize child vulnerability rather than agency and resilience. Children are described as "vulnerable, passive beings who need to be protected and cared for" instead of active community members.[4] On the other hand, the tendency is to depict youth, especially male youth, as spoilers and threats to peace. Robert D. Kaplan, for example, describes youth in post-conflict contexts as "out of school, unemployed, loose molecules in an unstable social fluid that threaten[s] to ignite."[5] An example of this dichotomy between children and youth is reflected in the outreach guidelines for the Special Court for Sierra Leone, which explains that

> the Outreach Section, together with the Press and Public Affairs Section, has specifically designed initiatives to reach three main categories of people: socially disempowered groups (women, victims, children, and the disabled), potentially destabilizing groups (ex-combatants, military, and youth), and law enforcement agencies and civil society leaders (the judiciary, religious leaders, the police, prison officers, and traditional leaders).[6]

Between the extreme perceptions of children as needing protection and youth as dangerous spoilers, we seek in this chapter to find a balance, recognizing the potential agency of children and youth while also acknowledging the need for certain standards to ensure safe and meaningful participation.

While we draw from experiences in different places in the world, unlike the other chapters in part 1, this chapter is not a case study. Important efforts have been made to include children and youth in outreach programming both by transitional justice measures and by civil society groups; however, the area remains underexplored. In this chapter, therefore, we aim to establish a guiding framework on how to conduct outreach for children and youth, offering ideas and examples of how to design and implement these types of activities. The final goal is to raise awareness about the participation of younger generations in TJ measures and to provide guidance on how to make that a reality.

OUTREACH AND ITS ROLE IN TRANSITIONAL JUSTICE PROCESSES

The establishment of TJ measures opens a political process that is public in nature. Although their justification stems from backward-looking considerations—that is, they are first and foremost attempts to redress previous violations of human rights that occurred on a massive scale—transitional justice processes are also future-oriented initiatives. To a great extent, redressing past violations is seen precisely as a way to help build a future according to democratic standards and respect of human rights.[7]

Although transitional justice measures primarily operate at the institutional level, both political and judicial, they also have a key symbolic dimension that, related to their capacity to establish a break with the repressive and conflictive past, importantly resonates at the social level. This dimension is not only one manifested through the establishment of a new set of norms that—enshrining the ideas of respect for the rule of law and human rights—contrast old repressive and abusive practices, but it is also one linked to the beliefs and perceptions that the affected societies have of such change. If TJ measures are to be relevant and have positive impact, they need to resonate widely and deeply within the societies in which they operate. That is, for the changes that TJ measures promote at an institutional level to have broader transformative potential, they need to have effect also at the social level. Indeed, those societies in which transitional justice processes have been more successful are arguably the ones in which the broader society has been more engaged in the process.[8]

However, neither society's understanding, support, nor engagement around transitional justice measures should be taken for granted. Transitional justice processes institute new practices that lead in turn to establishing novel institutions with complex mandates and rules that are far from self-explanatory. Moreover, the postauthoritarian and post-conflict contexts in which transitional justice measures develop are usually characterized by strong political and economic deficits, including lack of democratic practice and transparency, as well as huge competing social needs in terms of economic investment. While in some cases the successful implementation of TJ measures has to overcome generalized attitudes of indifference, distrust, or bitter opposition, in others their creation alone may quickly generate extremely high expectations.

In an effort to overcome some of these challenges, many transitional justice measures—including truth commissions, criminal justice processes, and reparations programs—have established outreach or public education and engagement programs. Such programs, using a variety of strategies and activities, aim broadly at creating awareness and understanding about the work of the transitional justice measure, while crafting a message of recognition to victims and promoting public participation in the process. From a programmatic perspective within TJ contexts, *outreach* thus refers to the set of tools that a given measure puts in place in order to foster these aims—including but not limited to

- Producing and distributing printed and audiovisual informational materials
- Organizing public events and interactive forums in which questions and criticisms can be raised
- Establishing consultation processes with affected groups in order to guarantee that stakeholders have a voice in the process
- Adopting context-based and participatory approaches, such as using traditional communication means and local cultural practices, enhancing national staffing opportunities, or involving local organizations in the implementation of outreach activities[9]

Beyond this programmatic outlook and understood in broader functional terms, outreach programs should aim at building an open and inclusive two-way communication process in order to promote public engagement and contribute to building a local sense of ownership of the transitional justice process. Only if TJ measures are seen as relevant to the affected population and responsive to their concerns will they be perceived as meaningful and legitimate processes and hence increase their social impact.[10]

THE JUSTIFICATION FOR CHILD- AND YOUTH-TARGETED OUTREACH

Activists and practitioners in the field are increasingly recognizing the need for and importance of outreach in transitional justice contexts. For example, neither of the ad-hoc international tribunals—the International Criminal Tribunal for the former Yugoslavia (ICTY) nor the International Criminal Tribunal for Rwanda (ICTR)—included outreach programs during the early stages of their operations in the mid-1990s; presently, that transitional justice measures need to put in place specific programs to explain their process and build direct channels of communication within the societies in which they work is generally accepted. Since the South African Truth and Reconciliation Commission broke new ground with its public hearings, every truth commission that has followed has included an outreach component in its work. Tribunals including the Special Court for Sierra Leone and the Extraordinary Chambers of the Courts of Cambodia have also learned that, without a public engagement strategy, the impact of the trials will be very limited. Tribunals have thus made efforts to reach out to the populations they seek to serve. Reparations programs, however, still have been pretty weak on outreach strategies.

While outreach is starting to take hold among TJ practitioners, given the great demands and limited resources that transitional contexts normally face, these programs often suffer from a lack of clear strategy and insufficient resources. In response to recommendations or pressures to integrate a child and youth focus, some who are struggling with these choices may be reluctant to take on another focus or special-needs category. However, effective outreach is vitally important for children and youth as they tend to be marginalized and excluded from general communication channels. Even without an outreach program, adults will more likely be able to access the information they need in order to take part in the process as compared to younger generations. If children and youth are not specifically included in outreach efforts they probably will be left out of the TJ process. Recognizing this need, some TJ measures have developed specific outreach for children and youth. For example, the Special Court for Sierra Leone, looking to foster a "two-way communication between Sierra Leoneans and the Special Court..., targets the general population as well as specific groups," including among them children and youth.[11] Likewise, some truth commissions, including the Peruvian and the Liberian truth commissions, have specifically undertaken youth- and child-tailored outreach activities.[12]

Developing outreach programs that target children and youth can enhance the effectiveness of TJ measures. A targeted approach to outreach is important on three levels: (1) for the children and youth themselves, (2) to strengthen the TJ measure, and (3) to enhance the potential of the TJ measure to benefit society as a whole. Conversely, excluding this important category of stakeholders may weaken (or threaten) efforts to address past violations in order to build a future based on democratic standards and respect for human rights.

FOR CHILDREN AND YOUTH THEMSELVES

The specific type and consequence of victimization of children and youth should be considered and factored into the way a TJ measure is set up and the way its outreach targets them. Children and youth are among those most vulnerable to conflict and its consequences in physical, psychological, and socioeconomic terms.[13] Children are not only subject to direct violence (including torture, displacement, forced recruitment, or sexual assault), but they also suffer indirectly the violations committed against their caretakers as well as their access to basic services, including health and education.[14] The 1996 report on the impact of armed conflict on children submitted by Graça Machel to the UN secretary-general put the international spotlight on this issue.[15] Two years later, the impact of conflict on children was reflected in the South African TRC final report: "Children and youth were the dominant victims in all categories of gross human rights violations described in the Act. For almost every adult that was violated, probably two or more children or young people suffered. Children and young people were killed, tortured, maimed, detained, interrogated, abducted, harassed, displaced as well as being witnesses to these abuses."[16]

In some cases, as a consequence of the type of violence, children and young people suffer cultural loss,[17] and depending on their age when the violence erupts, they might not even remember having lived during peaceful times. Despite their significant level of victimization, in many contexts children and youth will not necessarily see themselves as citizens whose rights have been violated. TJ measures must therefore send a targeted message and open channels of communication with those who have been victimized as children so that they understand that what they experienced was a violation of rights rather than a normal occurrence or some form of punishment, and they are aware of what is being done to address that violation. In the context of reparations programs, for example, for those who are victims and have a benefit to claim, outreach is important to inform them of that right, as they may not see themselves as rights bearers. ICTJ's research in Colombia found that "it took time for children and those working with children to understand that they were eligible for reparations and to mobilize to apply."[18] In part due to a lack of targeted outreach, many eligible children did not realize they could claim reparations until after the deadline passed.

Beyond those who are direct victims, in general terms, children and young people have a right to be involved in matters that affect them, as stated in Article 12 of the Convention on the Rights of the Child (CRC).[19] Furthermore, in many contexts they have shown the desire to take an active part in these processes. Children and youth are vulnerable, however; "while war's effects on youth are complex, resilience is their most prominent shared characteristic."[20] Part of that resilience manifests itself in a desire to participate in transitional justice measures and, broadly speaking, in efforts to help prevent what they themselves suffered. In Colombia, for example, former recruits expressed a need to warn others of the harsh realities of recruitment. Stella María Duque, the director of Taller de Vida, an NGO working directly with demobilized children, explained how girls have expressed their desire to tell their stories, even those of ill treatment and sexual abuse, and why they ended up joining armed groups.[21] Child ex-combatants wanted to share information about mass gravesites where armed groups buried friends and family members. They felt responsible for "not leaving them there."[22] The participation of children in the truth commissions of Sierra Leone and Liberia further highlights that interest.

In addition to fulfilling a rights obligation, child and youth participation in outreach can often prove beneficial in the long run to their development as engaged citizens, contributing to their civic education. In speaking about the youth volunteer program launched by the Peruvian truth and reconciliation commission (PROVER, Promotores de la Verdad [Promoters of Truth]), the president of the commission, Salomón Lerner, explained:

> The work of the volunteers has served as a powerful vehicle for them to discover their humanity. The experience they have lived not only has made them more compassionate, but it has also allowed them to fully assume their Peruvianess at a very young age. In this time, not only have they been able to understand our country in its light and shadows, but they have also been able to feel with greater intensity, the pain of the poorest, of the forgotten, who have suffered violations of their human rights.[23] (authors' translation)

In recognition of a child's right to participation delineated in Article 12 of the CRC, a TJ measure should implement child- and youth-specific outreach, taking into consideration the particular consequences of violations on children and youth. Making this right a reality can help build their capacity as citizens, a crucial component of building a solid and lasting peace.

FOR THE TJ MEASURE

At the next level, focused outreach to children and youth can help strengthen the TJ measure itself. One of the main goals of TJ efforts is to help lay the foundation for a future based on democratic standards and respect for human rights. In that sense they aim to advance new social norms of what is acceptable and contribute to civic trust. In order to have this effect on a societal level, TJ measures need to have a broad base of support. Since, in many countries with TJ measures, youth constitute close to half (if not more) of the entire population, they are a key sector that needs to be engaged if the message of social change is to take hold. Outreach programs for TJ measures should be as inclusive as possible (as a democratic requirement) and thus include children and youth. Furthermore, if a TJ measure aims to develop a clear understanding of past violations, the testimonies of those victimized as children will enrich the story and provide a more complete vision of the violations that occurred and their impact on society.

Targeting outreach activities to children and youth not only effectively informs a key segment of the population of the message of "never again," but this process can also create support groups that help transmit the work and aims of the TJ measure, thus further strengthening its impact, even after its mandate ends—as in Peru, for example, with the youth volunteers who were part of PROVER, as explained in greater detail later in this chapter. The aim was to teach youth about the conflict so that they could better understand the truth-seeking process. Many of the volunteers came from urban areas and had not directly experienced the conflict. Working with the Peruvian truth commission (CVR, Comisión de la Verdad y Reconciliación) helped them process and understand their country's past. Eventually these youth volunteers became active participants in taking testimony, disseminating information, and creating community forums. For example, they went with teams to regions to get the commission established, helped gather data for the commission (covering over sixteen thousand interviews), assisted in the exhumation process, and provided a valuable linguistic connection to remote communities.[24] The CVR's work was more effective as a result, as it had access to local languages that helped obtain information that would otherwise be inaccessible.[25] What was initially conceived as a modest youth volunteer program ended up being a significant source of support for the truth commission during its operation and in the follow-up phase.

FOR SOCIETY

Transitional justice measures have a forward-looking aim, notably to address past violations in a way that can help prevent their recurrence and lay the foundation for a stable peace. In order to fulfill that longer-term aim at the societal level, outreach efforts are a crucial link between transitional justice measures and society. By opening channels of communication and engagement, outreach can contribute to a broader understanding of the past and its significance in terms of shaping future society. In thinking of the future-oriented, preventative aims of transitional justice, youth must be targeted through outreach efforts specifically geared toward them, for two principal reasons: (1) if overlooked there is a risk of return to violence, and (2) youth are generally forward looking with the potential to be agents of change. In the long run, the success of a transitional justice effort and its impact on society depends on the extent to which future generations internalize the key findings of TJ mechanisms and put into practice some of the recommendations for reform and non-recurrence. As a key part of civil society, "youth can enforce 'a renegotiation of the social contract' and thus become a cornerstone for societal transformation."[26] As noted by the outreach work of the Documentation Center in Cambodia, in order to fight against the possibility of future genocide and other crimes against humanity, young generations of Cambodians have to understand how and why the genocide happened. Genocide education also helps promote moral and civic values, advancing democracy and rule of law in a culture long accustomed to impunity.[27]

While not wanting to fall into the paradigm of innocent children and dangerous youth, marginalized youth can potentially destabilize the peace if their needs are not sufficiently considered and addressed, research has shown. The most striking example is the case of children associated with armed forces and armed groups (CAAFAG). Deprived of formal education and thus lacking job skills and options for civilian life, "child soldiers often maintain their military identity and resort to violence as a means of meeting their basic needs and asserting their desire for power, wealth, and identity."[28] As a result, they "have difficulty constructing a meaningful role and engaging in meaningful activities in communities."[29]

Even for those who were not directly involved in the violence, they are likely to have witnessed it and may see it as normal. Furthermore, if the situation of violations prevented them from accessing schools (if schools were shut down, too unsafe, etc.), they are left without the skills to make a positive contribution to society and thus can be more likely to resort to violence. In the case of South Africa, for example, with unemployment rates soaring and poverty levels still high, many youth switched identities from political activism to criminal activity as a means of survival and due to a lack of other options.[30] For the younger generations who may not have known a time of peace without human rights violations, violence may been seen and understood as the normal way of resolving daily conflicts both at an individual and societal level. For transitional justice efforts to be effective at a societal level, that perception has to be addressed and alternatives need to be presented to the youth through targeted outreach initiatives that facilitate their engagement in the TJ process.

Excluding youth not only runs the risk of jeopardizing peace but also deprives societies of "a potential driving force for peace and development."[31] Since the next generation of leaders will come from the current cohort of young people, "their engagement in the peace process/peace building and the shaping of their political attitudes and skills in the post-conflict period will have important long-term implications."[32] Khamboly Dy of the Documentation Center of Cambodia (DC-CAM) explained that teaching Khmer Rouge (KR) history to young generations of Cambodians serves the collective interest of all Cambodians and all humanity. Putting KR history into the history book for students is not only to acknowledge the suffering of the old generation but also to shape a young generation's attitude about being future leaders. Understanding the full dimension of Khmer Rouge history will help enable young generations of Cambodians to physically, emotionally, legally, morally, culturally, and psychologically engage in solving social problems and participate in the process of national development.[33]

Youth need to hear the message "never again," see institutions responsible for violations acknowledge the harm caused, hear firsthand accounts of past violations, understand what led to that situation, and have a sense of how to prevent its recurrence in order to be able to envision a new future and contribute to that vision of peace. Both because of the risk they can pose if excluded and the role of youth as potential peacemakers, for a TJ measure to effectively meet its forward-looking aims, its outreach should directly target and engage youth for the long-term benefit of society as a whole.

OUTREACH TAILORED TO CHILDREN AND YOUTH: FOUR LEVELS OF ENGAGEMENT

After having considered the different reasons that children and youth should be specifically targeted in outreach programs for TJ measures, in this section we establish a potential framework for how to craft outreach activities to best facilitate child and youth participation in transitional justice measures. By examining outreach programming for transitional justice measures (including truth commissions, trials, and reparations programs), we can identify four different levels of communication: dissemination of information, establishment of interaction and dialogue, consultation exercises (feedback to TJ measures), and direct engagement in the operations of a TJ measure.[34] This classification aims to establish a gradient of depth in different levels of engagement that should be seen as cumulative and interconnected. While each of these levels has different aims and characteristics, when properly implemented to foster child and youth participation, they can all be genuine and important exercises.

DISSEMINATION OF INFORMATION

The first and more basic level for targeting children and youth through outreach programs relates to the dissemination of information, which can be done both through the organization of child-sensitive informational activities and the production of specific materials adapted to their capacities and needs. While accessing information is in general the most basic level of outreach programming, it is also a precondition or a necessary first step to ensuring child and youth participation in TJ processes, in terms of their being able to directly take part in the proceedings (e.g., providing testimony or accessing reparations benefits), as well as their having the possibility to engage in different ways with the process as members of the transitional society and citizens of the country.

In terms of their potential direct involvement in TJ proceedings, the ability to access reliable information is a necessary condition to inform children and youth and ensure that they have the capacity to make choices and facilitate their agency as rights holders. However, the world of adult communication is not primarily designed for children and adolescents. They may not have access to adult communication channels, and even if they do, such information may be conveyed in a manner ill adapted to their needs, or it may include content that is not relevant to them. For example, in Sierra Leone, the lack of information about the TRC mandate left many children affected by conflict fearful of participating: "in particular children associated with the fighting forces and child mothers were apprehensive to talk about their experiences for fear of community discrimination or stigmatization."[35] In order to prevent the lack of information from undermining their capacity to make choices regarding their interest in participating, those working in TJ measures need to proactively convey information to children and youth.

When undertaking dissemination activities with children who may be potential participants in transitional justice proceedings, the TJ measure needs to provide complete information about the overall process, their options and rights for participation, and the potential consequences of their involvement, so that they can make informed and free decisions. In this respect, putting forward specific messages tailored to the children's and youth's expectations and fears might also be necessary. In Sierra Leone, for example, the question of whether the Special Court should prosecute child soldiers caused distrust among former child soldiers who were fearful that they would be prosecuted and hence were afraid to come forward and participate in the proceedings. As the court took the position that child combatants should be viewed primarily as victims and therefore not be prosecuted, the first chief prosecutor of the court, David Crane, addressed this issue, stating unequivocally at town hall meetings that he was "not interested in prosecuting children" because they could not bear the "greatest responsibility."[36]

In addition to focusing on children who may have an option and desire to participate directly in the proceedings, information dissemination should also take into account those other children who, as members of a society overcoming conflict, also want to know about and have a direct stake in the overall process, including its goals, developments, and results. Indeed, outreach around transitional justice measures offers an excellent opportunity to raise awareness among children and youth, as both rights claimants and society members, about topics such as democracy, the rule of law, and human rights. Adopting a more educational lens, outreach activities can bolster the knowledge of children and youth about the history of their country and democratic citizenship.

Dissemination of information tailored toward children and youth can take place through materials and informational events. For example, the Truth and Reconciliation Commission of Sierra Leone—the first commission of the sort to significantly involve children in its proceedings—engaged children in dissemination activities from its inception; the commission of Liberia later did so as well by convening a series of regional awareness-raising workshops with children.[37] Child-friendly materials can be based on previous materials produced for the general public or can be created from scratch for children. As an example of the first method, the Truth and Reconciliation Commission of Sierra Leone collaborated with the UN Children's Fund (UNICEF) and the UN Mission in Sierra Leone (UNAMSIL) to produce a child-friendly version of its final report, *TRC Report for the Children of Sierra Leone*, an official document from the commission that, recognizing children's contribution to the truth-seeking process, specifically aimed to report directly back to them. Additionally, the

TRC prepared a secondary-school version and a video version of the report.[38] As for the second method, the International Criminal Tribunal for Rwanda (ICTR) published a comic book titled *100 Days—In the Land of a Thousand Hills.* Aimed at children eight years old and up, the book explains the 1994 Rwandan genocide in a child-accessible way, detailing the stories of two children affected by the violence.[39]

FOSTERING INTERACTION AND DIALOGUE

A second level of engagement is establishing spaces for dialogue and discussion in which children and youth can directly address personnel working at transitional justice measures as well as discuss relevant issues among themselves. Beyond the dissemination of information, interactive exercises give children and youth the opportunity to pose questions and engage in a conversation with adults and peers. When thinking about discussions around transitional justice, interactive exercises within outreach programming can be especially important for children and youth for at least three reasons. First, the possibility of asking questions about what children and youth have learned is the best way to ensure that the information has been understood. Moreover, clarifying doubts or learning from questions posed by others can also contribute to a discussion that yields a more nuanced understanding. Second, dialogue is also important in terms of fostering the autonomy of children and youth: by being given the chance to ask questions of adults in decisionmaking positions, they are treated as equals and as subjects capable of expressing their opinions and concerns freely and in their own manner. This is significant in countries overcoming conflict or authoritarianism in which there may still be little culture of dialogue, both in society and particularly within schools. Finally, establishing a conversation can also become a tool for learning about mutual respect and resolving conflict. Participating in a dialogue can be instructive in terms of sharing different opinions and eventually becoming aware of the other's position. In this sense, interaction is about promoting not only children's self-awareness of their right to express themselves but also the recognition that others have opinions as well. Moreover, when opinions differ, children may be challenged to question their own beliefs or to develop more nuanced ideas in order to justify their own claims. Engaging in such a deliberative exercise and eventually looking for ways in which to make commitments as a group can become a valuable experience in itself.

Facilitating dialogue, however, is not an easy thing to do, especially in transitional justice contexts, given the conflictive nature of the topics that are part of such exercises. While adults should seek to give as much space as possible for the children to articulate their own voices, adults also play a key role in facilitating such discussions by giving some structure to the debate, clarifying misconceptions or doubts, and ensuring the respectful nature of the exercise. Dialogues between children and youth and the staff working as part of a transitional justice measure (either a truth commission, a criminal tribunal, or a body established to implement a reparations program) can take different forms, such as small focus groups and workshops, or larger events, such as forums, conferences, or community gatherings. When planning interactive exercises, a fundamental difference exists between quality and reach. While smaller exercises guarantee a much more nuanced understanding, there might be pressure to invest resources to reach and involve as many children as possible. As an example of small-scale events, some international tribunals—including the International Criminal Court (ICC), the Special Court of Sierra Leone, and the Extraordinary Chambers of the Courts of Cambodia—have implemented different types of interactive activities with schoolchildren, in which senior officials from the court explain the mandate and work of the tribunal, followed by a question-and-answer session. As for larger events, in Nepal, the human rights NGO HimRights and the Partnerships for Protecting Children in Armed Conflict (PPCC) organized a series of public hearings in 2007 that brought children and youth affected by the conflict together with local leaders and decisionmakers. The organization assisted children and youth with developing questioning techniques—including how to use a microphone, project their voices, and overcome their fears of public speaking—and organized a gathering in which children and youth were given the space to pose their questions and receive responses directly. As part of the training, they also worked with artists on how to express their vision for Nepal's future and how to portray the suffering they had experienced. All of the artwork was later exhibited in a community center and compiled in a book.[40] When organizing activities with large groups, having a good facilitator is essential, and adults in decisionmaking positions should be present to listen to the debate, provide youth with feedback, and represent their interests at levels of society to which the youth do not typically have access. Adult organizers must ensure that youth do not come away with the impression that such activities are only decorative in nature.

GATHERING INFORMATION AND FEEDBACK THROUGH CONSULTATIONS

Consultation exercises, including surveys, focus groups, and discussion forums, can be designed in order to collect different types of information from the affected population, including children and youth.[41] Consultation and opinion-gathering methods allow those working in transitional justice measures to learn about preferences, demands, and opinions that are relevant to their work. In the most immediate sense, gathering information from children and youth is fundamental to shaping programs that, to the extent possible, address their concrete needs and demands. Moreover, consultations and other opinion-gathering methods give children and youth the opportunity to have their voices heard in transitional justice processes—in many instances, because of their age and social roles, for the first time in the public sphere. These exercises are important in terms of treating children and youth as stakeholders capable of having opinions and expressing their own needs and views. By requesting their opinions and ideas, consultations can also promote their sense of social belonging and raise awareness about their right to participate as citizens in processes affecting them.

Unfortunately, almost no examples exist of consultations led by TJ bodies that have specifically included children and youth. While some transitional justice measures have put in place consultation processes—for example, to help inform the mandate of a truth commission or craft a reparations program—these processes have been targeted exclusively to adults. One exception is the Children's Consultation on the Truth and Reconciliation Commission Bill, held in Nepal in November 2009 by the Ministry of Peace and Reconstruction, with the mediation of UNICEF. The dual aim of the consultation was to gather information about how children's issues should be included in the TRC bill and to provide an opportunity to involve children in deliberations about establishing the truth commission. In coordination with civil society organizations and child protection groups, thirty-two children affected by conflict from sixteen districts in the country were selected to participate. While this initiative was positive, the results of the exercise were not ultimately incorporated in the truth commission's draft bill. "As a result, advocates feel that children's input was ultimately not seriously considered and that the consultations were more a formality than a genuine effort to hear the concerns of children and incorporate them into the TRC bill."[42]

This example is useful for illustrating the difficulty of carrying out genuine consultation processes that, absent adequate will and planning, can be formalities and examples of tokenism.[43] In order to prevent such misguidance when organizing consultations, being transparent about the reality of the decisionmaking process and the degree to which the input gathered would be taken into consideration is fundamental. Second, providing full information about the consultation process and its aims is also essential, in order to avoid raising unrealistic expectations that can lead to further disappointment. A third important challenge is to ensure broad inclusion and representation. Failure to plan adequately and reach out widely to different communities may result in some groups being excluded from the process in favor of those who have had more opportunities to access certain networks. Moreover, when conducting consultations with children and youth, paying attention to how the representation mechanisms are established and who is choosing the representatives is especially important: while adult involvement may be necessary, the youth's capacity to choose their own representatives should also be considered. Finally, particularly when planning consultations with children and youth, devising creative strategies to convey information in a way that will not unduly influence decisions and gathering information using different strategies—such as art, role-play, and songs—may be necessary to facilitate children's and youth's capacity to express their views.

DIRECT ENGAGEMENT IN THE OPERATIONS OF TRANSITIONAL JUSTICE MEASURES

Finally, outreach programs can facilitate child and youth involvement through their direct participation in some aspects of the work of a transitional justice measure, when activities are put in place in which they play a key or even leading role in design and implementation. Some examples include creating youth advisory bodies within a TJ measure to oversee and provide recommendations on youth involvement policies; implementing justice-related programs by children and youth, such as planning and constructing memorials; or opening opportunities for volunteer work and direct collaboration with the TJ measure.

Activities that promote the direct involvement of children and youth represent the deepest level at which they can take part in outreach programming for TJ measures, and hence such activities offer the most genuine means for participation. In this respect, the more space for youth to take part in their design, the more participatory the activity will be. While direct experience and longer-term involvement in the work of a transitional justice measure is an excellent way to guarantee understanding of the process and its goals, the mere act of participating is an important learning experience. As Hart has argued, "An understanding of [democratic] participation and the confidence and competence to participate can only be acquired gradually through practice; it cannot be taught as an abstraction."[44] Thus, this sort of participation serves as civic education, as well as a capacity-building exercise that will likely have results in the long term. Firsthand experience is also important in order to promote engagement; indeed, these forms of participation can help to build a sense of ownership of the process among younger generations, while developing their capacity for civic engagement.

Although this type of programming has been less common, some outreach activities organized by TJ measures have given youth the opportunity for direct involvement in some aspects of the process. Among these examples is the case of PROVER, a youth volunteer program organized by the Truth and Reconciliation Commission of Peru from January 2002 until July 2003.[45] The program's main aim was to engage youth from all over the country in the truth commission process and ultimately to promote civic consciousness and active participation in society. The original idea for the program came from the president of the commission, Dr. Salomón Lerner Febres—a member of the academic community; its purpose was to educate young volunteers about the Peruvian conflict and its legacy and to train them to assist the commission in a variety of ways. The commission hoped that the young volunteers would enrich the commission's work while acquiring significant experience for their personal development and future careers, not to mention the program's importance in terms of promoting civic education.[46]

What began as a creative but limited idea soon became a large and sophisticated project, with approximately 1,200 participants ages eighteen to twenty-five in cities all over the country. Just in the capital of Lima, there were more than 250 volunteers.[47] The program was directly managed by the Communications and Education Department of the commission, which established partnerships with universities throughout the country as well as other social networks and NGOs that worked closely with the commission.[48] Through these groups, the commission was able to identify potential young participants and also get some assistance in developing a mandatory training program for the youth to complete before becoming volunteers.[49] The fact that the commission used different intermediaries, including religious and secular universities, along with civil society groups, resulted in a wide pool of youth from different backgrounds, especially important in a country like Peru, in which significant social, cultural, and economic divisions exist.[50] The volunteers supported the commission's work and contributed to its accomplishments. Through PROVER, youth volunteers became genuine participants in the commission's work as they took part in such activities as taking testimony and processing it, disseminating information, and creating community forums; they even assisted an exhumation process in Lucanamarca.[51] The program also served as a space for them to take initiative and propose ideas, enriching the work of the commission.

PROVER gave opportunities to youth from all over the country to strengthen their commitment to affected communities while taking part in a longer process of recovery for Peru. The experience of volunteering became an effective way of sensitizing the youth, providing them with knowledge about the country's history, and giving them a chance to participate. As a young volunteer explained, "I thought it was a process that was going to be unique in the history of my country. In the previous years I knew many things happened through the television or the radio, but it is different when you see it so close.... I didn't know there were so many disappeared in Peru, for example. I knew that people disappeared, but never that it was on such a scale" (author's translation).[52]

After the PROVER program officially ended, young volunteers became memory workers and continued to use other means, including arts and memorialization initiatives, to promote the commission's legacy. Although the capacity to follow the group was limited after the TRC dissolved, the civil society association Instituto del Bien Común created another volunteer program for university students who wanted to contribute socially to the country. It operated in parallel to the citizen movement Para Que No Se Repita (So That It Never Happens Again), which was mainly tasked with following up on the commission's work and monitoring the implementation of its recommendations. In addition, in 2005 the Catholic University of Peru launched a national training/academic program on democratic leadership that seeks to connect democracy and human rights topics with memory issues, which was conceived as a natural follow-up to PROVER.[53]

The Accountability Now Clubs (ANCs) organized by the outreach unit of the Special Court of Sierra Leone are another example of a participatory outreach program that has given youth the opportunity to become involved more deeply in a transitional justice effort. The rationale of the program was to train university-level students on the functions of the court—as well as issues of transitional justice, governance, human rights, and international law—so that they could in turn disseminate information about the Special Court to secondary-school pupils and to their broader communities—hence contributing to the sensitizing activities of the outreach unit as well.[54] While in the short term the program's goal was to promote student participation in the court's process, the founders ultimately aimed to develop a corps of young people sensitized to issues of accountability who would eventually become an active force for promoting human rights and the rule of law in the country. By 2011 there were fourteen ANCs in Sierra Leone and seven in Liberia.[55]

In a country as severely shattered by conflict as Sierra Leone, university-level students were targeted because literacy was low and university education rare; people who are highly educated are respected in their communities.

Indeed, the ANC organizers believed that the Special Court had the ability to frame their message most effectively through the support of such individuals.[56] So far, the relationship between the club's members and their communities has proved to be positive. People can identify with the club members, which helps greatly in transmitting the court's messages.[57]

These two examples of direct engagement of youth in TJ processes as facilitated by outreach programs represent the deepest level of participation. The first three levels are not less important; in fact, in a sense they provide the foundation for genuine engagement.

PUTTING IN PLACE A CHILD-SENSITIVE APPROACH TO PARTICIPATION

In order to implement different levels of outreach with children and youth safely and adequately, a child-sensitive approach is also necessary. Taking the Convention of the Rights of the Child as the fundamental normative framework, a child-sensitive approach balances children's right to protection and considers a child's individual views and needs while trying to maximize the empowering potential of involvement in different activities. This approach entails a set of conditions that can be conceived first as part of the protection framework and rights that children enjoy, and that importantly outline the principle of "do no harm"; second, but equally important, these conditions could also be understood as enabling factors to make such participation, even if guided by adults, relevant and meaningful for children.[58] Hence, these conditions are important not only for protection but also for facilitation and support—and eventually, as we discuss later in more detail, for promoting their empowerment and capacity for agency. At times, however, given their differing aims, tensions arise between the principles of participation and protection, calling for a delicate balance.

In order to understand how to apply a child-sensitive approach to transitional justice outreach programs, we need to consider two different issues: (1) the type of activity we are talking about and its particular aims—that is, the engagement of children and youth in TJ processes through outreach programming—and (2) the specific context in which such activities take place—that is, transitional justice processes that generally aim to deal with a legacy of human rights abuses and contribute to establishing a democratic regime in the aftermath of authoritarianism or conflict. Considering these two factors, in this section we use the international protection framework outlined in the CRC as a point of reference, adjusting it to the nuances of outreach programming in TJ contexts.

A series of context-related factors must be considered before engaging children in outreach programming. As with other activities involving children in post-conflict situations, outreach programming around TJ processes deals with complex and often extremely difficult topics—including violence, conflict, and grave human rights violations.[59] Taking this point into account, a number of factors or variables should be considered, including the type of conflict and its proximity in time, the role that different children played in it, and finally the children's immediate environments and sociocultural contexts. For example, for children directly affected by the conflict (e.g., children associated with armed forces or child victims of sexual abuse), participation in outreach activities can bring back frightening and traumatic memories. This situation may be additionally problematic when trying to engage children and youth who are in vulnerable situations and lack social support networks—situations that will be even more acute in countries that, in the aftermath of conflict, have huge infrastructural deficits, including the lack of reliable health and education systems. Finally, the community and social environments in which children and youth live are also fundamental. In places in which sharp social divisions remain after conflict, and in which TJ measures are not generally supported, participation in outreach activities can be socially disruptive for children and youth. Likewise, cultural factors may be in tension with promoting children's participation in transitional justice measures. Depending on a culture's perceptions of childhood, some societies do not recognize children's rights to information and expression, which may be even more acute in the case of girls, whose participation may challenge the status quo in societies in which women are not supposed to have a voice.

As an overarching consideration, the *best interest of the child* should always be the guiding principle when engaging young people, including in outreach programming. This approach entails ensuring, on a case-by-case basis, the well-being of the child and granting the child agency in determining the level and manner of participation according to one's own needs and capacities. Within that, key factors to consider include planning and protection, psychosocial support, and evolving capacities. These considerations are important not only to protect children participating in outreach activities but also as a means of supporting their meaningful participation.

PLANNING AND PROTECTION

When involving children and young people in outreach programming for TJ measures, certain safeguards are needed to guarantee their physical safety and well-being. For starters, outreach activities conducted with children and youth should be based on a reliable and stable organization. While the final aim of outreach activities is to provide children with a space to develop their own capacities for participation around transitional justice processes, adults also play a fundamental role in offering guidance and support.[60] Thus, programmers should put in place from the beginning some sort of formal structure that can guarantee adult supervision and eventually be capable of conducting follow-up with children and young participants as needed.

In terms of configuring the outreach team to carry out the activities' design and implementation, involving professionals specifically trained in education and child development is advisable, as is having personnel qualified to evaluate the psychological risks of children's participation and respond to emergent situations.[61] In contexts of scarce resources where a TJ initiative cannot hire professionals with these areas of expertise, partnering and coordinating with other organizations or networks that can contribute specific expertise may be possible. For example, educational institutions such as schools and cultural institutions or memory museums can significantly contribute to this supervision and assist in preparatory and follow-up activities. In regard to psychosocial attention, collaboration can be established with child protection organizations or different health and social services groups. In some cases, relying on adults whom children know and trust, including family members, friends, teachers, or mentors, may also be sufficient. Together with immediate relatives and friends, community-based structures that are a natural part of the daily environment and lives of children and youth can play a key role in terms of facilitation and support.[62] Considering the context to which youth belong, the Cambodian organization Youth for Peace regularly involves community members in the activities they conduct with youth. For example, the so-called Village Dialogues bring young people together with survivors of the Khmer Rouge regime so that they can share stories and promote intergenerational dialogue. Monks are generally included in the discussion groups, as they are important and well-respected figures in the community.[63]

When establishing collaboration frameworks with different networks and community structures, support for organizing activities may be easy to obtain, but guaranteeing adequate follow-up can be much more challenging. For example, in October 2010 ICTJ organized a four-day youth retreat in collaboration with the Canadian TRC, with the aim of engaging a group of Canadian youth in the truth and reconciliation commission process and assisting them with preparing videos that would be submitted to a national event planned for Inuvik in June 2011. During the retreat, the youth learned about the history of residential schools in Canada and the role of the truth commission, and they were provided with tools and guidance to start their own video production. However, finalizing the films in time for their presentation in Inuvik depended on the mentors who had come to the retreat and were assigned the role of supervising the process. While the retreat was a valuable experience for most of the youth, only one of the four groups from the retreat was able to complete its submission in time to present it to the TRC. Despite an agreement to follow up, all but one of the mentors were not in a position to provide follow-up support as they had committed.

Another important consideration when planning outreach activities with children and youth is the need to guarantee informed consent and the protection of privacy. Youth participation in TJ outreach activities should be informed, voluntary, and with the least amount of interference in the child's private life. In some instances, specific measures to ensure the protection of privacy and confidentiality are necessary. For example, the use of social media, such as Facebook, Twitter, and other sites, may in principle be attractive for outreach purposes; however, it can put the child's privacy and security at risk. Likewise, one needs to consider the immediate environment of children and youth to ensure that they are not at risk of being targeted as a result of their participation. In countries in which conflict is still recent, participation in outreach activities for transitional justice measures may place the youth in difficult situations when they return to their communities. For example, in Bosnia and Herzegovina, where tensions from the war period are still present, the youth-based NGO Youth Initiative for Human Rights realized the importance of having professional psychological support available during some of their activities. In one instance, after participating in an event organized at the Memorial Center in Potočari, a youth participant changed his own profile picture on a social media website to one of the Serbian war leader Ratko Mladić, an alleged war criminal facing trial at the ICTY. While this youth may have had some nationalist sentiment, the organizers suspect that his peers questioned his loyalty to his community and thus pressured him, directly or indirectly, perhaps creating an uncomfortable situation in which he felt the need to prove his belonging to the group.[64] Psychosocial counseling or attention is important to provide support or help youth cope in such instances.

In cases in which gathering opinions, images, and video footage from child and youth participants is of interest, organizers should take the necessary steps to inform children and youth in advance about the aims of such documentation processes and to ensure explicit consent from the children and their guardians by providing them with release forms that offer a choice among graduated levels of confidentiality (e.g., permitting the inclusion of their stories, image, voice, footage, or name). In early 2012, in collaboration with the Nepalese child protection agency Child Workers in Nepal (CWIN), ICTJ organized a series of outreach workshops with youth that aimed to train them on and foster discussions about transitional justice processes, specifically the development of the process in Nepal. Originally, ICTJ planned to record these meetings to produce additional training materials. However, after discussing this plan with CWIN and the young participants at the first event, given the sensitivity of the topics being discussed, the team ultimately decided not to film the events. While media access can be a powerful experience and platform, failure to sufficiently research local laws, consult with children and guardians, and design and complete appropriate consent forms can result in the inability to document children's participation. During the Halifax National Event organized by the Truth and Reconciliation Commission of Canada in October 2011, numerous youth were on site and actively engaged in the proceedings. The TRC media teams as well as local and national news outlets were interested in recording interviews with the youth. Unfortunately, due to limited knowledge of the age at which minors may consent to release their images and the lack of an appropriate consent form, few of the youth were interviewed; the opportunity to publicize their involvement was lost. Advance preparation of a form designed in accordance with relevant legal standards and allowing for varying levels of release ensures children's protection and offers them the chance to voice their ideas to a broad audience.[65]

PSYCHOSOCIAL SUPPORT

Psychosocial considerations are another fundamental element when facilitating outreach activities with children and youth. As Michels has argued, psychosocial factors are "a necessary component of any discussion about children's participation in transitional justice mechanisms. These factors affect children's ability to participate and their needs for protection and support."[66] Psychologically, children and adolescents are still in a developmental stage of their lives; they may be more vulnerable when confronting certain topics, especially when they have lived through the conflict and have experienced or witnessed abuses, or they may have a tendency to be less realistic when framing their expectations—especially when they have limited access to information. In this respect, when thinking about psychological considerations, paying attention to specific psychological situations that need evaluation on a case-by-case basis is important—for example, when conducting outreach with children who have suffered sexual abuse or been associated with armed forces. More generally, when conducting outreach activities, organizers need to build a space in which children and youth feel comfortable and free to express their views to adults and peers.

In order to account properly for psychosocial support issues in outreach programming, several options should be considered, including establishing specific rules, protocols, guidelines, and measures to protect and support children; conducting trainings on children's rights with the personnel involved; offering direct support or counseling; and setting up long-term support mechanisms.[67] In terms of organization, any outreach activity organized with children and youth should be viewed as a process, understanding that psychosocial support might be necessary before, during, and after the activity. Again, especially in instances in which outreach is directly geared toward gathering testimony from children and youth or when outreach is targeted toward a particularly vulnerable group, referring participants to follow-up support structures is a basic consideration. As with general planning issues, however, special attention may be necessary, since experience has shown that adequate follow-up is a recurrent challenge. For example, looking for ways of supporting children's participation in its proceedings, the Truth and Reconciliation Commission of Sierra Leone partnered with several local child protection agencies. While such attention and support were available during the proceedings, after the processes ended, "follow-up activities to monitor psychosocial well-being of children that participated in the commission appeared limited."[68]

Before implementing any outreach activity, preparatory meetings are helpful not only for planning and coordination but also for identifying potential risks and opportunities. During the activity, a healthy and emotionally safe environment is a precondition for conducting outreach activities with children and youth. Creating such an environment implies that making an extra effort is necessary to guarantee the participants' well-being. Creating a safe, respectful, and child- and youth-friendly space in which participants can express their concerns in their own language, freely and with mutual respect, is important. Depending on the outreach activity's type and duration, some techniques to create a more relaxed atmosphere and build trust both vertically (between the adults and the youth) and horizontally (among the youth themselves) may be important as well. These techniques can include working together to establish a set of rules of behavior, conducting some icebreakers and team-building exercises, combining substantive programming with leisure activities, and ending the meetings with debriefing exercises. For example, as part of its educational programs, the US Holocaust Memorial Museum in Washington, DC, regularly organizes school visits to the museum. Because of the sensitivity of the exhibit's content, and also considering that for some children this may be the first time they have learned about the German concentration camps during World War II, the educational team always conducts debriefing exercises with the youth at the end of the tour in the museum's Hall of Remembrance—a large six-sided room with a flame in the center—to help them to process anger or other emotional reactions.[69]

DEVELOPMENT AND EVOLVING CAPACITIES

The *children and youth* category reflects a continuum that comprises a heterogeneous group in terms of age. While important differences exist between early childhood, adolescence, and youth—what are referred to in general terms as a child's *evolving capacities*—each individual child also has singular capacities and abilities. The stage or degree of a child's development—which encompasses not only intellectual aptitudes but also emotional, moral, and social development and maturity—affects their capacity to behave as autonomous agents.[70] In post-conflict situations, and as a direct consequence of violence and missed educational opportunities, the natural course of children's development may have been seriously affected. Accordingly, "exposure to extreme violence, displacement and/or separation from parents and the loss of family and friends can all hinder children's well-being and development. The lack of access to education and health care, as a direct result of the war, also influences the capacity of children to cope and develop further."[71] Yet, in some cases, the experience of conflict may strengthen children's resilience and endurance as well as their motivation to contribute to society in positive ways.

Although adults generally tend to undervalue the competence of children—including their capacity to understand and assimilate difficult topics, as well as their ability to respond to them and make decisions accordingly—children and youth are capable of understanding difficult and sophisticated topics, especially when the topics affect the societies in which the children and youth live. The challenge then becomes putting adequate methods and techniques in place that recognize the different developmental stages and maximize children's and youth's ability to understand and speak about issues in a manner most comfortable to them.[72] In this respect, an emphasis on overprotection may hinder opportunities to participate.

Evolving capacities should also be factored in when conducting outreach with children and youth in terms of developing specific materials and activities that are adapted to their needs and capacities—that is, by considering issues such as format and length or the accessibility of the language employed, and also by making efforts to put in place pedagogical approaches that can contribute to making outreach activities a learning process. While some TJ projects have developed child-friendly materials, another possibility is to design materials for teachers or facilitators that they can present to children. Teacher-oriented materials can provide useful guidance to education professionals and other adults involved in education activities on how to convey the TJ process in their classrooms and other venues.[73] A good example is the work in Canada of the Legacy of Hope Foundation and the nation's truth and reconciliation commission, which have collaborated with "curriculum developers to create curricula on the history and legacy of the residential school system in Canada for grades 9–10 and 11–12, as well as for post-secondary students and lifelong learners."[74]

Finally, beyond achieving educational aims, the content of the materials and activities has to be relevant and interesting to children and youth, anticipating what children can, or need to, take away from the process. For example, in contexts in which children have lived through a violent period, they might still have difficulties understanding why the conflict took place. By participating in outreach activities for TJ processes, children and youth may be better able to understand their own experiences as they relate to a broader context of conflict and recovery. In other cases, especially in TJ processes that take place long after the conflict is over, or when working with children not directly involved in violent episodes, the interest of children and youth in the past may not be obvious. Julia Paulson, the former coordinator from the Instituto de Defensa Legal (IDL) in Peru, argued for children's need to engage with the past as something specific within their broader social context: "Two things impressed us during the entire process of the CVR: how little many people knew about what had happened and the sentiment that once the period of violence was over, it was seen as something that happened to other people, that it wasn't their problem. So we thought that especially younger generations, youth, must be seeing this period as even more distant."[75] In these cases, outreach personnel need to make special efforts to engage with youth—for example, by trying to make connections between transitional justice and topics of current relevance for them, such as corruption or current criminality, so that they can also understand the exercise of addressing the past as a future-oriented endeavor.

FOSTERING AGENCY: TOWARD MEANINGFUL PARTICIPATION

The final consideration has to do with the concept of participation as such. In this respect, because outreach in TJ contexts aims to engage children and youth in the general social process of overcoming human rights abuses and constructing a democracy, well-planned outreach activities can offer a unique opportunity to strengthen children's and youth's capacity for critical thinking and self-awareness as citizens. Participation, as a "process of sharing decisions which affect one's life and the life of the community in which one lives," is a fundamental right of democratic citizenship.[76] If outreach activities are to be meaningful in terms of bolstering children's and youth's participation in TJ processes, taking seriously children's status as rights holders and their capacity as active citizens who can creatively and positively contribute to societal change is crucial.

While adults face challenges in exercising their right to participation even in well-developed democracies, for children and youth the challenge is even greater. In a political world designed by adults and for adults, children and youth may not be able to identify themselves as rights-bearers. Because they are not organized or genuinely represented, children and youth may find it more difficult to articulate their own interests and exercise their civic rights. On the other hand, a generalized lack of awareness exists among adults about the need for and competence of children and adolescents to contribute their views and ideas in ways that nurture their capacity for agency. When facilitated, child participation often runs the risk of being based on a naïve image of children, integrated as part of a checklist of groups to include or, even worse, as an exercise in tokenism or manipulation. Finally, in some cases, even when efforts are well intentioned, an excess of protection and an inability to see children and youth as decisionmakers and agents in their own right can curtail their capabilities to take an active part in the process. Children and youth are not passive victims or mere passive-recipient members of a society. They are agents and citizens who have their own views, and they need spaces and methods to help articulate their own voices.

On the notion of children's participation, Roger A. Hart has identified four criteria that can be understood as minimum requirements for a project to be participatory, reflecting an intention to treat children as equals:

1. Children should be provided with enough information and explanation to understand the project.

2. Children need to know who made decisions concerning their involvement and why.

3. Children should play a meaningful rather than decorative role.

4. Children should be given the chance to volunteer after the project is made clear to them.[77]

When children and youth participate in outreach activities in TJ contexts, reporting back to them at the end of the process is also fundamental. Once this set of minimum conditions is met, the more space that children and youth have to take initiative, be involved in a decisionmaking process, and carry out specific projects, the more participatory the activities will be. Indeed, projects that are participatory in nature—such as PROVER or the ANCs—are the most effective way for youth to learn how to be responsible citizens. Directly experiencing involvement in political and social matters gives children and youth the opportunity to develop their civic agency.

CONCLUSION

Children and youth are a fundamental part of the societies in which TJ processes operate. While arguments around the importance of involving them in such processes are usually future oriented—because children and youth represent the future generation—the children and youth themselves also have a role to play in the present as citizens and stakeholders. As victims and members of the society in which transitional justice processes unfold, children and youth have their own particular experiences and views that adults cannot fully represent but which, instead, children and youth should articulate directly. In order for children and youth to understand and have a say in the TJ process, outreach programs must explicitly take them into consideration.

In this chapter we established a framework of different ways in which TJ outreach programs can involve children and youth—including disseminating information, establishing a dialogue, holding consultation exercises, and opening venues for children's and youth's engagement in TJ operations. We also looked to a series of specific considerations to make such a process child- and youth-sensitive. In addition to putting in place protection measures—including planning, psychosocial support, and respect for children's evolving capacities—we have also argued that meaningful outreach exercises must ensure that attempts to foster children's and youth's participation in them are genuine and honest.

The balance between participation and protection is a difficult one to find in the context of transitional justice. Overemphasizing protection may limit the potential of children and youth to learn from and contribute to TJ processes. However, pushing for participation without sufficient support and protection may cause harm to children and youth. In cases in which younger generations have been involved in outreach, there seems to have been a greater emphasis on protection, at times to the detriment of their genuine participation. We should not limit to peripheral activities such as drawings, songs, and games the role that children can play in TJ. When given the space and proper support, they are capable to take on much more. Thus, the challenge for transitional justice advocates is to find ways to facilitate more meaningful participation. The first step is through child- and youth-sensitive outreach, as we have outlined here. Information and the establishment of two-way dialogue between the TJ measure and children and youth lays the foundation for them to exercise their agency—and in that process strengthen efforts to address past violations for a future based on democratic standards and respect for human rights.

NOTES

The authors wish to thank all of the participants of the meeting on the "State of the Field: Children and Transitional Justice," organized by ICTJ on March 23–24, 2011, including Cecile Aptel, Jean Francois Basse, Charlotte Cole, Elizabeth Cole, Bix Gabriel, Marzia Gigli, Iris Jave Pinedo, Maria Kamara, Khamboly Dy, Long Khet, Karen Murphy, Mandy Sanger, Saji Prelis, Liz Silkes, Saudamini Siegrist, and Mohamed Suma, as well as the different persons interviewed for the drafting of this chapter, including Alma Masic, Mario Mazic, Maja Micic, and Jesse Nickelson. Patrick Fatoma and Iris Jave Pinedo generously shared very useful materials and information. At ICTJ, the authors are thankful to Pablo de Greiff, Roger Duthie, and Valerie Waters for comments on earlier drafts of this document and to the interns, Jessica Coffey, Brian Jacobi, and Katie Jessup, who contributed to the research at different stages of the process. This chapter does not necessarily represent the position of ICTJ.

1 UN Convention on the Rights of the Child, General Assembly Resolution 44/25, UN Doc. A/RES/44/25, November 20, 1989, art. 1.

2 The United Nations defines *youth* as those between the ages of fifteen and twenty-four. See "United Nations Youth Agenda FAQ," accessed May 6, 2013, http://social.un.org/

index/Youth/FAQs.aspx, Question 1; see also UN General Assembly and Economic and Social Council, *Report of the Secretary General: Implementation of the World Program of Action for Youth: United Nations System Coordination and Collaboration Related to Youth*, UN Doc. A/66/61, November 22, 2010, in which the secretary-general consistently refers to youth as ages fifteen to twenty-four. UNICEF has used the term to refer to people from the ages of ten to nineteen: Rakesh Rajani, "The Participation Rights of Adolescents: A Strategic Approach" (working paper series, UNICEF, New York, 2001), uses the terms *adolescents, youth,* and *young people* interchangeably to refer to the ten- to nineteen-year-old age group; for a discussion of the choice in doing so, see "Terms" on p. 8. UNESCO has distinguished between *youth*, ages fifteen to twenty-four, and *young people*, between the ages of ten and nineteen (UNESCO, *UNESCO's Contribution: Empowering Youth through National Policies*, Paris, March 1, 2004, 10).

3 In some cultural contexts, especially those that use biological markers, women are often excluded from this category: "The fact that female youth as a category in many cultures scarcely exists, if at all, constitutes a serious and direct challenge to everyone engaged in youth programming" (Marc Sommers, *Youth and Conflict: A Brief Review of Available Literature* [Washington, DC: USAID, 2006], 4).

4 Carola Eyber, and Ager Alastair, "Researching Young People's Experience of War: Participatory Methods and the Trauma of Discourse in Angola," in *Children and Youth on the Frontline*, ed. Jo Boyden and Joanna de Berry (New York: Berghahn Books, 2004), 189.

5 Robert D. Kaplan, *The Ends of the Earth: A Journey at the Dawn of the Twenty-First Century* (New York: Random House, 1996), 5.

6 Special Court for Sierra Leone, *Special Court Outreach Report 2003–2005* (Freetown: Special Court of Sierra Leone, 2007), 17.

7 For a nuanced normative understanding of transitional justice, see Pablo de Greiff, "Theorizing Transitional Justice," in *Nomos LI: Transitional Justice*, ed. Melissa Williams, Rosemary Nagy, and Jon Elster (New York: NYU Press, 2012), 31–77.

8 Success is a slippery concept, and not only the context but also a wide range of variables are important to explaining the success or failure of TJ measures, including the performance of the measures themselves. Still, experience shows that in countries in which there was a strong push from civil society to look into the past, as in the case of Argentina, the impact of TJ measures has been deeper than in places such as in the former Yugoslavia, in which a great majority of the population for a very long time opposed the creation of internationally devised mechanisms such as the ICTY.

9 See Clara Ramírez-Barat, *Making an Impact: Guidelines on Designing and Implementing Outreach Programs for Transitional Justice* (New York: ICTJ, 2011), http://ictj.org/sites/default/files/ICTJ-Global-Making-Impact-2011-English.pdf.

10 For more on the understanding of outreach as a function, see ibid. See also Victor Peskin, "Courting Rwanda: The Promises and Pitfalls of the ICTR Outreach Program,"

Journal of International Criminal Justice 3, no. 4 (2005): 950–61 and Norman H. Pentelovitch, "Seeing Justice Done: The Importance of Prioritizing Outreach Efforts at International Criminal Tribunals," *Georgetown Journal of International Law* 39, no. 3 (2008): 445–94.

11 See Special Court for Sierra Leone, "Outreach and Public Affairs," accessed December 2012, http://www.sc-sl.org/ABOUT/CourtOrganization/TheRegistry/OutreachandPublicAffairs/tabid/83/Default.aspx.

12 See UNICEF and ICTJ, *Children and Truth Commissions* (Florence: UNICEF and ICTJ, 2010).

13 For example, research in Colombia mentions the "differentiated impact" on children and youth, and describes the consequences of the violence on children in terms of fear, anguish, and trauma (Comisión Nacional de Reparación y Reconciliación [CNRR]), Grupo de Memoria Histórica, *La masacre de El Salado: Esa guerra no era nuestra* [The El Salado massacre: This was not our war] (Bogotá: CNRR, 2009), 165.

14 UNESCO, *The Hidden Crisis: Armed Conflict and Education*, EFA Global Monitoring Report (Paris: UNESCO, 2011).

15 UN Secretary-General, *Note by the Secretary-General: Promotion and Protection of the Rights of Children: Impact of Armed Conflict on Children*, UN Doc. A/51/306, August 26, 1996.

16 Truth and Reconciliation Commission of South Africa, *Truth and Reconciliation Commission of South Africa Report*, 5 vols. (Cape Town: Truth and Reconciliation Commission, 1998), 3:270.

17 Cultural losses may include the loss of both language and traditions, as occurred in Canada as a result of the Indian Residential School System, which forcibly removed Aboriginal children and placed them in church-run, state-sponsored boarding schools intended to "kill the Indian in the child."

18 Cecile Aptel and Virginie Ladisch, *Through a New Lens: A Child-Sensitive Approach to Transitional Justice* (New York: ICTJ, 2011), 31.

19 UN Convention on the Rights of the Child, art. 12: "States Parties shall assure to the child who is capable of forming his or her own views the right to express those views freely in all matters affecting the child, the views of the child being given due weight in accordance with the age and maturity of the child."

20 Sommers, "Youth and Conflict," 2.

21 Stella María Duque, April 26, 2010, interview with ICTJ researcher, Bogotá, Colombia.

22 Patricia Hernández, justice and peace prosecutor, interview with authors, May 5, 2010, Bogotá, Colombia.

23 Comisión de la Verdad y Reconciliación Oficina de Comunicaciones e Impacto Publico, "Culmina el programa de voluntariado 'Promotores de la Verdad' PROVER" [Truth and Reconciliation Commission Communications and Public Input Division, "The volunteer program Promotores de la Verdad (PROVER) comes to its end"], press release 222, Lima, July 21, 2003: "El trabajo de los voluntarios ha constituido un medio privilegiado para que descubran su humanidad, sin embargo la experiencia que hanvivido

no solo los ha hecho más humanos sino que esta experiencia les ha permitido asumir con plenitud su peruanidad en una edad muy temprana. En este tiempo no sólo han podido entender mejor a nuestro país ahondando en sus luces y en sus sombras, sino que han logrado sentirlo con mayor intensidad, comprometiéndose con el dolor de los más pobres, de los olvidados que son los que han sufrido las violaciones a sus derechos humanos."

24 Iris Jave Pinedo, *State of the Field: Children and Transitional Justice*, ICTJ meeting summary, New York, March 23–24, 2011.

25 Ibid.

26 Yvonne Kemper, *Youth in War-to-Peace Transitions: Approaches of International Organizations* (Berlin: Berghof Research Center for Constructive Conflict Management, 2005), 38.

27 Khamboly Dy, *Teaching Genocide in Cambodia: Challenges, Analyses, and Recommendations* (Phnom Penh: DC-CAM, 2008), http://dccam.org/Projects/Genocide/Boly_Teaching_Genocide_in_Cambodia1.pdf, 1.

28 Michael Wessels and Davidson Jonah, "Recruitment and Reintegration of Former Youth Soldiers in Sierra Leone: Challenges of Reconciliation and Post-Accord Peacebuilding," in *Troublemakers or Peacemakers? Youth and Post-Accord Peace Building*, ed. Siobhan McEvoy-Levy (Notre Dame, IN: University of Notre Dame Press, 2006), 27–28.

29 Ibid., 39.

30 McEvoy-Levy, *Troublemakers or Peacemakers?*, 6.

31 Kemper, *Youth in War-to-Peace Transitions*, 3.

32 McEvoy-Levy, *Troublemakers or Peacemakers?*, 7.

33 Khamboly Dy, *Teaching Genocide in Cambodia*, 20.

34 See Ramírez-Barat, *Making an Impact*, 7–9.

35 Cheryl Heykoop, "Child Participation and Agency in the Sierra Leone TRC," in UNICEF, "Expert Discussion on Children and Transitional Justice" (background paper, UNICEF Innocenti Research Center, Florence, June 12–13, 2008), 16.

36 Special Court for Sierra Leone, "Special Court Prosecutor Says He Will Not Prosecute Children," news release, November 2, 2002, http://www.sc-sl.org/LinkClick.aspx?fileticket=XRwCUe%2baVhw%3d&tabid=196.

37 Heykoop, "Child Participation and Agency in the Sierra Leone TRC," 15; Theo Sowa, "Child and Adolescent Participation in the Liberian TRC," in UNICEF, "Expert Discussion on Children and Transitional Justice," 43.

38 The three versions of the report are at the Sierra Leone TRC website, http://www.sierraleonetrc.org/.

39 Available at http://www.unictr.org/News/ICTRCartoonBook/tabid/2225/Default.aspx.

40 Himalayan Human Rights Monitors and Partnerships for Protecting Children in Armed Conflict, *Child Public Hearing 2007: The Impact of Armed Conflict on Children* (Kathmandu: HimRights and PPCC, 2007).

41 Consultation exercises may focus on facts (e.g., the demographic profile of victims), preferences (e.g., specific forms of reparations), or expectations (e.g., general views of justice). These exercises can serve to guide and inform the work of TJ measures in terms of their design, monitoring, and evaluation.

42 Aptel and Ladisch, *Through a New Lens*, 13–14.

43 An interesting account of different levels of participation at which children and youth can be involved in relation to the capacity of decisionmaking can be found at Roger A. Hart, *Children's Participation: From Tokenism to Citizenship*, UNICEF Innocenti Essays no. 4 (Florence: UNICEF, 1992), 11–14.

44 Ibid., 5.

45 Truth and Reconciliation Commission, *Reglamento de organización y funciones del programa de voluntariado de Promotores de la Verdad "PROVER" de la Comisión de la Verdad y la Reconciliación* [Rules of implementation and functions of the volunteer program Promoters of Truth (PROVER) of the Truth and Reconciliation Commission] (Lima: CVR, 2002).

46 Iris Jave Pinedo, *El impacto público de la Comisión de la Verdad y la Reconciliación, 2001–2003: Apuntes des de la comunicación política* [The public impact of the Truth and Reconciliation Commission, 2001–2003: Notes on political communication] (Lima: Tesis de Licenciatura, Universidad Nacional Mayor de San Marcos, 2003), 67.

47 Comisión de la Verdad y Reconciliación, "Culmina el programa," press release.

48 See, for example, the agreement signed by the Truth and Reconciliation Commission and Peru's Consortium of Universities, according to which the consortium agreed to provide training for young volunteers in workshops organized in coordination with the commission (Convenio de Cooperación Institucional entre el Consorcio de Universidades y la Comisión de la Verdad y la Reconciliación, Lima, May 2002).

49 This training covered a range of issues, including the mandate, goals, and working procedures of the TRC; specific training in the different areas of work that were to be assigned to the volunteers, especially regarding outreach; and, finally, a module on the meaning and role of volunteer work. See Truth and Reconciliation Commission, *Reglamento de organización y funciones*, chap. 3.

50 Iris Jave Pinedo, "The Volunteer Program of the Truth and Reconciliation Commission of Peru, PROVER"; Jave Pinedo, *State of the Field.*

51 Jave Pinedo, "Volunteer Program of the Truth and Reconciliation Commission of Peru."

52 Truth and Reconciliation Commission, *Boletín de la Comisión de la Verdad y Reconciliación* 1 (April 2002): 8: "Pensé que es un proceso único que se va a dar en la historia de mi país. En los años que pasaron yo me había enterado de muchas cosas viendo el televisor o escuchando la radio, pero no es lo mismo que cuando lo ves de cerca" [. . .] "Yo no sabía que había tantos desaparecidos, por ejemplo. Sabía que hubog ente que desapareció en el Perú, pero nunca imaginé que en esa magnitud."

53 More information on the program is available on the website, http://idehpucp.pucp.edu.pe/index.php?option=com_ content&view=article&id=49&Itemid=140 (in Spanish).

54 Mohamed Suma, "The Special Court of Sierra Leone: Accountability Now Clubs," in *State of the Field: Children and Transitional Justice*, ICTJ meeting summary, New York, March 23–24, 2011.

55 Special Court of Sierra Leone, *Eighth Annual Report of the President of the Court of Sierra Leone: June 2010 to May 2011* (Freetown: Special Court for Sierra Leone, 2011), 44.

56 Suma, "Special Court of Sierra Leone," 6.

57 ANC Fourah Bay College, "Fight against Violence and Corruption in Schools and Knowing the Role of the Special Court in Pursuing Justice" (project description, ANC Fourah Bay College, Freetown, March 2010).

58 While some of these are necessary conditions, others can be perceived as guiding principles that contribute to making such participation as genuine as possible. In this respect, failure to properly take into account this set of considerations not only raises ethical and legal concerns but also undermines the aim of the participatory exercise and the positive impact it may have in children's and adolescents' lives.

59 The special situation of children in post-conflict situations is explicitly recognized in Article 39 of the Convention of the Rights of the Child, according to which, "States Parties shall take all appropriate measures to promote physical and psychological recovery and social reintegration of a child victim of: any form of neglect, exploitation, or abuse; torture or any other form of cruel, inhuman or degrading treatment or punishment; or armed conflicts. Such recovery and reintegration shall take place in an environment which fosters the health, self-respect, and dignity of the child." For the topic of children's involvement in armed conflict, see also UN General Assembly, "Annex 1: Optional Protocol to the Convention on the Rights of the Child," UN Doc. A/RES/54/263, May 25, 2000.

60 See UNICEF, *Fact Sheet: The Right to Participation* (New York: UNICEF, 2005), http://www.unicef.org/crc/files/Right-to-Participation.pdf.

61 See An Michels, "Psychosocial Support for Children: Protecting the Rights of Child Victims and Witnesses in Transitional Justice Processes" (Innocenti Working Paper, IWP 2010–14, Innocenti Research Center, UNICEF, Florence, 2010), 2.

62 Local leaders and groups that have access to children and youth can also help by providing information about cultural context and practices, especially how those affect children or what roles children traditionally play.

63 Long Khet, "Youth for Peace (YFP)," in *State of the Field: Children and Transitional Justice*, ICTJ meeting summary, New York, March 23–24, 2011. See also the YFP website, http://www.yfpcambodia.org/.

64 Mario Mazic and Maja Micic, Youth Initiative for Human Rights, interview with authors, Sarajevo, June 2011.

65 Clara Ramírez-Barat, *Engaging Children and Youth in Transitional Justice Processes: Guidance for Outreach Programs* (New York: ICTJ, 2012).

66 Michels, "Psychosocial Support for Children," 1.

67 Ibid.

68 Heykoop, "Child Participation and Agency in the Sierra Leone TRC," 15.

69 Jesse Nickelson, director, youth and community initiatives, US Holocaust Memorial Museum, interview with authors, November 2011. In the Hall of Remembrance an inscription reads, "Only guard yourself and guard your soul carefully, lest you forget the things your eyes saw, and lest these things depart your heart all the days of your life. And you shall make them known to your children, and to your children's children" (Deuteronomy 4:9).

70 The concept of child development was first elaborated in Jean Piaget's work, including *The Moral Judgment of the Child* (London: Routledge and Kegan Paul, 1932) and *Origins of Intelligence in the Child* (London: Routledge and Kegan Paul, 1936). More generally, see also Carol Garhart Mooney, *Theories of Childhood: An Introduction to Dewey, Montessori, Erikson, Piaget and Vygotsky* (St. Paul, MN: Redleaf Press, 2000).

71 Michels, "Psychosocial Support for Children," 3. See also UN Secretary-General, *Note by the Secretary-General: Promotion and Protection of the Rights of Children*, note 18.

72 Hart, "Children's Participation," 15.

73 Although teacher-oriented materials are valuable resources in themselves, training exercises that help educators effectively teach these difficult topics ideally should accompany them.

74 For more information about Legacy of Hope, see http://www.legacyofhope.ca/home. The curriculum is at http://www.wherearethechildren.ca/en/bookcase/.

75 Julia Paulson, "Truth Commissions and National Curricula: The Case of Recordándonos in Peru," in *Children and Transitional Justice: Truth-Telling, Accountability, and Reconciliation*, ed. Sharanjeet Parmar, Mindy J. Roseman, Saudamini Siegrist, and Teo Sowa (Cambridge, MA: Harvard University Press and UNICEF, 2010), 345.

76 Hart, "Children's Participation," 5.

77 Ibid., 11.

PART 2

Conflict, Media, and Justice

CHAPTER 5

Democratization of Media in Post-Conflict Situations: Reporting on ICTY War Crimes Trials in Serbia

Nidžara Ahmetašević and Tanja Matić

More than twenty years ago, the Socialist Federal Republic of Yugoslavia (SFRY) began to disintegrate. Starting with Slovenia, Croatia, and Macedonia in the summer and fall of 1991, and followed by Bosnia and Herzegovina in March 1992, the former Yugoslav republics, one after the other, proclaimed their independence.[1] While the root causes for the dissolution of the Yugoslav Federation are still a matter of scholarly debate, the unspeakable horrors of the series of wars that resulted, lasting from 1991 to 2002, were broadcast worldwide through the international media.[2] Massive violations of human rights and humanitarian law were committed during the wars, including crimes against humanity and genocide.[3] According to the International Criminal Tribunal for the former Yugoslavia (ICTY), from 1992 to 1995, more than 104,000 people were killed in Bosnia and Herzegovina alone (out of a total population of about 4 million).[4] Exact numbers of victims from other countries, including Serbia, have still not been officially established.

In response to the crimes that were then ongoing in the former Yugoslavia, in 1993 the UN Security Council decided to establish an international tribunal to prosecute the highest-ranking political and military leaders, in accordance with its powers under Chapter VII of the UN Charter to preserve international peace and security.[5] The ICTY was the first war crimes tribunal created by the United Nations and the first international war crimes tribunal since Nuremberg and Tokyo. As of August 2012 the ICTY had indicted a total of 161 people for war crimes, including heads of state, prime ministers, military chiefs of staff, interior ministers, and leaders in the military and police forces.[6] At the time of the ICTY's founding, the Security Council stated that the tribunal's main aims were "to bring to justice the persons who are responsible" for crimes perpetrated in the former Yugoslavia, to deter further crimes, and "to contribute to the restoration and maintenance of peace" by "promoting *reconciliation*" in the region.[7] Although the current version of the ICTY's statute (which has been amended several times over the years) no longer refers to its potential role in contributing to reconciliation, many people would still consider reconciliation as one of its central goals. To a great extent, the tribunal's capacity to bring closure to the region's people and help them come to terms with the past was dependent on its ability to properly inform the population about the causes and consequences of the war through its findings and decisions. Accordingly, whether to bring justice or to advance peace and reconciliation in the former Yugoslavia, information about the trials needed to be carefully and responsibly disseminated to the region's public.

Unfortunately, however, even though the facts established in the trials were technically "public," they were not well publicized within the Balkans; worse, they were often subject to misinterpretations or clear manipulations by politicians and their allies within the media. Since 2004 the Belgrade Center for Human Rights and the Organization for Security and Cooperation in Europe (OSCE) Mission to Serbia have been conducting a periodic survey in Serbia to assess public knowledge and attitudes about the ICTY.[8] In the 2011 survey, about 41 percent of respondents said that they were familiar with the tribunal and its work only "to a little extent," while only 10 percent said that they were "very much" familiar with it.[9] Moreover, 66 percent of the respondents considered the tribunal to be unnecessary,[10] and 40 percent felt that the ICTY's primary function was "to put the blame for war sufferings on Serbs."[11] The same survey showed that 49 percent of those asked believed that the ICTY could not "help establish the truth about events in the wars in the former SFRY" since the information "will never reach ordinary citizens."[12] The survey's results in its assessment of factual knowledge were not much more encouraging. For example, only 40 percent of respondents believed that "a large number of Muslim/Bosniak civilians were killed in Srebrenica."[13] Regarding the statement that "Sarajevo was under siege by Serbian forces for more than a thousand days," 53 percent of respondents said they had heard of it, 37 percent believed it had happened, and only 12 percent thought that it was a war crime.[14]

Among all the factors that might explain this survey's results, the Serbian media's perpetuation of the population's fears and biases after the conflict's end was significant and should be carefully examined. Our aim in this chapter is both to examine the media's role in Serbia in spreading hatred and warmongering before and during the wars in the former Yugoslavia, as well as to show how, after the wars, the legacy of the deeply flawed media structures in the region—formed under Communist control and never properly democratized after the war—influenced the media's reporting on the prosecutions of war criminals. We also show how the attitude and approach of the ICTY toward the media failed to take the structural shortcomings of the ex-Yugoslav media and the social and political landscapes into consideration, and thus failed to prevent or address their negative effects. Using the Serbian experience as a case study, our final aim is to contribute to the broader question of the media's role in investigating and disseminating information on past abuses in countries that are trying to recover from conflict and establish a democratic form of government. Also we discuss how war crimes tribunals should best approach the media and the public sphere in order to contribute positively to this process.

In the next part of this chapter, we give a short background of the conflict in the former Yugoslavia and provide an overview of the media environment before the wars erupted. Then we analyze the current media scene in Serbia, including the ongoing reforms and the still prominent role of politicians in shaping the media's portrayal of the past. We address the ICTY's approach toward the media, aiming to show through a series of concrete examples how the ICTY's attitude, on the one hand, and the media's spread of political propaganda, on the other, contributed to public opinion about Serbia's past. To further illustrate this process, we analyze the mainstream media's reporting on three of the most complex and, according to many, most important cases of the ad hoc tribunal: the trials of Slobodan Milošević, former president of Serbia; Radovan Karadžić, the political leader of the Bosnian Serb rebels during the war; and Ratko Mladić, a military commander in the Bosnian Serb Army. All three were arrested in Serbia, but while Milošević was imprisoned in 2001, Karadžić and Mladić both managed to hide within the country for several years with the help of local supporters, until their respective arrests in 2008 and 2011. Given the significant time that elapsed between the three arrests, we are also able to show the evolution of attitudes toward the ICTY among politicians and the media, as well as of the tribunal's approach toward the media. Finally, we conclude by considering some of the lessons that should be learned from the Serbian case regarding the influence of the media's reporting on war crimes trials in post-conflict societies, and the damage that uninformed and biased reporting can cause for a nation's process of coming to terms with its past.

THE MEDIA IN THE FORMER YUGOSLAVIA AND THE DEVELOPMENT OF WAR PROPAGANDA

THE MEDIA UNDER TITO'S REGIME

From the end of World War II until his death in 1980, Marshal Josip Broz Tito led the communist regime that governed Yugoslavia. As in many other Communist countries during that period, the media were controlled by the

Communist Party—the League of Communists (Savez Komunista, SK)[15]—of which most journalists, especially editors, were members.[16] While the formal chain of command from the party propaganda structures to journalists was not as strict as under some other communist regimes, Tito's Yugoslavia still had very little freedom of the press. Until the mid-1960s Yugoslavia had a federal Ministry of Information, along with a Department for Propaganda and Agitation that the League directly controlled.[17] In addition, as the ruling party, the League of Communists had direct influence over establishing media outlets and appointing directors and editors, and it explicitly considered the task of journalists to be promoting the ideas and goals of the Communist Party.[18] For example, according to the Official Code of Journalists of Yugoslavia—originally adopted in 1965 and later revised in 1969—a journalist was obligated to fully engage in political life, while supporting the policy of reform and "struggle against bureaucratic, monopolistic, chauvinist, nationalist, anti-self-governing aspirations, as well as against all phenomena which are considered as retarding to the development of socialist democracy."[19] Structurally, the system included prepublication censorship, although it was never officially labeled as such; publishers were required to provide the local public prosecutor with two copies of every publication before it was sent to stores and kiosks.[20] Moreover, media content was further controlled by editorial councils, whose members were mostly drawn from outside the media. A large number of external bodies, most of them attached to the League of Communists, also monitored the media. Ultimately, though, the most powerful censors were the journalists themselves, who were so afraid of repercussions that they were extremely cautious about what and how they reported. In many cases, journalists considered self-censorship to be an act of patriotism.[21]

In the early 1970s, journalists' groups began to call for more freedom to conduct their work. Some of these demands were eventually reflected in the Constitution of 1974, which, in its Article 166, recognized "freedom of the press and other media of information and public expression, freedom of association, freedom of speech and public expression."[22] However, as Mark Thompson has stressed, the same constitution also established limitations on the use of these loosely defined freedoms, to the extent that Article 203 stated, "No one may use the freedoms and rights established by the present Constitution in order to disrupt the foundations of the socialist self-management democratic order."[23] At the same time, as part of the media reforms undertaken during the 1970s, control over the media was passed from the federal-level Communist Party to its branches within each of the Yugoslav republics, which from that point on had the authority to appoint editors and directors and monitor the work of journalists.[24] Thus, rather than establishing a free press, the reforms of the 1970s effectively decentralized political control over the media, so that the media now reflected the attitudes of the local politicians and enabled them to promote the specific interests of their individual republics, as we show now in more detail.

MEDIA FRAGMENTATION AND EVOLUTION DURING THE WARS

After Tito's death in 1980, a timid debate regarding freedom of the press was opened, and journalists and editors started to look for ways to avoid censorship. The most progressive coverage during this time came from youth media. Though still associated with the League of Communists, the youth began to broach issues that had never before been addressed publicly in the federation—such as the crimes committed by the Communists in the aftermath of World War II—and thus indirectly started to question the legacy of Tito and the Communist Party. Such efforts briefly gave the impression that some media outlets and journalists were taking on new, more independent roles within the system, and helping to foster a more democratic public space by offering critical perspectives and a wider variety of information, thereby giving people the opportunity to discuss and make their own judgments on certain issues. With support from the public, these same journalists started to ask for new laws and regulations, demanding more freedom and the establishment of independent, private media outlets.

Finally, in 1989 came the passage of laws that allowed for increased media freedom and also granted city governments, municipalities, and individuals the ability to establish media outlets.[25] In this same period, however, the recently passed media reforms that had ceded authority over the media to the branches of the Communist Party within each republic had opened the door for local leaders to establish close connections with journalists and media outlets. One effect was powerful and unforeseen: in the years after Tito's death, the economic and political situation in the SFRY had worsened, and instead of assuming responsibility, the leaders of the different republics started blaming each other for their problems—using their new power over the media to promote these ideas. As Noel Malcolm has written, during this time, "Non-stop bombardment of misinformation and fear-mongering, through the media and local politicians,"[26] was used in Serbia, as well as in the rest of the SFRY, to radicalize the populations. The media in each republic waged campaigns against the other republics, blaming each other for the nation's problems. Local politicians advocated for more autonomy from Belgrade, the SFRY's capital, which instead sought to impose stronger restrictions.

Slobodan Milošević began his climb to power in this context, in part by establishing close connections with the media world, especially in his native Serbia, the largest republic and the one with the most influential media. According to Radivoje Cvjetićanin, the war began when Milošević decided to take control of the media,[27] which Cvjetićanin claims occurred as early as when Milošević started his political career in 1983 as a member of the Presidium of the League of Communists of the Yugoslavia Central Committee (CKSKJ). He subsequently became the head of the Belgrade Communist Party organization from 1984 to 1986. Cvjetićanin argues that Milošević used this time to familiarize himself with the media landscape and to cultivate friends who would later become his loyal followers. In exchange for their allegiance, he nominated them to be directors and editors of the most important media conglomerations in Serbia, including TV and radio outlets and some of the most popular daily newspapers—including *Politika* and *Večernje Novosti*—but also other types of publications such as women's magazines, children's publications, and general entertainment periodicals.

Milošević's control over the media became apparent in 1986, the year he became president of the League of Communists of Serbia (Savez Komunista Srbije, SKS). According to Kemal Kurspahić, "Milošević was the first politician from the League of Communists . . . who understood and respected the power of the media."[28] He used the media not only to build a myth about himself as a leader but also to spread a message of fear and the portents of war, to radicalize people, and to incite hatred. The media were accustomed to serving those who held power throughout decades under Communist rule and were easily persuaded to become a tool of Milošević's brand of political propaganda. As Bennett explains, through his rigid control of the media, Milošević organized a powerful campaign that portrayed Serbia as the victim of the other republics' media attacks, while emphasizing the need to "readjust" Yugoslavia due to its alleged bias against Serbia.[29]

Following this pattern, in September 1986 the Belgrade daily newspaper *Večernje Novosti* published parts of a draft document later known as "the Memorandum,"[30] prepared by the members of the Serbian Academy of Sciences and Arts (Srpska Akademija Nauka i Umetnosti, SANU), that became "the ideological underpinning of the Serbian nationalist program."[31] The Memorandum's ideas were then incorporated almost "word for word in the nationalist platform that Milošević put into effect between 1988 and 1991 . . . In Milošević's hands, the notion of Serbia-as-victim became one of the regime's major psychological and political props."[32] The main themes of the

Memorandum focused on how the Communist-initiated decentralization processes had led to Yugoslavia's disintegration and on the alleged discrimination against the Serbs within the SFRY. For example, the Memorandum's paragraph on self-determination argued, "All nations are not equal: the Serbian nation, for example, did not obtain the right to its own state. Unlike national minorities, portions of the Serbian people who live in other republics in large numbers do not have the right to use their own language and alphabet, to organize politically and culturally, or to develop the unique culture of their nation."[33] *Večernje Novosti* accompanied excerpts of the Memorandum with supportive commentary and opinion pieces from one of its editors, stressing even further the notion of the victimization of Serbs and other nations within the SFRY. Subsequent "reports" continued to reinforce this idea and spread fear among the public, to the extent that, as Christopher Bennett has argued, "The key events in Yugoslavia's disintegration took place not in the distant past, or in [World War II], or even during Tito's rule, but in the years immediately preceding the outbreak of the war. ... It is a tale not of 'ancient hatreds' or centuries of ethnic strife and inevitable conflict, but of very modern nationalist hysteria which was deliberately generated in the media."[34] The narrative of Serbian victimhood that the media emphasized played a significant role in Milošević's rise to power and fueled division among the Yugoslav republics.

At the beginning of the 1990s the mainstream media in Yugoslavia were deeply divided, operating under the heavy influence of the leading politicians in each republic. The few media outlets that were newly established or under new management were either not strong enough to promote rigorous journalism or were mostly apolitical and focused on entertainment reporting. The gradual process of opening and liberalization, with the creation of a multiparty system and calls for free elections, did not bring significant changes in the mainstream media, since even the newly elected politicians—most of whom had previously been active in the Communist Party—continued to use the media as a propaganda tool.

When the war erupted in Slovenia in 1991, and as the conflict developed throughout the collapsing SFRY until the war in Kosovo in 1999, journalists were at the front lines with the soldiers, sometimes even dressed in uniforms and armed. The journalists glorified the soldiers, announcing the "liberation" of cities that the armies occupied and, in effect, justifying war crimes. Hate speech and what was called *patriotic journalism* became the predominant way of reporting all over the SFRY—and later on in its successor republics.[35] Indeed, the ICTY officially recognized in its proceedings the role of the media during the wars:[36] some media materials were used as evidence against some of the accused or to issue indictments against some high-ranking officials.[37] Among the charges brought against him, for example, Milošević was indicted for his use of propaganda.[38] Still, not one journalist or editor was ever brought to the court, as happened after the genocide in Rwanda.[39] The closest attempt to hold members of the media criminally accountable came from the Serbian independent union of journalists, which filed a complaint in 2009 against some of its colleagues for their roles during the wars and spurred local prosecutors to initiate an investigation; to date, this activity has not yielded any results.[40]

THE SERBIAN MEDIA TODAY

Although the wars in Serbia officially ended in 1999, transformation of the media system in Serbia began only after the fall of Milošević's regime in 2000. Until the last moment that his government retained power, Milošević controlled most of the media in Serbia and would appoint editors and directors, as well as directly involve himself with editorial policy. Fifteen years after the war's end, Serbia's media system is still undergoing transformation; while some progress in terms of pluralism and quality control has been made, many observers still perceive that the media suffer from a lack of professionalism and independence. The media remain entrenched in the legacy of long-term control and manipulation and are considered highly susceptible to political influence. As a recent report from the Anti-Corruption Council of Serbia argues, "There is no longer a medium from which the public can get complete and objective information because, under strong pressure from political circles, the media pass over certain events in silence or report on them selectively and partially."[41]

Unlike the laws of Communist Yugoslavia, the current laws in Serbia recognize freedom of the press and provide protections for journalists. Nevertheless, actual implementation of these laws remains a problem in the region. While, as occurs anywhere, journalists are sometimes openly members of political parties or explicitly promote the interests of certain economic groups, a greater problem in Serbia is that the ownership or loyalty of media outlets is often unclear. According to the latest data, there are currently 523 print media publications, 201 radio stations, 103 television stations, and 66 online media outlets in Serbia, a country with a population of 7.2 million people as of 2011.[42] These numbers may be even higher, however, since they do not include the hundreds of media outlets operating without permits. The huge number of competing outlets produces a struggle for economic survival, stress that exposes the media to various kinds of pressure and influence. Media outlets thus continue to maintain close ties with political elites at the local and national levels, who are often successful in making use of the media to advance the elites' own agendas and interests. Foreign investments, where they exist, are mostly concentrated in entertainment media.

In addition, many of the people who had worked as journalists before or during the war are still active members of the media, often holding managerial positions or professorships, and have not gone through any serious transformation process. Schools of journalism are far from meeting internationally established professional standards and provide little or no practical training for their students, resulting in a shortage of journalists capable of carrying out their jobs with a reasonable degree of professionalism and skill. Serious, in-depth investigative journalism, which can play a critical role in exposing key issues to the public, hardly exists; the media outlets that do wish to undertake such reporting lack the capacity for it, as they are faced with the exigencies of surviving in an oversaturated media market while staffed by young, inexperienced, and inadequately trained journalists.

In 2010 several European Union (EU) institutions and international journalism associations expressed concern about the media situation throughout the Balkan region. For example, according to the Reporters without Borders Press Freedom Index of 2010, although legislation for the media-related reforms required for accession to the European Union had been adopted in most Balkan countries, "their implementation is still in the embryonic—if not non-existent—stage. . . . In a precarious situation, caught in a vice between the violence of ultranationalist groups and authorities who have not yet rid themselves of old reflexes from the Communist era, an increasing portion of journalists are settling for a calculated self-censorship or a mercenary journalism which pays better, but gradually ruins the profession's credibility."[43] In its 2012 report the organization continued to stress that "self-censorship by a growing number of badly paid journalists" remains a problem in the region. The media are exploited for "private or criminal interests" and often have little recourse against those who seek to control them: many of the country's judicial officials are unprofessional, "allied with the government and often corrupt," and "seem more interested in harassing the media than ending impunity for those who threaten or physically attack journalists."[44]

According to an analysis carried out by the European Journalism Center (EJC), television news programs are still the primary source of information in Serbia today, with 85 percent of citizens obtaining news and information from television, compared with 11 percent from print media, 2 percent from radio, and 2 percent from the Internet.[45] Radio Television Serbia (RTS) remains the most influential media outlet in Serbia today. Although RTS was formerly under state control and served as the main propaganda tool for Milošević's regime—during which it was dubbed *TV Bastille* by the opposition—it has undergone significant reforms since becoming a public broadcaster in 2006. Despite these formal changes, however, RTS still faces a number of challenges in its administration and reporting, including a lack of accountability and transparency, as well as underpaid and undertrained journalists. As the EJC analysis notes, in contrast to RTS under Milošević's regime, "Today's RTS respects professional standards of balanced reporting but lags behind the commercial station B92 in the amount and influence of investigative reporting."[46] While RTS is not under the same level of state control as during the 1990s, its focus on entertainment programming has minimized its influence in creating a public dialogue about national issues. The private TV station TV B92, which grew out of the fierce opposition movement against Milošević, used to produce informative programming. However, although they still broadcast some news programs, due to the exigencies of survival in the market, the majority of their programming now also consists of reality and other entertainment shows. As a result, TV B92 has lost the loyalty of many of its former viewers, who used to make up the better-educated minority within Serbia. Other commercial stations are even less concerned about independent news programs, given that they do not generate as much financial gain and viewership as entertainment programs. Additionally, many of the daily tabloids only produce content for entertainment, and the political tabloids are often short-lived, raising questions about ownership. According to the same analysis from the EJC, the tabloids' "editorial policies are characterized by conservatism, nationalistic ideology, hate speech, and disregard of professional and ethical norms. Their sources often remain murky, and their possible ties with secret services and shadowy businesses are frequently discussed in professional and public circles."[47] Of course, sensationalism in the media is not an issue unique to the region; the problem in the Balkans is the lack of virtually any alternative. Sensationalist media constitute most of the commercial media in the region and can hardly be counted as news media or adequate primary sources of information, leaving public broadcasters as the only sources of news programs that are not entertainment. Lacking any real competition, these broadcasters have little incentive to produce high-quality journalism. Thus, the ICTY has had to face clear challenges to efforts to disseminate accurate and adequate information through the media.

THE ICTY AND ITS APPROACH TOWARD THE MEDIA

In 1993 the UN Security Council established the ICTY with the aim of holding war criminals accountable and helping to restore peace and security in the region. When the tribunal began its operations in 1994 the Balkan wars were still raging in Bosnia and Croatia, and then in Kosovo (1998–99) and Macedonia (2001)—with Serbia and Montenegro deeply involved in all of these events. In this context, the tribunal had to face important operational challenges during its first years. Located in The Hague—at a great distance from the region itself—and lacking enforcement powers, the ICTY depended almost entirely on Yugoslav leaders' cooperation to carry out its work. However, the strong opposition of the region's leaders hindered its capacity to conduct tasks as important as gathering evidence or making arrests. At the same time, as most politicians had strong biases regarding the issues that the tribunal addressed, the politicians were hardly interested in having stories about the war crimes tribunal presented to the public, and they used their significant influence over the mainstream media to prevent such coverage. In Serbia, the media's general approach was indeed to ignore as much information about the ICTY as possible. When they did cover the tribunal, the media minimized the crimes committed and misrepresented the role of the Belgrade government. Moreover, the media contributed to undermining the tribunal in the eyes of the public by diminishing and trivializing its role and by propagating the idea that the ICTY was a political, Western-based institution established only to prosecute one side of the conflict: the Serbs.

Today, twenty years after the ICTY's creation and fourteen years after the war's end—and despite the fact that the tribunal has already sentenced sixty-nine people and legally established fundamental facts about the crimes committed in the former Yugoslavia—the Serbian media still disagree with the ICTY's portrayal of the war. Unsurprisingly, the majority of the population still does not support the work of the tribunal, even while acknowledging their lack of knowledge about its work.[48] While the serious deficits of the Serbian media and the country's difficult political landscape have played leading roles in the tribunal's failure to effectively engage the region's population—important points to recognize—a more complete analysis that may also prove helpful for future efforts in justice mechanisms of this sort requires a look at the broader picture.[49] Specifically, we consider two additional factors here: the attitude of the court itself regarding the problematic reception of its trials in the region and the challenges that the few independent outlets faced—and continue to face—when attempting to cover the proceedings.

The ICTY was the first international tribunal that the United Nations established and the first tribunal of its sort after Nuremberg and Tokyo. As such, the ICTY was in many ways an exceptional and novel institution. The ICTY was given a complex mandate that drew from numerous sources of international law, and its procedures were (and still are) difficult for the general public to understand. In this respect, if the tribunal was to accomplish some of the broader goals stated in its founding charter, its capacity to impact the region would depend to a great extent on its ability to be understood by, and to secure the support of, those affected by the crimes it was meant to prosecute. However, those people at the Security Council in New York who designed the tribunal—who, to be fair, also lacked previous experience with institutions of this sort—unfortunately tended to understand the tribunal's significance mainly in regard to the evolution of international criminal law, and not necessarily in terms of its impact in the immediate context of its operations. Thus, they failed to anticipate the importance of the relationship between the court and the population of the countries of the former Yugoslavia.[50]

The court consequently began its operations without establishing any sort of direct communication with the population or the local media outlets of the former Yugoslavia. As Lal C. Vohrah and Jon Cina have argued, "Although a public relations capacity has existed since very early in its creation, the court's primary constituency—the population of the former Yugoslavia—was typically not its principal focus. Instead, efforts focused on States, academics, human rights organizations, and international law activists worked to ensure that the tribunal's potential effect on the development of those fields was maximized."[51] For example, as many commentators have already pointed out, until 1999 the ICTY's indictments and judgments were issued only in English or French—the official languages of the United Nations and accordingly of the tribunal—and its first press release in Serbian was not issued until 2000.[52] Indeed it was only in 2010 that, with support from the European Union and the OSCE, the ICTY launched a project to translate into local languages a selection of the most relevant transcripts from its hearings.[53] Moreover, if one examines the relationship between the Balkans and the ICTY, court officials for a very long time seemingly could not find a way to build a productive association with the media in the region or make its proceedings accessible to the public. Even more important, court officials were unable to understand the critical nature of this connection with the rest of society in order for the tribunal to have any positive impact in the region. Perhaps most damagingly in this respect, the ICTY's failure to provide explanations or summaries of its decisions left to the media or to politicians the task of explaining the court's judgments. Even today, when asked to comment on a particular judgment, officials from the Office of the Prosecutor widely default to the phrase, "Judgments speak for themselves."[54] This passive attitude left unfettered space for politicians and the subordinated media to construe the judgments' meaning without any official statements to counter their interpretations.

In contrast to the mainstream media's portrait of the country, since the early stages of the ICTY's operation, some important initiatives have aimed at providing alternative information about its proceedings to the countries of the region—for example, since 1998 South East News Service Europe (SENSE) News Agency provided daily coverage of all trials and produced a weekly television program from The Hague, while the Institute for War and Peace Reporting (IWPR) produced and still produces weekly reports about the trials.[55] In Serbia, the work of international groups, such as the SENSE Agency and the IWPR, has accompanied that of a relatively small group of independent media outlets that have also tried to help disseminate information about the cases before the ICTY and counter biased local reporting about the tribunal's work. Despite these efforts, local independent media have met with important challenges themselves, mainly related to scarcity of resources. For example, given the physical distance to the tribunal, for local media outlets, it was—and still is—a huge burden to send journalists to The Hague; most simply cannot afford to do so. Moreover, adequate reporting of the tribunal's work requires not only impartiality but also adequate access to a large volume of complex information and a high level of specialized knowledge. Even today, many journalists in Serbia lack a basic understanding of international human rights and humanitarian law, the work of international courts, and transitional justice. Indeed, despite the topic's relevance for the region, until recently many of the nation's most influential media sources did not have journalists who specialized exclusively in war crimes reporting. While, thanks to the support of a number of international organizations, some of the independent media in Serbia do have journalists specializing in this type of reporting, and who are even able to spend time at the ICTY or investigating wartime events,[56] fewer and fewer donors have been willing to help cover these costs as time has passed.[57]

Although the court began its operations in 1994, its outreach program was only established in 1999, when, after the judgment of the Bosnian-Serb Duško Tadić, the senior officers of the court started to take seriously the consequences of the tribunal's failure to reach out to the concerned populations.[58] In particular, Judge Gabrielle Kirk McDonald, in the last year of her term as ICTY president, decided to establish an outreach program stressing the importance of making the proceedings accessible to the region's people.[59] Today, the outreach program has become a fundamental part of the ICTY, with a team of permanent specialized staff and regional offices in Serbia and Bosnia and Herzegovina, while the offices established in Croatia and Kosovo were closed by the end of 2012 as part of the general downsizing efforts of the tribunal.[60] Having been operative for thirteen years, the program has contributed to making the tribunal's work accessible to the populations of the region by providing information directly to the people as well as to interested media outlets. An interesting example of its work was a series of events organized in 2004–5 that intended to bridge the gap between the ICTY and the communities in Bosnia and Herzegovina most affected by the war crimes. The events highlighted in a straightforward and succinct manner—in order to promote the local visibility of served justice and prevent historical revisionism—the facts that had been proved beyond a reasonable doubt.[61] In 2005 the outreach program merged with the press and information services section.[62] Since then, the outreach program has showcased on its website the voices of the victims and the guilty pleas of the accused. The victims' statements have generated a great deal of discussion and debate, but the guilty pleas have been generally perceived as lacking in sincerity and having a deliberately narrow scope.[63] In addition, a section of the ICTY's website on victims of sexual crimes created in 2011 provides information for the media in language that general audiences can readily understand. This section of the site presents stories of the victims, video testimonies, and segments of documentaries about prosecuting rape as a weapon of war.[64] Such approaches make it easy for the media to pass on stories about victims in a language that is familiar to their audiences and that the media themselves should model in the future.

However, despite its important contributions to the ICTY's work, the outreach program still continues to face important challenges, many of which are legacies of the early lack of attention the program received from decision-makers. For example, the program is not covered by UN funds and has always depended on external contributions. According to some commentators, this fact "illustrates the view that the tribunal's impact on the region in general, let alone the region's justice system, [was] of marginal interest to UN policy-makers."[65] Moreover, its initial years of disinterest in working directly with the local media, lack of any kind of strategy for communicating with the region, and inability to provide information to the public in a way that would make its decisions accessible and easy to understand all helped to establish a pattern of underreporting its work that has had longstanding effects, especially in light of the strong regional opposition that the tribunal encountered. The lack of an active outreach program and engagement with the press during the tribunal's early years not only contributed to the inaction of the local media in explaining what the ICTY was meant to be, how it would work, or what its mandate was to the public. Also—and more importantly—this lack of an active outreach program and engagement with the press created a vacuum of discourse surrounding the tribunal that politicians and local media were able to exploit and fill with their own misinformation and biased criticisms. Over time, some of these practices and misconceptions were altered and improved, but some of the damage has been irreparable.[66] Many of the ICTY's decisions never reached the region's broader public, and many of the objective facts established in the proceedings and judgments of this international institution are still treated as matters of interpretation. Even a well-thought-out communications strategy would likely have met with a certain degree of resistance from the population, due to the long-lasting effects of misinformation spread during and before the wars, as well as the region's imbalance between news and entertainment media. The more general problems of democratization within the region's media are also an issue. But while the relationships between media actors and audiences, especially in the case of privately owned media outlets, are always informed by the drive to gain larger audiences or by explicit or undeclared political interests, the extent of misinformation and ignorance of the trial's work suggests that these obstacles (its poor initial impression among the population and the disinterest of local media) and the ways in which the tribunal might have overcome them were never properly considered.

Of course, before concluding this analysis, we should mention that the ICTY's failure to implement an outreach program during its early years does not on its own explain the challenges and problems that reporting on the war crimes trials has faced in the former Yugoslavia; indeed, such an explanation falls quite short. However, considering the case of the ICTY from the perspective of media and transitional justice processes more broadly, the experience highlights the importance of taking seriously the context in which justice mechanisms operate. Especially considering that these institutions aim at promoting a broader social change, they cannot afford to ignore the media. In order to achieve the long-term goals of their mandate—such as promoting peace or security in the region, as in the case of the ICTY—these sorts of mechanisms need to acknowledge the importance of adopting a strong approach to outreach from the outset. They also need to take into consideration the media landscape of the country in which they operate—in terms of providing support to those media outlets that are genuinely interested as well as paying more attention to the power of entrenched biases among other media on the impact of their work. We turn to this last point in the next section, providing some more concrete examples of the ways in which the Serbian media have reported on the ICTY and exploring how such reporting has evolved in relation to the broader political contexts in the region.

THE EVOLUTION OF WAR CRIMES REPORTING IN SERBIA: THE COVERAGE OF THE MILOŠEVIĆ AND KARADŽIĆ ARRESTS AND TRIALS

The ICTY indicted Milošević in Kosovo in May 1999, while he was still in power in Serbia, for crimes against humanity. After the fall of his government in 2000, Serbian authorities arrested him in April 2001, which the ICTY then used as an opportunity to request his extradition to The Hague by the end of June. While the newly elected president, Vojislav Koštunica, strongly opposed the extradition on legal grounds, the Serbian prime minister at the time, Zoran Đinđić, was willing to cooperate with the Western powers, as Serbia was then opening up to the possibility of beginning the long procedure of gaining access to the European Union; he ordered the extradition.[67]

Milošević's transfer to The Hague brought the ICTY to the front pages of regional newspapers, and the proceedings against him remained one of the media's leading stories until he died in prison in March 2006—before a verdict had been issued. As anti-Hague propaganda in the country was at its peak at the time of Milošević's arrest, Đinđić's government, which had handed Milošević to The Hague, needed to take a strong public stance to support its decision. In a televised statement addressed to the nation, Đinđić justified his action by arguing that there would have been "negative consequences for the future of our country" if it had failed to cooperate with the tribunal.[68] In addition, on the very same day that Milošević was extradited, Serbian police investigators exhumed dozens of bodies of Kosovo Albanians, including those of children, from a mass grave near Belgrade.[69] This revelation sparked public disgust over the crimes of the regime. According to the international media's coverage, the local press reports around the arrest exposing the war crimes committed by Milošević's regime "[began] to change the way ordinary people in Serbia feel about co-operation with the international war crimes tribunal,"[70] which helped promote higher approval for the ICTY's work.

The change in Serbian public opinion did not last long. While Milošević's trial offered an excellent opportunity for the media to pursue more rigorous reporting on war crimes, government elements loyal to Koštunica halted the flow of information about the crimes to the state-run media.[71] As his predecessor Milošević had, President Koštunica repeatedly characterized the ICTY as an anti-Serbian tribunal and often publicly cast it as an obedient tool of US foreign policy.[72] Such statements, however, conflicted with Prime Minister Đinđić's position, as he was a strong advocate of European integration and thus was publicly in favor of extraditing Milošević and cooperating with the ICTY.[73] Koštunica's approach brought him more public support in Serbia while Đinđić continued to lose popularity, until he was assassinated in 2003 by former members of a paramilitary unit that had participated in the wars under the auspices of the state's secret police.[74]

According to Michael Scharf, during the first couple of weeks of the trial, "Five channels carried the proceedings live, and more than half of all Serbian households were tuned in,"[75] but as time passed only the independent TV B92 kept broadcasting the proceedings within Serbia. While, again quoting Scharf, in 2002 the US Agency for International Development (USAID) was "convinced that exposure to the Milošević trial would have a cathartic effect on the Serb population,"[76] the truth is that the real effects of this live broadcast on the general public are still a matter of dispute today. While some claim that the broadcasting of the proceedings helped the country face its violent past, others argue that by taking charge of his own defense and representing himself, Milošević was actually able to gain popularity in Serbia. The courtroom became a stage from which Milošević sent messages to his fellow citizens and once again gave speeches justifying the decisions that he made during the wars. Thus, as the UK-based newspaper *The Guardian* reported, the trial, "instead of revealing to Serbs the enormity of the crimes committed in their name," served "to reinforce the widespread Serbian prejudice that the tribunal is an anti-Serb kangaroo court and that Milošević will emerge, as he has already declared, as the 'moral victor.'"[77] According to the same article, in a poll conducted in Serbia, 41.6 percent of the respondents gave Milošević a "five out of five" for his performance in the courtroom. In her analysis of the effects of the trial, Jelena Tošić explains that the media's coverage of Milošević's defense actually allowed for the perpetuation of local myths and conspiracy theories: "In his narrative, Milošević's extradition to and indictment by a representative of international justice became not only the climax of his battle against the 'new world order'; in fact, Milošević also interpreted the ad-hoc Tribunal as a sign of the decay of global justice and the system of the United Nations, confirming and legitimizing the imperialism of the great powers, thus allowing itself to become an instrument for achieving their ends."[78] Before and during the trial,

Milošević frequently accused the ICTY of having been established with the aim of persecuting exclusively Serbs, due to Western conspiracies and hatred toward them—adopting a strategy that, as Doder has argued, "was designed to play on Serbia's psychological vulnerabilities and continued Serb resentment of the 1999 NATO bombing."[79]

The strategy's success also received a boost from the way in which the media covered Milošević's speeches in court. While the media invited various experts and human rights activists to comment on the ongoing trial, their interlocutors were chosen carefully to reflect the attitudes of their management and editorial boards. For example, one of the regular studio commentators was Ljiljana Smajlović, a controversial journalist from Belgrade who was the head of *Politika Daily* at the time and was close to Vojislav Koštunica,[80] the staunchly anti-Hague president of the Federal Republic of Yugoslavia (which comprised Serbia and Montenegro). Through this choice of guests, the media could manipulate and spin Milošević's appearances in the courtroom. At the same time, the public shrugged off the comments of human rights activists expressing different views as the opinions of those who were "foreign mercenaries" paid by the West and who worked against Serbian national interests.[81] Even when the activists were not dismissed, they reached a much smaller audience than those spokespersons who appeared on state media or were allied with leading politicians. Comments regarding human rights often stimulated a renewed backlash of extreme nationalism in Serbia, "bringing a revival of hate speech in the media and death threats against liberals."[82]

In hindsight, the journalists interviewed for this study generally agreed that there was very little knowledge in the region about the court's procedures at the time of Milošević's trial. Today, some of the journalists who covered the trial argue that while live transmission was important, more could have been achieved at certain stages if reports aiding public comprehension had accompanied the broadcasts.[83] The Helsinki Committee for Human Rights in Serbia analyzed the impact of Milošević's trial on the public in 2002 and concluded that it was a "major source of controversy in the country."[84] They also found that the public's reactions demonstrated "that Serbia had not broken with his policy and was not ready to confront the warlike policy and war crimes."[85]

Two years after Milošević's death, the arrest of Radovan Karadžić in July 2008 posed a huge challenge for the Serbian media. Although the arrest had been anticipated for a long time, it was the biggest war crimes–related event since Milošević's transfer to The Hague and soon fueled the country's well-developed political propaganda machinery. President of the Republika Srpska since 1992, Karadžić was indicted in 1996 for war crimes against Bosnian Muslims during the Bosnian conflict, as well as for ordering the massacre of Srebenica. He was one of the last men indicted by the tribunal who remained at large; given the severity and notoriety of the crimes he had allegedly committed, over the years the media, human rights organizations, and various EU institutions had closely monitored the efforts to find and apprehend him. Although Serbian politicians had long used the potential arrest of Karadžić as a political tool, especially during negotiations with NATO and the European Union over the country's possible membership in both organizations, an important part of the population still supported Karadžić. His arrest was a highly sensitive issue that many feared would incite violence.

In keeping with the importance of the case, as with Milošević's, Karadžić's detention was featured on the covers of major newspapers all over the world soon after the local police reportedly arrested him on a bus in Belgrade, where he lived in hiding under the name "Dragan Dabić" and worked as an alternative medicine doctor. Representatives of Serbia's Ministry of Internal Affairs and the Office of the State War Crimes Prosecutor in Belgrade, however, were not very forthcoming in sharing details about the capture, and the first picture of his detention did not come out until more than twenty-four hours after the arrest. Immediately, the "secret life of Dr. Dragan Dabić" became a topic of sensationalist speculation all over the Serbian media, but hardly any serious investigative stories resulted. Initially, the media relied entirely on the official sources, which offered only minimal information on Karadžić's life in hiding. While some journalists wrote supportive stories and published interviews with Karadžić's family members,[86] the majority focused primarily on the details of Karadžić's life as a fugitive under a false name. These stories generally ignored the actual indictment and the crimes listed in it, and the justifications for his arrest were thus often pushed to the background.[87] Svetlana Logar of the Ipsos agency, a public opinion polling agency in Serbia, stated that according to one of the polls they conducted at the time about the arrest, most people were still unaware of what he had been indicted for, in spite of all the media coverage.[88]

Like Milošević before him, Karadžić was very much aware of the power of the media and the attention he was given, and when his trial started in March 2010 he also used the courtroom as a platform for his political declarations. The ICTY granted him wide access to the media, providing him with further opportunities to disseminate propaganda.[89] Furthermore, because his interviews could only be conducted in written form, journalists were unable to ask him for clarification on the points that he asserted or confront him with the inconsistencies in his answers. Although ICTY officials did sometimes edit parts of the interviews, mainly in order to censor issues related to his life in the UN detention center or the ICTY itself, they did not interfere in any form when Karadžić's answers referred to wartime events or to victims, even in cases of blatant political propaganda and misinformation. Likewise, it was also left up to journalists to decide whether to simply publish his answers unedited in the interview format or to include the commentary of other interlocutors who could raise questions about his statements. Even today, three years after the beginning of the trial, the Serbian media have not yet shown any interest in regular coverage of the testimonies of the prosecution's witnesses. When the media do cover news from the court, they usually rely on short news agency reports rather than investing additional resources to research and produce more in-depth stories that include the testimonies of victims and prosecution experts.[90]

On April 15, 2011, while the main accusation of Serbian critics of the ICTY was still that the tribunal was biased and anti-Serbian, the ICTY delivered a first-instance guilty sentence against two Croatian generals for war crimes committed against Croatia's ethnic Serb population during the military's "Operation Storm" in the summer of 1995.[91] The declaration that the Croatian generals were members of a joint criminal enterprise headed by late Croatian president Franjo Tuđman was welcomed by the Serbian public and temporarily helped to counter arguments that the ICTY was an anti-Serbian institution. Indeed, the verdict made it possible to hear for the first time in Serbia positive public speech about the ICTY.[92] For example, in his comments in the Croatian daily *Jutarnji list*, Vuk Drašković, a former leader of the opposition against Milošević, noted that many people in Serbia would have to be more cautious after the judgment when tempted to call the ICTY an anti-Serbian institution.[93] Moreover, this judgment gave wings to the former Serbian president, Boris Tadić, to boost public support for cooperation with the ICTY[94] and to justify the arrest and extradition of Ratko Mladić. Mladić, who had been the chief commander of the main staff of the Bosnian Serb Army,[95] was "discovered" after sixteen years at large in the house of a close relative in a small village in Serbia in May 2011, just a month after the judgment against the Croatian generals was issued.[96]

Ratko Mladić was first indicted by the ICTY in 1995 for the Srebrenica genocide and for various war crimes in Bosnia and Herzegovina committed by Serb forces from 1992 to 1995.[97] Following his arrest, the media's treatment of the story was clearly different from that of previous extraditions. Most of the national media followed the approach taken by the government, which by mid-2011 was clearly expressing its support for the court and willingness to cooperate. After officially applying for EU membership on December 22, 2009, Serbia was required to demonstrate its full cooperation with the ICTY—including arresting all those indicted and granting the tribunal access to all requested documents and evidence; such cooperation is one of the main preconditions for EU membership for all of the countries from the region.[98] In this respect, one might argue that, by 2011 and after Karadžić's arrest, the Serbian state had actually learned some lessons. However, an important margin of ambivalence remains regarding the state's motives and whether the transparency with which Mladić's detention was handled was not a response to its "moral obligations toward the victims,"[99] but triggered by its self-interest in fulfilling the European Union's demands.

During the first two days after Mladić's arrest,[100] the media's reports were more rigorous and far less trivia-filled than those they had done on Karadžić, although there were also some comments about "the strawberries and books" that Mladić requested while in custody, as well as on his demand to visit his daughter's grave.[101] The biggest change was visible on state TV, which broadcast a documentary about the Srebrenica genocide and Mladić's hiding on the day of the arrest. For the government's part, in comparison to the official reticence surrounding Karadžić's arrest, information this time came directly from President Tadić, leaving far less space for speculation. By making a public appearance to provide information about the arrest, Tadić presented his government to the international community as open and ready to face the past. Indeed, several days after the arrest took place, President Tadić directly asked the European Union to support Serbia's efforts to join the union. In his own words, "I simply ask the EU to fulfill its part. We fulfilled our part and we will continue to do so."[102]

Despite the more general and official positive atmosphere surrounding the Mladić case, opposition to the tribunal in Serbia still remains high. Three days after Mladić's arrest, *Novosti Press*, a right-wing nationalist print media outlet, published several articles that portrayed Mladić as an inoffensive "old man" that helped garner him sympathy among the Serbian public. Mladić was suddenly perceived as sort of a celebrity, and the media put him on about the same footing as a *Big Brother* contestant.[103] Competing for readers, numerous media outlets in Serbia preferred to offer their audience more entertaining and superficial stories rather than focus on the crimes listed in the indictment or the victims Mladić had harmed. In a matter of days, reporting turned to whether he wanted to eat the strawberries he had allegedly asked for while in detention in

Belgrade or if he liked Russian classics, a devotion he had expressed during his first appearance in the Belgrade courtroom.[104] Still, in contrast with previous cases, even in these reports, there were no outright denials during the first days after his arrest of the crimes he had committed. Such denials, however, were easily found among the reader comments on most Serbian media websites.

CONCLUSION

As we have tried to show in this chapter, political interests in Serbia have played a dominant role in shaping the media's coverage of the war crimes trials for over a decade. In particular, political elites' manipulation of public opinion throughout the Milošević era left severe consequences that can be felt even today. Except for the short-lived attempts of Đinđić's administration, not one of the governments that followed Milošević's has made a serious effort to open a space to deal with the past. This environment has fostered a circular process of negative reporting on the ICTY: the unpopularity of the Hague tribunal among people in Serbia after the conflict made it an unsupported cause among political elites, insisting that cooperation with ICTY would not gain them votes. In this context, the media have often failed to fulfill their fundamental function of providing an acceptable level of accuracy in transmitting factual information,[105] which, as a basic principle of journalism, is necessary if the audience is to make their own judgments about actors and events. As Ristić has argued, media in the region "focu[s] primarily on relations between former enemies and not on crimes ... There are memories of trial but not of judgments."[106] According to the Helsinki Committee for Human Rights in Serbia, the media have "relativized the crimes committed in the name of the Serb people, in order to foil the discussion on moral responsibility," through various mechanisms—including discrediting witnesses, belittling the importance of admissions of guilt, ignoring the charges of the indictment, romanticizing war crimes indictees, showing empathy toward the families of war crimes indictees, or offering their daily commentary on the trials exclusively from the standpoint of the accused's lawyers.[107] Correspondingly, the media have shown a tendency to avoid reporting about victims and their courtroom testimonies. Acting in this way, the effect is to minimize their sufferings and loss. By refusing to make an issue of them, committed war crimes are easily pushed aside as if nobody had suffered from what has been done.

Writing about the role of the media in transitional justice, Marija Šajkaš argues that in the Balkans, independently of which side the victims were on,

"What matters is to publicly reveal what has happened so that the victims may continue with their lives and society may ensure such grave mistakes are never repeated. This is certainly a process that calls for the engagement of political elites, opinion makers, legislators and members of this sector, a process that will eventually call for mobilization of [the] entire society."[108] Unfortunately, many journalists in the region have not seen it as their task to promote the process of dealing with the past, but have instead left this to NGOs and state institutions. Given, however, the necessity of the media's role as an intermediary in disseminating information and a space for public discussion, the media must recognize the importance of their contribution and have the capacity and resources to adequately perform it. Media outlets should give substantial space to coverage of trials in different journalistic forms to help maintain the audience's interest in war crimes trials. Journalists should also provide in-depth analysis, be well informed and prepared for coverage of the trials, and make connections with specialized NGOs that can provide more information and access to victims' communities.

At the same time, people involved with the different transitional justice measures implemented in the region, especially the courts where war crimes are prosecuted, frequently neglect the media's integral function in this process—a role that the media must recognize if they are to address the effects of previous missed opportunities to make justice visible. Such missed opportunities have diminished the potential impact of the trials while leaving a vacuum in which politicians can spread their own biased interpretations. Tribunals and other transitional justice initiatives must make an effort to engage with the public as much as possible by making their rulings and decisions easily accessible and widely disseminated to the public through cooperation with local media and NGOs. Outreach departments must be established and begin their operations simultaneously with the courts. Outreach personnel must speak the languages of the region, be trained to use nonlegal language that broader audiences can understand, and count on the support of judges and prosecutors to conduct their operations. Moreover, outreach departments should put in place a media strategy and seek to establish cooperative relations with national press outlets.

On a more general level, the case of the Balkans also raises broader questions about the role of the media sector in societies undergoing transition. On the path to constructing a democratic and peaceful society, media reports on efforts to deal with the past, whether through trials or other transitional justice measures, are of extreme importance. By representing to the wider public what happens in the court or during a public hearing, the media can have a fundamental influence in facilitating and shaping the public debate about the past. As Zandberg argues, journalists shape the collective memories of each community: "Journalists choose which stories or facts have importance. They select facts, construct them into cultural-interpretative frames, and thus give them meaning. In summary, journalists 'lean' on the past in order to give meaning to the present."[109] In this way, media coverage serves to do more than simply disseminate the facts established during court proceedings; rather, the media takes an active role in shaping the narrative—and thus the meaning—of these facts as they are relayed to the public.

In countries emerging from a period of conflict and undemocratic rule, however, the public sphere is often as weak and fragmented as the society itself. The state of the media in the former Yugoslav republics and the corresponding problems in the coverage of the ICTY's proceedings demonstrate the potential negative consequences in such contexts. In cases in which the historical narratives of a recent conflict are vehemently contested by different sectors of a society, an even greater need is present to convey the facts about past human rights violations within a professional media environment in which the moral narratives established by justice measures can be represented fairly. While the media's role is not to establish a unified account of the past, they can and should play an important part in setting the ground rules of public discourse—by deciding which ideas to present as credible, broadly disseminating established facts and treating them as such, and setting norms regarding myths or attitudes that fall beyond the boundaries of mainstream public discourse. For example, within Serbia, the media outlets that covered the ICTY's proceedings could have contested the nationalist narratives surrounding the crimes committed by former leaders, such as Milošević and Karadžić, instead of passing on the narratives uncritically, giving platforms to their supporters, or focusing on sensationalist or trivial discourse. Of course, problems in media coverage typically have their roots in broader societal problems, and even the fairest and most capable media sector could not sufficiently resolve these issues. But to develop a democratic discourse about justice processes, the media must provide the public with accurate and complete information, including a balance of reasonable perspectives, so that individual citizens can evaluate the facts and come to their own conclusions.

While more research is needed to determine the best relationship between transitional justice measures and the media in different post-conflict or post-authoritarian situations, the status of the media sector after the conflict will likely have an impact on its ability to provide effective and balanced reporting on transitional justice measures. As Lisa J. Laplante and Kelly Phenicie have argued, "The habits, customs, and political orientations of the past carry over into the transition unless the media itself receives special consideration during the transitional justice process."[110] As with other sectors in post-conflict societies—such as the security forces or the judiciary—the media is a sector often in need of substantive reform, a process made more complicated by the need for transition within the field often coinciding with the establishment of transitional justice mechanisms that require adequate media coverage. People who want to promote media reform must also respect the freedom of the press and take into account concerns that outside interventions may raise, particularly if such interventions seek to control or restrict the media's coverage. Finding strategies for effective media reform that can support the development of a healthy and democratic public sphere is an essential task for societies attempting to address legacies of past conflict and division.

NOTES

The views presented here are from the authors alone and are not intended to represent those of the International Center for Transitional Justice.

1 In May 2006, ten years after the Dayton Agreement (or Dayton Accords), Montenegro also became independent. Finally, in February 2008, Kosovo declared its independence. Regarding the disintegration of Yugoslavia and the causes and consequences of the wars, see Laura Silber and Alan Little, *The Death of Yugoslavia* (New York: Penguin, 1996), and Misha Glenny, *The Balkans: Nationalism, War and the Great Powers, 1804–1999* (New York: Penguin, 2001).

2 See, for example, "The Scholars' Initiative: Confronting the Yugoslav Controversies," Purdue University, http://www.cla.purdue.edu/history/facstaff/Ingrao/si/scholars.htm.

3 See, for example, the ICTY cases relating to Srebrenica: Judgment, Radislav Krstić (IT-98-33-T), Trial Chamber, August 2, 2001, and (IT-98-33-A) Appeals Chamber, April 19, 2004; and the case of Popović et al. (IT-05-88), http://www.icty.org/cases/party/764/4. Authors including Edina Bećirević claim that genocide was committed in a much broader territory than Srebrenica. See Edina Bećirević, *Na Drini genocid* [Genocide on the Drina River] (Sarajevo: Buybook, 2009).

4 Nedim Hasić, "Bosanska knjiga mrtvih" [Bosnian book of death], *Slobodna Bosna*, May 20, 2010, 26. See also Research and Documentation Center, "Bosnian War Atlas," accessed October 3, 2012, http://www.idc.org.ba.

5 UN Security Council, Resolution 827, UN Doc. S/RES/827 (1993), May 25, 1993.

6 See ICTY, "Key Figures," last updated December 12, 2012, http://www.icty.org/sections/TheCases/KeyFigures. Note that thirty-six persons have had their indictments withdrawn or died before the completion of their trials.

7 See *The First Annual Report of the International Tribunal for the Prosecution of Persons Responsible for Serious Violations of International Humanitarian Law Committed in the Territory of the Former Yugoslavia since 1991 to the General Assembly and Security Council of the United Nations*, UN Doc. S/1994/1007; A/49/342, August 29, 1994, 11–12, emphasis added.

8 OSCE and Beogradski Centar za ljudska prava [Belgrade Human Rights Center], "Attitudes towards War Crimes Issues, ICTY, and the National Judiciary," conducted by Ipsos Public Affairs, October 2011, http://www.osce.org/serbia/90422. The OSCE Mission to Serbia also conducted a survey in 2001, in cooperation with TV B92; see OSCE and Beogradski Centar za ljudska prava, "Attitudes towards War Crimes Issues," 2.

9 Ibid., 13.

10 Ibid., 15.

11 Ibid., 16.

12 Ibid., 108.

13 Ibid., 84.

14 Ibid., 82.

15 The League of Communists of Yugoslavia, founded in 1919, was the major Communist party in Yugoslavia. Josip Broz Tito was the party's secretary-general (and later president) from 1939 until his death in 1980.

16 Sabrina Petra Ramet, *Balkan Babel: Politics, Culture and Religion in Yugoslavia* (Boulder, CO: Westview Press, 1992), 71.

17 Ministarstvo informisanja [Ministry for Information] and Odjel za agitaciju i propaganda [Department for Agitation and Propaganda], known as AGITPROP. See Bruno Vekarić, ed., *Reči i nedela: Pozivanje ili podsticanje na ratne zločine u medijima u Srbiji 1991–1992* [Words and misdeeds: Incitement to war crimes through the media in Serbia, 1991–1992], Historical Framework (Belgrade: Istorijski okvir, Centar za tranzicione procese [Centre for Transitional Processes], 2011).

18 For more on the role of the media in the breakup of Yugoslavia, see Mark Thompson, *Forging War: The Media in Serbia, Croatia and Bosnia-Hercegovina* (London: Article 19, 1999).

19 See Zdenko Antić, "Yugoslav Journalists' Code Emphasizes Ethical and Professional Standards" (Radio Free Europe Research, Communist Area, Yugoslavia, Information media, August 12, 1969), http://www.osaarchivum.org/files/holdings/300/8/3/pdf/78-4-320.pdf.

20 Ibid.

21 Milica Pešić, "Manipulation on Television in Belgrade" (master's thesis, City University, Department of Journalism, London, 1994), 10.

22 Quoted in Thompson, *Forging War*, 9–10.

23 Ibid.

24 Vekarić, *Reči i nedela* [Words and misdeeds], 24.

25 Thompson, *Forging War*, 9–10.

26 Noel Malcolm, *Bosnia: A Short History* (New York: New York University Press, 1996), 217.

27 James Gow, Richard Peterson, and Alison Preston, eds., *Bosnia by Television* (London: British Film Institute, 1996), 71.

28 Kemal Kurspahić, *Zločin u 19.30: Balkanski mediji u ratu i miru* [Prime-time crime: Balkan media in war and peace] (Sarajevo: Mediacentar, 2003; Belgrade: Dan graf, 2004), 37.

29 Christopher Bennett, *Yugoslavia's Bloody Collapse: Causes, Course and Consequences* (New York: New York University Press, 1995).

30 Tim Judah, *Kosovo: War and Revenge* (New Haven, CT: Yale University Press, 2002), 49–50.

31 James Gow, *The Serbian Project and Its Adversaries: A Strategy of War Crimes* (London: Hurst and Company, 2003), 40.

32 Louis Sell, *Slobodan Milošević and the Destruction of Yugoslavia* (Durham, NC, and London: Duke University Press, 2002), 46.

33 Serbian Academy of Arts and Sciences, "Serbian Academy of Arts and Sciences (SANU) Memorandum, 1986," *Making the History of 1989*, item no. 674, accessed September 28, 2011, http://chnm.gmu.edu/1989/items/show/674.

34 Bennett, *Yugoslavia's Bloody Collapse*, 298.

35 For more information on the role of the media in the breakup of Yugoslavia, see Thompson, *Forging the War*.

36 For example, the ICTY acknowledged the Radovan Karadžić and Slobodan Milošević cases, as well as those involving the massacre of Srebrenica and the Prijedor camps (Omarska, Keraterm, and Trnopolje).

37 SENSE News Agency, Video dokazi srebreničkih zločina [Video proofs of Srebrenica's crimes], March 19, 2010, http://sense-agency.com/tribunal_%28mksj%29/video-dokazi-srebrenickih-zlocina.25.html?cat_id=1&news_id=7972.

38 According to the prosecutor, "Slobodan Milosevic, acting alone and in concert with other members of the joint criminal enterprise, participated in the joint criminal enterprise in the following ways: ... controlled, contributed to, or otherwise utilised Serbian state-run media outlets to manipulate Serbian public opinion by spreading exaggerated and false messages of ethnically based attacks by Croats against Serb people in order to create an atmosphere of fear and hatred among Serbs living in Serbia and Croatia. The propaganda generated by the Serbian media was an important tool in contributing to the perpetration of crimes in Croatia" (Second Amended Indictment, "Croatia,"

Slobodan Milošević [IT-02-54-T], July 28, 2004, para. 26[m], http://www.icty.org/case/slobodan_milosevic/4#ind). See also "Expert Report of Renaud de la Brosse, "Political Propaganda and the Plan to Create a 'State for All Serbs': Consequences of Using the Media for Ultra-Nationalist Ends" (report compiled at the request of the Office of the Prosecutor of the International Criminal Tribunal for the Former Yugoslavia by Renaud de la Brosse), February 4, 2003, http://hague.bard.edu/icty_info.html.

39 For more on the role of the media during the Rwandan genocide, see Timothy Longman's chapter in this volume.

40 In July 2009 the Independent Journalists Association of Serbia (Nezavisno udruženje novinara Srbije, NUNS) filed a case with the state prosecutor's office against journalists who instigated war crimes and genocide. See Nidžara Ahmetašević, "Yugoslav Media War Mongers Evade Justice," *Justice Report*, Balkan Investigative Reporting Network, June 24, 2009, http://www.bim.ba/en/172/10/20499/.

41 Anti-Corruption Council, Government of the Republic of Serbia, *Report on Pressures on and Control of Media in Serbia*, September 19, 2011, http://www.antikorupcija-savet.gov.rs/Storage/Global/Documents/mediji/IZVESTAJ%20O%20MEDIJIMA%20PRECIS-CEN%20ENG..pdf, 2.

42 World Bank, "Serbia," accessed August 8, 2012, http://data.worldbank.org/country/serbia.

43 Reporters without Borders, "2010 World Press Freedom Index: Europe Falls from Its Pedestal, No Respite in the Dictatorships," October 20, 2010, http://www.rsf.org/IMG/CLASSEMENT_2011/GB/C_GENERAL_GB.pdf.

44 Reporters without Borders, "Press Freedom Index 2011/2012: Syria, Bahrain, and Yemen Get Ever Worse Rankings," January 25, 2012, http://en.rsf.org/press-freedom-index-2011-2012,1043.html.

45 European Journalism Center, "Media Landscape: Serbia," last updated November 8, 2010, http://www.ejc.net/media_landscape/article/serbia/#l3.

46 Ibid.

47 Ibid.

48 See Belgrade Center for Human Rights, "Attitudes toward International Criminal Tribunal for the Former Yugoslavia (ICTY) 2009," http://english.bgcentar.org.rs/index.php; and OSCE and Beogradski Centar za ljudska prava [Belgrade Center for Human Rights], "Attitudes towards War Crimes Issues." According to another survey of attitudes toward the ICTY among the people living in the states and entities of the former Yugoslavia (Serbia, Croatia, the two entities in Bosnia and Herzegovina, Montenegro, and Kosovo), conducted in 2002 by the International Institute for Democracy and Electoral Assistance, "The popularity of the ICTY in the former Yugoslavia is inversely proportional to the number of accused that come from these countries, entities and particularly ethnic communities." This condition arguably is a result of the coverage by Serbian TV

stations, which care only about the Serbian accused and sidestep the victims of Serbian aggression. The same holds true for Croatian TV stations. See Mirko Klarin, "The Impact of the ICTY on Public Opinion in the Former Yugoslavia," *Journal of International Criminal Justice* 7, no. 1 (March 2009): 91–92, 94.

49 See Katarina Ristić, "War Crimes Trials as a Site of Memory?" (presentation at the conference "Reconstruction, Reconciliation, and European Integration of the Western Balkans," University of Graz, Graz, Austria, February 25–26, 2011); Diane Orentlicher, *That Someone Guilty Be Punished: The Impact of the ICTY in Bosnia* (New York: Open Society Justice Initiative, 2010); and Klarin, "Impact of the ICTY on Public Opinion in the Former Yugoslavia."

50 "I am afraid that people who were involved with the tribunal were concentrated mostly on their historical role, [and the] history of the international law, but less on effects their work should have on the people from the region" (Florence Hartmann, former spokesperson for the Office of the Prosecutor of the ICTY, interview with Nidžara Ahmetašević, Graz, Austria, February 25, 2011, author's translation).

51 Lal C. Vohrah and Jon Cina, "The Outreach Program," in *Essays on the ICTY Procedure and Evidence: In Honor of Gabrielle Kirk McDonald*, ed. Richard May et al. (The Hague: Kluwer Law International, 2001), 550.

52 Diane Orentlicher, *Shrinking the Space for Denial: The Impact of the ICTY in Serbia* (New York: OSJI, 2008), 65.

53 ICTY, "ICTY Delivers First Transcripts in Local Languages to Serbia," press release, November 5, 2010, http://www.icty.org/sid/10483. The timeliness of the delivery of information, however, is still far from ideal, as it takes seven days for the ICTY to post transcripts even in English. Public hearings are broadcast over the Internet, yet the still limited penetration of the Internet in the region diminishes its impact for the general audience.

54 See, for example, the interview with the ICTY chief prosecutor in "TV Tribunal 495," SENSE News Agency, April 22, 2011, http://sense-agency.com/tv_tribunal.27.html?vid=484.

55 For SENSE's TV program, see "Sense Tribunal," http://www.sense-agency.com/tv_tribunal/tv_tribunal.15.html. See also SENSE's documentaries at http://www.sense-agency.com/documentaries/documentaries.37.html. For IWPR, see, for example, "IWPR Films Prompt Debate among Mostar Schoolchildren," http://iwpr.net/report-news/iwpr-films-prompt-debate-among-mostar-schoolchildren.

56 The only donor activity that helps to send journalists from the region to the ICTY is implemented by the OSCE Mission in Serbia's Media and Rule of Law and Human Rights Departments. Since 2008 the departments have organized six study visits for a total of fifty-one media professionals: journalists, camera operators, and representatives of key Serbian media associations. The visits last for up to one week and provide an opportunity for journalists to familiarize themselves with the functioning of the ICTY.

However, upon returning to their media organizations, these journalists have been burdened with other tasks; none have gone on to specialize in war crimes reporting. Still, these visits did lead to temporarily increased reports on the ICTY and opened the door for the production of ICTY-related content in local and regional media.

57 Dejan Anastasijević, Brussels correspondent for the Serbian news agency Tanjug, email correspondence with author, April 2011.

58 See Vohrah and Cina, "Outreach Program," 547–57. For more information on the ICTY outreach program, see Stephanie Barbour's chapter in this volume. See also Donna E. Arzt, "Views on the Ground: The Local Perception of International Criminal Tribunals in the Yugoslavia and Sierra Leone," *ANNALS of the American Academy of Political and Social Science* 603 (January 2006): 226–39, and Ralph Zacklin, "The Failing of the Ad Hoc International Tribunals," *Journal of International Criminal Justice* 2, no. 2 (June 2004): 541–45.

59 See Gabrielle Kirk McDonald, "The International Criminal Tribunal for the Former Yugoslavia: Making a Difference or Making Excuses" (speech at the Council on Foreign Relations, New York, May 12, 1999), http://www.tpiy.org/sid/7766.

60 See http://www.icty.org/sections/Outreach/OutreachProgramme.

61 See "Bridging the Gap Project," http://www.icty.org/sid/10164.

62 See *Report of the International Tribunal for the Prosecution of Persons Responsible for Serious Violations of International Humanitarian Law Committed in the Territory of the Former Yugoslavia since 1991*, Annual Report, UN Doc. A/60/267–S/2005/532, August 2005, paras. 201–10.

63 Refik Hodžić, "Living the Legacy of Mass Atrocities: Victims' Perspectives on War Crimes Tribunals," *Journal of International Criminal Justice* 8, no. 1 (March 2010): 113–36.

64 See ICTY, "Crimes of Sexual Violence," accessed September 2012, http://www.icty.org/sid/10312.

65 "The authors of the tribunal statute not only created the tribunal as quite separate and apart from the region with the local authorities legally obliged to defer to the tribunal prosecutor, but also made no provision for creating sustainable links with the region" (David Tolbert, "The International Criminal Tribunal for the Former Yugoslavia: Unforeseen Successes and Foreseeable Shortcomings," *Fletcher Forum of World Affairs* 16, no. 2 [Summer/Fall 2002]: 15).

66 For example, Orentlicher quotes an interview with one of the first outreach officers of the Tribunal, Olga Kavran, who recognized, "[It] is much more difficult to dismantle already established misperceptions and propaganda than it would have been to start from the outset with updated and accurate information about the Tribunal" (Orentlicher, *Shrinking the Space for Denial*, 66).

67 Slobodan Milošević was overthrown by a one-day uprising on October 5, 2000. The uprising occurred about ten days after Milošević and the opposition both declared victory in the general elections. After protesters took over the National TV and Parliament buildings, Milošević accepted his electoral defeat and resigned the presidency. He was

arrested on March 31, 2001, on suspicion of corruption and abuse of power and extradited to the ICTY to stand trial for war crimes on June 28, 2001. At the time, the Serbian Constitution prohibited the extradition of citizens to the ICTY.

68 "Milosevic Extradited," *BBC News*, June 28, 2001, http://news.bbc.co.uk/2/hi/europe/1412828.stm.

69 More than one thousand bodies were removed from Kosovo as part of a cover-up operation allegedly ordered by Milošević during Serbia's military campaign in Kosovo in 1999. See Marlise Simons, "Danube's Grisly Tale, Staring Milosevic in the Face," *New York Times*, August 26, 2002, http://www.nytimes.com/2002/08/26/world/danube-s-grisly-tale-staring-milosevic-in-the-face.html?pagewanted=all&src=pm; and Rory Carroll, "Serbs Split over Fate of Milosevic," *The Guardian*, June 5, 2001, http://www.guardian.co.uk/world/2001/jun/06/balkans.

70 "Mass Grave Discoveries Shift Serb Mood," *BBC News*, June 28, 2001, http://news.bbc.co.uk/2/hi/europe/1402605.stm.

71 According to a report from the Helsinki Committee for Human Rights in Serbia (one of the most reputable and well-known human rights NGOs operating in the country),

> after the June 2001 hand-over of Slobodan Milošević to the Hague Tribunal, all the state-run media attempts to more seriously deal with or probe into war crimes committed against non-Serb civilians were foiled. For example, the state-run RTS suspended live broadcasts of the Milošević trial. It turned out that articles on discovery of mass graves in Serbia were used only to bolster public support for Milošević's hand-over. Politicians and elite opted for bowing to the prevailing public opinion, instead of exacting changes thereof. This prompted many independent media to follow suit. They realized that their struggle for frequencies, large distribution, and ads would be more successful if they did not rock the boat too much. (Helsinki Committee for Human Rights in Serbia, *Human Rights in the Shadow of Nationalism: Serbia 2002* [Belgrade: Helsinki Committee for Human Rights in Serbia, 2003], http://miris.eurac.edu/mugs2/do/blob.html?type=html&serial=1052147292684)

72 The Serbian public still held bitter resentments toward the United States for ordering the North Atlantic Treaty Organization (NATO) bombing over Belgrade in 1999. See Nick Thorpe, "Analysis: Milosevic's Trials," *BBC News*, October 8, 2000, http://news.bbc.co.uk/2/hi/europe/961486.stm. See also Ian Fisher, "Milosevic Trial 'Sickens' Leader," *New York Times*, March 29, 2002, http://www.nytimes.com/2002/03/29/world/yugoslavia-milosevic-trial-sickens-leader.html?src=pm.

73 "Zoran Đinđić, Architect of the Extradition," *Time*, July 2, 2001, http://www.time.com/time/world/article/0,8599,166161,00.html.

74 According to some, the assassination was intended to halt Đinđić's efforts to improve cooperation with the ICTY. Ian Traynor, "Security Chiefs Charged over Djindjic Murder," *The Guardian*, April 29, 2003, http://www.guardian.co.uk/world/2003/apr/30/balkans.

75 Michael P. Scharf, "The Legacy of the Milosevic Trial," *New England Law Review* 37, no. 4 (2003): 930.

76 Ibid.

77 Tim Judah, "Serbia Backs Milosevic in Trial by TV," *The Guardian*, March 2, 2002, http://www.guardian.co.uk/world/2002/mar/03/warcrimes.balkans.

78 Jelena Tošić, "Transparent Broadcast? The Reception of Milošević's Trial in Serbia," in *Paths to International Justice: Social and Legal Perspectives*, ed. Marie-Bénédicte Dembour and Tobias Kelly (Cambridge: Cambridge University Press, 2007), 91.

79 Duško Doder, review of *Slobodan Milosevic and the Destruction of Yugoslavia*, by Louis Sell, *The Nation*, May 27, 2002, 25, quoted in Michael P. Scharf, "Legacy of the Milosevic Trial," 930.

80 Smajlović, a journalist at the weekly *NIN*, argued the following in defense of the work of ICTY correspondents: "It is not true they are acting in an unprofessional manner, that is, that they are rooting for Milosevic.... Journalists are only transmitters of messages from The Hague. They are not responsible for failures of the Prosecution, cynicism of the accused, falseness of witnesses" (quoted in Izabela Kisić and Seska Stanojlović, "Post-2000 October Media Situation in Serbia," Helsinki Committee for Human Rights in Serbia, May 2008, http://helsinki.org.rs/reports.html [in Serbian, http://helsinki.org.rs/serbian/doc/Mediji%20u%20postoktobarskoj%20Srbiji.pdf]).

81 Građanska Inicijativa, "Percepcija i stavovi javnosti o nevladinom sektoru u Srbiji u 2009. godini" [Citizen's Initiative, "Public perceptions and attitudes about the NGO sector in Serbia in 2009"], a survey conducted in Serbia in 2009. According to this survey, 4 percent of respondents still considered workers in the NGO sector as people who were paid from the outside to interfere with Serbian domestic politics. See www.gradjanske.org.

82 See Milanka Šaponja-Hadžić, "Regional Report: Milosevic Trial Inflames Serbs," Institute for War and Peace Reporting, February 22, 2005, http://iwpr.net/report-news/regional-report-milosevic-trial-inflames-serbs.

83 Miloš Milić, interview with author, June 2011. Milić is a journalist at the Serbian public broadcast service, RTS, who has specialized in war crimes trials at the ICTY for the past ten years.

84 Helsinki Committee for Human Rights in Serbia, *Human Rights in the Shadow of Nationalism*.

85 Ibid.

86 The daily newspaper *Politika* published a report on July 22, 2011, from the village in Montenegro where Karadžić was born. After describing the atmosphere in the village after

the arrest ("As if heaven collapsed on the day, this area was surprised by the news that Radovan Karadzic had been arrested in Belgrade"), the journalist proceeded to quote members of Karadžić's family as saying that they were still "proud of their relative." *Večernje Novosti*, another daily in Serbia, went a step further in fueling speculation about Karadžić's life as "Dr. Dabić," publishing that he used to buy "water in 5-liter packs" since he did not like to drink water from the tap (July 24, 2011).

87 See Aleksandar Roknić, "Serbia: Difference between Tabloids and Serious Media Erased by Trivia," and Nidžara Ahmetašević, "Bosnia and Herzegovina: Criminal or a Poet?," both in *History Overshadowed by Trivia: Regional Media Coverage of Radovan Karadžić's Arrest* (Sarajevo: Balkan Investigative Reporting Network, 2009, 13–18 and 9–12, respectively).

88 Ognjen Zorić, "Hag u kasnim večernjim terminima" [The Hague Tribunal in late-night news], *Radio Slobodna Evropa*, February 26, 2011, http://www.slobodnaevropa.org/content/tema_sedmice_haski_tribunal_icty_sudjenja_mediji/2321544.html.

89 See Denis Džidić, "Interview—Radovan Karadzic: Vehicle for Establishment of Truth," *Justice Report*, Balkan Investigative Reporting Network, December 21, 2010, http://www.bim.ba/en/250/10/31399/.

90 Only one news agency from Serbia, Beta News Agency, covered the case on a regular basis, aside from the SENSE news agency, which specializes in covering all ICTY proceedings.

91 See Judgment, Ante Gotovina, Ivan Čermak, and Mladen Markač (IT-06-90-T), April 15, 2011. For comments on the impact of the verdict in Serbia, see "No Room for Gloating over Hague Verdict," B92, April 22, 2011, http://www.b92.net/eng/news/politics-article.php?yyyy=2011&mm=04&dd=22&nav_id=73954, and Amnesty International, "Croatia: Praise for 'Operation Storm' Creates Climate of Impunity," public statement, EUR 64/010/2011, August 9, 2011, http://www.amnesty.org/en/library/info/EUR64/010/2011/en.

92 Ian Traynor, "Croatian Generals Jailed for War Crimes against Serbs," *The Guardian*, April 15, 2011, http://www.guardian.co.uk/law/2011/apr/15/croatian-general-jailed-war-crimes.

93 Snježana Pavić and Nikolina Šajn, "Vuk Drašković: Ne možete više tvrditi da je Haag antisrpski" [You can no longer claim that The Hague is anti-Serb], *Jutarnji list*, April 16, 2011, http://www.jutarnji.hr/draskovic--ne-mozete-vise-tvrditi-da-je-haag-antisrpski/939456/.

94 "Očekivana i pravedna presuda" [Expected and just verdict], B92, April 15, 2011, http://www.b92.net/info/vesti/indexphp?yyyy=2011&mm=04&dd=15&nav_category=64&nav_id=506435.

95 Miloš Milić, interview with author, June 2011.

96 "Ratko Mladić Arrest—Thursday 26 May 2011," *News Blog, The Guardian*, May 26, 2011, http://www.guardian.co.uk/news/blog/2011/may/26/ratko-mladic-arrest. Unfortunately all this effect disappeared by the time of this writing, after the final judgment was

delivered that found the generals not guilty. The sentence again aroused strong anti-tribunal sentiments—probably even stronger than before, because this time they were accompanied by criticism from international human rights and law professionals. One of the reactions came from Vuk Jeremić, minister of foreign affairs in the government of Serbia from 2007 to 2012 and current president of the UN General Assembly, during an interactive thematic public debate convened on April 10, 2013. The debate was organized after the ICTY acquitted Ante Gotovina and Mladen Markač for inciting the war crimes against Serbs in Croatia. Some countries attempted to boycott this debate, and some of the invited participants—for example, the president of the ICTY—cancelled their participation. Jeremić emphasized that he does not shy away from criticizing the ICTY, which has "convicted nobody for inciting crimes committed against Serbs in Croatia" (Rick Gladstone, "Serb Defends U.N. Meeting Boycotted by the U.S.," *New York Times*, April 16, 2013). The debate on "The Role of International Criminal Justice in Reconciliation" aroused many controversies internationally. Almost at the same time that the verdict was delivered in The Hague, the outreach program planned to hold a conference on the court's legacy in Belgrade, which was then rescheduled. To date, the conference hasn't yet been organized, and any announcement about it has been removed from the ICTY website. Once again, rather than going to Belgrade, confronting the negative comments, and explaining the decision made by the trial chamber, the tribunal remained silent, leaving ample space for biased propaganda.

97 Initial Indictment, Radovan Karadžić and Ratko Mladić (IT-95-5-I), July 24, 1995; Initial Indictment, Radovan Karadžić and Ratko Mladić (IT-95-18-I), November 14, 1995. The second indictment is amended with crimes committed in Srebrenica in July 1995.

98 Human Rights Watch quotes former prosecutor of the ICTY Carla del Ponte, who estimates that "90% of all indictees brought to justice are a direct result of conditionality applied by the EU." See "Letter Commending Belgian Commitment on SAA with Serbia," February 13, 2008, http://www.hrw.org/news/2008/02/12/letter-commending-belgian-commitment-saa-serbia#footnote1.

99 Republic of Serbia, Office of the War Crimes Prosecutor, Public Relations Service, "Press Release," May 26, 2011, http://www.tuzilastvorz.org.rs/html_trz/VESTI_SAOPSTENJA_2011/S_2011_05_26_ENG.pdf.

100 "Ratko Mladic Arrested: Bosnian War Crimes Suspect Held," *BBC News*, May 26, 2011, http://www.bbc.co.uk/news/world-europe-13561407.

101 The Belgrade daily *Blic* regularly reported on Mladić's arrest, giving space to details such as his requests to visit his daughter's grave, to read books, to meet with relatives, etc. See "Mladić tražio da poseti grob svoje ćerke" [Mladić wanted to visit his daughter's grave], *Blic*, May 27, 2011, http://www.blic.rs/Vesti/Hronika/256392/Uzivo-Mladic-trazio-jagode-i-televizor.

102 See "Tadić Wants EU 'to Do Its Part Now,'" B92, May 31, 2011, http://www.b92.net/eng/news/politics-article.php?yyyy=2011&mm=05&dd=31&nav_id=74662.

103 Radoša Milutinović, interview with author, June 12, 2011. Milutinović has been reporting on the ICTY trials since 2001 as the Hague correspondent for Belgrade-based Beta News Agency.

104 Tanja Tagirov, "Krv i jagode" [Blood and strawberries], *Vreme*, May 31, 2011, http://www.vreme.com/cms/view.php?id=993489.

105 "Journalism should give information about important things, events, and the only selection should be the one that will give possibility to the public to learn more about the basics. [A] journalist does not have a right to completely change information, but just to make it simple enough to be easily understandable for anybody. But they know that. We talk about manipulations here" (Hartmann, interview with author, February 25, 2011).

106 Katarina Ristić, "War Crimes Trials as a Site of Memory?" (presentation at the conference "Reconstruction, Reconciliation, and European Integration of the Western Balkans," University of Graz, Graz, Austria, February 25–26, 2011).

107 Kisić and Stanojlović, "Post-2000 October Media Situation in Serbia."

108 Marija Šajkaš, "Transitional Justice and the Role of the Media in the Balkans" (discussion paper, International Center for Transitional Justice, New York, August 2007), http://ictj.org/sites/default/files/ICTJ-FormerYugoslavia-Media-Justice-2007-English_0.pdf, 17.

109 Eyal Zandberg, "The Right to Tell the (Right) Story: Journalism, Authority, and Memory," *Media, Culture and Society* 32, no. 1 (January 2010): 5.

110 Lisa J. Laplante and Kelly Phenicie, "Media, Trials, and Truth Commissions: 'Mediating' Reconciliation in Peru's Transitional Justice Process," *International Journal of Transitional Justice* 4, no. 2 (July 2010): 208.

CHAPTER 6

The Uses and Abuses of Media: Rwanda before and after the Genocide

Timothy Longman

The role of the media figures prominently in explanations of the 1994 genocide in Rwanda.[1] Analysts blame extremist publications and radio broadcasts for inciting hatred of Rwanda's Tutsi minority and mobilizing the Hutu population for violence. While some researchers challenge the assumption of an unproblematic causal link between hate media and ethnic violence in Rwanda,[2] most observers agree that "the use of sophisticated propaganda techniques" was an important factor in the violence, and that the media played a crucial role in disseminating the anti-Tutsi propaganda.[3] In particular, commentators argue that hate radio encouraged people to participate in the genocide and, in at least a few cases, gave information on where targets could be found. Most important, the radio made clear to Rwandans that genocide was government policy. In an unprecedented move, the International Criminal Tribunal for Rwanda (ICTR) indicted four individuals for their use of the media to organize and incite the genocide, signaling the seriousness with which the international community viewed the media's part in the violence.[4]

In postgenocide Rwanda, the government has implemented a variety of transitional justice instruments, including trials in both Western-style tribunals and the grassroots *gacaca* courts,[5] memorialization initiatives, and a project for developing a new official historical narrative. In promoting and supporting these initiatives, the government has regularly employed the media. The government has also, however, restricted radio, television, and the print media—partly because of the complicity of hate media in the genocide, but also, as I argue, as a means of maintaining its hold on political power. As a result, the government's tight controls on the media have undermined the impact of transitional justice, particularly by hampering the media's effectiveness in promoting national unity and reconciliation. These same political considerations have also limited the media's role in publicizing the work of the ICTR, thereby greatly impairing the domestic impact of this major international judicial program.

In this chapter I review the dual role of the media in Rwanda prior to 1994, looking into the key part that certain sectors of the press played in promoting moderate, pro-democratic, political reform in the country and also the contribution that a small number of extremist publications and radio broadcasts made in setting the stage for the genocide. Then I consider the trials of some media members who were prosecuted for their involvement in the genocide, as well as the debate among analysts over how much direct responsibility for the genocide can be attributed to the media. Although the media clearly helped to make genocide possible and radio broadcasts in particular actively sought to fan the flames of violence, evidence suggests that the direct impact of the hate media during the genocide was more limited than the usual narratives of the genocide suggest, including those put forth in Rwandan and international courts.

Next I explore the media landscape in postgenocide Rwanda. In the aftermath of the genocide, the media sector has been quite weak, largely because of tight government restrictions on freedoms of speech and the press. Despite this impairment, the international community and the Rwandan government have both sought to use the media to promote reconciliation—through media-based reconciliation programs, such as radio soap operas designed to promote conflict resolution, and through the media-based promotion of other reconciliation programs, like gacaca trials. Research I conducted in 2004–5 to evaluate a particular media program demonstrated that the media could indeed have a major effect on popular attitudes toward transitional justice processes. Yet the restrictions on press freedom and the government's extensive attempts to use radio and print press for its own political purposes have undermined the media's credibility and limited their ability to promote reconciliation. Like people everywhere, Rwandans are not merely passive recipients of media messages but are discerning consumers, and the obvious bias and politicization of Rwanda's postgenocide media have made the public skeptical of any ideas that the media hope to promote, including ideas about justice and reconciliation.

HATE MEDIA AND THE RWANDAN GENOCIDE

In 1994 the small East African country of Rwanda experienced one of the most intense waves of organized ethnic violence in modern history. Rwanda's three ethnic groups—Hutu, Tutsi, and Twa—had been deeply divided by German and Belgian colonial policies that concentrated power and wealth in the hands of the minority Tutsi, about 14 percent of the population. Frustrated at their economic and political exclusion, the Hutu, about 85 percent of the population, had risen up in 1959 and driven many of the Tutsi chiefs into exile, precipitating a shift in ethnic control over the country. Rwanda gained independence in 1962 with a Hutu government led by Grégoire Kayibanda, while Tutsi became the targets of exclusion and discrimination. Anti-Tutsi attacks throughout the early 1960s drove thousands more Tutsi into exile, and the destabilizing effects of another wave of ethnic violence in 1973 helped propel the military to power, led by General Juvénal Habyarimana. As president, Habyarimana promised to stop ethnic conflict and focus on economic development.

For over a decade, the Habyarimana regime maintained peace and promoted an image of competent leadership and good governance that built the economy by attracting substantial foreign aid. By the late 1980s, however, an economic downturn and frustration with Habyarimana's authoritarian rule fed growing public discontent. In this climate, the Catholic newspaper *Kinyamateka* began to openly criticize Habyarimana's regime in 1989, inspiring a profusion of new publications. These new independent press outlets helped fuel a nascent pro-democracy movement that began to push for greater political rights and freedoms in early 1990. Because most of Habyarimana's policies favored his home region in northern Rwanda, the pro-democracy movement gained significant support from both Tutsi and Hutu from southern Rwanda. In October 1990, an invasion by the Rwandan Patriotic Front (RPF), a rebel group based in Uganda and comprising mostly Tutsi refugees from the ethnic violence that began in 1959, further destabilized the political situation.

In response to these developments, a group of influential politicians, military officers, and businesspeople with close ties to Habyarimana, widely known in Rwanda as the Akazu ("little house" in Kinyarwanda), sought to reinforce their political influence by reviving ethnic tensions and portraying themselves as defenders of the Hutu majority. Their open policy of scapegoating the Tutsi minority culminated in 1994 with a plan to wipe out all opposition under the cover of ethnic violence. For the three months following the assassination of President Habyarimana in a plane crash on April 6, 1994, Hutu extremist leaders organized the military, the police, and civilian militias to slaughter Rwanda's Tutsi, first in large-scale massacres in public places where the Tutsi fled seeking protection—such as churches, schools, and government offices—and then in a systematic search for survivors using roadblocks and community patrols. While some moderate Hutu were also targeted, the vast majority of victims were Tutsi. Between April 6 and July 18, 1994, five hundred thousand to seven hundred thousand people were killed in the violence, including an estimated 80 percent of the country's Tutsi.[6]

THE RISE OF HATE MEDIA AND THE GENOCIDE

The role and implication of the media in Rwanda's genocide has garnered particular public attention and debate.[7] For most of Habyarimana's regime, the government maintained a near-monopoly on the print media and a complete monopoly over radio broadcasts within the country.[8] The profusion of publications that emerged in the early 1990s as part of the pro-democracy movement, during a period that Jean-Pierre Chrétien has called the "springtime of Rwanda's press,"[9] forced the regime to liberalize the media sector, largely because journalists simply ignored attempts at censorship and published despite harassment and arrest.[10] Although most of these new publications were founded by opponents of the regime, supporters of the Akazu also turned to the newly free press to defend the status quo and promote their anti-Tutsi ideology in an effort to appeal to the Hutu majority. In this vein, in May 1990 the Akazu supported the formation of *Kangura*, a newspaper meant to respond directly to other publications' criticisms of the government while decrying those critics as Tutsi or Tutsi sympathizers. The continuing RPF attacks on Rwanda also provided fodder for the anti-Tutsi rhetoric that appeared in *Kangura* and increasingly also in other pro-regime publications.[11] In a move that gained particular notoriety, in December 1990 *Kangura* published a text titled "The Hutu 10 Commandments" that sought to build on popular resentment of the RPF invasion to inspire fear and hatred of Tutsi; the text accused Hutu who befriended or cooperated with Tutsi of being traitors.[12]

Pressure from the pro-democracy movement and the RPF, however, forced the Habyarimana regime to accept political reforms, including the legalization of opposition parties in 1991 and, in April 1992, the installation of a multiparty coalition government headed by a prime minister from an opposition party, the Democratic Republican Movement (Mouvement Démocratique Républicain, MDR). At the same time, the Akazu directly supported the formation of a new, more extreme political party, the Coalition for the Defense of the Republic (CDR), which openly embraced the anti-Tutsi ideology developed in the extremist press. In the midst of an open conflict in the country and with the RPF increasingly successful on the battlefield, the extremist Hutu media proliferated and intensified their rhetoric against regime opponents. Expanding on themes from "The Hutu 10 Commandments," the pro-regime press started warning Hutu against the treacherous character of Tutsi and accusing Tutsi of seeking to regain control over the Hutu majority. During this period, the pro-government media commonly published calls on Hutu to remember their persecution under Tutsi rule prior to the 1959 revolution, claims that the RPF planned to slaughter and enslave the Hutu, and warnings that Tutsi still living in Rwanda were secretly allies of the RPF—including Tutsi women who, it was insisted, would use their beauty to seduce Hutu men. These publications also painted reformist Hutu as traitors, claiming that the reformists were selling out the Hutu people to the RPF.

Maintaining its tight relationship with pro-regime political groups, by mid-1993 the Hutu extremist press had helped drive a wedge through the opposition parties; factions split off and allied themselves with the National Revolutionary Movement for Development (*Mouvement Révolutionaire National pour le Developpement*, MRND) and CDR in a new multiparty movement called Hutu Power. Moreover, some of these publications played an active role in rallying support for Hutu Power in response to two events in particular: (1) the Arusha Accords, a peace agreement in August 1993 between the Rwandan government and the RPF that many Rwandans felt conceded too much to the RPF, and (2) the assassination of Melchior Ndadaye, the first Hutu president of neighboring Burundi, by Tutsi army officers in October of the same year.[13]

Given the low level of literacy and the expense of purchasing publications, during the period before the genocide, the printed press was mainly read by Rwanda's elite, while radio was by far the most widely accessible medium in the country. In contrast to the proliferation of independent printed publications, the government controlled the country's only radio station, Radio Rwanda, which actively promoted the interests of Habyarimana's party, the MRND. While less inflammatory than extremist publications like *Kangura*, Radio Rwanda clearly broadcast news that favored the regime, including biased reporting about the ongoing war with the RPF. According to Des Forges, Radio Rwanda reports had by March 1992 helped incite anti-Tutsi massacres in the Bugesera region south of Kigali. This situation, however, briefly receded in the following month when Habyarimana installed the new coalition government. Ferdinand Nahimana, who was a strong Habyarimana ally, was replaced as director of Radio Rwanda by Jean-Marie Vianney Higiro, a member of the opposition who quickly worked to transform the station into a more reliable, less politicized news source.[14]

With Radio Rwanda no longer reliably serving their cause, a group of individuals with close ties to the Akazu came together to found a new radio station that they hoped would influence the general public more effectively. Headed by former Radio Rwanda chief Nahimana, the group set up Radio Télévision Libre des Mille Collines (Free Radio Television of the Thousand Hills, RTLM). While nominally private, RTLM's connections with the regime were apparent to everyone in Rwanda; the founding shareholders included in-laws of President Habyarimana, the ministers of communication and planning, and officials from the MRND and CDR.[15]

After nearly a year of preparation, RTLM began broadcasting in July 1993 with a format similar to "Western-style radio talk shows, complete with audience participation, offensive jokes, and popular participation."[16] RTLM's entertaining, modern style attracted a wide audience, particularly in Kigali, where its signal was strongest and where its sometimes crude content was least likely to shock.[17] For the first few months, the broadcasts focused mostly on music, interspersed with light banter from the disc jockeys, but after the assassination of Burundi's president Ndadaye in October 1993, RTLM began to run clearly inflammatory, anti-Tutsi commentary, equating Ndadaye's Tutsi killers with the RPF. During the following months of its programming, presenters sometimes read articles from the pro–Hutu Power press—warning, for example, that ethnic violence in Burundi, which they erroneously depicted as exclusively Tutsi violence against Hutu, could spread to Rwanda. Politicians who did not support Hutu Power, civil society activists who opposed ethnic violence or supported the Arusha Accords, and opposition journalists—Hutu or Tutsi—were also denounced on air. Once again, reformist Hutu in particular were accused of being traitors to their people and allies of the RPF.[18]

From 1990 to 1994, the printed press and radio both actively helped to develop and disseminate the ideology that motivated Hutu Power in Rwanda. Directly allied with the MRND and CDR, the hate media promoted the myth—first developed to justify the system of indirect rule during colonialism—that Tutsi were an outside ethnic group, probably Nilotic or Hamitic, that had conquered and subjugated the Hutu population several hundred years earlier.[19] They revived the rhetoric of the 1959 revolution, popular under Rwanda's first president, Kayibanda, that emphasized the subjugation of the Hutu masses to the Tutsi minority, warning that Tutsi wanted to reestablish their rule over the Hutu. The hate media claimed that there was solidarity among all Tutsi, warning that Tutsi within Rwanda were *ibiyitso* (collaborators) who secretly worked for the RPF, which was, after all, a largely Tutsi rebel army seeking to gain control of the country. The hate media further claimed that the RPF wanted to carry out genocide against the Hutu, as they asserted the Tutsi in Burundi had done. Hutu who opposed Hutu Power were accused not simply of being traitors to their own people but also of having suspect ethnic origins, allegedly hiding their Tutsi ancestry.[20]

In this climate, by the time President Habyarimana's plane was shot down, the media had already helped the Akazu and Hutu Power lay the groundwork for the genocide that was about to take place, dividing the population along rigid ethnic lines and isolating the Tutsi by sowing fear and uncertainty among the Hutu that their Tutsi neighbors might be *ibiyitso*. RTLM was the first radio station to announce the downing of Habyarimana's plane only half an hour after it crashed; two days later RTLM was the first station to announce the formation of a new interim cabinet, including reporting as missing the names of several ministers in the former cabinet who had in fact fled or been killed by government troops loyal to Hutu Power. As an important news source, RTLM was able to spread disinformation effectively within Rwanda and exploit Habyarimana's death to heighten public anxiety about the RPF, the ongoing war, and Tutsi still in the nation. At the same time, RTLM spread the coded language that made genocide more palatable, such as references to the supposed RPF attacks on the Hutu majority and the need for civil self-defense. More specifically during the genocide, as the ICTR later established, "RTLM broadcasting was a drumbeat, calling on listeners to take action against the enemy and enemy accomplices, equated with the Tutsi population."[21] RTLM also broadcast more specific details about how to carry out the genocide, telling those manning roadblocks, for example, to check identity cards and assume that those without cards were RPF infiltrators.[22] Moreover, in a few cases RTLM broadcast specific information about places where Tutsi were hiding, helping to direct militias on where to hunt down survivors, and identified specific individuals as *ibiyitso*. Finally, Radio Rwanda, while less obviously inflammatory than RTLM, also contributed to spreading disinformation and creating a general climate of fear at a time in which most print media had ceased publication.[23]

HOLDING HATE MEDIA ACCOUNTABLE: THE ICTR AND DOMESTIC MEDIA TRIALS

Just as the organizers of the genocide recognized the media's importance, using the media to recruit and inspire supporters while systematically silencing alternative voices, since the end of the war in 1994 the government of Rwanda and the international community have both made clear their recognition of the media's ability to influence public opinion and mobilize a population regarding genocide. Breaking new legal ground, the ICTR and the national courts of Rwanda have sought to promote responsible publishing and broadcasting by holding accountable those who abused the media to promote the genocidal violence. In a groundbreaking case in 2003 the ICTR convicted two of the directors of RTLM and the editor of *Kangura* on charges of conspiracy to commit genocide, incitement to commit genocide, and crimes against humanity. For its part, the Rwandan government has also prosecuted a number of individuals involved in hate media. The most prominent case was against Valerie Bemeriki, a radio personality on RTLM whose anti-Tutsi rhetoric was particularly harsh. In transcripts of Bemeriki's broadcasts entered into evidence at the ICTR, she portrayed the Tutsi in terrible terms, even accusing them of cannibalism. She was arrested in the Democratic Republic of Congo (DRC) in 1999, convicted in a Rwandan court, and sentenced to life in prison in 2009.[24]

The attention given to the role of the media in promoting hate speech can be traced to the first days of the ITCR's trials. In one of the international tribunal's earliest cases, the 1998 guilty plea of Jean Kambanda, the prime minister during the genocide, the judgment stated that Kambanda "acknowledges the use of the media as part of the plan to mobilize and incite the population to commit massacres of the civilian Tutsi population."[25] In another guilty plea in 2000, Georges Ruggiu, a Belgian national who had been an announcer on RTLM, admitted to incitement to genocide and crimes against humanity for his role in calling for Hutu to continue the 1959 revolution.[26]

With these precedents set, in a groundbreaking case decided in 2003, the ICTR convicted three defendants—Ferdinand Nahimana, the former National Bureau of Information and Broadcasting (ORINFOR) director and RTLM founder; Jean-Bosco Baraygwiza, an RTLM board member; and Hassan Ngeze, the founder and editor in chief of *Kangura*—on charges of genocide, incitement to commit genocide, conspiracy to commit genocide, and crimes against humanity.[27] According to Gregory Gordon, this so-called media trial "stands as a landmark in the jurisprudence of hate speech. Not since the International Military Tribunal (IMT) at Nuremberg tried the Nazi propagandists Julius Streicher and Hans Fritzsche in 1945–1946 had an international tribunal been called upon to decide whether the media's free expression prerogative had degenerated into war crimes."[28] In a fourth case, popular musician Simon Bikindi, a strong Hutu Power supporter and founding member of RTLM's board of directors, was prosecuted for writing nationalistic anti-Tutsi music that inspired participation in the genocide. Although the ICTR convicted him for incitement to commit genocide because of a public speech that he gave in June 1994 calling on people to kill Tutsi—whom he referred to as "snakes"—the court found that even though some of his songs clearly incited anti-Tutsi sentiments, they had been written prior to 1994, and he could not be shown to have participated *directly* in their dissemination during the genocide.[29]

Their legal innovation notwithstanding, the contradictory conclusions of the media and Bikindi trials—with one considering the dissemination of propaganda via the media to be direct incitement to genocide, and the other treating it as general incitement—highlight the difficulty in conclusively proving the legal charge of incitement, because of the real difficulty of demonstrating the causal link between the inciting rhetoric and the actual genocidal acts. The official legal charge applied in both cases was "direct and public incitement to commit genocide." In the case against the RTLM officials, the court accepted the radio station's claims of general responsibility for the violence but also relied heavily on evidence of direct causation, as calls over the radio to locate specific Tutsi were followed by their murder. Demonstrating direct causation for print media was, however, more challenging, given the time lag between publication and actions.[30] While *Kangura* published highly incendiary attacks on Tutsi, the newspaper's direct link to the genocidal violence was less clear, since the prosecution relied on editions published before the genocide began. Nevertheless, the court found, "Through fear-mongering and hate propaganda, *Kangura* paved the way for genocide in Rwanda, whipping the Hutu population into a killing frenzy."[31] The appeals chamber concurred, stating that "it is not necessary to show that direct and public incitement to commit genocide was followed by actual consequences," dismissing Ngeze's objections that the publications had appeared well before the violence began and thus could not be found to have directly incited genocide.[32] In the Bikindi case, however, the court took a more conservative approach. While noting, when considering two of his songs, that "the only reasonable inference in the Chamber's opinion is that Bikindi composed [them] with the specific intention to disseminate pro-Hutu ideology and anti-Tutsi propaganda, and thus to encourage ethnic hatred," and also noting that "the songs inspired action" among militia members,[33] the court nevertheless resolved that "the Chamber does not find that there is sufficient evidence to conclude beyond reasonable doubt that Bikindi composed these songs with the specific intention to incite such attacks and killings, even if they were used to that effect in 1994."[34] While Bikindi's songs met the same relaxed standard of causation used in the Nahimana case, the court concluded that it could not demonstrate genocidal intent when he wrote the songs.

Another interesting issue that these cases raise is over how far free speech can be limited to prevent potential violence. As Schabas notes, "The crime of incitement butts against the right to freedom of expression, and the conflict between these two concepts has informed the entire debate on the subject."[35] While Gordon claims that "the Nahimana decision goes a long way toward answering significant questions regarding the proper legal standard for distinguishing between permissible speech and criminal advocacy in the context of massive violations of international humanitarian law,"[36] exactly how much hate speech can be tolerated remains uncertain. As I discuss in the next section, this issue is still quite relevant in Rwanda today. According to Parker Patterson, "The Trial Chamber was careful to differentiate censorship designed to subordinate minority populations or opposition political groups from the present situation, which involved punishment of hate speech advancing majority domination and violence."[37] Some observers, though, feel that the court went too far in its verdict. Diane Orentlicher, for example, claims, "In a departure from established jurisprudence the Chamber convicted all three defendants of persecution as a crime against humanity based upon speech that constitutes incitement to racial hatred but not incitement to violence."[38]

While today no one doubts that the media spewed hatred of Tutsi and reformist Hutu, the degree to which the genocide can be blamed directly on the media remains a topic of academic debate. Indeed, some scholars have challenged the soundness of the ICTR convictions on the grounds that they assume too direct a connection between hate speech in the media and the murderous actions that the perpetrators of the genocide committed.[39] Although before April 1994 the media clearly helped to create the conditions for genocide by disseminating Hutu Power's anti-Tutsi propaganda and isolating the Tutsi, the media's role during the actual killing was more limited. Scholars claim that the image of "the killers [with] a radio in one hand and a machete in the other"[40] has become central to the narrative of the genocide, but it exaggerates and distorts the media's actual involvement in the violence. The RPF-dominated postgenocide government itself—in part seeking to justify its own authoritarian practices that restrict Hutu engagement in the political process—has helped promote this image of the media's responsibility by repeatedly asserting that the genocide—in which, they claim, participation was extremely widespread—was driven by hatred of the Tutsi and rooted in Hutu Power's anti-Tutsi ideology. Several of the best-known texts on the genocide and many casual observers of Rwanda have unquestioningly embraced this premise.[41]

Empirical research on the genocide has demonstrated, however, that far from being a spontaneous reaction driven by passion over the killing of President Habyarimana, the Akazu organized and directed the genocide. Most of the killing was done not spontaneously but by relatively small groups of killers in each community, many of whom were trained and armed well in advance of Habyarimana's death.[42] Moreover, recent research into the motivations of those who participated in the genocide indicates that hatred of Tutsi was not among the principle reasons that people killed. Instead, people acted primarily out of fear and because of social ties and local dynamics.[43]

The role of RTLM in directly inciting violence has come under particular scrutiny, as scholars have challenged the iconic image of killers acting at the behest of the radio, as portrayed in films such as *Hotel Rwanda* and *Sometimes in April*. For example, using several empirical methods to test the claim that the RTLM broadcasts led people to kill, Scott Straus persuasively shows that the tie between the RTLM broadcasts and genocidal violence in most of the country was more nuanced and less direct.[44] According to Straus, it is unclear how far-reaching the broadcast range of RTLM was outside of the capital, Kigali, but it was certainly less extensive than Radio Rwanda, meaning that many rural residents could not have heard the RTLM broadcasts. The oft-cited examples of RTLM giving specific instructions on Tutsis' locations followed by attacks on them are quite limited and restricted geographically to the Kigali area.[45] Furthermore, while content analysis indicates that RTLM did broadcast incendiary anti-Tutsi messages, the assumption that people simply accepted these messages without question contradicts current research into the ways that populations respond to the media. Indeed, applying this literature to the Rwandan case, Charles Mironko challenges the view of rural residents as passive and obedient subjects who simply carried out any actions demanded of them on the radio. He writes, "As active (re)interpreters of RTLM's message, many ordinary peasants in the ranks of the low-level perpetrators did not swallow everything they heard whole. For most ordinary Rwandan peasants (*abaturage*), radio was viewed as a medium for the urban, the educated, and the elite."[46]

While direct causal relation between the media and the genocide has thus been seriously challenged, the role that the media played in Rwanda remains fundamental in understanding or explaining how it happened. According to an important body of comparative studies of genocide, many scholars understand it as a process that requires a series of steps, beginning with a clear definition of groups moving toward their increasing isolation.[47] Accordingly, and as Frank Chalk has stated, "The media do not make ideologically motivated genocide happen, but they facilitate and legitimate it."[48] The hate media's identification of the Tutsi as aliens with distinct cultural characteristics, such as arrogance and deviousness, did not necessarily convince most Hutu to hate Tutsi, but it did help to draw a clear line between Hutu and Tutsi in public discourse. The naming of Hutu activists and politicians opposed to Hutu Power as *ibiyitso* forced Hutu to decide their loyalties and helped to increase the polarization between Hutu and Tutsi. Even though most of the population was not driven to hate Tutsi by the propaganda, among a segment of elite Rwandans who had benefitted from the Habyarimana regime and found their social and political dominance challenged by the changes taking place in the early 1990s, arguments that blamed their diminishing status on Tutsi resonated. The media additionally helped to create a general atmosphere of crisis and fear in the country, which was immersed in a war between the government and the RPF at that time. As a researcher living in Rwanda during 1992 and 1993 (prior to the radicalization of RTLM's content), I found indeed that the proliferation of anti-Tutsi publications clearly instilled fear in people—both in Tutsi, who felt themselves increasingly targeted and vulnerable, and in Hutu, whose hatred of the RPF was intensified and whose suspicions of their Tutsi neighbors were raised by the hate media.

Research indicates that during the genocide, the media did play an important contributing role. While in most of the country, RTLM and other media were not directly responsible for inciting violence, "In the capital, RTLM's broadcasting of names and locations as well as its generally hostile tone inspired attacks and were a factor in the hard-liners' ability to assert dominance."[49] More broadly the media helped to promote an atmosphere of fear and uncertainty that contributed to motivating individuals to participate in the killing. As Straus explains, "At the micro level, most individuals chose to enter the violence because they were afraid of the consequences of disobeying or afraid of what a rebel victory meant. In articulating hard-liners' positions, signaling who had power, and setting a tone of war and belligerence, hate radio narrowed the choices some individuals believed they had and reinforced the choices they faced in their communities—at least where RTLM was heard."[50]

The media's control of information was important in the context of an ongoing war, as the RPF advanced across the country displacing thousands of people and creating fear and uncertainty. By distorting information about the war and exaggerating the RPF's attacks on civilians (which were common enough to lend credence to reports), the radio helped to create the paranoia necessary to inspire many people to believe that their participation in the killing was a means of defending themselves and their families. Finally, as Straus indicates, the media were also important as a means for disseminating the government's official support of the genocide: "The main effect of the radio broadcasts was to help establish killing Tutsis as the new order of the day—as the new 'law,' as the new basis for authority—after Habyarimana's assassination and after the civil war was resumed."[51]

THE MEDIA IN POSTGENOCIDE RWANDA: COPING WITH A COMPLEX LEGACY

A day after Hutu Power supporters launched the genocide, the RPF broke the cease-fire that the August 1993 Arusha Accords had put in place. Over the next several months, RPF troops swept across the country, quickly occupying territory and displacing much of the population. The RPF declared victory on July 18, 1994, after they drove the last government troops—accompanied by nearly 1 million Rwandan civilians—across the border into the Democratic Republic of Congo (then called Zaire). While the RPF stopped the genocide in the areas they occupied, RPF troops also engaged in extensive violence against civilians. After taking power, the RPF faced the daunting task of governing a deeply divided country. As a movement made up overwhelmingly of members of the Tutsi minority group, the RPF sought to appear moderate and inclusive by naming a multiethnic, multiparty government, but real power remained in the tight control of RPF leaders. The RPF gradually took more direct and open control of the country beginning in 2000, when RPF military leader Paul Kagame assumed the presidency; their ascendancy culminated in the 2003 presidential and parliamentary elections, in which opposition parties and candidates were severely constrained. In recent years the RPF government has gained international praise for its good governance practices and effective economic management, but the regime is in many ways authoritarian and tolerates little dissent.[52]

Like much of Rwandan society, the media sector was devastated by the 1994 genocide. The leaders who launched the genocide—members of the Akazu and other Hutu Power leaders—had clearly viewed the media sector as an important area in which to exert their control. Within hours after President Habyarimana's death, Faustin Rucogoza, the minister of information and a moderate Hutu, was arrested; he was assassinated the next day. Indeed, Tutsi and pro-opposition journalists were among the first to be targeted in the genocide, as the Presidential Guard and other elite troops went through the capital searching out people whom they regarded as key opponents of Hutu Power. The Committee to Protect Journalists counts twenty-four journalists killed in the genocide, more than half in the first week of the violence.[53] Other sources list as many as forty-seven killed.[54] ORINFOR leader Higiro and many other Tutsi and Hutu opposition journalists fled into exile.

As a result, in the aftermath of the genocide, few experienced or trained journalists remained in Rwanda. In addition to the Tutsi or moderate Hutu writers, editors, and broadcasters killed in the genocide and those who were threatened and then fled, dozens of others—mostly Hutu—fled the country as soon as the RPF took power, fearing retribution for their involvement in the hate media. Lacking qualified personnel and without financial backers, only a few of the publications from the 1990–94 period of relative press freedom reappeared. The country's oldest newspaper, the Catholic Church's *Kinyamateka,* returned to twice-monthly publication but studiously avoided politically sensitive topics (in contrast to the mid-1950s, when president-to-be Kayibanda was the editor, and 1989, when *Kinyamateka* helped to launch Rwanda's democracy movement under the editorship of Father André Sibomana). *Le Tribun du Peuple* also reappeared, after its editor, Jean Pierre Mugabe—who had fled Rwanda in 1993 to work for the RPF's radio station, Radio Muhabura—returned to the country. The new government also restarted the ORINFOR publications *Imvaho* and *La Nouvelle Relève,* and the army publication *Ingabo.* Other private publications slowly began to appear. In 1995 a group of returned Tutsi refugees from Uganda with close ties to the RPF leadership founded the English-language paper the *New Times.* A private news service, the Rwanda News Agency (RNA), was established in the same year.[55] Due both to problems of financing and to harassment from the government—problems that are, as I describe in more detail below, connected—many publications have appeared, published a few editions, and then disappeared again. A few newspapers, such as *Umuseso,* which published from 2000 to 2010, have lasted longer. Yet the print media have not yet achieved the number of titles or the diversity of voices of the years prior to the genocide.

Not surprisingly, given the media's role in the genocide, the government put in place by the RPF in July 1994 soon started establishing strict controls on all forms of media, controls that have been maintained ever since; the regime has generally justified this repression as necessary to prevent the media from fueling future ethnic conflict. However, human rights groups and other observers have contended that the RPF has since 1994 consistently harassed, arrested, and even killed journalists who criticize the regime.[56] For example, Hervé Deguine reports that in January 1995, at a conference on "The Role of the Media in National Reconstruction," the new minister of information warned that the media would be tightly controlled: "The warning was thus issued: 'The new information policy is the promotion of unity and reconciliation among Rwandans. For this, nothing will be held back in the pursuit of this new policy.' The message was firm: 'We will not tolerate any deviations.'"[57] That same month, a group of armed men attacked Edouard Mutsinzi, the editor of *Le Messager,* after he published articles criticizing abuses by RPF soldiers.

In April 1995 a cabinet-level report on the media claimed that the private press was publishing biased information and promoting "divisionism," and the Ministry of Information shut down *Le Messager* the following month.[58]

Since 1995, attacks on the press have followed a similar pattern. Official public denunciations of the press, often mentioning specific publications, have been combined with arrests and sometimes physical attacks on journalists and editors, as well as the seizure or closure of recalcitrant publications. Few of these actions have been based on real evidence of promoting ethnic hatred. Instead, the government has simply equated criticizing the RPF with promulgating anti-Tutsi rhetoric. Several journalists have disappeared or been killed, and many others have been arrested—sometimes on specious genocide charges, sometimes on charges of supporting divisionism—and journals have regularly been seized or entirely shut down.[59]

Since 2001 the government has gradually built a legal framework to justify the suppression of the independent media in the name of fighting hate media. The 2001 Law on Prevention, Suppression, and Punishment of the Crime of Discrimination and Sectarianism[60] has been used to authorize the arrest of journalists on charges of divisionism. The 2003 constitution criminalizes negation or trivialization of the genocide,[61] a provision used in practice to justify silencing those who mention RPF war crimes. The 2008 Law Relating to the Punishment of the Crime of Genocide Ideology[62] gives the government further authority to suppress legitimate dissent, as vague language in the law allows the government to define what is meant by *genocide ideology*. Finally, a 2009 media law[63] gives the government wide latitude in its authority to license publications and also forces journalists to register with the government, requiring a college degree as a minimum standard, which effectively prevents the vast majority of the population from publishing.[64]

These laws have effectively created a system for severely constraining the media through legal means; extralegal means continue to be used to silence the media as well. For example, in the lead-up to the 2010 presidential elections, the government launched a major crackdown on the press: arresting a number of journalists, closing the newspapers *Umuseso* and *Umuvugizi*, and then, a week before the elections, suspending thirty publications and radio stations for supposedly failing to meet registration requirements. The deputy editor of *Umuvugizi* was murdered after his newspaper's online edition published information about an attempted assassination of one of President Kagame's erstwhile allies in South Africa.[65] In November 2011 Charles Ingabire was killed in Kampala, where he edited an online journal critical of the Kagame regime. Ingabire was a Rwandan Tutsi genocide survivor who had been in exile in Uganda since 2008. He had previously written for *Umuvugizi*, and in recent months he had sought to leave Uganda due to death threats connected to his criticism of the Rwandan government.[66]

The broadcast media have been subject to even tighter control by the government than the written press in postgenocide Rwanda, both because of the role of the radio in encouraging the genocide and because of its much larger audience in a country where illiteracy remains high and few people can afford to purchase publications.[67] Until a decade ago, the Rwandan government did not allow private radio stations, so Radio Rwanda was the only domestic radio station broadcasting. The British Broadcasting Corporation (BBC), Radio France Internationale (RFI), Voice of America (VOA), and Deutsche Welle, however, have transmitted from within Rwanda since the end of the genocide, although the government has shut down the BBC and RFI at various times. From February 1995 to March 1996 the UN Mission for Rwanda (UNAMIR) ran a radio station with broadcasts in English, French, and Kinyarwanda. The BBC and VOA both offer one hour of news in Kinyarwanda each day, providing an important alternative news source. A 2002 media law authorized the creation of private domestic radio stations, and although an extended delay of a few years took place before the government began to actually issue new licenses, a number of new stations have since been established. These include religious broadcasters such as the Catholic Church's Radio Maria, commercial music stations such as Radio 10 and Radio Flash, and regional community radio stations used for educational broadcasts. While the independent radio stations that have emerged since 2004 have been almost entirely apolitical or pro-regime, they have still faced tight scrutiny.

Television has been very slow to develop in Rwanda. Despite its name, RTLM never established a television station, although just before the genocide ORINFOR did launch Rwanda Television, a public channel that broadcast a few hours a day. Since 1994 Rwanda Television has greatly expanded its broadcasts, adding a variety of locally produced programming. A small minority of Rwandans have satellite dishes that give them access to stations from South Africa and elsewhere, but no private television stations have been authorized in the country to date. Nevertheless, television has swiftly become an important source of information for many Rwandans. In our 2005 survey, 11.7 percent of respondents listed television as a source of news, despite the rural location of the survey sites. A 2009 study of the media found that 33 percent of respondents listed television as a source of news.[68]

Given the media's role in promoting ethnic division and promulgating the Hutu Power ideology leading up to the 1994 genocide, concern over their role in postgenocide Rwanda is certainly understandable. Critics assert, however, that the government's policies go far beyond what is necessary to prevent ethnic conflict. As an Amnesty International report states,

> Prohibiting hate speech is a legitimate aim, but the Rwandan government's approach violates international human rights law. Rwanda's vague and sweeping laws against "genocide ideology" and "divisionism" under "sectarianism" laws criminalize speech protected by international conventions and contravene Rwanda's regional and international human rights obligations and commitments to freedom of expression. The vague wording of the laws is deliberately exploited to violate human rights.[69]

Whether they are justified, the effect of these policies has been to create a highly constrained media sector. According to a 2004 assessment of the progress of Rwanda's postgenocide transition, of the thirty-seven publications officially registered with the Ministry of Information in 2004, "Only eight can be described as regular publications that address political, economic, and social issues."[70] Of these, six were published by the government or controlled by RPF supporters. Only *Kinyamateka* and *Umuseso* were fully independent, and only *Umuseso* dared to criticize the government. Largely because of government harassment, a number of publications that have appeared since 1994 and published for a time have been forced to close down when the regime, taking offense at some issue, arrested or drove into exile their publishers, editors, or reporters. As I argue below, the postgenocide government's censorship of the press has not only stymied efforts to develop a vibrant independent media sector but has also undermined the potential to use the media to promote reconciliation.

THE USE OF MEDIA IN POSTGENOCIDE RECONCILIATION PROGRAMS

Since taking control of the country, the RPF has sought to radically transform Rwandan society, in part to prevent future anti-Tutsi violence. Their government has sought to promote a new unified national identity that would supersede ethnic identities and has developed numerous programs to confront the legacies of past violence and promote reconciliation. While the government has regularly used the media to promote its programs and disseminate its ideas, it has not developed programs specifically designed to use the media themselves to promote reconciliation. Ironically, although the regime has recognized the power of the media to influence the population, it has focused more on limiting and controlling the media to prevent them from doing harm than on exploiting the media's potential to promote social reconstruction. While the government has effectively used the media to inform the public of government policies and official positions, the failure to use the media to build real national unity represents a missed opportunity.[71]

As an example of the ways in which the government has made use of media, one important basis for the RPF's social project is a revised version of Rwandan history that seeks to correct the colonial-era distortions promoted by the Belgian authorities—who portrayed the Tutsi as foreign invaders—and instead strongly emphasizes the historical unity of all Rwandans. Politicians, including President Kagame, have consistently drawn on historical themes in their public lectures, which are repeatedly broadcast on Radio Rwanda and on Rwanda Television, and history has also been an uncharacteristically common topic for discussions in newspapers and on radio talk shows.[72] In several research projects that I directed in Rwanda from 2001 to 2003, we found that the population had an impressive grasp of the government's ideas, even if people did not fully embrace them. For example, people knew that ethnic labels were taboo long before the government passed laws that effectively banned their usage. When asked their identity, many people told us, "We are all Banyarwanda now."[73] In another example the National Unity and Reconciliation Commission (NURC), a government body established in 1999 to develop programs to unite Rwandans, has regularly taken to the airwaves to disseminate information about its activities. It consistently broadcasts its conferences, workshops, and other events on radio and television, yet the NURC has not developed any media-specific reconciliation programs.

A few initiatives undertaken by international NGOs in Rwanda demonstrate the potential for the media to more effectively promote reconciliation. Several projects have focused on directly using entertainment to promote reconciliation, an approach sometimes called *edutainment*.[74] Radio La Benevolencija Humanitarian Tools Foundation, a Dutch NGO initially founded to respond to the crisis in Bosnia-Herzegovina in the mid-1990s, developed a radio soap opera that has broadcast twice a week on Radio Rwanda since 2004. The program, titled *Musekeweya* (New dawn), uses a diverse cast of characters living in two neighboring farming villages and confronting life in modern Rwanda to promote tolerance and encourage peaceful modes of conflict resolution.[75] According to the NGO's website, their objective for 2011–13 is "deepening reconciliation and trust in post-Gacaca Rwanda." They intend to focus *Musekeweya* and other activities on themes such as the following:

- Sensitizing the population on the importance of equal justice in a post-genocide society
- Sensitizing the population on the role of free speech and danger of hate speech
- Sensitizing the population on the importance of empathy for others
- Sensitizing leaders to beware of the possible influence of survivor trauma on their decision making processes[76]

Other organizations have also created edutainment programs. Health Unlimited began a radio soap opera in 1998 as part of its Well Women Media Project. Titled *Urunana* (Hand in hand), the program is focused on women's issues, particularly reproductive health, and is broadcast on the BBC and Radio Rwanda. An independent Rwandan NGO, Urunana Development Communications, was eventually set up to produce the program and provide supporting services. As another example, the Population Media Center created the radio soap opera *Umurage Urukwiye* (Brighter future) in 2007 to focus on AIDS and other public health issues.

These programs are highly popular in Rwanda, and many observers credit them with effectively using accessible means to promote positive social values. However, a yearlong experimental study by Elizabeth Paluck on *Musekeweya*'s impact found that the program did not successfully change individual beliefs about issues such as the causes of violence. Still the study confirmed that the program did help to promote positive social values. Paluck concludes,

> It is interesting to note that the present evidence for disparities between private beliefs and public behaviors parallels findings from studies of ethnic violence, including the Rwandan genocide [e.g., Fujii and Straus]. Scholars emphasize that violence often did not reflect the killers' personal prejudices but that along with other factors, their authorities, peers, and the media made killing seem socially appropriate and necessary.... The nuanced and sobering suggestion raised by these analyses is that normative pressure—applied in a targeted manner through the media and other sources—can promote or restrain ethnic violence.[77]

The use of the media primarily to report news and disseminate the government's official perspective rather than to creatively promote social change has been particularly pronounced in the extensive justice initiatives undertaken by both the Rwandan government and the international community. In the aftermath of the genocide, the Rwandan government believed that legal accountability for those who committed genocide crimes was essential to fighting impunity and ultimately making reconciliation possible. As a result, shortly after taking power in 1994 the RPF began to arrest large numbers of Hutu, with around 130,000 people imprisoned on genocide charges by 1999.[78] After working to rehabilitate the national judicial system and adopting new laws to govern genocide prosecutions, the government launched its first genocide trials in December 1996.

Given the massive number of perpetrators, however, trials in the classical judicial system proceeded at such a slow pace that prosecuting all of those incarcerated could, one estimate showed, take more than one hundred years.[79] To speed the process for the tens of thousands of people languishing in prison, the government created a new grassroots court system in 2001, drawing loosely on gacaca, Rwanda's traditional community dispute resolution mechanism. The gacaca courts were a massive undertaking, involving a committee of nineteen popularly elected judges in each community in the country, charged with trying all but the most serious genocide crimes. The judges were common citizens, not professional jurors, and they received only limited training. The National Gacaca Jurisdiction office depended heavily on radio broadcasts to explain not only to the general public but also to the judges themselves how the gacaca courts should work. This office also used the radio to promote participation in the gacaca process. The courts began with a trial phase in a few areas in June 2002 and were expanded later in the year, but they were not launched nationally until 2005, with most of their work wrapping up by 2009. Throughout the process, the government repeatedly revised its rules and organization, using the radio to help explain changes to the process. Government leaders also used the radio to address perceived problems, such as low levels of participation and the acquittal of too many defendants.

Despite the incredible focus on postgenocide transitional justice in Rwanda, the potential for the media to support transitional justice measures and to promote justice as part of the reconciliation effort has been little developed in the country. The government has used the media extensively to provide information about gacaca and other judicial initiatives but has not developed programs to use the media to promote justice. The same is true of the international community's judicial interventions in Rwanda, but they have arguably performed worse in terms of disseminating basic information about their mandates and operations. Although the ICTR has been the international community's most important and extensive contribution to transitional justice in postgenocide Rwanda, the ICTR itself has done very little to inform the Rwandan public about its work. In spite of being specifically called in its mandate to "contribute to the process of national reconciliation and to the restoration and maintenance of peace" in Rwanda,[80] the ICTR had no outreach program in its first several years of existence, and its press and public affairs offices had no focus on promoting the work of the tribunal within Rwanda. Even after its establishment, the outreach program was allocated a very limited budget and therefore conducted few activities. Based in Arusha, Tanzania, the tribunal did open an office in Kigali in 2002, five years after the first ICTR judgments were handed down, but this office had few specific outreach programs beyond a library with limited public accessibility.[81]

The job of publicizing the ICTR's work has been left largely to international NGOs. Foundation Hirondelle's ICTR project has been the primary source of reliable news about the tribunal, eclipsing the work of the ICTR's small press office. Efforts to disseminate news about the ICTR within Rwanda have been hampered by tense relations between the Rwandan government and the ICTR.[82] Radio Rwanda has been reluctant to broadcast positive news about the ICTR. At the same time, the ICTR has never partnered with the BBC or VOA or any local publications to help disseminate its work. As a result, the Rwandan population has only limited information about the ICTR. In a survey conducted in 2002, we found that only 0.7 percent of respondents claimed to be "well informed" about the ICTR, compared to 55.9 percent who said they were poorly informed and 31.3 percent who claimed to be "not informed at all."[83]

One internationally sponsored program has used the media creatively to promote transitional justice. In 1998 the US-based NGO Internews began a project to help raise public knowledge about the ICTR. According to its website, Internews "is an international media development organization whose mission is to empower local media worldwide to give people the news and information they need, the ability to connect, and the means to make their voices heard."[84] In several dozen countries around the world, it provides training, works with local journalists to produce programming, supports media infrastructure development, and helps promote revision of media laws. In the Rwandan case, Internews noted the weakness of the media sector and the failure of the ICTR to adequately report on its activities; in response, Internews created a project to produce documentary newsreels. Internews producers videotaped ICTR sessions and interviewed judges and others, then created short documentaries that they took to locations throughout Rwanda, including prisons, to show to local populations who often lacked access to television. Following the viewings, individuals from Internews would lead public discussions. In some cases, the Internews team took questions from the Rwandan public back to the ICTR and then included the answers from judges and other

ICTR officials in subsequent newsreels. Over time, Internews expanded its focus to include reporting on Rwandan national genocide trials and the gacaca courts. They have produced thirty newsreels that have been shown to more than two hundred thousand Rwandans, including eighty thousand prisoners. English, French, and Kinyarwandan DVDs of the films have also been widely distributed.[85]

In an assessment of the Internews Newsreel Project conducted in 2004 and 2005 I found that people who had watched Internews films felt better informed about the ICTR, Rwandan trials, and gacaca. People who had attended the films were also better informed about the specific issues covered in the films. Whereas a plurality of informants who had not seen the Internews films did not have opinions about questions such as whether the trials were contributing to reconciliation or were functioning fast enough, people who had viewed the films were much more likely to articulate clear opinions. Significantly, the films—which attempt to provide unbiased information—did not lead viewers to have uniformly positive opinions about the courts but rather enabled people to feel well enough informed to formulate opinions. The benefits of the films were made clear in key informant interviews and viewer focus groups. Prisoners, for example, mentioned how important it was to see that even the powerful, not just the common people, could be judged. One prisoner in Gikongoro told us, "You could see the seriousness of events, because pictures provide more information than simple words." Another added, "There were things [in the film] that reminded me of what happened in 1994. That made me ashamed, and I don't want this [violence] to ever happen again."[86]

The results of this assessment of the Internews project indicate, perhaps not surprisingly, that when more information is disseminated about trials, they can have a greater influence within communities. The ICTR's failure to take seriously its mandate to promote reconciliation within Rwanda has meant that the greatest impacts of the trials were on international justice rather than on the process of rebuilding within the country itself. More concerted use of the media to provide information about the conduct of trials, the facts being presented in cases, and the judgments rendered could vastly increase the positive impact of trials or other transitional justice mechanisms on social reconstruction. The primary limitation of the Internews project was the limited audience exposed to its films, but the content of the films represented an excellent example of the sort of unbiased reporting needed in the conflict's aftermath. In the Rwandan case, the potential of the media to support transitional justice has been sorely neglected. The fact that the media were such an important tool in the genocide makes it all the more tragic that effectively rebuilding the media—rather than merely constraining them—has not been a goal of the social reconstruction process.

The limited use of the media to promote reconciliation in postgenocide Rwanda is directly related to the regime's suspicion of the media, and the politicization of the radio, television, and printed press has undermined their ability to contribute to reconciliation. In my research on Internews, I found that people generally regarded the domestic media with suspicion and considered foreign radio broadcasts the most reliable sources for news. In seeking to maintain very tight controls on the media and heavily regulating speech, the regime has pushed journalists into self-censorship, which not only compromised the quality of reporting but also discouraged the sort of creative uses of the media that might make them an effective tool for social reconstruction. The effectiveness of even the limited reporting on reconciliation and transitional justice that has taken place in Rwanda is undermined by the public's lack of faith in the Rwandan media.

CONCLUSION

The Rwandan case demonstrates the potential and the limitations of the media in relationship to conflict and post-conflict rebuilding. Rwanda also shows the fundamental role that the media play in relation to political and social processes. On the one hand, in the early 1990s the press played a major role in promoting democracy and political reform in Rwanda, but on the other, the proliferation of media during this period allowed a relatively small number of extremist publications and radio stations to support efforts to use ethnic violence to stop political transition. Even if the hate media cannot be held responsible for direct incitement to genocide, RTLM and extremist newspapers like *Kangura* clearly did help set the stage for genocide by contributing to an environment in which genocidal acts were made to seem acceptable or even encouraged.

In the aftermath of the 1994 genocide the government has opted to control the media tightly. While justifying its actions by appealing to a legitimate fear of the media's potential to inspire social disruption, the government has also been motivated by the desire to prohibit criticism and exclude news that might cast the regime in an unflattering light. Government restrictions have precluded the emergence of a vibrant, free, and independent media sector and limited the media's ability to support reconciliation. While the media have been used in a few innovative reconciliation programs organized by NGOs or international actors, the media's potential to support reconciliation has generally not been realized.

As a concrete example, the research that I conducted on the Internews Newsreel Project in 2005–6 demonstrates some of the media's potential for promoting public engagement and increasing the impact of transitional justice initiatives. By providing information about the various judicial processes undertaken in response to the Rwandan genocide and showing them in operation, the Internews films raised the awareness of audiences about the attempt to build accountability for the genocide. Whereas people in general felt poorly informed about all judicial initiatives, people who viewed the films were better able to form opinions about the trials' desirability and effectiveness. With all of the time and money spent on pursuing accountability after the 1994 genocide, the failure to inform the public adequately about the various trials seriously diminished their potential to affect Rwandan society—whether as a warning against future violence or to provide a basis of information about what happened. As Lord Gordon Hewart once famously wrote, "Not only must justice be done; it must also be seen to be done."[87] Sadly, the untapped potential for the media to support transitional justice in the Rwandan case meant that, for most people, justice was not seen to be done.

US Supreme Court justice Louis Brandeis also famously wrote in defense of free speech, "If there be time to expose through discussion the falsehood and fallacies, to avert the evil by the processes of education, the remedy to be applied is more speech, not enforced silence."[88] Yet he acknowledges in his opinion that some circumstances may warrant restrictions on speech. The difficult challenge growing out of the Rwandan case is to know how much potentially dangerous speech can be allowed. While the lesson that many people take from the Rwandan genocide is that hate media must be suppressed, the important contributions that the progressive press made to promoting democracy and human rights prior to the genocide need to be recognized as well. Any control of the press in the 1990–94 period would have been carried out by the very authoritarian regime that was supporting the hate media, and would thus likely have targeted the progressive pro-democracy media rather than *Kangura* or RTLM. In postgenocide Rwanda the regime has opted to keep a tight lid on the press, yet in doing so, they have gone well beyond the requirements of suppressing hate speech to silencing a considerable amount of legitimate speech. Not only has disproportionate control of free speech in postgenocide Rwanda hampered the possibilities for the media to contribute to reconciliation but it has also undermined the country's development in a broader sense. Free speech is a key to democratic development, and Rwanda was unfortunately not a democracy before the genocide and has not since transformed into a democracy. Having lived in Rwanda in the period leading up to the genocide I would argue that the problem then was not an excess of free speech and democracy but an excess of authoritarianism. Having lived and worked in Rwanda extensively since the genocide I would contend that the primary threat to peace and social harmony today comes not from the potential for dangerous speech but once again from too much authoritarianism. Until Rwandans are able to speak freely and openly about their society and politics—including through a free press—the scourge of ethnic division will never be effectively addressed and real reconciliation will remain elusive.

NOTES

The ideas here presented do not necessarily represent those of the International Center for Transitional Justice.

1 Alison Des Forges, *Leave None to Tell the Story: Genocide in Rwanda* (New York: Human Rights Watch, 1999), 65–95; Gerard Prunier, *The Rwanda Crisis: History of a Genocide* (New York: Columbia University Press, 1995); Helen M. Hintjens, "Explaining the 1994 Genocide in Rwanda," *Journal of Modern African Studies* 37, no. 2 (June 1999): 241–86.

2 Linda Kirschke, *Broadcasting Genocide: Censorship, Propaganda, and State-Sponsored Violence in Rwanda, 1990–1994* (London: Article 19, 1996); Scott Straus, "What Is the Relationship between Hate Radio and Violence? Rethinking Rwanda's 'Radio Machete,'" *Politics and Society* 35, no. 4 (December 2007): 609–37.

3 Hintjens, "Explaining the 1994 Genocide," 280–81.

4 Indictments were handed down in 1998, 1999, and 2000. Georges Ruggiu pleaded guilty, and the other three accused were subsequently combined into a single case that began in 2000. International Criminal Tribunal for Rwanda, *The Prosecutor vs. Ferdinand Nahimana, Jean-Bosco Barayagwiza, Hassan Ngeze*, "Judgement and Sentence," ICTR-99-52-T, December 3, 2003; International Criminal Tribunal for Rwanda, *The Prosecutor vs. George Ruggiu*, "Judgement and Sentence," ICTR-97-32-I, June 1, 2000.

5 As described below, the gacaca courts were a system of courts set up in every community throughout Rwanda; nonprofessional jurists were popularly elected to organize genocide trials in their communities. They developed records of all the genocide crimes

committed in their communities, listed those believed to be responsible, and sat in judgment over all but the most serious cases. Although loosely based on a traditional Rwandan system of dispute resolution in which people brought their conflicts to a group of respected community elders for judgment, the modern gacaca courts were governed by national law and structured according to Western judicial principles.

6 Des Forges, *Leave None to Tell the Story*; Prunier, *Rwanda Crisis*; Timothy Longman, *Christianity and Genocide in Rwanda* (New York: Cambridge University Press, 2010).

7 Jean-Pierre Chrétien, ed., *Rwanda: Les médias du génocide* [Genocide's media] (Paris: Karthala, 1995); Allan Thompson, ed., *The Media and the Rwandan Genocide* (London: Pluto Press, 2007); Kirschke, *Broadcasting Genocide*; William Schabas, "Hate Speech in Rwanda: The Road to Genocide," *McGill Law Journal* 46, no. 1 (2001): 141–71.

8 No television broadcasting occurred in Rwanda until after the genocide with the exception of Rwanda Television, a public channel launched by the National Bureau of Information and Broadcasting (ORINFOR) just before the genocide that broadcast for a few hours a day. Although no private domestic radio stations broadcast in Rwanda, Deutsche Welle and Radio France International had broadcast posts in Rwanda.

9 Chrétien, *Les médias du génocide* [Genocide's media], 29.

10 Longman, *Christianity and Genocide in Rwanda*, 126–33; Catharine Newbury, "Rwanda: Recent Debates over Governance and Rural Development," in *Governance and Politics in Africa*, ed. Goran Hyden and Michael Bratton (Boulder, CO: Lynne Reinner, 1992), 212–14.

11 Kirschke, *Broadcasting Genocide*, 62–70; Chrétien, *Les médias du génocide* [Genocide's media], 19–29; Prunier, *Rwanda Crisis*, 74–92.

12 Chrétien, *Les médias du génocide* [Genocide's media], 141–42.

13 Ibid., 139–208; Prunier, *Rwanda Crisis*, 144–206.

14 Des Forges, *Leave None to Tell the Story*, 66–68.

15 Ibid., 68–71; Kirschke, *Broadcasting Genocide*, 70–78.

16 Kirschke, *Broadcasting Genocide*, 84.

17 In the style of Western radio, the banter among disc jockeys often included sexual innuendo, bawdy jokes, and other adult content, which was new to media broadcasts in historically conservative Rwanda.

18 Kirschke, *Broadcasting Genocide*, 84–100; Chrétien, *Les médias du génocide* [Genocide's media], 70–73.

19 The best explanation of how the Tutsi came to be depicted as Hamitic is given in Edith Sanders, "The Hamitic Hypothesis: Its Origin and Function in Time Perspective," *Journal of African History* 10, no. 4 (October 1969): 521–32.

20 Des Forges, *Leave None to Tell the Story*, 72–86; Chrétien, *Les médias du génocide* [Genocide's media], 183–208.

21 International Criminal Tribunal for Rwanda, *The Prosecutor v. Jean Kambanda*, "Judgement and Sentence," ICTR 97-23-S, September 4, 1998.

22 Mary Kimani, "RTLM: The Medium That Became a Tool for Mass Murder," in Thompson, *Media and the Rwandan Genocide*, 110–24; Kirschke, *Broadcasting Genocide*; Chrétien, *Les médias du génocide* [Genocide's media].

23 Chrétien, *Les médias du génocide* [Genocide's media].

24 Dele Olojede, "When Words Could Kill," *Newsday*, May 4, 2004; "Rwanda Jails Journalist Valerie Bemeriki for Genocide," *BBC*, December 14, 2009, http://news.bbc.co.uk/2/hi/africa/8412014.stm.

25 International Criminal Tribunal for Rwanda, *The Prosecutor v. Jean Kambanda*, "Judgement and Sentence," ICTR 97-23-S, September 4, 1998.

26 ICTR, *Prosecutor v. Ruggiu.*

27 ICTR, *Nahimana, Barayagwiza, and Ngeze.*

28 Gregory S. Gordon, "A War of Media, Words, Newspapers, and Radio Stations: The ICTR Media Trial Verdict and a New Chapter in the International Law of Hate Speech," *Virginia Journal of International Law* 45, no. 1 (Fall 2004): 140–99.

29 International Criminal Tribunal for Rwanda, *The Prosecutor v. Simon Bikindi*, "Judgement and Sentence," ICTR 01-72-T, December 2, 2008.

30 Charity Kagwi-Ndungu, "The Challenges in Prosecuting Print Media for Incitement to Genocide," in Thompson, *Media and the Rwandan Genocide*, 330–42.

31 ICTR, *Nahimana, Baraygwiza, and Ngeze*, 318.

32 International Criminal Tribunal for Rwanda, *Ferdinand Nahimana, Jean-Bosco Barayagwia, and Hassan Ngeze v. the Prosecutor*, "Judgement," Appeals Chamber, ICTR-99-52-A, November 28, 2007, 248.

33 ICTR, *Bikindi*, 61, 60.

34 Ibid., 61.

35 Schabas, "Hate Speech in Rwanda," 149.

36 Gordon, "War of Media," 142.

37 Parker Patterson, "Partial Justice: Successes and Failures of the International Criminal Tribunal for Rwanda in Ending Impunity for Violations of International Criminal Law," *Tulane Journal of International and Comparative Law* 19, no. 1 (Winter 2010): 369–95.

38 Diane F. Orentlicher, "Criminalizing Hate Speech in the Crucible of the Trial: Prosecutor v. Nahimana," *New England Journal of International and Comparative Law* 12, no. 1 (Fall 2005): 18.

39 Straus, "What Is the Relationship between Hate Radio and Violence?"; Orentlicher, "Criminalizing Hate Speech"; Gabriele Della Morte, "De-Mediatizing the Media Case: Elements of a Critical Approach," *Journal of International Criminal Justice* 3, no. 4 (September 2005): 1019–33.

40 Human Rights Watch, "Rwanda," in *World Report 1995* (New York: Human Rights Watch, December 1994), http://www.hrw.org/reports/1995/WR95/AFRICA-08.htm#P397_139563.

41 Philip Gourevitch, *We Wish to Inform You That Tomorrow We Will Be Killed with Our Families* (New York: Farrar, Straus, and Giroux, 1998); Mahmoud Mamdani, *When Victims Become Killers: Colonialism, Nativism, and the Genocide in Rwanda* (Princeton, NJ: Princeton University Press, 2002).

42 Longman, *Christianity and Genocide in Rwanda*; Des Forges, *Leave None to Tell the Story*.

43 Scott Straus, *The Order of Genocide: Race, Power, and War in Rwanda* (Ithaca, NY: Cornell University Press, 2007); LeeAnn Fujii, *Killing Neighbors: Webs of Violence in Rwanda* (Ithaca, NY: Cornell University Press, 2009).

44 Straus, "What Is the Relationship between Hate Radio and Violence?"

45 Ibid., 620.

46 Charles Mironko, "The Effect of RTLM's Rhetoric of Ethnic Hatred in Rural Rwanda," in Thompson, *Media and the Rwandan Genocide*, 134.

47 Helen Fein, *Accounting for Genocide: National Responses and Jewish Victimization during the Holocaust* (New York: Free Press, 1979).

48 Frank Chalk, "Intervening to Prevent Genocidal Violence: The Role of the Media," in Thompson, *Media and the Rwandan Genocide*, 375–80.

49 Straus, "What Is the Relationship between Hate Radio and Violence?," 632.

50 Ibid.

51 Straus, *Order of Genocide*, 281.

52 Timothy Longman, "Limitations to Political Reform: The Undemocratic Nature of Transition in Rwanda," in *Remaking Rwanda: State Building and Human Rights after Mass Violence*, ed. Scott Straus and Lars Waldorf (Madison: University of Wisconsin Press, 2011), 25–47.

53 "17 Journalists Killed in Rwanda since 1992 / Motive Confirmed," Committee to Protect Journalists, accessed August 21, 2012, http://www.cpj.org/killed/africa/rwanda/.

54 "Casualties Recorded in 1994: Journalists and Media Workers Killed in War Zones and Other Hostile Areas in 1994," International News Safety Institute, accessed August 21, 2012, http://www.newssafety.com/casualties/1994.htm.

55 International Crisis Group, "Rwanda at the End of Transition: A Necessary Political Liberalization," International Crisis Group, Brussels, November 13, 2002, 14–15.

56 The RPF denies involvement in attacks on journalists, consistently blaming them on simple criminality or other causes, but Amnesty International, Human Rights Watch, Reporters without Borders, and the Committee to Protect Journalists have all suggested strong evidence of RPF involvement. See, for example, Amnesty International, "Safer to Stay Silent: The Chilling Effects of Rwanda's Laws on 'Genocide Ideology' and 'Sectarianism,'" AFR 47/005/2010, August 31, 2010; Amnesty International, "Unsafe to Speak Out: Restrictions on Freedom of Expression in Rwanda," AFR 47/002/2011, June 3, 2011; and Human Rights Watch, "Rwanda," in *World Report 2011* (New York: Human Rights Watch, December 2010), 154–59.

57 Hervé Deguine, "La communauté internationale et la question des médias au Rwanda" [The international community and the media question in Rwanda], in *Restructuring the Media in Post-Conflict Societies: Four Perspectives, the Experience of Intergovernmental and Non-Governmental Organizations*, ed. Monroe E. Price (Geneva: UNESCO, May 2000), 40–52.

58 Ibid., 44.

59 Lars Waldorf, "Censorship and Propaganda in Post-Genocide Rwanda," in Thompson, *Media and the Rwandan Genocide*, 404–16.

60 Rwanda, Law no. 47/2001 on Prevention, Suppression, and Punishment of the Crime of Discrimination and Sectarianism, December 18, 2001.

61 The Constitution of the Republic of Rwanda, adopted May 26, 2003, art. 13

62 Rwanda, Law no. 18/2008 Relating to the Punishment of the Crime of Genocide Ideology, July 23, 2008.

63 Rwanda, Law no. 22/2009 on Media, August 12, 2009.

64 Amnesty International, "Safer to Stay Silent"; Enrique Armijo, "Rebuilding Rwanda: Current Prospects for Media Reform," GlobalMediaLaw.com, January 20, 2010.

65 Lars Waldorf, "Instrumentalizing Genocide: The RPF's Campaign against 'Genocide Ideology,'" in Straus and Waldorf, *Remaking Rwanda*, 48–66; Reporters without Borders, "Around 30 News Media Closed a Few Days Ahead of Presidential Election," August 2, 2010, http://en.rsf.org/rwanda-around-30-news-media-closed-a-few-02-08-2010,38076.html.

66 Human Rights Watch, "Uganda/Rwanda: Investigate Journalist's Murder," press release, December 6, 2011, http://www.hrw.org/news/2011/12/06/ugandarwanda-investigate-journalist-s-murder.

67 In a survey of 727 people in three representative communities that I conducted for the International Center for Transitional Justice in 2004, 72.9 percent of respondents said that radio is how they find out what is happening in Rwanda, compared to 22.4 percent for publications and 11.7 percent for television. Additionally, 61.5 percent of respondents claimed that they listened to the radio daily, and another 23.5 percent claimed that they listened to the radio several times a week. In contrast, only 2.5 percent of respondents claimed that they read a newspaper or magazine daily, 8.4 percent several times per week, and 16.5 percent at least once per week. Only 5.8 percent of people said that they never listened to the radio, compared to 51.4 percent who claimed that they never read a newspaper or magazine. Furthermore, 68.3 percent of respondents claimed that the radio was the most reliable source of information for what was happening in Rwanda, compared to 5.4 percent who regarded newspapers and magazines as most reliable. See Timothy Longman, "Evaluation of Internews Newsreel Project," International Center for Transitional Justice, 2006. These results are consistent with a survey conducted with a more urban population by Search for Common Ground in 2009; according to

this survey, 93 percent of respondents said that radio was a source of information, compared to 33 percent for television and 32 percent for newspapers. They found, however, a much lower level of trust in the radio and higher level of trust in print media than in our research. Search for Common Ground, "Rwanda: Media Mapping Baseline Report," Washington, DC, March 2010.

68 Search for Common Ground, "Rwanda," 1.

69 Amnesty International, "Safer to Stay Silent," 7.

70 Jean-Paul Kimonyo, Noël Twagiramungu, and Christopher Kayumba, "Supporting the Post-Genocide Transition in Rwanda: The Role of the International Community" (Working Paper 32, Democratic Transition in Post-Conflict Societies Project, Conflict Research Unit, Clingendael [Netherlands Institute of International Relations], The Hague, December 2004), 77.

71 For an extensive discussion of the ways in which media can be put to use not merely to inform populations but to generate discussion, see the chapter by Wanda Hall in this volume.

72 Timothy Longman and Théoneste Rutagengwa, "Memory, Identity, and Community in Rwanda," in *My Neighbor, My Enemy: Justice and Community in the Aftermath of Mass Atrocity*, ed. Eric Stover and Harvey M. Weinstein (Cambridge: Cambridge University Press, 2004), 162–82.

73 Ibid.; Timothy Longman, Phuong Pham, and Harvey Weinstein, "Connecting Justice to Human Experience: Attitudes toward Accountability and Reconciliation in Rwanda," in Stover and Weinstein, *My Neighbor*, 206–25.

74 Elizabeth Levy Paluck, "Reducing Intergroup Prejudice and Conflict Using the Media: A Field Experiment in Rwanda," *Journal of Personality and Social Psychology* 96, no. 3 (2009): 574–87.

75 Franziska van Scheven, "Rwanda Radio Soap Opera Casts a Healing Spell," *New York Times*, January 6, 2008; Paluck, "Reducing Intergroup Prejudice and Conflict Using the Media."

76 "La Benevolencija in Rwanda," Radio La Benevolencija Humanitarian Tools Foundation, accessed August 21, 2012, http://www.labenevolencija.org/2010/12/the-task-of-la-benevolencija-in-rwanda/.

77 Paluck, "Reducing Intergroup Prejudice and Conflict," 583.

78 Alison Des Forges and Timothy Longman, "Legal Responses to Genocide in Rwanda," in Stover and Weinstein, *My Neighbor*, 49–68.

79 Ibid.

80 UN Security Council, Resolution 955, Statute of the International Criminal Tribunal for Rwanda, November 8, 1994.

81 Des Forges and Longman, "Legal Responses to Genocide in Rwanda"; Victor Peskin, "Courting Rwanda: The Promises and Pitfalls of the ICTR Outreach Programme," *Journal of International Criminal Justice* 3, no. 4 (September 2005): 950–61.

82 For discussion of some of these tensions, see Des Forges and Longman, "Legal Responses to Genocide in Rwanda."

83 Longman, Pham, and Weinstein, "Connecting Justice to Human Experience," 213.

84 "About Us," Internews, accessed August 21, 2012, internews.org/about-internews.

85 "Rwanda," Internews, http://www.internews.org/regions/africa/rwanda.shtm (this web page is no longer available, but general information about the project can be found at "Extending Coverage of Genocide after Rwanda," Internews Europe, accessed August 21, 2012, http://www.internews.eu/projects/extending-coverage-justice-after-genocide-rwanda).

86 Longman, "Evaluation of Internews Newsreel Project."

87 English King's Bench Divisional Court, *R v. Sussex Justices*, 2 KB 475, 1927.

88 Louis Brandeis, Concurring Opinion, *Whitney v. California*, 1927.

CHAPTER 7

The Media's Potential in Developing Social Awareness for Justice: The Example of Interactive Radio for Justice

Wanda E. Hall

Reaching out for public support is essential when trying to establish justice after periods of massive abuse or a fundamental breakdown of basic norms.[1] Proponents of transitional justice and international criminal justice recognize this need, using terms like "ending impunity," "complementarity," "prevention," and "reconciliation" to explain and promote endorsement for truth commissions, encourage victims' participation in such processes, and garner support for international tribunals. Slogans of "Never Again" are the cornerstone of many international campaigns against human rights violations, nongovernmental organization (NGO) projects, and defenses of human rights law in general. In contrast, such campaigning for the public support of justice is rarely seen at the national level, even in countries in which the justice system is seriously flawed. Social understanding of the existence of and respect for citizens' rights and trust in the adequate functioning of the rule of law is taken for granted in such contexts; populations are familiar with the language of justice and generally do not question the official roles of the police, lawyers, and judges in their society; and although they may well criticize actors who do not fulfill their roles properly, or claim that the system is corrupt or inadequate, people still embrace the concept of how the process should function. However, international justice mechanisms and alternative justice concepts that try to incorporate peacebuilding instruments such as truth commissions and amnesty laws present a different challenge. Populations may not be familiar with the rationale and functioning of such measures, informed about how they can participate in these processes, or aware of the impact that these measures might have on their country and their daily lives. Moreover, in post-conflict contexts, societies are often deeply shattered; development deficits such as widespread poverty, lack of infrastructure, and low education and literacy rates go hand in hand with the consequences of conflict, including strong divisions along political or ethnic lines, a grave legacy of human rights abuses, and the collapse of adequate state functions.

Against this backdrop, I explore in this chapter the ways in which the media—and more specifically radio—have been used to explain and promote international criminal justice processes taking place in different countries of sub-Saharan Africa. As a practitioner I focus on projects in which I have been personally involved and those with which I have direct experience as examples of how the media have been used to educate, engage, and ultimately create avenues of participation for communities affected by international criminal justice mechanisms after years of conflict. From this perspective, I present the argument that while more traditionally conceived media projects such as training journalists and supporting a professional and independent press are beneficial in order to encourage responsible and objective reporting in post-conflict situations, projects that use media tools in less conventional, more participatory ways can have a sustained and profound impact on building social awareness about the rule of law and transitional justice processes in such environments.

To begin, I discuss the need for transitional justice measures to implement outreach initiatives that can foster such social awareness and the potential for radio to serve this function as a primary means of communication in many sub-Saharan Africa countries. Next I offer an overview of traditional approaches to media that focus on training and support for journalists and discuss afterward less conventional efforts that seek to foster public discussion and awareness of justice issues. I then provide a detailed review of the activities developed by Interactive Radio for Justice (IRfJ) in the Democratic Republic of Congo (DRC) and the Central African Republic (CAR) as examples of this type of approach. Finally I explore some of the issues that arise when working with media in such challenging and volatile environments.

THE NEED FOR OUTREACH FROM INTERNATIONAL TRIBUNALS

Public perception of the International Criminal Tribunal for the former Yugoslavia (ICTY) and the International Criminal Tribunal for Rwanda (ICTR) has tended to be more negative than positive, especially among the affected communities. Proponents of these types of mechanisms thus slowly started to adopt language that underlined the importance of public information and outreach activities, focusing primarily on target populations but also directed to the international community at large.[2] Such refocusing served as a reminder for some, and a new awareness for others, that the criminal justice process is only as viable as people are prepared to honor it and use it. A well-functioning justice system requires not only good law and good practitioners but also a society that understands it, participates in it, and trusts it. In the case of international criminal justice, this reality is even more pronounced. Not only is the criminal justice process normally a foreign concept, and thus sometimes perceived as imposed, but its rationale and modus operandi are also difficult to understand. Moreover, in many post-conflict situations, the state and the associated systems that naturally guarantee the adequate function of the rule of law and socialize a population about its role—the education system, a working court system, an accountable security sector, and a thriving civil society—have been profoundly damaged. Presumably, international justice mechanisms wouldn't be there if the systems were properly in place.

Learning from the experiences of the two ad hoc tribunals and the huge challenges they faced in their attempts to engage with populations in the former Yugoslavia and Rwanda, the Special Court for Sierra Leone (SCSL)[3] and the International Criminal Court (ICC) have both invested considerably in their public information and outreach programs in an effort to promote understanding and garner support for their work among the affected populations. Aware of the important role that the press plays in disseminating information among affected communities, both institutions have developed specific media-oriented strategies as part of their outreach and public information activities. These strategies have normally been designed around two basic tenets: (1) reach out to the local media in order to efficiently disseminate information, and (2) train journalists so that court activities are covered in the press with more interest and competence.[4]

Media-oriented outreach strategies can be crucial for garnering public attention and promoting well-informed and reliable reporting. However, regardless of how well these strategies are crafted and implemented, conventional journalism—and media activities in general—falls short of creating social awareness on its own. While integrated and dynamic mass media are necessary to inform public discussions around political issues and problems, using media as a tool to promote a politically active and engaged civil society where it doesn't yet exist, or has been badly damaged, is much less sure. Accordingly, in some post-conflict settings where the general conditions for a well-functioning public sphere are extremely weak or even absent, a strong incentive is present to look for other approaches that might have a clearer focus on strengthening social awareness. Among these approaches, the means of media—their technical capacity—may have an interesting potential to engage a public that has been deprived of more systemic forms of socialization, not necessarily by being reported on or reported to, but with projects in which people can interact with each other with some technological assistance.

From this perspective, the question is not primarily how to guarantee a professional journalistic approach but rather whether media technology—by increasing the speed and impact of information flow—can jump-start a public discussion process that helps to build a broader understanding of and support for the rule of law and its role in democratic societies overcoming conflict. Indeed, the media's uses and capabilities have gone through such a transformation over the last ten years that one could view the media as an all-powerful and all-changing force—limitless and even revolutionary.[5] At the same time, however, we should keep in mind the societal conditions that influence people's experiences that are not media-driven—cultural relations, social structures, education, stability, and safety—all of which allow people to process, critique, learn from, and essentially use media as they conventionally exist in peaceful and well-established democratic societies. In short, while traditional media-oriented outreach efforts tend to reflect preexisting social conditions, in post-conflict contexts the participatory use of media—and radio more specifically—may challenge these conditions and promote their reformulation and strengthening. As a result, two interrelated questions are raised: Can participatory uses of media promote a social self-reflection process on the conditions that led to conflict and the possible adjustments to be made in order to create a more inclusive society, aware of its rights and willing to support and oversee the sound functioning of the rule of law? Second, can the media actually be used as an instrument to influence such processes rather than merely mirroring the current state of society?

RADIO AS A TOOL FOR COMMUNICATION IN AFRICA

To date, much of the focus of international criminal justice has been on countries in sub-Saharan Africa. The International Criminal Tribunal for Rwanda (ICTR), established by the United Nations in response to the genocide in 1994, was followed by the establishment of the Special Court for Sierra Leone, an ad hoc hybrid court mandated to try those most responsible for serious crimes committed in Sierra Leone since November 30, 1996.[6] The ICC, a permanent court established in 2002 with jurisdiction over the 121 countries who have currently signed the Rome Statute, has active investigations only in Africa: Uganda, the DRC, the CAR, Sudan, Kenya, Libya, and Côte d'Ivoire.[7] These areas share certain important media characteristics: while weak or nonexistent infrastructure limit the influence of television and the Internet, and high illiteracy rates inhibit the viability of printed media in most of sub-Saharan Africa,[8] no one can dispute radio's huge influence on this part of the continent.[9] In eastern Congo, for example, a survey found that radio is the primary mode of communication for 67 percent of respondents, with 66 percent stating that they have never read a newspaper.[10]

Radio's influence in Africa is also apparent because of those people who exploit it to gain and retain power. In Rwanda in 1994, for example, a single radio station, Radio Mille Collines, played a frighteningly effective role in encouraging people to kill their neighbors.[11] Its shadow is still felt on the continent, and the station has been compared in very recent discussions to the role that Kass-FM played in Kenya in the aftermath of the gross violence following that country's last presidential elections. Joshua Sang, a popular broadcast journalist at Kass-FM, is the only nonpolitician among the six Kenyans named by the ICC prosecutor as the alleged masterminds of the country's postelection violence. Former chief prosecutor Luis Moreno Ocampo has accused Sang of "us[ing] coded language disseminated through radio broadcasts to help coordinate the attacks."[12] While Sang made his initial appearance before ICC judges on April 7, 2011, the broadcaster has denied the charges, continuing to host his show and even campaigning for a senate seat until October 2012, when he stepped down from both the campaign and his position as a radio presenter to focus on his legal defense.[13]

At the same time, however, radio can serve to promote positive endeavors and has been widely used to do so. Indeed, radio has been employed on the continent by humanitarian and civil society NGOs and by UN agencies to promote everything from condoms and mosquito nets to registering to vote, in addition to traditional news programming. For example, Radio Okapi, a station born as a collaboration between the Swiss Agence Hirondelle and the UN Organization Stabilization Mission in the DRC (MONUSCO), has contributed enormously by providing reliable and relatively unbiased information throughout the DRC—news that most Congolese had no access to before the station's establishment.[14] In addition, small community radio stations that may only broadcast five to ten kilometers function as the heartbeat of rural communities—allowing people to communicate from village to village and informing communities on a variety of topics from purifying water to the next visiting clinic, the movements of armed militia, the birth of a child, or a marriage in the village. Radio's impact as arguably the most effective means of mass communication on the continent is clear to anyone who has lived or worked in sub-Saharan Africa.

Still, discussions on human rights, justice, and the rule of law—especially in regions that are reeling from the most extreme destruction and violence a society can experience—are very slippery endeavors. Simply informing the public that justice has arrived is not particularly effective, at least not in the DRC, Uganda, the CAR, Kenya, or Sudan. In such contexts, imposing a set of standards on people without taking into consideration the complexity of the conflicts, as well as the cultural and political implications of that imposition, is impossible; too many questions, too many sides, and too many interests have been involved in these long-term and complicated conflicts for the application and public acceptance of justice to be a straightforward matter. Why had the ICC not arrested Bosco Ntaganda when an arrest warrant had been issued against him and he continues to live openly in—and hold much control over—the city of Goma? Indeed, Ntaganda's walking into the US Embassy in Kigali to turn himself in on March 18, 2013, was a complete surprise and undoubtedly a result of a contextual situation of which the ICC is only a small part. Why are the forces of international justice not holding leaders accountable in the countries that have pillaged the DRC? Why has the ICC arrested no one in power in Kinshasa? Congolese on the ground are asking these questions. Who will answer them? Not the media on their own, surely. And if these concerns aren't addressed, the communities that are targeted by the ICC will likely have reason to perceive justice as selective. Moreover, what about the role of victims at the ICC? How will these communities get information about participating in trials, and how will they take part in the ongoing debate about what constitutes a victim in the eyes of the court? These questions have not even been decided definitively by the ICC itself, so it is hardly sufficient for journalists to merely inform people on policies that will hopefully be decided with the input of these same communities. If target communities are not involved in this debate, they will not be engaged enough to make full use of the dramatic evolution in international justice that the ICC offers. These questions demand input and consensus from a variety of participants, and while conventional media can facilitate the flow of information, the target communities and the responsible authorities—not the media—must be in charge of this conversation.

TRADITIONAL MEDIA APPROACHES: PROMOTING GOOD JOURNALISM TO PROMOTE GOOD JUSTICE

A host of international NGOs specialize in training journalists on reporting on international justice, and these organizations themselves often report on the work of international tribunals—for the target audiences where tribunals are investigating and for the international community at large. These NGOs undertake their activities in the belief that responsible reporting on international justice helps target populations to understand and respect the rule of law and to support the functioning of international criminal justice by following and even participating in the proceedings. These NGOs work either in parallel or in direct collaboration with international tribunals to encourage an increased level of professionalism among journalists and more prominent news coverage by media outlets in target communities on the work of international tribunals. The main groups currently working in regions involved with international justice are presented here, as examples of the traditional approach to working with media in such contexts.

Fondation Hirondelle is a Swiss NGO that has been operational since 1995, training journalists in conflict and post-conflict situations in areas such as newswriting, content programming, and media management.[15] Fondation Hirondelle procures funding for and serves as a consultant to local radio stations; at times the NGO creates its own stations, seeking to offer local journalists the means to report independently in contexts where doing so is difficult because of poor infrastructure as well as political instability. As stated in its charter, Hirondelle seeks to promote the human right to information in places where it is threatened by a lack of impartiality, rigor, and professionalism.[16]

Since its establishment, Hirondelle has worked in Kosovo, Nepal, and Timor Leste, among other nations. Currently, the NGO has projects in Tanzania, the DRC, the CAR, Liberia, Sierra Leone, and Sudan. For example, Hirondelle works in the pressroom at the ICTR in Arusha, Tanzania, where it has covered trial activity for more than ten years; in early 2011 Hirondelle began to cover the ICC's trials for the DRC, the CAR, and Sudan. In addition, through a collaboration with MONUSCO, in 2002 the two organizations created Radio Okapi, the DRC's first national radio station, which, as already mentioned, has been instrumental in raising awareness about the UN mission's work. Hirondelle projects are often carried out in close partnership with UN agencies and other international actors, such as the International Committee of the Red Cross (ICRC).

The Institute for War and Peace Reporting (IWPR) is a British/US NGO that dedicates itself to training and reporting in war zones and post-conflict situations.[17] The institute's work focuses on promoting high standards of journalism, supporting local media outlets, and providing a platform for local voices to contribute to international policy debates. In order to do so, the IWPR offers an apprentice-style mentoring program in which experienced journalists accompany local reporters as they investigate and develop stories in the field; the institute also provides training on specific issues such as human rights and elections reporting.

The IWPR has specialized in international justice reporting, with projects that focus on the ICTY and the ICC. For example, the institute holds training seminars for Balkan journalists on covering the work of the ICTY and offers internships in The Hague for Congolese journalists to learn how to report on ICC trials. The stated aim of the institute is to "[increase] the level of public information and responsible debate ... forge skills and capacity of local journalism, strengthen local media institutions and engage with civil society and governments to ensure that information achieves impact."[18]

Internews Network is a US NGO that was founded in 1982 and operates in more than seventy countries to train and support journalists' work.[19] Internews works in conflict and post-conflict zones and in countries with poor track records for independent journalism; the network has also operated projects specifically around transitional justice processes, including broadcasting the proceedings of the ICTY. Most of its activities involve training and support for journalists who work in difficult environments. For example, the Internews Reporting for Peace program has trained "hundreds of print and radio journalists how to move beyond the 'body count' style of war reporting," developing local reporters' understanding of conflict dynamics and causes in order to improve the quality of their work.[20] Internews also provides production grants for new journalism projects focused on promoting human rights, and the group has supported fair-media legislation in several countries.

The BBC World Service Trust is the British Broadcasting Corporation's international charity organization.[21] The trust engages in training and providing technical support for journalists worldwide. Between 2007 and 2009 the BBC World Service Trust ran a Communicating Justice project in partnership with the International Center for Transitional Justice (ICTJ) and Search for Common Ground (SFCG) to train journalists in Burundi, the DRC, Liberia, Sierra Leone, and Uganda. The project's purpose was to raise awareness and enhance debate about transitional justice mechanisms, including international tribunals, the ICC, and various truth and reconciliation commissions.[22] As part of this project, the BBC World Service Trust and the ICTJ, seeking to improve coverage on the subject, published a handbook for journalists that provides a "quick-reference manual on key TJ issues."[23] The BBC World Service Trust also carried out a project to support a team of Liberian and Sierra Leonean reporters covering the trial of former Liberian president Charles Taylor from the courtroom in The Hague and to promote the development of local media outlets in these countries to produce their own content about the trial.

An independent and professional press that provides timely and accurate information while facilitating informed discussions of public interest issues is essential for the proper functioning of a strong civil society in democratic countries. By informing citizens about a justice system's proceedings and monitoring the system's performance, an independent press plays a key role in ensuring that the rule of law functions properly and that it is respected by and protects the powerful and the powerless. But does training journalists and increasing the quality and quantity of reporting about justice have an actual impact on justice in places where international justice operates? This question becomes even more difficult to answer in places where those who are in power inhibit or even, as in Rwanda, outlaw the independent press through legal or extralegal means.[24] However, journalists who have received training from these NGOs clearly do produce better and more copy on justice, demonstrating that such strategies succeed in provoking more thinking and a stronger focus on justice issues among those who work in the press. In so doing, these trained journalists help create more opportunities for the general public to be informed at some level, even if much of what is produced is censored.

NONTRADITIONAL APPROACHES: USING MEDIA AND TECHNOLOGY TO FOSTER A PUBLIC AWARENESS ON JUSTICE

Working side by side with organizations and people operating traditional media projects are a handful of NGOs that for years have employed less conventional approaches for using media to support the strengthening of civil society. I note their work here to provide a model of creative strategies that can inspire appreciation and respect for the rule of law and participation in nonviolent forums for resolving conflicts. By using traveling video and community radio, for example, people who don't normally have a voice in their societies can ask the questions and make their own decisions as to what to talk about on air. The media are also attractive as tools for encouraging participatory social discussions. Tens of thousands of people can be invited simultaneously into a dialogue with a radio program, and hearing neighbors rather than a journalist or some distant authority speak on subjects of concern to them encourages people to participate in the dialogue themselves as protagonists and not as mere passive observers.

I briefly present several examples of organizations that have adopted nontraditional approaches to the use of media to foster social change, social participation, and respect for human rights.

Witness is a US NGO begun in 1992 by British musician Peter Gabriel, who realized the powerful potential for average citizens with handheld video cameras to document human rights violations. The organization has distributed cameras and trained people to document, publish, and archive records of human rights violations in more than seventy countries, in order to support efforts to end and redress abuses, including the prosecution of crimes and truth-telling processes. Witness also helps local organizations publicize and disseminate such footage through international media outlets and among government officials, international organizations, and activist networks. Its stated mission of using "video to open the eyes of the world to human rights violations . . . [and] to empower people to transform personal stories of abuse into powerful tools for justice, promoting public engagement and policy change,"[25] explains succinctly why Witness represents a unique and dynamic model for using media to encourage engagement with justice. Of specific relevance to transitional justice processes, Witness ran a special campaign on gender-based violence in the midst of armed conflicts. The project produced video footage to be submitted as evidence to the ICC to support its investigations on the Central African Republic.[26] The Witness Media Archive preserves all footage recorded by the organization or its partners, making it available to human rights advocates, prosecutors, and the general public.

SFCG is another US NGO founded in 1982. Its core focus is conflict management, but its strategy of leveraging popular opinion to forge peaceful dialogue lends itself to media projects, which have been part of SFCG's work since the early 1990s. The crossover into projects that touch on transitional justice has come naturally for SFCG over the last decade. As mentioned earlier, SFCG partnered with ICTJ and the BBC World Service Trust to implement a series of training sessions for journalists on transitional justice. SFCG projects use "innovative tools and wor[k] at different levels of society" to "engage in pragmatic long-term processes of conflict transformation." Its "toolbox includes media production—radio, TV, film, and print—mediation and facilitation, training, community organizing, sports, theater, and music."[27] Through its Common Ground Productions unit, the Radio for Peacebuilding Africa project operates in eight African countries, providing resources for African journalists to produce radio programming that fosters dialogue and peaceful problem solving; the unit also produces a number of TV programs seeking to promote intercultural understanding and impart conflict resolution skills. For example, the TV series *The Team*, which has been produced and aired in a number of African countries, uses a soccer squad comprising players from diverse backgrounds as a metaphor for cooperation and understanding in pursuit of common goals. Search for Common Ground works in seventeen countries, many of which have been seized by international justice—that is, formally identified by justice institutions for investigation—or have ongoing transitional justice initiatives in progress, including Angola, Burundi, Côte d'Ivoire, the DRC, Guinea, Indonesia, Iran, Liberia, Macedonia, the Middle East (with offices in Jerusalem and Amman), Nigeria, and Sierra Leone.

Radio La Benevolencija Humanitarian Tools Foundation (La Benevolencija) is a Dutch NGO that focuses its activities on grassroots projects to combat divisive responses to conflict, such as hate speech, prejudice, and violence. The NGO also has worked in regions devastated by war and seized by international justice, including Rwanda, Burundi, and the DRC. According to its mission statement La Benevolencija works using media to empower groups and individuals who form the target of hate speech and its ensuing acts.[28] In Burundi and Rwanda, for example, La Benevolencija airs radio soap operas that seek to promote peaceful discussions on the history of confrontations between Hutus and Tutsis without falling back into ethnic stereotypes. Soap operas in the DRC also provide listeners with tools for conflict prevention and resolution. Additionally, the organization broadcasts news, talk shows, and debates, often inviting local leaders and officials to respond to questions from listeners and the general public. All of La Benevolencija's projects are reviewed by experts and advisors in the fields of psychology, trauma, and education, in order to promote healing and avoid causing unintended harm when addressing sensitive issues.

Internews Network, as mentioned earlier, is an NGO that specializes in journalist training in places where an independent media is lacking, usually in societies experiencing serious social and political transition. In contrast to the projects discussed earlier, its Justice after Genocide project was unique in its effort to engage directly and interactively with Rwandan citizens regarding the country's ongoing transitional justice processes. The strategy was to screen throughout the country using mobile cinema an informational video about the ICTR and the ways that it functions within the national justice system; the project was an effort to spark discussions among Rwandans regarding the different justice recourses available to them after the genocide of 1994.[29] The target audiences included the accused and people who considered themselves victims of genocide. The official goal was the transfer of information, but the most compelling part of the project was its use of the films to give voice to and encourage conversations among people in Rwanda who had lived through the genocide, whether they identified themselves as perpetrators or victims. After each screening, which would highlight recent activity in the ICTR and national courts, the team would film a discussion with the audience in which they had the chance to pose questions and concerns. These films became a channel for communication between citizens and authorities; if someone posed a question, the organization would follow through by recording an authority's response for the next film. The films also facilitated communication between prisoners and victims—many times former neighbors—and family members who had been separated for years.

As the project was implemented, the most important factor in building a consciousness about the role of justice in Rwandan society was apparently not what the authorities said—and not even what the ICTR was doing—but what the people said about it, asked about it, and gained by having their voices heard. The project made uniquely beneficial use of the media: most authorities working at the ICTR never went to Rwanda, and most Rwandans had no access to either their national or ICTR authorities. The films were the only available means to enable contact and make discourse possible. The project screened these bimonthly films at the ICTR in Arusha (Tanzania), in all of the sixteen provincial prisons in Rwanda, and in at least two Rwandan villages in each province. The films averaged twenty thousand viewers per month.

Projects that adopt an unconventional, participatory approach can offer unique and substantive contributions to transitional justice processes. The line between conflict management and transitional justice becomes blurred in these regions, where conflict runs so deep and has become so violent, and citizens search for creative ways to forge peace and justice. Soap operas on the radio that address real conflicts, such as those produced by SFCG and La Benevolencija, are developed as truth-finding and reconciliation mechanisms. They are designed to present the reality of people's suffering in a nonviolent, nonthreatening way that encourages dialogue. In addition to promoting peacebuilding and conflict resolution in the midst of violence or in post-conflict settings, La Benevolencija, SFCG, Witness, and Internews can arguably be seen as facilitating or promoting the goals of transitional justice interventions, as they are each, through their own models, using dialogue to help wounded societies face the concerns that divide them. Each of these projects uses media in a nontraditional way—outside of classic journalism or reporting—to engage their target communities. The reason that these projects are successful is that they place the media's tools in the hands of the citizens with whom the projects are attempting to engage. The media become public in the truest sense, and people start to see media as a tool that is relevant to their lives. Giving ownership of the media to the public through journalism can be risky, but the strategy is a natural one if the goal is to support the strengthening of participatory civil society on issues as inherently social as justice and respect for the rule of law.

USING RADIO TO PROMOTE DIALOGUE ABOUT JUSTICE: THE CASE OF INTERACTIVE RADIO FOR JUSTICE (IRFJ)

> Interactive Radio for Justice is a very, very new, interesting tool, because basically, what I see is international institutions failing to enrich local communities in a way that [they] will appreciate, that's local—no formal messages, no Western messages. And I think in this sense, the Interactive Radio program is very, very useful and interesting. In part today, six years later, I'm here in Bunia, and we organized this visit through this radio project. Because we had a dialogue with the local leaders and they invited me to come.
>
> —Luis Moreno Ocampo, chief prosecutor for the International Criminal Court, Bunia, Ituri, Democratic Republic of Congo

> There's no education on the law here. And yet, they say that every citizen is supposed to know the law. In this setting, Interactive Radio for Justice on Radio Canal Révélation arrived at the right moment, because it makes the laws accessible. If there are questions that you're struggling with, that you can't answer, then you ask this question on Radio and the specialists try to answer your question.
>
> —A listening group member at Lopa, outside Bunia, Ituri, Democratic Republic of Congo

> We have recognized that soldiers did not adequately know the law with regard to certain infractions that they have committed. . . . The IRfJ project aids us enormously in bringing down the number of infractions committed (sexual violence, arbitrary arrest by military, etc.).
>
> —Innocent Maymbe, judge president for the military garrison tribunal in Bunia, Ituri, Democratic Republic of Congo

Interactive Radio for Justice (IRfJ) is an independent project that launched in June 2005 in Ituri, DRC, with the goal of creating an interactive and consistent opportunity for communication between communities targeted by ICC investigations and the national and international authorities responsible for administering justice for these communities. The IRfJ project was active for more than six years, closing in July 2011. Although independent of the ICC—IRfJ was financed by private foundations—the project followed the path of ICC investigations, expanding into the CAR in 2008 and in the Kivus region of the DRC in 2009.

Community radio was the project's principal medium. As we have already seen, radio is the most available and reliable tool for mass communication in these regions. Radio was chosen as the most effective means for creating this conversation because IRfJ worked in regions where land mines and armed groups pose a serious threat to security on the roads—making mobile video, for example, too dangerous—and where radio is already an established, viable, and popular source for information. At the same time, the use of radio makes it possible to create an interactive dialogue in different languages, so that all participants in the process can effectively communicate with each other, even if separated by distance, language, and real time. Programs were broadcast in French and in local languages over radio partner organizations in target regions, and listening groups were organized so that people had the opportunity to discuss justice issues among themselves as well as with national and international authorities through the programming. The project provided listening groups with radios so that they could follow the programs together, and the IRfJ teams were in regular contact with them so that listening club members could pose their questions and give feedback on programming. The listening clubs were also essential as focus groups for IRfJ to evaluate its impact in target communities.[30] Other activities supplemented the radio programs, including public meetings in target communities with high-level justice officials and the Music for Justice initiative, which engaged youth to write and perform music on justice and human rights themes.[31]

The IRfJ project was designed around five fundamental concepts that guided all activities and policy decisions:

1. A functioning justice system and respect for the rule of law are fundamental to guaranteeing a safe space for civil society to exercise its political and participatory rights. In turn, an active civil society can be an important guarantor and promoter of justice and respect for the rule of law. IRfJ therefore promoted the concept of civic participation around justice issues, believing that a more involved and educated

public would have an increased respect for the rule of law. Additionally, IRfJ worked to inform people sufficiently about the law so that the public would be able to use it as a tool to strengthen their rights as citizens and members of a democratic civil society.

2. The ICC is a public institution, financed with public funds and therefore accountable to the public—specifically to the public in all member states and symbolically to the public of all states. In this way, ICC employees are first and foremost global public servants.

3. Justice authorities and citizens living in regions under investigation both benefit from interactive dialogue. Justice authorities are more effective—their public relations projects, their investigations, their judgments, and their diplomacy initiatives all work better—if they understand and appreciate the views and concerns of citizens in target communities. Target communities are more likely to obey the law and use the law when they need it if they understand it and feel that those who uphold it are accountable.

4. IRfJ's priority was to honor the concerns of citizens living in regions under ICC investigation. The priorities and the level of knowledge of the target populations determined the rhythm of the dialogues. Questions were raised and issues discussed as they became important to the target populations, rather than as authorities deemed them important. The IRfJ motto in this regard was, "It's not about the experts—it's about the people who suffered most and who will benefit most from justice."

5. IRfJ created the space for dialogue but did not advocate on its own. Programming was initiated by citizens' questions, which IRfJ would record to address later to the relevant authorities, officers, or experts, depending on the particular question, and then continue the conversation by soliciting follow-up questions. IRfJ's role was moderating the dialogue, playing neither the role of a journalist deciding what questions to ask nor that of an expert answering questions or taking an advocacy stance.

IRfJ was not a journalistic project as much as a project aimed to strengthen civil society, creatively using media technology to achieve its goal. Journalists on its local teams were trained to use their medium to listen to and engage citizens, rather than reporting on or to them. Programming was designed by consensus with the local teams and evolved along with the current of public interest, in order to attend to the concerns and needs of the target communities. This model showed that questions from listeners became more nuanced and sophisticated over time as their knowledge of the law increased; their trust in international justice officials also increased as they followed the programs over the years, posing questions and hearing responses that officials offered through the programming.[32] The different series of programming produced by IRfJ local teams—which were created in Bunia, Goma, and Kasugho in the DRC, and in Bangui (the capital city) and five rural towns in the CAR—were all interactive in nature and addressed a variety of justice and human rights concerns in the target communities:

1. *Base Series:* The basic idea for this series was to record questions from citizens on local, national, and international justice issues, and then record responses to each question from relevant justice officials. Programs were subsequently edited to sound like a conversation between citizens and authorities. Questions were as diverse as the listening public. Within one program, officials might address questions such as, "What are my rights to visit my husband in the local prison?"; "If I sleep with a prostitute who is under eighteen, will she be arrested for prostitution or will I be arrested for rape?"; and "Why does the prosecutor for the ICC not investigate the crimes that members of our government are committing in Kinshasa?"[33] The novelty of this format was that citizens who had never had a voice in their society had the opportunity to hear themselves on the radio and to hear authorities at local, national, and international levels acknowledge and respond to their questions. This aspect made the series very popular in all of the places where IRfJ worked. The team in Bunia would visit different villages in the Ituri region each month so that citizens in rural communities who heard the programming could feel that these programs were "theirs," since they featured their voices and questions.

2. *Debating for Justice:* In this series, one repeatedly asked or particularly controversial question was addressed by four or five authorities through a debate. IRfJ then invited international and local authorities to discuss the issue together (by conference-call-type technology), each putting forth their own perspective so that listeners were more informed about the diversity of viewpoints on the same question, and hopefully could feel after listening to the program that they had a sufficient understanding to form their own opinions. Questions that IRfJ dealt with in this

series included, "Why does the international community insist that using children as soldiers is a crime against humanity?" and "What are civilians' rights against military and police abuse and extortion?"

3. *A Child: Yesterday in the Bush, Today Part of Our Community:* Each program in this series was dedicated to the personal story of one former child soldier. The child recounted his or her story in the first person. The project made an effort to include children from all groups that fought during the war and to feature children from each ethnic group implicated in the conflict, as well as having boys and girls tell their stories. This series was launched shortly after the ICC arrested Thomas Lubanga on three counts of using children in war.

4. *Our Reconciliation:* Communities that had reconciled on their own initiative without outside assistance told their stories in this series through the voices of community members. These stories of grassroots conflict resolution were presented as possible models for communities still in conflict within the region. An additional result of broadcasting the success stories of these rural communities was that international organizations working in the region heard the programs over the radio and were inspired to invest in these isolated villages in order to support their efforts to reconstruct their lives in a peaceful manner.[34]

5. *Our Dialogue for Peace and Justice:* After following the concerns of Iturians through the base series, ICC chief prosecutor Luis Moreno Ocampo joined the dialogue with this community by posing questions to the Ituri leadership. In a sequential process, he would raise a question that IRfJ then brought to political, military, religious, and judicial leaders in order to record their responses. The prosecutor's question and the various responses were then broadcast as a radio program. The prosecutor listened to the responses via the programming and then posed a follow-up question for the next program, and hence the dialogue would continue. This series, which produced four programs, played an important role in the prosecutor's first visit to Ituri in 2009 as he was invited to come to Bunia through a consensus of local leaders. The invitation was broadcast in this series.

6. *On the Track of Justice:* IRfJ journalists were brought to the ICC during key points in the trials to produce programming in local languages. The first programs in this series covered the start of Thomas Lubanga's trial in January 2009. The second group focused on the opening of the

trial of Germaine Katanga and Matthieu Ngudjolo in November 2009; the third visit was organized for the start of Jean Pierre Bemba's trial in November 2010. This programming was produced using trial footage recorded directly from the courtrooms, as well as interviews with relevant ICC authorities and questions from the listening public in target communities.

7. *Justice Magazine:* This series addressed a variety of justice-related questions through a multigenre production, in which IRfJ used drama, listener commentary, and responses by a justice official who was invited to the studio for each program in the series. An integral part of these programs was person-on-the-street recordings, in which a variety of citizens' voices were heard with regard to a particular question.

WORKING RESPONSIBLY IN VOLATILE ENVIRONMENTS

Whether using traditional or more experimental approaches to media to address the issues of international criminal law, transitional justice, or the rule of law, practitioners must be conscious of the volatility of peace and justice issues and the divisions that exist in war-torn communities. In these contexts, only objective, balanced, and rigorous reporting makes it possible to engage these topics without exacerbating the existing unrest or instability. One important goal in the immediate aftermath of conflict is to provide the population with the tools to learn about important human rights and justice questions that concern them and that have long been neglected in their immediate contexts. For a classic journalist, this approach may feel at times like a compromise; a journalist, after all, is trained to learn and understand objective facts and present them as such. But the objective facts, such as they are, usually vary drastically from one person to another, depending on personal circumstances, history, and perspective. Such differences may be even more pronounced in strongly divided post-conflict societies. Therefore, when working in such environments, journalists who seek to establish justice-related projects must be aware of the role they play in order to not cause more harm.

Another important challenge in this respect may derive from the media landscape itself. While editorial programming plays an important role in promoting discussion and shaping public opinion, its impact may be diminished or especially negative in places where the average listener has limited access to diverse views and alternative information sources. For example, a survey conducted in eastern Congo found that only 4 percent of respondents read newspapers on a daily basis, compared to 67 percent who relied on radio and 23 percent who relied on informal channels of communication with other community members. Moreover, a majority did not trust newspapers or believe that journalists had more than "a little" freedom to report openly on social and political issues.[35] In such contexts, individuals have little recourse to secondary sources of information and opinions, leaving them unable to confirm or contradict the few sources they can access, and offering few opportunities to gain experience in assessing the reliability of reporting in general. While problems of real or perceived media bias and self-selecting audiences are widespread in all societies, these issues are arguably qualitatively more extreme in areas with more profound divisions and where a lack of infrastructure severely curtails the number and range of sources that the population can access. As a result, the kinds of editorial and opinion journalism that might be used to promote awareness of justice issues will be less effective in this context, because they are already viewed as biased or divisive. A Lendu in Bunia is typically skeptical of anything he hears on a radio station affiliated with a Hema political party, for example. A Tutsi in Rwanda would probably still be hesitant to listen to a Radio Hirondelle report, almost twenty years after this station was accused of allowing pro-Hutu hate speech into its programming. Finding neutral media outlets to work with and gaining the trust of communities that feel unfairly targeted by the media are constant challenges for journalists reporting on such divided communities. Overcoming these challenges might well require a long-term process.[36]

When using media in civil society–strengthening projects in regions where international or transitional justice processes are taking place, the focus should remain on how to use the media to give voice to community members in a manner that does not isolate or aggravate any particular group. Many times, these projects not only offer a new and different form of communication but also provide the only channel of communication available that is nonconfrontational and promotes a sustained and peaceful dialogue. This ability to provide a channel for peaceful dialogue is an important advantage for projects that are interactive and sustained versus projects that train journalists to responsibly report and present information. In IRfJ's activities, for example, the prerecorded talk show has emerged as an excellent genre for allowing two groups to talk with each other; the protective buffer of time and space allows each side the chance to process what the other says and to formulate responses that move the dialogue forward. Journalists trusted on both sides of the conversation as neutral intermediaries relay between the two groups—recording questions from citizens and responses from authorities, and then broadcasting the exchanges in languages that everyone involved can understand.

Once a minimum level of trust exists between communities, live participatory talk radio could become an interesting tool because it allows each group to experience the other in an immediate sense, giving the listeners a heightened feeling of engagement. Conversations in which the focus is on past crimes or specific present problems—rather than on the members of a group that committed these crimes—might contribute to establishing an interactive approach in which individuals on different sides of a conflict can engage with each other as people rather than as opposing group members. Through this type of immediate dialogue, rapport can be established, and citizens can feel that they are on the same team, working to establish respect for their country's rule of law. In order for a live exchange to be productive and viable, however, a common desire must be present for genuine dialogue, as well as a common understanding of the priorities of the discussion, a certain level of trust, and a common language. This type of live dialogue was not possible for the IRfJ project, mainly because of logistical restraints—notably the distance and languages that separate the people between whom IRfJ aimed to forge a dialogue. The project tried to compensate by organizing public meetings that were held in communities targeted by ICC investigations and by inviting high-level ICC officials to come to the regions to respond directly to citizens' questions. In this way IRfJ created a live debate facilitated through translators on site and then recorded these meetings in order to broadcast them in local languages. As a result, the general listening audience could have access to the information exchanged.[37]

CONCLUSION

The media—the press and the technology that the press traditionally uses—offer seductive and powerful tools for fostering social innovation and public dialogue. The evolution of communications over the last fifteen years has completely transformed how we view control over the media and the potential to effect social change. The mobile phone and Internet have become tools for public assembly and disseminating images of social unrest and human rights abuse. As organizations like Witness have shown, these images can be used to bring justice as well as to build international support for social revolutions (as we have seen most recently in Tunisia, Egypt, Yemen, Syria, and Libya).

The training of journalists and increased reporting on international criminal justice and transitional justice issues certainly represents a positive resource in societies reeling from violence and destruction. A professional and independent press is essential for a peaceful democracy to form and thrive. Reading or hearing information that one can trust offers solace and hope that cannot be dismissed. However, adding the use of media tools to engage average citizens so that they can participate in and even direct public dialogue can jump-start a meaningful conversation on the rule of law and respect for human rights. These types of initiatives need to be created and managed with vigilance and responsibility, especially in societies in which general access to the media is limited and independent media practices are still nascent.

Even when using the media, at least a generation may pass before real change develops from the seeds of social awareness on justice, human rights, and the rule of law, because social awareness demands more than an immediate image or message sent over the Internet. From my own experience I have felt the impact when people are touched, inspired, and motivated by productive dialogue.

It is encouraging that listening groups in the DRC showed an evolving understanding and appreciation of the law over their six years of participating in the IRfJ project, that listeners expected their local authorities as well as international authorities to respond in earnest to their questions, and that impact analysis showed an increased knowledge level and strong participation in its programs among authorities at local, national, and international levels.[38] Will IRfJ's programs bring significant social change in communities gutted by war, violence against civilians, destitute poverty, and virtual impunity for not only corruption but also crimes against humanity? The programs definitely cannot make such an impact on their own. IRfJ understood that people hearing their own voices on the radio and hearing high-level authorities acknowledge and respond to their concerns would give target communities the information, confidence, and encouragement they needed to continue to try to build the kind of society they desire.

To further that goal in the regions where IRfJ operated, no tool is more effective than radio. Becoming discouraged is easy when, after years of international intervention, impunity and violence still reign. But what has kept IRfJ and so many imaginative and dynamic projects working and growing is that the local partners believe that these projects—*their* projects—will make a difference in their communities. For projects like Interactive Radio for Justice, another key driving force was that listeners kept asking questions.

Returning to one of the opening questions in this chapter's introduction, I conclude by answering that, indeed, media can become an important factor in engaging people in the wake of massive conflict to help them create their own realities, have their voices as citizens heard, and honor the rule of law.

NOTES

The views expressed in this paper are my own and are not intended to represent the opinions or perspective of any organization that I have worked for in the past, nor do they necessarily reflect the views of the International Center for Transitional Justice.

1 My own experience in this realm focuses specifically on developing methods to engage average citizens in a dialogue on the rule of law and justice in places that have suffered massive crimes, including Rwanda, Burundi, the Democratic Republic of Congo (DRC), and the Central African Republic (CAR). My work in the Great Lakes Region of Africa dates from 2000, when I worked with Internews Network as country director for the Justice after Genocide project, discussed in this article. I also worked as outreach advisor for the prosecutor at the International Criminal Court during the time in which he initiated investigations in northern Uganda and the DRC, and as a development consultant for Radio Publique Africaine in Bujumbura, Burundi, before launching the Interactive Radio for Justice project in 2005, which I founded and led as its director until July 2011.

2 No Peace without Justice, "Outreach and the International Criminal Court" (NPWJ International Criminal Justice Policy Series no. 2, No Peace without Justice, New York, 2004), http://www.npwj.org/sites/default/files/documents/File/NPWJOutreachPolicyICCSep04.pdf, 1.

3 The Special Court for Sierra Leone was created in 2002, and its outreach program has been operating since its inception (Special Court for Sierra Leone, "Outreach and Public Affairs," accessed February 2011, www.sc-sl.org/ABOUT/CourtOrganization/TheRegistry/OutreachandPublicAffairs/tabid/83/Default.aspx). For more on the outreach program at the Special Court, see Maya Karwande's chapter in this volume.

4 International Criminal Court, "Outreach," accessed February 2011, www.icc-cpi.int/Menus/ICC/Structure+of+the+Court/Outreach/. For an overview of the different media activities normally organized by outreach programs, see Clara Ramírez-Barat, *Making an Impact: Guidelines on Designing and Implementing Outreach Programs for Transitional Justice* (New York: International Center for Transitional Justice, 2011), 31–33.

5 For a general account, see, for example, Gerald W. Brock, *The Second Information Revolution* (Cambridge, MA: Harvard University Press, 2003). On the other hand, some observers have also warned that although the Internet, mobile phones, and other types of new media can help citizens express their views and mobilize for political and social change, nondemocratic actors can also exploit these technologies. See Larry Diamond, "Liberation Technology," *Journal of Democracy* 21, no. 3 (2010): 69–83; and Evgeny Morozov, *The Net Delusion: The Dark Side of Internet Freedom* (New York: Public Affairs, 2011). See also Camille Crittenden's chapter in this volume.

6 See Agreement between the United Nations and the Government of Sierra Leone on the Establishment of a Special Court for Sierra Leone, January 16, 2002, http://www.sc-sl.org/LinkClick.aspx?fileticket=CLk1rMQtCHg%3d&tabid=176 and Sandesh Sivakumaran, "War Crimes before the Special Court for Sierra Leone," *Journal of International Criminal Justice* 8, no. 4 (2010): 1009–34. See also the SCSL's website, http://www.sc-sl.org.

7 See the ICC's website, http://www.icc-cpi.int.

8 The UNESCO Institute for Statistics (UIS) estimates that adult literacy rates in sub-Saharan Africa average 62 percent, with women disproportionately constituting more than 60 percent of illiterate adults in the region (UIS Statistics in Brief, "Regional Literacy Profile—Sub-Saharan Africa," 2011, http://stats.uis.unesco.org/unesco/TableViewer/document.aspx?ReportId=367&IF_Language=eng&BR_Region=40540).

9 See Lishan Adam and Frances Wood, "An Investigation of the Impact of Information and Communication Technologies in Sub-Saharan Africa," *Journal of Information Science* 25, no. 4 (1999): 303–18. Radio's reach throughout sub-Saharan Africa is not universal, however. It is, though, the most powerful and far-reaching mass media in the region by far. For example, a lack of radios and the batteries necessary to operate them may prevent many people from accessing radio broadcasts in regions such as the eastern DRC (Human Rights Watch, "Courting History: The Landmark International Court's First Years" [New York: Human Rights Watch, 2008]), and a survey conducted in the CAR found that 41 percent of respondents never have access to a radio at all, including 52 percent of women (Patrick Vinck and Phuong N. Pham, "Outreach Evaluation: The International Criminal Court in the Central African Republic," *International Journal of Transitional Justice* 4 [2010]: 433).

10 Patrick Vinck, Phuong Pham, Suliman Baldo, and Rachel Shigekane, *Living with Fear: A Population-Based Survey on Attitudes about Peace, Justice, and Social Reconstruction in Eastern Democratic Republic of Congo* (Berkeley: Human Rights Center at the University of California, Berkeley; Payson Center for International Development at Tulane University; and International Center for Transitional Justice, 2008), http://ictj.org/sites/default/files/ICTJ-DRC-Attitudes-Justice-2008-English.pdf, 53.

11 See Timothy Longman's chapter in this volume. See also Allan Thompson, ed., *The Media and the Rwandan Genocide* (London: Pluto Press, 2007).

12 Linawati Sidarto, "RTLM Ghost Looms over Kenya," *International Justice Tribune*, February 2, 2011, www.rnw.nl/international-justice/article/rtlm-ghost-looms-over-kenya.

13 Nicholas Wamala, "Kenya: Sang Pulls Out of Senator Race," *The Star* (Nairobi), hosted on the AllAfrica website, October 15, 2012, http://allafrica.com/stories/201210161236.html.

14 Studies have also found that of those in northern Uganda and the CAR who were aware of the ICC, 87 and 90 percent, respectively, had heard of it through the radio. See Phoung Pham et al., *When the War Ends: A Population-Based Survey on Attitudes about Peace, Justice,*

and Social Reconstruction in Northern Uganda (Berkeley: Human Rights Center at the University of California, Berkeley; Payson Center for International Development at Tulane University; and the International Center for Transitional Justice, 2007), 38; and Vinck and Pham, "Outreach Evaluation," 433.

15 Fondation Hirondelle, accessed February 2011, www.hirondelle.org/category/la-fondation-hirondelle/.

16 See "La charte de la Fondation Hirondelle," *Fondation Hirondelle*, accessed February 2011, http://www.hirondelle.org/la-charte-de-la-fondation-hirondelle.

17 Institute for War and Peace Reporting, accessed February 2011, http://iwpr.net. See also Institute for War and Peace Reporting, *Reporting Justice: A Handbook on Covering War Crimes Courts* (Johannesburg: IWPR, 2006).

18 "What We Do," Institute for War and Peace Reporting, accessed November 2012, http://iwpr.net/what-we-do.

19 Internews Network, accessed February 2011, www.internews.org.

20 "Global Issues," Internews Network, accessed February 2011, http://www.internews.org/global/conflict/default.shtm.

21 BBC World Service Trust, accessed February 2011, www.bbc.co.uk/worldservice/trust.

22 Communicating Justice, accessed February 2011, http://www.communicatingjustice.org.

23 See *Reporting Transitional Justice: A Handbook for Journalists* (London: BBC World Service Trust and International Center for Transitional Justice), http://www.communicatingjustice.org/files/content/file/TJ%20Handbook%20-%20Jan%2008.pdf.

24 See, for example, *Amnesty International, Safer to Stay Silent: The Chilling Effects of Rwanda's Laws on "Genocide Ideology" and "Sectarianism,"* AFR 47/005/2010 (London: Amnesty International, 2010); Amnesty International, *Unsafe to Speak Out: Restrictions on Freedom of Expression in Rwanda* (London: Amnesty International, 2011); and Lars Waldorf, "Censorship and Propaganda in Post-Genocide Rwanda," in Thompson, *Media and the Rwandan Genocide*, 404–16. For an in-depth discussion of the media restrictions in Rwanda, see Timothy Longman's chapter in this volume.

25 Witness, accessed February 2011, www.witness.org.

26 "Gender-Based Violence in the Context of Armed Conflict Campaign," Witness, accessed February 2011, http://www.witness.org/campaigns/gender-based-violence-context-armed-conflict.

27 "About Search for Common Ground," Search for Common Ground, accessed February 2011, http://sfcg.org/sfcg/sfcg_intro.html.

28 Radio La Benevolencija, www.labenevolencija.org, accessed July 21, 2013.

29 I worked as country director for Tanzania and Rwanda with Internews Network from 2000 to 2003.

30 IRfJ engaged an impact assessment analyst to document the project's impact on its focus groups through quantitative and qualitative data collection. Listening clubs in

the field were an important source for this data collection, as they regularly completed questionnaires for the project and spoke in person with the analyst or assistants who made periodic visits to the groups. See Interactive Radio for Justice, "Executive Summary of First Impact Assessment Report," August 2010, http://web.archive.org/web/20120425200100/http://www.irfj.org/the-project/impact-assessment/; Interactive Radio for Justice, *Executive Summary of Second Impact Assessment Report,* May 2011. The IRfJ website has been taken down, but an archived version of the site from June 19, 2012, is available through the Wayback Machine Internet Archive (http://archive.org/web/web.php). All links are to the archived site.

31 See Interactive Radio for Justice, accessed February 2011, http://web.archive.org/web/20120619042047/http:/www.irfj.org/. The IRfJ website allowed the international community to follow and engage in its activities as well.

32 See Interactive Radio for Justice, "Executive Summary of First Impact Assessment Report."

33 All programs produced by IRfJ are available as mp3 files at http://web.archive.org/web/20120619042047/http:/www.irfj.org/ (in French with accompanying English transcripts).

34 The UN Educational, Scientific, and Cultural Organization (UNESCO) and the International Federation of Red Cross and Red Crescent Societies both contacted the local team in Bunia to reach out to villages highlighted in these programs. One village was given assistance putting in a paved road between two former combating communities, and another received aid to build a school for Lendu and Hema children in the village.

35 Vinck, Pham, Baldo, and Shigekane, *Living with Fear,* 53.

36 For a discussion of similar problems in the former Yugoslavia, see the chapter by Nidžara Ahmetašević and Tanja Matić in this volume. See also the chapter in this volume by Timothy Longman on the media in Rwanda.

37 ICC officials who participated in the three public meetings that IRfJ organized included the ICC registrar, deputy prosecutor, chief prosecutor, and the chief counsel for Thomas Lubanga, the first person to be put on trial at the ICC.

38 According to impact assessments, the project's greatest strength lay in prompting change in listeners' knowledge about their national and international authorities and improving their perceptions about those authorities' work. See Interactive Radio for Justice, *Executive Summary of Second Impact Assessment Report.* See also Interactive Radio for Justice, "Executive Summary of First Impact Assessment Report."

CHAPTER 8

Using Media to Foster Mutual Respect and Understanding among Children in a Post-Conflict Region: The *Rruga Sesam/Ulica Sezam* Project in Kosovo

Charlotte F. Cole and June H. Lee

Sesame Street is arguably the world's best-known educational children's television program.[1] Created by Sesame Workshop (then known as the Children's Television Workshop, CTW) in 1969 the television series had a simple mission: to use television to help children, especially boys and girls from low-income families, to gain the skills needed in preparation for school entry. *Sesame Street* aimed to have a transformative effect and aspired to be an equalizer by helping to provide children from low-income homes with the same preparation as their peers from wealthier households. The series broke new ground in many important respects in the early 1970s[2] by employing television, then a relatively new technology, to simultaneously entertain and educate. *Sesame Street* was also the first children's television show to depict people of different ethnicities and backgrounds living in the same neighborhood. This racial integration concept was so controversial at the time that when the series first aired in the United States, one state—Mississippi—vetoed the broadcast on Mississippi public television of *Sesame Street*, citing racial grounds.[3] Forty-one years later, *Sesame Street* continues its efforts to help children reach their highest potentials through television and other media—now on six continents around the world.

In this chapter we provide an overview of Sesame Workshop's international work, with a focus on its projects in regions subject to prolonged conflict. We begin by outlining the organization's work in this content area and then describe the process by which Sesame Workshop engages in international coproductions (i.e., locally created or adapted versions) of *Sesame Street*. We also include a more in-depth review—as a case study example—of the background and impact of one project: a coproduction in Kosovo. We conclude with a discussion of the lessons learned from the project, the critical elements that accounted for its effectiveness, and its applicability in transitional justice settings.

SESAME STREET IN POST-CONFLICT ENVIRONMENTS

The media have historically played an important role in transitional societies, from reporting on conflict to mediating post-conflict dialogue and sustaining transitional justice measures. In such settings, however, media efforts have rarely made children the target audience. Researchers have found that children as young as preschoolers begin to form stereotypical perceptions of members of different cultural groups.[4] Given the prominence of the media in many children's lives, carefully designed media programs can be powerful tools to aid in building a culture of peace and respect for human rights.

Sesame Workshop's work in the post-conflict arena has centered on introducing children from oppositional groups to one another. The program seeks to provide concrete ways for children from different life circumstances to appreciate their differences and to experience their common humanity. With local adaptations in more than thirty countries, *Sesame Street* has addressed many relevant issues that confront children and families around the globe. In some parts of the world, the series concentrates on promoting social inclusion among children from different backgrounds and mutual respect and understanding across divides. These efforts manifest themselves in different ways on various projects. For example, the focus might be reducing prejudice and improving race relations in the United States; encouraging and providing role models for girls in Egypt, India, and elsewhere; destigmatizing people infected or affected by HIV/AIDS in South Africa and Tanzania; highlighting the individuality and skills of children with physical disabilities in Bangladesh, Canada, and France; and, of particular relevance to transitional justice frameworks, introducing children from different cultural backgrounds to each other in Israel, Palestine, Kosovo, and Northern Ireland.

Many of Sesame Workshop's efforts in this arena take place in regions affected by protracted conflict. Focused work in this area began with projects in the Middle East, including a cooperative effort between Palestinian and Israeli producers who created the *Rechov Sumsum* (the Hebrew translation of *Sesame Street*) and *Shara'a Simsim* (*Sesame Street* in Arabic) programs, which aired in the late 1990s on Israel Educational Television (IETV) and the Ma'an Network in the Palestinian Territories, respectively. The joint project was conceived at a time of new hope and optimism about the situation in the Middle East prompted by the 1993 Oslo Accords and the famed handshake on the White House lawn that took place between Yitzhak Rabin and Yasser Arafat during the Clinton administration.

The success of *Rechov Sumsum/Shara'a Simsim* and other projects led Sesame Workshop to pursue additional efforts, including *Takalani Sesame*, a series in

South Africa that embraced the country's rich diversity and aimed to introduce children of different racial backgrounds to one other; *Sesame Tree* in Northern Ireland, which was designed to help build a shared future among children living in a post-conflict region; and the *Rruga Sesam/Ulica Sezam* program in Kosovo, which sought to introduce children from the Albanian, Serbian, Turkish, and Roma ethnicities—who were living in a region of conflict and ethnic discord—to one another and help humanize the face of the other.

Research examining the educational effectiveness of these projects has found measurable changes in children's perceptions of the other after exposure.[5] Notably, the greatest documented benefit has been for children from the least disenfranchised groups, pointing to a need—as articulated further in the Kosovo case study we present later in this chapter—for efforts that more specifically target the different needs of all the groups in the viewing audience. Underpinning these efforts is the importance of building bridges across cultural divides for children living in regions of conflict. Helping children see the common elements of their human experiences is a large part of *Sesame Street*'s intent. With live-action films that feature a diversity of children engaged in everyday activities—such as going to school, playing in a park, visiting a grandparent, observing a parent executing a craft, celebrating a holiday, or practicing a religious ritual—children from different groups learn about the aspects of their lives that are similar and those that are different. Such segments are presented as an antidote to negative images—coming from journalistic and other media—that dominate the screen and that highlight conflict and struggle. The producers' hope is that, in building an understanding of the ways that other children live, viewers will begin to respect others and gain a more positive perception of them.

PROMOTING RESPECT AND UNDERSTANDING: LOCAL APPLICATION OF THE SESAME WORKSHOP MODEL

Sesame Street travels internationally in a variety of ways. Originally crafted for English-speaking audiences, in some countries where it has been exported, such as Australia and the United Kingdom, viewers see essentially the same version of the program as broadcast in the United States (with some shifts to accommodate differences such as the pronunciation of the letter "z" from the US "zee" to the local "zed" and reductions of episodes' length to accommodate broadcast scheduling time constraints). On the other end of the continuum are full coproductions, which feature their own sets, characters, and educational plans as devised by local partners. Between the two ends of the continuum is

FIGURE 8.1.
Sesame Street Coproduction Localization Range.

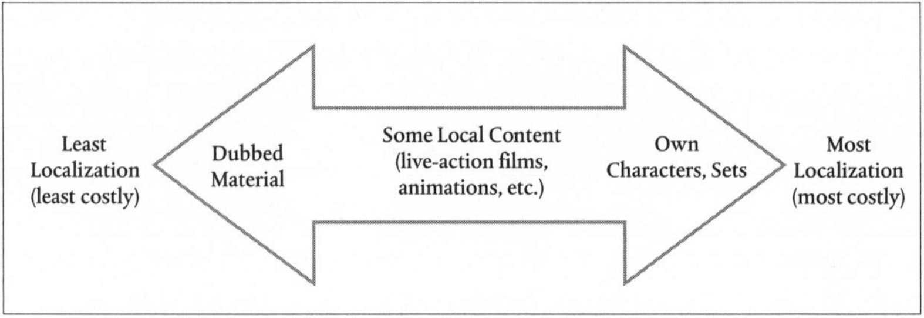

a range of other options depending upon the scale of a project, available funding, and production capacity within a region. The varying range of localization (from dubbed to more fully produced) is graphically depicted in Figure 8.1.

The value of a localized approach comes from the understanding that children learn best when educational opportunities match their own cultural context. Aspects of culture influence what skills children acquire, what they think about, how they attain information, when they are allowed to participate in certain activities, and who is allowed to participate.[6] Thus, for the purposes of learning, the more localized and culturally relevant the content, the better. Greater localization, however, comes with greater costs (money, time, and resources) and is not always the most feasible option. Sesame Workshop balances practical budgetary constraints with the need for and efficacy of culturally specific content by determining at the onset of a project the location on the continuum that brings together the capacity to develop local content with the funding available to support its creation. In general, material dubbed from Sesame Workshop's international library of already-produced content lowers the cost of a given project but does not offer a great degree of localization. Conversely, developing characters and sets locally raises the costs yet provides for material that is more meaningful and salient. Localization allows for *Sesame Street* to become, for example, a plaza in Mexico (*Plaza Sésamo*) and a train station in Norway (*Sesam Stasjon*); the characters populating the neighborhoods can be as diverse as a Bengal tiger in Bangladesh (named Halum), a meerkat (Moishe) in South Africa, and a brown bear (Samson) in Germany.

The internationalization of *Sesame Street* began soon after its inception in the United States in 1969. In the early 1970s, producers from Brazil, Mexico, Canada, and Germany saw *Sesame Street*'s value and approached Sesame Workshop (then the Children's Television Workshop) about creating a version of *Sesame Street* that would specifically meet the educational needs of children in their respective countries. To achieve this objective, Sesame Workshop devised a production model that parallels the one in the United States but is tailored to the cultural context of a specific country.[7]

Over the course of the production process, experts in production, educational content, and research work collaboratively to develop programming for television, print, radio, or digital media. The producers and writers are responsible for the production's creative elements, such as characters, sets, and story. Educational content specialists set the curricular priorities and maintain the educational integrity and age appropriateness of the content. Researchers bring the voice of the child into the production process by testing content that is in development with children (and with adults, parents, or caregivers as necessary) to ensure its comprehensibility and appeal. Findings from such formative research help to inform and refine the production. This process ensures that the project benefits from the unique perspective that each party brings; through this collective expertise, the projects achieve a blend of education and entertainment that no single party can accomplish on its own.

In international coproductions of *Sesame Street*, this process takes place in-country, involving local production personnel, educators, and researchers. Sesame Workshop owes its international success to the principle that, while the Workshop may have knowledge on how to create a *Sesame Street* project, the expertise on how to create a media program that will resonate with children in a given country resides with local experts. Accordingly, at the onset of each international coproduction project, Sesame Workshop's local partners convene a seminar or series of seminars that bring together educational experts who define the parameters of a given project. As the production process advances, educators consult on the development of characters, settings, scripts, and other production elements, helping to interpret findings from formative research and guide their practical application. In turn, local producers develop content for the series.

The international application of the Sesame Workshop model allows for the flexible adaptation of a production process in a manner that has worked successfully in different countries throughout the world. While specifics differ across productions, the steps engaged in to complete a project are similar. As highlighted in Figure 8.2, Sesame Workshop productions begin with a feasibility assessment and proceed with the development of an educational framework, conceived by local educational specialists, that serves as the educational vertebrae for all material developed for the project. As material is produced, researchers test prototypes for their appeal and comprehension with members of the target audience. After distribution, if funding permits, Sesame

FIGURE 8.2.
The Production Process.

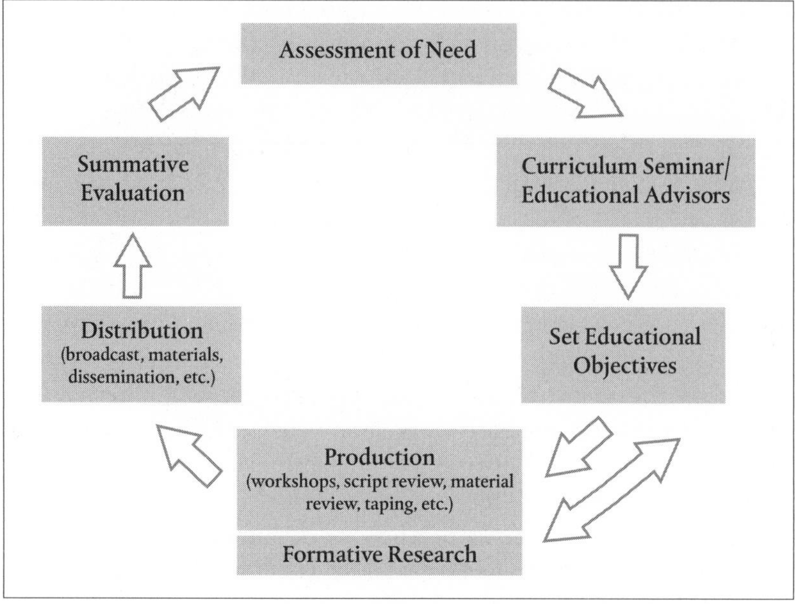

Workshop commissions an outside research vendor to study the impact of the program, looking at its reach and educational effectiveness. The information gained from that assessment is then used to enhance the quality of future productions. Then the steps start again with the creation of a new season of material.

The process results in productions that maintain the essence of *Sesame Street* in their format, structure, and approach, while presenting identifiably as from the country or region in which they are produced. A key advantage of this approach is that local production teams lead the development of their own content. Rather than merely using material dubbed into another language, local producers create content that features their own characters and sets. In addition, the program format is diverse, as each element affords different educational opportunities. Studio scenes with the well-known Muppet characters offer a lively and attractive way for producers to provide scripted, age-appropriate messages as prescribed by educators. Animations, which are inherently attractive to children, offer an alternative way to hone messages. Live-action segments, featuring children and families in real-life contexts, provide a window into daily routines and special events that take place in a given region. Such segments are particularly valuable when presenting messages designed to promote respect and understanding. They provide viewers with positive images of children like themselves or from other groups in a context that is meaningful and relevant to their own lives. Key to this element is the ability to provide authentic representations on the screen with stories told from the perspectives of real children, rather than actors, in their real and current homes and communities. On projects that are specifically oriented toward promoting respect and understanding across cultural divides—such as in the Middle East, Kosovo, Northern Ireland, and elsewhere—the use of live-action films is critical to their educational salience. Often in such places, the depictions that children typically view on the screen are those emphasizing negative views of a conflict. *Sesame Street*'s live-action films document children's daily lives, providing engaging, relevant stories that present positive images of their cultures. The films provide an opportunity for children to view themselves and their neighbors through an aperture specifically directed toward the ways that they and others nearby them live.

The *Rruga Sesam/Ulica Sezam* project in Kosovo provides an example of an attempt to provide a high-quality early education experience to young children living in a post-conflict region. In the following pages we provide an overview of the specifics of that project, highlighting its strengths and weaknesses and outlining what an independent evaluation showed about its educational effect. We chose this project as an example of Sesame Workshop's educational efforts in a transitional justice context, using multiple media (television and print) as conduits for building respect and understanding in a young audience in an effective way. *Rruga Sesam/Ulica Sezam* falls in the middle of the localization continuum presented in Figure 8.1. Less elaborate and less costly than a full coproduction, the series uses a base of material dubbed from *Sesame Street*'s international production library but also, importantly, includes as an integral element of each episode live-action documentaries filmed throughout Kosovo. We describe its conception, development, and impact with an eye toward highlighting the benefits as well as limitations of such a project so that other educators might use lessons learned as a point of departure in their own endeavors.

THE NEED FOR *RRUGA SESAM/ULICA SEZAM*

When the *Sesame Street* project was launched in Kosovo in 2004, the country had been administered by the UN Mission in Kosovo (UNMIK) for about five years.[8] At that point, Kosovo had been mired in a prolonged conflict between its Albanian and Serbian populations[9] and faced a range of challenges in educational, economic, and social development—endemic challenges in post-conflict settings. Moreover, ethnic tensions in Kosovo among Serbians and Albanians have played out over the past decade in an education system with dual infrastructures, separately servicing the ethnic Albanian and Serbian sectors. In 1991 the central government from the previous administration imposed a strict Serbian curriculum in all schools by ceasing to finance Albanian schools and companies publishing Albanian textbooks. In response, the Albanian population created a parallel education system that effectively divided the Serbian children, who kept attending the small number of publicly funded official schools, from the Albanian children, who studied in a larger, unofficial, privately financed system. Because of the limited resources flowing into the Albanian system, quality inevitably suffered and enrollment decreased, especially among girls.[10] Today, children in Kosovo live in an environment in which the established government is seeking to improve the education system with the help of the international community and nongovernmental organizations (NGOs). However, coupled with housing problems, unemployment, lingering anger among groups, and other issues,[11] the task of educating a country's youngest citizens is daunting when the nation is still suffering from years of civil unrest.

This situation is further compounded because the country does not have a strong history of structured early childhood education. The previous administration did not provide state-run early childhood education services, and little cumulative knowledge in the country exists on children's learning processes during their early years of development.[12] Although formal early childhood education efforts were renewed in 1999 through funding by international agencies and NGOs, most children in Kosovo do not have access to these early childhood programs.[13] Only 3 percent to 5 percent of children attended early childhood education programs in 2004.[14] Available programs were concentrated in urban centers. Given that roughly 60 percent of the population resides in rural areas,[15] access to early education is clearly limited for a large sector of the population. The lack of access is particularly troubling in light of the economic and social benefits of early childhood education, which have been well documented in the development literature.[16]

This backdrop of educational need is coupled with relatively high access to television. An estimated 85 percent of Kosovo's population has access to television, which serves as a primary source of entertainment given that few other recreational options are available. Few programs were available for children, however, and none specifically for the preschool age group.[17] Thus, a *Sesame Street* project was well poised to contribute to education in the preschool sector and make a difference in Kosovo's rebuilding process.

PROJECT ORIGINS

Sesame Workshop's project in Kosovo began with a trip jointly sponsored by the UN Development Program (UNDP) and the UN Children's Fund (UNICEF). The UNDP and UNICEF invited Sesame Workshop to conduct a fact-finding mission to determine the desire for, value of, and feasibility of a *Sesame Street* project in Kosovo.[18] The funders' interest in the potential project stemmed from the belief that a focus on Kosovo's youngest citizens could be a significant step in the reconciliation process and contribute to the peacebuilding process by helping young children from different groups gain a more positive perception of one another. In that respect, Sesame Workshop brought history and experience uniquely suited to such a context. The trip was an opportunity for two senior executives (vice presidents of international production and international education) to meet with a range of stakeholders in the education, government, and media fields to talk about the project's potential and whether the local community would welcome it. The two-person team traveled throughout Kosovo and met with teachers, visiting schools and other institutions to assess the project's viability.

A critical aspect of Sesame Workshop's approach is the time and attention paid to the introduction of a given project. As we already mentioned, *Sesame Street* works with the understanding that success is best secured when championed locally and when resident individuals have a hand in the content provided. The trip resulted in a desire to move forward with a project designed with a dual purpose: (1) to provide greatly needed, high-quality early education materials to young children living in Kosovo and (2) to introduce children from different ethnic backgrounds to one another in an effort to engender respect and understanding across a cultural divide.

Set against this backdrop of the need for early childhood education and a means to meet that need with a media project, Sesame Workshop embarked on a coproduction in Kosovo that followed the process outlined in Figure 8.2. As with all *Sesame Street* coproductions, the project's educational goals—its curriculum—were determined by Kosovar educators and expert advisors during a seminar convened in-country. Delineated along the domains of cognitive, emotional, physical, and social development, as well as core educational goals of respect and understanding, these objectives reflected what the advisors saw as the most critical educational needs of Kosovo's children (see Table 8.1 for a summary of the project's Statement of Educational Objectives).

The resulting multimedia educational project comprised a television broadcast component and a community outreach component. Although best known for television, many Sesame Workshop projects consist of both a broadcast TV and a community outreach element. Each component draws on the strengths of the medium and delivery mechanisms. The television platform enables the educational content to reach a large segment of the population that has access to the broadcast; community outreach initiatives add an extra dimension to the project through creating and distributing materials (usually in print form, such as books, posters, games, guides, and, more recently, digital technologies) to settings such as schools, community centers, or other environments that serve young children or their families. Outreach projects typically address a topic in depth and provide accompanying caregiver-targeted materials so that adults can mediate and facilitate children's learning.

THE TELEVISION SERIES

Fifty-two half-hour episodes over two seasons wove together segments featuring Muppets and animations dubbed from Sesame Workshop's library of existing content, as well as fifty-two live-action films (twenty-six in each season) that were coproduced in Kosovo by CMB, a Pristina-based production company. The episodes were presented in two language versions: Albanian (*Rruga Sesam*) and Serbian (*Ulica Sezam*). The segments from Sesame Workshop's library were carefully chosen for their appropriateness for children living in Kosovo.

As previously noted, the locally produced live-action films were the heart of the project and the primary carriers of the mutual-respect messages. Creation of these live-action films drew on Sesame Workshop's experience with *Rechov Sumsum/Shara'a Simsim*, *Sesame Stories*, and other projects, as well as knowledge regarding best practices for using media to forward messages on mutual respect. Cole, Labin, and Galarza synthesized these approaches,[19] which built off a body of research suggesting that children at young ages begin to form stereotypes about members of other groups.[20] Children appear susceptible to the political turmoil around them and are, as Connolly, Smith, and Kelly explain, not "too young to notice"; they readily absorb negative references to other groups that they overhear from adults and then apply these references in their own interactions.[21] The idea behind *Sesame Street* is to counter these effects by providing positive, authentic representations of others that meaningfully offer a different perspective and give children an age-appropriate venue for formulating judgments. Additionally, a core rationale behind the *Rechov Sumsum/Shara'a Simsim* project was that children needed to learn about themselves in order to be more respectful of others. Just as promoting positive portrayals of

Table 8.1.

Statement of Educational Objectives for *Rruga Sesam/Ulica Sezam*

COGNITIVE	EMOTIONAL	PHYSICAL	SOCIAL	RESPECT AND UNDERSTANDING
A. Literacy	A. Emotions	A. Hygiene and Health Care	A. Social Interactions	A. Human Diversity
1. Reading	1. Labeling emotions	1. Health	1. Friendship	1. Appreciating similarities
2. Writing fundamentals	2. Expressing emotions	2. Nutrition	2. Conflict resolution	2. Ethnic or cultural diversity
3. Library		3. Dental care	3. Cooperation	3. Religious diversity
4. Computer awareness	B. Coping with Emotions	4. Exercise	4. Helping	4. Gender
	1. Empathy		5. Sharing	5. Children with special needs
B. Mathematics	2. Overcoming obstacles	B. Safety	6. Turn-taking	6. Language appreciation
1. Number sense	3. Task persistence	1. Traffic safety	7. Entering social groups	
2. Number operations	4. Self-confidence	2. Fire safety	8. Basic interactions	B. Emotions
3. Measurement		3. Lead awareness		1. Recognizing and expressing emotions
4. Geometric forms			B. Group Relations	2. Self-control and appropriate emotional expression
			1. Social units	
C. Science			2. Diversity	3. Self-esteem
1. Living things				
2. Our world				C. Social Groups and Institutions
3. Light and shadows				1. Family and home
				2. The neighborhood
D. Arts				3. Culture, sports, and the arts
1. Appreciating the arts				4. The natural environment
2. Creating art				5. The human-made environment
E. Appreciating Arts				D. Health
1. Observation				1. Doctor
2. Visual discrimination				2. Prevention
3. Asking questions				
4. Listening				E. Safety
5. Auditory discrimination				1. Safety practices
6. Classification				
7. Problem solving				
8. Planning				
9. Predicting				
10. Cause and effect				
11. Guessing from clues				
12. Remembering				
13. Imagining				

the other culture is important, the project also needed to help children learn about their own culture. Therefore, a critical aspect of the project was to present scenarios from everyday life that rang true, so that children could see themselves on screen and build a positive self-image and group identity.[22]

Developing content to meet the dual need of building pride in one's own culture as well as respecting that of another is a challenge. Representations of the other culture that are too subtle may elude young children[23] because the differences are not concretely visual (as they are, for example, in race relation projects in the United States). For a preschool-age audience, cues such as spoken language accents, landmarks, and names—which may be directly linked to a given group for adults—may be too elusive as indicators of the other. While such signals can be helpful, additional signifiers, such as more concrete cultural symbols, may be necessary. Accordingly, depictions of the other's ethnic background need to be explicit for a young audience.

The live-action films in *Rruga Sesam/Ulica Sezam* were developed with such intent. They featured children from different ethnic groups in Kosovo: Albanian, Serbian, Turkish, Bosniak, Croatian, Ashkalia, Roma, and Gorani. Many of these films focused specifically on ethnic Albanian and Serbian children. They were the window through which children could see both themselves and the other. These segments portray the varied settings in which children live and the traditions and holidays that different ethnic groups celebrate. The films also focus on the similarities that different ethnic groups share by showing children from a range of backgrounds engaging in activities with their families, learning to master a task, handling daily challenges, and experiencing daily joys. For example, one of the films shows an ethnic Albanian girl with her grandfather learning to make a *qifteli*—an Albanian musical instrument; the film ends with the grandfather and the girl playing the instrument together. Such a film depicts an experience that all children share—family, learning a new skill—but simultaneously underscores elements that are unique to a particular group (in this case, the *qifteli*). The films are sometimes woven into a montage showing children from different ethnic groups talking about the same topic or engaged in the same activity while speaking in their own languages. Through these approaches, the films aim to engender mutual respect and understanding by celebrating diversity.

Another innovative feature of the *Rruga Sesam/Ulica Sezam* project was the creation of a visual dictionary, a live-action format where children from different ethnic groups are featured on screen pronouncing the same vocabulary word (e.g., "glasses") in their own languages. The statement of the word is then paired with a creative visual, such as the child wearing a pair of crazy-looking glasses. Viewers then see four renditions of the same word in different languages: Albanian, Siberian, Roma, and Turkish. The visual dictionary was conceived less as a tool to promote language learning than as a means for using language as a window into another culture and a way to engender an understanding of similarity and difference.

Once the dubbing of the library material and the production of the live-action films were completed, the series premiered in 2004 on RTK, which aired the Albanian- and Serbian-language versions throughout Kosovo. Additionally, three regional Serbian-language broadcasters aired *Ulica Sezam*: DTV Šilovo/Shillovë, TV Most Zvečan/Zveçan and TV Herc Štrpce/Shtërpcë. While the series was produced successfully with collaboration from Albanian and Serbian production teams, other issues arose that highlighted the many challenges associated with developing a program of this nature in a region of ethnic tension. Even seemingly simple circumstances can take on unintended political weight. Such an issue emerged during the broadcast of the first season of the series regarding the presentation of the *Sesame Street* street sign—the icon used for all coproductions—that appears in the opening sequence of the program.

As *Rruga Sesam/Ulica Sezam* was to broadcast in two languages, the team had developed "Sesame Street" signs for the Albanian- and Serbian-language versions. The Serbian sign used Cyrillic text, as advocated by many of the native Serbian speakers; the problem was that Cyrillic text was offensive to some in the ethnic Albanian community. The issue went unsolved in the first season of broadcast, which aired with two versions of the sign—the Serbian-language sign in Cyrillic and the Albanian-language sign in Latinic text.

As the project moved into the second production season, many members of the team voiced a concern that Cyrillic signage was being used. The team held a project meeting, but the situation seemed impossible: whatever was done—Cyrillic or no Cyrillic—would result in one group being offended. The solution came, as is so often the case when compromise seems unlikely, from turning the problem over and looking at it from another direction. Someone in the group reminded the team that *Sesame Street* is for young children who do not yet read. Rather than using the street sign as the icon of the program, the group suggested using a verbal signature instead. Members of the ethnic Serbian and Albanian communities liked the idea. In the second season, the team developed an auditory "sign" that consisted of young children in the opening sequence shouting out the program names.

THE OUTREACH COMPONENT

In addition to the television broadcast, Sesame Workshop formed a partnership with UNICEF to extend the reach of *Rruga Sesam/Ulica Sezam*. Using additional media platforms, Sesame Workshop and UNICEF developed print materials (in Albanian and Serbian languages) that were distributed throughout Kosovo. Prior to finalizing the materials, the team conducted formative research in ethnic Albanian, Serbian, Roma, and Bosnian communities to ensure that the content in the materials was relevant to children and caregivers in the region.

The materials included two children's books and a facilitator guide (see Figure 8.3). The books extend the *Rruga Sesam/Ulica Sezam* project's messages of diversity, mutual respect, and understanding. One of them is a storybook about a young girl's first day of school, highlighting messages about community, making new friends, safety, and the excitement of learning in school. The second book—a picture book—centers on topics that range from cognitive development to caring for the environment and playing with children who look different. The facilitator guide—targeted at parents and teachers—helps the adults use the books effectively in the home and in the classroom; the guide also offers tips on how to foster adult-child interaction and learning through the *Rruga Sesam/Ulica Sezam* books and television series. Providing information for adults on ways to interact with children and facilitate their learning through child-centered educational materials can be important in view of the lack of history and foundation in early childhood development in Kosovo, as discussed earlier.[24]

The team distributed the materials throughout Kosovo via a network of facilities that served children and families: preschools, family health-care centers, women's literacy centers, early childhood education centers, and parent-teacher organizations. The materials were printed in three different languages: Albanian, Serbian Cyrillic, and Serbian Latin. A total of 38,000 storybooks (30,000 in Albanian, 5,000 in Serbian Cyrillic, and 3,000 in Serbian Latin); 38,000 picture books (30,000 in Albanian, 5,000 in Serbian Cyrillic, and 3,000 in Serbian Latin); and 12,000 facilitator guides (7,000 in Albanian, 3,500 in Serbian Cyrillic, and 1,500 in Serbian Latin) were disseminated in 2007.[25]

RRUGA SESAM/ULICA SEZAM'S IMPACT

Sesame Workshop commissioned a small-scale study in 2005 to document children's responses to the first season of *Rruga Sesam/Ulica Sezam* as well as

FIGURE 8.3, a–c.
Outreach Materials in Albanian, Serbian Cyrillic, and Serbian Latin.

a. Children's storybook.

b. Children's picture book.

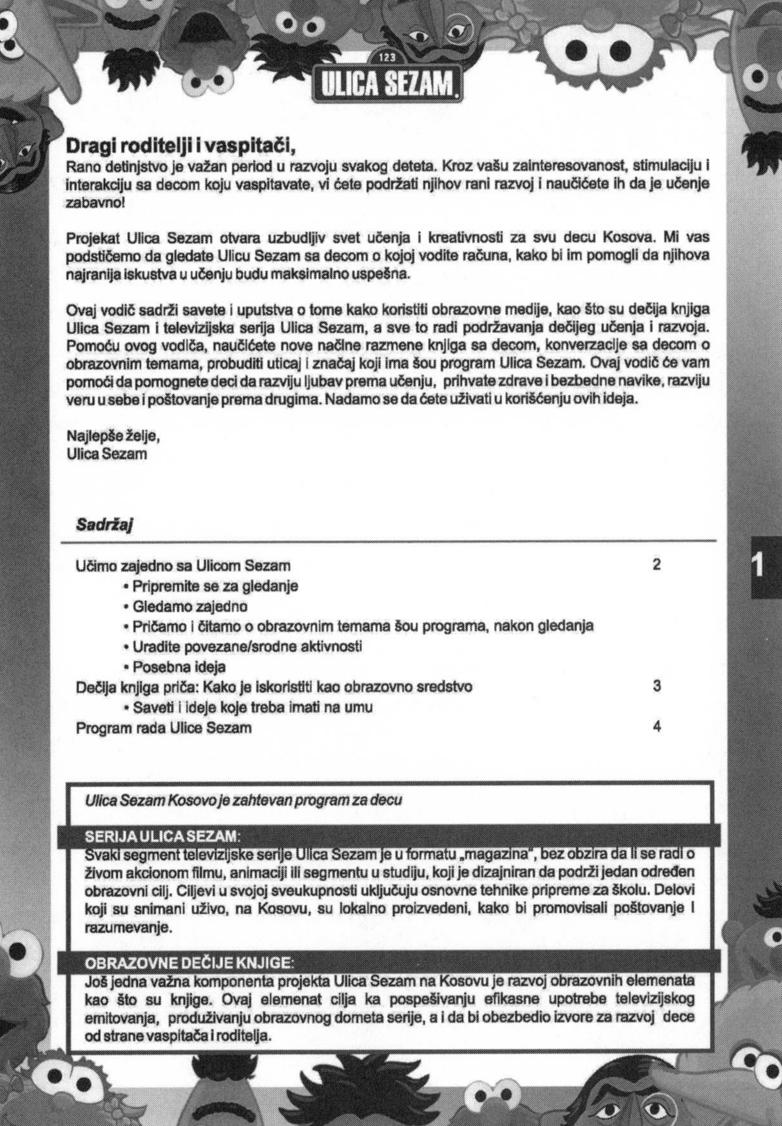

123 ULICA SEZAM

Dragi roditelji i vaspitači,

Rano detinjstvo je važan period u razvoju svakog deteta. Kroz vašu zainteresovanost, stimulaciju i interakciju sa decom koju vaspitavate, vi ćete podržati njihov rani razvoj i naučićete ih da je učenje zabavno!

Projekat Ulica Sezam otvara uzbudljiv svet učenja i kreativnosti za svu decu Kosova. Mi vas podstičemo da gledate Ulicu Sezam sa decom o kojoj vodite računa, kako bi im pomogli da njihova najranija iskustva u učenju budu maksimalno uspešna.

Ovaj vodič sadrži savete i uputstva o tome kako koristiti obrazovne medije, kao što su dečija knjiga Ulica Sezam i televizijska serija Ulica Sezam, a sve to radi podržavanja dečijeg učenja i razvoja. Pomoću ovog vodiča, naučićete nove načine razmene knjiga sa decom, konverzacije sa decom o obrazovnim temama, probuditi uticaj i značaj koji ima šou program Ulica Sezam. Ovaj vodič će vam pomoći da pomognete deci da razviju ljubav prema učenju, prihvate zdrave i bezbedne navike, razviju veru u sebe i poštovanje prema drugima. Nadamo se da ćete uživati u korišćenju ovih ideja.

Najlepše želje,
Ulica Sezam

Sadržaj

1

Ulica Sezam Kosovo je zahtevan program za decu

SERIJA ULICA SEZAM:
Svaki segment televizijske serije Ulica Sezam je u formatu „magazina", bez obzira da li se radi o živom akcionom filmu, animaciji ili segmentu u studiju, koji je dizajniran da podrži jedan određen obrazovni cilj. Ciljevi u svojoj sveukupnosti uključuju osnovne tehnike pripreme za školu. Delovi koji su snimani uživo, na Kosovu, su lokalno proizvedeni, kako bi promovisali poštovanje I razumevanje.

OBRAZOVNE DEČIJE KNJIGE:
Još jedna važna komponenta projekta Ulica Sezam na Kosovu je razvoj obrazovnih elemenata kao što su knjige. Ovaj elemenat cilja ka pospešivanju efikasne upotrebe televizijskog emitovanja, produživanju obrazovnog dometa serije, a i da bi obezbedio izvore za razvoj dece od strane vaspitača i roditelja.

c. Facilitator guide.

their knowledge and attitudes toward Albanian and Serbian groups.[26] This study had the goal of informing subsequent season(s) of production. Although the sample for the study was small ($N = 66$), it yielded information regarding children's knowledge and attitudes that was useful in informing the project's educational approach, helping to set the stage for a larger, more comprehensive evaluation (described later in this chapter).[27] Ethnic Albanian and ethnic Serbian children ages four to seven participated in the research. They watched an episode from the first season of *Rruga Sesam/Ulica Sezam* and participated in one-on-one interviews that assessed their comprehension of the content. The study found that both groups of children liked the program and demonstrated good recall of what they had watched. Perhaps more important was what researchers discovered about children's knowledge and attitudes toward their own and the other cultural group before exposure. Researchers learned that, while each group had more knowledge about its own culture than the other group's, both groups had minimal knowledge about each other. Furthermore, when asked about their perceptions of the other, children's responses were striking. Although many of the responses were neutral (e.g., "she is a bit older") or positive ("her eyes, face, hair, and pants are like mine"), there was a substantial portion of negative statements (e.g., "they kill children"). Albanian children offered more negative comments about Serbians than Serbian children did about Albanians (see Table 8.2): 65 percent of Albanian children's responses about Serbians were negative, compared with 10 percent of Serbian children's responses about Albanians. Interestingly, Albanian children also offered more negative comments about their own group (31 percent) than Serbian children did about theirs (6 percent). These findings underscored the continued need for a project like *Rruga Sesam/Ulica Sezam* in Kosovo.

To extend what was learned from the preliminary study, Sesame Workshop commissioned an independent evaluation in 2007 of the impact of *Rruga Sesam/Ulica Sezam*.[28] The project had launched three years before the study, and it was an opportune time to examine its educational impact. This study built upon research on other Sesame Workshop projects focusing on mutual respect and understanding,[29] as well as the smaller-scale study[30] of the Kosovo project described earlier in this chapter.

The study used what some regard as the gold-standard research approach: a randomized control trial (RCT)[31] design that enables researchers to attribute to the intervention rather than confounding factors differences in the performance of the two groups after intervention (in this case, watching *Sesame Street*). They included a sample of 536 children ages five and six, approximately evenly split between ethnicities, ages, genders, and settlement types (see Table 8.3). Half

TABLE 8.2.
Perceptions of Children about Their Own Group and the "Other" Group (**N**=66)

	POSITIVE	NEUTRAL	NEGATIVE
"What is an Albanian?"			
Serbian responses	10%	80%	10%
Albanian responses	41%	29%	31%
"What is a Serbian?"			
Serbian responses	61%	33%	6%
Albanian responses	16%	19%	65%

of the participants were randomly assigned to the intervention group, which saw the *Rruga Sesam/Ulica Sezam* series over a period of six weeks; the other half were assigned to the control group, which did not see the show. Caregivers of children in the intervention group were instructed to have their child view the show as they would naturally at home, at least twice a week for six weeks. Those in the control group were instructed not to watch the show.[32]

The study assessed outcomes that were part of the project's educational objectives, which included five domains covering a range of cognitive, physical, and social-emotional skills (see Table 8.1). Most pertinent to this paper are the data related to one of the social-emotional domains: mutual respect and understanding. In this area, the study not only provided insight into the contribution that the *Sesame Street* program made toward prompting positive change but also advanced academic knowledge of how to study children's perceptions of the other. While a number of relevant examples of tests of cognitive and physical abilities are available, those in the social-emotional realm are generally more scarce and often more challenging to administer, particularly with young children. It is, for example, simpler and more straightforward to measure how high a child counts (a skill in the cognitive domain of the program's curriculum) than to measure a child's level of empathy or respect for someone from another group (elements included in the social-emotional sections). To our knowledge, at the time of the study, there were no standardized (what social scientists would call *normed*) research instruments designed to examine changes in the social inclusion attitudes of preschool-age children living in Kosovo.

Building on the work of others, the researchers created a measure specifically designed to study the mutual respect and understanding skills outlined in the program's curriculum. Inspired by measures that other researchers had developed, the researchers used a scenario-based questioning technique, similar in format to one developed to study a *Sesame Street* project in the Middle East that had analogous curricular goals. Known as the Social Judgment

TABLE 8.3.
Description of Sample ($N=536$)

	INTERVENTION	CONTROL	TOTAL
ETHNIC GROUP			
Albanian	134	138	272
Serbian	119	145	264
GENDER			
Boys	129	156	285
Girls	124	127	251
AGE			
Five Years Old	134	139	273
Six Years Old	119	144	263
SETTLEMENT TYPE			
Urban	112	158	270
Rural	141	125	266
TOTAL	253	283	536

Interview, the measure uses a question/answer format in which researchers present children with a scenario aided by illustrations or a picture of a child and ask a series of questions based on the scenario or the child in the picture.[33] Children's responses to the questions are then coded to yield a score on the outcome of interest.

For the Kosovo study, researchers used the program's curriculum to guide the aspects of children's perceptions that they tested. They looked at elements such as children's receptiveness to children from another country and receptiveness to a child who does not speak the same language. For instance, to study children's receptiveness to a foreign child, children saw a picture of a same-gender child with physical features associated with people of Asian descent. Children then responded to a series of questions about the degree to which they would want to interact with the child: whether they would want to meet the child, play with him/her, befriend him/her, go to his/her house, and so on. The extent to which a child reported being willing to interact with the child pictured constituted an indicator of the child's receptiveness, with higher scores indicating greater receptiveness. While admittedly a far-from-perfect measure of the respect and understanding concept, scenario-based questioning gave researchers a window into children's thinking.

Using standard statistical procedures—analysis of covariance and logistic regression—to analyze the data, the researchers found notable[34] effects of exposure on five key aspects related to promoting respect and understanding across group divides:

1. Recognition of similarities
2. Receptiveness to a foreign child
3. Receptiveness to a Roma child
4. Receptiveness to a child who does not speak the same language
5. Receptiveness to a child who speaks Serbian (for Albanian-speaking children) or Albanian (for Serbian-speaking children)

To talk about the findings more succinctly, the researchers grouped the responses to the latter four questions and created a composite measure[35] of mutual respect and understanding that showed that after exposure to the series, children were, remarkably, 74 percent more likely than those from the control group to demonstrate strong mutual respect and understanding attitudes.[36] Furthermore, the effects held when pre-exposure scores and ethnicity were considered.

While the actual degree of change in these children's attitudes—or effect size—was classified within the study parameters as "small,"[37] it is still noteworthy that a media intervention can at least move the needle on important attitudes and knowledge among a preschool-age audience. The researchers concluded that the program was effective in delivering messages on mutual respect and understanding. Perhaps one of the most key findings of the study, though, was the evidence that the program's impact was not uniform. While, on average, children who viewed the series demonstrated positive change, data also indicated that ethnic Serbian children who watched the series expressed stronger attitudes of mutual respect than did their Albanian peers. The authors suggested that the pattern may be linked to the amount of prior exposure that children had to the show, which differed for the two groups due to factors such as intricacies of the broadcast schedule, network reach, and viewer access. Alternatively, the difference may have been associated with variation in the sensibilities of the two groups and the ways that their respective histories influenced the receptiveness of viewers at the onset of—and over the course of—the intervention. The latter explanation fits with findings from other research, according to which children from the least disenfranchised groups are more likely or are quicker to make positive gains in perceptions than their peers from more marginalized groups.[38] Further research on other interventions is needed to disentangle the effect of receptiveness versus access. Regardless, the findings point to the need in the future for educators and producers to consider the varying needs of opposing groups and factor in the differences in their starting points when crafting an intervention and in the study effects.

This point aside, the study extends prior research about *Sesame Street*'s impact in engendering positive change in children's attitudes toward those of another culture. Cole et al. found that exposure to *Rechov Sumsum/Shara'a Simsim* enhanced positive perceptions of the other among Arab-Israeli and Jewish-Israeli children, but not among Palestinian children.[39] The researchers concluded that these differences were partly due to differential exposure to content about the other in the versions of the series that Palestinian and Israeli children saw (i.e., Palestinian children were exposed to less content depicting Israeli culture compared with Israeli children's exposure to content about Palestinian culture). In the Kosovo study, the two versions of *Rruga Sesam/Ulica Sezam* differed only in the language in which they were broadcast, not in content; differential impact was still evident. While determining the reasons for this pattern is difficult to do, children's preexisting attitudes may yield a clue. The study did not specifically examine prior differences between the Albanian and Serbian samples in the range of measures of mutual respect, but an informal examination reveals that a smaller proportion of Albanian children expressed strong mutual respect attitudes compared to Serbian children, echoing previous research findings that Albanian children held markedly more negative attitudes toward Serbians than Serbian children did toward Albanians.[40]

That the effects of the series did not have equally positive impact in both groups was disappointing, but the outcome points to the possibility that some degree of receptivity may be necessary for such messages to take root. It confirms the conclusions from an earlier study examining the impact of *Sesame Stories* on similar outcomes. Fox et al. found a high level of prosocial attitudes among the sample at baseline and speculated that having a predisposition toward being prosocial was perhaps a necessary condition for the series to have an effect; "Without some initial baseline level of social perspectives, viewing a show such as *Sesame Stories* would have minimal impact."[41]

CONCLUSION

Taken together, the body of research on *Sesame Street* points to the potential for media projects to shift attitudes about the other in post-conflict settings. *Sesame Street*'s approach to education around such potent issues has its underpinnings in experience from multiple projects around the world. *Sesame Street* has succeeded in shifting attitudes in challenging sociopolitical contexts such as Northern Ireland, Israel and Palestine, and Kosovo. These projects have specific principles for content development and production that contributed to their effectiveness for a preschool-age audience:

1. Adopt a child-oriented approach.
2. Present the audience with real-life, positive images of both themselves and others.
3. Create portrayals that are concrete and explicit.

In addition to the content of the projects, the process through which Sesame Workshop engages local partners is also an important contributor to its impact across different contexts and places. Each project differs in its context, resources, and capacity, but they share the following elements:

1. The educational and creative vision for each project is driven by local experts and production partners.
2. The formative research that informs content development is conducted with the target audience (children and their caregivers) in-country.
3. Local partners are supported in their desire to shape the project in a way that makes sense for them.

Education around issues of mutual respect and peace involves the participation of multiple agents[42] and consists of formal processes, such as schools, and informal processes, such as mass media and communications. Mass media, including television, are powerful tools for these efforts not only because of the media's compelling nature but also because of their reach. In a post-conflict setting, educational efforts are critical aids in supporting institutional and legal reforms. Mass media have the potential to reach broad audiences, effecting change on a large scale, and addressing issues that may not be emphasized in the formal education system. While educational media projects do not purport to supplant or replace formal education, they can enhance other educational efforts, formal and informal. Realizing this potential, however, also requires content that is engaging and resonant. The *Rruga Sesam/Ulica Sezam* project has endeavored to ensure the cultural relevance of its educational content through a process that supports local voice and local opinion; such a process is integral to the project's legitimacy and impact.

Educational media, however, are only one piece in the complex interplay of factors that shape behaviors and attitudes. While the research indicates that *Sesame Street* can contribute to broader social change, true transformation will best occur with greater alignment among the various institutions serving children. Children living in post-conflict regions are, perhaps, the best hope for the future. Just as learning the alphabet helps to promote a child's future literacy, there is a need for multiple efforts, such as those embedded in Sesame Workshop's projects in regions of conflict, to present the fundamentals for reconciliation. Helping children from different groups to learn about each other builds a greater sense of shared humanity and mutual respect and understanding across cultural divides. The impacts of a given *Sesame Street* project, while positive, are modest, but perhaps they plant a seed of hope for other similar endeavors.

APPENDIX: DETAILS OF STATISTICAL ANALYSIS OF THE STUDY OF *RRUGA SESAM/ULICA SEZAM*'S IMPACT

Researchers used analysis of covariance (ANCOVA) and logistic regression to examine the differences between the intervention and control groups.[43] Table 8.4 shows the results from the ANCOVAs, analyzing the effects of the intervention on measures of mutual respect and understanding. Main effects and significant interactions are presented. In all instances, the main effect of condition (exposure to the program) was significant: Children who watched *Rruga Sesam/Ulica Sezam* received higher scores in all five outcomes compared with children who did not watch. The effects of the intervention remained significant over and above children's performance at pre-test. Interaction effects with ethnicity also emerged in four out of the five measures: The analyses revealed that effects of exposure were primarily evident among Kosovar-Serbian children; the effects were weak among Kosovar-Albanian children.

TABLE 8.4.

Results from ANCOVAs Analyzing the Effects of Condition on Mutual Respect and Understanding Outcomes

MEASURES	*F* STATISTIC (1,531)	COHEN'S d FOR MAIN EFFECT OF CONDITION	STANDARDIZED GROUP MEANS AT POST-TEST		COHEN'S d FOR SIGNIFICANT INTERACTION EFFECTS
			INTERVENTION	CONTROL	
1) Recognition of Similarities	6.84**	0.25	51.2	49.1	Serbian: $d=0.46$ Albanian: $d=0.08$
2) Receptiveness to a Foreign Child	13.93***	0.25	53.5	50.3	Serbian: $d=0.46$ Albanian: $d=0.08$
3) Receptiveness to a Roma Child	10.82**	0.23	53.5	51.1	Rural: $d=0.35$ Urban: $d=-0.05$
4) Receptiveness to a Child Who Does Not Speak the Same Language	8.57**	0.21	53.6	51.3	Serbian: $d=0.42$ Albanian: $d=0.03$
5) Receptiveness to a Child Who Speaks Serbian (for Albanians) or Albanian (for Serbians)	7.27**	0.20	53.3	50.8	Serbian: $d=0.42$ Albanian: $d=-0.05$

$^{**}p < .01$, $^{***}p < .001$

NOTES

The authors wish to thank Nellie Gregorian, William Sandy, and Craig S. Rosen, PhD, from Fluent Opinion + Market Research, as well as the research team from SMMRI, Kosovo, for their valuable work on the impact assessment of *Rruga Sesam/Ulica Sezam*. This paper does not necessarily represent ICTJ's position.

1 The *Rruga Sesam/Ulica Sezam* project has benefited from a diverse funding base. Funding for Season 1 was provided by the Netherlands Ministry of Foreign Affairs, the Organization for Security and Cooperation in Europe (OSCE), the UN Children's Fund (UNICEF), the Canadian International Development Agency (CIDA), and the German Institute for Foreign Cultural Relations (IFA). Funding for Season 2 came from the Swedish International Development Cooperation Agency (SIDA), the OSCE Mission in Kosovo, and the US Agency for International Development (USAID).

2 Gerald S. Lesser, *Children and Television: Lessons from* Sesame Street (New York: Random House, 1975).

3 "Mississippi Agency Votes for a TV Ban on 'Sesame Street,'" *New York Times*, May 3, 1970.

4 Paul Connolly, Alan Smith, and Berni Kelly, *Too Young to Notice? The Cultural and Political Awareness of 3- to 6-Year Olds in Northern Ireland* (Belfast: Northern Ireland Community Relations Council, 2002), http://eprints.ulster.ac.uk/19237/1/Connolly,_Smith_and_Kelly_%282002%29_Too_Young_to_Notice.pdf.

5 Charlotte Cole, Cairo Arafat, Chava Tidhar, Wafa Zidan Tafesh, Nathan A. Fox, Melanie Killen, Alicia Ardila-Rey, et al., "The Educational Impact of *Rechov Sumsum/Shara'a Simsim*: A *Sesame Street* Television Series to Promote Respect and Understanding among Children Living in Israel, the West Bank, and Gaza," *International Journal of Behavioral Development* 27, no. 5 (September 2003): 409–27; Fluent Research, "Assessment of Educational Impact of *Rruga Sesam* and *Ulica Sezam* in Kosovo: Report of Findings" (unpublished manuscript, Fluent Research, New York, 2008); Emma Larkin, Paul Connolly, and Susan Kehoe, "A Longitudinal Study of the Effects of Young Children's Natural Exposure to *Sesame Tree* on Their Attitudes and Awareness" (unpublished manuscript, Queens University, Belfast, 2009).

6 Barbara Rogoff, *The Cultural Nature of Human Development* (New York: Oxford University Press, 2003).

7 Charlotte F. Cole, Beth A. Richman, and Susan A. McCann Brown, "The World of *Sesame Street* Research," in *"G" is for Growing*, ed. Shalom M. Fisch and Rosemary T. Truglio (Mahwah, NJ: Erlbaum, 2001), 147–79.

8 Kosovo subsequently declared its independence in 2008.

9 According to the Statistical Office of Kosovo, as of 2005, the population consisted of 88 percent Albanians, 7 percent Serbians, and 5 percent from other ethnic groups (Bosniaks,

Goranis, Turks, and Roma); "Kosovo in Figures 2005," January 2006, http://esk.rks-gov.net/ENG/publikimet/doc_view/509-kosovo-in-figures-2005?tmpl=component&format=raw.

10 Statistical Office of Kosovo, *Statistics on Education in Kosovo: Version 2* (Pristina: Statistical Office of Kosovo, 2001), http://esk.rks-gov.net/ENG/publikimet/doc_details/662-statistics-on-education-in-kosova-2001.

11 UN Development Program, *Second Millennium Development Goals Report for Kosovo* (New York: UNDP, 2007), http://www.ks.undp.org/repository/docs/English.pdf.

12 UNICEF, "Profile 2010: Education in UN-Administered Province of Kosovo," 2010, http://www.unicef.org/ceecis/Kosovo_2010.pdf.

13 Ministry of Education, Science, and Technology (MEST) and Ministry of Agriculture, Forestry, and Rural Development (MAFRD), *A Strategy for Education for Rural People in Kosovo (2004–2009)*, Pristina, UN Doc. TCP/KOS/2901, 2004, http://www.fao.org/sd/erp/ERPkosovoenglish.pdf.

14 UNICEF, "Profile 2010."

15 MEST and MAFRD, *Strategy for Education.*

16 See, for example, Robert Lynch, *Exceptional Returns: Economic, Fiscal, and Social Benefits of Investment in Early Childhood Development* (Washington, DC: Economic Policy Institute, 2004), http://www.epi.org/publications/entry/books_exceptional_returns/; Save the Children, *What's the Difference? An ECD Impact Study from Nepal: A Summary of Findings regarding the Impact of Participation in ECD Programs on School Enrollment, Achievement, and Retention*, 2003, http://www.ecdgroup.com/pdfs/nepal_impact_study.pdf; and Jacques van der Gaag and Jee-Peng Tan, *The Benefits of Early Child Development Programs: An Economic Analysis* (Washington, DC: World Bank, 1997), http://www.ecdgroup.com/download/gw1becdi.pdf.

17 Sesame Workshop, "Report of Sesame Workshop's Fact-Finding Trip to Kosovo" (unpublished manuscript, Sesame Workshop, New York, 2002).

18 Ibid.

19 Charlotte F. Cole, Daniel B. Labin, and Maria Del Rocio Galarza, "Begin with the Children: What Research on *Sesame Street*'s International Coproductions Reveals about Using Media to Promote a New More Peaceful World," *International Journal of Behavioral Development* 32, no. 4 (July 2008): 359–65.

20 Frances E. Aboud and Maria Amato, "Developmental and Socialization Influences on Intergroup Biases," in *Blackwell Handbook of Social Psychology: Intergroup Processes*, ed. Rupert Brown and Samuel L. Gaertner (Oxford: Blackwell Publishers, 2001), 65–88; Daniel Bar-Tal, "Development of Social Categories and Stereotypes in Early Childhood: The Case of 'the Arab' Concept Formation, Stereotype, and Attitudes by Jewish Children in Israel," *International Journal of Intercultural Relations* 20, nos. 3–4 (Summer–Autumn 1996): 341–70; and Connolly, Smith, and Kelly, *Too Young to Notice?*

21 Connolly, Smith, and Kelly, *Too Young to Notice?*

22 Cole, Labin, and Galarza, "Begin with the Children."

23 Snjezana Kojic Hasanagić, Selma Kapo, and Vigan Behluli, "Research about the Reception of *Rruga Sesam* and *Ulica Sesam* in Kosovo: Children's Assessment Report" (unpublished manuscript, Prism Research, Pristina, 2005).

24 UNICEF, "Profile 2010."

25 UNICEF, "Sesame Workshop Extends beyond Television to Reach Children and Their Families in Kosovo," press release, September 28, 2007, www.unicef.org/kosovo/Press_release_Sesame_Street_PR.eng.doc.

26 Hasanagić, Kapo, and Behluli, "Children's Assessment Report."

27 Fluent Public Opinion + Market Research, "Report of Findings."

28 Ibid.

29 Cole et al., "Educational Impact of *Rechov Sumsum/Shara'a Simsim*"; N. A. Fox, M. Killen, L. A. Leavitt, A. Raviv, S. Masalha, F. Mura, et al., "An Evaluation of the Educational Impact of *Sesame Stories*" (unpublished manuscript, University of Maryland, Baltimore, 2005).

30 Hasanagić, Kapo, and Behluli, "Children's Assessment Report."

31 A randomized controlled trial is a research design characterized by random assignment of research participants to a "treatment/intervention" group that receives the treatment (in this case, watching *Rruga Sesam/Ulica Sezam*) and a control group that does not receive the treatment (i.e., does not watch the series). Random assignment ensures that any differences between the intervention and control group are not systematic and are due to true change.

32 Ideally, the research would have included an evaluation of the outreach component, but such a study would have added a layer of complexity to the design and implementation of the research that was outside the range of available resources.

33 N. A. Fox, M. Killen, and L. A. Leavitt, "The Social Judgment Interview Coding Manual" (unpublished manuscript, University of Maryland, Baltimore, 1999).

34 Technical details related to the statistical analysis of the findings are presented in the appendix to this chapter.

35 The four measures were interrelated and showed fairly good internal consistency (Cronbach's $\alpha = 0.67$). For ease of interpretation, researchers converted the score to a scale of 0 ("no appreciation of mutual respect and understanding") to 100 ("full appreciation of mutual respect and understanding"). They considered children who received a score of 80 or higher to have a "strong" appreciation of mutual respect and understanding.

36 Odds ratio = 2.5, $p < .001$.

37 Jacob Cohen, *Statistical Power Analysis for the Behavioral Sciences*, 2nd ed. (Hillsdale, NJ: Lawrence Erlbaum Associates, 1988).

38 See, for example, Cole et al., "Educational Impact of *Rechov Sumsum/Shara'a Simsim*."

39 Ibid.

40 Hasanagić, Kapo, and Behluli, "Children's Assessment Report."

41 Fox et al., "Educational Impact of *Sesame Stories,*" 69.

42 Daniel Bar-Tal, "Nature, Rationale, and Effectiveness of Education for Coexistence," *Journal of Social Issues* 60, no. 2 (June 2004): 253–71.

43 Fluent Public Opinion + Market Research, "Report of Findings."

CHAPTER 9

"Friend" of the Court: New Media and Transitional Justice

Camille Crittenden

The International Criminal Court and Facebook were born at the same time.

—Luis Moreno Ocampo, chief prosecutor, International Criminal Court (2002–12), personal communication with author, June 1, 2011

New media and social networking increasingly pervade public life.[1] In addition to chatting, shopping, and playing games online, Internet users can follow breaking headlines, view satellite footage of disaster areas, and donate to causes that move them. The online world offers great potential for the field of transitional justice, which aims, among other things, to promote civic trust and to demonstrate to victims of human rights violations that justice has been done.[2] In moments of political change and transformation, new media can enable international tribunals, truth commissions, or civil society organizations (CSOs) to educate and engage broader communities than ever before.

To be sure, substantial gaps remain in the degree of online access available across geographic regions and among groups of varying socioeconomic and educational levels. This participation gap suggests that many of these tools are better suited for advocacy campaigns and external relations by institutions to peer organizations, journalists, and members of the connected public rather than direct outreach to populations emerging from violence or repressive rule. Still, the reach and capacity of these strategies—and the creativity of those who employ them—hold potential for bringing the justice process closer to victims and affected communities.

The disadvantages or vulnerabilities of social media are also apparent, since rumors and incitement to violence can spread just as quickly as reliable information. It seems particularly important, then, that international courts recognize the utility of social media for communicating their work and render their materials accessible over time and between countries and regions. Quick adoption of these strategies—and investment in staff to deploy them—can counter the possibility of misinformation and promote transparency in the courts' work.

In this chapter I explore the promising contributions of new media to international criminal justice institutions and consider also some challenges and potential hazards. Within this broad and rapidly evolving field, I highlight a few key areas. First I describe the extent to which the six main international, ad hoc, and hybrid criminal tribunals use new media and social networking.[3] Next I turn to the efforts of advocacy organizations and others to engage with these courts or the constituents they serve. I then look at the implications of the rapidly expanding use of social media for the judicial process itself and for documenting and preserving the courts' legacies. I conclude with a discussion of issues that cut across institutional lines—such as audience, technology, and resources—as well as a consideration of the promise and challenges of new media to contribute to the goals of transitional justice.

A BRIEF BACKGROUND

Social media applications have evolved along a continuum and often work in tandem with earlier means of mass communication. Traditional or legacy media, such as newspapers, radio, and television, now exist alongside new media, digital media, or multimedia. These applications, known collectively (and retrospectively) as Web 1.0, include Internet-based tools that are largely channels for one-way distribution of information, such as websites with video, interactive maps, podcasts, and the like. These sites served as a basis for the development of social media (Web 2.0), tools that invite user-generated content and participation. Examples include Facebook, Twitter, and FourSquare, as well as social applications and crisis mapping, such as Ushahidi or FrontlineSMS, for emergency contexts.[4] Within the field of human rights and transitional justice, many institutions, such as international tribunals and truth commissions, are using new media quite effectively to publicize information by posting text documents and video footage. In comparison, nongovernmental organizations (NGOs) working in the same field are usually more in the vanguard of using social networking (see Figure 9.1). None of these means are mutually exclusive. Indeed, information presented in one mode frequently refers to another for further detail.

Much has been written about the use of social media to catalyze political change, starting with Howard Dean's US presidential campaign in 2004.[5]

FIGURE 9.1.
Relationship between Traditional Media, Web 1.0, and Web 2.0.

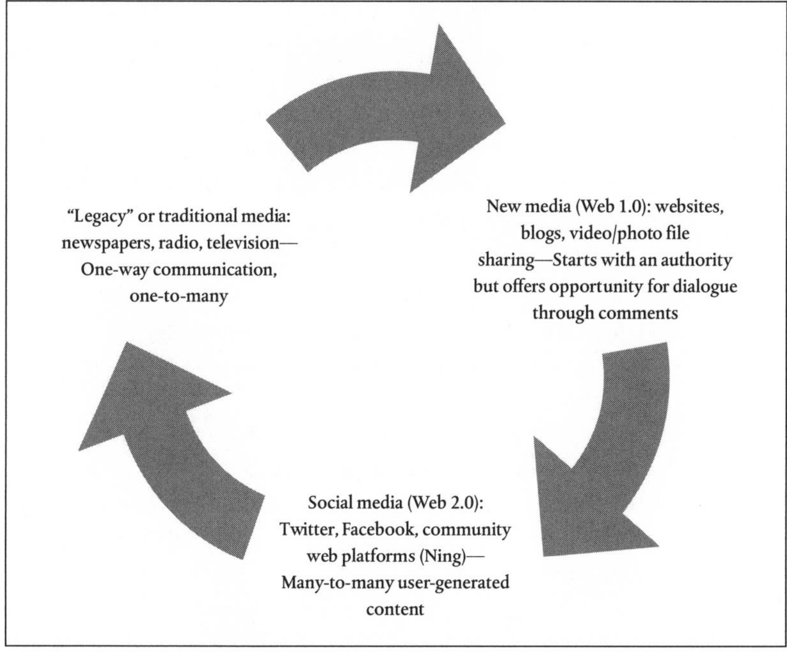

Since then, advocacy organizations have used the power of the Internet to bring attention to injustice and human rights violations around the world. Groups like MoveOn.org, Avaaz, and Change.org have emerged specifically to pursue online advocacy, while brick-and-mortar organizations like Amnesty International and the Southern Poverty Law Center have incorporated online tactics into their offline suite of tools. Examples are also growing of the Internet as a tool for organizing political resistance or building democracy. Antigovernment activists turned to online methods to mobilize their constituents in Eastern Europe in 2009 (e.g., Moldova's "Twitter revolution"[6]) and in Tunisia and elsewhere in the Middle East in the spring of 2011.[7] Numerous articles and blog posts have described the use of social networking tools for organizing dissidents and sharing information.[8] Upon closer examination, however, scholars have recognized that a relatively small number of activists with links to international media actually used these tools, cautioning against a broad-brush impression of the Internet as a tool for advancing democracy.[9] Indeed, repressive regimes frequently have an equal appreciation for the power of the Internet and have gone to great lengths to slow, censor, or shut down access. Still, the widespread attention to use of these channels has increased awareness and acceptance of them within more bureaucratic institutions, such as government agencies, courts, and universities.

In addition to emerging political parties and charismatic candidates, established institutions and politicians have embraced the idea of new media as a vehicle to advance foreign policy or their own agendas. The US State Department, for example, has an Office of eDiplomacy with nearly 150 full-time staff members working at State's headquarters and hundreds more in diplomatic missions around the world.[10] Products of this activity include the State Department's tech@State initiative and *dipNote*, its official blog.[11] Many governments and world leaders have their own online presence and, increasingly, their own Twitter accounts.[12] The use of such tools by transitional justice institutions—tribunals, truth commissions, informal or traditional courts, and the like—has not yet gained such broad popularity, and has not been explored in detail.

How might social media contribute to the goals of transitional justice? Transitional justice measures are meant to bring accountability for perpetrators of massive violations of human rights and provide public redress for victims. Outreach measures play a central role in creating or restoring social cohesion following mass atrocities. Public engagement is meant to inform potential participants in the justice process, give affected populations a voice, publicize the goals and results of justice measures, promote inclusiveness and transparency, and build a sense of local ownership.[13] New media have the capacity to address or contribute to most of these goals, and therefore should be part of the tool kit for public information officers and outreach practitioners.

NEW MEDIA STRATEGIES AND TOOLS OF THE TRIBUNALS

Like many large, bureaucratic organizations, the international and hybrid criminal tribunals are grappling with how best to use new media to communicate their work and engage constituents.[14] On the one hand, such tools make public information campaigns more powerful and cost-effective than ever before. With a simple video camera, staff can record footage of court proceedings or interviews with practitioners and upload it to YouTube for public viewing. Yet the interactive aspect of social networking also creates an opportunity to express opposition to the courts' activities or sow suspicion regarding their motives. The discussion below examines each of the six courts and their approach to new media.[15]

INTERNATIONAL CRIMINAL COURT (ICC)

For international tribunals, new media tools are largely an extension of the courts' public information and outreach offices.[16] The ICC distinguishes between public information, outreach, and external relations:

> The Court defines *public information* as delivering timely and accurate information to the public at large and target audiences through various channels of communication. It aims to contribute to global understanding and respect of the principles ruling the system established by the Rome Statute at the national, regional, and international levels. *Outreach* activities are directed toward communities affected by situations and cases before the Court to build awareness and understanding of the Court's role and activities and provide access to the Court's judicial proceedings. Outreach aims to address specific information needs of communities engaged and to contribute to their participation in the process. *External relations* is a dialogue between the Court and States Parties, non–States Parties, international organizations, nongovernmental organizations (NGOs), and other key partners that have direct roles in the activities and the enabling environment of the ICC.[17]

Among the goals of the Public Information Section are helping the court to deliver "public and transparent justice" and "increasing the broader impact of the Court, contributing to lasting respect for and enforcement of international justice."[18]

The ICC website offers a number of multimedia resources, including a virtual tour, downloadable video coverage of trial proceedings, and opportunities for users to pose questions that are then answered in a weekly broadcast by court staff ("Ask the Court"). The site includes links to text-based public communications like newsletters and press releases, as well as over forty-four thousand legal texts and tools regarding the ICC and international justice in general. The court's YouTube channel offers an archive of nearly 385 videos (as of April 2012), including press conferences, courtroom coverage, interviews, and statements from court officials. The ICC also has a Twitter account, which it uses to alert its nearly twenty-two thousand followers in English, French, and Arabic to new posts on its website—updated newsletters, press releases, and the like. The Public Information Office also uses Twitter for short announcements that may not merit a full press release or to alert journalists of forthcoming news, giving them advance notice about stories before the full details are released.[19]

The court has a limited presence on Facebook. An unofficial "Interest" page offers basic information about the court drawn from Wikipedia, and the Employment and Recruitment Office has its own page with staff and internship job postings.[20] As of summer 2011 the Public Information and Outreach Offices have hesitated to establish an official page because of the staff resources necessary to maintain it, especially if the comment feature were available. A staff member would need to monitor the site and respond to comments that users may post. The court's YouTube channel does provide the opportunity for comment, however, which offers a window into popular support and criticisms of the court. Recent comments have come primarily from Kenya and are divided between those supporting the court's investigation—against the perceived corruption of national politicians—and those opposing it for investigating only African countries.

According to its public information strategy for 2011–13, the court planned to "improve use of Internet-based technology including [the ICC] website, web-based social networks and blogs."[21] However, lack of resources has delayed implementation of these strategies.[22]

Other court organs use new media tools to fulfill their own communications goals. For example, the Trust Fund for Victims has its own website (http://trustfundforvictims.org), and the Office of the Prosecutor has its own Twitter account (@OTP_ICC), created in May 2011. (New media projects developed by outside organizations related to the ICC are discussed below.)

INTERNATIONAL CRIMINAL TRIBUNAL FOR THE FORMER YUGOSLAVIA (ICTY)

The ICTY offers extensive multimedia resources on its website, including an interactive map, extensive case documents in an online database, and video coverage of much of the proceedings. Over 1,125 videos appear on the ICTY YouTube channel, and analysis of the traffic shows that, on average, 40 percent of viewers come from the former Yugoslavia.[23] Indeed, online video is the only way to see many of the proceedings without actually being in the courtroom. The tribunal actively uses Twitter to alert its nearly twenty-seven hundred followers to breaking news or event announcements.

As in the case of the ICC, an unofficial Facebook page includes basic information about the ICTY. Nerma Jelacic, head of communications, is eager to launch an official Facebook page but wants to gain the support of all three organs of the court. Although the various sections of the court could pursue their own communications strategies, as in the example of the ICC, a unified and coordinated message may ultimately better serve the court's interests as a whole. A Facebook page would be staff-intensive to maintain and respond to comments and questions, but "it will be useful for promoting the Court's accomplishments and mission and countering misinformation,"[24] especially considering that groups in the region have already been actively engaged on Facebook and elsewhere expressing their opinions of court decisions.[25]

The Yugoslavia tribunal, perhaps more than other ad hoc or international tribunals, faces a challenge of making information available in multiple languages. The court's website offers parallel pages not only in English and French, the official languages of the court, but also Bosnian-Croatian-Serbian (BCS) and Russian.[26]

The court's legacy plan takes into account the capacity for storing documents and trial footage and making them available to the public online.[27] Considerations of online tools and audience engagement should also be taken into account as cases are transferred to the national war crimes chambers and the international tribunal is closed. The national body should continue investing in new media tools as an integral part of its outreach and public information strategy.

EXTRAORDINARY CHAMBERS IN THE COURTS OF CAMBODIA (ECCC)

The ECCC has been a leader among tribunals in implementing social media tools. These strides were made largely under the leadership of Reach Sambath, head of public information, until his untimely death in May 2011. The ECCC website includes up-to-the-minute news stories, photos, press releases, and publications. It also features a section, "Follow Us in Social Media," with links to the ECCC's Facebook, YouTube, Flickr, and Twitter pages. The ECCC is the only tribunal with a Flickr account, a useful service for journalists, teachers, participants, and court officials to exchange photographs. A weekly television show, *Facing Justice,* began in December 2011 to help explain the proceedings of Case 002 to a wide audience. Broadcast on the top television channel and posted on YouTube, the show is in Khmer with English subtitles.[28]

Unlike the ICTY's unofficial Facebook page, which offers only an excerpt from the Wikipedia article about the court, the commenting feature is enabled on the ECCC Facebook page, and a handful of people regularly respond to items posted by the court. Representatives from the Public Affairs Section clarify questions raised in this forum, where critics of the court can also make their views known. For example, seven people "liked" an announcement of the June 2011 decision by the Co-Investigating Judges to reject the request for extension for filing Civil Party Applications in Case 003. Among the comments, a user noted, "7 people like impunity for crimes against humanity." These online tools, along with radio, television, and public events, will undoubtedly continue to engage the media and offer a public forum for discussion of the court's work.

SPECIAL COURT FOR SIERRA LEONE

The Special Court for Sierra Leone (SCSL) has been a pioneer in conducting outreach to affected communities. In early years, outreach programs were primarily conducted in person, with visits by court staff to town hall meetings and the like. Since the proceedings moved from Sierra Leone to The Hague, online outreach has become increasingly important for maintaining a connection to local populations. The website for the Special Court includes press releases, newsletters, video summaries, and photographs, and featured live coverage of the Charles Taylor trial when it was underway in The Hague.[29] It also helps to increase awareness of international justice mechanisms and the history of Sierra Leone's conflict through its "More Info" page, which includes links to Sierra Leone legislation, ceasefire and peace agreements, international conventions and treaties, and legal organizations such as the international ad hoc tribunals, the ICC, and others.

Social media use is limited in Sierra Leone, where Internet connections are very slow, but it is helpful for reaching international audiences of journalists and civil society. For example, the court uses Twitter for brief announcements that do not merit a press release.[30] The Open Society Justice Initiative's blog about the court has reached a broader online audience, including many members of Sierra Leone's diaspora community. I discuss more about this blog below.

SPECIAL TRIBUNAL FOR LEBANON (STL)

The STL, established in 2006, began operations in the Netherlands in 2009 and offers a number of multimedia resources on its website (which has English, French, and Arabic versions), including a virtual tour of the courtroom and live video streaming of court sessions.[31] By early 2012 the tribunal had launched a suite of social media initiatives, including a YouTube channel, Twitter account (which has a feed on the tribunal's homepage), Flickr page, and Scribd page, all of which are prominently featured under a "Stay Connected" heading on its website. Scribd, a website that enables users to upload and search for documents (as Flickr does with photos), may be a particularly useful resource for transitional justice measures; the tribunal has used it to post its annual reports, fact sheets, and other publications in English, French, and Arabic, making them easily accessible for users worldwide.

INTERNATIONAL CRIMINAL TRIBUNAL FOR RWANDA (ICTR)

The ICTR was established in 1994, before the Internet was widely available or used by international organizations. Today, the ICTR website offers extensive textual resources, including judgments, press releases, and event announcements in English, French, and Kinyarwanda. Video coverage is available by satellite for television (not online), and social media are not part of the court's communication strategy. Since the court's activities are winding down, it seems unlikely that social media will be developed as part of its outreach strategy. Perhaps other organizations, such as the Virtual Tribunal or museum collections described below, will archive its material and make it available online.

The informality and immediacy of social media seem at odds with the formal, highly structured institutions of international courts, where judges and prosecutors still wear traditional robes and cravats. Yet clearly many court public information officers have recognized the utility of these tools for communicating their work and countering misinformation. Materials being gathered and organized online today will become the archives of tomorrow. These repositories will serve as vital resources for disseminating the finished work of tribunals and preserving their accomplishments and controversies for future generations (see Table 9.1). Legacy projects are discussed in greater detail later in the chapter.

Table 9.1.

The Courts and Social Media at a Glance (as of December 2012)

TRIBUNAL	FACEBOOK	TWITTER	YOUTUBE	OTHER
International Criminal Court	No official page	@IntlCrimCourt 40,000 followers 600 Tweets @OTP_ICC 1,284 followers 11 Tweets	http://www.youtube.com/user/IntlCriminalCourt (created October 6, 2009) 1,300 subscribers 490,000 video views	
Extraordinary Chambers of the Courts of Cambodia	http://www.facebook.com/krtribunal 6,000 likes	@KRTribunal 2,300 followers 450 Tweets	http://www.youtube.com/krtribunal (created November 19, 2009) 91 videos 122 subscribers 164,000 video views	Flickr: http://www.flickr.com/photos/krtribunal/
International Criminal Tribunal for the Former Yugoslavia	No official page	@ICTYnews 3,750 followers 5,000 Tweets	http://www.youtube.com/user/ICTYtv (created August 2, 2010) 1,428 videos 750 subscribers 1.2 million video views	
Special Court of Sierra Leone	No official page	@SpecialCourt 2,700 followers 650 Tweets	No official account, but some trial footage available.	
International Criminal Justice for Rwanda	No official page	No account	http://www.youtube.com/ICTRTPIR (created February 3, 2012) 10 subscribers 3,360 video views	
Special Tribunal for Lebanon	No official page	@STLebanon 7,000 followers 1,400 Tweets	http://www.youtube.com/stlebanon (created January 26, 2011) 107 videos 48 subscribers 12,500 video views	Flickr: http://www.flickr.com/photos/stlebanon Scribd: http://www.scribd.com/STLebanon

VIEW FROM THE COURTROOM

> The more we can do to open the process to the public, the greater the public understanding—the more legitimacy the public system will have in the eyes of the public.
>
> —US district judge J. Thomas Marten, concerning the use of Twitter in the courtroom

New media's allure and utility—as well as the controversies surrounding its use—have extended to courtrooms in the United States and abroad. A federal district judge in Iowa made news in 2009 when he allowed a fraud case to be blogged live from the courtroom.[32] Since then, judges and legal professionals have grappled with the implications of widespread use of social networking tools and Internet availability in the courtroom.[33] An experiment in social media coverage was launched in May 2011 when the Quincy District Court in Massachusetts began livestreaming proceedings, installed WiFi in the courtroom, and allowed full access to bloggers and citizen journalists. Funded in part by the Knight Foundation, OpenCourt is a pilot project to explore the technical and policy issues of increasing new media coverage of the legal process.[34]

The US federal courts recently formed an Ad Hoc Subcommittee on New Media under the Judicial Branch Committee of the Judicial Conference of the United States, the policymaking body for the federal courts.[35] A report on new media and the courts, sponsored by the Conference of Court Public Information Officers, finds that more than one-third of state court judges and magistrates use social media sites like Facebook, while less than 10 percent of courts as institutions use social media for public outreach and communication.[36] In this sense, the international tribunals are ahead of US domestic courts in the percentage using at least some form of social media.[37]

Outside the United States, journalists have been allowed to use Twitter in UK courtrooms since December 2011.[38] Tweeting from the courtroom is also allowed in France, where many judges and lawyers have built their own sizable followings.[39] Information about the use of social media in courtrooms internationally is scarce, but online platforms are contributing to innovations in the rule of law through the Hague-based Innovating Justice Forum.[40]

The desire to make judicial proceedings publicly available in a timely fashion must be balanced in the age of multimedia with questions of witness protection. Victims or witnesses who testify in The Hague, even in open court, may not want their participation or details about the crimes known to their home communities, especially if the crimes are sensitive or carry social stigma, such as sexual assault. Increasingly widespread use of social media also brings ethical considerations: Can judges "friend" a prosecutor on Facebook? What access should juries have to social media during the trial or deliberations? What privacy concerns of the accused or victims should be heeded regarding social media use in the courtroom?[41] These issues need to be considered when developing policy regarding new media and formal justice mechanisms, for they raise not just procedural questions but also influence public perceptions of the court and the fairness of due process.

ADVOCACY ORGANIZATIONS, GOVERNMENT AGENCIES, AND INDEPENDENT GROUPS

Free from the layers of bureaucracy inherent in most official international justice institutions, civil society organizations have often enjoyed the flexibility to be more entrepreneurial in their use of new media and social networking tools. Since many of these organizations have an explicit advocacy agenda, online and social media strategies have taken a prominent role in their communications plans. Social media offer institutions a means to educate, engage, and mobilize new audiences. At the same time, these tools offer opportunities for independent supporters or opponents of transitional justice measures to express their views and catalyze their own communities outside of an institutional framework.[42]

One innovative online effort to support the work of international justice is IJCentral, "a resource for concerned citizens around the world who want an effective International Criminal Court to prosecute perpetrators of crimes against humanity, war crimes, and genocide."[43] The site offers blog posts, videos, geo-located Twitter feeds about the International Criminal Court, and other international justice news. It also has a community section (run on the Ning platform) in which members can upload their own content, comment, post, and "Ask the Prosecutor," a section that promises answers from the ICC prosecutor to questions posted on the comment wall. The site was created as an outreach component to the film *The Reckoning: The Battle for the International Criminal Court*, by Paco de Onís and Pamela Yates of Skylight Pictures, and first produced at the Bay Area Video Coalition's Producers Institute for New Media Technologies in 2008.

IJ Central currently has about fifteen hundred active members, primarily from the United States and Europe.[44] In the next phase, cofounder de Onís says, "We want to move [IJ Central] from being primarily an aggregator of information to facilitating more interaction among its members. We want to create a platform for a global discussion of international justice."[45] Plans for additional staff will help to facilitate this more active engagement.

The Coalition for the International Criminal Court (CICC) is a collection of twenty-five hundred civil society organizations in 150 countries working "to strengthen international cooperation with the ICC; ensure that the Court is fair, effective, and independent; make justice both visible and universal; and advance stronger national laws that deliver justice to victims of war crimes, crimes against humanity, and genocide."[46] Since 2009 the coalition has been an active user of social media, including Facebook, Twitter, and Flickr (links to these accounts are available on its homepage), and now has nearly 14,000 followers on Facebook and 2,066 on Twitter (@_CICC). The coalition uses Twitter not only to make its own announcements but also to stay abreast of news from its member organizations.[47]

However, the CICC still publishes printed newsletters and other publications; its *Monitor*, for example, is sent to nearly twenty thousand organizations or households, and it also produces other newsletters with a regional focus. The organization hosts a blog, "In Situ," launched at the beginning of the Thomas Lubanga trial in January 2009. It proved difficult to get information from the Democratic Republic of Congo over the course of the trial, and the blog was suspended for a time to reexamine its effectiveness and purpose. The group continues to post updates and live blogging sessions intermittently.[48] Learning experiences like these are essential for groups testing new strategies for outreach and communications.

The Open Society Justice Initiative (OSJI) produces five blogs that monitor ongoing trials of defendants at the International Criminal Court and Special Court for Sierra Leone (see the appendix to this chapter for a list of the blogs' website addresses and dates of operation). The blogs are excellent sources of information, providing a front-row seat to the proceedings and background on the issues unfolding in the courtroom. The audience for these websites includes journalists tasked with covering the trials from the regions, as well as members of affected communities, whether in Africa or abroad.

In the convention of blogs, they offer an opportunity for interaction through comments. On the Charles Taylor trial blog (http://www.charlestaylortrial.org), for example, a lively exchange ensued following the announcement of the verdict on April 26, 2012. More than one hundred comments were posted within the following two weeks, with many readers commending the verdict for bringing justice to victims of Taylor's crimes while others regarded the result as further evidence of colonialism and European prejudice against Africa. Some raised the question of culpability of multinational corporations for the trade in blood diamonds that, in part, fueled the conflict. Others questioned whether this precedent would facilitate prosecution of US president George W. Bush or UK prime minister Tony Blair for war crimes in Iraq. The comments on this and subsequent posts offer insight into the highly charged views of Sierra Leone and Liberia's online constituents, both in the region and abroad.[49] Despite divergent and strongly stated opinions, several commenters expressed appreciation to the blog's moderators for offering the platform to inform them of the court's proceedings and exchange their views.[50]

The Center for Accountability and Rule of Law in Sierra Leone (http://www.carl-sl.org) provides some resources related to transitional justice in that country, including links to the Special Court for Sierra Leone and the Truth and Reconciliation Commission report. The center also sponsors a blog (http://carlsl.wordpress.com) that provided weekly summaries of the Charles Taylor trial until September 2010.

Rwanda's *gacaca* courts, authorized to try cases unaddressed by the ICTR related to the 1994 genocide, have an extensive website with resources in English, French, and Kinyarwanda (http://www.inkiko-gacaca.gov.rw/). Maintained by the National Service of Gacaca Jurisdictions, the site includes information on the applicable laws, activities completed by the courts, and data about the accused and the status of their trials or sentences.

The accessibility of new media tools also creates opportunities for those outside of formal institutions to inform and create momentum for causes related to justice in specific countries or situations. A Facebook group dedicated to investigating forced disappearances in Syria during the 1970s and 1980s was established in 2010 and now has more than three thousand members.[51] The administrator of the group said it "was created by the National Committee of the Disappeared in Syria, which was established in 2000 as an underground movement after the death of president Hafez al-Assad." He said he hoped the group would "encourage the families of the disappeared to participate in the discussions online without fear because of the anonymous cover offered by the internet."[52]

Similarly, social networking can also be useful for diaspora communities to stay abreast of developments regarding transitional justice measures. For example, the Darfurian diaspora community in Europe is very active online. Since mid-2011 the ICC Outreach Officer for Darfur has been helping to coordinate a project with the UK-based Darfur Watch, the Sudanese Democratic

Forum in the Netherlands, and the Sudan Contemporary Center for Studies and Development in Egypt, to develop projects using social media tools to disseminate information on the ICC's work and mandate, including information on victims' rights to participation and reparations. The groups have created platforms on Facebook, Twitter, YouTube, and Flickr with the legal content reviewed by the outreach staff for accuracy. Although these projects operate independently of the court, the outreach officer supports their work by providing informative public documents, fact sheets, case information sheets, and responses to frequently asked questions on the situation in Darfur, in addition to audiovisual materials provided on the ICC YouTube channel (summaries of hearings and cases, explanatory videos on the situation, and the like).[53]

Shortly after the 2008 post-election violence in Kenya, comments on a plethora of blogs in that country highlighted persistent ethnic divisions and spoke to questions of peace versus justice. On Mashada.com, an online forum frequented by Kenyans at home and abroad, user DaDon complained about the endemic corruption of the politicians, writing, "I do not want peace if the status quo is going to remain the same." Other blogs followed the unraveling of the electoral process and subsequent mediation efforts.[54] The topic arose again on message boards as the ICC summoned the six possible defendants for hearings in The Hague in fall 2011 and throughout the judicial process that followed. OSJI's blog, *Kenya Monitor*, offers summaries of proceedings, links to Kenyan online media, and a forum for comments on updates and decisions.[55]

In addition to situation-specific blogs, a number of blogs, often based at academic centers or law schools, are devoted more broadly to international criminal justice and human rights. These outlets provide an increasingly important channel for public discussion of transitional justice issues. More timely and nimble than peer-reviewed journals, they offer a space for academics and practitioners to discuss and comment on new developments at the international tribunals. Examples include the Human Rights & International Law Online Forum, a joint project of the ICC Office of the Prosecutor and the UCLA School of Law (http://uclalawforum.com/); *IntLawGrrls*, a blog written by women who teach and work in international law, policy, and practice (http://intlawgrrls.blogspot.com/); *Grotian Moment*, "the international war crimes trial blog," hosted by Case Western Reserve University's School of Law (http://law.case.edu/grotian-moment-blog/); and the Foreign Policy Association's blog on war crimes (http://foreignpolicyblogs.com/category/warcrimes/), among others.

LEGACY AND EDUCATION

New media and online social networking allow up-to-the-minute access to breaking news posted by institutions, journalists, and activists on the ground. At the same time, these posts and uploaded materials serve to document the history of a conflict and efforts toward its resolution through transitional justice measures. Websites created by courts or through special agreements with universities or other organizations become excellent archival sources, memorializing tribunals' accomplishments and challenges.

The Virtual Tribunal Project, a joint project of UC Berkeley's War Crimes Studies Center and Computer Science Department and Stanford University's Hoover Institute, recognized an untapped resource in the materials available at the ICTY in the mid-2000s. The court had produced ample trial materials, such as transcripts and video, but these were poorly organized and difficult to use, since the United Nations had conducted no advance planning for their storage or organization.[56] In this absence, UC Berkeley professors David Cohen and Ruzena Bajcsy envisioned an electronic resource, eventually to be available online, that would re-create the courtroom environment and preserve trial information and make it accessible for later use by judges, lawyers, academics, and the general public. For the ICTY, they have created a model for organizing information left by the court through aligning courtroom video with transcripts and making the transcripts searchable by keyword, date, speaker, and the like.

The trials of Khmer Rouge leaders in Cambodia by the ECCC offered another opportunity for the Virtual Tribunal Project to work with the court—in this case, from the beginning—and make the complete materials available online. The site will be fully searchable in English and Khmer, and innovations in computer programming will allow text and video footage to be synchronized. Users can search for a particular keyword and have the video cued up to display the specific moment of the trial. The site will include cross-references to motions and judgments, as well as links by record number to documentary and physical evidence. The website will also offer external materials such as newspaper articles, broadcast interviews and coverage, photographs, and more. Its 2012 launch has been delayed, but eventually the Virtual Tribunal will be a valuable resource for research and education about the trials, defendants, and victims of the crimes.[57]

Several libraries and archives devoted to human rights collections are also preserving their holdings electronically and making them available to a broad public. Not only are the catalogs and finding aids available online, but in many cases archival materials have been digitized and made freely available. A leading example is the Open Society Archive (OSA), based at the Central European University in Budapest (see http://www.osaarchivum.org). In addition to collecting documents related to recent history and human rights, the archive "continue[s] to experiment with new ways to contextualize primary sources, developing innovative tools to explore, represent, or bridge traditional archival collections in a digital environment."[58] Among the materials available online are transcripts of Radio Free Europe broadcasts and documents on the activities of the UN Special Committee on the Problem of Hungary from the 1950s, extensive materials related to Hungary's democratic transition in 1989, and the Digital State Security Archive (in Hungarian). Finally, OSA also hosts a server for Martus, the documentation program developed by Benetech for secure reporting on human rights violations. HURIDOCS (Human Rights Information and Documentation Systems) is another international NGO using information technology to monitor and document violations.[59]

Online tools offer opportunities to reach young people, inside and outside the classroom, through innovative use of interactive websites and games. The field of video games for social change has been led by the organization Games for Change (G4C), based in New York.[60] G4C is helping to develop several projects related to international human rights and justice, including a multimedia platform based on the book by Nicholas Kristof and Sheryl WuDunn, *Half the Sky*. The organization is spawning international chapters; the first, in South Korea, has facilitated funding of a new game based on the demilitarized zone between North Korea and South Korea. The keynote address at G4C's 2010 annual conference was given by former US Supreme Court justice Sandra Day O'Connor, who has promoted this strategy to educate students about civics and the courts. Her project, iCivics (formerly Our Courts), offers games such as Court Quest, Do I Have a Right? and Supreme Decision, which explore the three branches of the US government.[61] Similarly, a website sponsored by Arizona's state court, Law for Kids, had 22 million hits in the first six months of 2008 (apparently reaching a more active online audience than seniors, as the parallel Law for Seniors website had only 368,000 hits during the same period).[62] In the United Kingdom, the Education Service of the Parliament has launched a number of online games in recent years, in order to inform young people about their government and engage them in the democratic process. These include the Campaign Trail, which explores active citizenship; Get the Houses in Order, which explores the buildings and functions of Parliament; MyUK, which enables players to create their own version of the country and pass their own laws; and MP for a Week, which simulates the job of a parliamentary representative.[63] These have enjoyed significant success: MyUK drew 60,000 plays from 40,000 unique visitors in the first six months after its launch,[64] and MP for a Week received over 125,000 visits in its first year, along with four educational awards.[65] The gaming model holds promise for engaging new audiences in the complicated issues of transitional justice and educating them about ongoing investigations and cases.

New media also provide resources for educators teaching the complicated histories of genocide, whether in their own countries or elsewhere. The international organization Facing History and Ourselves uses video and social networking tools, as well as more traditional resources, to help educators talk with their students about genocide and mass violence in order to draw lessons for their own moral choices. The organization has developed materials on international human rights and justice mechanisms, including an extensive guide for teaching the documentary *The Reckoning* in the classroom.[66]

A similar project is the interactive website launched in June 2010 by the Youth Initiative for Human Rights (YIHR) in Sarajevo. "Srebrenica Mapping Genocide" is a multimedia project that uses "documentary animation" to present the chronology of events between July 6 and 19, 1995, in Srebrenica. Materials in English and BCS (Bosnian/Croatian/Serbian) are divided into seventeen "maps" that guide the user through the chronology of the genocide.[67] Alma Mašic, director of YIHR, plans to use the website to expand understanding of the genocide among youth through the formal education systems and reduce the space for denying the atrocities.[68] If education is a component of the transitional justice toolbox, new media and social networking are well suited to support that strategy.

CROSS-CUTTING ISSUES

Despite the great potential offered by new media and social networking, transitional justice institutions and affiliated organizations share a number of challenges related to effective implementation of these tools. Some of the considerations highlighted here include multiple languages of organizations and users, evolving technology, the sociodemographic profile of their audiences, and financial and human resources.

Most social media tools were created and developed for English-speaking audiences, but courts and international justice NGOs must also communicate in French, Khmer, Arabic, and other local languages. Many of the online tools can be used in these languages—Twitter and Facebook support Khmer and Arabic fonts, for example—but posting in all relevant languages poses challenges. Should a court have one Facebook page with the same messages in multiple languages? A different page for each language? Tweet only in English but with links to pages in local languages? (This has been the solution of the ICTY to date, while the STL tweets in English, French, and Arabic.) Each of these decisions has political as well as staffing implications.

Context is paramount. Where Internet connections are well developed and relatively uncensored, social media are more effective than in contexts in which Internet access is slow or unavailable. Internet penetration in Cambodia, for example, is extremely limited, which is paradoxical, considering the pioneering use of social media by the ECCC. The court's investment in these strategies may speak to its commitment to inform international audiences of journalists and diaspora communities. Just over 3 percent of Cambodians (or 449,160 people) had access to the Internet in December 2011,[69] while in Kenya access is more widespread (almost 10.5 million users, or 25.5 percent of the population).[70] Kenya also had 17.5 million mobile phone subscribers by 2009.[71] Internet infrastructure is growing rapidly but unevenly, and areas affected by war and mass atrocities are less likely to have access to online resources and tools.

Geographic and technological context must be considered when developing use of these tools for outreach or data collection. In some areas, especially in developing countries, cell phones are more ubiquitous and cost-effective than the Internet. For example, as of April 2010, mobile phones represent more than 90 percent of all phone lines in Africa,[72] and mobile penetration on the continent reached 50 percent later that year.[73] Text messaging (SMS) is already being used for agricultural updates, public health interventions, and mobile banking in some areas and could be incorporated more widely into court outreach plans—such as announcing court decisions or events.[74]

Justice practitioners, whether in courts, advocacy organizations, or ad hoc groups, must consider the audience they are reaching through online tools. A useful analysis would include more than metrics such as the number of visitors or geographic distribution of visits to their websites, which are easily gained through Google Analytics or other software. For a more nuanced understanding of online audiences for transitional justice issues, empirical research or surveys could distinguish between types of activity—whether passive consumption (e.g., visiting websites, following on Twitter or Facebook, reading blogs) or active creation of content (e.g., tweeting or re-tweeting, commenting on blogs or Facebook, creating websites or Facebook pages, entering data into mapping software), according to level of education, socioeconomic status, gender, ethnicity, and other parameters.

Studies of the digital divide have suggested a participation gap, determined by frequency of access to hardware, software, and the Internet. Studies of youth with low-quality home access to the Internet in the United States show that they are more task-oriented and less creative in their online pursuits than high-access, high-autonomy peers.[75] Producing content online also requires time: "Online content production, such as posting to a daily blog or maintaining a Web site, is labor intensive and requires more leisure time since this commodity is often 'free labor' in the digital economy."[76] Both of these considerations—access to tools and the Internet, as well as time for production and consumption—have implications for understanding the actual and potential audiences for transitional justice projects. Recent surveys in the United States, conducted by the Pew Internet and American Life Project, suggest that Internet users who visit social networking sites (MySpace, Facebook, LinkedIn, Twitter) are much more likely to be involved in civic and political life than users who do not visit such sites, even controlling for other demographics, such as age and education.[77]

What about gender? *Foreign Policy* magazine's list of the "FP Twitterati 100: A Who's Who of the Foreign-Policy Twitterverse in 2011" included fewer than 20 women.[78] This reflects academic studies showing that although women constitute just over half of online users, they are significantly less likely to post their own creative content on the Web.[79] In low- and middle-income countries, studies show that women are 21 percent less likely to own a mobile phone.[80] Considering this gender gap will be important when creating and assessing transitional justice projects.

If courts and NGOs intend to include new media as part of their strategies for communications and outreach, they must invest adequately in staffing and infrastructure. A misconception persists in some quarters that because an Internet connection is relatively low-cost and online services like Facebook and Twitter are free, the work of social media engagement requires little investment. This is true, when compared to the cost of printing glossy publications or producing polished television segments. But effective use of these new platforms requires dedicated, knowledgeable staff to work within the communications team to develop and implement online strategies.

PROMISE AND PERIL OF NEW MEDIA IN TRANSITIONAL JUSTICE

New media channels have the power to influence and engage opinion leaders, advocates, and the online public. In the connected world, online tools are helping to facilitate communication, raise awareness, increase transparency, and build political will. Such tools can make these sometimes daunting and bureaucratic institutions more engaging and approachable. The disadvantages or vulnerabilities of social media are also apparent. Misinformation and propaganda can spread just as quickly as reliable information.[81] The same open platforms that facilitate community-building can also serve as forums for criticism and sow ethnic division. Similar hopes and suspicions have recurred with each new wave of innovation in communication technology; the telegraph was extolled in 1858 as a tool to "remov[e] causes of misunderstanding, and promot[e] peace and harmony throughout the world," but at the same time was recognized as a key to colonialism and blamed for the deterioration of public intelligence because it dispensed news in brief snippets (echoed in criticisms of Twitter today). Likewise, in the 1920s the radio was thought to promote democracy and transparent government, only a few years before Hitler and Mussolini effectively employed it.[82]

Careful analysis of online social networks can suggest to what extent they are aiding or confounding efforts to repair post-conflict societies. Questions that could be addressed through survey research or link analysis include: Do new media foster or undermine connections between like-minded people or groups? Do new media help reinforce group identity in pre-conflict and conflict situations? Can new media be used to further cross-community engagement in post-conflict situations?[83] Armed with a more nuanced understanding of current uses and effectiveness of these networks, transitional justice scholars and practitioners can develop more targeted interventions using these tools.

In the transitional justice sphere, perhaps the most promising technologies are those that offer interoperability between platforms. Smartphones or even conventional cell phones may be used to upload data to a website, ask questions or receive information via SMS, or access social networks through Facebook or Twitter. All these activities could contribute to the goals of investigating and documenting atrocities and war crimes and communicating about justice mechanisms. International tribunals like the ICC, ICTY, STL, and ECCC are to be congratulated for the investments of time, finances, and personnel they have made in new media. Online audiences are growing, especially in countries where Internet access is high, and such channels provide multiple opportunities for courts and advocacy organizations to reach out to scholars, donors, practitioners, and—in some cases—affected communities. Efforts to memorialize the courts' work not only contribute to current understanding of transitional justice measures but will also serve as a record of the justice process well into the future.

New media will undoubtedly be part of the battle for the global narrative about transitional justice. But new communication tools are no panacea for engaging communities struck by human rights violations or for building political will to intervene or protect them. Behind every gadget or app must be a person willing to use it. Perhaps the most promising—and empowering—use of new media is not on behalf of institutions like courts or truth commissions at all but rather among groups struggling to emerge from repressive governance and establish democratic systems. Events during 2011 and 2012 in Syria, Burma, and elsewhere suggest that when ICT infrastructure is available, local populations arrive at resourceful solutions for organizing and advocating for the future they want. Transitional justice scholars and practitioners could look to the emerging field of community informatics for relevant research on the confluence of social media, community organizing, and participatory governance. Likewise, transitional justice would be a worthwhile context in which to apply and test ideas arising in domestic studies of online behavior, political beliefs, and personal development.

To be effective, courts and related organizations must plan and invest accordingly to integrate these strategies into their public information and outreach programs. Entrepreneurial individuals with a grasp of the opportunities and liabilities posed by new media should be encouraged to explore the application of innovations in communications technology and social media to the work of the courts and the organizations that support them. Ultimately, the same degree of care, creativity, and investment must be brought to this area of transitional justice work as to other activities meant to provide accountability for the perpetrators and redress for the victims.

APPENDIX OF ONLINE RESOURCES

INTERNATIONAL AND HYBRID TRIBUNALS

The black and white boxes are QR codes, two-dimensional codes that people can scan with the QR code readers on their smartphones or other devices that can capture the image and access the Internet. Scanning the codes links the user to the websites of the respective court.

International Criminal Court: http://icc-cpi.int/	International Criminal Tribunal for the former Yugoslavia: http://icty.org
International Criminal Tribunal for Rwanda: http://www.unictr.org	Extraordinary Chambers in the Courts of Cambodia: http://www.eccc.gov.kh/
Special Court for Sierra Leone: http://www.sc-sl.org/	Special Tribunal for Lebanon: http://stl-tsl.org

NGOS AND RELATED ORGANIZATIONS

Transitional Justice in the Arab World: http://www.arabtj.org
International Center for Transitional Justice: http://www.ictj.org
Coalition for the International Criminal Court: http://www.iccnow.org
IJ Central: http://www.ijcentral.org
National Service of Gacaca Jurisdictions: http://www.inkiko-gacaca.gov.rw/index_.html
Open Society Justice Initiative: http://www.soros.org/initiatives/justice

COVERAGE OF SPECIFIC TRIALS

ICC trial of Jean-Pierre Bemba: http://www.bembatrial.org/
ICC trial of Thomas Lubanga (since January 2009): http://www.lubangatrial.org/
ICC trial of Jean-Pierre Bemba (since November 2010): http://www.bembatrial.org/
ICC trial of Germain Kataga and Mathieu Ngudjolo Chui (since February 2011): http://www.katangatrial.org/
ICC trials of defendants in Kenya's post-election violence (since April 2011): http://www.icckenya.org/
SCSL trial of Charles Taylor (since June 2007): http://www.charlestaylortrial.org/

NOTES

I would like to thank Eric Stover and John R. Palmer for their helpful comments on this chapter. I also thank the court officials and NGO representatives interviewed for generously sharing their time and expertise.

1 In this chapter I use *new media* to refer to any tools or applications available via the Internet, from information posted on a website (text or multimedia) to more interactive applications (blogs or commenting/sharing features). Unless otherwise specified I use *new media* also to encompass *social networking*, the range of applications that allow for user-generated content (Facebook, Twitter, etc.) that can be consumed, created, and shared from a standard computer as well as from most smartphones or other mobile devices.

2 *Transitional justice*, as defined earlier in this volume, refers to the range of judicial and non-judicial mechanisms used by states emerging from conflict to redress massive human rights violations. These measures may include criminal prosecutions, truth commissions, reparation programs, institutional reform, memorials, and education programs.

3 Although criminal tribunals are only one of many transitional justice mechanisms, they tend to be better funded and more fully staffed than truth commissions or programs for reparations or memorialization, for example, and are often better able to utilize new media resources. Lessons learned from their successes and challenges can be relevant for other transitional justice organizations.

4 The boundary between 1.0 and 2.0 is not always distinct, as some sites offer users the chance to manipulate or combine given data sets for applications like creating word clouds or mashups. In these cases the raw data are given, but the user creates something new from them.

5 Gary Wolf, "How the Internet Invented Howard Dean," *Wired*, January 2004, http://www.wired.com/wired/archive/12.01/dean.html.

6 See Evgeny Morozov, "Moldova's Twitter Revolution," *Net Effect* (blog), *Foreign Policy*, April 7, 2009, http://neteffect.foreignpolicy.com/posts/2009/04/07/moldovas_twitter_revolution. See also successive blog posts analyzing the roles that Twitter did and did not play in the Moldovan uprisings.

7 Ethan Zuckerman, "The First Twitter Revolution?," *Foreign Policy*, January 14, 2011, http://www.foreignpolicy.com/articles/2011/01/14/the_first_twitter_revolution. See also Catherine Smith, "Egypt's Facebook Revolution: Wael Ghonim Thanks the Social Network," *Huffington Post*, February 11, 2011, http://www.huffingtonpost.com/2011/02/11/egypt-facebook-revolution-wael-ghonim_n_822078.html.

8 See, for example, Jennifer Preston, "Seeking to Disrupt Protesters, Syria Cracks Down on Social Media," *New York Times*, May 22, 2011: "With foreign journalists barred from the country, dissidents have been working with exiles and using Facebook, YouTube and Twitter to draw global attention to the brutal military crackdown on protesters that has killed more than 700 people and has led to mass arrests in the last nine weeks. The Syrian Revolution 2011 Facebook page, which now has more than 180,000 members, has been a vital source of information for dissidents." See also Clay Shirky, "The Political Power of Social Media: Technology, the Public Sphere, and Political Change," *Foreign Affairs*, January/February 2011, 28–41.

9 See Evgeny Morozov, *The Net Delusion: The Dark Side of Internet Freedom* (New York: Public Affairs, 2011).

10 Fergus Hanson, *Revolution @State: The Spread of Ediplomacy* (Sydney: Lowy Institute for International Policy, March 2012), 3.

11 "Tech@State connects tech innovators and those interested in diplomacy and development to enable 21st-century statecraft by improving education, health, and welfare of the world's population. This site was created by the U.S. State Department's Office of eDiplomacy." The site has 734 members. See http://tech.state.gov. For *dipNote*, see http://blogs.state.gov.

12 For an excellent discussion of Twitter diplomacy, see Brian Solis, "How World Leaders Use Social Media: Why the @WhiteHouse Doesn't Follow @BarackObama and Other Idiosyncrasies," *Brian Solis* (blog), May 16, 2011, http://www.briansolis.com/2011/05/how-world-leaders-use-social-media-why-the-whitehouse-doesn't-follow-barackobama-and-other-idiosyncrasies/.

13 See Clara Ramírez-Barat, *Making an Impact: Guidelines on Designing and Implementing Outreach Programs for Transitional Justice* (New York: International Center for Transitional Justice, January 2011), 3.

14 Lists of website addresses for the tribunals and other institutions cited in this chapter are available in the chapter's appendix.

15 As mentioned above, I do not consider in this article new media regarding informal justice mechanisms or truth commissions, some of which have extensive websites with archival documentation of their work, but few of which use social networking tools. One exception is Liberia's Truth and Reconciliation Commission (LTRC), which benefited from the MOSES project (Mobile Story Exchange System), an initiative to collect video testimony and share footage of the LTRC with those in remote areas using a Jeep outfitted with video equipment. See Shawn Pelsinger, "Liberia's Long Tail: How Web 2.0 Is Changing and Challenging Truth Commissions," *Human Rights Law Review* 10, no. 4 (December 2010): 730–48.

16 Aside from their implementation in communications programs, online tools continue to be developed for judicial purposes. New models for e-courts are emerging for adjudicating civil cases. The Netherlands has pioneered such a court; see "E-Court, the First Private Online Court," *Innovating Justice*, http://www.innovatingjustice.com/innovations/e-court-the-first-online-private-court. Although international and domestic courts have developed electronic tools for internal operations, such as cataloging documentary evidence and witness testimony (the "eCourt Protocol" at the ICC), these tools are not intended to serve the public.

17 International Criminal Court Assembly of States Parties (ICC-ASP), "Report of the Court on the Public Information Strategy, 2011–2013," Doc. No. ICC-ASP/9/29, November 22, 2010, http://www.icc-cpi.int/iccdocs/asp_docs/ASP9/ICC-ASP-9-29-ENG.pdf.

18 International Criminal Court, "Integrated Strategy for External Relations, Public Information, and Outreach," 2006, http://www.icc-cpi.int/NR/rdonlyres/425E80BA-1EBC-4423-85C6-D4F2B93C7506/185049/ICCPIDSWBOR0307070402_IS_En.pdf.

19 Fadi El-Abdallah, spokesperson and associate legal outreach officer, personal communication with author, June 1, 2011.

20 See https://www.facebook.com/#!/pages/International-Criminal-Court/106219979409522, and https://www.facebook.com/#!/iccemp.

21 ICC-ASP, "Report of the Court on the Public Information Strategy, 2011–2013."

22 Claudia Perdomo, head of the outreach unit, ICC, personal communication with author, May 10, 2011.

23 Nerma Jelacic, head of communications, personal communication with author, July 1, 2011.

24 Jelacic, personal communication with author, May 31, 2011.

25 Jelacic related the story of a Facebook page created in Croatia upon the court's controversial indictment of former general Ante Gotovina on war crimes charges in mid-April 2011. The I F*** Your Mother on All Counts of Indictment page had several thousand followers within days.

26 Transcripts of key proceedings available in BCS were made possible by the War Crimes Justice Project, funded by the European Union.

27 See below for a discussion of assistance provided by UC Berkeley's Virtual Tribunal Project.

28 The show is produced by an independent production company with funding from the US State Department. (Case 001 was covered in a similar series, funded by the British Embassy in Phnom Penh.) See http://www.youtube.com/watch?v=2fhtRqbnRNw.

29 See http://www.sc-sl.org.

30 Peter C. Andersen, chief of outreach and public affairs, Special Court for Sierra Leone, personal communication with author, May 18, 2011.

31 Several courts that offer streaming of court proceedings online actually delay transmission of the broadcast by thirty minutes in order to redact any information that could pose a danger to victims or witnesses or should otherwise be stricken from the record.

32 Debra Cassens Weiss, "Judge Explains Why He Allowed Reporter to Live Blog Federal Criminal Trial," *ABA Journal*, January 16, 2009, http://www.abajournal.com/news/article/bloggers_cover_us_trials_of_accused_terrorists_cheney_aide_and_iowa_landlor/. See also Michael Tarm, "Courtroom Tweet Ban? Judges, Journalists Clash over Social Media in High-Profile Upcoming Trial," Huffington Post, April 18, 2012, http://www.huffingtonpost.com/2012/04/17/courtroom-tweet-ban-judge_n_1432686.html.

33 The role of new media in investigations and prosecutions could be the subject of another discussion, beyond the scope of this article. To what extent can user-generated evidence such as crowdsourced maps of violations or video of witness testimony be admissible in court? The video advocacy organization WITNESS has developed training programs and guidelines in this regard. Other sources of crowdsourced evidence may come from crisis-mapping applications developed by Ushahidi.

34 See http://opencourt.us/about/faq/.

35 New Media Committee, Conference of the Court Public Information Officers (CCPIO), "New Media and the Courts: The Current Status and a Look at the Future" (report presented at the CCPIO 19th Annual Meeting, Atlanta, Georgia, August 26, 2010), http://www.ccpio.org/documents/newmediaproject/CCPIO_newmedia_execsumm.pdf, 12.

36 Ibid.

37 Two resources from the United States include "Social Media and the Courts: Resource Guide," National Center for State Courts, accessed April 29, 2013, http://www.ncsc.org/Topics/Media/Social-Media-and-the-Courts/Resource-Guide.aspx, and the Reynolds National Center for Courts and Media, University of Nevada, Reno (http://courtsandmedia.org/journal/).

38 Laura Dugan, "UK Journalists Can Now Tweet from Any Courtroom without Getting Permission First," Mediabistro, December 14, 2011, http://www.mediabistro.com/alltwitter/uk-journalists-use-twitter-in-courtroom_b16765.

39 "'Could We Slap a Witness?' French Judge Tweets from Court," France 24, February 12, 2012, http://www.france24.com/en/20121202-french-judges-courtroom-tweets-murder-twitter.

40 See http://www.innovatingjustice.com/.

41 New media raises a host of questions about its impact on jurors, from doing independent research online to communicating details about the case via social networking. Since jury trials are not typically the case in transitional justice measures, these questions are only touched on here. For a fuller discussion, see Derrick Harris, "How Social Media Is Pushing the Limits of Legal Ethics," Gigaom, February 26, 2011, http://gigaom.com/2011/02/26/how-social-media-is-pushing-the-limits-of-legal-ethics/.

42 For a good example of this, see Wanda Hall's chapter in this book.

43 See http://ijcentral.org.

44 Paco de Onís, personal communication with author, March 3, 2011.

45 Ibid.

46 See http://www.iccnow.org.

47 Oriane Maillet, CICC head of communications, personal communication with author, May 30, 2011.

48 See http://www.coalitionfortheicc.org/blog/.

49 See http://www.charlestaylortrial.org/2012/04/26/charles-taylor-found-guilty/#comment-.

50 The OSJI blogs are lightly moderated to ensure that the comments adhere to guidelines of civility. All users who post comments must agree to the site's Terms and Conditions, which include specific rules of conduct that prohibit threatening or harassing speech, among other guidelines (see, e.g., http://www.charlestaylortrial.org/about/terms). Moderators also respond to questions of fact and procedure posed by the commenters.

51 See http://www.facebook.com/SyrianEnforcedDisappearances.

52 Institute for War and Peace Reporting, "Group to 'Break Silence' on Disappeared," Transitional Justice in the Arab World, May 5, 2010, http://www.arabtj.org/english/news.php?id=76&idC=11.

53 Diale Chehade, ICC legal outreach coordinator for Sudan, personal communication with author, April 26, 2012.

54 See Juliet Njeri, "Battle of the Blogs in Kenya," BBC Monitoring, January 16, 2008, http://news.bbc.co.uk/2/hi/africa/7189291.stm.

55 See http://www.icckenya.org/.

56 Comments summarized from personal communications with the cofounders, as well as a presentation, are available at http://iis-db.stanford.edu/evnts/5731/The_Virtual_Tribunal_Project.pdf, accessed April 29, 2013.

57 Information in this paragraph comes from Penelope van Tuyl, senior program officer at the War Crimes Studies Center, personal communications with author, August 25, 2011, and April 17, 2012.

58 "What Is OSA," Open Society Archives, accessed April 29, 2013, http://osaarchivum.org/index.php?option=com_content&view=article&id=48&Itemid=59&lang=en. This collection and others are related to efforts to create virtual museums, which make images

and information about their collections available free on the Internet. For a list of more than three hundred virtual museums and exhibits, see http://www.virtualfreesites.com/museums.museums.html.

59 See http://benetech.org/human_rights/ and http://www.huridocs.org. The video advocacy group WITNESS is also concerned with preservation of audiovisual materials and has compiled a list of human rights archives on its website at http://hub.witness.org/ArchivesHumanRights.

60 See http://gamesforchange.org.

61 See http://www.ourcourts.org or http://www.icivics.org.

62 "The 'New Media' and the Courts: Journalists and Judges Consider Communications by and about Courts in the Internet Era" (conference report, Rehnquist Center, the Governance Institute, University of Arizona, May 2009), 22. See http://lawforkids.org and http://lawforseniors.org.

63 See www.parliament.UK/education/online-resources/games/.

64 Joshua Rice, "MyUK: Engaging Youth with Parliament and Politics: A Very Informal Evaluation Paper," Parliament Education Service, July 5, 2012, http://museumgames.pbworks.com/f/MyUK%20informal%20evaluation%20-%20Engaging%20youth%20with%20politics%20and%20Parliament.pdf, 3.

65 Peter Stidwell, Joshua Rice, and Emma-Jane Watchorn, "MP for a Week: An Immersive Game De-mystifying the UK Parliament" (presented at "Museums and the Web 2011," Philadelphia, April 6–9, 2011), http://www.museumsandtheweb.com/mw2011/papers/mp_for_a_week_an_immersive_game_de_mystifying_.

66 In 2010, Facing History's website had 740,000 visits from 211 countries and territories, and the organization has an active Facebook page and YouTube channel. See http://facinghistory.org/reach

67 See http://www.srebrenica-mappinggenocide.com.

68 YIHR, "Interactive Web Site of 'Srebrenica Mapping Genocide' Presented Today in Sarajevo," press release, Sarajevo, June 17, 2010, on file at the Human Rights Center.

69 See http://www.internetworldstats.com and http://www.internetworldstats.com/facebook.htm.

70 Ibid.

71 Steven Livingston, "Africa's Evolving Infosystems: A Pathway to Security and Stability" (Research Paper no. 2, Africa Center for Strategic Studies, Washington, DC, March 2011), 10.

72 Michael Schwartz, "Research and Markets: 50% Mobile Penetration in Africa This Year," Developing Telecoms, April 9, 2010, http://www.developingtelecoms.com/research-and-markets-50-mobile-penetration-in-africa-this-year.html.

73 See "Africa and Middle East Mobile Operator Statistics," Africa and Middle East Telecom News, accessed March 9, 2012, http://www.africantelecomsnews.com/Africa_Subscriber_Data.html.

74 The International Criminal Court Outreach Unit planned to pilot this service in Uganda in 2009. See its Outreach Report 2008, http://www.icc-cpi.int/NR/rdonlyres/AE9B69EB-2692-4F9C-8F08-B3844FE397C7/279073/Outreach_report2008enLR1.pdf, 28.

75 See Laura Robinson, "A Taste for the Necessary," *Information, Communication, and Society* 12, no. 4 (2009): 488–507.

76 See Jen Schradie, "The Digital Production Gap: The Digital Divide and Web 2.0 Collide," *Poetics* 39, no. 2 (April 2011): 151. Schradie finds a strong class divide among Internet activities, even controlling for age, race, and gender.

77 Keith Hampton, Lauren Sessions Goulet, Lee Rainie, and Kristen Purcell, "Social Networking Sites and Our Lives" (report by the Pew Research Center's Internet and American Life Project, June 16, 2011), http://www.pewinternet.org/~/media//Files/Reports/2011/PIP%20-%20Social%20networking%20sites%20and%20our%20lives.pdf, 40–41. A number of earlier studies on the relationship between online activities and civic engagement have come to sometimes contradictory conclusions; see the discussion of research variables in M. Kent Jennings and Vicki Zeitner, "Internet Use and Civic Engagement: A Longitudinal Analysis," *Public Opinion Quarterly* 67, no. 3 (Fall 2003): 311–34.

78 Posted June 20, 2011, http://www.foreignpolicy.com/articles/2011/06/20/the_fp_twitterati_100.

79 Eszter Hargittai and Gina Walejko, "The Participation Divide: Content Creation and Sharing in the Digital Age," *Information, Communication, and Society* 11, no. 2 (2008): 239–56.

80 "Women and Mobile: A Global Opportunity: A Study on the Mobile Phone Gender Gap in Low- and Middle-Income Countries," GSMA Development Fund, 2010, http://www.cherieblairfoundation.org/uploads/pdf/women_and_mobile_a_global_opportunity.pdf.

81 A rumor that South Carolina's governor Nikki Haley was to be indicted for tax fraud spread across the Internet in minutes on March 29, 2012, and was taken up by mainstream journalists before the governor could react to the false allegation. See "A Lie Races across Twitter before the Truth Can Boot Up," *New York Times*, April 9, 2012.

82 See Morozov, *Net Delusion*, 276–80 (see n. 10).

83 See Sean Aday, Henry Farrell, Marc Lynch, John Sides, John Kelly, and Ethan Zuckerman, *Blogs and Bullets: New Media in Contentious Politics* (Washington, DC: US Institute of Peace, 2010), 10.

PART 3

Art, Culture, and Transitional Justice

CHAPTER 10

From Tears to Energy: Early Uses of Participatory Theater in Afghanistan

Nadia Siddiqui and Hjalmar Jorge Joffre-Eichhorn

> The theater can help us to turn our tears into energy to keep fighting for justice.
>
> —Dr. Sharif, Afghan actor and political activist

Storytelling within the realm of cultural expression (including oral, written, visual, and performative practices) in ongoing and post-conflict settings provides opportunities for portraying the narratives of war and war-related experiences. Such expression can serve as an important step not only toward individual healing but also more broadly toward restoring collective memory and repairing the social fabric in which individuals are embedded.[1] Reconstructing narratives of past events and telling stories in collective forums can provide a certain sense of normalcy and closure. At the same time, and perhaps more importantly for transitional justice aims, reclaiming truths through the sharing of stories can also serve as a means to foster collective change; it can be a political process.

In contexts in which human rights frameworks are beginning to (re)emerge and transitional justice measures are nascent, theater can be used as an alternative, informal method to push for rights claims and help ensure recourse for survivors of human rights violations. Arts-based forms for storytelling—in particular, the use of what is known as *participatory theater*—are a potentially useful means for addressing the need for self-articulated, personal, and shared narratives, opening space for people to collectively share their stories and create "meaning about what happened in the community."[2]

Paying heed to the political dimensions of participatory theater, our aim in this chapter is to situate these methodologies within the context of arts-based and memory-related efforts to promote transitional justice, specifically raising awareness around truth-seeking opportunities in Afghanistan, by examining the results of projects initiated between 2008 and 2009, first in conjunction with the Afghanistan Independent Human Rights Commission (AIHRC) and the UN Assistance Mission in Afghanistan (UNAMA), and subsequently expanded upon by the International Center for Transitional Justice (ICTJ) and the Afghanistan Human Rights and Democracy Organization (AHRDO). We explore the potential benefits and risks of the use of participatory theater by human rights groups to promote transitional justice in societies during and after conflict. We do not present an exhaustive analysis of such efforts, but rather we intend to contribute to further discussions about the potential for theater as a means of dealing with the past in transitional societies. In examining the possible role of theater within transitional justice, we first describe the links between transitional justice and cultural expression broadly, before more specifically presenting the performative processes implemented in Afghanistan, and then analyzing how this work is helping to broach transitional justice topics at cultural and community levels in the country. In conclusion we offer some concrete recommendations for taking participatory theater methodology forward for its capacity to support transitional justice aims in conflict, post-conflict, or transitional settings, in particular through two complementary conceptual triads—the first geared toward people involved in facilitating the performance process, and the second toward theater audiences or spectators.

TRANSITIONAL JUSTICE AND PARTICIPATORY THEATER

While recognized as an entertaining form of re-creation, theater has traditionally held a deeper purpose than storytelling alone: it functions as a vital act of transfer, conveying social knowledge, memory, and a sense of identity through reiterated behaviors.[3] Because performance in general and theater in particular operate on a number of cognitive registers simultaneously, including reason and emotion, they can be powerful methods for cultural transmission, particularly social critique and cultural analysis.[4]

According to the late playwright and theater theorist John McGrath, theater functions "at the interface between the creative and the political, calling together audiences of citizens to contemplate their society or its ways."[5] As such, it can play an important role in giving voice to the excluded and to minorities, as well as in demanding the right to speak publicly without fear.[6] Theater can further serve to demonstrate the "commonality of living and the importance of seeing the world through the eyes of others."[7] The ideas of universality and impartiality onstage, already key aspects of Greek tragedy, extend into its political purpose in revealing a society's limitations as well as its possibilities.[8] This potentiality is particularly important in times of crisis and change, such as in conflict and post-conflict contexts, where members of communities are pitted against each other for any number of reasons. Showing not only the universal capacity and experience of suffering but also that the world is changeable allows spectators to empathize with the protagonists onstage and may contribute to empowering them to address their own suffering.

A related but more active and collective interpretation of the political aims of theatrical experience can be connected to the understanding of compassion as "an unstable emotion. It needs to be translated into action, or it withers."[9] The aim is to create disequilibrium inside spectators not only so that they will empathize with the protagonist onstage but also to prepare the way for concrete actions to address injustices and bring about transformation. Having audiences actively participate in the transformation process is a central principle of what is known as *community-based theater*.[10] Community-based theater aims to offer participants an aesthetic instrument to analyze their past in the context of the present, and to invent and shape their futures according to their needs, which participatory theater exercises and games help them to determine, without having solutions imposed on them by experts.[11] The underlying assumption inherent in this technique is that people are all equipped to be actors and to take center stage. The main theatrical focus is on dialogue, with the explicit aim of allowing participants to take control of situations rather than simply having things happen to them.

Community-based theater is most closely identified with Brazilian theater director Augusto Boal and his "Theater of the Oppressed," which became an international movement in the 1970s that used his techniques as vehicles for participatory social change. For Boal, many ordinary citizens feel powerless and are in fact blocked in the face of oppression and injustice. With the aim of addressing this problem, he developed a process whereby "theatrical means of both showing what needs to be changed and imagining and deliberating how it might be changed" guide citizens into action.[12] In this process, audience members—so-called spect-actors—can, for example, stop a performance and assume a protagonist role onstage to change the dramatic action, propose various solutions, discuss plans for change, and train themselves for social action.[13] The theatrical act itself thus becomes a conscious intervention and a rehearsal for social action, based on previous collective analysis.[14] Among the components of Boal's method are (1) Image Theater, a basis for other participatory theater work that asks participants to transform their own or others' bodies into representations of particular situations, emotions, or ideas, and (2) Forum Theater, which allows audience members to stop a scene or play showing a conflict that the characters do not know how to resolve or transform and suggest and try out possible solutions. In Forum Theater, "Joker" characters serve as neutral moderators between the actors and the spect-actors.

Playback Theater is another widely used technique in community-based theater. Developed in the United States in 1975 by Jonathon Fox and Jo Salas, this method enables an audience member to tell a story from his or her life and then watch as actors and musicians immediately re-create the scene, giving it artistic shape and coherence.[15] Its main tenet is that human beings need to tell their stories in order to construct meaning. Any story that is significant to the teller, whether happy or sad, mundane or transcendental, can be a part of a performance. Playback Theater celebrates individual experience and the connections between people through their stories. Similar to Theater of the Oppressed, this methodology is open both to professional actors and those with no acting experience, promoting the idea that artistic expression is the domain of all people.

A Playback Theater performance usually includes a variety of short and long forms to respond to audience input, with the three most common being "fluid sculptures," short, abstract sounds and movements expressing the spectators' emotional states; "pairs," an improvisation based on spectators' experiences of simultaneously occurring conflicting emotions; and "stories," in which audience members share longer personal stories of their pasts. Improvised music is an essential element as well, and an array of different instruments is usually available with which the performers can experiment. Finally, a conductor plays the role of host and interviewer and helps to frame and shape the stories told by the audience, thereby effectively cocreating them.

Unlike Boal's Theater of the Oppressed, Playback Theater was not originally devised with an explicit collective political agenda in mind. However, human rights activists and theater practitioners used both methodologies to raise social justice concerns in post-conflict and transitional contexts, including Burundi,[16] the Democratic Republic of Congo,[17] Kosovo,[18] and more recently Afghanistan, among others. The use of these theater forms in such contexts is not entirely surprising given that a central tenet of transitional justice is to give voice to the victims of trauma and human rights violations.

Two of the most well-known transitional justice measures—trials and truth-telling exercises—have among their direct aims providing forums for testimony in an effort to bring accountability and uncover truth in violent contexts where both have been absent. As such, these measures require voices from communities that have in many cases been silenced. For example, Catherine M. Cole argues in her 2007 essay, and in more detail in her chapter in this volume, that the South African Truth and Reconciliation Commission's (TRC) live public hearings functioned in essence as performances, and were effective, however imperfectly, in facilitating transition from a racist, totalitarian state to a nonracial democracy because they were *affective*.[19]

Despite this, official transitional justice initiatives, due to mandate and resource limitations, can only include a select and limited number of victims as participants, leaving a larger number of individuals and groups to feel excluded; certain truths thus remain taboo or silenced.[20] Furthermore, in criminal justice settings, participants are constrained in their responses, given the structures of formal proceedings, and may face adversarial questioning of their experiences. Rather than set the scene and express themselves freely, victims must confine their explanations to the questions asked, as their testimonies are requested to demonstrate culpability (or not) of the accused.

At the same time, in the absence of any formal processes for justice and truth, communities seek their own means for remembering past violations. Recent research in Colombia indicates, for instance, that a number of arts-based initiatives have been undertaken locally by residents of conflict-affected regions in the absence of formal, national processes.[21] These unofficial and alternative truth-seeking projects serve to "repudiate past violence... demand remembrance... and insist that violence not be repeated."[22] In utilizing their own forms of expression and traditions for commemoration and mourning, tellers of truths form, in effect, informal networks of "watchdogs against new encroachments... speak[ing] their truths to power, to themselves, to their compatriots, to anyone who might be listening."[23] These unofficial processes can present stories about specific communities or groups but cannot in and of themselves capture the "complex truths" inherent in a broader historical narrative of a given conflict—a narrative necessary for rebuilding a more just society.[24] Cultural expressions outside of formal proceedings can, however, inform transitional justice processes aimed at capturing a national record because they are densely packed with meaning, having been polished by centuries of transmission from one generation to the next.[25] This meaning may not be apparent in literary or historical documents or straightforward testimony alone, but rather is found in performed, expressive behaviors, as was evident within the South African TRC, where "some truths could be contained within the commission's mandate and procedures [and] other truths constantly erupted in the live, embodied experience" of its public hearings.[26]

Put another way, by examining post-conflict and transitional contexts through a frame of performance, "What would we know that we do not know

now? Whose stories, memories, and struggles might become visible? What tensions might performance behaviors show that would not be recognized in texts and documents?"[27] These questions are about truth and accountability; they are questions for transitional justice. In this chapter we explore these issues as well as the potential benefits and risks of using theater, specifically participatory theater, as a way to facilitate transitional justice in the particularly complex context of Afghanistan by examining concrete projects centered on performance of a scripted play and Theater of the Oppressed and Playback Theater methodologies implemented in the country during 2008 and 2009.

THEATER IN AFGHANISTAN

After more than three decades of war, many Afghans have lived with conflict and abusive political leadership all their lives. Hopes for a more peaceful and just future, which grew in the country after the US-led military intervention in 2001, have been shattered with the reemergence of abusive leaders, corrupt institutional structures, and recurrent violent conflict. Lack of accountability has enabled warlords—politico-military leaders with continued links to illegal armed groups—to become part of the new national and community-level elite. Many of these leaders are alleged perpetrators of war crimes or other serious human rights violations, and their continued access to power contributes to an atmosphere of fear. As a consequence, transitional justice issues are politicized and highly sensitive in Afghanistan today. Opportunities for expressing opinions about past and present violations are diminishing by the day, and public space in which to talk about the legacies of war is fast disappearing.

In this context, formal transitional justice measures may not be immediately viable. Alternative ways must be identified to encourage opportunities to discuss experiences of conflict and explore accountability beyond the traditional mechanisms used in postwar contexts. Theater is one powerful alternative entry point for this process. Afghanistan has a longstanding tradition of oral storytelling and performance, but modern Afghan theater was born in the early twentieth century as a practice and form of entertainment. It was originally started by a few Afghan men who began translating the Western canon and training performers in romantic acting styles in the 1930s, but in just twenty years, modern theater had gained the attention of prominent Afghans and evolved into a collective of about a dozen playwrights whose original works dealt with relevant social, political, economic, domestic, and religious problems facing society.[28] By 1960 Kabul housed two public theaters subsidized by the Ministry of Press, Information, and Culture and by the municipality.

While traditional and modern performance practices were suppressed during years of conflict by a combination of violence and opposition by political and religious leaders, theater and storytelling have in recent years started to slowly and naturally reemerge in Afghan cultural life.[29] Given Afghanistan's low levels of literacy, theater and other unwritten means of outreach are ideal for communication and interaction that can foster public understanding, engagement, and participation around justice-related topics. While the use of participatory theater techniques specifically to broach issues surrounding the legacies of war and accountability is a recent innovation, it has already helped create positive impulses for peacebuilding and the promotion of transitional justice in Afghanistan.

Theater projects specifically oriented around transitional justice began in earnest in Kabul in 2008, initiated jointly by AIHRC and UNAMA, and followed up with support from ICTJ. This initial work consisted of introducing traditional and participatory theater techniques to a group of independent Afghan human rights activists who, tired of working with national and international organizations in Afghanistan at a remove from ordinary citizens, wanted to develop cultural approaches to help foster transitional justice in-country. This group of activists went on to formally establish AHRDO, whose aim is to build a theater- and arts-based transitional justice and gender platform in Afghanistan, serving to bring war victims' concerns to the fore by documenting narratives of war and providing appropriate space for robust policy and strategy debates among victims' groups. Members of AHRDO served as the main theater interlocutors in the initial processes described below—specifically, the adaptation and performance of a scripted play, Playback Theater workshops, and Theater of the Oppressed workshops.

ADAPTATION AND PERFORMANCE OF A SCRIPTED PLAY: *AH 7808* (*AH 6905*)

To begin discussions of accountability with Afghan citizens in their own communities, the Afghan theater team—which was entirely made up of independent Afghan human rights activists—decided to first present a theatrical form that more closely resembled traditional Afghan oral storytelling techniques, and therefore chose to perform a one-man stage play examining the notions of history and justice in a divided society. *AH 7808* is based on a script written in 2005 about the Troubles by the Northern Irish playwright Dave Duggan. The original work, titled *AH 6905*, was adapted to the Afghan context (primarily through changes to names, places, and dates), translated into Dari and Pashto, performed in eleven provinces in Afghanistan through the summer of 2008, and then revived by AHRDO in 2009 with several performances in Kabul.

The play is about conflict, violence, harm, and healing through truth recovery, using a medical metaphor to relay these concepts: the pains of the past conflict are embodied in us, and the truth of them must be "cut out" in order to move on. The title of the piece itself is a reference to the main character Sardar's medical record number and is symbolic, as it comprises the dates of the start of conflict in Afghanistan (1978) and when the piece was first performed (2008).[30] In *AH 7808* Sardar is haunted by ghosts who, reciting their own lives through poems, represent victims of violence from decades of conflict in Afghanistan. Sardar wants to rid himself of these voices and needs to know what it is that they, the victims of conflict, want, so that he may live in peace and move on. Do they want knowledge or information? Do they want truth? Prosecutions? Justice? Revenge? Peace? Sardar explores these questions in a one-way dialogue with the audience, a fictionalized audience of individuals who are, in the action of the play, visiting him on the eve of his scheduled surgery. He is not sure whether the operation is a good idea, and the play ends with Sardar uncertain about whether to go into the past to try to find the truth of individual victims. Sardar effectively turns over to the audience the decision of whether to delve into the past or to leave it untouched.

By and large, *AH 7808* deals with transitional justice in a symbolic and powerful manner. It presents many thematic aspects relevant to transitional justice interventions, including truth, memory, prosecutions, and reparations, by raising the demands that people may have vis-à-vis past human rights abuses and the ways the victims would like them to be addressed. However, because there is very little will in Afghanistan for discussing these issues at the political level and because these issues are so sensitive even among ordinary citizens, many specific attempts were made to ensure understanding, engagement, and ownership of the theatrical productions among Afghan communities.

First, beyond seeking to expose Afghan war victims to a theatrical form that would resonate with them culturally, the theater team understood from the outset that war victims' participation would be absolutely crucial throughout the project. They were the target audience and were also sought to be part of the performance and production crew. Specifically, invitations were extended to two Kabul-based victims' groups to take part in almost every aspect of the production, despite their lack of any major theatrical experience; among many forms of engagement, victims participated in translating the play into Dari and Pashto, providing pictures of disappeared or killed relatives for use in the set and invitations, and reciting the poems of the ghosts of the past in the play. After every performance a facilitated discussion with the audience opened up a space not only to talk about the content of the play but also to give audience members the opportunity to speak their minds and mourn their relatives. A twenty-page booklet that summarized the play, elaborated questions of transitional justice, and described the overall purpose of the project was also distributed to every member of the audience. The booklet was accompanied by a small gift in the form of a tiny bottle filled with rocks and debris from destroyed buildings in Kabul.

Second, an attempt was made to stimulate memories by connecting people to the places in which the play was performed. Generally speaking, the performances were well grounded in the locales and employed memories of places and events that had meaning for the audience. This point is particularly important to help ensure that the performance does not forget the audience it is addressing, and thus reduce the discrepancy in power while simultaneously increasing reciprocity between actors on stage and spectators.[31] To this end, the *AH 7808* premiere, for example, took place in the destroyed former Russian Cultural Center in Kabul, a symbol of the war between the Soviet-backed Afghan government and mujahedeen groups that is now home to several hundred heroin users. Subsequent performances were organized around equally symbolic ruins, including the former king's palace north of Kabul and near the remains of the ancient Buddha statues in Bamyan Province, which the Taliban destroyed in 2001.

Third, several artistic attempts were made to connect the audience to the play's themes and to establish individual and collective bonds to the truth of the past. In addition to employing a symbolic title comprising meaningful dates for the production, the theatrical props that were used were meant not only to enhance the plot but also to serve as memory-inducing, symbolically independent, and valid stage presences in and of themselves. For example, several chunks of meat were scattered around the stage to metaphorically represent the embodied memories referred to in the play and to evoke associations of the constant presence of body parts throughout the country. Other objects onstage were also used to stimulate the audience on multiple sensory levels, including pieces of rock from destroyed buildings, empty chairs marking the absence of the victims among us, and the cords tying the protagonist Sardar's arms to those empty chairs and thus to the past. The idea was to provide a theatrical experience that enabled the possibility of both an embodied and an intellectual engagement with the content of the play. The latter was attempted mainly through exhibiting what German playwright Bertolt Brecht called the "alienation effect," a theatrical technique designed to distance the audience from emotional involvement in the play, and instead become consciously critical observers.[32] In one such moment, just before the end of the play, the audience is confronted with a collective pause in which Sardar directly asks them to connect their own memories of the past with the immediate future and to think about whether the trauma and violence that have been part of everyday life in the past should be carried over to new generations of Afghans. The play ends with the audience obliged to look at itself in seven mirrors placed onstage, while Sardar spills a jar of (animal) blood across these reflections.

Generally, a wide range of emotions were displayed in response to the play as witnessed by the theater team and reported in a later assessment exercise, including tears and sobbing, outbursts of anger, spontaneous applause, and most commonly silence and emotional paralysis. The last was particularly palpable in the transition period between the end of the play and the facilitated discussion that followed, with many visibly distressed audience members temporarily incapable of moving and unwilling to engage in reflective activity as part of the post-performance discussion. This response was understandable given that for many people, the performance represented the first public confrontation and engagement with the thirty years of conflict and abuse they had experienced.

As a production, *AH 7808* aimed to at least start the conversation on accountability. By exposing the absurd and dehumanizing effects of violence in the country, the play raises the possibility that ignoring past violence may be a reason that political change has not materialized. Because victims of war were heavily involved in the production, it also asks why they have so far been ignored or marginalized by those officially proclaiming to redress the past. These conversations are difficult to have, given that the conflict in Afghanistan is ongoing and many in power today have a strong interest in moving on and avoiding the reopening of old wounds.

PLAYBACK THEATER

The lack of opportunities for marginalized groups to engage in "'public discussion' of vital issues central to their communities, as well as [of] an arena for gaining visibility and staging their identity"[33] makes Playback Theater an appealing tool, particularly in Afghanistan, where most victims are deemed invisible. The vast majority are confined to lives of hardship and impoverishment, without any public identity or social status that could help provide validation of their experiences. While the *AH 7808* performances helped raise questions as to why victims in Afghanistan have been ignored and marginalized, the Playback Theater sessions that were organized as part of a joint AHRDO-ICTJ initiative aimed to rectify this slight on a small scale by providing opportunities to be not only heard but understood.

In order to facilitate this validation, throughout 2009 AHRDO staged twenty-four Playback Theater workshops and performances for a variety of audiences, totaling around three hundred people, in different community settings in Kabul. These journeys deep into the heart of Kabul were in part pedagogical, with some actors entering these communities for the first time; many areas of Kabul are strongly divided along ethnic lines. These actors openly admitted their prejudices about the places and their inhabitants, and later they expressed their astonishment and happiness about having come to know new communities and people, all of whom were ultimately their fellow Afghan citizens. This perspective was especially important given that the Afghan Playback Theater performance ensemble consisted of a gender-mixed group of up to nineteen people of different ethnicities, ages, and abilities—groups that generally do not come together in Afghanistan. To strengthen this interaction, one specific Playback Theater ritual that was routinely applied in Afghanistan was to invite audience members and actors to spend time together after each performance drinking tea, sharing, and building upon the climate of trust created during the performance.

While telling stories can provide victims of human rights abuses with a way back from atomization and disconnection, storytelling can also be an extremely painful renewal of their past trauma. Both types of experience were witnessed during the performances with victims' groups in Kabul, yet the overall feedback from those who told their stories during Playback sessions was overwhelmingly positive. Participants felt a deep sense of gratitude that the actors had come to visit their communities and that they exhibited genuine interest in getting to know them as people and understand their experiences, without forcing them to share. Concretely, as reported by AHRDO, two widows who shared their experiences during a performance expressed afterward that they had not been able to tell their stories when approached by researchers as part of a more formal conflict-mapping exercise. When asked why, the women indicated that they had not felt enough trust to do so and bemoaned the formality of the questioning procedure.

That this type of interaction happened in an environment where the vast majority of people have never seen or even heard of theater, and certainly have not participated in it, suggests that Playback Theater can help in creating the spaces of trust and respect needed for community-building and more formal truth-seeking processes as well.

THEATER OF THE OPPRESSED

If the *AH 7808* performances served to start conversations on accountability in Afghanistan and the Playback Theater stagings helped to create spaces for affirmation and validation of individual experiences, then the Theater of the Oppressed workshops aimed to begin engaging Afghan war victims in not only creating new narratives but also developing ways to start problem-solving around agreed-upon injustices. Such actions are in keeping with Theater of the Oppressed founder Augusto Boal's original intent to create a methodology that served as "an effective tool for the comprehension of social and personal problems and the search for their solutions."[34]

In starting this process in Afghanistan, twelve Theater of the Oppressed workshops were conducted with Kabul-based victims', widows', and women's organizations during 2008 and 2009. The workshops lasted between four and twelve days, with an average of sixteen participants in each workshop, the majority of whom were women between twelve and seventy years of age. A requirement for all workshops was assembling a group of participants affected by different periods of conflict and comprising different ethnic groups. This makeup was especially important as the Theater of the Oppressed focuses on dialogue established by participants engaging in progressively complex games and exercises, in a physically, emotionally, and intellectually safe space to experiment with the different perspectives and philosophies of other members of the group, including the facilitators.

The workshops culminated in participants developing short plays based on issues raised throughout the process. These plays would then be presented as semipublic Forum Theater performances in nontraditional venues, often close to the participants' places of residence. More than a dozen of these performances took place, including one during a conference on transitional justice in Kabul. Examples of these plays include *Tears into Energy*, made up of six scenes: a prologue, four main scenes (on female schooling/forced marriage, freedom of expression/torture, the years of civil war, and escape/migration), and an epilogue; and *Light in Dark Nights*, comprising five scenes: a prologue, three main scenes (on the demise of the communist regime and the circumstances of former regime supporters, female schooling under the Taliban, and land usurpation/displacement), and an epilogue.

A conscious effort was made to include the different participant groups in as many aspects of workshop preparation as possible, which included taking the time to explain the entire workshop methodology in detail, sending out invitations to prospective participants that served as a basis for informed decisionmaking about participation, and giving participants full control of the workshop process. Each group was allowed the opportunity to terminate the workshop at any moment if they felt that there was sufficient reason to do so. The group also agreed that a collective decision would be made regarding whether a Forum Theater play would be developed and performed, and who would be invited should a performance take place.

Approximately 80 percent of the initial Theater of the Oppressed participants were women, many of whom participated without the explicit consent of their families. The vast majority of female participants came from extremely low socioeconomic backgrounds with little to no education and no conceptual knowledge of theater. Despite this, the women seem to have embraced the idea of theater as a tool to address their own conflicts and struggles.

There were, nonetheless, many moments where one could not help but wonder how much preliminary social work, for lack of a better term, must be done with people directly affected by violent conflict before one can even think about addressing transitional justice measures in a more formal and traditional way. In one striking example, a workshop group was asked to make images of war and then images of an ideal or dream Afghanistan. To the facilitators' dismay, no one came forward to make a positive image. The participants were, in their words, "too busy surviving" and had "forgotten," indeed had "given up dreaming of a better Afghanistan." However, when given the opportunity to engage with a concrete example of oppression as part of a Forum Theater scene on the last day of the workshop, many of the same women came up onstage to undermine the abuse, thereby arguably working toward a very practical dream: transforming their own respective existences.

THEATER AND TRANSITIONAL JUSTICE: LESSONS FROM AFGHANISTAN

The projects and methodologies we have described have fostered discussion, laughter, and tears among heretofore unheard and unconnected victims' voices in Afghanistan. While it is too early to say whether such work has had or will have an impact on broader transitional justice discourse in the country, we can already make some connections from the groundwork that theater is starting to lay in broaching transitional justice issues within communities and cultural production in Afghanistan.

Perhaps the most obvious of these initial connections between theater and transitional justice in Afghanistan lies in memory and truth-seeking. Central to repairing both individual and community bonds is the ability to remember, commemorate, mourn, and tell truths. The act of remembering, however, is fraught, as "formations of memory carry implicit and/or explicit assumptions about what is to be remembered, how, by whom, for whom, and with what potential effects."[35] As a result, the performance of memory is inevitably a political act that can serve not only as a way of achieving stability and of maintaining a particular political order but also to challenge official accounts of history by raising awareness of alternative perspectives. This form of historical representation could account for what Michel Foucault called "counter-memory," referring to a process by which popular memory embedded in the experience of everyday life might be exhumed and the voices of the subordinated or silenced be heard.[36] Following this account, theater then creates an opportunity to reconstruct public history as it allows for both the shared experiences and the discontinuities and differences inherent in a conflict setting to emerge. As a witness before the Special Court for Sierra Leone noted, in the courtroom each witness speaks for him- or herself, but in the context of a play, participants are able to present their stories simultaneously to show how different elements of their respective experiences are linked.[37] In Afghanistan such a perspective is important; social as well as geographic barriers, to say nothing of more than three decades of continuing conflict, have prevented individuals from understanding their suffering in a broader context—that is, from understanding that they are not alone, and that their stories, most told publicly for the first time, make up a part of the collective history of Afghanistan.

This countermemory narrative can thus honor the voices of marginalized groups while helping to promote a sense of belonging to community life, because this narrative reconstructs multiple histories. One notable example is the work of el Grupo Cultural Yuyachkani, a Lima-based theater collective. The Yuyachkani collective has been performing in Peru for more than thirty years, using the country's own archive and repertoire with the aim of "imagining Peru"[38] as a coherent nation despite the pervasive violence of the civil war through "cultural engagement with the indigenous and mestizo populations and with complex, transcultured ways of knowing, thinking, remembering."[39] This work addresses Peru's many populations and elucidates its multiply constituted history.[40] The Afghan context considered here is similar in terms of its continuous violence, civil war, and divided ethnicities and ways of understanding. In an effort to start grappling with the idea of Afghanistan as a coherent nation, a requirement of each theater initiative was including individuals from differing social and ethnic groups who have lived through different periods of conflict. That the group of Playback Theater actors, for example, who performed a variety of stories together consisted of a diverse representation of Afghanistan and had men and women sharing the stage had considerable symbolic value, with many audience members expressing approving astonishment that something they thought impossible was actually happening in their community. In this regard, the theater can indeed become a "rehearsal for reality," in which concrete alternatives and strategies for different situations and conflicts can be explored and tested prior to transferring them into real life.[41]

While many workshop participants initially were unable to imagine a better Afghanistan in the future—free of conflict and injustice in a broad sense—they were able to engage in games and create short performances based on their own immediate situations that required actors and audience members to take on new roles and attempt different solutions to resolve conflicts. These workshops and performances, being participatory in nature, perhaps have allowed those involved to begin to awaken from what Diana Taylor terms "percepticide": the metaphorical (and sometimes all too literal) blinding of the population on behalf of those who have an interest in hiding the truth from view, usually members of abusive political regimes.[42] In Afghanistan, percepticide specifically means not seeing what has happened and is still happening, and not seeing that those who committed mass crimes are still in positions of power; it means accepting that the time has come to move on without any further distractions; it means being "too busy surviving" to consider what a future without impunity could look like or to demand one's rights.

Countries that have gone through long years of violent conflict lack physical and emotional spaces to gather, to share, or to simply exist; they also lack spaces to have fun, to play, and to enjoy being in the company of others and laughing together. Theater can provide space in which those affected by war can recover their smiles, let go of fear, and simply have a good time, while simultaneously empowering individuals to find the space within their tragic circumstances to celebrate life and discover new possibilities for living together. By offering a space where taking risks and making mistakes is expressly encouraged, theater can create an atmosphere of freedom that challenges imposed norms, where realities opposed to war and violence can be experienced.[43]

Theater also creates elastic spaces for self-expression that allow people to address difficult feelings of fear, anger, pain, and suffering. While these emotions are important to express, risks are involved in reenacting violent and traumatic narratives. This work demands tough ethical reflection on behalf of everyone interested in working with theater in a place of war. What happens to performers and audience members before, during, and after a performance that deals with past violence? How does one contain the emotions and energies provoked? How likely is retraumatization? How can theater effectively justify its participation in a society's search for justice and reconciliation?

Sensitivity on the part of those working with theater is of the utmost importance. One can attempt to at least inform conduct by involving the audience and participants in a way that allows for a genuine appraisal of the goals, benefits, and potential side effects of theater in a place of war. Such an assessment can be facilitated by pre-performance staged readings and post-performance discussions, as well as the involvement of victims and survivors in the development of the script and mise-en-scène, and in the actual performance as actors, technicians, or directors. In a context like Afghanistan, working with communities to provide support for women may also be important so that women may participate without putting further burden or risk on the individual or her family.

In addition, in its participatory form, standard theatrical practice prescribes participant involvement in the event in such a way that the participants themselves drive virtually the entire range of theatrical activities. Through a prior active engagement of the community in the selection of the theatrical event's specific objectives, facilitators support this freedom on behalf of the participants. In a way, whether in its participatory or more conventional form, working with theater in a transitional context requires that the audience/participants be aware of their ownership of the entire process.

Appropriately crafted theater initiatives ensure that nothing is imposed on participants, inviting them throughout the process to become an integral part of the staging and interpretation of what happened. This approach is intended to lead to a greater understanding of the full scope of experiences in the community, informing strategies for active engagement in local problem solving and dispute resolution. Despite this, performance can "create tension, a sense of dis-ease . . . in a place where tension has frequently erupted into open violence."[44] This tension was palpable in many Playback Theater performances organized in Afghanistan, particularly as transitional justice-focused Playback events contain highly fragmented, partial, and seemingly incomplete truths of the past that may not reconcile with other participants' narratives or perceptions. Trauma specialist Judith Herman argues that "remembering and telling the truth about terrible events are prerequisites both for the restoration of the social order and for the healing of individual victims,"[45] and allowing for simultaneously opposing and complementary accounts to emerge within a contained space may help to expose the different identities that people take on in conflict settings (i.e., victim/perpetrator) and may promote collective memory. These concepts can be difficult for people to process, especially in fragile communities. The responsibility of theater facilitators is to guide participants in resolving these tensions, helping them to connect the dots, as it were, in relating the performance to the broader contexts of justice, accountability, and identity. AHRDO has also taken to inviting psychologists to larger performances to provide additional help for those feeling distress.

While a majority of the participants in the Afghan theater initiatives have reported feeling a sense of empowerment, heightened self-esteem, and emotional relief, particularly after sharing stories in Playback Theater sessions, for these feelings to have a more lasting effect they need to be sustained and supported outside of the theater context and in communities at large. Individual theater practices may not in and of themselves provide more permanent healing, but they can help lead to renewed cultural production and community life, which can foster and sustain agency and closure.

Cultural expression is rarely neutral, and during civil conflicts like those in Rwanda and the former Yugoslavia, cultural artifacts—radio pieces, poetry, music, and so on—were used by warring parties to incite hatred and violence. In some conflict contexts, the production of cultural expression on behalf of minority or discriminated groups is severely limited or repressed, whereas in countries like Afghanistan, decades of war have contributed to a general reduction in and even a complete disappearance of certain cultural activities. The increased commodification of cultural activity, the development of art as a product of consumption, and the ownership and production of the mainstream media in a very few hands exacerbate these factors. Taken together, these factors pose a serious threat to cultural production as a generally accessible, democratically accountable, and genuine expression of community life. In countries where community life has been severely altered by violent conflict, the reclaiming, reevaluation, and reappropriation of the cultural means of production can be an important tool for societal reconstruction. It can be a way to develop new norms for rights and justice at a local level and to allow individuals the opportunity to "feel recognized once more as people, not only as victims."[46]

The initial intent of transitional justice theater work in Afghanistan was to open up spaces for discussion on justice issues, document narratives of war, and begin to bring the nascent and disparate victims', women's, and widows' groups together. The hope, for example, in casting a member of a victims' group (and theater activist) as the protagonist in *AH 7808* was to develop between the actor onstage and an audience made up of victims a theatrical relationship that could have potentially transformative consequences. Because audiences might better relate to this actor given his background, their personal encounter with someone unwilling to accept the general silence about what happened and continues to happen in the country would perhaps lead some spectators also to feel encouraged and empowered to take action. In building on this performance with participatory theater workshops, the aim was to start developing new repertoires to perform and new ideas to experiment with and share beyond the workshop setting.

This cultural production has in small ways begun to take shape in Afghanistan: women participating in a Theater of the Oppressed workshop of their own accord developed and altered theater games to better reflect the Afghan context; theater participants requested that their own stories be developed into a stage play, incorporating traditional Afghan symbols and poetry; and perhaps most tellingly, people have begun organizing themselves more formally in victims' *shuras* or councils within their respective communities. While these developments are important, they are limited in scope if not connected with other processes. As one theater activist reported, "Participatory theater ... is a very useful and effective means which would need to be accompanied by complementary means in order to mobilize civil society on transitional justice."[47] This view recognizes that participatory theater is but one method of raising transitional justice issues, and that it is unlikely to trigger significant change unless accompanied by other initiatives.

At the same time, the use of a largely symbolic tool—the production of a play—in place of more traditional transitional justice approaches can crucially preserve safety for activists who would otherwise be at risk. The fact that, at least in Afghanistan, the transformative potential of theater in all its forms is for the most part underestimated and sometimes even ridiculed may be a comparative advantage. It may empower people, particularly women, to participate in the formation of an outlet where what happened to them individually and collectively can be dealt with openly and respectfully. Consequently, as both a creative process in which to problem solve and a creative solution to security concerns, theater may help keep alive the struggle for justice in Afghanistan.

CONCLUSION AND RECOMMENDATIONS

These initial and connected projects carried out by different human rights groups in Afghanistan signal, in a small, targeted way, that participatory theater has the capacity to explore the legacies of conflict and to establish spaces for discussion and action, thus supporting transitional justice aims in contexts in which more formal processes are nascent. The projects have also allowed for significant female participation, providing a modicum of agency to victims in general and women in particular. These gains are small, but in a context where movement on accountability is nearly at a standstill, they are worth building upon and pursuing. In order to do so, these processes must employ every tool available in order to ensure that justice is pursued in a way that promotes permanent peace and development rather than brief interludes of peace before a return to conflict. In terms of their practical implementation, two separate but ultimately complementary models—presented here as conceptual triads—can support transitional justice processes in conflict and post-conflict settings. The first, centering on conscientization, documentation, and mobilization, is directed toward those involved in facilitating the performance process. The second, revolving around contemplation, telling and interpretation, and mobilization, is focused on theater audiences or spectators.

CONSCIENTIZATION, DOCUMENTATION, AND MOBILIZATION

This conceptual grouping is aimed at further engaging and activating the individuals who have chosen to take on roles within various theater methodologies and serve as facilitators for these processes. They may be performing in stage plays, telling their stories and acting through Playback Theater, or involved in developing and performing Theater of the Oppressed techniques. Individuals here are learning through direct experience.

CONSCIENTIZATION

Conscientization refers to an in-depth understanding of the world, allowing for the perception of and exposure to social and political contradictions; it also involves taking action against oppressive elements that are illuminated through this understanding. A play with transitional justice content such as *AH 7808* creates spaces for the discussion, better understanding, and exploration of accountability and justice in an uncontroversial environment. As such, the play allows for conscientization of audience members. More importantly, post-performance presentations, lectures, and discussion groups allow for a critical, pedagogical engagement with the material, while allowing ordinary people to gain a deeper conceptual comprehension of transitional justice and a more profound understanding of their own role in this process.

DOCUMENTATION

Playback Theater is informed by the notion that "survivors . . . not only need to survive to tell their stories, they also [need] to tell their stories in order to survive."[48] It is a method for the documentation of human rights abuses and the organization of historic memories—what Beatrice Pouligny has called a narrative-building process.[49] The core objective is to establish a physically and emotionally safe environment for people to tell stories about themselves, their loved ones, and their communities. While this goes on, someone at the performance records these events in order to establish an account of what happened. These accounts are shared with a wider audience, using theater to convert personal, internalized, traumatic history into openly accessible public memory. Playback Theater serves as an "incubator for the creation of historical events" by highlighting those that are unrecognized or suppressed by official history.[50]

MOBILIZATION

Theater of the Oppressed is based on the notion that victims of violence are survivors and need psychosocial healing and empowerment in order to recover a sense of appreciation for their own existence. Active participation in workshops or performances provides a sense of achievement and "improves the quality of suffering"[51] by providing a space of mutual respect and recognition as well as fun and entertainment. It offers participants an opportunity "to experience themselves in multiple ways" and encourages them to diversify their ideas of self by deconstructing their often-demobilizing self-identity as victim. If "each genuinely new experience [in the theater] offers the promise of expanding who we are," then this expansion of one's existence may well lead to further empowerment in the form of more active participation in addressing the conflicts in one's society.[52]

CONTEMPLATION, TELLING AND INTERPRETATION, AND ACTION

In addition to the triad of conscientization, documentation, and mobilization, the three theater methodologies can be viewed and applied as a progressive continuum of contemplation, telling and interpretation, and action, in which the audience experiences three different forms of spectatorship and ultimately citizenship.

CONTEMPLATION

Conventional theater plays like *AH 7808* constitute an opportunity for the audience to objectify and contemplate the particular situation of their own country. They provide for a kind of witnessing to the reporting and remembrance of events—both those presented onstage and those from their own lives. They allow the witness "to experience what we experience, to see what's in front of us, to allow the truth in, with all its sorrow and brutality, because in the theater we are not alone in our worried and stained beds. We are there, for these moments together, joined by what we see and hear, made stronger, hopefully, by what opens us."[53] The intent is that this witnessing will lead to deeper reflection on the events and themes presented onstage and their relation to one's own life and the life of the individual's community at large.

TELLING AND INTERPRETATION

The next step is to build on this involved, informed, caring-yet-critical form of spectatorship. Playback Theater can provide spaces to tell and interpret historical events; it is a means for inviting multiple accounts of individual experiences of the truth of the past. By establishing these manifold truths, performances become radical social and ethical encounters. We come face to face with the other, with knowledge that encourages relationships based on openness, dialogue, and a respect for difference. As a result, theater for awareness-raising or contemplation gives way to performance as ethical practice in which broken relationships can be repaired and reconfigured into a new sense of community. The expectation is that "in telling one's story, civilian to civilian, the technique of terror is undermined and the telling can become a countering force to stigmatize violent actions."[54] In addition, working toward the third phase of the continuum, these multiple accounts of history can mediate between contemplation of the past and the search for future actions to address the past in a way that does justice to the population's individual and collective needs, paving the way to a peaceful future.

ACTION

Having contemplated, shared, and interpreted both past and present, the Theater of the Oppressed and particularly Forum Theater can be a means to identify justice-oriented actions. These theater styles can present established transitional justice scenarios—such as prosecution, truth commissions, institutional reform, memorials, or reparations—while always remaining open to indigenous techniques for conflict change. The audience, by proactively exploring practical strategies and solutions, may eventually be able to complete their transformation. They transform from witnesses, to tellers and interpreters, to a combination of actors, activists, creators, and shapers of their own futures. In doing so, they give an example of democracy in practice and practiced democracy.

MAXIMIZING POTENTIAL

Regardless of the theatrical triad or combination thereof one begins with, based on the case study above, we can stress three particular lessons to maximize theater's potential to play an active role in shaping transitional justice processes. First, people need to understand why theater might be a useful tool. Awareness must be raised among potential participants—victims, widows, civil society actors, and others—and potential international partners. For many of those involved, theater would normally be considered a form of entertainment rather than an innovative and creative tool for social change. Second, though having an ostensibly objective outsider lead the work can have short-term advantages, for theater to become an effective tool in a potentially slow, drawn-out process of transitional justice, the means of creative production need to be in the hands of those expected to lead this process nationally and locally. Finally, the question of what follows needs to be addressed. Target groups expected to be the main protagonists of a theatrical work should not be cut loose once the project activities have come to an end. Theater is a component of a holistic approach to transitional justice that includes other activities that guarantee the pursuit of human dignity and some form of justice in a post-conflict setting.

Context is important when considering judicial and artistic or theatrical methods for truth-seeking and accountability: if one approach is relatively weak, the other may become more central to national healing.[55] This is certainly the case in Afghanistan, where impunity is rampant and the space for accountability continues to shrink. Formal transitional justice mechanisms beyond documentation seem a long way off, but an arts-based approach may be suitable even when large-scale, public discussion about the past is not yet possible. Theater provides for the expression, verbal and embodied, of collective feelings in the public realm. In a repressive environment, self-articulation is itself an act of defiance aimed at the established order, a rebellion against official attempts at silencing alternative accounts of history. Performance in this type of setting can serve not only to denounce but also to defamiliarize the violence that people live with every day, exposing its absurd and dehumanizing effects in a coherent fashion.[56]

Participatory theater methodologies can be suitable tools for enriching transitional justice mechanisms' efforts to deal with the painful truth of the past. These methods can create spaces for discussion and allow for local ownership of the process of remembering by taking into account religious, ethical, cultural, social, and psychological dimensions of memory, and addressing individual and collective needs.[57] This last point is important, as approaches to memory that privilege the individual fail to do justice to the cumulative and collective nature of trauma suffered by communities, literate or not.[58] By enabling participants to investigate the possibilities of life after violence and mass crime, theater can contribute to laying the groundwork for transitional justice, indeed turning tears into energy.

NOTES

Some of the material contained here also appears in a different form in Nadia Siddiqui, Hadi Marifat, and Sari Kouvo, "Culture, Theatre and Justice: Examples from Afghanistan," in *The Arts of Transitional Justice*, ed. Olivera Simic and Peter Rush (New York: Springer, 2014), 113–34. The views reflected in this chapter are of the authors alone and do not reflect those of the International Center for Transitional Justice.

1 Shanee Stepakoff, "Telling and Showing: Witnesses Represent Sierra Leone's War Atrocities in Court and Onstage," *Drama Review* 52, no. 1 (2008): 26.

2 Beatrice Pouligny, "Understanding Situations of Post–Mass Crime by Mobilizing Different Forms of Cultural Endeavors" (panel contribution, Nineteenth International Political Science Association World Congress, Durban, South Africa, July 1, 2003).

3 Diana Taylor, *The Archive and the Repertoire: Performing Cultural Memory in the Americas* (Durham, NC: Duke University Press, 2003), 2.

4 Catherine M. Cole, "Performance, Transitional Justice, and the Law: South Africa's Truth and Reconciliation Commission," *Theatre Journal* 59, no. 2 (2007): 179.

5 John McGrath, "Theatre and Democracy," *New Theatre Quarterly* 18, no. 2 (2002): 137–38.

6 Jonothan Neelands, "Acting Together: Ensemble as a Dramatic Process in Art and Life," *Research in Drama Education: Journal of Applied Theatre and Performance* 14, no. 2 (2009): 180.

7 Ibid., 185.

8 Ibid.

9 Susan Sontag, *Regarding the Pain of Others* (New York: Farrar, Straus, and Giroux, 2003), 101.

10 See John Fletcher, "Identity and Agonism: Tim Miller, Cornerstone, and the Politics of Community-Based Theatre," *Theatre Topics* 13, no. 2 (2003): 189–203.

11 UN Assistance Mission in Afghanistan (UNAMA), "Tears into Energy: Community-Based Theatre and Transitional Justice" (unpublished report, Kabul, 2008).

12 Neelands, "Acting Together," 185–86.

13 UNAMA, "Tears into Energy."

14 Arvind Singhal, "Empowering the Oppressed through Participatory Theater," *Investigación y Desarrollo* [Research and development] 12, no. 1 (2004): 146.

15 Bev Hosking and Christian Penny, "Playback Theatre as a Methodology for Social Change" (paper presented at the DevNet Conference, Wellington, New Zealand, December 2000).

16 Search for Common Ground, *Acting Out, Together: The 2010 Theatre Festival*, Special Update (Washington, DC: Search for Common Ground, 2010), http://www.sfcg.org/sfcg/evaluations/BDI_AX_Mar12_Annex%20II%20Theater%20Festival%20Highlights.pdf.

17 Ibid.; and Search for Common Ground, *Participatory Theatre for Conflict Transformation: Training Manual* (Kinshasa: Search for Common Ground, n.d.), http://www.sfcg.org/programmes/drcongo/pdf/Participatory-Theatre-Manual-EN.pdf.

18 Jonathan Chadwick, "Working in Kosovo on a Participatory Theatre Project on Missing Persons," AZ Theatre, November 24, 2005, http://www.aztheatre.org.uk/index.php?page=war-stories-kosovo.

19 Cole, "Performance, Transitional Justice, and the Law," 179.

20 Ksenija Bilbija, Jo Ellen Fair, Cynthia E. Milton, and Leigh A. Payne, eds., *The Art of Truth-Telling about Authoritarian Rule* (Madison: University of Wisconsin Press, 2005), 3.

21 See Marcela Briceño-Donn, Félix Reátegui, María Cristina Rivera, and Catalina Uprimny Salazar, eds., *Recordar en conflict: Iniciativas no oficiales de memoria en Colombia* [Remembering during conflict: Unofficial memory initiatives in Colombia] (Bogotá: International Center for Transitional Justice, 2009).

22 Bilbija et al., *Art of Truth Telling about Authoritarian Rule*, 3.

23 Ibid.

24 Judy Barsalou, *Trauma and Transitional Justice in Divided Societies*, Special Report (Washington, DC: US Institute of Peace, 2005), 1.

25 Cynthia E. Cohen, "Creative Approaches to Reconciliation," in *The Psychology of Resolving Global Conflicts: From War to Peace*, ed. Mari Fitzduff and Christopher E. Stout, vol. 3, *Interventions* (Westport, CT: Greenwood Publishing Group, 2005), 72.

26 Cole, "Performance, Transitional Justice, and the Law," 186.

27 Taylor, *Archive and the Repertoire*, xviii.

28 George H. Quimby, "Theatre in Iran and Afghanistan," *Educational Theatre Journal* 12, no. 3 (1960): 203.

29 Wahid Omar, "From Storytelling to Community Development," in *Telling Stories to*

Change the World: Global Voices on the Power of Narrative to Build Community and Make Social Justice Claims, ed. Rickie Solinger, Madeline Fox, and Kayhan Irani (New York: Routledge, 2008), 194.

30 In the original work, *AH 6905*, the numbers in the title represent the beginning of the Troubles (1969) and date of the script itself (2005).

31 Taylor, *Archive and the Repertoire*, 199.

32 Bertolt Brecht, *Brecht on Theatre: The Development of an Aesthetic*, trans. and ed. John Willet (New York: Hill and Wang, 1992), 121–29.

33 Dwight Conquergood, "Rethinking Ethnography: Towards a Critical Cultural Politics," *Communications Monographs* 58, no. 2 (1991): 189.

34 Augusto Boal, *The Rainbow of Desire: The Boal Method of Theatre and Therapy* (London: Routledge, 1995), 15.

35 Roger I. Simon, Sharon Rosenberg, and Claudia Eppert, *Between Hope and Despair: Pedagogy and the Remembrance of Historical Trauma* (Lanham, MD: Rowman and Littlefield, 2000), 2.

36 Michel Foucault, *Language, Counter-Memory, Practice: Selected Essays and Interviews*, ed. Donald F. Bouchard, trans. Donald F. Bouchard and Sherry Simon (Ithaca, NY: Cornell University Press, 1977).

37 Stepakoff, "Telling and Showing," 23.

38 Francine A'ness, "Resisting Amnesia: Yuyachkani, Performance, and the Postwar Reconstruction of Peru," *Theatre Journal* 56, no. 3 (2004): 400.

39 Taylor, *Archive and the Repertoire*, 192; A'ness, "Resisting Amnesia," 399.

40 Taylor, *Archive and the Repertoire*, 193.

41 Boal, *Rainbow of Desire*, 15.

42 Diana Taylor, *Disappearing Acts: Spectacles of Gender and Nationalism in Argentina's "Dirty War"* (Durham, NC: Duke University Press, 1997), 72.

43 Ibid., 151; see also Nick Rowe, *Playing the Other: Dramatizing Personal Narratives in Playback Theatre* (London: Jessica Kingsley Publishers, 2007), 49.

44 James Thompson, *Digging Up Stories: Applied Theatre, Performance, and War* (Manchester: Manchester University Press, 2005), 156.

45 Judith Herman, *Trauma and Recovery: The Aftermath of Violence—from Domestic Abuse to Political Terror* (New York: Basic Books, 1997), 1.

46 Pouligny, "Understanding Situations of Post–Mass Crime."

47 ICTJ Assessment, "Transitional Justice Theatre Training of Trainers Project" (unpublished report, ICTJ, New York, August 2009).

48 Shoshana Feldman and Dori Laub, *Testimony: Crises of Witnessing in Literature, Psychoanalysis, and History* (New York: Routledge, 1992), 78.

49 Pouligny, "Understanding Situations of Post–Mass Crime."

50 Jodi Kanter, *Performing Loss: Rebuilding Community through Theater and Writing* (Carbondale: Southern Illinois University Press, 2007), 127.

51 William Sloane Coffin, *The Collected Sermons of William Sloane Coffin: The Riverside Years*, 2 vols. (Louisville, KY: Westminster John Knox Press, 2008), 2:475.

52 Kanter, *Performing Loss*, 161.

53 Eve Ensler, *Necessary Targets: A Story of Women and War* (New York: Villard Books, 2001).

54 Carolyn Nordstrom, *A Different Kind of War Story: The Ethnography of Political Violence* (Philadelphia: University of Pennsylvania Press, 1997), 168.

55 In Cambodia the arts served as the main vehicle for victims of the genocide to communicate their experiences, because the tribunal was slow to be established. See Stepakoff, "Telling and Showing," 23–24. Colombia is another context in which the arts are being used as a main vehicle for truth and memory; see n. 21, this chapter.

56 A'ness, "Resisting Amnesia," 400.

57 Ly Daravuth, "Notes on Pchum Ben" (working paper, Recasting Reconciliation through Culture and the Arts, Coexistence International, Brandeis University, Waltham/Boston, 2005), 4.

58 Taylor, *Archive and the Repertoire*, 193.

CHAPTER 11

Reverberations of Testimony: South Africa's Truth and Reconciliation Commission in Art and Media

Catherine M. Cole

Christopher Colvin notes that South Africa's Truth and Reconciliation Commission was the centerpiece of "the most publicized and celebrated post-conflict transition process undertaken in the last fifty years."[1] This sentiment is widely shared internationally, as seen in Priscilla B. Hayner's most recent (and revised) edition of *Unspeakable Truths: Transitional Justice and the Challenge of Truth Commission*, where, one decade after publication of the original book, she still identifies South Africa's Truth and Reconciliation Commission (SA-TRC) as one of the five strongest truth commissions out of the forty that have been held to date internationally.[2] Given Hayner's comprehensive coverage of the field of transitional justice, her assessment of the legacy of the South African TRC is particularly persuasive.

While Priscilla Hayner singles out the SA-TRC as one of the most successful internationally, we must also recognize that local perceptions of the TRC within South Africa are far more ambivalent. Such ambivalence is to be expected; truth commissions are no panacea for the vast wounds and unfathomable damage that gross violations of human rights and systematic, state-sponsored terror perpetrate. An endeavor that goes by the Orwellian-sounding name "Truth and Reconciliation Commission" must surely be judged at least by how well it produces truth and reconciliation. In this regard, the jury on South Africa's TRC is divided. Reading the print media coverage of the TRC, it would appear that the majority of South Africans did not view the process well. As James L. Gibson says of the media coverage, "Complaints and condemnation of the truth and reconciliation commission far outnumber laudatory assessments."[3] Yet Gibson's empirical research among South Africans sheds light on a much different perspective on the commission. In 2000–2001 he conducted surveys with a representative sample of thirty-seven hundred South Africans. The results demonstrated that "vast racial differences existed in how people evaluate the TRC, with the extremes being defined by blacks and whites. For instance, while roughly three-quarters of black South Africans approve of the work of the commission, only slightly more than one-third of white voters are so inclined."[4] What accounts for this largely favorable view of the commission among the general public when the print media was so often critical and condemnatory of the proceedings?

I think part of the answer to that question can be found by considering broadcast media, which had a much larger circulation and was able to convey the affective and narrative richness of the live hearings in a way that neither the print media nor the TRC's own written report could. The weekly television digest *TRC Special Report*, which aired for two years, announced itself as being the place where viewers could find the "stories behind the stories" of the TRC. Hence it was narratively driven, even as the reporters for this series also provided astute analysis that often moved beyond simply telling a story to providing examinations of structures and systemic forces of violence. Television and radio both gave their audiences experientially rich access to those who gave testimony. Whether that access was conveyed largely through sonic dimensions of timbre, tone, gasps, and silence through radio, or through the added visual registers such as body language, clothing, and facial expressions that are conveyed through television, broadcast media made manifest the people who were at the center of the public hearings—including victims giving testimony, perpetrators asking for amnesty, spectators in the hall, and commissioners presiding over the proceedings. Broadcast media provided a personalization and particularization of the stories that the commission called forth—stories that in aggregate could otherwise be mind-numbing in magnitude, scale, and sheer brutality. The hearings and their promulgation via broadcast coverage focused on individuals, whereas print coverage and the TRC's own summary report privileged information divorced from its more human element.

The extensive broadcast media coverage of the SA-TRC is just one aspect, however, of its impressive public engagement of South African citizens in the transitional justice process. The country was also blessed with a particularly rich tradition of journalism and a community of gifted writers, photographers, and artists who dedicated themselves to covering, amplifying, and critically engaging with the SA-TRC process. As soon as the commission began its work in 1996, many journalists, but also artists working in different genres, immediately rose up to respond to and transform the stories, images, characters, insights, themes, mysteries, and epiphanies of the TRC. While not technically employed by the commission, and thus beyond its control, artists and journalists were key interlocutors and intermediaries between the commission and South African society, providing framing and forums for the reception of the TRC testimony. As with journalism, the arts provided crucial mediation between the givers and receivers of testimony, between the work of the commission and the larger public, and between the fleeting moments of testimony in real time and the collective memory of the TRC extending into the future. News programs, memoirs, and artistic works based on TRC testimony generated critical public engagement and amplified the communicative impact of this extraordinary transitional justice process so that its stories and themes reverberated long after the commission had formally concluded its work.

But how did journalists and artists amplify and complicate the commission's work? How do we critically evaluate their contributions? What is the status of truth when testimony moves between nonfiction and fiction, from spoken utterance to transcript or film, and finally into genres such as music or theater? And what ideas can we glean from the South African experience that might apply to the design of future truth commissions elsewhere? In this chapter I examine these questions by building upon my previous research and also presenting new analysis about how one particular story—Father Michael Lapsley's—coursed through several different modes of representation, from print to broadcast media, from memoir to cantata.[5] I begin by contextualizing the TRC's public dimensions—the pivotal choices the commission made in allowing its proceedings to be publicly accessible. I then trace Father Lapsley's testimony as it moved from spoken word to transcript, from embodied utterance to television, from nonfiction to fiction, from text to music. What becomes evident by tracing the reverberations of one particular TRC testimony is that each interlocutor brought different expectations, biases, insights, and distortions. In the gaps between these various representations we come closest to seeing how the truths of any transitional justice process remain elusive, even as many important truths and insights are revealed.

GOING PUBLIC

In considering the public profile of the SA-TRC, we might be tempted to begin by examining the commission's own final report, the first five volumes of which were published in 1998; two more appeared in 2003. This massive text is an important primary document of the commission's work as well as a fulfillment of the commissions' legislative mandate to provide "as complete a picture as possible of the causes, nature and extent of the gross violations of human rights" committed during a thirty-four-year period of apartheid.[6] For many years after the conclusion of the SA-TRC, scholars focused on this report as being the most authoritative and relevant representation of the commission's work. For instance, one of the best critical scholarly engagements of the commission is the edited volume by Deborah Posel and Graeme Simpson, *Commissioning the Past*. Many essays in this collection focus on the TRC's summary report as a definitive text and representation of the SA-TRC.[7] However, as I have argued elsewhere, the SA-TRC report is so voluminous and expensive that few in the country have read it, even those closely involved with the commission itself.[8] The report costs a hefty sum, well over two hundred US dollars, which is prohibitively expensive for most South Africans. In addition, the report is not especially user friendly. Written by multiple authors, the report's tone and style are uneven, and it favors quantitative social science methods that trace patterns of violence. Only occasionally does the report represent the specificity, complexity, and narrative potency of testimony—qualities that tend to be far more efficacious in reaching a general readership. The relative scarcity of narrative in the SA-TRC report was particularly unfortunate; by exiling story from its pages, the report failed to capture one of the four key types of truth that the commission itself defined as its goal: factual/forensic, personal/narrative, healing/restorative, and social.[9] Despite the prominence of personal and narrative truth in the TRC's mandate and the role it played in the public hearings, the commission's summary report was overwhelmingly factual and forensic in focus.

We must therefore look beyond the commission's own official public document for answers as to why the SA-TRC had such widespread public impact. The public hearings of the commission and their broadcasting generated widespread public engagement and were the primary means by which the commission's work was made manifest to the nation.[10] As a massive state-sponsored endeavor, South Africa's TRC was designed to weave discrete experiences into a larger national narrative about the past. Yet while the TRC was mounting this national project of reckoning and memory, its public hearings also had a quite local specificity and resonance. Hearings moved geographically throughout the country, and the cases heard in any particular region were homegrown. Of the many statements taken in a particular region, a few were selected for public hearings. Commission staff chose cases based upon multiple criteria, including the degree to which a story represented the types of violence perpetrated in that place, or the racial, ethnic, and gendered patterns of violence and gross violations of human rights under apartheid that had happened in that specific place and over decades of apartheid. The hearings were held in a range of venues, from large cavernous stadiums and churches in major cities to intimate town halls and school auditoriums in smaller municipalities. Spectators could attend the TRC public hearings in person, and many did; transcripts of these hearings were also made and posted online.[11] But as I explain in more detail here, far more South Africans witnessed the TRC proceedings from their homes, offices, cars, taxi ranks, and other spaces of daily life by tuning in to radio and television.[12]

South Africa made the historically unprecedented and controversial decision to give television cameras full access to document the proceedings. Inasmuch as amnesty hearings, in particular, resembled a court of law, judges presiding over the amnesty process were especially loath to have TV crews in hearings, feeling strongly that cameras distort and bias the judicial process. Negotiations about the scope and nature of broadcast coverage for the TRC led to specific protocols for shooting, such as where cameras could and could not be placed, what they could shoot, how they would use close-ups and long shots, and so on.[13] Yet within these constraints, the South African Broadcasting Corporation (SABC) enjoyed relatively wide-ranging access to the proceedings with an understanding of reciprocity: the SABC could shoot the hearings if they did so fully, donating the unedited raw footage as an archive. This footage was subsequently given to the Department of Justice, the "owner" of the material, with the National Archives serving as custodian. In total, the SABC shot over fourteen thousand hours of footage; only a small fraction was used in nightly news bulletins and weekly digests. This material is an extraordinarily rich repository of primary evidence for future researchers.

In the reciprocity of this arrangement, we see television's liminal status as it participated in the TRC process: it was an outside force of journalism charged with presenting an objective view of the proceedings to the larger South African public, but it could also be viewed as an inside participant within the TRC's apparatus, literally serving as documentarian. Because so many people in South Africa experienced the truth commission primarily through the SABC programs, some audience members not surprisingly came to confuse television coverage of the TRC with the commission itself. People wishing to make formal statements as victims or perpetrators before the TRC sometimes contacted journalists. Such requests happened so often that journalists periodically had to publish disclaimers, such as when the television digest *TRC Special Report* noted in a May 1997 broadcast that if viewers wished to make a statement to the TRC, "Here are the phone numbers. Please don't write to *Special Report*. We are a completely independent agency. We just report on the commission."[14] Such confusion is not uncommon with media events, which Daniel Dayan and Elihu Katz define as historic occasions of state that are broadcast live and transfix a nation. *Media events* are "hailed as historic; they strive to mark a new record, to change an old way of doing or thinking, or to mark the passing of an era."[15] Media events involve three main participants: the people who organize the event, the broadcasters who reproduce it, and the audiences. By reproducing the event, broadcasters become organizers and audience. Their role is analogous to that of the Greek chorus—part of the play but standing outside the action. They witness and comment on the unfolding stories and themes; they are thus performers onstage and surrogates for the audience. In their metadiscursive commentary as well as the framing and focus on the evolving action they provide, the chorus (and the media) is a critical force in shaping audience perceptions and reception.

As a result of the public dimension that the SA-TRC adopted, the regional specificity of the hearings was translated through broadcast coverage into a national discourse about the past and about the TRC. Through this decision to go public—which was quite controversial at the time, although it became standard practice in the truth commissions that came later—the SA-TRC was transformed from a discreet governmental investigative commission into a national phenomenon, a media event, a ritual of epic proportions that had widespread reach within and outside South Africa. But broadcast media also served as a critical interlocutor in modulating between the local and the national, the personal and the political, individual and collective memories. This act of transformation and translation, or interlocution, was absolutely critical in achieving the degree of public impact and engagement for which the South African TRC is known. Television and radio gave the public access to stories—stories told in the first person and conveyed not just in words but also through a full, embodied expressivity: a pause, a gasp, a wail, or a frown; the unflinching deadpan of an unremorseful perpetrator; the sunken, anguished grimace of a bereaved survivor. Manifest in the hearings and their broadcast was precisely the centrality of narrative truth to the TRC's process and experience, in contrast to the forensic and factual truth captured in the report. By personalizing the stories that came forth through the TRC process, the hearings and their broadcast coverage performatively realized a key animating principle of South Africa's Truth and Reconciliation Commission: *ubuntu*, a Zulu principle that can also be expressed in the phrase *umuntu ngumuntu ngabantu*, which means, "A person is a person through other people," or "I realize my humanity only when I also realize your humanity," or "I am what I am because of who we all are." Since a core goal of the commission was to restore the humanity of people who had been brutalized as well as those who had perpetrated brutality, ubuntu was manifest in human-to-human encounters that were most evident through public hearings. There needed to be a speaker giving voice to stories of gross violations of human rights, and a receiver of these stories also needed to be present. In the public hearings, the receiver was at least threefold: the commissioners, the spectators in the audience, and the television cameras and radio microphones that recorded and transmitted this testimony. Through broadcast media the larger nation was thus woven into the larger process of ubuntu as performed through the hearings. These broadcasts brought millions of viewers and listeners into the process as receivers of the testimony and, by extension, as witnesses to the atrocities that the testimony narrated. While dozens or perhaps as many as a couple of hundred people might attend a public hearing, millions more witnessed remotely, listening to live coverage of the hearings on the radio or watching the nightly news summary or the weekly digest *TRC Special Report*. Of the extensive media coverage the TRC enjoyed, the commission's deputy chairperson Alex Boraine has written,

> Never in my wildest imaginings did I think that the media would retain its insatiable interest in the Commission throughout its life. Not a day passed when we were not reported on radio. We were very seldom absent from the major television evening news broadcasts, and we were, if not on the front page, on the inside pages of every newspaper throughout the two and a half years of our work.... Unlike many other truth commissions, this one was center stage, and the media coverage, particularly radio, enabled the poor, the illiterate, and people living in rural areas to participate in its work so that it was truly a national experience rather than restricted to a small handful of selected commissioners.[16]

TRC Special Report as a series and television document of the TRC is a particularly notable instance of broadcast coverage. This weekly news digest was produced by Afrikaans journalist Max du Preez, a notorious gadfly of the apartheid state and founder of *Vrye Weekblad*, an Afrikaans-language weekly newspaper. The *Vrye Weekblad* team of renegade investigative journalists published important exposés during the apartheid years on topics hidden from the public at the time: death squads, assassinations, and the clandestine activities of the South African Defense Force. Du Preez's apartheid-era journalism made him the target of death threats, but in the tumultuous years of regime change as South Africa transitioned to democracy, du Preez suddenly found himself in unlikely surroundings. Not only was he now working for the formerly loathed

SABC, which had been a mouthpiece for apartheid government propaganda, but he was also changing platforms from print to television journalism—with its very different genre expectations, potential, exigencies, capabilities, and limitations.

During the period of political transition in the wake of the 1994 democratic elections and on the eve of the launch of the SA-TRC, du Preez himself became an advocate for creating a special television show dedicated to the TRC. He felt strongly that the truth commission could not be done justice through brief stories on the nightly news hour. His perseverance with his supervisors at the SABC eventually resulted in the creation of *TRC Special Report,* a current affairs program that produced eighty-seven episodes lasting thirty to sixty minutes each. Du Preez served as executive producer along with Jacques Pauw. They were joined by an exceptionally talented crew of journalists; among them were Jann Turner, Benedict Motau, Anneliese Burgess, René Schiebe, Shenid Bhayoo, and Bronwyn Nicolson. Like du Preez, most of the crew was far more experienced with print journalism and had relatively little or no experience working in television. But what they lacked in technical experience, they made up for in craft and knowledge. These journalists were chosen for their gifts as storytellers and for their experience of working on past news stories about violence and atrocity perpetrated under the previous regime. Since most mainstream journalists working under apartheid had not covered these events, the *Special Report* journalists had an advantage when they needed to find quickly background and context for stories and incidents that came to light through the SA-TRC. Cases that appeared before the TRC public hearings often arrived in an abrupt way, without the commission providing important framing. Yet because so many *TRC Special Report* journalists had previously covered these stories for the opposition press, they were prepared to generate in-depth analysis on short notice. This experience and background knowledge of the *TRC Special Report* team helped the series counterbalance what can be a main limiting factor of television as a medium: it tends to be better suited to the compelling image and emotional engagement rather than substantive analysis and critique as well as content-rich analysis.

Soon after the TRC began its hearings, *TRC Special Report* was established as a primary means for getting a compact summary of the week's events. Alex Boraine, in his memoir recounting his service as deputy chairperson of the commission, paid tribute to the program, commending du Preez and his crew "for the sensitive and professional way" they covered each week's proceedings.[17] Du Preez claims, "Everybody knew that this is where the story is going to be told, not the thirty-second bits on the news bulletins.... People knew that this story will unfold on Sunday afternoons or Sunday evenings. There's going to be a good hour and the main stories will be there. And the nation was listening."[18] In its first year, *TRC Special Report* achieved an estimated viewership of 1.2 million people weekly. The program eventually topped television ratings across all channels, surpassing even the obsessively watched soap opera *The Bold and the Beautiful*.[19] For its quality, *TRC Special Report* garnered critical acclaim: a Pringle Award and the 1996 Award for Outstanding Journalism from the Foreign Correspondents' Association of South Africa. The first program aired on April 21, 1996, and weekly installments concluded on March 29, 1998. The programs subsequently have been digitized by the Yale School of Law's Lillian Goldman Library and can be viewed online at the library's website. In early April 2011 and as I write this chapter, the SABC appears to have begun its own digitization project, with many episodes of *TRC Special Report* now on YouTube.[20] To watch the entire series in succession is quite a remarkable retrospective experience; the viewer gets a keen sense of the evolving process of the TRC: how the commission represented itself to the public over time, what kinds of controversies and issues seemed most urgent at particular historical moments, and the unfolding questions about key investigations—some of which were never answered. Some evolving mysteries were solved later in the series when the TRC's own focus shifted from Human Rights Violation Committee hearings to those of the Amnesty Committee.

At times, *TRC Special Report* and its team of investigative journalists would conduct their own shadow investigations into issues that the TRC was not tackling but perhaps should have been. Sometimes perpetrators chose to give their testimony to *Special Report* rather than the TRC, and those disclosures occasionally had an impact on how TRC investigations unfolded. Hence, this is a dynamic archival document, one that captures well the experience of the truth commission as an ongoing process rather than a dry record of conclusions and findings. Many years after the TRC finished its work, Max du Preez distilled key episodes and segments from the series to create a DVD for educational use in South Africa's high schools. The series—called *Truth, Justice, Memory*, and produced by the Institute of Justice and Reconciliation in Cape Town—is used in the history curriculum as well as in Life Orientation classes.[21]

One might assume that television was a problematic medium for covering such complex and emotionally volatile subject matter as testimony about gross violations of human rights—that television would tend to pull in the direction of sound bites and sensational and graphic fragments rather than sophisticated and nuanced analysis. It would be so easy for a television producer to turn TRC testimony into a trauma spectacle. While all of these potential dangers were real and genuine for *TRC Special Report,* I would argue that through careful management of decisions about staffing, firm guidelines about cinematography, clear protocols for camera operators, and an evolving sophistication of the show's own particular style and genre—the way it implemented its mission of providing "the story behind the stories"—the program managed to produce an ongoing critical documentary of the TRC process that provided far more in-depth analysis and critical engagement than perhaps any other single representation of the SA-TRC. The show had to walk a fine line between advocating for public participation in the process and acting as an outside critical voice. It did so deftly. *TRC Special Report* resisted neat conclusions for stories that were far too complex and ambiguous to be resolved in a single episode or even in many months of hearings. What becomes evident through watching this series in chronological succession is that the full story, the "true" story, or what "really happened" continually elude the commission as well as *TRC Special Report.* The series demonstrated this lack of resolution, even as it doggedly searched for and demanded answers. The program thus made palpable the fact that truths of the apartheid past were rarely singular, and reconciliation would be neither easy nor ever final. Yet the show also demonstrated that pursuing truth and reconciliation, however elusive they proved to be, brought everyone closer to a new South Africa—one that was surely better than the old.

TRC Special Report journalists prioritized storytelling from the beginning. Executive Producer du Preez chose his team of journalists precisely for their narrative abilities. He did not consider the lack of television experience of the many former print journalists on his staff to be a barrier; he chose them because they were good storytellers. His team of journalists was "put together under pressure with very little means, with fairly inexperienced people—well, not inexperienced, but inexperienced in terms of television skills." He continues:

> But they were good journalists. They were good storytellers, and that's how I picked them: People who were storytellers. People who have experience in journalism in telling a story, because we knew right from the start: this is about storytelling.... That's the essence of what I believe we should be doing. From the beginning we knew this [program] is ... beyond a documentary.... We have to reflect all the natural drama of this story, and it's a big dramatic story that we told. It was a very dramatic story. It was the most dramatic story in the world at the

> time. It's about love and hatred and violence and bravery and patriotism and prejudice and cruelty. So it was good material to work with in terms of storytelling. But you had to give the story an interesting beginning and you have to build a structure for the story: a beginning, a middle, and an end. And you have to save some punch for the end.[22]

Exactly how journalists working on the series shaped the narrative; how they found the beginning, middle, and end of any particular tale; how they decided in what order to convey these and what information was to be revealed and what should be withheld—the *TRC Special Report* team actively and thoughtfully engaged all these matters. Of course, those who worked on the commission also, like reporters, routinely faced ethical and technical challenges of condensation. They had to transform reams of testimony and evidence from expansive investigative processes into some kind of coherent document for the summary report. Likewise every artist who works with the TRC material has to face the question of what to select and what to leave out. Shot through all of these reverberations of the TRC process are ethical questions about what it means to work selectively with stories that have been told at such personal cost—and to receive these stories as spectators, readers, viewers, and listeners.

THE CIRCULATION OF TESTIMONY

In order to illustrate the challenges of representing testimony and engaging a larger public in the TRC process, I trace one particular story from the commission as it moved between different modes of representation: from public testimony to the commission's summary report, from a television news program to a popular memoir, and finally to the story's incorporation within a major musical work. What we see in these reverberations from a single act of testimony is how much the selection and format of representation shape the experience for the receiver of the testimony—whether that audience is sitting in a hall where the personal testimony is being given, listening on the radio to simultaneous coverage, reading a report issued by the commission many years later, reading a journalist's semifictional memoir, or listening to a cantata that uses material from the commission's sonic archive. Each reverberation has its own potentials and perils, and each genre and medium elicit particular terms of engagement—not all of which the interlocutor may self-consciously realize. My goal here is not to suggest in a categorical or doctrinaire way how to undertake such representations. Rather, I think that this particular case study illustrates the capacity for certain approaches to the process of interlocution to promote public engagement and the restoration of humanity, as well as the potential pitfalls of representing such fraught material. Reverberations of testimony can work to enhance as well as to undermine the overarching ambitions of restorative or transitional justice. In a way, writers of reports and official documents for truth commissions face challenges that are not inherently different from those that journalists and artists face, even if each interlocutor operates with distinctive parameters and mandates, as well as genre expectations, methodologies, and moral responsibilities. Each of these interlocutors makes choices about content and form and, in so doing, sets a certain horizon of expectation about the nature and terms of public engagement.

I wish to focus on the case of Father Michael Lapsley, an Anglican priest who was an antiapartheid activist forced to live in exile in Zimbabwe. In 1990 Lapsley was the recipient of a parcel bomb that, when detonated, blew off both of his hands and seriously damaged his vision and hearing. Lapsley's story is an iconic one in South Africa partly because of his public visibility and longstanding commitment to fighting apartheid as a non–South African (he is from New Zealand). Like the US Fulbright student Amy Biehl, whose story also became an iconic one from the SA-TRC,[23] Lapsley was an expatriate who chose to dedicate himself to the South African liberation struggle, a choice that obviously came at tremendous personal cost. Lapsley's story also captured public attention because of the miracle of his survival given the magnitude of the blast and the profound damage that his body sustained. In the face of that trauma and loss, Father Lapsley remained steadfast in his commitment to restorative justice. He has been a dramatic visible symbol of sacrifice and survival, an iconic status often conflated with his distinctive body—in particular, his metal prosthetic hands. As disability studies have shown, disability provides what David Mitchell and Sharon Snyder call an "opportunistic metaphorical device," a kind of shorthand that both facilitates and disguises constructions of "normal," "abnormal," and "deviance."[24] Because of its narrative potency, disability is a recurring device in novels and in narrative constructions of a nation, such as one sees in the TRC process.

OFFICIAL TESTIMONY

Father Lapsley gave public testimony before the SA-TRC in Kimberley on June 10, 1996, accompanied by his colleague Father Michael Worsnip.[25] I urge readers to peruse the online transcript.[26] Father Lapsley tells what happened to him on that day in April 1990 when he innocently opened a parcel containing what he thought were religious magazines, only to detonate a hidden explosive device. As with many SA-TRC transcripts, the record shows the stops and starts of spoken testimony, the qualifications and repetitions of verbal speech, the immediacy of the first-person narration, and the dynamism of the interaction between various interlocutors in the TRC hearings. As is typical of the genre of testimony, the transcript begins with a welcoming address (in this case by Deputy Chairperson Alex Boraine), followed by the swearing in of the witness. What follows is the witness's extensive first-person testimony. Father Lapsley speaks, and Father Worsnip provides corroboration. Several commissioners then question the witnesses, both of whom respond, and the record ends with a homily by Chairperson Archbishop Desmond Tutu.

The case of Father Lapsley appears in the TRC summary report in several different sections. Each time, the testimony is put into the service of some larger rhetorical point, exemplifying a particular pattern of violence or a historical period. The case first appears in volume 1, in a section on concepts and principles, as evidence relevant to a discussion of reconciliation and forgiveness: "Father Michael Lapsley, who lost both arms [*sic*] and an eye in a near fatal security police parcel bomb attack in Harare in 1990, told the Commission: 'I need to know who to forgive in order to endeavor to do so.'"[27] The most extensive entry on Lapsley appears in volume 2, in a section titled "Political Violence in the Era of Negotiations and Transition." Here his story becomes emblematic of the escalating and intensifying violence during a period when negotiations toward a peaceful political transition were well underway:

> On 28 April 1990, Father Michael Lapsley [CT00654], a New Zealand citizen but long-time resident of Southern Africa, and well known for his support of the South African liberation movement, was severely injured in a parcel bomb explosion at his home in Harare, Zimbabwe. The explosive was contained in a registered package in a large manila envelope with a Dobsonville, Soweto postmark. A colleague in the room at the time, Mr. Andrew Mutizwa, was slightly injured by the blast.
>
> In his appearance before the Commission, Lapsley stated that the security authorities in Zimbabwe had warned him in 1988 that his name was on a South African hit list of targets for elimination. Given the recent spate of attacks on targets inside Zimbabwe, the warning was taken seriously and Lapsley was given a twenty-four-hour guard and warned not to open large packages. After the unbannings in South Africa in February 1990 and a statement by General Malan that there

> would be no further attacks in the front-line states, the protection was relaxed. The Lapsley case is the last known incident of an attempted cross-border or external killing in the mandate period.
>
> Christoffel Nel, who had no direct knowledge of this operation, confirmed that Lapsley had been a DCC [Directorate of Covert Collections] "target" (for intelligence attention and not necessarily killing) since 1987, and that whenever Leon Nefdt (DCC operative responsible for Zimbabwe) . . . presented his targets to the Generals, Father Michael Lapsley was included in the so-called support infrastructure of the Zimbabwean machinery and part of the political machinery. . . . There was at one stage a discussion about doing something to Father Michael Lapsley . . . before I joined the CCB [Civil Cooperation Bureau], about the possibility of sending him a parcel. Leon Nefdt in my presence had a discussion with a certain Colonel Hekkies van Heerden. He was known as "Colonel Hammer" because it was jokingly said that he would use a hammer to kill a fly. . . . I think that's exactly what happened in the case of Father Michael Lapsley, that he received a parcel.
>
> The one question that puzzled Nel was the timing of the operation—post–February 1990—which made him feel that it was neither a DCC nor Special Forces/CCB operation. Joe Verster [AM5471/97], the CCB's general manager who appeared before the Commission, deviated only once from his position that he would not discuss external operations when, under oath, he denied that Lapsley was a CCB project.
>
> Nel speculated that the Lapsley bombing was possibly a NIS [National Intelligence Service] operation. He argued strongly that NIS had an operational division with a strong presence in Zimbabwe. Its key operative, Danie du Plessis, was said to have had an intimate knowledge of the situation, particularly in relation to what was known as the "white left." There is other supporting evidence that NIS monitored Lapsley closely. The Commission received source reports on Lapsley dated 29 January and 8 May 1990.[28]

The TRC report's summary of Lapsley's story provides factual details about the case and weaves together information garnered from his own testimony as well as from Joe Verster and Christoffel Nel. The first-person voice evident in the transcript transforms into the depersonalized third person. Narrative becomes subservient to investigative findings, which are ultimately inconclusive. We do not learn the full extent of Lapsley's bodily damage: in addition to loss of both hands and an eye, he suffered a broken arm, extensive burns, and shattered eardrums. The affective register of his testimony is absent entirely, as is any sense of the nonlinguistic features—hesitations, revisions, pauses, or physical gestures.

A fuller description of the damage that Father Lapsley sustained is not provided in the summary report until several volumes later—in volume 5 in a chapter titled "Consequences of Gross Violations of Human Rights." On page 133 appears a brief passage from Father Worsnip, who reported how Father Lapsley woke repeatedly in the hospital, screaming as he remembered the bomb blast. Page 139 offers a summary of Lapsley's physical injuries, and on page 154 we see brief testimony about the difficulties of life during rehabilitation, when Lapsley says, "I returned to Zimbabwe to joblessness in that the Bishop who was supposed to employ me had said, 'Well you're disabled now, what can you do?'"[29]

Fragments of one victim's testimony from a single day thus appear strewn across pages, chapters, and volumes in the summary report. In each case, the testimony is used to exemplify some larger pattern or philosophical point. While one of the primary goals of the TRC was to restore the humanity, integrity, and personhood of victims, the summary report performed its own kind of violence to individuals by fragmenting and dispersing their testimony in the text and then invoking this testimony in an instrumentalist fashion; portions are reproduced as examples, significant only because they demonstrate larger patterns and overarching concepts. One might quite legitimately argue, though, that as far as the government report genre goes, this text is remarkable for including any direct testimony at all. As a genre, government reports are dull. The TRC summary report departs from expectation. As Justice Albie Sachs notes, some of the sections of the TRC summary report are "written in a very lively way. It's spirited. It's not a boring summing up for the board of activities for the last year. It probes. It asks questions. It illustrates with examples. It's philosophical. And very well structured, and I think quite a literate document."[30] Yet one cannot help but notice that when measured against the commission's own typologies and valuations, the summary report is at odds with the TRC's stated commitment to personal and narrative truth.

TELEVISION

TRC Special Report covered Father Lapsley's story in ways that sharply contrasted with the commission's summary report. The program suggests a different model for how nonfiction representations of TRC material might be able to simultaneously value narrative/personal and factual/forensic truth, treating them as mutually enriching and compatible rather than arenas that must be segregated. Father Lapsley's story is covered in episode 6, which the reader can watch on YouTube.[31] The episode covers a tremendous amount of information, context, storytelling, and interpretation in a way that is coherent, accessible, and personal. Lapsley himself is at the center of the piece, with the segment's structure being informed largely by key thematic threads that Father Lapsley had raised in his own narrative before the commission. The segment begins with host Max du Preez in the newsroom quoting Lapsley: "They got my hands and my eye. But they didn't get my most powerful weapon: my tongue." After this hook, the segment then cuts away to news footage covering the immediate aftermath of the 1990 bombing of Father Lapsley's house, followed by a segment of Father Lapsley's 1996 TRC testimony. The editors chose to focus on his first-person account of the bombing and his own description of the experience, in which he narrates the subjectivity of trauma and conveys his memories of pain. Then an excerpt of Father Worsnip's testimony describes and further corroborates the injuries that Lapsley sustained. The testimony is intercut with photographs of Lapsley lying in a hospital bed, gazing in a stunned way at the camera, his body wrapped in bandages.

Next is an excerpt of Max du Preez interviewing Father Lapsley specifically for *TRC Special Report*. Du Preez notes that Lapsley is an expatriate from New Zealand who came to live in South Africa for altruistic reasons, yet "this is what we have done to you." Du Preez asks, "Why are you still here?" Father Lapsley answers by talking about his faith, his views on justice, and his commitment to fight apartheid in the old regime and be an agent of restorative justice in the new South Africa. The segment then shifts gears to ask about the motives of Father Lapsley's attackers: Why was Lapsley seen as such a threat? This brief, ten-minute piece carefully and deftly modulates between personal profile and investigative journalism. A du Preez voiceover accompanies news footage showing various potential perpetrators who are now in prison for other charges. Could these men have been responsible for the bombing? While the program cannot answer these questions, du Preez's voiceover succinctly and concisely references a whole host of other similar cases of parcel bombs, when they happened, what is known of their perpetrators, and the vast network of agencies involved in such nefarious deeds. While *Special Report* cannot answer the whodunit question, the program provides meaningful empirical evidence that should guide the investigation.

The program at that point cuts to Lapsley's TRC testimony, where he provided his own interpretation about where culpability ultimately rests: "I have always been clear that the person I hold responsible for my bombing is F. W.

De Klerk," the last state president of apartheid-era South Africa. Father Lapsley then explains and justifies this charge. Here Lapsley's testimony is intercut with shots of the spectators in the hall at the public hearings listening with rapt attention. These spectators are surrogates for us—those watching remotely on television or, in the case of the present reader, those experiencing the testimony at a greater temporal distance via text. The program cinematically made clear that *we* are the ultimate witnesses to Lapsley's testimony. Only rarely did *TRC Special Report* focus on how the TRC commissioners received the testimony, although they technically were the primary audience to whom victim testimony was addressed. *TRC Special Report* thus made an argument through its editing: the public is the primary audience, the ones charged with receiving victim testimony.

The Lapsley episode concluded by focusing on philosophical concerns—in particular, the topic of forgiveness. Lapsley is shown explaining before the TRC why, in his view, forgiveness could not yet "be on the agenda." He draws attention to the fact that, to that point in the TRC process, very few voices had come from the community of perpetrators. He also talks about whether he would want to meet the person who made or sent the letter bomb and what his attitude would be toward that person, depending upon whether the bombing incident troubled that person's life or was considered now of no consequence. In a brief sequence, *TRC Special Report* covered a tremendous amount of ground—moving from the empirical to the affective, from findings to narrative, from facts to philosophy.

Witnesses who appeared before the commission typically spoke for thirty minutes, and they had great latitude to shape their narratives as they wished. Particularly notable about the way *TRC Special Report* represented and retold Lapsley's testimony is that the segment's major thematic threads and structure are entirely consistent with Lapsley's own structuring of his testimony. The piece operated in so many different registers, as did Lapsley's official comments. A complex narrative surrounds the circumstances of the bomb's planting, discovery, and impact on Lapsley's body and life. Larger questions of motive are also present: Lapsley's for being in South Africa at all, both during and after apartheid, and also the issue of the motivation of his perpetrator. For what reason did someone make and send this bomb? Who authorized this act? Important pieces of the plot are missing. Beyond this issue is an even larger frame: an expansive discussion about the underlying philosophical and spiritual issues of accountability, justice, and forgiveness—and how these framed the commission and Lapsley's own life before and after the bombing. In all regards, *TRC Special Report* honored the complexity and range of Lapsley's testimony before the Human Rights Violation Committee hearings. The most dramatic visual marker of his loss—the two metal hooks that now form his prosthetic hands—occasionally came into the visual frame as Lapsley gestured while giving testimony. At the very end of the *TRC Special Report* episode, a brief clip appears of Lapsley drinking a glass of water that he holds nimbly in his metal hands, but the camera operators and editors do not dwell on this one mechanical feature of this remarkable person. They do not reduce Father Lapsley to his disability, nor do they make this feature of his body an opportunistic metaphorical device.

In total, the *TRC Special Report* segment on Lapsley lasts just over ten minutes, yet the piece covers succinctly a remarkable breadth of storytelling, investigative journalism, and philosophical reflection. Aided by news footage and archival photos of the bombing and of Lapsley's life as a priest, as well as footage from a newly commissioned interview and ample excerpts of video from Lapsley's appearance before the TRC, the episode honors the integrity of Father Lapsley as a whole person and as he chose to represent himself before the commission. Father Lapsley's life intersected with large, elaborate, and sinister forces at work in the nation, yet in narrating that larger web that perpetrated crimes against humanity, the program never loses sight of Lapsley's humanity and never reduces him to his loss.

THE ARTS

We have examined thus far the transcription of Father Lapsley's testimony before the TRC and the way in which this testimony was re-presented in the commission's own summary report as well as on *TRC Special Report*. I wish to turn now to another layer of representation, that of the arts. Artistic representations about the SA-TRC include theatrical productions such as the collectively devised play *Ubu and the Truth Commission* by Jane Taylor, William Kentridge, and the Handspring Puppet Company. Other plays about the commission include John Kani's *Nothing but the Truth*, *The Story I Am About to Tell* by Duma Khumalo, and *He Left Quietly* by Yael Farber; novels such as *Red Dust* by Gillian Slovo and Sindiwe Magona's *Mother to Mother*; visual arts such as Judith Mason's *The Plastic Blue Dress* and Sue Williamson's *Truth Games* series; films such as the documentary *Long Night's Journey into Day* as well as fictional features such as *Forgiveness*; and musical works such as Philip Miller's *REwind* cantata or the audio documentary *South Africa's Human Spirit*, a multidisc oral memoir produced by journalists who covered the TRC for the SABC. There is also the memoir by poet and SABC journalist Antjie Krog titled *Country of My*

Skull, a work of creative nonfiction whose ambiguous genre status has been the source of much controversy.[32] In these various representations and iterations, one finds innovative storytelling, compelling and critical engagement of the TRC, and an overall composite image of the process in which one sees the multiple and conflicting truths that the TRC brought into view. This complexity of representation helped shape and complicate collective memory, regardless of whether all the works were successful artistically. Even as some of these works were deemed quite controversial or politically problematic, such controversy often provokes a healthy level of public engagement with the TRC process.

Country of My Skull, Antjie Krog's memoir of her years covering the TRC for SABC radio, quickly became one of the most widely circulated representations about the commission. The text is masterful and engaging. Krog is a gifted and celebrated novelist and poet, and she managed to weave the great dispersion and surfeit of material that the TRC generated into a coherent, poignant, compelling, and accessible story. What is odd is the degree to which the book—which is marketed as "nonfiction" and categorized by the publisher as "current affairs/international"—takes huge liberties with empirical facts. One can find evidence throughout *Country of My Skull* of ways in which Krog took poetic license with the TRC material, and she has subsequently defended her right as an artist to do so.[33]

In Krog's book, Father Lapsley's story appears in a chapter titled "Blood Rains in Every Latitude," and the book presents the text in a way that appears to be verbatim testimony. Close comparative analysis with the transcript of Lapsley's June 10, 1996, appearance before the TRC shows some points of convergence. However, Krog's presentation is odd in two respects: first, the order of the material is jumbled; second, the quotations from Lapsley and Father Worsnip (identified only as "a friend from Lesotho") are intercut in ways that have little bearing to the actual SA-TRC transcript. More strangely and inexplicably, finding any single sentence in the Krog text that corresponds to what Lapsley actually said before the commission is difficult. Sometimes the modifications are minor and are clearly edits made for clarity or efficiency, yet other modifications are more substantive. For example, in his testimony Lapsley said,

> It's one of the moments I remember when I was called into this office and told that the Government of South Africa wishes to kill you. And I remember the loneliness in the way of the moment because it was very personal—it wasn't simply that they wanted to kill members of the ANC [African National Congress] but it was me in particular.[34]

In *Country of My Skull,* Krog transforms Lapsley's words as follows:

> That moment I remember. I was called in and told: "The South African government wants to kill you." And I remember the indescribable solitude of the moment...because it was so personal....They didn't want to kill the ANC members, but me specifically.[35]

The changes are in some ways minor: phrasing, syntax, punctuation, and small excisions of words. But to change "loneliness" to "indescribable solitude" seems far more invasive. Words are being put into his mouth and without any cloak of excuse about issues of translation in a radically multilingual South Africa: Lapsley is a native English speaker. This ventriloquism is disturbing but well-disguised. Readers generally do not do the sort of cross-referencing with the archival record that I suggest, nor would overt clues in the text prompt them to do so. Given the profound price that Father Lapsley paid to tell his story, seeing such liberties taken with his testimony is disturbing and mystifying. Is this done for poetic effect? The changes often diminish rather than enhance the testimony's poetic qualities. For instance, in the actual TRC hearings Father Lapsley described the period immediately after the loss of his hands as follows:

> I should also say that I was helpless as a newborn baby for three months. There was literally nothing that I could do for myself but I also said to myself that I—my struggle now is a struggle to get well—a struggle to return—a struggle to live my life as fully, as joyfully, as completely as possible and that would be my victory. I also realized that [if] I was filled with hatred, bitterness, self-pity, desire for revenge that they would have failed to kill the body, but they would have killed the soul. That I would be a permanent victim and today I would say that I [am] not simply as a survivor but I'm a victor over all the evil and hatred and death that apartheid represented. And the sign of the triumph of good.[36]

In *Country of My Skull* this passage appears quite differently:

> I do not see myself as a victim, but as a survivor of apartheid....This is part of my triumph of returning to South Africa and living my life as meaningfully and joyfully as possible....I am not captured by hatred, because then they would not only have destroyed my body, but also my soul.[37]

The second phrasing is certainly more succinct, but it's far less poignant. Lapsley's real testimony draws our attention first to his helplessness, the vulnerability of losing his hands. The next passage focuses on his decision, his determination, his choice to embrace "struggle," a word he repeats several times, with the temporal signifier "now" referring both to the aftermath of the bombing and also to the present moment of testimony. His struggle is continuous. Yet the rhetorical thrust of his testimony does not stop with struggle but rather builds to his assertion of triumph. By way of contrast, Krog's text has Lapsley self-identifying merely as a "survivor." However, his actual words move beyond mere survival to herald himself a "victor" and a "sign of the triumph of good." These renderings are profoundly different.

Interrupting the direct quotation in *Country of My Skull*, the narrator briefly inserts an editorial commentary, drawing the reader's attention to a particular visual detail—Father Lapsley's prosthetic hands, or "pincers" as they are called here:

> It is these stainless-steel pincers that Father Lapsley raised to take the oath before the submission to the Truth Commission: "So help me God..." But it is also these pincers that prevent him from wiping away his tears like other victims. When their stories cut too close, victims often bury their faces in their hands, and wipe their eyes with tissues. But how do you hold the fragile veil of a tissue in such pincers? How do you complete the simple action of blowing your nose? Several times the pincers move toward his face in a reflex action—and every movement flashes the inhumanity of South Africa's past into the hall... hard, shiny, and sterile.[38]

Here a sign of disability becomes what Mitchell and Snyder call "narrative prosthesis"; Lapsley's mechanical hands become in Krog's narration a metaphor for the inhumanity of South Africa's past—"hard, shiny, and sterile." The narrator does not take up—or even apparently see—the actual physical and social experience of disability that is being performed by Lapsley in his appearance before the commission, as is evident in the video footage used by *TRC Special Report* when he drinks a glass of water quite capably using his prosthetic hands. There is also a disjunction of affect: Lapsley appears in the video footage to be emotionally composed during his testimony before the TRC. While his testimony does narrate that in the immediate aftermath of the bombing back in 1990 he was "as helpless as a newborn baby," by the time of the TRC in 1996, Lapsley's competence with his prosthetic hands is quite high. Surely if he can manage a glass of water, he can also now manage to wield a tissue.

What *Country of My Skull* appears to provide is a verbatim reproduction of actual TRC testimony. But upon closer inspection and comparing the text with the archival record, we see that Krog's book is rather a document of reception.

It records the narrator's subjectivity, the narrator's/Krog's jumbled and foggy memory of that testimony. The interlocutor transforms Father Lapsley from victor to victim, from a competent person to someone so helpless he cannot wipe a tear from his face. The fragile tissue of testimony is vulnerable to such manipulations, for once in the public domain, testimony can be shredded, maimed, crushed, and reassembled into forms quite unrecognizable in comparison to the original. Obviously this transposition of testimony is highly problematic, raising a host of questions about truth and the ethics of interpreting and manipulating such testimony. Had the memoir provided more overt clues that the narrator was an unreliable witness, Krog's ethics of engagement would have significantly shifted. Her radical transformation of victim testimony masquerades as verbatim speech, which is what is so morally problematic. The masquerade is performed at Father Lapsley's expense.

CANTATA

The last representation of Father Lapsley's testimony that I wish to examine is its appearance in Philip Miller's *REwind* cantata, a musical work created in 2006. *REwind* is subtitled *A Cantata for Voice, Tape, and Testimony*. Miller used the archival sound record of the public TRC hearings as a source of inspiration. He built the cantata around not just the recorded words of testimony but also the sighs, gasps, wails, technical glitches, and many languages heard in the TRC's hall. All of this material was seen as generative for this formidable work of art. I have written at length elsewhere about the cantata,[39] but I have not before discussed the particular song in which Father Lapsley's testimony appears—"Liza Lis'indinga Lakho," an adapted well-known hymn that the composer translates as "Confession of Sins Makes Us Whole."[40] The song appears twice in the cantata; the first time is a straightforward rendition sung by a large chorus in a major key. It begins in a regular, on-beat tempo. Partway through this first version, the chorus shifts rhythm, adding syncopation and a distinctly South African element with whistles and foot stomping that begin to suggest anti-apartheid struggle music and dancing such as the *toyi-toyi*. The second rendering of the hymn is rather as a trio, and the entire song is transposed to a minor key. The piece begins with spoken words, Father Lapsley's recorded testimony:

> I came upon this manila envelope that had been among the accumulated mail
> Um...
> I opened it...and it was addressed to me
> And inside were two religious magazines

And they…the magazines were wrapped in plastic, sealed in plastic.
So I ripped open the plastic. I took out the magazines.
And I opened the English magazine
And the act of opening the magazine was the detonating device for a bomb.
Um…I um…

Until this point, there is no music, singing, or instrumentation. Music enters just at the point where Lapsley narrates the bomb exploding. Strings play a slow, sustained note, and then a second pitch emerges. Then there is a silence. After a pause, more strings enter, and the pitch deepens with resonant bass notes. This pitch is sustained for many seconds. Then silence. After a moment, the first singer is heard, contralto Sibongile Khumalo singing the first line of the hymn, "Liza Lis'indinga Lakho." The phrase is familiar because we heard a conventional rendering of the song earlier in the cantata. But in the trio version, the song becomes warped and distorted. The pacing is off, and the harmonics slide into dissonance. The strings keep going lower, underscoring the gravity of the situation. The tempo is uneven, and then a second voice enters: a sonorous bass. When these two singers complete the first musical phrase, the recording of Father Lapsley's testimony resumes. Strings underscore his narration:

The ceiling and three rooms blew out.
There was a hole in the floor.
And I can still remember…what happened.
Ah…
The actual explosion is still…is still…is still something with me.

Lapsley's testimony is interwoven with music—vocal and orchestral. The piece takes us on a guided journey that conveys an emotional experience through music and a narrative experience through Lapsley's spoken words. Miller, like Krog in her book and du Preez in his television series, has made editorial selections and manipulated Lapsley's testimony. The libretto focuses with an almost surgical precision on specific details: a simple letter, the exact moment of the detonation of the bomb, a conjuring of the image of someone making the bomb. Lapsley had, in his testimony, speculated about what this person did when he or she returned home that night. What did this person say to his or her family about the work done during the day? The totality of Father Lapsley's testimony is severely reduced, and the composer's incisive selectivity expands the impact.

Miller draws our attention to subjectivity, both Lapsley's—his subjective experience of the moment of the bomb blast, the pain and trauma of that moment—and the perpetrator's. What is the state of his or her soul now? Lapsley did indeed pose this question at the TRC, yet the question did not find its way into the TRC report, the segment of *TRC Special Report*, or *Country of My Skull*. The libretto highlights Lapsley's speculation about whether and under what circumstances he would want to meet the person who made the bomb. He wonders: Does that person still make letter bombs today, and if so, what would that say? Finally, is it possible for Lapsley to imagine forgiving the person who made the bomb? Under what conditions would such forgiveness be possible? Miller has selected this through line of testimony, a thread united by its focus on quotidian details and intersubjectivity.

Where Miller's musical iteration of Father Lapsley's testimony surpasses the others is in its ability to orchestrate an affective response through time and sound. The site of engagement is inherently intersubjective, located between sound issued through voice and music and sound received in the listener's ears. Amplifying the encounter into the visual realm is a dynamic projection from designer Gerhard Marx (see Figure 11.1). A plain brown envelope appears but is made strange by immersion in water. Slowly an inky black substance bleeds out from the edges of the envelope, wafting and smoldering. We expect the quotidian object to be static, but the streams of black fluid suggest a sinister dynamism that will unfold in unexpected ways.

The beauty of the musical form and its accompanying image is that the space of the intersubjective encounter with verbatim testimony is open, not literal. This approach is quite different from Krog's false memory of Lapsley—the way her misquotations transformed him from an affectless witness into a sobbing one, from a physically capable person who happens to have a disability to one incapable of performing basic tasks such as wiping a tear. As a durational and time-based art form, the cantata has capacity to create openings in the testimony, spaces to be filled by music, or silence, or by the listener's own emotion and thought. Lapsley's TRC testimony narrated memories about his emotions at the time of the bombing, but the testimony itself was not particularly emotionally expressive. Father Lapsley spoke in a consistent, even, uninflected tone. The contrast between his tone and the music makes this song so effective. The music is dynamic, changing rapidly in volume and tempo. It is sometimes gentle and plaintive with a long, sustained lack of resolve. At other times the music becomes turgid, suddenly loud or fast, hitting unexpected pitches or changing key. The music provides a richly textured and

FIGURE 11.1.

REwind performed at the Market Theatre, Johannesburg, in 2008. The image behind the soloists is a film of a letter impregnated with dye that slowly bleeds ink when submerged in water. The projection, designed by Gerhard Marx, accompanies a song that uses the TRC testimony of Anglican priest Father Michael Lapsley. Photograph by John Hodgkiss, courtesy of Key Films in association with the Market Theatre, 2008.

unpredictable emotional terrain that serves as a counterpoint to the flatness of Lapsley's delivery. Suggesting the volubility under this story's surface, the music does not, however, determine or proscribe any particular interpretation.

As with Krog's memoir and du Preez's television program, as well as the TRC's own summary report, Miller had to make editorial decisions about what to include. He has freely edited the text, removing digressions, qualifications, and extraneous details. An inherent disruption of the testimony occurs in that process, and one could argue that an inherent violence is done to the testimony's integrity. But the poetic license that Miller has taken in selecting passages for inclusion in this libretto seems consonant with the rhetorical arc and thrust of Lapsley's original testimony. Also, the brevity of Miller's selections combined with the musical arena in which these words are uttered allow us—the listeners—to react, digest, absorb the unimaginable circumstances, and connect empathetically with a story that is almost beyond one's imagination. We are led to dwell not on the loss of Father Lapsley's hands but rather on people, relationships, the ordinary acts of daily life, and extraordinary acts of evil, as well as Lapsley's extraordinary grace and focus. He invites us all to imagine: How does the bomb maker live today? What is the state of that person's conscience today? Under what conditions could these two lives converge again? In ruminating on these questions, the music amplifies, sustains, and evades resolution. It shifts in key. We are constantly kept off guard. We are surprised by what wells up. While Lapsley's voice conveys an almost clinical distance on the actions he narrates, the music suggests another emotional landscape that surely lies behind the TRC's deceptively clean and sterile words: "truth," "reconciliation," and "forgiveness." They are so easy to say, so very hard to do.

CONCLUSION

As stories from the SA-TRC move from the first-person, embodied testimony of victims and perpetrators at the hearings to re-presentation on television and in an official government report—or in memoirs and artistic productions—each iteration brings new resonances, insights, distortions, and truths. Each version—like a turn of the kaleidoscope—allows us to see different details while obscuring or erasing others. Each has its own meanings, silences, omissions, suppressions, distortions, insights, and violence. Some narrators guide audiences to see the testimony as exemplary of patterns or historical periods. Others prompt us to ask investigative questions: What happened, who did it, and why? Other interlocutors focus on isolated details and the affective registers they provoke: How do we feel when we see stainless-steel prosthetics replacing a man's hands? What does it mean when an ordinary envelope—something that you might receive every day at your home, something that may contain a magazine, a bank statement, or a letter from a friend—becomes an agent of catastrophic destruction?

Which of these representations is the best or the most truthful? Which most respects the person who gave testimony? Which is the most effective at engaging the public in a transitional justice process, and what are the terms of that engagement? What aspects of reception are triggered or privileged through different modalities, genres, and media forms? I have, of course, my personal preferences. I think that Miller's cantata and the *TRC Special Report* episode on Father Lapsley do justice to the rhetorical thrust of Father Lapsley's testimony while taking the story in quite different directions. The cantata and the television show both made radical excisions from Lapsley's testimony, but in ways that are consonant with the testimony's entirety, using Lapsley's own structuring and delivery of his story before the TRC. The *TRC Special Report* episode adds on top of Lapsley's own narrative a densely layered analysis that points to larger issues, investigations, findings, political forces, and questions. Hence, while the episode uses Lapsley's personal truth as a foundation, the program does not limit itself to this one register but freely moves in the direction of investigative journalism on a national scale as well as toward philosophical reflection about the nature of forgiveness. While modulating between the personal and the political, the individual and the national, the physical and the metaphysical, the program maintains an unwavering commitment to the victim's integrity.

This approach stands in sharp contrast to the TRC's summary report, which seems to have been written with the assumption that personal/narrative truth was incompatible with factual/forensic truth, despite the fact that the TRC's own mandate was charged to honor both registers equally. As a result, the report renders the case of Father Lapsley in a fragmented way, with bits and pieces of his story strewn over many volumes. The report utterly fails to provide any sense of the actual person who gave testimony, or what key themes and structuring devices the witness provided. Thus I would say that in thinking ahead to the design of future commissions, the SA-TRC example raises the issue of how to express a commission's values—in this case, the commitment to a victim-centered process—in the final work product. Enlisting the collaboration of more scholars who work in the humanities, artists, and gifted storytellers in the crafting of the summary document may help provide a counterbalance to the quantitative, social science, and legalistic directions in which truth commission summary documents are inevitably pulled.

In assembling a team of journalists to work on *TRC Special Report,* du Preez looked for people who were good storytellers. In doing so, he was not seeking those with a gift for fabricating details or taking poetic license with the facts. Rather du Preez believed that the television program needed to capture the TRC's narrative potency because narration was one of the main ways that the commission would engage with the public. This *desire* for public engagement is, of course, a key difference between a truth commission and a court of law. If the people and institutions in South Africa were to be caught up in the TRC process, du Preez felt, stories would be the hook. Hence, as interlocutors of those stories, the journalists he hired for *TRC Special Report* had to have gifts as narrators while also being dogged journalists who corroborated evidence and tirelessly pursued leads. In short, they had to be equally adept in following the protocols, expectations, and methodologies of both narrative and factual/forensic truth.

Krog's *Country of My Skull,* a work of creative nonfiction, succeeds very well as a compelling narrative account of the commission, but this story was often told at the cost of the victims themselves, for whom the text sometimes literally put words in their mouths. The uncertain status of this text was highly problematic because the narrator's editorial hand took such dramatic liberties. Is the book fiction or nonfiction? Are excerpts from the TRC verbatim testimony or the author's invention? Had Krog tipped her hand a bit more, revealed more explicitly the suturing and manipulation of testimony, or more effectively raised questions about the reliability of the text's narrator, one can imagine a very different outcome—one that would not be such an affront to the victim whose testimony has been so radically manipulated.

Artistic and fictional works answer, of course, to a different set of protocols and genre expectations than either a TRC summary report or a television news digest program. In the arena of art, one is beholden to other truths; they may be emotional, affective truths, or expectations and possibilities unique to a particular medium (text, video, music, theatre, visual art) or genre (poetry, cantata, film documentary, memoir). In Philip Miller's *REwind* cantata, Father Lapsley's story appears in highly compressed form. Miller selected very particular quotidian details and then guided the listener into a narrative and emotional experience using the sonic capacities of music as well as its durational possibilities. Listeners must endure in real time the pauses, the silences, and the spaces between words. No skipping ahead. His score sets up a conversation between Father Lapsley's voice and the images that the story conjures, just as it imagines a hypothetical conversation or encounter between Lapsley and his would-be killer. The unspeakable moment of the bomb detonating is rendered in such a way that we are forced to imagine it, as unimaginable as it is. As with the *TRC Special Report* episode on Father Lapsley, Miller's editorial selections of inclusion and exclusion arise quite organically from key structuring devices that Lapsley himself used in his testimony. Here again, then, is an example of a representation of testimony that I would argue is victim-centered in terms of the care with which editorial liberties are taken in transposing full spoken testimony into a condensed, highly altered musical form. The musical work performs its own kind of restorative justice: the tonal and durational features that were inevitably silenced when Father Lapsley's spoken testimony was turned into a typed transcript by the TRC staff are, in Miller's musical rendering, once again presented for public consumption.

The big ethical question that this range of representations raises is whether those who give testimony in public formats before truth commissions fully realize what putting their words into circulation in the public domain means—whether they understand that testimony given at a public hearing can then be manipulated, reproduced, and interpreted in so many different ways. Do they understand that they will have little or no control over these representations? I corresponded with Father Lapsley while writing this chapter, and he expressed irritation with the ways his TRC testimony has been misquoted. He is also frustrated with the frequent tendency toward reductionist and crude views in regard to his disability. Lapsley added, "I am often taken aback when even to my face people quote me, but it is something I never said, and occasionally in flat contradiction to what I have said. But I guess it is part of the privilege and challenge of living in the public domain."[41] Father Lapsley was an unusual witness before the commission in that he had long been a public figure in South Africa. He was in a position to fully appreciate the ways in which his words might circulate, often quite independent of his agency. But many other witnesses may not have appreciated this capacity that their public testimony could unleash. How should future truth commissions deal with these questions?

The reader is urged to peruse the source material cited here—to read the original testimony given by Father Lapsley, to watch the *TRC Special Report* episode about his case, to listen to Philip Miller's cantata, and to read Krog's *Country of My Skull* and the entries in the TRC's summary report that focus on this one case. In doing so, readers are invited to form independent opinions about which version is the most truthful or effective or successful, or which truths brought into focus by these various iterations of testimony are most deserving of our allegiance. My own allegiance rests with Miller's *REwind* cantata and du Preez's television program, because I think they provide exemplary models of how artists and journalists can simultaneously honor the integrity of witness testimony while deftly navigating the rules of engagement of medium (music and television, respectively) and genre (cantata and news program, respectively) to produce a new and sophisticated yet accessible form of public engagement.

The work of journalists and artists is not something that can or should be orchestrated or controlled by people who mount truth commissions. Indeed, the independence of artists, writers, and journalists is key to building civil society in the aftermath of state-sanctioned terror and violence. Each interlocutor brings different expectations, biases, insights, and distortions. Each genre and medium also inherits particular terms of engagement that may or may not be negotiable. In the gaps between these various representations we come closest to seeing how the truths of any transitional justice process remain elusive, even when so many important facts and insights are revealed.

NOTES

A version of this paper was presented at the conference "Things Unspeakable: Theatre and Human Rights" at the University of York, October 7, 2011. I would like to thank participants in that conference for their excellent feedback. I am also grateful to Father Michael Lapsley and Stephen Karakashian for their thoughtful reflections on earlier drafts. Clara Ramírez-Barat deserves special thanks for inviting the essay and ministering to it throughout the publication process. This chapter does not necessarily represent the views of the International Center for Transitional Justice.

1 Christopher J. Colvin, "Overview of the Reparations Program in South Africa," in *The Handbook of Reparations*, ed. Pablo de Greiff (New York: Oxford University Press, 2006), 176–214.

2 Priscilla Hayner, *Unspeakable Truths: Transitional Justice and the Challenge of Truth Commissions*, 2nd ed. (New York: Routledge, 2011), 27–32.

3 James L. Gibson, *Overcoming Apartheid: Can Truth Reconcile a Divided Nation?* (New York: Russell Sage Foundation, 2004), 2.

4 James L. Gibson, "The Truth about Truth and Reconciliation in South Africa," *International Political Science Review* 26, no. 4 (2005): 347.

5 I have written about media coverage of the TRC in my recent book *Performing South Africa's Truth Commission: Stages of Transition* (Bloomington: Indiana University Press, 2010), esp. chap. 4. Some of this material is also reprinted in a revised format with additional analysis in Catherine Cole, "Mediating Testimony: Broadcasting South Africa's Truth and Reconciliation Commission," in *Documentary Testimonies: Global Archives of Suffering*, ed. Bhaskar Sarkar and Janet Walker (New York: Routledge, 2010), 196–214.

6 Truth and Reconciliation Commission in South Africa, *Truth and Reconciliation of South Africa Report*, 7 vols. (Cape Town: Truth and Reconciliation Commission, 1998), 1:55 (hereafter SA-TRC, *TRC Report*).

7 Deborah Posel and Graeme Simpson, eds., *Commissioning the Past: Understanding South Africa's Truth and Reconciliation Commission* (Johannesburg: Witwatersrand University Press, 2002).

8 Cole, *Performing South Africa's Truth Commission*, 7–8.

9 SA-TRC, *TRC Report*, 1:110–14; Cole, *Performing South Africa's Truth Commission*, 163–69.

10 While public hearings were a notable and distinguishing feature of the South African TRC, much of the commission's actual work was done behind closed doors. The first layer of statement taking, corroboration, and investigation was done away from the glare of television lights. Of the 21,000 victim statements and the 7,115 applications for amnesty taken by the TRC, only about 10 percent were chosen to have public hearings. Transcripts from the public hearings are available at http://www.justice.gov.za/trc/index.html. For background on how particular cases were chosen for public hearings, see Cole, *Performing South Africa's Truth Commission*, 9. See also Lars Buur, "Monumental Historical Memory: Managing Truth in the Everyday Work of the South African Truth and Reconciliation Commission," in Posel and Simpson, *Commissioning the Past*, 66–93.

11 For access to transcripts, see the official SA-TRC website, accessed September 20, 2011, http://www.justice.gov.za/trc/index.html. Both the simultaneous-language interpretation at the hearings as well as the transcriptions of the recordings were done in haste, and much was lost in translation from spoken utterance to written text. The recent work by Krog, Mpolweni, and Ratele is exemplary in demonstrating the potential for a deeper rendering, interpretation, and engagement with TRC testimony long after the commission has ended and despite all of the flaws in the commission's archival record (Antjie Krog, Nosisi Mpolweni, and Kopano Ratele, *There Was This Goat: Investigating the Truth Commission Testimony of Notrose Nobomvu Konile* [Scottsville, South Africa: University of KwaZulu-Natal Press, 2009]).

12 Certainly some citizens experienced the commission through print media coverage, although readership and circulation of newspapers in South Africa are limited. Radio

had the most extensive coverage, often broadcasting proceedings live and continuously in the original language of testimony to audiences spread all over South Africa. In a country with limited literacy and access to technology, radio had the greatest geographic and socioeconomic reach. During the mid-1990s, South African Broadcasting Corporation (SABC) radio stations had an audience of 3.3 million Zulu-speaking listeners, 1.6 million Xhosa speakers, 1.5 million SeSotho speakers, 1 million SeTswana speakers, 700,000 Afrikaans speakers, 450,000 English speakers, and 116,000 Venda speakers (SA-TRC, *TRC Report*, 1:357). For the English speakers alone, the figure of 450,000 far surpassed that of any English-language newspaper (Antjie Krog, "Manipulator or Human Rights Facilitator?" *Nieman Reports* online exclusives [Winter 2009], http://www.nieman.harvard.edu/reports/article-online-exclusive/100012/Manipulator-or-Human-Rights-Facilitator-Extended.aspx). Although television had a smaller reach, it arguably had a longer-lasting impact because it provided searing moments that became iconic through both visual and aural signification: images, sounds, faces, gestures, speeches, and encounters that resonated and reverberated widely. Television also became a documentarian and archivist of the commission, charged literally with creating a moving-image archive of the TRC process as it unfolded over time. Broadcast coverage was particularly potent because of its geographic and multilinguistic reach.

13 For background, see Cole, *Performing South Africa's Truth Commission*, 102–4.

14 Max du Preez, *TRC Special Report*, South African Broadcasting Corporation, tape 46, episode 46, aired May 4, 1997, accessible online at the Yale Law School Lillian Goldman Library, http://trc.law.yale.edu/. Viewers should be aware that the links for this collection on the Yale website are not always accurate: sometimes a click on one episode launches one from an entirely different date, and some of the episodes are incorrectly numbered—a detail that becomes evident through close readings of dates in relation to the TRC summary report about locations and dates of hearings. There were also discrepancies in dates between the set of tapes for this series that I purchased from SABC and what Yale showed in its catalog. These inconsistencies and inaccuracies aside, the Yale *TRC Special Report* archive is enormously useful and deserves to be studied widely.

15 Daniel Dayan and Elihu Katz, *Media Events: The Live Broadcasting of History* (Cambridge: Cambridge University Press, 1992), 12.

16 Alex Boraine, *A Country Unmasked: Inside South Africa's Truth and Reconciliation Commission* (New York: Oxford University Press, 2000), 89.

17 Ibid., 272.

18 Max du Preez, interview with the author, Napier, December 18, 2006.

19 Annelies Verdoolaege, "Media Representations of the South African Truth and Reconciliation Commission and Their Commitment to Reconciliation," *Journal of African Cultural Studies* 17, no. 2 (2005): 191; Zubeida Jaffer and Karin Cronjé, *Cameras, Microphones, and Pens* (Cape Town: Institute for Justice and Reconciliation, 2004), 13.

20 See, for the first episode, "TRC: Episode 01, Part 01," *TRC Special Report*, South African Broadcasting Corporation, aired April 21, 1996; posted April 6, 2011, http://www.youtube.com/watch?v=yTnY5SQYAro.

21 Max du Preez, email message to author, May 29, 2011.

22 du Preez, interview with the author, Napier, December 18, 2006.

23 For background on the story of Amy Beihl, see the website of the Amy Beihl Foundation, http://www.amybiehl.org/, accessed September 20, 2011.

24 David Mitchell and Sharon Snyder, *Narrative Prosthesis: Disability and the Dependencies of Discourse* (Ann Arbor: University of Michigan Press, 2000), 47.

25 *Truth and Reconciliation Commission: Day 1–10 June 1996* (Testimony of Father Michael Lapsley and Father Michael Wilsner [*sic*], Victims Hearings, Human Rights Violations, Kimberley, June 10–11, 1996), http://www.justice.gov.za/trc/hrvtrans/kimber/ct00654.htm. The TRC transcript erroneously names this person as Father Michael *Wilsner* instead of *Worsnip*. I am grateful to Stephen Karakashian for providing this correction (Karakashian, e-mail message to author, June 29, 2011).

26 Ibid.

27 SA-TRC, *TRC Report*, 1:107.

28 Ibid., 2:592–94.

29 Ibid., 1:154.

30 Justice Albie Sachs, interview with the author, Johannesburg, June 29, 2007.

31 See "TRC Episode 06, Part 05," *TRC Special Report*, South African Broadcasting Corporation, episode 6, aired June 16, 1996; posted April 12, 2011, http://www.youtube.com/watch?v=TfM766RVGvc.

32 Cole, *Performing South Africa's Truth Commission*, 80–82.

33 See Antjie Krog, "Last Time, This Time," LitNet, March 20, 2006, http://oulitnet.co.za/seminarroom/krog_krog2.asp; Ashleigh Harris, "Accountability, Acknowledgment, and the Ethics of 'Quilting' in Antjie Krog's *Country of My Skull*," *Journal of Literary Studies* 22, no. 1/2 (2006): 31, 33; and Laura Moss, "'Nice Audible Crying': Editions, Testimonies, and *Country of My Skull*," *Research in African Literatures* 37, no. 4 (2006): 87.

34 *Truth and Reconciliation Commission* (Testimony of Father Michael Lapsley).

35 Antjie Krog, *Country of My Skull: Guilt, Sorrow, and the Limits of Forgiveness in the New South Africa* (1998; repr., New York: Three Rivers Press, 1999), 275.

36 *Truth and Reconciliation Commission* (Testimony of Father Michael Lapsley).

37 Krog, *Country of My Skull*, 177.

38 Ibid., 176–77.

39 See Cole, *Performing South Africa's Truth Commission*, 135–62.

40 Philip Miller, "REwind: A Cantata for Voice, Tape, and Testimony" (libretto), in *Dramaturgy of the Real World on Stage*, ed. Carol Martin (London: Palgrave, 2010), 104. Loren Kruger, in a review essay on recent books on South Africa's TRC, takes issue with this

translation of the hymn title (Kruger, "Beyond the TRC: Truth, Power, and Representation in South Africa after Transition," *Research in African Literatures* 42, no. 2 [Summer 2011]: 190). However, composer Philip Miller has provided this translation within his published libretto, so I cite this title here.

41 Father Michael Lapsley, e-mail message to author, September 14, 2011.

CHAPTER 12

Photography and Transitional Justice: Evidence, Postcard, Placard, Token of Absence

Eduardo González Cueva and M. Florencia Librizzi

In this essay we argue that the use of photography in transitional justice initiatives raises significant opportunities but also challenges well beyond those assumed by a noncritical view of photography as mere technology. We suggest here that photography is a form of discourse that cannot be easily aligned to the narratives proposed by justice initiatives and that—on the contrary—photography can be destabilizing and unpredictable. Transitional justice practitioners may be drawn to photography due to its aura of authenticity and fixation of reality; however, the actual use of photographs shows that their interpretation and decodification are indeed critical elements of the medium. In that sense, we do not follow a descriptive route about photography as a technology subject to certain functions. Rather, we examine photography as a discursive practice whose inherent invitation to interpretation can strengthen but also challenge the aims of transitional justice, and pose significant dilemmas to institutions and stakeholders.

Photography could be described as no more than technology, ancillary to the stated objectives of transitional justice policies—a tool to disseminate knowledge, generate dialogue, and inspire social change. From this solely functional point of view, photography would be similar to technologies such as printing or recording, with the difference that photography dispenses with two characteristic elements that those other technologies are well suited to convey: verbal communication and sequential narratives. That difference, however, is fundamental. The visual, nonnarrative discourse of photography makes its actual interpretation contingent on the cultural values prevalent in any given society in which photography is used. Whether employed in the context of presenting evidence or in the context of memorializing the victims of human rights abuses, photography provides a space for interpretation, disagreement, and often polyphonic conclusions.

We explore the idea of photography primarily as an evidentiary discourse: the interaction between photographer, subject, and witness through a claim of authenticity, corroborated by technical and supposedly neutral means.

We examine how such an authenticity claim, when successful, is able to gain iconic status. In addition, we offer some examples in which photography has been used for outreach and communication purposes. First we analyze some of photography's characteristics, posing questions around its use in transitional justice; then—mimicking the nature of photography—we propose four snapshotlike reflections illustrating some questions that the use of photography raises in societies going through the application of transitional justice policies. Next, we turn to the *Yuyanapaq* photograph exhibition in Peru in order to consider a concrete case in which photography is used to tell the story of the victims. Finally, we present some tentative conclusions to open and stimulate debate.

PHOTOGRAPHY IN TRANSITIONAL JUSTICE

Photography proposes images that invite decoding. In a transitional justice context, that exercise takes place in a tense institutional environment. During transitions, certain fragile equilibria are being negotiated between the requirements of political expediency, moral demands, and legal principles. The fate of justice lies in the balance and can be tipped in different ways and by different factors, including photographic discourse.

Discussing photography as a communication practice requires identifying the roles of the agents producing photographic images and the role of the people receiving and decoding the images. Further, photography requires an understanding of the cultural and political demands that such a societal context imposes on the production and reception of a photographic image. Susan Sontag has described the complex interactions between photographer and subject: "A photograph is not just the result of an encounter between an event and a photographer; picture-taking is an event in itself, and one with ever more peremptory rights—to interfere with, to invade, or to ignore whatever is going on. Our very sense of situation is now articulated by the camera's interventions."[1]

The photographer is our first agent, inasmuch as he or she is the initiator of the communicative act. The most primordial form of the photographer's agency is the act of selection of the visual field, based on certain assumptions regarding what is significant and what is not. Whether it occurs on the spur of the moment or as a result of careful observation, the operation of aiming and clicking is an act of selection and—conversely—deselection.

The work of the photographer becomes relevant for transitional justice when representing atrocities such as torture, forced disappearances, genocide, and other gross human rights violations. The photographer, whether a spontaneous witness or a trained documentary specialist, is not necessarily an expert on defining what constitutes a "human rights violation" or a "victim";[2] those legal categories are often too abstract for common sense to distinguish or too desiccated for empathy. However, the photographer pays tribute to certain cultural coordinates and their claims of what constitutes an outrage; otherwise, the photographer would never be there, aiming the camera, in the first place.

At the other extreme of the camera, as the targeted one, resides the victim. Let's remember that the concept of *victim* of a human rights violation inevitably evokes the notion of a disabled agent: somebody whose ability to act freely has been destroyed and needs restoration by some external agent. Photographers not only convey the notion of victimhood in their selection of what reality to show, but they may also intervene and perform it in their relationship with that reality. If human rights abuse is fundamentally an act that denies agency by reducing a subject to the position of an object, photography entails the possibility of a compounding denial of agency. Indeed, the victim, reduced to powerlessness, does not have control over the uses of his or her own image. The victims, even if they are opposite the photographer, are not necessarily party to the act of photographic communication. In fact, the victim rarely becomes the viewer of photography. More commonly, victims only provide their images, emerging from an otherwise indistinguishable mass of suffering humanity for just an instant, to become icons and then disappear. When a famous photographer "discovers" the model of a famous picture, decades after a war or a disaster, such an event becomes an extraordinary occurrence, and it often leads to abundant soul-searching on the divergent fates of the photographer and photographed.[3]

As much as it is an act of intervention, photography can also be an act of nonintervention, as Sontag reminds us: "To take a picture is to have an interest in things as they are, in the status quo remaining unchanged (at least for as long as it takes to get a 'good picture'), to be in complicity with whatever makes a subject interesting, worth photographing—including, when that is the interest, another person's pain or misfortune."[4] Sontag's claim is particularly interesting from the standpoint of photographing atrocity, as we expect the images to constitute some form of denunciation, or a step toward justice—that is, a change of the current, atrocious status quo. The freezing effect of the photographic technology is a paradoxical counterpoint to the mobilizing impact we expect it to have; taking a photograph to denounce a situation is an act of significant optimism—and a strong belief in the possibility of the pictures being decoded in a univocal way, in favor of the cause of human rights.

How would that work? Why do we think photography can be favorably consequential in a context of transitional justice? Apparently, we expect that since photography is a representation of reality that offers itself directly and with a sense of immediacy, photography will become evidence in the purest etymological sense: what is directly in front of our vision, thus becoming undeniable. Photography in a context of transition would then act as an iconic force against denial and forgetting, rising against both of these mechanisms of impunity.

That optimistic program has to be examined soberly. We have mentioned, for example, the risk of photography instrumentalizing the victims in one direction or another, and we have indicated the necessarily selective character of the photographer's gaze. However, perhaps the most critical issue is that the faith in photography as an evidentiary discourse is based on a naïve epistemology that purposefully chooses to ignore matters of interpretation and technical manipulation. That photography of atrocity will always be decoded as atrocity, a supposedly universal concept synonymous with revulsion, is not guaranteed. Otherwise, we would not get to know about some atrocities documented by perpetrators who did not see anything abnormal or revolting about taking photographs of their actions. The truth that remains in dispute in transitional justice contexts is the conflictive construction of a narrative, mediated by language and culture,[5] and as such it must deal with multiple views, fragmentation, and indeterminacy.[6]

What happens in transitional justice is that certain institutions are established with the mandate of building a truthful narrative. Those institutions seek to balance out the ingrained injustices of society by opening the agenda to sectors of that society that are normally excluded or rendered invisible; transitional justice creates certain extraordinary, perhaps fleeting circuits of communication. Truth commissions and courts of law working with photographs do not participate—as photographers do—in the foundational act of framing, selecting, and shooting. They work with the product the photographer presents—with archives that represent, in a certain way, the atrocity they purport to study. However, just like photographers, truth commissions and courts do select and build a narrative. The act of selecting photographs as exhibits in a criminal case or for an exhibition by a truth commission becomes a performance. Such an exhibit of photographs will by no means have an assured single interpretation or even the effects desired by the transitional justice institution making use of it. Postmodern thinkers have fruitfully called our attention to the linkages that take place in interpretation between presence and presentation, authorship and authority, archive and performance, and the irreducible role of some aspect of volatility and randomness.[7] Those reflections are worth keeping in mind.

As we have already suggested, the authenticity of photography becomes an evidence issue. Transitional justice processes—such as those conducted in courts of law but not limited to them—are based on information deemed authentic and faithful to the reality of past outrages. In trials, photography has laid claim to authenticity of record, often subverting rules of procedure or leading the tactics of prosecutors and defenders down a certain road. An exemplary snapshot is evidence, but given its powerful iconic potential, it is also more than that. Another concern is focused around the idea of witnessing or advocating. Photography can be seen as a statement of fact, for which technique is supposed to give a guarantee of authenticity. However, since photography is by definition selective, one of the most corrosive doubts that can arise about it is that the photographer is not merely an objective, disinterested witness but instead an intentional advocate.

The tasks of decoding and encoding involve another challenge in photography and transitional justice that is particularly important to consider when outreach measures aim to generate reflection by disseminating iconic photographs. The authenticity effect of photography resides partly in the generalized assumption that its meaning is evident for every possible public, and the corresponding notion that the public is a mere passive decoder of the message. However, situations of transition make evident that the different publics are far from being passive; instead, they are capable of appropriating images and resignifying them, infusing them with meanings and connotations perhaps alien to the original intention.

Photographs, the objects that constitute the sign of the interaction between photographer and viewer, do not entail a direct or intrinsic relationship between the physical objects and their meaning; that relationship is culturally informed and open to debate. The viewer is not a passive decoder of some intrinsic and univocal message; different viewers see different things and build a meaning only by confronting their perceptions with those of others.

Photographs are also not only intelligible in different ways but they are also the possible objects of varied forms of reproduction, which entails the possibility of falsification—that is, the intentional suppression or alteration of represented elements. Prior to the computer revolution, photographs were reproduced by mechanical means; developing original film, printing, and reprinting were specialized crafts. Depending on the materials or methods used in those tasks, the results would be different and unique; at that stage, deceptive interventions could take place. In the era of digital photography and inexpensive, easy-to-use software, manipulation is no longer easily identifiable or the result of a specialized craft.[8]

Photography, like the notion of human rights, is fundamentally modern—that is, conceptually problematic, open to a multiplicity of interpretations and value systems, and fraught by contradiction. Transitional justice, as the set of policies that try to apply human rights principles to the fluid environment of a transition, is a clear setting for those contradictions. Transitional justice lies at the intersection of policymaking, moral argument, and legal procedure. Specific measures in any country are the result of a case-by-case balancing of political constraints, societal pressure, and legal capacity. Such a balance is never satisfactory or stable, depending on the skills of and power differentials among different agents, such as political leaders, victims' organizations, and judicial institutions. Photography in transitional justice is an invitation to instability within instability.

What questions, then, does photography raise in a transitional justice context? At the very least and not being comprehensive, three fundamental issues need examining: authenticity, which is paradoxical, given that photography is always selective and decontextualized; agency, which is also paradoxical, given that the photographer's intentions lose control of the object once it goes out into the world; and iconicity, which is the capacity of certain readings of photography to become, in certain social contexts, the gold standard of interpretation, even defying the original sense of the photographic object. By interrogating some selected snapshots, we examine the difficulties posed for transitional justice in managing the communication potential of photography, channeling it, or subjecting it to pre-existing procedure. While transitional justice institutions may use photography to propose or support a certain narrative, the propensity of the medium to catalyze unexpected interpretations and uses exceeds the capacity of stakeholders to fully control it.

SNAPSHOTS: EVIDENCE, POSTCARD, PLACARD, TOKEN OF ABSENCE

VISUAL DISCOURSE: FIKRET ALIĆ BEHIND THE WIRE

In the summer of 1992, a murderous campaign was taking place against Muslim communities in Bosnia and Herzegovina during the former Yugoslavian wars. What little international sympathy existed toward the persecuted civilians derived from press reports that caused a sense of outrage among Western publics that was difficult for governments, unsure about what steps to take, to manage. The Serbo-Bosnian leader in the war, Radovan Karadžić, seems to have felt confident that he could deal with scandalous press stories by staging carefully led tours to discredit victims' stories. Regrettably for his plans—if indeed they were plans and not plain bravado—some bold journalists, armed by Karadžić's promises of transparency, were already on the ground before the public relations operation could be prepared. On August 5, British television teams were able to visit prisoner camps at a mining installation in Omarska, and a school compound in Trnopolje. The names of both sites would later become references for twentieth-century atrocity as a result of what these reporters witnessed. The camps were used to process Muslim civilians from villages in the surrounding area, which had been forcibly evacuated after Serbian troops arrived. An apparent use of the camps was to neutralize military-age males, either by keeping them in captivity or executing those deemed most dangerous to the Serbian project. Today, the International Criminal Tribunal for the former Yugoslavia (ICTY) has established beyond doubt that the Serbian actions in the region were crimes against humanity. A dozen Bosnian politicians and combatants have been tried and sentenced for their responsibilities regarding what happened in camps like Omarska, Trnopolje, and Keraterm; some people have actually confessed to their crimes.[9]

Back at the time of the war, the story that Karadžić wanted to propagate—and hence his promise of transparency—was that the camps were collection centers to support refugees whom the hostilities would otherwise endanger. However, journalists Penny Marshall and Jeremy Irwin were shocked by what they saw: thousands of prisoners, some of them emaciated, surrounded by armed guards in an open-air yard partially fenced with wire, a few hundred yards from a railway connection. The evocation of similar, not-too-distant European horrors was too strong to be ignored. Out of the video material taken that day, what would mark the conscience of the Western public was a series of stills published in major magazines and newspapers all over the world—particularly a photo of one young man, Fikret Alić, a skeletal phantom standing behind the barbed wire (see Figure 12.1).

The physical condition of Fikret Alić, malnourished and stripped to the waist, in combination with the wire created a picture that evoked other pictures: those of the Nazi concentration camps at the time of their liberation by the triumphant Allies in the spring of 1945. Northern Bosnia evoked Buchenwald, Auschwitz, and Bergen Belsen. The symbolic link between the

FIGURE 12.1

Muslim prisoners in Serbian detention camp, *Daily Mirror* front page, August 7, 1992. Reproduced with permission from Mirrorpix.

DAILY Mirror

Friday, August 7, 1992 NEWSPAPER FOR THE NINETIES Last month's daily sale: 3,596,544 (INCORPORATING THE DAILY RECORD) 27p

THE PICTURE THAT SHAMES THE WORLD

STARVING AND DESPAIRING: Bosnian prisoners at the Omarska concentration camp run by Serbs dedicated to their barbaric policy of "ethnic cleansing" Picture: ITN

BELSEN 92

By MARK DOWDNEY
Foreign Editor

HOLLOW-EYED and haggard, row upon row of men without hope stare out from a barbed wire cage.

The haunting picture of these skeletal captives evokes the ghosts of the Nazis' Belsen concentration camp during the Second World War.

But this is European barbarism in 1992, filmed at one of the Serbian "detention" centres in northern Bosnia.

The picture was part of a harrowing ITN report by newsgirl Penny Marshall, screened last night. Many prisoners at the Omarska camp are thought to have futures no brighter than an executioner's bullet.

Others face the agony of slow death by starvation.

And as the men die, world leaders dither about what – if anything – they will do to halt the unspeakable atrocities which shame humanity.

HORROR OF THE NEW HOLOCAUST PAGE 2 AND CENTRE PAGES

photographs of the Holocaust and the Fikret Alić picture is evident. In that sense, not only do the images of the Holocaust come to mind when viewing the latter picture but so does the whole discourse attached to the photography of Nazi crimes. We could say that the photograph taken of Alić in 1992 had become a "visual discourse" inasmuch as it attached with the image the text—a very well-known narrative—of the resembled Buchenwald photograph (see Figure 12.2). This logic of evocation is not dissimilar to those we often see in narrative contexts; once established, a photograph steps away from the mere image that "does not explain anything," as Sontag pointed out, and suddenly brings an entire narrative into play, requiring little to gain its own iconic status.

British papers immediately made the same connection: "Belsen 1992" was the headline in both the *Daily Mirror* and the *Daily Star*, referring to the infamous Nazi concentration camp. Naming one atrocity after another is a way to escape the fundamental problem that atrocity cannot really be represented, because it defies sense. Even the original referent for what was taking place in Bosnia—Nazi extermination—sometimes has to be named after something else that is more understandable—for example, the geographic location of the crimes.

The reference to the Nazi camps invoked the symbolic constellation of the Holocaust and concepts that, although having origins in law, have achieved an almost fetishistic status—chief among them the concept of genocide. The images of the Serbian camps together with other horrors of the war became a fundamental discourse for the transitional justice project implicit in the establishment of the ICTY, informing all the debates that have followed the tribunal's actions. To the victims, the pictures that the British teams took that afternoon are incontrovertible proof that the victims suffered genocide, even though the ICTY has not come to that conclusion.

For ultranationalistic Serbs and their sympathizers, the pictures are a successful falsification. Using other videos taken the same day by journalists sympathetic to the Serbian cause, they try to demonstrate that Marshall and Irwin fabricated their stills, seeking the perfect location and the perfect victim. According to this view, the journalists purposefully went behind a wire, even though it did not surround the entire camp, in order to evoke the idea of a concentration camp; they used the emaciated Fikret Alić as a prop. The ICTY has debunked this revisionist version, as discussed at the beginning of this section, and, in fact, the journalists won a libel suit against those who accused them of falsification. However, the Serbian conspiracy theory about the images is instructive: it used to its advantage the fact that the pictures were stills from a

FIGURE 12.2

Prisoners in Buchenwald, April 16, 1945. Photograph by H. Miller, 1945, US Office for Emergency Management, Office of War Information, Overseas Operations Branch, New York Office, News and Features Bureau.

video to raise suspicion in general about photography and to make the act of selection an inherent act of bad faith.

The snapshot of Fikret Alić shows us that "photographs invoke deduction, speculation, and fantasy,"[10] but that such interpretive activities are not inherently illegitimate or deceptive. The British journalists or their editors were looking for the best shot, and they did it by invoking a well-established iconic tradition. Such an expressive exercise was useful to convey what was happening in northern Bosnia, as many other pictures of the time showed—and the reality conveyed by the pictures was vindicated by massive evidence in several ICTY trials. Even if Alić's picture may not be representative in a descriptive, statistical sense of the entirety of the male population of the camp, it represented in a symbolic manner the experience of persecution; it stood for the population of the camp.[11]

TOURISM OF ATROCITY IN ABU GHRAIB

Photography is one of the most emblematic modern technologies; it is eminently portable and becomes ever simpler to use. With cameras incorporated into cell phones, photography has also become easily transmittable and omnipresent. Where there is a human action, there is the possibility of photography. Given the present ubiquity of cameras, the very plausible possibility exists that someone might consider virtually any event relevant and photo-worthy. At the same time, photography is directly connected with another important modern activity: leisure travel or tourism. Wandering, the activity of the *flâneur,*[12] has been saluted by modernist writers as a liberating experience through which the individual shows a capacity to break the feudal attachment to land and tradition and fulfill the insatiable capacity to create ever-changing scenarios for the performance of life.

In this activity, photography becomes a form of collection. Wandering and performing are not enough; it is necessary to somehow gather evidence of those actions. Photography frames, flattens, and desiccates experience. Sontag points out that photography disfavors experience by transforming it into a compulsive search for the "photogenic"—whether beautiful or horrible—"converting experience into an image, a souvenir."[13] The massive proliferation of images has become a common phenomenon, whether during travel for leisure or work, in a safari expedition or in a world-class city, and even in the midst of war.

Early on, Sontag pointed out the relative ease of producing photo documents, given the accessibility of affordable cameras and the possibility of manipulating images without much skill or training:

> That age when taking photographs required a cumbersome and expensive contraption—the toy of the clever, the wealthy, and the obsessed—seems remote indeed from the era of sleek pocket cameras that invite anyone to take pictures....Manufacturers reassure their customers that taking pictures demands no skill or expert knowledge, that the machine is all-knowing, and responds to the slightest pressure of the will. It's as simple as turning the ignition key or pulling the trigger.[14]

The proliferation of social media networks along with increasing Internet use throughout the world has provided another space in which the massiveness of the use of photographs becomes apparent. As a result, everyone who knows how—and it does not take much—can upload a photograph in seconds, no matter where they are. Often these images become some sort of "postcards" that travelers secure as proof of their adventures. In our society, which is saturated (or perhaps not) by images,[15] certain motifs are judged trivial by the educated critical eye. Postcards of New York are identical to one another, and tourist photographs posed in front of the Statue of Liberty are nothing more than a banal reproduction of an exhausted model. However, the cynical view of the critic is obviously not shared by the millions of tourists who shoot exactly the same images every day, while grinning and showing the thumbs-up.

Perpetrators who record their deeds as extraordinary, image-worthy events in their lives represent an extreme case of this photographic tourism. However, a paradox is inherent in this action: the persons who took pictures of themselves participating in lynchings, or the Nazi soldiers who took pictures of executions, recorded scenes that they considered extraordinary but not outrageous. The scene is not something that you see every day, but it is possible within the moral compass of the photographer-perpetrator; administering mob justice or annihilating a certain kind of population is permissible, even if the annihilation event is notable in a similar sense as the Great Pyramids, the Eiffel Tower, and other settings.

The torture of Iraqi prisoners by their US captors was the object of journalistic reports during 2003, as the speedy invasion of Iraq gave way to an amorphous guerrilla war, where the prisoners were often no longer identifiable soldiers but instead were civilians identified by intelligence as possible members of resistance groups. However, not until April 2004 did those reports become suddenly credible, as the US media widely disseminated a set of pictures taken by soldiers acting as guards in an old prison—Abu Ghraib—originally used by the Saddam Hussein regime (see Figure 12.3).

US soldiers posed in the pictures next to torture victims or dead bodies, often flashing a smile and the thumbs-up symbol of optimism. One of the soldiers implicated in the ensuing scandal, army reservist Sabrina Harman, was asked about her smile and the thumbs-up gesture. Her answer was, "Whenever I would get into a photo, I never know what to do with my hands so in any kind of photo, I probably have a thumbs-up because it's just—I just picked it up from the kids. It's just something that automatically happens. Like when you get into a photo, you want to smile. It's just, I guess, something I did."[16]

The apparent lack of reflection surrounding the production of those photographs is striking. According to her, she does the same gesture—smile and thumbs-up—in "any kind of photo." Just like Sontag warned, photography replaces actual experience and itself becomes the experience: a repetitive, automatic ritual. The trivialization of the action of posing for a photo—an action now learned in early childhood in nearly all cultures and all countries on Earth—in the case of Abu Ghraib constitutes the trivialization of atrocity.

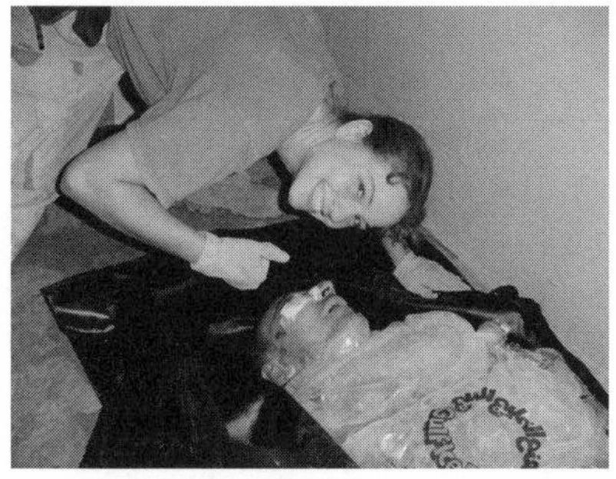

FIGURE 12.3
Sabrina Harman posing over the body of Manadel al-Jamadi, Abu Ghraib Prison, November 2003. Photograph by US military personnel at Abu Ghraib prison.

If Hannah Arendt attached the notion of banality to bureaucratic evil,[17] we can see that this notion can also be attached to the infinitely variegated experience of the wanderer, the *flâneur*. Photography, transformed into an ever-present eye, has anchored the originally liberating experience of traveling into a repetitive ritual: aim at something universally and banally considered ordinary; ask for a smile; shoot.

The life of the Abu Ghraib pictures in a context of justice was stillborn. Accountability has been limited to those low-level personnel directly implicated in the torture of prisoners, through military trials lacking the normal guarantees of transparency that civilian trials provide. The upper echelons conducting US aggression in Iraq have been spared, and as much as the Abu Ghraib photographs created awareness of torture, the political context was not the same as in World War II or Bosnia. While the direct perpetrators, the likes of Sabrina Harman, were convicted, the higher-ups have so far not been vulnerable to criminal justice.

PASSPORT PHOTOS: UNIFORMITY AND UNIQUENESS

Passport photos have become probably the most trivial use of photography. Different from the triviality of personal use, this use is bureaucratically sanctioned: in most countries, every citizen must be accountable to his or her specific facial characteristics in order to be registered as a unique individual, enjoying the rights and bearing the obligations recognized by the state.

In several contexts of atrocity, that modest instrument of citizenship, the passport picture, has become the sole evidence that relatives of the disappeared have to indicate that their relatives indeed existed and that the state, which required the person to be registered visually, is at once witness and perpetrator. The claim of the passport picture that relatives laminate and use as a placard—or show in one public institution after another—is the following: "This person, the one you yourself recognized as existing, as having human rights under the laws of this country, has disappeared. You cannot deny the disappearance by saying that he did not exist, that we have invented this outrage to shame you. Here he is. Where is he?" (See Figure 12.4.) Passport photos are photographs of the face. More explicitly, they are photographs of a gaze. In a passport photo, the disappeared look at us, as the state originally wanted. In this configuration also resides its power: Passport pictures represent us as we want to be seen in our official documents or in a work interview—with clean, crisp clothes, makeup, hair carefully combed, all centered in a purposeful look: a frontal gaze.

Of course, since the state is the party requesting the passport photos for its official purposes, these pictures are a variation on a motif we examined earlier: the perpetrator taking pictures of its victims. In some cases, this is literal: the pictures of concentration camp inmates in Auschwitz, prisoners in extermination camps in Cambodia, and Muslim women forced to unveil in front of French colonial authorities during the repression of the Algerian war for independence. In those three cases, we are not in front of pictures of persons hoping that the picture is a step toward citizenship, but instead we are seeing pictures of victims knowing that the photographs are actually part and parcel of their victimization—victims who cannot do anything but look intently and transfer to us their cold fear of imminent atrocity.

The use of the individual passport photo as evidence of existence is in essence an affirmation that there was a "here," but there is no longer. However, in the case of pictures of the disappeared, an additional use generates intriguing questions, when individual pictures serve as an instrument of recognition and an aggregation of relatives' interests. Soon enough the individual pictures become a collage, a mass of pictures, one next to the other in some sort of placard.

From far away, the numerous pictures of the disappeared, brought together by their relatives to demonstrations, all with the same look as required by their original use, convey an idea of uniformity and pattern. The quantitative totality produces something more than mere aggregation and becomes something new: the affirmation that, for disappearance to have happened on such a scale, there must have been a certain calculation, a modus operandi, a system.

On the other hand, once we get closer to the photographs, we can appreciate their faces and connect with the qualitative aspect of the atrocity—the fact that each of those photographs represents a unique human being whose life was truncated by gross human rights violations. This contemplation evokes a similar response as Peter Eisenman's Memorial to the Murdered Jews of Europe.[18] The memorial's design includes a rigid grid structure of some twenty-seven hundred concrete pillars. The pillars are spaced about ninety-five

FIGURE 12.4
Adelina García holds up the picture of her disappeared husband, Zósimo Tenorio, Ayacucho, Peru, May 2010. Reproduced by permission from Marina García Burgos.

centimeters apart, enough space to allow people to walk between them. The apparent massivity and uniformity of the pillars reflects the idea of human beings being depersonalized, losing their dignity and identities by becoming victims of a holocaust such as the one to which this memorial is dedicated. On the other hand, as soon as we approach the memorial and start looking closely, we see that each of the pillars has a different shape and height, and the layout produces a unique sense of movement. This design seems to be an attempt to represent how victims recuperate their individuality, a story that was not told but that we can intuit of a unique human being whose dignity and life should never have been lost. In a similar way, the aggregation of pictures of the disappeared becomes a powerful form of memorialization.[19]

The generalization of the pictures of the disappeared as passport photos has seared a certain notion of absence and presence into public discourse. Since we cannot represent the disappeared as tortured, destroyed bodies because we do not know their ultimate fates and whereabouts, we represent them as they were before the state so profoundly violated its contract with them.

PHOTOGRAPHY AS A TOKEN OF ABSENCE

Photography owes much of its power to our naïve epistemology—attributing reality to what is visible—and also to its capacity to represent the extraordinary. However, we also find that photography of the ordinary can achieve a symbolic status in contexts of transitional justice; surprisingly, such photography of the ordinary can indeed be representative not of what is there but of what is not. In particular, for photography of those missing, as Sontag says, "A photograph is both a pseudo-presence and a token of absence."[20]

Pursuant to remembering victims, and moreover to represent their painful absence, the Argentinean photographer Gustavo Germano has created a series of images titled *Absences* (in Spanish, *Ausencias*),[21] on the disappearances that took place in his country during the 1976–83 military dictatorship, making the absence visible by showing the hole left in the family by those whom power plucked from them. Germano's photographs evoke the idea of temporality, producing a sort of illusive parallel in which the absence of the other conveys the weight of what it means that a human, a presence, has vanished—leaving a hole of pain but also the presence of memory in their absence. The project is built in series of two photographs: first, the original photograph, in which the disappeared person and relatives or friends are together, not knowing of their future unfortunate fate (see Figure 12.5). The second picture is cast with the

FIGURE 12.5

Maria Irma and Maria Susana Ferreira. Reproduced by permission from Gustavo Germano, *Ausencias (Argentina)* (Absences [Argentina]), 2007, http://www.gustavogermano.com/.

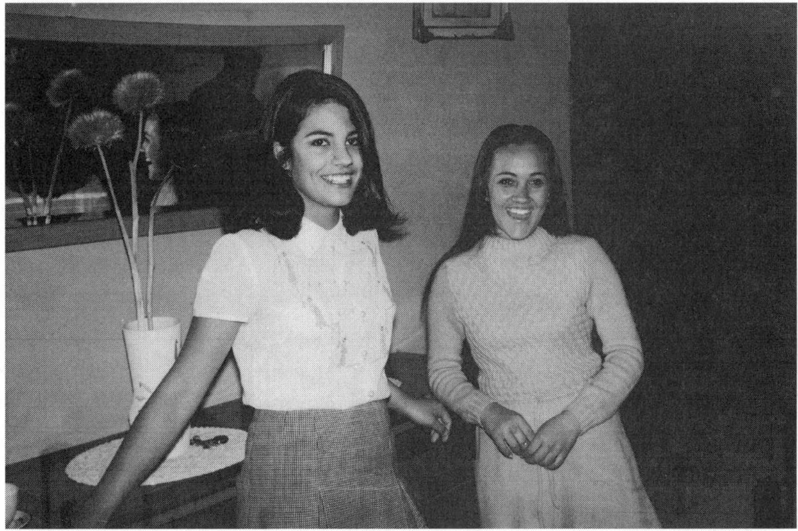

a. Maria Irma Ferreira and Maria Susana Ferreira, 1970.

b. Maria Susana Ferreira, 2006.

relatives, the ones who survived, with the disappeared present through their very absence. In some cases, no one remained, and the second photograph shows an isolated place—a witness of what has been and will not be any more in the most patent way. Both photographs are taken in the same place, emphasizing this parallel and making the loss even more evident—something that is obvious for the victim's relatives but that society as a whole has to remember, in order not to fall in the same hole again and again. The simplicity and the exactness of the photographs generates a profound emotion for those who dare to engage with this exhibition.

Germano has experienced in his own life the absence reflected in his pictures. He was eleven years old when his eighteen-year-old brother, Eduardo, was kidnapped. It took Gustavo Germano ten years to start exploring photography as an exercise of memory and sublimation. In the Argentinean case, as Germano explains, the relatives of the victims are almost always available to pursue projects that "mantienen viva la memoria" (keep alive the memory) of the disappeared.[22] Germano also points out the importance of trust in these initiatives, as relatives have often given photographs of their loved ones to some projects that were never concluded, and the photos have never been returned,[23] leaving them without the most tangible remaining representation of their loved ones.[24] In a way, then, Germano's project is quite different from other forms of documentary photography because it attempts to put the victims in control: deciding whether to engage in the project, choosing the scenarios and settings, and consequently limiting the role of the photographer, who is a survivor himself.

The present absence of Germano's works might illuminate communities' understandings of these extremely complex and painful situations and encourage each community to restore the victims' and relatives' dignity through a public acknowledgment that those absent should still be present.

TELLING A STORY IN PHOTOGRAPHY—"*YUYANAPAQ*: TO REMEMBER"

If a single picture can spark a prairie fire, what about a permanent, itinerant exhibit? The Peruvian Truth and Reconciliation Commission (Comisión de la Verdad y Reconciliación, CVR) took that bold step in 2003 when it decided to release the photographic collection *Yuyanapaq* (To remember), together with its comprehensive final report.[25] This unique exhibition has generated different reactions among viewers and received multiple and diverse analyses from scholars.[26]

The CVR was created after the fall in 2001 of Alberto Fujimori's authoritarian government. The CVR had a mandate to clarify the process and facts of—and responsibilities for—the violence that scourged Peru between 1980 and 2000. The commission was in many ways innovative compared to previous truth-seeking initiatives in Latin America, and it is considered to be one of the strongest examples within the transitional justice field. During its tenure, the commission organized public hearings at which victims of illegal armed groups as well as state counterinsurgency recounted their stories to be broadcasted nationally. Its final report—a comprehensive nine-volume text supported by seventeen thousand testimonies—methodically examined the strategies of the actors of the conflict, charted the patterns of abuse, and laid the blame squarely at the feet of political elites and fanatical insurgents.[27]

During its work, the CVR called on all photojournalists who had been active during the conflict to share their archives with the commission. More than eighty journalists and news media outlets responded, giving the commission access to millions of images that a group of curators examined, selecting about seventeen hundred pictures from which three products were created: a web page, an itinerant exhibit, and a book, all sharing the Quechua-language name *Yuyanapaq*.[28] The Peruvian truth commission was probably the first to make extensive use of photography as an avenue to promote feelings of shame and national solidarity.[29] By using iconic pictures—the most symbolic or representative photographs taken during that period—the exhibition tried to trigger a profound reflection among individuals and the community regarding Peru's violent past.[30] Hundreds of thousands have visited the exhibit in different cities around the country, and its success has forced the commission, which originally thought it would be a temporary exhibit, to work hand in hand with the national authorities to house it in the National Museum in Lima, and then create itinerant versions to be shown in the rest of the country. Its continued popularity has spawned a new project, a National Site of Memory, to permanently host it and other artifacts from the conflict period.[31]

An interesting aspect of the Peruvian exhibition was its combination of two different and probably contradictory objectives: (1) encouraging the audience to analyze the images critically, providing it with accurate contextual information, and (2) memorializing the country's losses, proposing a narrative of shared national shame and pain. Another significant issue regarding *Yuyanapaq* is that the collection proposes a narrative that is related but not ancillary to the written final report. Indeed, *Yuyanapaq* was the result of the work of curators only marginally associated with those writing the report, and the curators finished their work before the written report was released. One could argue that the strong reactions and debates sparked by *Yuyanapaq* impacted the report writers as they drafted their final conclusions. Also, just like the final report, *Yuyanapaq* was vigorously criticized from all sides of the cultural and political spectrum. The right-wing press, far more powerful than the small Peruvian left, saw it as "one sided" and believed it promoted a "pro-terrorist" agenda.[32] Some conservative legislators even accused the commission of faking specific pictures in order to malign the honor of the armed forces and soil their victory over the Shining Path. Mirroring the controversy in the Fikret Alić case, an ultraconservative legislator suggested in Parliament that the picture of a specific survivor, Edmundo Camana, had been posed in order to defame the armed forces (see Figure 12.6).

Camana's picture—taken by Oscar Medrano, one of the most celebrated Peruvian photojournalists—is a close-up of a man whose head is partially covered by a coarse piece of cloth acting as a bandage, dressing unseen wounds. The strength of Camana's gaze is not reduced but actually intensified by the fact that one of his eyes is covered by the improvised bandages, and his facial expression conveys profound desolation and perplexity.[33] The image does not show blood or signs of violence, except for some swelling in Camana's lips.

The infuriated legislator argued that he had seen the entire series of negatives from which the picture of Camana was selected, and some pictures showed that Camana's wounds were only superficial. The ominous bandage was a prop, proving that the photographer was looking for the "best shot" as part of a conspiracy against the country. The accusation was not only absurd but misdirected, since Camana was actually a survivor of Shining Path violence, not an army attack on civilians. Even if the picture had been the result of some act of expressive exaggeration, the commission had no way to control its composition, which took place during the war—well before the existence of the CVR.

As absurd as it was, the accusation against *Yuyanapaq* showed the desperation of those groups that perceived the exhibit as a powerful instrument wresting away their control of the conflict's memory. Averting the eyes from the photography of atrocity is simply impossible, particularly as in the case mentioned, where the image is not particularly grotesque or graphic but rather subtle and connotative. The chairperson of the CVR, Salomon Lerner, has stated that the complexity of truth resides not just in the multiplicity of versions of it but also in the multiplicity of means to accede to it, and he has also recognized the limitations of description. Truth has to be not just narrated in written form, but demonstrated and expressed through the iconic power of photography:

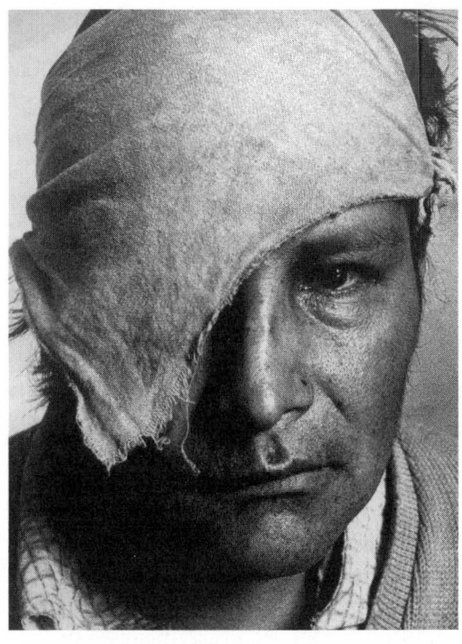

FIGURE 12.6
Edmundo Camana Sumari, survivor of the massacre of Lucanamarca (taken at the Hospital of Ayacucho, 1983). Reproduced with permission from Oscar Medrano Perez (*Caretas*).

> We discovered that truth—a polyedric reality, irreducible to a single dimension—needs to be recovered not just in a discursive, intelligible dimension, but also in its demonstrative strength, in aspects that talk to our emotions and our sensibility and that cannot be exhausted in a reconstructed history, since it continues in human suffering and in the testimony of this suffering—past, but simultaneously alive—as it is preserved in the images of violence and human resistance.[34]

Doubtlessly, far more persons have visited the exhibit than have cared to read even a small fragment of the CVR's four-thousand-page report. The commission's gamble of unleashing the power of photography was handsomely repaid in terms of public awareness: *Yuyanapaq* has helped destabilize the status quo of memory in the country, where conservative sectors are dominant in the political arena. Its improvised character and the spontaneous reception it obtained from the population demonstrate that photography can upset the logic of a truth commission. It was not the agglomeration of data or written argument that signaled the work of the commission and gained visibility and strength for it. Rather, performance and memorialization served that function: the first-person oral accounts of the public hearings and the subtle force of photography.

TRANSITIONAL JUSTICE: WRITING WITH LIGHT

Transitional justice institutions, such as truth commissions or courts, may be seduced by photography since it activates what we have portrayed here as a naïve epistemology. Commissions and courts seek evidence and may use photography as proof of reality, but photography is much more than a neutral, technically mediated reflection of the world; photography is hardly a univocal discourse, its decodification by an audience is difficult to foresee, and its demonstrative and expressive force outlasts its evidentiary value.

Transitional justice institutions are predicated on the value of the written word; their practice is diametrically opposed to that of photographers. Truth commissions, courts of law, and reparation boards are part of the lettered city, eminently accessible to the reading classes and transmitted in the archival language of power. That such constituencies will embrace photography is not a given. But nor is it apparent that transitional justice institutions would adopt any form of performance or connotative discourse—yet they have done so. As many other chapters in this volume show, transitional justice measures have made use of performance from the first moment in which they put victims on the stand in front of an audience.[35] Additional uses of cultural means—such as theater, cinema, and literature—have just followed suit. So has photography.

However, by embracing photography and other cultural practices, transitional justice transforms itself. It must renounce at least partially its assumption of and its project of supporting an enlightened public sphere that rationally discusses arguments presented in a scientific, forensic manner; as we have pointed out, this assumption is unrealistic and insufficient. Transitional justice is also an exercise of directing one's gaze toward the inexpressible and accepting the presence of a certain irreducible darkness in humanity's experience. In our opinion, the power of transitional justice resides precisely in that it is not, and cannot be, the ordering of the world or the enthroning of a new, incontestable truth; instead, transitional justice is the opening of an arena for contestation. Transitional justice's democratic character resides in the fact that it does not replace one official, status-quo truth with another; it would be an Orwellian piece of machinery if it were to do so. As we explained at the opening of this chapter, transitional justice merely empowers certain marginalized voices and sectors, giving them the space in an agenda and a public sphere that would otherwise be closed to them.

Photography, etymologically, means "writing with light," as Derrida reminds us.[36] But that light is only able to leave an imprint because it works in a camera obscura of absolute darkness. Let us recall one more time photography's original nature, before the time of digitalization: transitional justice practices are—like any instrument of civilization—just an attempt to use a certain illumination in the obscurity and chaos of the world. Transitional justice cannot aspire, unless in a display of extreme naïveté, to fully enlighten human nature.

The images that a transitional exercise offers, just like those of photography, are only fleeting slices of a reality that cannot be fully grasped: intentional actions of framing, selection, and deselection; and desperate actions to cope with the ever-fluid nature of time and the inevitability of absence. As transitional justice becomes more juridicized, and possibly desiccated into sets of best practices, lessons learned, or normative principles, establishing a linkage to photography and other cultural practices may introduce a welcome, enriching destabilization.

NOTES

The views presented here are the authors' and do not represent those of the International Center for Transitional Justice.

1 Susan Sontag, *On Photography* (New York: Picador, 1990), 11.

2 The UN General Assembly, *Basic Principles and Guidelines on the Right to a Remedy and Reparation for Victims of Gross Violations of International Human Rights Law and Serious Violations of International Humanitarian Law*, UN Doc. A/RES/60/147, March 21, 2006, paras. 8–9, defines *victims* as "persons who individually or collectively suffered harm, including physical or mental injury, emotional suffering, economic loss or substantial impairment of their fundamental rights, through acts or omissions that constitute gross violations of international human rights law, or serious violations of international humanitarian law. Where appropriate, and in accordance with domestic law, the term 'victim' also includes the immediate family or dependents of the direct victim and persons who have suffered harm in intervening to assist victims in distress or to prevent victimization." The notion of victimhood is always problematic in reality, often causing confusion even within the legal community. On the controversy of the victimhood notion, see Heidy Robouts and Stef Vandeginste, "Reparations for Victims of Gross and Systematic Human Rights Violations: The Notion of Victim," *Third World Legal Studies* 16 (2003): 89–114.

3 The possibility of revictimization should be a key ethical consideration for documentary and journalistic photographers. Revictimization also becomes an issue, quite

obviously, for transitional justice institutions that gain access to photography. However, such a discussion is outside the boundaries of this essay. We examine below the case of a victim "rediscovered" by the photographer when discussing the case of the photographic exhibit *Yuyanapaq*.

4 Sontag, *On Photography*, 12.

5 Terry Barret, "Modernism and Postmodernism: An Overview with Art Examples," in *Art Education: Content in a Postmodern Era*, ed. James Hutchens and Marianne Sugges (Washington, DC: National Art Education Association, 1997), 18.

6 In addition, we cannot assume that the evidentiary basis of photography is untainted. Photography was eminently open to manipulation when it was the result of a mechanical process, and it has become even more open to manipulation in the digital era.

7 See Gerhard Richter, introduction to Jacques Derrida, *Copy, Archive, Signature: A Conversation on Photography* (Palo Alto, CA: Stanford University Press, 2010), xxvii.

8 Naturally, fraudulent interventions need to be distinguished from the good-faith lies that we know as artistic fiction. Following an implicit pact of coding between photographer and public, nobody hides the fact that the image has been altered in order to enhance a certain concept—for example, in the political photomontage that German antifascist artist John Heartfield made in the 1930s.

9 At the time of writing this essay, the ICTY was trying Radovan Karadžić himself.

10 Sontag, *On Photography*, 23.

11 On the distinction between descriptive and symbolic representation, see Hanna Pitkin, *The Concept of Representation* (Berkeley: University of California Press, 1967).

12 The French term *flâneur* has the basic meanings of "stroller," "lounger," "saunterer," or "loafer." The *flâneur* is a literary type from the nineteenth century in France, associated with any picture of Parisian streets as well as the urban explorer or the connoisseur of the street. Taking the poetry of Charles Baudelaire as a model, the German philosopher Walter Benjamin made the *flâneur* an object of scholarly interest as an emblematic figure of modern urban experience. See Benjamin, *The Writer of Modern Life: Essays on Charles Baudelaire*, ed. Michael Jennings (Cambridge, MA: Harvard University Press, 2006).

13 Sontag, *On Photography*, 9.

14 Ibid., 7, 14.

15 The idea of massivity of photographs could lead us to consider some sort of visual pollution that makes it difficult for us to engage in a meaningful reflection about the important topics to which the photographs might refer. In that sense we could examine the idea of "photo-zapping," whether compulsively taking pictures without seeing or seeing pictures taken by others without observing. Gerard Wajcman describes this reality and goes further, stating that photography even hides the "real." See Gerard Wajcman, *El ojo absoluto* [The absolute eye] (Buenos Aires: Manantial, 2011). However, such a discussion goes beyond the boundaries of this essay.

16 Errol Morris, "The Most Curious Thing," *Opinionator* (blog), *New York Times*, May 19, 2008, http://opinionator.blogs.nytimes.com/2008/05/19/the-most-curious-thing/.

17 See Hannah Arendt, *Eichmann in Jerusalem: A Report on the Banality of Evil* (New York: Penguin Classics, 2006). Even though Arendt has been criticized for the phrase "banality of evil," she has provided an interesting basis for reflection on how human beings often renounce their critical thinking, whether encouraged by systems of bureaucracy (as she posited) or by other mechanisms of social control, such as peer pressure or fashion mandates. This idea (without discussing the original meaning of the controversial "banality of evil" phrase, which is outside of the scope of our essay) is closely related to the lack of reflection regarding the often massive use of photography that we discuss in this paper.

18 See "Memorial to the Murdered Jews of Europe," accessed November 2012, http://www.stiftung-denkmal.de/en/memorials/the-memorial-to-the-murdered-jews-of-europe.html#c694.

19 On memoralization, see the chapter in this volume by Louis Bickford.

20 Sontag, *On Photography*, 16.

21 See "Ausencias: 30.000 Detenidos/Desaparecidos y asesinados por la dictadura militar Argentina entre 1976 y 1983" [Absences: 30,000 Detained/disappeared and assassinated by the Argentinean military dictatorship between 1976 and 1983], accessed November 2012, http://www.gustavogermano.com/.

22 Agustin Marangoni, "Gustavo Germano: Fotografías de la Ausencia," interview with Gustavo Germano, *Pixelicia*, April 2, 2011, http://pixelicia.com/gustavo-germano-fotografias-ausencias/.

23 Ibid.

24 Again, this issue may be significant in terms of photographers' ethical responsibilities when working in transitional justice settings.

25 See "Exposición 'Yuyanapaq: Para recordar'" [Exhibit: *Yuanapaq:* To remember], CVR, accessed November 2012, http://www.cverdad.org.pe/apublicas/p-fotografico/e_yuyanapacha.php.

26 See, e.g., Lizbeth Arenas Fernández, "El Sendero de la Fotografía: Una aproximación al análisis de las fotografías sobre la violencia política del Perú, 1980–2000" [The path of photography: An approximation to the analysis of photography of the political violence in Peru, 1980–2000], *Memorias de las XI Jornadas Nacionales de Investigadores en Comunicación* 11: "Tramas de la comunicación en América Latina contemporánea. Tensiones sociales, políticas y económicas" [Memories of the Eleventh National Congress of Communicational Researchers: Communication plot in contemporary Latin America. Social, political and economic tensions], Facultad de Ciencias Políticas y Sociales [Faculty of Political and Social Sciences], UNCUYO, Mendoza, 2007; Fernández, "Cuanto más

cerca, más lejos: Las víctimas en las fotografías de violencia de la Comisión de la Verdad y Reconciliación del Perú" [The closest, the furthest: The victims in the photographs of violence of the Truth and Reconciliation Commission of Peru] (paper presented at the 2009 Congress of the Latin American Studies Association, Rio de Janeiro, Brazil, June 11–14, 2009); Cynthia E. Milton, "Images of Truth: Art as a Medium for Recounting Peru's Internal War," *A Contra Corriente* [Against the flow] 6, no. 2 (Winter 2009): 63–102; Margarita Saona, "The Knowledge That Comes from Seeing: *Yuyanapaq* and the Peruvian Truth and Reconciliation Commission," *Hispanic Issues On Line* 4, no. 1 (2009), http://hispanicissues.umn.edu/assets/pdf/saona.pdf; Robin Hoecker, "Painful Pictures: Photojournalism and Reconciliation in Peru" (paper presented at the 2007 *Association for Education in Journalism and Mass Communication* Conference, Chicago, IL, 2007), http://www.robinhoecker.com/writing/yuyanapaq_quant.pdf, and others.

27 See "Informe Final," CVR, accessed November 2012, http://www.cverdad.org.pe/ifinal/index.php.

28 See "Proyecto Fotográfico. Presentación" [Photographic project: Presentation], CVR, accessed November 2012, http://www.cverdad.org.pe/apublicas/p-fotografico/index.php.

29 Deborah Poole and Isaías Rojas Pérez, "Memories of Reconciliation: Photography and Memory in Postwar Peru," *Emisférica* 7, no. 2 (Winter 2010), http://hemisphericinstitute.org/hemi/en/e-misferica-72/poolerojas.

30 "Proyecto Fotográfico."

31 See "Lugar de la Memoria, la Tolerancia y la Inclusión Social" [Site of memory, tolerance and social inclusion], accessed November 2012, http://lugardelamemoria.org/.

32 Poole and Rojas Pérez, "Memories of Reconciliation."

33 Salomón Lerner Febres, "The Visual Legacy," CVR, accessed November 2012, http://www.cverdad.org.pe/ingles/apublicas/p-fotografico/index.php.

34 Ibid.

35 See especially Catherine Cole's chapter in this volume.

36 Richter, introduction to Derrida, *Copy, Archive, Signature.*

CHAPTER 13

Visions of Justice and Accountability: Transitional Justice and Film

Carolyn Patty Blum

Film promises a unique capacity to envision transitional justice. While transitional justice is normally thought of as a process of social and political transformation, repair and reconstruction,[1] film opens a window into its emotional, human, and personal sides. Especially in narrative feature films, but at times in documentaries as well, the stories of the human impact of abusive regimes and the attempts to respond to these abuses in their aftermaths, and the failures and pitfalls of these attempts, are at their most visceral. One fundamental aspect of film is its capacity to depict the past; film offers a lens to what it was like during the period in which a country was controlled by an authoritarian government or colonial power, or suffered in the throes of civil conflict and war.[2] This reconstruction of the past plays a key role not only in raising awareness about the conditions extant before a transition but also during the process of transition itself. In the subsequent task of reckoning with the injustices left in conflict's wake, film communicates a message that can reach a broader public, including those within a society who may have never seen these experiences depicted, about what remains to be done. As an enduring art form, film becomes one small part of the larger cultural expression of how the past is constructed and remembered in the collective consciousness.

Because of its capacity to re-create or imagine situations and stories, film can present the emotions that may linger after a conflict subsides. For example, films may portray characters along a broad spectrum, from those seeking vengeance to those capable of or promoting forgiveness and the range of emotions in between.[3] Film can dramatize the complexities of assigning moral or legal blame or responsibility to individuals in the aftermath of a period of extreme violence. Film probes these "positional portrayals" of perpetrators, commanders, collaborators, aiders, rescuers, helpers, bystanders, and victims.[4] Understanding these roles within a torn society can contribute to its social reconstruction.[5] Beyond the personal narratives and interpersonal dynamics, film can also capture the ways in which societies have addressed an abusive past or failed to do so.[6] Films look at justice, truth, repair, and political or institutional reform as responses to mass atrocity, and they are capable of showing the complexities, contradictions, and nuances involved in these processes. Films grapple with the ways in which the legacy of the past continues to linger into and affect the present and succeeding generations, thereby raising questions for the audience about their own relationships to the dynamics of transition and change.

In this chapter I explore each of these themes related to transitional justice on film. In each section of the chapter, I consider one exemplar film as the focus of discussion.[7] In the first section, using the film *Missing*, I focus on the way in which film may display the realities of creating and perpetuating an authoritarian society and its impact on one family. The next section analyzes the film *Divided We Fall*, which grapples with the complexities of individual complicity under Nazi occupation. I then consider four modalities of transitional justice in the third section. Examining the classic work *Judgment at Nuremberg*, I explore the ways in which criminal trials limit and expand our understandings of criminal accountability. My look at the documentary *Long Night's Journey into Day* shows how the South African Truth and Reconciliation Commission attempted to balance the experiences and needs of victims and survivors against its intention to provide amnesty to perpetrators who provided the "full truth." In considering the film *Cautiva*, I address the aftermath of military dictatorship and how attempts at social repair have sharp consequences for those in the present who unwittingly bear the burdens of the past. Finally, I discuss the film *The Lives of Others*, which portrays the ubiquity of the Stasi's intrusion into the private lives of East German citizens and elements of reformation in that regime's aftermath.

Each film simultaneously operates at dual levels—as a rendering of historical events and as a work of art with its own artistic choices and integrity. Each film illustrates the ways in which the medium has a unique capacity to show the stories of the lived human experience of state violence and its aftermath. Further, film can be a tool to represent post-conflict transitions and the mechanisms used to address and come to grips with the past. As such, film helps both to represent the fuller reality for citizens whose own history was hidden from them and to raise awareness globally about the character and consequences of state repression and the post-conflict means to address it.

ENVISIONING THE PAST: *MISSING*

The Greek director Costa-Gavras has a history of creating cinematic visions of authoritarian regimes and societies in conflict. *Missing*, which depicts events in Chile, was preceded by Z (about Greece) and *State of Siege* (about Uruguay).[8] These films present fictionalized versions of actual events. In *Missing*, Costa-Gavras tells the story of the military overthrow of the democratically elected socialist president Salvador Allende by chronicling the experiences of Charles Horman, a US citizen living in Chile, and his family.[9]

In the film, Horman and his wife, Beth,[10] are drawn to living in Chile because of the idealism, reformism, and energy of the Popular Unity government of President Salvador Allende. When Charles disappears soon after the 1973 military coup overthrowing that government, the movie changes its focus to the efforts of Beth and Charles's father, Ed, to find him. Unlike Beth, Ed—a patriotic, conservative Christian Scientist—is inclined to rely on US government officials to assist in this effort. But as the search takes them through the overflowing hospitals and morgues of post-coup Chile, Ed begins to confront the reality that harm likely has come to his son, and that the US government is not being truthful with him about his son's whereabouts.

Beth and Ed determine that Charles likely was taken to the National Stadium, where thousands of prisoners are being held. When Ed and Beth meet a Chilean Intelligence Service defector, they find out that a US citizen, held at the Ministry of Defense, was interrogated, roughed up, and taken to the stadium to be killed because he knew too much about US involvement in the coup. Ed and Beth's subsequent review of Charles's meticulously kept journals indicates his numerous conversations with US military personnel in Viña del Mar, the location where many believe the coup was prepared. Ultimately, Ed receives confirmation that Charles was murdered at the stadium. He confronts US Embassy officials, but they continue to prevaricate, claiming they have news that Charles was smuggled out of the country. The chief US military advisor emotionlessly tells Ed that if his son played with fire, he was going to get burned. Ed's evidence of his son's fate, however, forces the hand of reluctant US government officials. Charles's murder is confirmed, and his body is found in the morgue. In the final scene at the airport, Ed and Beth sign documents to ship the body to the United States within days; as the postscript reveals, the body did not arrive until seven months later.

Through the individual stories of Charles, Ed, and Beth, *Missing* vividly portrays the events during the important first month of the Chilean junta. In an attempt to silence opposition and terrorize the population, the Chilean military systematically and quickly sought out suspected opponents and subjected them to arbitrary detention, torture, disappearance, and murder. The film shows the militarization of Chilean society and the imposition of a state of siege with curfew, random arrests, and killings. When two other friends of the Hormans are arrested, the widespread nature of the arrests becomes visible. The National Stadium (as well as the Chile Stadium, a smaller sports arena) became a warehouse for the military to detain the arrested. The locker rooms in the basement became interrogation and torture chambers and, in all likelihood, the location of the murders of Charles Horman and many others. The use of the National Stadium as a locus of repression is a deliberate usurpation and control of a public space—especially one associated with joyful activities—and part of an explicit strategy to solidify the military's power.

In smaller ways, Costa-Gavras reveals the more pervasive, day-to-day aspects of the authoritarian project of the Chilean military. In one scene, women are removed from a bus line and roughly told that they must dress in skirts as soldiers cut off their pant legs. In another, young men are forced to paint over pro-Allende graffiti. These cinematic glimpses reveal the larger conservative aims of the military as well as its desire to erase from public space expressions of opposition. And when Charles tries to intervene to stop the arrest of a man in a restaurant, he is punched by the plain-clothed captor; the movie dramatizes the reality that "anything can happen at any time," a central tactic of state terror.[11]

The Chilean military implemented a systematic policy of disappearance, a phenomenon well depicted during the search for Charles. The Chilean military consistently denies any knowledge of Charles's whereabouts; instead, military leaders imply that he is in hiding or in the custody of leftists with whom he conspired to embarrass their government. Charles's father must buck these accusations and, in so doing, discard his own preconceived notion that if something has happened to his son, he must have done something wrong.[12] US officials engage in the same lies, obfuscations, and denials as the Chileans. Costa-Gavras makes central throughout the question of US political responsibility for toppling Allende.[13]

The film implies that Charles's body was identified only because of the intervention of his US relatives and their political contacts; had he been Chilean, he might have remained unidentified, like the hundreds of corpses that Ed and Beth see in the morgue. Costa-Gavras is ever mindful that while he has chosen to examine the meaning and consequences of the military takeover of Chile through the story of a US citizen, the audience should never forget that most of the victims were Chileans.

COMPLICATING INDIVIDUAL RESPONSIBILITY IN "POSITIONAL PORTRAYALS": *DIVIDED WE FALL*

Divided We Fall begins in 1939 in occupied Czechoslovakia.[14] The Wieners, an affluent Jewish family, are evicted from their home and move in with their accountant, Josef Cizek, and his wife, Marie. In 1941 the family is sent to the Theresienstadt concentration camp. The film then fast-forwards two years. Having escaped from the camp, young David Wiener, the family's sole survivor, returns to his hometown. One of the Cizeks' neighbors, Franta Simácek, sees David and calls out to have him arrested, lest the Germans kill everyone on the block. David hurries to hide in his old home. As a Nazi family is about to move in, the Cizeks take him in again. At first, Josef and Marie also fear the consequences and offer David only a night's refuge, but as circumstances change they agree to hide David in their pantry.

A regular visitor to the home is Horst Prohazha, who had worked for the Wieners as a driver. Horst now collaborates with the Nazis. He has access to food and other benefits that he shares with Josef and Marie, in part because he is enamored of Marie. Josef and Marie constantly fear that Horst will discover that they are harboring David. As a result, Josef exaggerates his anti-Semitic sentiments, assists the Nazi professor now residing in the Wieners' former home, and helps Horst in his duties. When Horst tries to molest Marie, she rebuffs him by declaring she is pregnant. Due to Josef's infertility, though, the couple has been unable to conceive, and if she does not become pregnant their situation will turn dire. They ask David to impregnate Marie.

The film moves intensively through the final days of the occupation as the Nazis and their Czech collaborators search each home, but Horst protects the Cizeks. The occupation ends, and a montage shows how the tables have turned: the Nazi professor is spit upon by a neighbor's child; female collaborators have their heads shaved; people are beaten and executed; and the Czech army-in-exile, the Russians, and the resistance are now in control. When Marie goes into labor and Josef seeks the assistance of his doctor, Josef comes under suspicion since the doctor from whom he is requesting assistance had collaborated in the Nazi sterilization program. Josef is brought to the local headquarters of the Russian Army. Simácek, his neighbor and an apparent resistance member, also is there. Josef pleads his bona fides by telling them that he has been harboring David. Finally, the Soviet commander allows Josef to look into the cells where collaborators are locked up. Seeing Horst there and knowing that he is facing death, but also knowing that Horst had assisted his own wife's births, Josef claims Horst is the doctor for whom he has been searching. At the house, Horst delivers Marie's baby. David vouches for Horst by asserting that Horst knew all the time that the Cizeks were hiding him. Simácek concurs. The cast of characters comes together joyfully at the birth scene.

Divided We Fall visually presents the ambiguities of assigning blame for actions during the Holocaust.[15] The film chooses not to focus on obvious villains—the Nazis who are deporting and exterminating Jews. Instead, *Divided We Fall* focuses on the townspeople of a small community and shows how they acted during and immediately after the occupation of Czechoslovakia.

The clearest delineation of positional portrayal is that of David. He is a victim; the film opens with his family's eviction and moves midway to David's poignant recitation of his family's horrible deaths. But the film ends with David engaging in an unexpected act of rescue. By vouching for Horst, David literally saves his life. David might be driven by a range of motivations—a genuine belief that Horst knew all along that the Cizeks were hiding him, a specific recognition of Horst's role in delivering his own son, or a broader humanistic or religious purpose. David also rescues the Cizeks in profound ways. He agrees to impregnate Marie to preserve the falsehood she has told Horst and does not betray that he is the father during the actual birth of the baby. The film shows that David's humanity survives despite the incredible inhumanity he has suffered.

Josef and Marie initially are not positioned as rescuers. On the first night David stays with them, they might best be characterized as helpers—persons who will engage in a singular act of compassion but little more. Marie overcomes her initial reticence as she gets to know David and recognizes his humanity and individual personhood. In order to create a plausible façade to shelter David, Josef engages in various acts of collaboration, including helping Horst in his duties of confiscating Jews' possessions and assisting the Nazi professor whose outrageous ideas fuel anti-Semitic Nazi ideology. One question the film poses is whether Josef's acts are justified because they facilitated a rescue.

The character of Franta Simácek presents a different dimension to the position of the bystander. The first time Simácek appears, he denounces David and declaims that the "whole street will be killed" if he is sheltered there. At the film's end, though, the audience finds out that Simácek was a partisan. Should he be seen, then, as having taken the steps necessary to preserve the larger anti-Nazi project of resistance even if David's life would have been sacrificed? Or was he simply afraid for himself and his neighbors—emotions that deserve some consideration?

The film's treatment of Horst is perhaps the most complex. Initially, one might read the film as tending toward the easy conclusion that Horst was a collaborator. He not only gains materially from the occupation but takes advantage of fascism to advance himself from his pre-occupation position as a driver. At several points, however, the audience must rethink whether Horst knew of David's presence in the Cizek house and provided cover for the three of them all along. Late in the occupation, Horst risks his own safety by preventing the Nazis from entering the Cizeks' home. Ultimately, he saves the day by delivering Marie's baby. The film queries, then, how to reckon with and determine the blameworthiness of a character who does bad as well as noble things and, by turns, is malevolent, decent, pathetic, and simply flawed.

Finally, the film's portrayal of the new Soviet occupation is disturbing. The film shows executions without trial and the humiliating and degrading treatment of Nazi collaborators. The audience develops deep sympathy for the people of this community and the suffering they have experienced. But when a child is encouraged by her mother to spit on the Nazi professor, the film questions whether acts of contempt like this merely perpetuate cycles of violence. This child's actions are counterposed to the film's ending. Marie's baby breathes new life into the community, and a new community is created of a Jew who rescues the collaborator (and is the baby's father), the two "righteous gentiles" who saved him, the collaborator who delivers the baby, the bystander who really was a partisan, and the Soviet Army officer with the broad smile. In the final scene, Josef takes the baby for a walk in his buggy and sees those who have died—the Wiener family, the young son of the Nazi professor, a beloved dog—and proudly shows them his new infant son. The film proffers the question of whether forgiveness must trump vengeance to truly reconstitute a community. After all, the film has signaled from its inception that "divided we fall."

ADDRESSING THE PAST: TRANSITIONAL JUSTICE

JUSTICE: *JUDGMENT AT NUREMBERG*

Judgment at Nuremberg is set in 1948 in Nuremberg, Germany,[16] and focuses on the criminal prosecutions of judges who enforced Nazi laws.[17] Judge Dan Haywood from Maine and two US colleagues are assigned to preside. Four defendants are on trial, but the film focuses particularly on Ernst Janning, a well-known professor and prolific author who served as a judge in the Nazi legal system, while claiming that he opposed the regime. The US prosecutor, Colonel Lawson, who helped to liberate the camps and is determined to vindicate those who suffered there, presents two key witnesses. One is a young Aryan woman who allegedly had sex with an older Jewish man; as a result, Janning condemned the man to death for violation of the Nazi Racial Pollution laws. Despite eyewitness evidence to the contrary from a Nazi sympathizer, she still denies the allegation. The defendants' lawyer ruthlessly cross-examines her. Janning, who has refused to recognize the legitimacy of the Nuremberg court and has remained silent throughout, intervenes and declares that he had decided at the time to condemn the Jewish man no matter the evidence against him. Another witness in the judges' trial is a man who was subjected to the Nazi forced sterilization laws. On cross-examination, the defense lawyer again treats the witness harshly. He asks the witness to pass the intelligence test for feeblemindedness. When the witness fails the test in court, the defense lawyer claims that his mental condition was the reason for his sterilization, not an invidious political motive, as the prosecution suggests.

In closing, the defense counsel argues that the defendants cannot be convicted as war criminals when they were simply doing their jobs: to enforce laws they had no hand in crafting. Further, he argues that Janning used his position to protect others and only accepted the position in order to stave off further, more horrendous damage by the Nazis. Finally, the defense counsel argues, if these defendants are guilty, so must be thousands of others.

As the judges contemplate their decision, they are subjected to increased political pressure. The Cold War is heating up, and Germany is needed as a postwar partner; the cases are no longer of interest and could be detrimental to the new alliance. Nonetheless, Haywood and one of his colleagues issue decisions condemning the defendants to life sentences. Haywood accepts Janning's invitation to visit him in his cell, and Janning once again protests that he had no idea where the Nazi enterprise ultimately was headed. Haywood responds, "You knew the first time you sentenced an innocent man to death." But as the defense lawyer predicted and the postscript indicates, the condemned are released within a few years.

Judgment at Nuremberg remains, more than fifty years after its release, a high-quality portrayal of the post-Holocaust tribunals as well as a provocative inquiry into the nature of criminal responsibility. By focusing on the cases of lawyers and judges, the film interestingly eschews the easy path to assessing responsibility for the Holocaust, which would have been presented more sharply in a film about the major Nuremberg International Criminal Tribunal or the cases against concentration camp officials.[18] Instead, the film chooses a more ambiguous subject matter through which to engage the question of criminal liability, as well as broader questions of individual and collective responsibility.

Focusing on judges and prosecutors raises the issue of whether individuals should be held responsible for laws they did not draft or pass but merely enforced. Thus, the film cuts to the core of individual accountability in two ways. First, the film emphasizes how various actors contributed to carrying out the crimes of the Nazis and, in this case, to providing them the veneer of legality. Second, by enforcing the law, the defendants denied the humanity of those who stood before them in the dock as surely as the Nazis denied the humanity of the victims exterminated in the camps.

This equation is made visual by the inclusion of newsreel footage of the death camps aired in the courtroom. Over the defense counsel's objections of relevancy—these defendants claim to have known nothing of the atrocities and played no role in them—the film-within-a-film's screening is a particularly harrowing moment for everyone in the courtroom and for the theater audience. Actual footage was used as evidence in the courtroom of the major war crimes trial in Nuremberg,[19] but for most filmgoers, this footage was the first from the camps that they may have seen. The film-within-the-film shows that the Nazis operated in the camps with impunity; *Judgment at Nuremberg* itself counterposes this complete lack of law with the reality that Jews and other victims were subjected, by the defendants, to the strictures of trials and their resulting swift condemnations.

A key issue when addressing the legacy of Nazism, as well as more generally in all societies overcoming mass atrocities, is the question of collective versus individual responsibility, a point that the film interrogates deeply. The defendants' lawyer constantly returns to this theme; the actions of these judges cannot be the basis for legal culpability when they should not be singled out from the rest of the German people and their collective responsibility for the Nazis' crimes. Through the actions of Judge Haywood, the audience also queries how the Holocaust could have happened, what role ordinary Germans played, how they could not have known what was going on, and why they did not stop it. These moral quandaries are represented most starkly in Haywood's relationship with Madame Bertholt, the aristocratic widow of a German officer executed for war crimes but who claims that she and her husband reviled the Nazis. After the documentary footage is shown, Madame Bertholt protests that no one knew women and children were being killed. Haywood retorts, "As far as I can make out, no one knew anything."

Ultimately the film warrants the conclusion that a courtroom can be a site for addressing mass violence. The guilty verdicts demonstrate a measure of legal justice, especially in the face of increased political pressure to forgive and forget. The verdict is also an affirmation of the value of each human life in the face of the Nazis' catastrophic mass assault on human dignity. The trial's use of witnesses and the screening of the documentary footage allow for a more complete truth and accurate historical record of the crimes of the Nazis and their legal henchmen. As a cultural product, the film continues to illuminate the necessity of holding individuals accountable for their own actions when they sustain and enhance large-scale repression.

TRUTH: *LONG NIGHT'S JOURNEY INTO DAY*

Long Night's Journey into Day tells the story of South Africa's Truth and Reconciliation Commission (TRC) by focusing on four cases in which amnesty is sought for the crime of murder.[20] The first involves the killing of US exchange student Amy Biehl. Slain in a black township as protests and violence escalated near the end of the apartheid era, she was pulled from her vehicle and beaten and stabbed to death. The three men responsible have served three years in jail and, according to the film, are among the first to seek amnesty. Biehl's parents support their application—to honor their daughter who embraced change in South Africa. They also meet with the mother and other family members of one of the perpetrators.

The second story is that of the Craddock Four, several of whom were activists within their Port Elizabeth neighborhood. Security forces abducted and murdered them, and the people responsible seek amnesty from the TRC. One of these men, Eric Taylor, explains how he was affected by viewing the film *Mississippi Burning* (which he describes as about apartheid)[21] and reading Nelson Mandela's autobiography.[22] He realizes that the police should have been protecting people, not assassinating them. The amnesty application turns on whether the police knew whether one of the victims was an activist; if not, then no political motive for killing him exists, and amnesty cannot be granted within the requirements of the TRC.

The third story is that of African National Congress (ANC) fighter Robert McBride. He served a prison term for carrying out the car bombing of the Why Not bar, frequented by military and police, and was released when Mandela came to power. Three people were killed and many injured. The sisters of one of the victims are angry that McBride may get amnesty for a "common crime." McBride apologizes for the deaths but locates them within his own quest for freedom and to "unshackle" himself from apartheid.

The final story is that of the Guguletu Seven. The official version of this crime is that seven terrorists engaged in an early-morning gun battle with the police and were killed, a version displayed in court in documentary footage. Of the twenty-five people implicated in carrying out the crime, two apply for amnesty, each telling different versions of the same events. The film focuses on Thapelo Mbelo, a black government infiltrator, trained as part of the notorious Vlakplaas, the secret government hit squad. Mbelo says that the victims were deliberately targeted and lured into a trap, and they were not armed. One person was surrendering with arms raised; Mbelo later killed him. Mbelo wants to meet with the families of the victims. He admits that he has "done evil" and asks for their forgiveness; ultimately one of the mothers offers her forgiveness, and Mbelo is seen shaking hands and hugging the woman. The final postscript notes that Biehl's killers received amnesty and that the other cases are pending.

Long Night's Journey into Day is about truth-seeking as a means of coming to terms with the past. But truth has a more specific meaning in the TRC context. An applicant for amnesty cannot receive its benefits without disclosing the "complete" truths and the political motives behind them.[23] In this framework, when five men come forward to seek amnesty for the killing of the Craddock Four, the question of eligibility for amnesty turns on whether they have been honest in their public confessions. Were they aware that the file of one of the victims indicated that his political activities were unknown? If so, then their motive was perforce apolitical, and they cannot benefit from amnesty.[24] Even though it is a nonjudicial inquiry, the film shows the reliance on the adversarial interrogation of the perpetrators to uncover this truth.

Truth also can be elusive, ambiguous, and subjective. Robert McBride's story captures this in a unique way. McBride expresses strength in his conviction that acts of violence, committed by the ANC's armed wing, were appropriate and justifiable responses to the violence and oppression of apartheid. Yet the young women who lost their lives in the bar bombing had no desire or intention to further that cause; as one of the victims' sisters states, "We can't be held accountable for apartheid. We were opposed to it." However, Mary Burton, a TRC commissioner, points out that part of developing a fuller truth is to identify how white South Africans, even if not supportive of the regime, benefited from apartheid and the price that others paid to secure the luxuries and safety of whites. This segment of the film asks whether the victims of the bombing were innocents or if they were somehow complicit.

The commentary by commissioners and journalists also frames the TRC truth-seeking process within a larger national narrative of reconciliation.[25] Archbishop Desmond Tutu, the chair of the commission, emphasizes that the TRC is contributing to the promotion of reconciliation as a "national project."

Tutu notes that justice must not be conceived solely as retributive; restorative justice—here in the form of full, public confessions of wrongdoing and absolution—is for him the underlying normative value of the TRC.[26] Truth-seeking not only is desirable to establish an accurate record of the history of apartheid, its victims, its perpetrators, and the role of the state apparatus but also as a method of healing.

How do apology and forgiveness fit into this project of truth-seeking? While the TRC does not require the amnesty applicant to apologize, the film seems to signal that the "most deserving" applicants are those who apologize and the most "healed" victims are those who can receive the apology and move on with their lives. The film portrays Amy Biehl's parents as moral exemplars because they can forgive, going so far as to visit the home of one of Amy's killers and physically and emotionally embrace his family. Later, when the families of the Guguletu Seven confront the informer Mbelo, the film suggests that the one mother who forgives him is somehow more praiseworthy despite the film's obvious sympathy and understanding for those who cannot.

Documentary film, too, has the pretense of a kind of objectivity that fiction film cannot claim. But the eye of the documentarian also is selective. Here, the four stories from the TRC amnesty process simultaneously tell *all* stories and *no other* stories. Even within each story, the filmmaker chooses to frame and therefore "stage" the viewers' attention. The use of broadcast documentary footage cleverly raises this issue. Government law enforcement officials staged the scene at the site of the killing of the Guguletu Seven, and journalists accepted and reported it as accurate. The replaying of the video purposefully is to force the witness-perpetrators to correct these falsehoods and tell the true story of the film-within-the-film. Simultaneously, it reminds the audience that documentary film has the capacity to perpetuate lies as well record truth.

REPAIR: *CAUTIVA (THE CAPTIVE)*

Set in 1994 Argentina, *Cautiva (The Captive)* opens with a joyful birthday celebration for fifteen-year-old Christina.[27] The next day, she is called from her classroom and taken to meet with a judge, Dr. Barrenechea. The judge tells her that she is old enough to be told the truth: DNA testing shows that she is not the daughter of her parents but of two architects, Augustin Lombardi and Leticia Dominich, who were kidnapped and disappeared in 1978. He introduces her to her maternal grandmother, Elisa Dominich. Christina is horrified by the news and runs back to the parents who have raised her. When the police find her, the judge determines she should live with the grandmother.

Slowly, over the course of the film, Christina begins to thread together everything she can find out about her new reality. She confronts her parents who, ultimately, admit that they could not conceive a child, and an officer friend knew this and brought her to them. She meets her biological mother's sister, who shows her a picture of her mother pregnant with her. She goes to the doctor, and he explains the DNA information to her. She attends the grandmothers' march in the Plaza de Mayo and visits the memorial to the victims of the Dirty War. She and a resourceful school friend, whose parents also were disappeared, try to find out what happened to Christina's parents. The friend determines where Christina's mother was held and locates a woman who worked in the hospital there and knew her mother. Via flashback, the audience sees Leticia, bruised and burned, giving birth to a baby. Before the baby is taken from her, she names her Sofia. With additional information, Christina/Sofia now realizes that her own godfather, Jorge, likely was responsible for abducting her and possibly also for her mother's torture and disappearance. She angrily confronts her parents about the lies they had told her: the date of her birth, that her biological parents had abandoned her, how she came to live with them. Her mother did not know the full truth, but evidently her father did. Christina returns to her grandmother and tells her she wants to live with her mother's sister and her cousins. Christina asks her, "About disappearance, is it forever?" We know, of course, it is.

Cautiva plays out the continuing effects of the Dirty War in Argentina on each generation. Christina/Sofia's grandmother, like many other grandmothers in Argentina and elsewhere, sought to locate the stolen generations of children and grandchildren. The grandchildren, many of whom had been given to military families to be raised, had no idea of their real heritage; in many cases, the children were raised in families with values diametrically opposed to those of their birth families. The return of their fraudulently adopted grandchildren becomes a measure of repair for the grandmothers. The judicial system enforces this mode of reparative justice.[28]

The judge has concluded that, now that Christina/Sofia is fifteen, she should know the truth about her real identity, but she is still treated as a child for purposes of making the choice as to where she will live. The legal reality—that her parents may have been complicit, or worse, in her kidnapping and appropriation—trumps her feelings that, for much of the movie, she would prefer to stay with her adoptive parents and have life go on as it was. Her world has spun out of control at a formative moment in her adolescence. The film interrogates whether her needs should be considered in the legal equation. How should they be balanced against those of her biological relatives? The court makes a straightforward legalistic choice, softened through the kindness and help of a social worker. The ultimate burden thus falls on Christina/Sofia to come to her own reckoning with the truth, a quest that becomes a kind of personal truth commission.

The metaphor of captivity operates on multiple levels in the film. Most directly, her biological parents were captured, held in one of Argentina's many clandestine prisons, tortured, and disappeared. Christina/Sofia then was captured from her mother. But the film also makes clear that Christina/Sofia experiences being taken from the safety of her home and school as a new form of capture. When she is forced to live with her grandmother, a woman she does not know, she experiences capture again. But mostly, her own identity and sense of selfhood have legally and personally been taken from her since birth. More broadly, the metaphor relates to the military junta holding all of Argentina captive during the Dirty War. In the grips of these captors, the Argentine people were deprived of their own identity. The loss of their children and grandchildren is a social as well as personal loss.

Metaphor is also operative on the level of repair, reconstruction, and reconciliation. Elisa's loss of her daughter is profound. Her reunion with her granddaughter cannot fully repair that loss or instantaneously reconstruct her family, but it is one step in that direction. The film cautions, however, that Christina/Sofia must find for herself the need to reconstruct her family, not simply have that imposed on her. As she comes to understand more profoundly what happened to her parents, she opens herself up to whom they were, where they had fit into their own families, and therefore where she might fit in, too. But Christina/Sofia returns again and again to the family that raised her—for nurturing and comfort, but more for explanation and understanding. Through the two families, the dual narrative of the Dirty War is implicated—the disappearance of innocents or the perceived necessity of thwarting a left-wing threat. The film asks, Can these narratives be reconciled? Should a young person like Christina/Sofia bear the burden of that reconciliation? By the end of the film, the audience is acutely aware that the painful personal and societal repair is only just beginning.

REFORM: *THE LIVES OF OTHERS*

The Lives of Others opens in East Berlin in the Orwellian year of November 1984, when the Stasi, the Democratic Republic of Germany (GDR) Security Services, employs one hundred thousand people and uses a network of two hundred thousand informants.[29] Their objective: "To know everything." At a training session for new Stasi agents, Gerd Wiesler, a dedicated and upright Stasi agent, plays the recording of an interrogation as an object lesson in how to break a detainee by persistence, skill, and sleep deprivation. That night Wiesler and an ambitious Stasi colleague, Anton Grubitz, attend a play by East German writer Georg Dreyman. When Dreyman and his lovely paramour, the actress Christa-Marie Sieland, dance seductively for the crowd at a party afterward, the minister of culture Hempf is smitten. A hint of suspicion—or is it a fabricated one?—regarding Georg's political leanings becomes an excuse to engage in surveillance of his home.

Wiesler is assigned to "listen in" and render daily reports on Dreyman's activities. However, as a result, he is exposed to a world of people, literature, music, friendship, love, and ideas previously denied to him in his sterile apartment, in which loneliness is alleviated only by the services of a prostitute who also works for the Stasi. When one of Georg's close friends, the blacklisted director Albert Jereska, kills himself, Georg is determined to write an homage and exposé in his honor. He and his fellow writers conspire to have the essay published in the West while Georg pretends that he is writing a play for the fortieth anniversary of the GDR. Meanwhile, Christa is coerced into a sexual relationship with Minister Hempf, who threatens to prevent her from acting and apparently is supporting her drug habit. After Georg's essay is published in West Germany, the Stasi obtains a copy of the original. Grubitz emphasizes to Wiesler that both of their careers depend on identifying who wrote it. When Christa is interrogated, eventually by Wiesler, she betrays Georg and his circle. Wiesler lets her return home so that she may act surprised when the Stasi find the typewriter in the spot she has identified. Wiesler leaves the interview with Christa quickly; the Stasi agents, with Grubitz in the lead, enter the apartment and go to the spot where the typewriter supposedly is hidden. It is not there. But before that moment, Christa runs into the street and stands in front of a vehicle to kill herself, unable to cope with her act of betrayal; Wiesler watches from his car as Georg runs to her limp body.

Four years later, a demoted Wiesler sits steaming open mail when he hears on the radio the news of the fall of the Berlin Wall. Wiesler and the other Stasi employees walk out. When Georg mounts his play again, he runs into Hempf, who tells him that he had been subject to surveillance under the GDR government. Georg returns home and finds the listening devices in his walls. Georg goes to the Research Site and Memorial, an institution set up for public access to Stasi files. Thousands of files are organized in long rows of steel cabinets.

Georg is handed a large pile of documents and sees that his surveillance even had a name, "Operation Lazlo," and that Minister Hempf had ordered it. He reads Christa's confession, including the exact time she was released from custody, realizing for the first time that she did not have time to return home and move the typewriter before the search; it must have been the Stasi agent who protected him. Cross-referencing the files containing the names of the agents on his case, he identifies Wiesler. After obtaining his address and going to find him, he is unable to approach him. Two years later, Georg's memoir is published. Wiesler sees it in a bookstore window, goes in to buy it, and sees that it is dedicated "in gratitude" to him.

The Lives of Others is a classic portrait of omniscient centralized power and control through close surveillance of the population. The Stasi, both through their own employees and their collaborators, are everywhere.[30] The film does not show beatings, murders, or torture. Instead, the pervasiveness of state control through the penetration of spheres of privacy leads to subordination. The audience knows the full extent of the surveillance on Georg Dreyman (which Georg suspects but cannot fully accept). When Georg's neighbor sees the Stasi planting the bugging devices, her daughter's place in the university is threatened. When a cadet makes a joke about President Hoenecker, Grubnitz treats him sadistically; later in the film, the former cadet appears in the basement mailroom with Wiesler. The important and the mundane are both controlled, thanks to the Stasi.

The film engages the issue of reform of the security sector on a personal and a societal level. First, the film tells the story of Wiesler's personal reformation. Can Wiesler listen in to the lives of people who are moved by literature, art, and music and not himself be moved by these same forces? His life as a Stasi apparatchik is a narrow, constrained, drab, and routinized one. Little by little over time, the audience sees the signs of reform. Georg cannot find his book by Brecht, and Wiesler is seen reading and enjoying Brecht's poetry. Wiesler listens in to the beautiful music that Georg plays; Georg asks, "Can anyone who has *really* heard this be a bad person?" Georg has posed for the audience the ultimate question: Is Wiesler evil or part of an evil system that he must take some action to escape? Is that even possible? The echoes of the Nazi era are surely in the wind here. Wiesler returns to his apartment building one evening, and a young boy in the elevator asks him if he is Stasi. Wiesler asks him to explain what that means, and the boy answers that his father has told him that Stasi are bad people who put people in prison. Wiesler stops himself before asking the boy his father's name, an action that he would not have thought twice about at the beginning of the film. He meets Christa in a bar and sees that she is a decent person struggling in an untenable situation; conversely, the minister is using his position of authority to oppress her. Ultimately, we sense that Wiesler has transformed, but in the context of opposing an oppressive government, will he be able to act on it? He does—he takes the typewriter from Georg's apartment and hides it so that his fellow Stasi agents cannot discover it and use it to justify Georg's arrest. Shaken, Wiesler sits in his car afterward and then watches in horror as Christa runs into the street to kill herself. He knows that he has played a major role in Christa's betrayal and consequent self-loathing. He will be demoted in the short run and purged in the long run—penalties that the film implies he rightfully should pay for his complicity in the state apparatus. But ultimately the movie is forgiving toward Wiesler. Georg's dedication of his book to Wiesler recognizes that all Stasi are not equal, and Wiesler's individual humanity must be acknowledged.

In the scenes after the dissolution of East Germany, the film depicts the inversion of the Stasi system of secrecy through the process of allowing access to the Stasi files.[31] In Timothy Garton Ash's review of the movie, he reports that "unprecedentedly swift, far-reaching, and systematic opening of the more than 110 miles of Stasi files occurred."[32] Georg can go into a state archive and request to read his own Stasi file, and the information will be delivered for his perusal, an essential element of the process of societal reform. The Stasi invaded the privacy of its own citizens; now state law endeavors to protect individual privacy where appropriate but require transparency to the greatest extent possible. Only by knowing exactly what was done in the past, to whom, and by whom can the new German society guarantee the kind of transparency that undergirds democratic institutions. The Stasi has been disbanded, and even the names of Stasi agents may be made available to the public. The reunified Germany, with its own policing mechanisms, has no need for these purveyors of fear, unlike in other transitional situations in which the state police apparatus is much more difficult to disband. These obedient servants of the East German state no longer have the power to wreak havoc on the lives of others.

CONCLUSION

Film has made and will always make an incomparable contribution to the discourses of transitional justice because of its capacity to portray viscerally the essential emotional dimensions of transitional justice processes. One of film's most enduring capabilities is the ability to present visually the conditions in a society during periods of civil conflict, war, mass violence, or authoritarian or dictatorial reigns. Thus, film becomes a mechanism to record that experience for the generations who lived through it as well as for succeeding generations. Even for those who lived through these experiences, they may not be aware of the full scope of the conflict from which their own society is emerging. While film locates itself in a specific time and place, the universality of mechanisms of social and political repression are evident in films like *Missing*, which focuses on the ways in which the military dictatorship in Chile quickly consolidated power through mass state terror, or *The Lives of Others*, which portrays the ubiquity of social and political control exerted by the intelligence services in Communist East Germany.

Survivors of gross human rights abuses and the families of victims find it understandably difficult to share their experiences; thus, films may serve the needs of victims and survivors by acting as a vehicle for portraying the unspeakable so that peers, family members, and others may understand and appreciate the full dimensions of their experiences. The underside of these portrayals of violence and state terror, however, are concerns about the exploitation of suffering and its consequent impact on audiences. For example, *Judgment at Nuremberg* uses graphic and upsetting footage from the Nazi concentration camps as a centerpiece of the criminal trial portrayed in the film, just as the major Nazi war crimes tribunals used documentary footage. In contrast, *Divided We Fall* eschews more than a minimal portrayal or description of Nazi persecution, yet Nazi oppression is pervasive. Critics have raised questions about portrayals of suffering and victimization particularly in an era when film routinely uses violence, torture, and mayhem in entertainment vehicles.[33] Thus, filmmakers engaged in producing works of art about mass violence and its aftermath must grapple with pressing ethical questions about their obligations to ensure that their works do not contribute to the re-exploitation or re-traumatization of victims.[34]

Feature and documentary films focused on individual stories highlight the roles that individuals play in carrying out violence and, thereafter, in assessing each person's culpability. In part due to its portrayal of Czechoslovakia both during the Nazi occupation and afterward as Soviet control became ascendant, *Divided We Fall* reveals the nuances of individual complicity and becomes a cautionary tale on easy and glib judgments about people facing excruciating choices. *Long Night's Journey into Day* displays varied portraits of individual perpetrators and challenges the audience to engage, as the TRC does, with the demands and needs of victims in the context of societal commitments to amnesty, forgiveness, and reconciliation.

The aims of justice, truth, repair, and reform are given personal and social manifestations in film. Some films, enumerated in the filmography appendix to this chapter, specifically depict the mechanisms of transitional justice, similar to the portrayals in *Judgment at Nuremberg* and *Long Night's Journey into Day*, discussed here. Films also serve as a tool of historical memory, setting out visions of how past traumatic events in the life of a nation are remembered and how the process of transition, social reconstruction, and reformation are recorded.[35] However, film selects how it directs the gaze of the audience—an assertion more transparently true with fiction films, yet applicable as well to documentaries. Documentary as a genre has the imprimatur of objective truth-making, therefore appearing to support one of the goals of transitional justice: obtaining the full truth and creating an accurate historical record. Documentary footage routinely is used in international criminal court proceedings as well.[36] A documentary's evidential value, however, must be tempered by the awareness that the film remains a creative cultural product, not unvarnished fact. Whether films are fictional or documentary, they are the product of the filmmakers' biases and artistic and political choices. Their use must include thought and discussion about their understandable but inevitable limitations and selective focus. This does not make them less valuable, but this reality must be considered when engaging with and using film in highlighting aspects of transitional justice.

The films discussed in this chapter and those in the accompanying appendix use individual stories to make accessible the realities of mass violence, armed conflict, and the ideals of transitional justice. They visualize what may be indescribable, bring forth new or hidden stories, and assist in the creation of a historical record. As such, they are invaluable tools. They can educate audiences globally, explore the past and address the ambitions of transitional justice locally, and serve as organizing and engagement tools.[37] With the creation, proliferation, and accessibility of digital technologies, film as a form of witness will continue to expand and shine its light on transitions and their aftermaths.

APPENDIX: SELECTED TRANSITIONAL JUSTICE FILMOGRAPHY

The list that follows is not comprehensive; it is intended as a useful resource for those interested in exploring films of relevance to transitional justice themes.[38] The films were selected with the goals of representing a wide variety of geographical areas and transitional justice issues and including works by local filmmakers wherever possible. The list comprises feature films and feature-length documentaries, is organized by region, and provides a very brief description of the topic of each film.

GENERAL/GLOBAL

Confronting the Truth. Directed by Steve York and Neil J. Kritz, USA, 2007. *Documentary about truth commissions and societies in transition.*

The Memory of Justice. Directed by Marcel Ophüls, UK/USA/France/Germany, 1976. *Documentary about atrocities committed during wartime (Nuremberg trials and Vietnam War).*

Prosecutor. Directed by Barry Stevens, Canada, 2011. *Documentary about former International Criminal Court prosecutor Luis Moreno-Ocampo and the ICC.*

The Reckoning: The Battle for the International Criminal Court. Directed by Pamela Yates, USA, 2009. *Documentary about the International Criminal Court.*

AFRICA

Courting Justice. Directed by Jane Limpan, South Africa, 2011. *Documentary about seven women judges and their role in the transition in South Africa.*

Ezra. Directed by Newton I. Aduaka, France/Nigeria, 2007. *Film about a demobilized child soldier accused of murdering his parents, testifying before the TRC in Sierra Leone.*

Grey Matter. Directed by Kivu Ruhorahoza, Rwanda, 2011. *Film about the aftermath of the genocide in Rwanda.*

The Last Just Man. Directed by Steven Silver, Canada, 2002. *Documentary about Romeo Dallaire, the commander of UN forces during the genocide in Rwanda.*

The Last King of Scotland. Directed by Kevin Macdonald, UK/Germany, 2006. *Film about Idi Amin's dictatorship in Uganda.*

Long Night's Journey into Day. Directed by Frances Reid and Deborah Hoffman, USA, 2000. *Documentary following four cases at the TRC in South Africa.*

My Neighbor My Killer. Directed by Anne Aghion, USA/France, 2009. *Documentary about* gacaca *in Rwanda.*

Pushing the Elephant. Directed by Beth Davenport and Elizabeth Mandel, USA, 2010. *Documentary about a woman who fled the Democratic Republic of Congo (DRC) with nine of her ten children, then returned ten years later to find her lost child and advocate for peace.*

The Redemption of General Butt Naked. Directed by Daniele Anastosion and Eric Strauss, USA/Georgia/Liberia, 2011. *Documentary about a former militia leader in Liberia responsible for war atrocities who is now a Christian preacher seeking to redeem his past.*

The Team. Directed by Patrick Reed, Canada, 2010. *Documentary about the television show* The Team *and reconciliation in Kenya.*

War Don Don. Directed by Rebecca Richman Cohen, USA, 2010. *Documentary about the Special Court for Sierra Leone.*

ASIA AND OCEANIA

Brother Number One. Directed by Annie Goldson, New Zealand, 2011. *Documentary about the Khmer Rouge and the Extraordinary Chambers of the Courts of Cambodia (ECCC), and the abduction and murder of a New Zealand sailor.*

Burma VJ: Reporting from a Closed Country. Directed by Anders Østergard. Denmark/Sweden/Norway/UK/USA/Germany/Netherlands/Spain/Belgium/Canada, 2008. *Documentary about the 2007 protests against the military junta in Burma, using smuggled footage.*

Enemies of the People. Directed by Rob Lemkin and Thet Sambath, UK/Cambodia, 2009. *Documentary about the Khmer Rouge, the ECCC, and the filmmaker's efforts to learn about the deaths of his family members.*

Rabbit-Proof Fence. Directed by Phillip Noyce, Australia, 2002. *Film based on a true story of three girls at a residential school who journey fifteen hundred miles to escape.*

Shadow Play. Directed by Chris Hilton, Australia/USA, 2002. *Documentary about Suharto's regime in Indonesia and its aftermath.*

S21: The Khmer Rouge Death Machine. Directed by Rithy Panh, Cambodia/France, 2003. *Documentary about two survivors of Tuol Sleng prison in Cambodia who return to meet their former captors.*

Total Denial—Doe vs. Unocal. Directed by Milena Kaneva, Bulgaria/Italy, 2006. *Documentary about the lawsuits against Unocal and Total for abuses during the construction of the Burmese pipeline.*

EUROPE

Au Revoir Les Enfants. Directed by Louis Malle, France, 1987. *Film (autobiographical) about a boy at a French boarding school during World War II, where three students are exposed as Jews in hiding.*

Back to Ararat. Directed by Pea Holmquist, Sweden, 1988. *Documentary about the Armenian genocide and the desire among the diaspora to return.*

Belvedere. Directed by Ahmed Imamović, Bosnia and Herzegovina, 2010. *Film about women survivors of Srebrenica living in a refugee camp fifteen years after the conflict.*

Black Book. Directed by Paul Verhoeven, Netherlands, 2006. *Film about the Occupied Netherlands and the Dutch resistance during World War II.*

The Blind Sunflowers. Directed by José Luis Cuerda, Spain, 2008. *Film about the Francoist repression in the aftermath of the Spanish Civil War.*

Bloody Sunday. Directed by Paul Greengrass, UK/Ireland, 2002. *Film about Bloody Sunday in Northern Ireland.*

Calling the Ghosts: A Story about Rape, War and Women. Directed by Mandy Jacobson, USA, 1996. *Documentary about women, sexual violence, and the conflict in Bosnia and Herzegovina.*

Carla's List. Directed by Marcel Schüpach, Switzerland, 2006. *Documentary about the International Criminal Tribunal for the former Yugoslavia (ICTY).*

Conspiracy. Directed by Frank Pierson, UK/USA, 2001. *Film about the Wannsee conference in Germany during World War II, at which the plans for the Final Solution were made.*

Divided We Fall. Directed by Jan Hrebejk, Czech Republic, 2000. *Film about a Czech couple that hides a young Jewish man during World War II and their interactions with a Nazi collaborator.*

Europa, Europa. Directed by Agnieszka Holland, France/Germany, 1990. *Film about a Jewish boy who joins the Hitler Youth, trying to conceal his identity in Nazi Germany.*

Hotel Terminus: The Life and Times of Klaus Barbie. Directed by Marcel Ophüls, USA, 1987. *Documentary about Klaus Barbie, a German SS captain who headed the local Gestapo in Lyon and his eventual deportation from Bolivia to stand trial in France.*

Judgment at Nuremberg. Directed by Stanley Kramer, USA, 1961. *Film about the Judges Trial at the Nuremberg Tribunal after World War II.*

Justice Unseen. Directed by Aldin Arnautovic and Refik Hodzic, Bosnia and Herzegovina, 2004. *Documentary about outreach at the ICTY.*

Katyn. Directed by Andrzej Wajda, Poland, 2007. *Film about the massacre of Polish soldiers and civilians in Katyn during World War II.*

Kawasaki's Rose. Directed by Jan Hrebejk, Czech Republic, 2009. *Film about memory and reconciliation after the Communist era in the Czech Republic.*

The Lives of Others. Directed by Florian Henckel von Donnersmarck, Germany, 2006. *Film about the Stasi surveillance of a playwright in East Germany.*

Milosevic on Trial. Directed by Michael Christoffersen, Denmark, 2007. *Documentary about the trial of Slobodan Milosevic.*

Night and Fog. Directed by Alain Resnais, France, 1955. *Documentary about Auschwitz and Majdanek (Nazi concentration camps during the Holocaust).*

900 Days. Directed by Jessica Gorter, Netherlands, 2011. *Documentary about the Siege of Leningrad during World War II and controversy over its memory in Russia today.*

Omagh. Directed by Pete Travis, Ireland/UK, 2004. *Film about the Omagh bombing in 1998 and victims' efforts to find the truth in Northern Ireland.*

The Pianist. Directed by Roman Polanski, France/Germany/Poland, 2002. *Film about a Jewish pianist who escapes the Warsaw ghetto and survives World War II in hiding, based on the memoir of Władysław Szpilman.*

The Rehearsal. Directed by Jules Dassin, UK/Greece, 1974. *Film about the student uprising at the Athens Polytechnic against the junta in Greece.*

Shoah. Directed by Claude Lanzmann, France, 1985. *Documentary about the Holocaust, with stories of survivors, bystanders, and perpetrators.*

The Sleeping Voice. Directed by Benito Zambrano, Spain, 2011. *Film about Francoist repression in Spain after the war and the role of the church in the kidnapping of babies.*

Sophie's Choice. Directed by Alan Pakula, USA, 1982. *Film about a woman who survived the Holocaust and lives in the United States traumatized by her memories.*
The Sorrow and the Pity. Directed by Marcel Ophüls, Switzerland, 1970. *Documentary about the French resistance during World War II.*
The Trial. Directed by Rob O'Reilly and John Murphy, Ireland, 2009. *Documentary about the trial of Ramush Haradinaj, former prime minister of Kosovo.*
Verdict on Auschwitz. Directed by Rolf Bickel and Dietrich Wagner, Germany, 1993. *Documentary on the trial of twenty-two former SS men in a German court in the 1960s.*
View from the Bridge: Stories from Kosovo. Directed by Laura Bialis and John Ealer, USA, 2007. *Documentary about the aftermath of conflict in Kosovo.*
Z. Directed by Costa-Gavras, France/Algeria, 1969. *Film about the assassination of Grigoris Lambakis and repression by the junta in Greece.*

MIDDLE EAST AND NORTH AFRICA

The Battle of Algiers. Directed by Gillo Pontecorvo, Italy/Algeria, 1965. *Film about the Algerian independence conflict, the use of terrorist tactics, and torture and repression by the French.*
Essaïda. Directed by Mohamed Zran, Tunisia, 1997. *Film about life in an impoverished neighborhood in Tunisia under Ben Ali in the 1990s.*
5 Broken Cameras. Directed by Emad Burnat and Guy Davidi, Occupied Palestinian Territory/Israel/France/Netherlands, 2011. *Documentary filmed by a Palestinian villager about the effects of settlements and the conflict regarding the wall around and through the West Bank.*
Gaza Strip. Directed by James Longley, USA, 2002. *Documentary about life in the Gaza Strip and the intifada.*
Tahrir: Liberation Square. Directed by Stefano Savona, France/Italy, 2011. *Documentary about the protests and revolution in Egypt (filmed in Tahrir Square).*
Voices of Iraq. Directed by People of Iraq [Martin Kunert], USA/Iraq, 2004. *Documentary about Iraq after the US invasion, filmed by Iraqi citizens.*
Words of Witness. Directed by Mai Iskander, Egypt/USA, 2012. *Documentary about a young woman who reports on the revolution in Egypt and the disillusionment that followed it.*

SOUTH AND CENTRAL AMERICA

Alonso's Dream. Directed by Danièle Lacourse and Yvon Patry, Canada, 2000. *Documentary about the Zapatista uprising and paramilitary violence in Mexico.*
The Battle of Chile [Parts 1, 2, and 3]. Directed by Patricio Guzmán, Venezuela/France/Cuba/Chile, 1975, 1977, and 1979. *Documentary trilogy about the coup against Allende in Chile.*
Cautiva. Directed by Gaston Biraben, Argentina, 2003. *Film about a student in Argentina who learns that she was adopted and that her real parents were disappeared.*
Death and the Maiden. Directed by Roman Polanski, USA, 1994. *Film about the aftermath of repression in an unnamed South American country.*

The Disappeared. Directed by Peter Sanders, USA/Argentina, 2007. *Documentary about a man's efforts to discover the truth about his parents, who were disappeared during the Dirty War in Argentina.*
The Fall of Fujimori. Directed by Ellen Perry, USA, 2005. *Documentary about the arrest of Fujimori in Peru.*
Granito. Directed by Pamela Yates, USA, 2011. *Documentary about the trial in Spain for the genocide in Guatemala, which used footage from* When the Mountains Tremble *as evidence.*
Impunity. Directed by Juan José Lozano and Hollman Morris, Colombia/France/Switzerland, 2010. *Documentary about the justice and peace trials to prosecute paramilitary members in Colombia.*
Innocent Voices. Directed by Luis Mandoki, Mexico/USA/Puerto Rico, 2004. *Film about a twelve-year-old boy trying to avoid forced recruitment during the conflict in El Salvador.*
Justice and the Generals. Directed by Gail Pellett, USA, 2002. *Documentary about trials held in Florida (USA) for generals charged with the murder of four US churchwomen during the conflict in El Salvador.*
Lucanamarca. Directed by Carlos Cárdenas and Héctor Gálvez, Peru, 2009. *Documentary about the TRC's arrival in a village in Peru where many people were massacred by the Shining Path.*
The Night of the Pencils. Directed by Héctor Olivera, Argentina, 1986. *Film about the kidnapping of seven students who participated in a protest for lower bus fares during the Dirty War in Argentina and their later disappearance.*
Nostalgia for the Light. Directed by Patricio Guzmán, France/Germany/Chile, 2010. *Documentary about relatives of the disappeared in Chile and the aftermath of the Pinochet regime.*
The Pinochet Case. Directed by Patricio Guzmán, France/Germany/Chile, 2010. *Documentary about efforts to bring Pinochet to trial in London.*
Romero. Directed by John Duigan, USA, 1989. *Film about the assassination of Archbishop Oscar Romero in El Salvador.*
The Siege. Directed by Angus Gibson and Miguel Salazar, Colombia/South Africa, 2011. *Documentary about the siege of the Palace of Justice in Colombia and efforts to obtain truth and justice.*
Silence in Paradise. Directed by Colbert Garcia, Colombia, 2011. *Film about civilians killed by the army but counted as guerrillas* (falsos positivos) *by the government in the conflict in Colombia.*
State of Fear: The Truth about Terrorism. Directed by Pamela Yates, USA/Peru, 2005. *Documentary about repression by Fujimori during the conflict against the Shining Path in Peru.*
State of Siege. Directed by Costa-Gavras, France, 1973. *Film based on a true story of a US official kidnapped and killed by guerrillas in Uruguay.*
The Tiniest Place. Directed by Tatiana Huezo, Mexico, 2011. *Documentary about rebuilding and memories of conflict in a village destroyed during the conflict in El Salvador.*
Tracing Aleida. Directed by Cristiane Burkhard, Mexico, 2007. *Documentary about the children of those disappeared during Mexico's Dirty War.*
When the Mountains Tremble. Directed by Newton Thomas Sigel and Pamela Yates, USA, 1983. *Documentary about the conflict in Guatemala.*
The Year My Parents Went on Vacation. Directed by Cao Hamburger, Brazil, 2006. *Film about a boy in Brazil who is left with his grandparents when his activist parents are forced to flee.*

UNITED STATES AND CANADA

Greensboro: Closer to the Truth. Directed by Adam Zucker, USA, 2007. *Documentary about the Greensboro Massacre and the TRC initiated by civil society in Greensboro, North Carolina (USA).*

Muffins for Granny. Directed by Nadia McLaren, Canada, 2007. *Documentary about residential schools in Canada and the Truth and Reconciliation Commission.*

Taxi to the Dark Side. Directed by Alex Gibney, USA, 2007. *Documentary about torture perpetrated by the United States in Afghanistan, Iraq, and Guantanamo Bay.*

We Were Children. Directed by Timothy Wolochatiuk, Canada, 2012. *Film about the true stories of two survivors of residential schools in Canada, including their actual testimony.*

NOTES

The views expressed in this paper are my own and are not intended to represent those of the International Center for Transitional Justice.

1 Laurel E. Fletcher and Harvey W. Weinstein, "Violence and Social Repair: Rethinking the Contribution of Justice to Reconciliation," *Human Rights Quarterly* 24, no. 3 (2002): 573–639.

2 Film can play a controversial role in the contest over how the past is understood and interpreted. See, e.g., Pacale Bonnefoy, "Hundreds Protest Screening of Pro-Pinochet Film in Chile," *New York Times*, June 10, 2012, http://www.nytimes.com/2012/06/11/world/americas/chileans-protest-pro-pinochet-film-screening.html.

3 Martha Minow, *Between Vengeance and Forgiveness: Facing History after Genocide and Mass Violence* (Boston: Beacon Press, 1998), 9–24.

4 See, generally, David H. Jones, *Moral Responsibility in the Holocaust: A Study in the Ethics of Character* (Lanham, MD: Rowman and Littlefield, 1999).

5 Fletcher and Weinstein, "Violence and Social Repair," 603–17.

6 "What Is Transitional Justice?" International Center for Transitional Justice, accessed June 8, 2012, http://ictj.org/about/transitional-justice.

7 A select filmography is appended at the end of the chapter. The films discussed in the chapter as well as those in the filmography do not fit neatly into the chapter's subsections; in the main, the films contain multiple relevant themes.

8 *Missing*, directed by Costa-Gavras (Universal City, CA: PolyGram Filmed Entertainment, 1982).

9 The film is based on Thomas Hauser, *The Execution of Charles Horman* (New York: Harcourt Brace Jovanovich, 1978).

10 The film changes Charles's spouse's name to Beth; her real name is Joyce. I refer to her as Beth here.

11 Nora Sveaass, "The Organized Destruction of Meaning," in *Pain and Survival: Human Rights Violations and Mental Health*, ed. N. Lavik, M. Nygåard, N. Sveaass, and E. Fannemel (Oslo and Cambridge, MA: Scandinavian University Press, 1994), 45.

12 Sveaass refers to this as the strategy of "No Smoke without Fire"; that is, "If something happens to you, you must be guilty of something" (ibid., 47).

13 Peter Kornbluh, *The Pinochet File: A Declassified Dossier on Atrocity and Accountability* (New York: New Press, 2003). In 2011 a Chilean judge indicted US Navy captain Ray Davis, depicted in the film and head of the US military group in Chile at the time of the coup, in connection with Charles Horman's death ("Chile Seeks Ray Davis Extradition over 1973 Coup Murder," *The World*, November 30, 2011, http://www.theworld.org/2011/11/chile-military-murder-missing/).

14 *Divided We Fall*, directed by Jan Hřebejk (2000 [in Czech]; Culver City, CA: Sony Picture Classics, 2001 [in English]).

15 The discussion here is indebted to the work of Jones, *Moral Responsibility in the Holocaust*, and Raul Hilberg, *Perpetrators, Victims, and Bystanders: The Jewish Catastrophe, 1933–1945* (New York: HarperCollins, 1992).

16 *Judgment at Nuremberg*, directed by Stanley Kramer (Los Angeles: United Artists, 1961). See also my previous discussion of the film in Carolyn Patty Blum, "Film, Culture, and Accountability for Human Rights Abuses," *Law and Popular Culture*, vol. 7, ed. Michael Freedman (Oxford: Oxford University Press, 2005), 504–59.

17 The trials were held according to Control Council Law No. 10, Punishment of Persons Guilty of War Crimes, Crimes Against Peace and Against Humanity, December 20, 1945, 3 Official Gazette of the Control Council for Germany, 50–55 (1946). For discussion of the *Justice* case, the trial on which the film is based, see Matthew Lippman, "The Other Nuremberg: American Prosecutions of Nazi War Criminals in Occupied Germany," *Indiana International and Comparative Law Review* 3, no. 1 (1992–93): 62–75.

18 The idea for the focus of the film was suggested to its writer, Abby Mann, by the Nuremberg prosecutor, Telford Taylor (Thomas Doherty, "Judgment at Nuremberg," *Cineaste*, Spring 2005, 57).

19 The seminal article on the subject is Lawrence Douglas, "Film as Witness: Screening 'Nazi Concentration Camps' before the Nuremberg Tribunal," *Yale Law Journal* 105, no. 2 (November 1995): 449–81.

20 *Long Night's Journey into Day*, directed by Deborah Hoffmann and Frances Reid (Berkeley, CA: Iris Films, 2000). Two feature films treat the same subject: *Red Dust*, directed by Tom Hooper (London: BBC Films, 2004), and *In My Country*, directed by John Boorman (New York: Sony Picture Classics, 2004).

21 *Mississippi Burning*, directed by Alan Parker (Los Angeles: Orion Pictures, 1988). The film concerns the FBI investigation of the murder of three civil rights workers.

22 Nelson Mandela, *The Long Walk to Freedom: The Autobiography of Nelson Mandela* (New York: Back Bay Books, 1995).

23 For fuller discussions of the TRC process, see Alex Boraine, *A Country Unmasked: Inside South Africa's Truth and Reconciliation Commission* (Oxford: Oxford University Press, 2000) and Richard A. Wilson, *The Politics of Truth and Reconciliation in South Africa* (Cambridge: Cambridge University Press, 2001).

24 After the film was completed, the TRC denied amnesty to the applicants responsible for the Craddock Four killings. "No Amnesty for the Killers of the Craddock Four," *IOL News*, December 14, 1999, www.iol.co.za/news/south-africa/no-amnesty-for-killers-of-cradock-four-1.23218#.UAtFlqCB_Ak.

25 See also *Invictus*, directed by Clint Eastwood (Los Angeles: Warner Bros. Pictures, 2009).

26 See, generally, Desmond Tutu, *No Future without Forgiveness* (New York: Doubleday/Random House, 1999).

27 *Cautiva*, directed by Gaston Biraben (2004; Port Washington, NY: KOCH Lorber Films, 2007). The filmmaker was inspired by Rita Arditti, *Searching for Life: The Grandmothers of the Plaza de Mayo and the Disappeared Children of Argentina* (Berkeley and Los Angeles: University of California Press, 1999).

28 See, generally, Laura Oren, "Righting Child Custody Wrongs: The Children of the 'Disappeared' in Argentina," *Harvard Human Rights Journal* 14 (2001): 123–95.

29 *The Lives of Others*, directed by Florian Henckel von Donnersmarck (New York: Sony Picture Classics, 2006).

30 Sveaass, "Organized Destruction of Meaning," 46: "The omnipotent power is strong because people know it is present, although not always identifiable."

31 For further discussion of the law on the disclosure of Stasi records, see John Miller, "Settling Accounts with a Secret Police: The German Law on the Stasi Records," *Europe-Asia Studies* 50, no. 2 (March 1998): 305–30.

32 Timothy Garton Ash, "The Stasi on Our Minds," *New York Review of Books*, May 31, 2007.

33 See Susan Sontag's seminal work on photography's representation of suffering, *Regarding the Pain of Others* (New York: Farrar, Straus, and Giroux, 2003).

34 See Carolyn Blum and Alicia Blum-Ross, "Film," in *The Encyclopedia of Human Rights*, ed. David Forsythe, 5 vols. (New York: Oxford University Press, 2009), 2:214–24, esp. 220–21.

35 Film may allow the viewing audience to witness successor generations as they watch films about a past that historically has been suppressed or inadequately visually portrayed. Two excellent examples are Patricio Guzman's documentary *Obstinate Memory* (Brooklyn, NY: Icarus Films, 1998), in which he shows the reactions of young Chileans to screenings of his masterful three-part documentary *The Battle of Chile* (1976; Brooklyn, NY: Icarus Films, 1998). Pamela Yates engages in a similar process in the documentary *Granito: How to Nail a Dictator* (Brooklyn, NY: Skylight Pictures, 2011), in which she

records the reactions of young Guatemalans to her first film about Guatemala, *When the Mountains Tremble* (Brooklyn, NY: Skylight Pictures, 1983). See the filmography appendix to this chapter for information on these films.

36 See, e.g., Human Rights Watch, *Weighing the Evidence: Lessons from the Slobodan Milosevic Trial* (New York: Human Rights Watch, 2006), http://www.hrw.org/en/reports/2006/12/13/weighing-evidence-0.

37 Some organizations explicitly create films as a means to raise awareness. One excellent example is Just Visions, which has produced films about Israeli-Palestinian efforts for nonviolent resolution of the conflict and has developed extensive resource and curriculum guides for each of its films. See www.justvisions.org.

38 The select filmography is a rearranged, updated, and substantially expanded version of one found in Carolyn Patty Blum and Alicia Blum-Ross, "Film," in Forsythe, *Encyclopedia of Human Rights*, 2:222–24.

CHAPTER 14

Memoryworks/Memory Works

Louis Bickford

In July 1995 almost eight thousand men and boys were taken into the hills surrounding a large field in Bosnia and Herzegovina. They were killed by units of the army of the Republika Srpska under the command of General Ratko Mladić, a war criminal who remained at large until May 2011, in what came to be known as the Srebrenica-Potočari massacre—an episode of genocide. Today, the Srebrenica-Potočari Memorial Center and Cemetery, with its hundreds of somber graves, stands on the site of the field below the hills (see Figure 14.1). An interpretive center includes an explanation of the massacre and haunting photographs of the disinterment of mass graves. A Genocide Study Center and Museum is planned for the site, to be housed in an abandoned factory across the road. Every year on the anniversary of the massacre, political figures and families of victims converge on the site to remember the terrible event and proclaim that nothing like it should ever happen again.

On a different continent, in Morocco, a truth commission finished its work in 2006 with a set of recommendations, including some that focused on eleven former detention centers, many of which were used for the brutal torture of putative opponents of the regime during the Years of Lead in the 1970s and 1980s under King Hassan II (see Figure 14.2). The commission recommended that these centers be developed as sites of historical memory, suggesting that it was important for Moroccan society to remember what had happened there.[1] In Liberia, West Africa, at the end of a cul de sac, down a dusty laterite-red dirt road on the outskirts of Monrovia, resides a mass grave in which untold dozens of unidentified corpses lie. This is the Duport Road Massacre site, where bodies were dumped and buried after an egregiously violent episode during the so-called Second Liberian Civil War (1999–2003). Nearby, the Cowfields massacre site, the James Sprigg Payne Airport massacre site, and the Lutheran Church massacre site, marked by a white star painted on the asphalt covering the mass grave, contain more human remains.

These mass graves remain unmarked or only partially visible but not unnoticed. At Duport Road, the town council has been vexed by how to deal with

FIGURE 14.1
Srebrenica-Potočari Memorial, 2006. Photograph by Louis Bickford.

FIGURE 14.2
Agdiz Pricipal. Originally a mansion belonging to the Glaoui Dynasty in southern Morocco, this building was used as a clandestine detention center during the Years of Lead in Morocco in the 1970s and 1980s under King Hassan II. Photograph by Louis Bickford.

a mass grave in their midst. Some members of the community prefer for it to remain somewhat invisible, because they fear that any official notice would be either too painful or would provoke more violence. On the other hand, some local officials suggest that it would be better to acknowledge the site for what it is and to teach their children about what happened. A grassroots community group, the Duport Road Community Development and Empowerment Organization, argues that recognizing and marking the site would help Liberia recover from the war. They are debating how to mark the grave in a way that can contribute both to learning about the past and to reconciliation.

MEMORY WORKS

Over the past twenty-five years, dealing with the past has become an important component of the ways in which many societies around the world have sought to build their futures.[2] By the second decade of the twenty-first century, confronting the legacies of past atrocities has become a recognized element of democratic and post-conflict transitions throughout the world. Some strategies, such as those under the heading of *transitional justice*—a term connected to international jurisprudence that is frequently understood as the "legal obligations of states in the aftermath of mass atrocity,"[3] such as the creation of truth commissions, pursuit of criminal accountability for former perpetrators in courts, and establishment of comprehensive reparations programs—have become widely accepted ways of dealing with mass human rights abuse, crimes against humanity, genocide, and war crimes that took place in the recent past.

Countless other strategies for confronting the past are available, including those situated in the realm of society, the arts, and culture.[4] Many of these focus on the idea of remembering the past in the collective consciousness and harnessing the power of social memory to come to grips with past abuse. In contexts as diverse as Argentina, Belgium, Bosnia, Cambodia, Canada, Estonia, Iraq, Morocco, Sierra Leone, South Africa, and the United States, significant and serious initiatives are underway to create public memorials—what I call here *memoryworks*. A new term—*memory museum*—has emerged, with major projects recently opened or currently being built under this name in Argentina,[5] Chile,[6] and Peru.[7] Hundreds of initiatives call themselves *sites of conscience*.[8]

I intend for the title of this chapter to have different but related meanings. On the one hand, throughout the world, there has been an outburst of what might be considered memoryworks similar to the examples above. These are memorials, museums, interpretive sites, sites of conscience, and monuments created to commemorate and learn from mass atrocity and human rights abuse. Previous sites of atrocity and genocide, former torture centers, mass grave sites, and other similar locations are being turned into public memorials in ways that draw innovatively on the memorialization of the Holocaust.[9] Memorials related to the Nazi atrocities were initially the most significant historical and global referent for these efforts. Beginning in the 1980s, a subsequent wave of remembering took place not only in Germany but also in developing countries such as Argentina and Chile. I call these *public memorials* and define them as "physical representations or commemorative activities that concern events in the past and are located in public spaces. They are designed to evoke a specific reaction or set of reactions, including public acknowledgment of the event or people represented; personal reflection or mourning; pride, anger, or sadness about something that has happened; or learning or curiosity about periods in the past." They "seek to engage and learn from the memory of past events and periods of societal trauma" in order to contribute to "guarantees of nonrepetition" of these kinds of crimes.[10] In this chapter I explore this new generation of public memorials and define this genre as an emerging and important type of initiative, similar and deeply related to mechanisms such as truth commissions and criminal trials of perpetrators.

Each of the initiatives I examine here is unique and emerges from a specific national context; indeed, various efforts in Cambodia, Chile, or South Africa, for example, demonstrate strong linkages to the histories and cultures of those places. But if their uniqueness and wide diversity are interesting, their similarities are equally so. These initiatives have taught and learned from each other. They have also emulated one another in content and form while retaining their national and cultural distinctiveness. Often they consciously draw on internationally known examples, such as the Vietnam Veterans Memorial in Washington, DC; the Robben Island Museum in South Africa; the Memorial to the Murdered Jews of Europe in Berlin; the Tuol Sleng jail in Phnom Penh, Cambodia; and the Memory Park in Buenos Aires, Argentina. Advocates and creators seek to learn from and contribute to debates about architecture, design, and public art. Perhaps the greatest similarity, however, is that those who commission and design these initiatives seem to believe that they accomplish certain specific results. These designers and commissioners make numerous claims, either implicitly or explicitly, about how these sites are understood to help redress or repair the damage of past abuse in the public domain and prevent future violations of human rights.

The second meaning of the phrase is to suggest that remembering mass atrocity and human rights abuse in this way *works*. To explore the role played by public memorials in the transitional justice process, I focus on the question of exactly how memory works. In my investigation I examine the explanatory claims, often implicit, of designers and commissioners of a set of public memorials, specifically those that create a common space of remembrance oriented toward engaging the public in dealing with their society's past. At the heart of my inquiry are two basic notions—redress and prevention. My particular goal is to explore how memoryworks function in terms of prevention. How can and do public memorials prevent mass atrocity and severe human rights abuse from happening in the future?

Methodologically, my focus is the explanatory logics of the protagonists involved in creating public memorials. These logics are not always explicitly presented; sometimes they are embedded deep in the materials that protagonists create. Reconstructing logics requires a close reading of materials that are intended not necessarily to explain but to convince audiences of the importance of these initiatives.[11] My purpose here, then, is to identify, extract, and explore those explanations when they can be found. Toward this end I have identified two basic categories of explanations: the private/reflective and the public/educative.[12] I only briefly examine private/reflective explanations. Although these explanations are indeed important to designers and commissioners of public memorials, I am less equipped to analyze these kinds of claims, which are better suited to psychologists, who have done much interesting work,[13] or perhaps to theologians.[14] Nonetheless, I offer some tentative conclusions on how reflective explanations are logically structured and what it would mean for public memorials to work according to these approaches.

THE ARGUMENT, IN BRIEF

In the realm of the public/educative, the theory of change is that creating a public memorial will lead to learning by citizens, as individuals and as organized groups,[15] and in particular by potential future bystanders—an important although often unarticulated target audience for these initiatives. The word *educative* in this context is meant in an aspirational and deeply optimistic sense—following a stream of thought from Aristotle to John Dewey[16]—suggesting that we can learn from tragedy and that such learning makes us better human beings.

According to this view, memorials teach by employing specific pedagogic strategies: generating empathy for victims, transferring facts and information, and asking existential questions. Memorials work, in terms of their public/educative side, in a way that is more analogous to universities and museums than to cemeteries, yet memorials derive much of their power to teach from the emotional connection with memory, which is why they do not work exactly the same as universities and museums. The memory of tragedy and the suffering of fellow human beings creates (or, more accurately, has the potential to create) an emotional, creative, empathetic kind of learning that is qualitatively different from the learning that takes place in a classroom or a museum. At the core of this idea is an assumption about the ways in which history can be used to make societies better—that we can and should learn from the past. This view of the relationship between past, present, and future is often contested, perhaps most often by professional historians,[17] but it remains a powerful notion—that by remembering history we can change our future.

Successful teaching of this sort can produce cultural shifts and institutional changes, such as reforms of the military or the creation of civilian oversight mechanisms, that in turn reduce the cultural or institutional likelihood (or both) that these kinds of events will happen in the future.[18] To be exact, these memorials are meant to create cultural or institutional disincentives toward the future behavior of those who would cause mass atrocity—for example, intellectual authors, leaders, and perpetrators—or people who would allow mass atrocity to occur by not intervening to stop it. Such bystanders arguably play a vitally important role in episodes of mass violence. Victoria Barnett, for example, writes that the Holocaust "would have been impossible without the active participation of bystanders to carry it out and the failure of numerous parties to intervene to stop it."[19] That being said, bystanders are obviously not fully responsible for mass atrocity. Since Nuremburg, the international justice movement has argued about the importance of holding individual perpetrators responsible, and international law is clear on the responsibility of states to hold the intellectual and moral authors of crimes against humanity responsible for their actions. However, prosecutions alone are a grossly insufficient response to mass atrocity,[20] not to mention the significant political difficulties and logistical challenges associated with prosecuting those most responsible.

Memorials designed with public/educative ends in mind are meant, therefore, to fill the spaces that prosecutions cannot reach: the questions of societal guilt and complicity as well as the broader issues of responsibility for mass atrocity.[21] Insofar as the broader public and cultural norms also played a role in enabling systematic violations of human rights, their roles must also be addressed. I do not think that protagonists overly exaggerate the importance of memorials. The argument I am making here is actually modest. Indeed, when memorials do work, they work by making a small but significant contribution to prevention by catalyzing a certain kind of social learning aimed at preventing future episodes of mass atrocity.

No one is suggesting that memorials alone can change the world or prevent genocide. Peter Novick, who is skeptical of memoryworks' ability to provide lessons about the past that can then be used for prevention, explains that the justification among US Jews for remembering the Holocaust was often the idea of creating a sensibility that would stop a future holocaust. I agree with Novick that preventing a future holocaust—given the contingencies at play—is an improbable goal. But the materials generated by the movement to create public memorials seem to hold out at least a hope that, in addition to the private/reflective goals of healing among victims, these initiatives will indeed create such a sensibility. I return to Novick's arguments at the end of the chapter.

In short, the people who create many of the memorials examined invest their time, creativity, and other resources building them because they believe that indeed they work, and they do so by affecting the public in this public/educative sense.

RECOGNITION AND EMPATHY

If done in certain ways, memory activists believe, acts of social remembering can recognize victims as fellow citizens in the public sphere[22]—more specifically, as fellow citizens who have been harmed and whose harm ought to be acknowledged. Ideally, this process of recognition humanizes victims, creates empathy for them, and raises the classic question, "Could this have been me?" This walk-a-mile-in-their-shoes approach creates equality between the victims being commemorated and the visitors to the memorial. The visitor is thus asked—albeit fleetingly, briefly, and superficially—to experience the pain of the victim and to empathize with him or her. Thinking about generations of future bystanders to atrocity is a vitally important step. The scholarship on bystanders suggests strongly that the ability to consider the victim as the other, either as physically distant—in another, faraway place—or distant in another way—by appearing different, such as of a different ethnicity—is a key variable in being able to witness atrocity as a bystander and not do anything to stop it.[23]

By creating empathetic experiences, the memorial seeks to force the observer to ask if he or she could become a bystander, a victim, or a perpetrator in a hypothetical future episode of violence. In this sense, these sites could raise potentially interesting questions about how one becomes a perpetrator, although in the sites I have examined, perpetrators tend to be somewhat invisible or at least minimally defined.[24] Still, a second set of questions also might emerge: Of what are we capable? What kind of human beings could do something so atrocious? This recognition, of victims and possibly of perpetrators, can contribute to a social consensus that rejects some kinds of violence and creates an aversion or a disincentive, represented in both institutions and culture, for a repetition of that violence.

A second result of social remembering, according to many supporters of these initiatives, can be to create discussion within society about why atrocities occur, why bystanders often fail to intervene, and what can be done to prevent future recurrence.[25] If channeled in constructive ways, this dialogue can catalyze, strengthen, and support better public policies and enhanced vigilance—both formal (through institutions such as ombudsman offices or civilian oversight mechanisms, or by supporting trials of perpetrators) and informal (through cultural norms that, at elite and popular levels, reject as abhorrent the idea of arbitrary state violence)—to prevent such atrocities from happening again.

THE NEGATIVE EFFECTS OF MEMORY

While the goals of the protagonists who create many of the public memorials examined here are intended to lead to happy results, they are far from guaranteed. Many memorials fail to create these kinds of educative experiences. We all know many memorials that have faded into the landscape and been forgotten: statues and monuments that no one notices. But far more significant than mere invisibility, public remembering can have seriously negative effects. It can cause pain, new forms of trauma, and even conflict. Too much memory, especially if presented as irreconcilable versions of the past, might hurt rather than help a society. The late Charles Tilly, one of the twentieth century's great sociologists, focused on memorials in his final book.[26] On the construction of monuments and memorials, he notes that the great monuments of Europe have hardly been benign. On the contrary, "The vengeance called for by the Hermann Monument [in Germany] helped bring on World War I and lead to the rise of Nazism." With regard to future memorials, Tilly warns that "struggles over collective memory pivot on credit and blame"; he suggests that "we had better be very careful about how we design those monuments and the stories of credit and blame that they invariably tell. We can only hope that, when all is said and done, we can tell stories about those monuments in a way that creates consensus and not separation."[27] Indeed, the stakes are high. Public memorials—such as many in the former Yugoslavia, Lebanon, or Estonia—can serve to prolong or reignite hostilities.[28] In other contexts, such as in Liberia, economic development and post-conflict reconstruction might hinge on resolving the deep divides over how the past is remembered and represented in public spaces.

NEW PARADIGMS OF PUBLIC MEMORIALIZATION

The numeric outburst of public memorials to victims of mass atrocity around the world—often driven by activists associated with human rights and democracy movements, including former victims of human rights abuse and their families—is simultaneously a cause and consequence of an invigorated attention to a particular kind of social remembering. The new trend, beginning tentatively in the 1950s and strengthening with Holocaust memorials in the 1980s—but only gaining global momentum in the early 2000s—represents a paradigm shift in public memorialization, following other major paradigm shifts in how societies represent the past in public spaces. The equestrian, heroic statues of the nineteenth century, for example, and the somber, mournful tombs to the fallen soldiers of World War I are increasingly seen as anachronistic forms of memorialization.

The current trend has a few notable characteristics. First, these public memorials do not celebrate the glories of the past. On the contrary, they commemorate the crimes perpetrated by the state itself, frequently against its own people. They commemorate, in other words, a shameful past, not a glorious one. In this sense, they look inward at national histories to identify and publicly repudiate the harm inflicted upon fellow nationals, and they try to understand horrible acts committed by people who often were entrusted with roles of leadership that were supposed to include the obligation to protect and govern.

Second, public memorials are increasingly being used by nonpowerful groups to wrestle their way into the national memory. That is, if it used to be true that, as the aphorism goes, "History is written by the victors," this assessment seems less true today as less powerful groups assert themselves and demand to be seen and recognized on the memoryscape.[29] The most obvious of these newcomers to memorialization are victims, but there are many others, too. For example, women are challenging the highly gendered nature of the memoryscape—the fact that memorials tend, in many societies, to focus on men, male stories, or male imagery. The stories of women are increasingly told in these public spaces.

Third, these public memorials assume important linkages and continuities between past, present, and future, specifically around the notions of vigilance and prevention. Such memorials link commemoration to prevention: only by remembering a past event can it be prevented from happening again. The refrain of "never again" is based on the assumption that repetition is possible and must be actively forestalled. Designers of pre–World War II memorials in many parts of the world did not have this concern.[30] The twenty-first-century idea that the past is embedded in the present and that the future depends on grappling with that embedded past can be contrasted with a more traditional, early- and mid-twentieth-century, progressive view of history that sees historical stages as building on each other, each ending in turn and replaced by a new one.

That being said, many memorials are created during moments of political transition in which successor regimes are significantly different from prior regimes, and indeed the past is being remembered in a specific way: as the end of an era or a period that can be encompassed as a conceptually distinct if not historically distinct unit of analysis.[31] Nonetheless, these public memorials are as much about preventing future abuse as they are about commemorating the past, which makes them significantly different from some of their predecessors.[32]

A fourth and related characteristic is that these memorials assume that we can learn from the past, that the past is itself a source of deep human knowledge and understanding. George Santayana's overquoted warning—"Those who do not learn from the past are destined to repeat it"[33]—is only a start. In fact, protagonists want more than nonrepetition. They want public memorials that draw on the past to teach lessons for democratic citizenship.

Fifth, the relationship between memorialization and public art has changed. Although some memorials—especially the great nation-building monuments of Western Europe—have frequently been constructed by famous and important artists, many public memorials represented here have drawn on avant-garde notions of the role of art and the artist in challenging authority, such as the authority of official history, and in articulating a vision for a better society. The now fifty-year history of Holocaust memorial art,[34] which itself has become increasingly conceptual and intellectual,[35] has been a major contributor to this shift; for many people, the change is epitomized in the Vietnam War Veterans Memorial in Washington, DC, designed by Maya Lin and now considered one of the world's most important memorials in terms of design.[36] Other experiments—from the Bruce Lee statue in Mostar to Horst Hoheisel's remembrance of "absence" to the marvelous AIDS quilt in the United States to

Gerz's "vanishing monument" in Hamburg—have sought to push the boundaries of art and remembrance in creative ways.

Moreover, many classic forms of memorialization (statuary, obelisks, etc.) seem not only anachronistic in the second decade of the twenty-first century but also naïve.[37] Peter Carrier, who focuses on a similar species of memorial in his exploration of 1990s Holocaust memorials in France and Germany, discusses the "postnational memorial paradigm."[38] This definition encompasses far more than aesthetic and form, but nonetheless the "language of archways, busts, columns, and inscriptions has been rendered obsolete by the apparently unbridgeable gap between the event being commemorated and the existing iconic repertoire....Forms of monumental art have been enriched and diversified by the language of contemporary art, including elements of conceptual art, installations, happenings, and even multimedia."[39]

WHY DO WE BUILD MEMORIALS?

I have just made the argument that a new paradigm of public memorialization is emerging and gaining strength.[40] The global human rights movement—which over the last twenty-five years has demanded, in the words of one of its most significant early protagonists, the Mothers of the Plaza de Mayo (Madres) in Argentina, the interlocking triad of "Truth, Justice, Memory"[41]—has been one of the great catalysts of this new approach to the way we remember atrocity. Before exploring the arguments offered not only by the Madres but by hundreds of other groups and human rights leaders in the last few decades, reviewing some of the classic rationales for memorializing that have emerged since World War II can be helpful. All of these rationales remain relevant today in different ways, at different times, and in different contexts. After reviewing some of these metatheoretical arguments, I move on to focus on the logics employed by the protagonists—creators, designers, and commissioners—of these memorials. As discussed earlier, I have called these the private/reflective approach, which focuses on redress, and the public/educative approach, which focuses on prevention. I then address the latter rationale of memorialization.

NATION BUILDING

One commonly heard explanation for why we build memorials involves nation building. In short, the argument is that the state builds memorials to create a sense of national identity that unifies the people in a single "imagined community."[42] Memorials "work," according to this approach, if they succeed in contributing to the creation of a unified community of nationals who are willing to fight, die, and pay taxes for the sake of the nation. In order to achieve this goal, memorials essentialize a dominant or hegemonic view of the nation that can create loyalty, patriotism, and pride in the (ostensibly shared) past, and then capture these iconic or archetypal forms in figures of public art. This explanation is prevalent among traditional theorists of nationalism such as George Mosse, who sought to explain the creation of World War I and II memorials as conscious, or perhaps subconscious, efforts by nation-states to consolidate a postwar national identity.[43]

A slightly different version of this argument is narrower and more straightforwardly instrumentalist: that the government of the day,[44] especially one that has been victorious in war or is a newly democratized state with high levels of legitimacy stemming from a successful transition, uses memorialization as a tool to rally together its subjects. More recent theorists of democratic transitions, for example, argue that "all new regimes must create their own myths in order to re-found the nation, either through recycling already existing material or through the creation of new commemorations, that is, by organizing new celebration dates and building new monuments through which to express attachment to the new regime."[45]

The idea that memorialization efforts are most likely a component of a larger nation-building strategy when the government is involved is especially relevant when the state is involved in building public memorials. For example, the ceremony at the inauguration of the Freedom Park Trust in South Africa was clearly aimed at creating a sense of a new democratic, postapartheid national identity. As then–deputy president Jacob Zuma put it, "Today's event is but one of the many processes that our government has engaged in since 1994, with a view to creating and fostering a new national consciousness among all South Africans of the common legacy that binds us as a nation."[46]

Similarly, consider the comments of the minister of public lands in Chile, Romy Schmidt, who also oversees the Bureau of Chilean National Monuments. In extensive public remarks about the reclassification of a clandestine mass grave site called Patio 29 into a "historic monument," Schmidt repeatedly emphasizes that "historical memory" requires that "we provide recognition and official protection" to the "public patrimony" that is associated with the "enormous pain of the past."[47] The implication of these statements is to disassociate the present government from the past and to signify that the current government continues to reject authoritarianism.

When civil society organizations drive the process, in contrast, the nation almost vanishes as an object of interest. Such protagonists focus on, for example, the victims and their experiences (such as the Trojan Horse Monument in Cape Town[48] or the Villa Grimaldi Peace Park in Chile[49]), the evil of the regime (such as the Paraguayan Memory Museum project[50]), or the damage caused to the local or municipal community, such as the K'laat Maguna and Agdiz prison memorialization efforts in Morocco.[51] Moreover, protagonists of the new paradigm of public memorialization are likely to be suspicious of state-run memorialization efforts, assuming that they will inevitably follow a nation-building logic.

REMEMBER *US*: MEMORY AND IDENTITY

An explanation for memorialization that is closely related to nation building has to do with identity more narrowly conceived—ethnic, political, gender, or racial identities, for example. That is, groups, subnational and smaller, self-consciously seek to create symbols that emphasize their self-definition and give meaning to shared experiences that tie them together—and, by extension, differentiate them from others. This kind of reasoning also appears in some of these texts, especially when ethnic or other minorities were severely victimized, as was the case for the Halabja Memorial in Kurdistan that highlights the targeting of Kurds under Saddam Hussein. Indeed, the planning of this memorial, carried out by Kurdish authorities, did focus on strengthening Kurdish identity and honoring Kurdish experience.

Plenty of memorials seek to bring into the national public conversation a specific experience of a group that had been oppressed on the grounds of identity. Obviously this is the case with the Memorial to the Murdered Jews of Europe in Berlin and Holocaust memorials more generally. That said, except to the degree that "victims" are a distinct identity, most of the memorials I examine here do not focus on subnational groups. A major memorialization effort in Lebanon, for example—planned for Martyrs Square in downtown Beirut but abandoned because of the 2006 conflict with Israel—was explicitly aimed at the experiences of all Lebanese who suffered during the civil conflict that lasted from 1975 to 1990, seeking to deemphasize ethnic identity in favor of the shared identity of victimization during conflict.[52] Even in the case of Srebrenica in Bosnia, for example, where one might expect to find ethnic identity foregrounded, it is quite conspicuously not. In the establishment of the Foundation of Srebrenica-Potočari Memorial and Cemetery, the justifications for creating the memorial are legal and moral. No mention is made at all of ethnicity or nationality—so conspicuously as to suggest that the omission was quite deliberate.

One fascinating, if complicated, example in Bosnia and Herzegovina is the Bruce Lee Statue in Mostar,[53] a small statue of the martial arts hero and movie star erected in the middle of the central Spanish Square, and since removed, that was intended to transcend identity. The designers of this conceptual art project understood it as a representation of commonality among them—the fact that Bruce Lee is ostensibly a hero whom everyone can agree on—and, as such, a repudiation of ethnic tension and violence. Although not exactly a public memorial, the designers saw this statue as an effort, drawing on satire, to learn from two elements of the past: first, a celebration of a shared childhood when everyone of a certain generation was watching and enjoying Bruce Lee movies, and second, a rejection of the violence of a more recent past when those same people were hating and even killing each other.

In spite of these observations, memorials can be at their most dangerously provocative when they do highlight subnational identities—when, in Tilly's words, they attribute either "credit" or "blame" to one group over another.[54] Interviews of Kosovo Albanians suggest that the monuments to fallen Kosovo Liberation Army (KLA) fighters that dot the landscape of Kosovo were very much about ethnic identity—unabashedly claiming Kosovo as an ethnic (Albanian) territory.[55] One doubts that the Serbian minority in Kosovo feels comfortable with so many public heroic representations of Kosovar Albanians.

PRIVATE/REFLECTIVE ARGUMENTS

If nation building is the most common explanation for state-driven memorialization projects, perhaps the most common explanation for victim-driven projects is the need to have a public space for mourning. This approach would suggest that memorials work when they provide solace, healing, and closure for victims. In fact, all of the public memorials examined here mention what I have called the *private* or *sacred* side of their missions. They exist, in part, to "honor the dead," to "show our respect for the victims," or to "provide family members and friends with a place to mourn."[56]

There are traditions and vernaculars to follow when creating memorials for this purpose—some ancient and some dating back to the early twentieth century—and most of the public memorials described here indeed draw on these formats, such as gravestone images; memorial walls with names inscribed; somber, meditative spaces; peaceful gardens resembling cemeteries; or, especially in recent years, memorial forms that represent absence.[57]

FIGURE 14.3
Un lugar para recordar (A place to remember). Photograph by Louis Bickford.

For example, the Vietnam Veterans Memorial in Washington, DC, remains, in spite of its important design innovations,[58] more similar to the World War I memorials in Britain, France, and Germany—such as the Cenotaph in Whitehall, London, in its emphasis on coming to grips with the enormity of loss—than it does about learning lessons from the Vietnam War, although certainly some observers think of it in this sense. As the designer Maya Lin put it, "I thought about what death is, what a loss is. A sharp pain that lessens with time, but can never quite heal over. A scar. The idea occurred to me there on the site. Take a knife and cut open the earth, and with time the grass would heal it. As if you cut open the rock and polished it."[59] Other memorials have sought to evoke absence through less traditional forms. For example, a memorial inaugurated in Chile in March 2006 marks with three enormous, starkly empty chairs the place where the mutilated bodies of three disappeared schoolteachers were found (see Figure 14.3). The purpose of the memorial is, among others, to provide a place to "remember and heal."

Throughout history, in many if not all societies, human beings have sought to deal with death, loss, and suffering by creating some form of memorial.[60] However, this impulse, as universal as it might be, does not seem to adequately explain many of the memorials examined here, perhaps because most of the events were on some level preventable, or at least conceptually seem different than a random or natural death, or suffering that occurs in disease or a so-called natural disaster, such as a hurricane. Most of the commemorated events have agents—perpetrators, victims, bystanders, institutions—that can, at least theoretically, be influenced or reformed in the future. For this reason, these sites seem designed to do more than aid in mourning and coming to grips with loss. The creators are also wrestling with the ostensible preventability of the events that took place. In this sense, even those memorials that are primarily centered on vernaculars of past-looking mourning—and many if not most of those studied here certainly are—have simultaneously a forward-looking purpose aimed at preventing similar events in the future.

PUBLIC MEMORY AS A BASIS FOR LEARNING

One of the most salient characteristics of the modern era is the notion that we continuously learn from, benefit from, and improve upon the lessons of history. At the same time, however, the experiences of the twentieth century seem to violently contradict this notion. The fact that presumably enlightened global consciousness about the evil of the Holocaust, for example, was insufficient to prevent other analogous tragedies was bitterly demonstrated in Cambodia (1975–79), Bosnia (1992–95), and Rwanda (1994), among other tragedies of what Hobsbawm called the "short century."[61] In spite of this contradiction, I believe that the single most important justification for creating many of these public memorials—at least among those who create them—is "to learn from the past" so as to "never again" repeat it. The basic idea, as I have suggested earlier, is that learning about the past will help create both culture and institutions that will contribute to the broader goal of nonrepetition. The logic of this idea—unmitigated, it seems, by the problem discussed above—is that cumulative, progressive learning over time will allow societies to create better ways to prevent mass atrocity from happening in the future. But how can memorials create public learning that leads to prevention? How do they seek to provide "lessons"[62] about the past?

First, these sites seek to create an experience of learning that transcends the ordinary. This experience is ultimately one meant to create empathy for the victims, seeing and understanding the victims not only as human beings—although that itself is a significant goal—but also as fellow citizens who ought to be seen, recognized, and acknowledged. Marguerite Feitlowitz explains that many of these projects were viewed in Buenos Aires in the 1990s "as part of our ongoing struggle to cement pluralism, democracy, and creativity in public life. And to accomplish this, we must document our painful history and cultivate collective memory."[63]

Second, they seek to convey key pieces of information, usually about brutality and harm, that will be unforgettable and will create a deep sense of disgust, anger, or sadness. For this reason, these sites draw heavily on the power of the site itself: the bloodstained walls, the presence of torture devices, the bars on the windows. The purpose here is to tell history, but a very specific kind of history—a history that focuses on pain—in the hopes that the visitor learns about the pain of victims. The further assumption here is that aggregated learning will ultimately contribute to "never again."

Finally, in varying degrees, these public memorials seek to develop an existential conversation: How did this happen? Why did this happen? How can we stop it from happening again? On the one hand, sites certainly encourage this kind of thinking. On the other hand, however, to a greater or lesser degree, sites control or circumscribe the kinds of answers that are likely to emerge. For example, according to one of the key figures in the creation of the Vietnam Veterans War Memorial, Jan Scruggs, "Future generations will look at the names engraved on the Memorial and ask 'Why did these people die in Vietnam?' The Wall will help answer this question. Because it will remind Americans of our history—and of the sacrifices made by those who served—for as long as our nation exists."[64]

Along all of these axes, it is reasonable to ask whether public memorials succeed in attaining these goals and to examine whether, in turn, these intermediate goals can or do lead to the final goals of prevention and nonrepetition. The inherent difficulties in measuring this form of efficacy should not prevent efforts to do so, although it must be acknowledged that such efforts must be qualitative and modest, since, for example, the success of preventing mass atrocity from occurring in the future is indeed impossible to determine.

I am not claiming that all of these memorials have only these goals in mind. In fact, I have emphasized that many memorials' designers, architects, and patrons have multiple objectives. The goal of redress, although not my focus here, remains vitally important. For example, the creators of the Vietnam Veterans Memorial in Washington, DC; the solemn hillside Halabja Memorial in Iraq; and the eight thousand graves at the Srebrenica-Potočari Memorial and Cemetery in Bosnia all saw these as ways to come to grips with the enormity of death—what I have called the *reflective* goals of public memorialization. Those who created the memorial in the small city of Paine, Chile, had a vision of social solidarity among the family members of victims. They wanted to build on the community of family members to create a project that would demonstrate the individuality of each victim and the love of the family members. More crass elements are sometimes at play as well. The creators of the Choeung Ek memorial in Cambodia, following a classic credit/blame nation-building strategy, originally saw it as a way to create a Cambodian narrative in support of the Vietnamese invasion of 1979 and the subsequent government and to vilify the Khmer Rouge forever in the national consciousness,[65] although teaching about the genocide was also a part of the strategy (as discussed below). Now the memorial has become a major revenue producer as a tourism site.

That said, however, the majority of the public memorials studied here do prioritize learning from the past, side by side with reflection and grieving. Just a few examples:

- As the Hiroshima National Peace Memorial Hall for the Atomic Bomb Victims puts it, "Mourning the lives lost in the atomic bombing, we pledge to convey the truth of this tragedy throughout Japan and the world, pass it on to the future, learn the lessons of history, and build a peaceful world free from nuclear weapons."[66]
- In Chile, Villa Grimaldi's primary objective is "to promote and defend a culture of respect for human rights that allows future generations to know the facts of the recent past so that they will not be repeated in this country or continent."[67] The postapartheid museums in South Africa—Robben Island, District Six, and the Apartheid Museum, among them—were created "as powerful tools for educating the young and old of all of South Africa's ethnic groups, as well as foreigners."[68]
- In Medellín, Colombia, a proposed House of Memory seeks to honor victims of violent conflict in the city from 1985 to 2005 through exhibitions, education programs, and an extensive documentation center comprising written and photographic records of human rights abuses by paramilitary and government forces, drug trafficking, gender-based violence, and peace settlement endeavors. The designers of the House of Memory intend these programs to be participatory, inspiring intergenerational dialogue and an ongoing examination of Medellin's violent history.[69]
- The original designer (in 1980) of the Tuol Sleng Museum of Genocidal Crimes, the Vietnamese "museologist" Mai Lam, said in an interview, "For seven years I studied . . . to build up the Museum . . . for the Cambodian people to help them study the war and the many aspects of war

crimes.... For the regular people who cannot understand, the museum can help them.... As a researcher I want them to go [to the museum]. Even though it makes them cry...The Cambodian people who suffered the war could not understand the war—and the new generation also cannot understand. This will help."[70]

- In Peru, a Museum of Memory is being designed to commemorate the deaths of nearly seventy thousand people lost in the violent conflict between Shining Path guerrillas and the Peruvian government that plagued the country between 1980 and 2000. Two million dollars in German government funding was initially rejected by the Peruvian government but eventually accepted following widespread domestic and international pressure. Mario Vargas Llosa, who is in charge of the museum's design committee, has suggested in interviews that the ultimate goal of memorialization is preventing recurrence.[71]
- In Monrovia, Liberia, in August 2009, St. Peter's Lutheran Church held a memorial service for victims of the July 29, 1990, massacre. Organizers have been working with the Memory Resource Group, a coalition of human rights organizations and others, to turn the site into a formal site of memory. At the memorial service a victims' fund drive was launched. The establishment of a Memorial Shrine was also announced in order to show present and future generations the horrors of war and teach that it should never be resorted to as a means of settling differences.

This emphasis on learning from the past suggests that, in addition to personal mourning, the most important aspect of public memorials is pedagogical: to teach.

TRANSFERRING THE GRIM FACTS

The most common way that public memorials seek to educate about the past is through the transfer of basic—often gruesome—information about victims, usually by using stark imagery or interpretive verbal narratives about the events that took place. As the African Burial Ground administrators put it in the mission statement, the goal is "to provide knowledge"[72] about the facts of what happened.

This approach often fits well with cemetery motifs or grave markers. For example, the Hillside Memorial and the Halabja Memorial Museum use this approach to convey the terror of the Ba'ath Party attack on the Kurds in northern Iraq on March 16, 1988, in which as many as five thousand people died instantly and additional thousands died over time as a result of it. The museum in particular uses exhibits of life-sized dioramas—very similar to those in the central portion of the Hiroshima (Japan) Peace Memorial Museum—that recreate the brutality of the attack. Oradour-Sur-Glane in southern France, by leaving the destroyed village unrepaired, conveys a sense of the devastation of the bombing. Although other parts of the museum demonstrate other methods of teaching and learning, the core of the museum is this basic information: *This village was totally destroyed.*[73]

Another example is the killing fields at Choeung Ek, half an hour from Phnom Penh in Cambodia. At this location, an estimated 20,000 people were killed between 1975 and 1979, the majority of them having passed through the notorious Tuol Sleng prison and detention center first.[74] Choeung Ek is one of the estimated five hundred killing fields found throughout Cambodia. In 1980, one year after the Vietnamese invaded the country, mass graves were discovered at Choeung Ek. A total of 8,985 skeletons have been exhumed at the site. The skeletal remains were treated with chemicals in order to preserve them and exhibit them in an open-wall memorial. There are 86 mass graves of the 129 discovered at Choeung Ek that have remained untouched.[75] In 1988, a new memorial was proposed at the site by the ministerial and municipal authorities. The skeletal remains were relocated to the newly constructed Buddhist shrine (stupa), and narrative explanations of the site were put in place. Since that time, little has changed within the site itself, except the addition of a few new signs near the entrance.

The basic strategy of the designers of Choeung Ek has been to transfer information about the manner in which people were killed at this site, which the design does in three ways. First, the visible skulls and bone fragments that are displayed in the stupa are evidence that genocide took place.[76] On the most basic level, the site is sending a clear message to its visitors: "This happened here." Second, small narrative plaques are placed at various sites within the killing fields; as visitors walk among the disinterred mass graves, stepping among fragments of clothes and even shards of bone and teeth from victims, they come into contact with smaller sites that have significance, such as the tree against which children's heads were bashed. The metanarrative of the site—captured in the signage, such as the explanatory sign in Figure 14.4—is the brutal moments before and during the deaths of victims. Today this narrative is at the core of how visitors experience the site. These plaques focus on the brutality of death, describing in intimate detail the manner in which victims died. The information being transferred is simple and horrible.

FIGURE 14.4
Narrative plaque at Choeung Ek. Photograph by Louis Bickford.

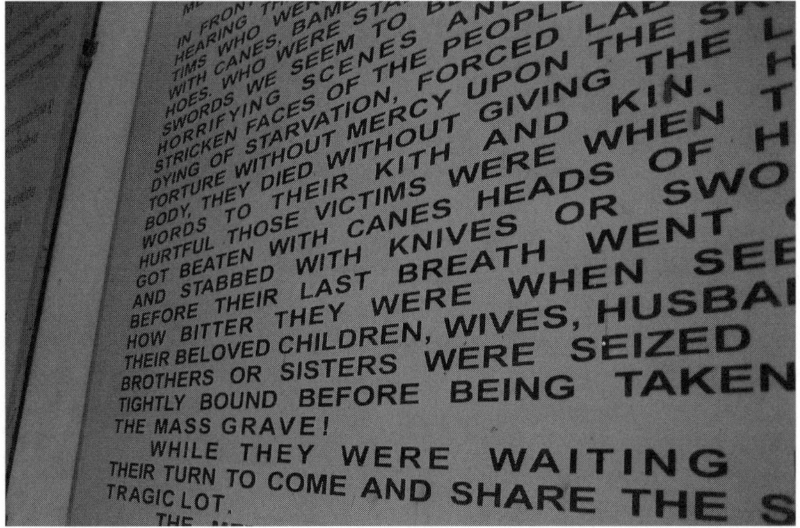

Much, however, is also left out. Representations of victims and perpetrators are thin, with hardly any discussion of either group. Victims are presented as nameless people who suffered tragic death but have no other story. Perpetrators are also represented as nameless individuals who committed gruesome crimes or, at a political level, as simply the "Pol Pot clique." Unlike, for example, the Holocaust Museum in Washington, DC, no effort is made to analyze or explain the logic of the system of genocide or of the Khmer Rouge as a political actor. Third, the site administrators provide guides who are available to take visitors around. Most guides speak English in addition to Khmer, and a few speak either Spanish or French. The guides, most of whom do not have formal training in history nor a direct connection with the site,[77] are required to take a brief course to learn the site's story. The guides' narrative follows the other forms of interpretation at the site, focusing on the brutality of death.

Transfer of information of this kind is the least sophisticated approach to teaching because it assumes a very basic relationship between authoritative source and recipient of information,[78] but such an approach can still work. Indeed, to explore the effectiveness of this site, the International Center for Transitional Justice organized and implemented a site survey in collaboration with the Choeung Ek administrators. The survey interviewed some one hundred visitors to the site in November 2007, most of them international tourists.[79]

The results of the survey were to show that visitors took away from their visit a very clear and particular message: the Cambodian genocide of 1975–79 happened and it was terrible. This message may be sufficient. Indeed, if the goal of such a site is to attract international tourists and teach them this very simple but important lesson, then the site works extremely well. The emotive power of seeing human remains, reading narratives of the brutality inflicted upon victims, and walking amid the bones and clothing fragments from mass graves is impossible to overestimate. The minimalist interpretation and almost nonexistent history-telling may serve the site well, since its audience is primarily international tourists who know nothing about the genocide and for whom Choeung Ek is another must-see destination on the journey recommended in their guidebooks—after the archaeological ruins of Angor Wat and, in Phnom Penh, the National Museum.

On the other hand, examining what is *not* learned at Choeung Ek is also useful. Because interpretation of the events is so thin and the focus is so exclusively on the brutality of death, the site does not teach visitors about the victims (no stories of individual victims are represented), the perpetrators (visitors also learn nothing about perpetrators except their methods of eliminating victims), the Khmer Rouge, the Cold War, the killing system of the regime, or about countless other contextual, historical, or biographical issues that could be raised at such a site. Moreover, not only is the content thin, the means of communicating that content—through the authoritative transfer of basic information—does not allow for alternative interpretations, visitor engagement, or a deeper intellectual questioning of, and concomitant learning from, the site. The narrative exchange is based on a take-it-or-leave-it assumption, with the insistence, because of the power of the site itself, that the only available option is to accept the story as told. In short, learning does indeed occur at Choeung Ek—learning that may help prevent genocide in the future, especially if we assume that the international community can learn from the past. But the learning is primarily limited to a single narrative message that conveys a simple, stark, brutal set of facts as information.

DEVELOPING PEDAGOGY

In addition to the transfer of information about the events that took place, designers of many public memorials pursue richer interpretation strategies or seek to develop experiential learning approaches. In some cases, for example, public memorials invite visitors to have an experience that imitates the traumatic experiences of victims, following a walk-a-mile-in-my-shoes approach to learning that can have a profound effect on the observer/participant.[80] For example, the Villa Grimaldi Peace Park on the outskirts of Santiago, Chile, includes the "water tower," a replica of an enclosed, two-story wooden tower with an internal staircase. On the second floor of the original tower had been a small rectangular room, about eighteen inches wide by twenty-four inches long, and about six feet tall, similar to a closet in shape, and a bit bigger than the size of a standing adult man. The entrance to this peculiar room was a crawl space at the bottom, about two feet off the ground. During the worst days of Villa Grimaldi, a common form of torture was to make two or even three people stand in this room for hours, even days, on end, unable to sit, unable to move comfortably, stuck without much air and with no toilet.

Although the water tower was destroyed along with most of the infrastructure at Villa Grimaldi, organizers have rebuilt it. On a tour of the site, visitors are encouraged to enter the water tower, climb to the second floor, and, two or three at a time, stand inside the small and miserable chamber just for a few moments to experience an inkling of the torture that took place there. The purpose of this exercise is obvious—and effective. In the stifling discomfort of the replica of the torture space, visitors can, in some small way, empathize with the victims' experience. Since tours at Villa Grimaldi are led by former prisoners—survivors—the experience is further enhanced by their presence and their anecdotes about their time incarcerated there.

TEACHING AS PROCESS

The greatest opportunity for learning about the past—for memory work—may be during the process of creating public memorials. James E. Young has highlighted this element of learning in his studies of, for example, the Topography of Terror Exhibit in Berlin. In this case, Young argues, "The best memorial to the fascist era and its victims in Germany today may not be a single memorial at all—but only the never-to-be resolved debate over what kind of memory is to be preserved, how to do it, in whose name, and to what end." It is, in short, this *debate* that is the most effective memorial in terms of learning from the past. Young continues, "Imagine, for example, a series of annual competitions, whereby the proposed designs and Jury's debate are exhibited in lieu of an installed winner.... Instead of a fixed figure for memory, the debate itself—perpetually unresolved amid ever-changing conditions—would be enshrined."[81] If adequately publicized in the media and brought out in classrooms and other venues, this debate could be substantially more productive, in terms of memory, than a fixed granite monument.

The idea that an *unfinished* public memorial would be the most valuable way to learn about the past emerges, in part, from realizing that the classic paradigm of memorials and monuments—in short, the building of statuary and sculptures in stone that are meant to be permanent fixtures on the landscape—might have the paradoxical effect of contributing to *forgetting*, not remembering, since they fade into the background and become invisible to passersby. In place of this stagnant vision of memory, some designers and artists, such as Horst Hoheisel in Germany, have substituted the idea of *active* memory—dynamic, engaged, dialogic, ephemeral, provocative—that aims *not* to solidify in stone an interpretation of memory but rather to use creative forms of public memorials to provoke a conversation about how and why we do or should remember the past.

An emphasis on process may mean more than simply the design phase of creating a memorial. For example, numerous public memorials are increasingly developing slower, more deliberative and consultative, and more participatory approaches to remembering the past. In my view, one of the world's most successful public memorials from this perspective is the AIDS Memorial Quilt.[82] This dynamic and tactile traveling exhibit is the opposite of a stone monument. It is constructed by thousands of family members who each create a single square of the quilt in memory of a single loved one. The quilt itself is then brought out in its entirety on certain occasions. The effect of the quilt as a tool of HIV/AIDS awareness cannot be underestimated. It has been arguably one of the most important consciousness-raising tools used by the AIDS activist movement, and it has helped to create both a backward-looking memory of loved ones and a forward-looking activism aimed at prevention.

In a similar way, the Paine Memorial to the Disappeared in Chile, a year-long project that brought Chilean art students to a small village to collaborate with family members to create table-sized mosaics, placed a similar emphasis on process. The art students encouraged family members to work with the community to design a powerful memorial space. Over a year, they chose an artistic approach and a set of guidelines for creating the memorial space. The resulting memorial in Paine can therefore be seen as both an empowering and meaningful *process*, as well as a profoundly moving *result*: a memory site that teaches and mourns at the same time and that is a significant contributing element in Chile's comprehensive efforts to come to grips with its past.

PUBLIC MEMORIALS AS CIVIC SPACE: DEMOCRATIC DIALOGUE AND CITIZENSHIP

These examples and many more suggest that learning from the past to avoid repetition is one of the primary goals of public memorials. At times, this goal might come into tension with other goals, such as mourning and other private/reflective goals. For example, for many family members these sites are *sacred* spaces where questions of appropriate behavior are important; visitors should come only with a spirit of reverence or sadness, and the family members themselves should have primacy in deciding how to design and use the space. On the other hand, when educative goals are the primary motivation, these sites can be seen as *civic* spaces in which teaching and learning ought to occur. Spatial differentiation within sites usually resolves the tension between civic space and sacred space. That is, part of the site is usually separated out as, for example, something resembling a cemetery; another part of the site may be designated as something more clearly resembling a museum.

In terms of civic space, these sites can indeed serve a powerful educative function, as some of the examples have shown. Bringing the discussion back to transitional justice, the Truth and Reconciliation Commission in Sierra Leone puts it this way in its recommendations: "By serving as a prism through which to examine past and present and to prepare for the future, memorials create a public space for lasting dialogue"[83] and can "[transform] a site of conflict and violence into a useful building or space for the community."[84] The specific ways that this transformation can happen are further elucidated in a report by the New Tactics Project of the Center for Victims of Torture, which explains that public memorials can

- Serve as an open forum. Raising both sides of an issue and encouraging debate stimulates citizen participation more effectively than teaching a single story to a passive audience. But [they] must find ways to do this without becoming moral relativists or appearing to excuse or condone perpetrators.
- Serve as an ongoing forum. Memorials must be active places where issues are constantly debated, where stories are told and retold. The site and program must be flexible enough to accommodate the ways the meaning of the past changes for each generation, to be constantly reinvented. A static narrative or permanent sculpture will foreclose dialogue and become obsolete in short order.[85]

In short, many of these memorials do indeed articulate a vision of themselves as part of a broader civic dialogue about the past, a place where existential questions can emerge and be debated, a place where people will be compelled to face the hardest questions a nation can address about its past.

CRITIQUES

The creators of public memorials to mass atrocity around the world often believe that these initiatives might be able to make significant contributions to "never again." They believe this, I have argued, because many of them have an often-unstated causal theory of how memoryworks *work*. They may be right. On the other hand, recognizing that the *preventive* aspirations of works of memory can also be criticized is also important. Peter Novick has questioned whether remembrance of the Holocaust has led to "never again." He constructs this question in a very specific way: Has the effort in the United States and globally to *remember the Holocaust* created incentives or pressures for the US government to intervene to stop ongoing genocides? Can it be said that "never again will the United States tolerate genocidal atrocities"?[86]

Glancing then at Cambodia, Bosnia, Rwanda, and other cases, he concludes that indeed this "never again" formula has failed. He tends to agree with a "disillusioned advocate of intervention in Bosnia" that "never again" seems to mean only that "never again would Germans kill Jews in Europe in the 1940s."[87] By constructing his argument almost entirely around military intervention,[88] however, Novick does not do service to the broader kinds of prevention claims that are implicit in many of these projects. For example, they may be premised on the idea of empathy with victims, of a long-term pedagogical project aimed at changing the hearts and minds of a wide range of people—from potential future bystanders to potential future perpetrators[89]—or of providing the basis for improved international or national law and norms on these questions.

Instead of arguing that Novick is right or wrong, however, I prefer to reframe his question. Is it possible that, if they were to be done *well*, these kinds of initiatives could create disincentives, cultural aversions, and other forms of rejecting future mass atrocity? Is it possible, if they were to be done well, that these efforts could provide the basis for changes in the way national and international affairs are conducted? If these things are possible, then the logical next question is what does it mean to do these initiatives *well*? If we understand the causal relationships, then the answer must reside in the world of pedagogy writ large: What does it mean to have an educated citizenry, and how can public memorials contribute to this?

CONCLUSION

How do memoryworks *work*? This question has at least two answers. Often, memoryworks work as spaces for goals such as mourning, solemnity, and healing. I have called this approach the *private/reflective* purpose of public memorials, which has redress as its goal, yet I have not focused on this aspect here. Public memorials can be said to work in a second way, which I have focused on here. Proponents and designers of public memorials—as is evidenced in their written materials about why they are pursuing these initiatives—suggest that a certain kind of public memorial can create a certain kind of learning experience that will contribute to the nonrepetition of atrocity in the long term. My purpose in this chapter was not to measure how well these initiatives work but rather to set the stage for that task by suggesting a set of alleged causal relationships that researchers can explore. This task requires critical analysis and a willingness to challenge the assumptions that protagonists make about "never again."

In the last few decades, on every inhabited continent in the world, public memorials have sprung up as a way to confront past atrocity, mass abuse of human rights, and conflict. (For a listing of some of these memorials, many of which I've mentioned here, see Table 14.1.) Drawing on well-established vernaculars and traditions in some places, or inventing or creating new ones in others, the trend toward memorialization overlaps deeply with another recent movement: transitional justice, which is an emerging legal doctrine concerning state obligation. Both of these trends focus on how to prevent mass atrocity from happening in the future by grappling with the past.

Public memorials are just one of many mechanisms for dealing with the past, but they seek perhaps most directly to engage the broader public in this process. Combined with other initiatives, such as truth commissions and war crimes tribunals, public memorials are infused by their creators with an optimism that they can help create a better world. In this chapter I have sought to begin a discussion about whether public memorials really do have that potential, and if they do, what we can learn from them to help them achieve it.

TABLE 14.1.

List of Memorials and Museums Examined

COUNTRY	SITE
Argentina	ESMA (Escuela Superior de Mecánica de la Armada)
Argentina	Parque de la Memoria, Buenos Aires
Bosnia	Bruce Lee Statue (Mostar) / conceptual art project
Bosnia	Srebrenica-Potočari Memorial and Genocide Museum project
Cambodia	Choeung Ek killing fields
Cambodia	Tuol Sleng genocide museum
Chile	Memorial / Cemeterio General
Chile	Paine memorial
Chile	Patio 29 historic site
Chile	Un Lugar Para Recordar (the three chairs memorial)
Chile	Villa Grimaldi Peace Park
Chile	Women's Memorial
El Salvador	El Mozote memorial
France	Oradour-Sur-Glane Monument and Historic Site
Germany	Cold War Tourist Trail (Berlin Wall section)
Germany	Memorial to the Murdered Jews of Europe/Berlin
Guatemala	Comalapa municipal memorial
India	Jallianwalla Bagh Massacre Martyrs' Memorial, Amritsar
Iraq	Crossed Swords / Parade Grounds (proposed)
Iraq	Halabja Museum and Memorial, Kurdistan
Iraq	Halabja Hillsite Cemetery and Memorial, Kurdistan
Japan	Hiroshima Peace Memorial Museum
Lebanon	Memorial to the victims of civil conflict (cancelled)
Mexico	Tlatelolco Square
Morocco	Agdiz (former detention center)
Morocco	Derb Moulay Cherif (former detention center)
Morocco	K'laat Maguna (former detention center)
Morocco	Tazmamart (former detention center)
Paraguay	Human Rights Museum / Stroessner Period (proposed)
Peru	The Eye That Cries (El Ojoque Llora) memorial
Russia	Butovsky Poligon (Butovo Shooting Range)
Rwanda	Rwanda Genocide Museum
Serbia	Milosovic trial traveling exhibit (proposed)
South Africa	District Six Museum
South Africa	Freedom Park

COUNTRY	SITE
South Africa	Robben Island Museum
South Africa	Trojan Horse Memorial (eliminated)
South Africa	Trojan Horse Memorial (second version)
South Africa	Voortrekker Monument
United States	African Burial Ground / New York
United States	AIDS Quilt
United States	Enola Gay Exhibit
United States	Ground Zero / New York
United States	International Freedom Center (cancelled), New York
United States	Vietnam Veterans Memorial

Note: This is not intended to be a comprehensive list of memorials and museums; it simply lists all the sites examined during the research for this chapter. It is organized alphabetically by country for ease of reading.

NOTES

I have benefited enormously from the comments of Pablo de Greiff, who read and engaged with various earlier drafts. I also gratefully acknowledge comments or various contributions to either this chapter or my thinking in general from Tal Avivi, Youk Chhang, Jon Connolly, Eduardo González, Samantha Hinds, Horst Hoheisel, Felix Reategui, Rollo Romig, Brigitte Sion, Amy Sodaro, Aaron Weah, Alex Wilde, James E. Young, and the members of the Documentation Affinity Group (DAG), who heard me try out many of these ideas at different times, as well as students in my graduate seminars at the Graduate Program in International Affairs (GPIA), New School for Social Research, and the Wagner School of New York University. I presented earlier versions of this paper and received very useful feedback for which I am grateful at the Interdisciplinary Memory Conference (February 2009) sponsored by the New School for Social Research and the Seminario Internacional, "Verdad y memoria en contextos de guerra" [Truth and memory in contexts of war], in Bogotá, Colombia. The ideas here presented are mine and do not necessarily represent those of the International Center for Transitional Justice.

1 A community association working on developing Agdiz Pricipal (the site featured in Figure 14.2), with funding from the European Union channeled through and coordinated by the Conseil Consultatif des Droits de l'Homme (CCDH), is interested in focusing not only on the victims but also on the ways in which the broader community was victimized by having the jail in its midst.

2 See Louis Bickford and Debra Schultz, "Memory and Justice: A Brief and Selected History of a Movement," The Memory and Justice Project, International Center for Transitional Justice, 2009, http://memoryandjustice.org/about/history/.

3 See United Nations, *Report of the Secretary-General on the Rule of Law and Transitional Justice in Conflict and Post-Conflict Societies*, S/2004/613, July 30, 2004. I have developed an alternative definition elsewhere, suggesting more broadly that transitional justice consists of "the ways that societies deal with the legacies of past human rights abuse and atrocity" (Louis Bickford, "Transitional Justice," in *The Encyclopedia of Genocide and Crimes against Humanity* [Independence, KY: Macmillan Reference USA, 2004], 3:1045–47). Also see International Center for Transitional Justice, "What Is Transitional Justice?," accessed September 2012, http://www.ictj.org/about/transitional-justice.

4 The best overview of the theoretical material on social remembering can be found in Marita Sturkin, *Tangled Memories: The Vietnam War, the AIDS Epidemic, and the Politics of Remembering* (Berkeley: University of California Press, 1997), 1–18.

5 The Museo de la Memoria [Museum of Memory] was created in 1998 and opened in its permanent location in Rosario in December 2010; see "Historia y Fundamentos," Museo de la Memoria, accessed November 2012, http://www.museodelamemoria.gob.ar/page/institucional/id/1/title/Historia-y-Fundamentos.

6 The Museo de la Memoria y los Derechos Humanos [Museum of Memory and Human Rights] opened in January 2010; see "Sobre el Museo," Museo de la Memoria y los Derechos Humanos, accessed November 2012, http://www.museodelamemoria.cl/el-museo/sobre-el-museo/.

7 The Lugar de la Memoria, la Tolerancia, y la Inclusión Social [Place of Memory, Tolerance, and Social Inclusion] is currently under construction; see http://lugardelamemoria.org.

8 According to the International Coalition of Sites of Conscience, accessed August 2009, www.sitesofconscience.org.

9 See Andreas Huyssen, *Present Pasts: Urban Palimpsests and the Politics of Memory* (Stanford, CA: Stanford University Press, 2003); James E. Young, *The Texture of Memory: Holocaust Memorials and Meaning* (New Haven, CT: Yale University Press, 1993); and Peter Novick, *The Holocaust in American Life* (New York: Houghton Mifflin, 1999).

10 Sebastian Brett, Louis Bickford, Elisabeth Sevcenko, and Marcela Rios, *Memorialization and Democracy: State Policy and Civic Action* (New York: International Center for Transitional Justice, 2008), 1.

11 The main source of information for this study is a collection of materials from approximately fifty public memorials, which are listed at the end of this chapter. For each of these public memorials, the collection includes most or all of the following: (1) mandate and terms of reference; (2) relevant legislation; (3) newspaper articles and clippings; (4) images of the memorial, either in video or photographs; (5) interviews with key actors, conducted either by me or a consultant working with me, or published in other sources; (6) scholarly articles; and (7) other supporting materials about the history and development of the memorial. In some cases, the research has been complemented by interviews and additional methods; in Cambodia, for example, using a site survey, some one hundred visitors were interviewed in November 2007 (see Louis Bickford, *Transforming a Legacy of Genocide: Pedagogy and Tourism at the Killing Fields of Choeung Ek* [New York: International Center for Transitional Justice, 2009]). This collection is not, of course, meant to be an exhaustive survey of all public memorials. On the contrary, the results here are anecdotal, and the goal is to provide some impressionistic, if tentative, conclusions from the cases examined. Many of these materials can be found at www.memoryandjustice.org.

12 Elsewhere I used the terms the *goal of solemnity* and the *goal of transitional justice* to connote the same idea. See "Human Rights, Justice, and the Struggle for Memory," in *Transitional Justice and Human Security*, ed. Alex Boraine and Sue Valentine (Cape Town: International Center for Transitional Justice, 2006).

13 See Brandon Hamber, "Narrowing the Micro and the Macro: A Psychological Perspective on Reparations in Societies in Transition," in *The Handbook of Reparations*, ed. Pablo De Greiff (Oxford: Oxford University Press, 2006), 560–88. More generally, for a seminal text, see Judith Herman, *Trauma and Recovery* (New York: Basic Books, 1997). An extremely interesting book that explores these topics—in particular, the way that

mourning and memorials have shifted over historical time—is Peter Homans, ed., *Symbolic Loss: The Ambiguity of Mourning and Memory at Century's End* (Charlottesville: University of Virginia Press, 2000).

14 For example, see Miroslav Volf, *The End of Memory: Remembering Rightly in a Violent World* (Grand Rapids: Eerdmans, 2006).

15 Protagonists, to the degree that they think through this question, tend to target individual observer/participants as the primary agent of change. That is, they assume that individuals will visit the memorials and have transformative experiences at those sites.

16 For an excellent explanation of this idea, see Hilde Hein, "Assuming Responsibility: Lessons from Aesthetics," in *Museum Philosophy for the Twenty-First Century*, ed. Hugh Genoways (New York: AltaMira Press of Rowman and Littlefield, 2006), 1–9.

17 For some insight into these debates, see Roy Rosenzweig and Dave Thelen, *The Presence of the Past* (New York: Columbia University Press, 2000).

18 As a final outcome, off in the distance, many of these initiatives articulate a set of ultimate ends that represent a broader vision that will fall into place, such as democracy, sustainable peace, or a reconciled society. But my purpose here is not to explore how memorials work in terms of those broader ends.

19 Victoria Barnett, *Bystanders: Conscience and Complicity during the Holocaust* (Westport, CT: Praeger, 1999), 11.

20 See Jaime Malamud Goti's discussion of the shortcomings of prosecution in Argentina in Goti, *Game without End: State Terror and the Politics of Justice* (Norman and London: University of Oklahoma Press, 1996).

21 Karl Jaspers identifies four kinds of guilt, only one of which criminal trials address. The other kinds of guilt—moral, political, and existential, in his terminology—can be addressed in other ways, such as through the creation of public memorials; see Jaspers, *The Question of German Guilt*, trans. E. B. Ashton (New York: Fordham University Press, 2001).

22 There is an echo here of an argument that Pablo de Greiff makes in "The Duty to Remember? The Dead Weight of the Past or the Weight of the Dead of the Past?" (draft manuscript), in which he summarizes his argument in favor of remembering as follows: "We have an obligation to remember whatever our fellow citizens cannot be expected to forget."

23 See Barnett, *Bystanders*, 118–31; see also Zygmunt Bauman, *Modernity and the Holocaust* (Ithaca, NY: Cornell University Press, 1989).

24 As discussed in more depth later, there is a potential problem—from the viewpoint of the public/educative function of memorials—with the tendency of many memorials to leave the perpetrator entirely out of picture, such as New York's Ground Zero (September 11) Tribute Center, which ignores the hijackers completely, as if they did not exist. Another problem is caricaturing the perpetrator as a monolithic force of evil, such as at Choeung Ek, where the crimes committed there are blamed on the "Pol Pot genocidal

clique" without further explanation. By creating a void in terms of the perpetrator, these memorials might fall short of their potential to truly teach about what happened and why.

25 Note that being a bystander can also describe international observers. If we do not act to stop genocide in another country, we are technically bystanders, even if far away. Of course, this moral category is not clear-cut, given questions of sovereignty, the complicated politics of intervention, and the difficulty in knowing how best to stop atrocity from happening.

26 Charles Tilly, *Credit and Blame* (Princeton, NJ: Princeton University Press, 2008).

27 Ibid., 151. Tilly and I might not entirely agree about what kind of consensus is desirable. I clarify later in this paper that the kind of consensus I am referring to is not necessarily a consensus about history. The more important and feasible kind of consensus refers to an agreement that history can and should be told in different ways, and that these different interpretations can represent democratic dialogue.

28 I would argue that the Srebrenica-Potočari Memorial mentioned above is an exception to this pattern.

29 Felix Reategui reminded me of this point, but made it more eloquently than I do, at the Conferencia Internacional Memoria y Reparaciones in Bogotá, Colombia, August 18–19, 2009.

30 Jay Winter argues that the memorials created in the immediate aftermath of World War I did not seek to create a narrative about prevention in the future; they were exclusively concerned with trying to come to grips with the enormity of loss in the recent past (Winter, *Sites of Memory, Sites of Mourning: The Great War in European Cultural History* [Cambridge: Cambridge University Press, 1995]).

31 For example, the Iraq Memory Foundation (IMF) justified its decision to focus on the Ba'ath Party period that ended with the US invasion, even though there was great political pressure for the institution to continue to focus on post-US-invasion human rights abuse. The latter argument was that human rights abuse did not cease after the invasion and in fact worsened; thus, such a dividing line was artificial. However, the IMF countered that the Ba'ath Party period in Iraq *does* represent a specific historical period with a particular regime logic that needs to be interrogated and understood as such. The IMF insisted that remembering the Ba'ath Party period was therefore a valuable exercise in long-term prevention of future atrocities, even if there were ongoing atrocities being committed all around them in the mid-2000s.

32 See Winter, *Sites of Memory*.

33 There are problems with this formulation, of course—most importantly that repeating the past is never possible under any circumstances. There are too many contingencies and specificities at any given moment in historical time for them all to be aligned in exactly the same way. But the spirit of Santayana's quote is the important part.

34 Beginning with the unveiling of Nathan Rappaport's Warsaw Ghetto Memorial in April 1948. See Young, *Texture of Memory*, 170 (see n. 2).

35 See the discussion of the "countermonument" movement in Germany (ibid., 27–48).

36 See Sturken, *Tangled Memories*, chaps. 2 and 3.

37 There are certainly exceptions. A monumental statue of Martin Luther King Jr. proposed for the National Mall in Washington, DC, for example, generated significant controversy. See Shalia Dewan, "Larger than Life, More to Fight Over," *New York Times*, May 18, 2008.

38 See Peter Carrier, *Holocaust Monuments and National Memory Cultures in France and Germany since 1989* (New York: Berghahn Books, 2005), esp. chaps. 7 and 8.

39 Ibid., 212–13.

40 I am convinced that we are undergoing a paradigm shift in terms of the way we think of memory and memorials globally. Those creating memorials are increasingly moving away from private/reflective modes and toward public/educative modes. I find support for this intuition in Homans, *Symbolic Loss*; Carrier's discussion of the postnational memorial in *Holocaust Monuments*; and even, though less directly, in Winter, *Sites of Memory*.

41 See, for example, Alison Brysk's analysis of the Argentinean human rights movement, *The Politics of Human Rights in Argentina* (Stanford, CA: Stanford University Press, 1994).

42 See Benedict Anderson, *Imagined Communities* (London: Verso, 1991).

43 George Mosse, *Fallen Soldiers: Reshaping the Memory of the World Wars* (Oxford: Oxford University Press, 1991).

44 Jenny Edkins, *Trauma and the Memory of Politics* (Cambridge: Cambridge University Press, 2003), 230.

45 Paloma Aguilar Fernandez and Carsten Humlebaek, "Collective Memory and National Identity in the Spanish Democracy: The Legacies of Francoism and the Civil War," *History and Memory* 14, no. 1/2 (2002): 121–64. Aguilar's masterful study of the memory of the Spanish Civil War in Francoist Spain, *Memoria y olvido de la guerra civil española* (Madrid: Alianza, 1998), is a key text in the field of collective memory. It was translated to English by Mark Oakleyu as *Memory and Amnesia: The Role of the Spanish Civil War in the Transition to Democracy* (Oxford: Berghahn Books, 2002), and a revised and updated edition was published as *Politicas de la memoria y memorias de la política* [Politics of memory and memories of politics] (Madrid: Alianza, 2008).

46 Jacob Zuma, "Address by Deputy President Jacob Zuma at the Launch of the Freedom Park Trust," Presidential Guest House, Pretoria, June 1, 2000, http://www.info.gov.za/speeches/2000/000601217p1001.htm.

47 See "Se firmó el decreto que declara monumento histórico el patio 29 del cementerio general" [Decree declaring Lot 29 of the general cemetery a historical monument signed] on the website of the Consejo de Monumentos Nacionales de Chile, www.monumentos.cl, under the subheading "noticias" (accessed September 26, 2007).

48 This memorial commemorates the so-called Trojan Horse incident when three youths

were killed in Athlone, a suburb of Cape Town, by security force officers hidden in barrels on the back of a truck. See Bickford, "Human Rights."

49 A former torture center (1973–78) near Santiago, Chile, that has been turned into a memory site. See Victoria Baxter, "Civil Society Promotion of Truth, Justice, and Reconciliation in Chile: Villa Grimaldi," *Peace and Change* 30, no. 1 (2005): 120–36.

50 This effort is spearheaded by Paraguayan human rights activist Martin Almada (interview with author, May 2004).

51 Tazmamart was a notorious prison where foiled coup plotters were incarcerated from 1971 to 1991. See Ahmed Marzouki, *Tazmamart Cellule 10* (Paris: Éditions Paris-Méditerranée, 2000), and Susan Slyomovics, *The Performance of Human Rights in Morocco* (Philadelphia: University of Pennsylvania Press, 2005).

52 Mémoire pour L'Avenir, a group headed by Lebanese journalist and public figure Amal Makaram, floated this proposal (interview with author, December 2005).

53 The next section is based on the author's interviews with Veselin Gatalo, president of Urban Movement Mostar, in Mostar, June 2005.

54 Tilly, *Credit and Blame.*

55 This conclusion emerged from interviews with staff members of the Kosovar Research and Documentation Institute and the Humanitarian Law Center during the author's visit to Pristina, June 2005.

56 These quotations could have been taken from almost any memorial mentioned here but were taken from, respectively, the African Burial Site, New York (text); Comalapa Memorial site, Guatemala (wall text); and Villa Grimadi (glossy report).

57 A good example is the design chosen for the September 11 / Ground Zero Memorial by Michael Arad. The memorial's most salient feature is the empty space where the towers stood.

58 There is no doubt that the design innovations of this memorial were profound, and in the sense of memorial *art*, Maya Lin's design was paradigm-shifting. Numerous memorials today imitate this sublime, haunting, and provocative design. One of the best descriptions of the design appears in Sturkin, *Tangled Memories*, 44–85.

59 Quoted in Robert Campbell, "An Emotive Place Apart," *A.I.A. Journal* 72, no. 5 (1983): 150–51.

60 See the useful anthology edited by Antonius C. G. M. Robben, *Death, Mourning, and Burial: A Cross-Cultural Reader* (Oxford: Blackwell, 2004).

61 Eric Hobsbawm, *The Age of Extremes: A History of the World, 1914–1991* (New York: Vintage Books, 1996).

62 Peter Novick uses this term somewhat disparagingly in *Holocaust in American Life* to refer to the goals of some Holocaust memory activists.

63 Jorge Tula discussing the proposed El Olimpo site, as quoted in Marguerite Feitlowitz, *A Lexicon of Terror: Argentina and the Legacies of Torture* (Oxford: Oxford University Press, 1998), 188.

64 Jan Scruggs, *The Wall That Heals* (Washington, DC: Vietnam Veterans Memorial Fund, 1992), 112.

65 See Judy Ledgerwood, "The Cambodian Tuol Sleng Museum of Genocidal Crimes," *Museum Anthropology* 21, no. 1 (1997): 82–98.

66 Wall text at the Hiroshima National Peace Memorial Hall.

67 "Quiénes Somos" [Who we are], Villa Grimaldi, accessed October 9, 2007, http://www.villagrimaldicorp.cl/.

68 Serena Nanda, "South African Museums and the Creation of a New National Identity," *American Anthropologist* 106, no. 2 (June 2004): 379–86.

69 See "Museo Casa de la Memoria," http://www.museocasadelamemoria.org/site/Default.aspx.

70 Quoted in David Chandler, *Voices from S-21: Terror and History in Pol Pot's Secret Prison* (Berkeley: University of California Press, 1999), 8–9.

71 For more information, see http://lugardelamemoria.org.

72 See "Elements Underlying Interpretation and Education," in *National Park Service Draft Management Recommendation Report*, African Burial Ground website, 2005, http://parkplanning.nps.gov/document.cfm?parkID=467&projectID=13667&documentID=12695.

73 See Sarah Farmer, *Martyred Village: Commemorating the 1944 Massacre at Oradour-Sur-Glane* (Berkeley: University of California Press, 1999).

74 Numerous works have been written on Choeung Ek. Although it focuses on Tuol Sleng, the Museum of Genocidal Crimes, David Chandler's 1999 book *Voices from S-21* is essential reading. Other works include Meng-Try Ea, Documentation Center of Cambodia, "Cambodian Memorialization: Tuol Sleng Genocide Museum and Choeung Ek Genocide Memorial" (draft manuscript, August 14, 2006); and Rachel Hughes, "Memory and Sovereignty in Post-1979 Cambodia: Choeung Ek and Local Genocide Memorial," in *Genocide in Cambodia and Rwanda: New Perspectives*, ed. Susan Cook (New Brunswick, NJ: Transaction Books, 2005). Also see Wynne Cougill, "Buddhist Cremation Traditions for the Dead and the Need to Preserve Forensic Evidence in Cambodia," Documentation Center of Cambodia, accessed November 2012, http://www.d.dccam.org/Projects/Maps/Buddhist_Cremation_Traditions.htm.

75 Paul Williams, "Witnessing Genocide: Vigilance and Remembrance at Tuol Sleng and Choeung Ek," *Holocaust and Genocide Studies* 18, no. 2 (Fall 2004): 234–54.

76 The slight ambiguity of the word *evidence* is intentional. Whether these remnants constitute *legal* evidence is not entirely certain, although the emerging consensus among international experts and, informally, staff of the Khmer Rouge Tribunal (according to author discussions, November 2007) is that they do not. The remnants could be replaced by facsimiles, and the actual bodily remains could be cremated, as the former king has called for. On the other hand, these remnants do constitute evidence in the nonlegal sense. Seeing these remains and denying that something terrible took place is impossible.

77 One of the guides, however, has been at the site for almost thirty years, starting as the original caretaker soon after the site was discovered in 1980.

78 See Genoways, *Museum Philosophy for the Twenty-First Century*.

79 See Choeung Ek Visitor Survey, reproduced in Bickford, *Transforming a Legacy of Genocide*. In this section I draw heavily on that document and that study.

80 See Gail Anderson, ed., *Reinventing the Museum: Historical and Contemporary Perspectives on the Paradigm Shift* (Walnut Creek, CA: AltaMira Press, 2004).

81 Young, *Texture of Memory*, 81.

82 See Sturkin, *Tangled Memories*, 145–83, and http://memoryandjustice.org/site/aids-memorial-quilt-atlanta/.

83 Truth and Reconciliation Commission of Sierra Leone, "Appendix 4: Memorials, Mass Graves, and Other Sites," in *Witness to Truth: The Final Report of the Truth and Reconciliation Commission of Sierra Leone* (Freetown: Truth and Reconciliation Commission of Sierra Leone, 1994), http://www.sierraleonetrc.org/, para. 7.

84 Truth and Reconciliation Commission of Sierra Leone, "Chapter 3: Recommendations," in *Witness to Truth: The Final Report of the Truth and Reconciliation Commission of Sierra Leone*, vol. 2.

85 Liz Ševčenko, "The Power of Place: How Historic Sites Can Engage Citizens in Human Rights Issues," New Tactics in Human Rights Project, Center for Victims of Torture, 2004, 14.

86 Novick, *Holocaust in American Life*, 257.

87 Ibid.

88 Also in this realm, Novick may be looking at too limited a time period. The UN General Assembly held a debate on July 29, 2009, on the emerging set of norms called the "Responsibility to Protect"—described at www.responsibilitytoprotect.org as "a new international security and human rights norm to address the international community's failure to prevent and stop genocides, war crimes, ethnic cleansing, and crimes against humanity." The debate did not result in definitive support for this new norm, as a number of nations in the Global South feared it would be an invitation to intervene, and they were able to argue in favor of sovereignty. But the fact that this was a serious matter for debate at that level may be indicative of a changing attitude toward stopping genocide.

89 I hesitate to exclude "potential future victims" from this list, but ultimately I think that they are a key target group in only a few cases—specifically those cases that celebrate resistance.

CHAPTER 15

Literature and Experiences of Harm

Carlos Thiebaut Luis-André

How does literature depict experiences of harm, particularly those of a public nature, that force societies to face the negativity of oppression, exclusion, dispossession, and pain—in a word, the loss of conditions for the dignity of human life? How does literature contribute to the efforts to define such harms and confront them, to attempt to understand their obscurities and effects, to oppose and address such harms—indeed, to the overall efforts of transitional justice processes? How does the descriptive, explicative, and interpretive power of literary expression help people to understand and relate their own experiences within the complex social, political, and juridical processes in which transitional justice efforts take place? What is the relationship between the two subjects involved—that is, between the reader of a narrative piece or a poem or the spectator of a play and the citizen who has lived through an experience of harm or who is confronting it by demanding a new experience of truth, justice, and reparation? In this chapter I intend to explore these questions and some possible answers to them. In order to do so, first I attempt to define the domain to which the questions pertain. Then I present a model for analyzing the role of literary works in relation to experiences of harm, and finally I offer a short, systematic reflection about the problem of how literature expresses, gives meaning to, and problematizes such experiences.

DEFINING A QUESTION OR A PROBLEM

The questions posed above obviously do not exhaust or even define what literary, writing, and reading experiences are. These questions also do not define the intricate experiences of harm from the standpoints of victims, perpetrators, and bystanders—nor from the perspective of some collective "us," from which a society or nation takes on the task of doing justice, providing reparations to victims, prosecuting perpetrators, and establishing institutional conditions to prevent harm from recurring in the aftermath of mass human rights violations. The relationship between literature and experiences of harm is problematic in terms of both of its component parts. On the one hand, literature is not defined only by its ability to name harm with the precision of its language or to create meaning, nor is literature defined solely by its role in interpreting the negative vicissitudes of the human condition. In the aesthetic context of today's world, defining a unique role or even a main role for writing and reading is not possible, even if these practices have diverse effects on personal and social life. Unless we adopt a reductionist concept of literary experience, singling out a defining feature is impossible: the experiences of writing and reading take on multiple forms depending on the historical and social context and—because they are artistic practices—on different aesthetic traditions. While literary theory has emphasized the autonomous dimension of texts, insofar as they enact forms and logics of meaning attached to different schools and traditions, we also know that the meaning of literary texts is closely related to their processes of reception: meaning mutates in different contexts and time periods in ways that cannot be reduced to the intentions that gave origin to a given text, if identifying such intentions could even be done. Last, the temporal process that accompanies experiences of harm—how they are experienced and transformed from the moment of suffering through their subsequent elaboration—is also fundamental for determining literary experiences that address them. Still, that same temporal process also influences and transforms the forms and meanings of literary works and their reception, as I explain later in this chapter.

Something similar occurs at the other end of the relationship between literature and experiences of harm. Experiences of oppression and repression under a dictatorship, crimes against humanity, racial discrimination, or economic and social exploitation also cannot be defined by a single feature, nor do they all fall under the same type of political and social processes. As with the different processes that fall under the transitional justice paradigm, which vary across geographic contexts and historical moments, the vast topography of harm is made up of countless ways in which individuals and societies inflict harm and respond to it. In some cases, processes of political change act as catalysts for addressing past harms; in other cases, judicial processes play this part; and in yet others, the only possibility is expressing the unfinished tasks of justice in symbolic terms. Some important differences also exist in the ways in which harm itself is collectively experienced. Some societies face their harms directly while others conceal them. Among the latter, some societies forget their distant or immediate pasts, and they continue on with their histories without any sign that justice might or should be done for the sake of victims; neither a judgment of the present nor an exercise of memory—individually or collectively—figures among societal priorities.

Not only are there countless different possible forms of harm depending on how they begin to be elaborated or on how their past or present reality is experienced, but even those experiences are different, depending on the social positions of the people involved in them. The demands for interpretation generated by experiences of harm take many forms: a victim's search for meaning in relation to what the person has undergone, a perpetrator's justifications, a concerned bystander's judgments (or the justifications of one who is morally undisturbed), and a moral and political community's search for emotional and motivational interpretations, as well as the ability to undertake the tasks of justice. Each demand configures different and asymmetric forms of subjectivity; the identities at issue cannot be reduced to any specific defining features, and the processes of identity creation are also diverse. In addition, one last element is at stake: the demands for meaning attached to the building of subjectivity in experiences of harm are not voiced in a single language or discursive form. These subjects turn to diverse languages, to interpretations of themselves in ordinary language as well as in various institutionalized languages—such as politics, law, economics, or history—and all of these languages contribute in equally diverse ways to the elaboration of experiences of harm. These languages and institutionalized forms contribute to the interpretation of what happened or is happening in terms of such experiences, how they can be resolved, and finally, how they can be turned into elements pertaining to the pursuit of justice. Yet, as I explain below, the expressive force of the symbolic in literary texts enhances the languages in which harm is expressed (the languages of politics, sociology, or law) by lending them a power of understanding that they naturally lack, insofar as it is a force that unveils the background of emotions, beliefs, and desires of persons affected by harm and sets in motion what I call the "fine grammar" of their experience.

The complexity of the multidimensional meanings of literature, on the one hand, and of the diverse forms and processes in which harm is caused as well as the different subject positions and demands for meaning of those who experience such harm, on the other, appears to make impossible answering in a simple way the questions I have posed. Some broad assertions, however, are certainly possible: literature allows human beings to voice and convey their pains and their joys; it reveals different facets of the human condition. Poems and plays shed light on the motivations underlying the actions of human beings, and they raise questions about those actions. As a result, the negative experiences of suffering that I call experiences of harm can be told and put to the test. Literature at times raises questions to which no answers can be found, but literary works can give a strong and peculiar voice to demands for truth, justice, and reparation in response to conditions of oppression, discrimination, or dispossession. Literary works can also showcase the difficulties and obstacles that those demands tend to encounter. One can also say, at the same level of abstraction—although this time focusing on experiences of harm themselves—that narratives, poems, or plays can offer the subjects of such experiences interpretations about their condition that, on an aesthetic or symbolic level, may be relevant for comprehending what their experiences mean to them. These works may also be helpful for subjects to assume particular positions through them; they can elaborate their emotions and their reasons, and literature can even suggest some actions that subjects can take to respond to their experiences.

General answers such as these could be offered through some of the existing theories of literature and literary criticism, which could also provide ways to analyze the relationships between literary forms and human experiences and explain the ways in which some specific literary works have played a role in the elaboration of harm. Such answers, first posited as hypotheses or general interpretations, would need to be tested and explicated for each particular case. Thus, one possible path to take, following literary criticism, would be to analyze each experience of harm, or at least the most significant ones, in order to identify the ways in which lived experiences have called for literary representation. Conversely, one could analyze how literature has contributed in each case to understand or obfuscate the experience of harm and its elaboration.[1] Although this option—a particularistic one, so to speak—may be illuminating in some ways, it may also distract from the fact that literature does not have a single meaning restricted to the particular context in which a text was written. A literary work can be read in different contexts, and its contributions can have transcontextual meanings; through its grasp or expression of what took place at a specific time and place, a work can capture and represent the reality of human experience in a way that extends beyond particular times and spaces.

To mention just a few examples, to which I return later, the meanings of a book such as *Requiem* by the Russian poet Anna Akhmatova are not limited to the ones its readers may have attributed to it during Soviet Russia as a testimony of resistance. The book also expresses the possibility of speaking about the human condition—and the struggle to do so—in situations of complete social and political obscurity. Similarly, J. M. Coetzee's *Age of Iron* gets much of its strength not only from the context of apartheid in South Africa; but its compelling depiction of the obscurity of social and personal identities in unjust societies can also be seen as accurate and appropriate beyond that specific context. The same author portrays in *Disgrace*—a novel set in South Africa after the official timetable of its political transition within the framework of the ideals of truth and reconciliation—the problematic conditions of people who have faced situations of harm, along with their private motives and experiences, which appear to be removed from the public realm; in that work Coetzee calls attention to the unresolved tasks of grief and the loose ends of the aspiration to overcome harm. Grief, Coetzee seems to tell us, is not a task that can be conceived of solely in public and institutional terms. This process may be much more complex and difficult if understood as a personal process of dispossession.

Likewise, as regards the protracted and paradigmatic cycle of the Holocaust, Primo Levi's expiatory witness accounts, Roger Antelme's harrowing meditation on the loss of trust in the world, Jean Améry's testimony of a victim's bold resentment, Imre Kertész's literary efforts against the difficulties of memory, and Paul Celan's convulsive depiction of terror and death in his poem "Death Fugue" have made the Shoah the foremost symbol of absolute negativity. In addition, these works depict the countless dimensions of the grieving process and, in doing so, determine the course of history in terms of exposing and representing evil. The cycle of the Holocaust and the experience of its negativity thus foster the emergence of guilt and resentment, of courage and cowardice, of not wanting to remember and resisting the impulses of memory—all of which constitute attitudes and emotions that we see played out in other experiences and processes.

Focusing on the relationship between victims and perpetrators as a site where demands for justice converge with the swifter option of revenge directs our attention to victims' struggles in facing their own injuries and in demanding that perpetrators be judged. Obstacles also arise in such a judgment, which falls on the shoulders of a moral and political community that must take on the always unfinished tasks of justice—for instance, in relation to torture, as depicted in the play *Death and the Maiden* by the Chilean writer Ariel Dorfman. Finally, the narratives of a society that has yet to face its grief, as captured by Alberto Méndez's *The Blind Sunflowers* on the subject of the Spanish Civil War, can not only help foster a society's historical memory but also bear witness to how a demand for dealing with tasks that remain pending is often voiced collectively in symbolic terms. One can also make a statement about the silences and absences that always accompany harm and that are reiterated as long as a society fails to confront its own past and postpones the work of memory. The making of such demands through fictions of an absent or silenced memory exemplifies literature's performative character—in Mendez's case, in the form of denunciation.

These and other examples indicate that criticism can identify the strength of literary efforts and see them as paradigm examples of the moments, processes, and dimensions that are present in the elaboration of harm. In such works we find the emotions, reactions, and reasons of different characters that encapsulate experiences of negativity; we find the difficulties of the experience itself and the elements that catalyze, hinder, complicate, or fully prevent its elaboration. We become aware of the strength of ideals such as grief, justice, reparation, and even social reconciliation, not just in relation to a specific case, but also more generally. Moreover, we comprehend how difficult or even impossible they are to realize. Perhaps we may even learn, above all, that such ideals are always unresolved but recurring demands.

One key element in our conception of literature and its function in relation to experiences of harm can serve as a guide for beginning to answer the questions I have posed. I want to emphasize the different roles that literary works assume in relation to experiences of harm based on the idea that literary texts not only express the ways in which an author perceives such experiences but also have an important performative dimension. Literature offers an avenue for understanding and interpreting the human condition in situations of harm. Such avenues, however, require and foster an active, autonomous reception on the reader's part. Fiction, especially the novel, provides a special mechanism for this to unfold. As Stanley Cavell has pointed out, "Novels . . . are meant to make private what is public and private business, make them mine."[2] In novels, the performative element invites, even requires, an interpretive response, although without forcing it. Fiction does so at a personal level, offering exemplary and emblematic life experiences marked by failure, pain, or resistance. The literary form allows for the fictionally portrayed world to become a site for envisioning the possibility of different forms of life in which emotions, beliefs, and desires become intertwined.

In order to consider more clearly the ways in which literature operates in relation to harm and to capture its transcontextual capacity to signify such harm, we should refer to some dimensions of experiences of harm in relation to which some representative literary works may play a performative role, calling for active responses on the part of readers. For this purpose, I concentrate on examples that refer to different processes and historical moments and that may have some emblematic and transcontextual significance. The examples belong to different literary genres, come from different aesthetic traditions, and can be analyzed within the contexts in which they were created. But these literary experiences can also be seen through the lens of the specific human experiences that originated them. At the same time, however, understanding their mutated and constantly mutating reception contexts is decisive for capturing the power of literature to describe, interpret, compel, or question—a power that gives literature its strength when naming and facing harm.

For didactic and interpretive purposes, we address through examples three idealized moments of the elaboration of harm. This analytical approach is based on the intuition that the timing of experiences of harm may determine the types of interpretive demands with which literary works may prove helpful. The first moment is the anticipation of a negative experience—in fiction, presenting the experience after the fact as something that was to be expected, as a sort of warning, or on the contrary, representing a past experience as a future peril. The second moment is the experience of harm itself, in the form of the testimony about that which has been suffered, or the occasion to express the reaction of resistance or admitting defeat, as it happened there and then. The third moment is a return to the experience of harm to flesh out its meanings in what one could call an elaboration of grief: on the one hand the materialization of calls for justice, and on the other the exercise of memory—sometimes denouncing that which has been forgotten or silenced, and at other times calling attention to the difficulty of such an exercise. In these cases it becomes clearer how the elaboration of harm is not only a matter of acknowledging its truth but also one of envisaging the possibilities, limits, and forms of remembering.

These tense exercises of memory bring to the fore other, more structural and important problems concerning the relationship between literature and experiences of harm. I return to them in the third section of this chapter, but one may help to frame my proposed analysis. Perhaps with the exception of militant or activist literature—marked by action, combat, and resistance[3] and characterized by an immediate connection between a text and the context of its reception—the act of reading always takes place after the fact. Further, reading is delayed in another sense, insofar as it comes after the experience and its elaboration, but also because the act of reading always comes after the act of writing. These delays—real temporal distances between the experience of harm, its symbolic elaboration in a text, and the moment of reading—frame even more temporal displacements within the text itself. The reader travels from one's own time—socially and historically situated—to the temporal forms, times, and the understanding processes that a work reveals and proposes. Navigating through such distances, as the performative conception of literature I have put forward suggests, is a reader's own task, making the reader the subject of the aesthetic experience. But what is the nature of the relationship that arises between the time of the reader-subject and that of the actor-subject who is tasked with elaborating the harm suffered—a task that, to the former, takes place in the realm of memory within writing, while to the latter, it takes place always in the present and in the memory of her life or society? I argue in the chapter's final section that the relationship between the reader (and that subject's access to the chronological elements of a text) and the citizen (and that subject's times of action and lived memories) is the site of cognitive, emotional, and motivational transfers that can be conceived of as a learning process.

TEXTS AS EMBLEMS OF HARM

A GLIMPSE OF HIDDEN EVIL: THE WARNING

In the first moment, literature offers a glimpse into hidden evil and could be seen as anticipating it—although, paradoxically, only after the fact. After some texts' reception, they became foreshadowers of evils that took place after their creation and dissemination. Franz Kafka and Walter Benjamin have been presented as *Feuermelder* (fire alerts) because those authors foresaw, among other things, the menace of Nazism. At the very least, their works and their aesthetic universes have become recurring references for facing evil: the writings of Coetzee, among others, illustrate Kafka's importance. What makes authors such as these relevant for anticipating future evils? What about them serves, in the aftermath, as an aesthetic and literary paradigm for representing and grasping harm? At least two elements can be singled out. First is the disclosure of a world that appears to us as incomprehensible, opaque, and oppressive and of the subjects who live in such a world. Kafka's imagined universes of oppression were not—nor would they ever be—the same as the hellish concentration camps, but his characters (for example, in *The Trial* or *In the Penal Colony*) astonishingly display some of the very same elements of incomprehension expressed by victims of the gulag or of Nazism. Years later Coetzee would also retrieve these elements to define the South African reality in *Life and Times of Michael K*. Such incomprehension on the part of a victim is accompanied by a dissection of its causes: the surprise brought about by a conviction or the sudden destruction of a world that makes harm—or evil as something inexplicable—an irruption, an unexpected and unjustifiable rupture of the normal course of life. The second relevant element of Kafka's texts is the expressive power of a language that breaks with the normalized cadence of an epoch's hegemonic literature: his literary expressionism became a paradigm of the clash between the world and the language available for capturing unexpected harms or evils. Even the ambiguity of expressionism as a vehicle for totalitarian politics—as Sigfried Kracauer noted in relation to German expressionist film in *From Caligary to Hitler: A Psychological History of the German Film*—speaks to the discrepancy between language and reality, a discrepancy that later works dealing symbolically with harm would recuperate.

Meditations on totalitarianism as a terrain where identities and understanding become distorted are recurrent elsewhere and in different historical contexts. Gabriel García Márquez's *The Autumn of the Patriarch* penetrates into the entrails of the beast and uncovers, using its own language, its dense, overwhelming, and oppressive obscurity. Coetzee's *Age of Iron* fleshes out its characters' fractured experience and the difficulties of their own awareness of living in a socially broken and unjust world, as though the obscurity of a social space resonated with a subject's own reality. All these texts explore the undefinability of evil and the innate complexity of its representation; as in Kafka's work, characters appear to oppose what remains partially unnamed even as they nonetheless reproduce its very obscurity. When they first appeared, these texts' reception—the exercise of reading them—seemed to be marked by a shared perception of the obscurity of present times and circumstances. Then, once tyranny and its political forms appeared to be things of the past, those same texts became emblematic sites of the disparity between the subject and the world—between language and the world—insofar as they were capable of depicting that which seemed incomprehensible. But the texts themselves continue to show the recurrence of social fractures and the collapse of identities.

Thanks to that power of depiction of social or political obscurity, of failures in comprehension and of powers of resistance, texts can be conceived of as an exercise of unveiling and evincing hidden evil that society barely notices at a given moment in time. Many of Mario Vargas Llosa's 1980s works (*Who Killed*

Palomino Molero? or *The War of the End of the World*) anticipated much of what has since been discovered—particularly after the publication of the Peruvian Truth Commission's report—about the cruelty of self-described revolutionary movements and state authorities. Literary work was able to perceive and unveil those dark Peruvian times through the precise and insightful description of particular cases or through the symbolic reconstruction of an institutional logic or policy for action.

Literature thus frequently takes on an admonishing role, which it can also adopt through fiction's imaginational and counterfactual power. Not only does fiction have a descriptive and anticipative role, it can also situate itself in the future to frame as negative prophecies the representations of situations and evils that have already come to pass. The dystopias of the 1940s and 1950s, such as George Orwell's *1984* or Ray Bradbury's *Fahrenheit 451*, are presented as admonitions about future dictatorships while portraying the real experiences of oppression under totalitarianism and warning about the threats to freedom in administered societies. Political and social criticism and denunciation make these texts testimonies of resistance. Their portrayal of obscurity and oppression complements the dissection of their characters' subjectivities, ambiguities, and contradictions, as well as their resistance and failures.

The heuristic and revealing capabilities of the symbolic make clear the discrepancy between language, the world, and the ways of interpreting experiences of harm. In the cases I have mentioned, the disclosure of that discrepancy serves both as a denunciation of past events and as a warning, highlighting the future dimension of the negative possibilities of human experience. Against assurances of the conventional and everyday taken-for-grantedness, the disturbing ambiguity of the relationship between fiction and reality calls to mind the lack of certainty and resolution, questioning the common expectation that life and the world will go on and all will be well in the end. The frustration of such expectations and the daunting destruction of confidence—a recurring characteristic of experiences of harm, especially in the twentieth century—also challenge a reader's understanding and destroy any notion about being able to avoid an experience of harm. Such texts—and, in particular, their ability to provide a glimpse of harm—force the reader to realize that the unexpected possibility of harm is always latent. In doing so, the texts also stress a crucial trait of every experience of harm: the ability to draw attention to the fragility and precariousness of the human condition, the ease with which a body is susceptible to being hurt, and the vulnerability of human dignity and respect to being undermined. Human beings' fragile helplessness is made evident and constantly recalled by showing not only that harm exists but also, as it happens in this first moment, its imminent possibility and latency.

NAMING HARM: TESTIMONY AND RESISTANCE

In addition to their interpretive power, literary works are also capable of fostering efforts to give a name and a description to that which causes harm, in addition to identifying and laying bare its meaning, even in the face of the difficulty or impossibility of doing so under conditions of social and political obscurity. A second moment, the moment of harm itself, is also one for testimony and resistance, a moment in which literature exerts its power to identify and name the evils experienced and to signify them with words and images. A literary text can demonstrate its relevance as an effective emblem of harm and as a testimony of its truth: it names, defines, and identifies victims' solitude, pain, abandonment, and the collapse of their world. It portrays victims' impotence, their defeat, and often their silence, but it also underscores their resistance (even when it takes place in forced silence) and supports their conviction and their strength. In doing so, literary works portray the depth of the harm suffered, the ways in which people experience it, and the unfolding of their reactive emotions and even their virtues.

Anna Akhmatova begins her *Requiem* with a small text, "Instead of a Foreword," dated on April 1, 1957. She narrates how she spent seventeen months waiting in line outside the prison in Leningrad during the time of the purges in Soviet Russia in the late 1930s. We know that she was there to drop off food for her son, who was being held prisoner there. One time, a woman with lips blue from the cold asked her in a whisper, "(everyone spoke in whispers there): 'Can you describe *this*?' And I said: 'I can.' Then something like a smile slipped across what once had been her face."[4]

A text's descriptive intent—cutting across multiple temporalities, as in the case of *Requiem*, which depicts a desolate interpretation of absences, namely a husband's death and a son's imprisonment—is anchored in a present of testimony and resistance. To unveil the lived experience of harm is to achieve a descriptively precise representation and to situate it within a web of meanings. The night, the threatening dawn, the anguish of waiting, the threat and final horror of death are all related to one another and to the symbolic language of culture—in this case, the motifs of crucifixion and of the shroud. *Requiem* is directed at women who stood in line outside of Soviet prisons and whose words, she says, the author has borrowed. That community of suffering is reiterated in every moment of harm, making the poet's voice that of hundreds of millions of others. What those voices express through the poet's fiduciary voice—although in this case she is also a victim, but let us recall other instances, such as Paul Celan—is not only the multidimensionality of an experience of harm but also different attitudes and reactions in response to it. The poem gives a human face to the wounded subjectivity of a person whom we may call a victim; it sets that subjectivity in motion and serves as a witness to its truth. Here the testimony is one of resistance and anger but also of defeat and desolation. In other cases the testimony may also express a loss of trust in the world in the aftermath—or as a consequence—of absolute negativity. All the different facets represent the indelible permanence of pain, one's own and that of others.

I have dwelled on some of the meanings of Akhmatova's poem and highlighted their semantic strength in order to underscore also the extent to which they are able to pin down the experience of harm in a precise, inimitable, and indispensable way. By giving harm a name, the text reclaims the truth of the lived experience and asserts that of its representation. The search for that truth—reiterated in every demand for every experience of harm to be exposed and recognized—connects the text to the experience of the reader, who also acts as recipient of the text's testimony. For this very reason, as made clear when we turn to the next moment, the reader is compelled to play an active role.

The truth of a testimony and its ability to compel the reader operate simultaneously on two levels. On the one hand, they are contingent on the truthfulness of the witness. Though truthfulness is a quality that can be understood in different ways, in testimony it always seems to transcend the text, and even in fiction it gives a special, indispensable quality and strength—the force of what we could call *reality*. On the other hand, the immediacy of that reality—even though it always appears as delayed in the text, as noted earlier—allows symbolic representations, which articulate the truth of testimony, to exert their power to call for an active response. In contrast to truth claims that are put forward in an objective fashion, as in historical knowledge or documentary evidence, which have a different type of testimonial strength, the testimonies of victims or of those who lend them a voice constitute truth claims that are (or seek to be) communicative demands of acknowledgment as well, even in the face of the abovementioned intervals between lived experiences, representations, and the act of reading.

The truth of testimony has other dimensions. Testimonies are also a form of struggle, not just against the difficulty of speaking, expressing, and representing, but also against forgetting. Experiences of harm, as it becomes evident in transitional processes, reveal the constant tension between the motives and reasons for forgetting and the motives and reasons for remembering. Several political, social, and personal pressures and needs lend weight to forgetting; victims cannot be forced to speak—it seems necessary to respect their own grieving processes and their right to silence—and sometimes societies cannot or do not want to make remembering a priority, especially in the immediate aftermath of harm. The reasons for forgetting are a point of contention, and appreciating them may require a more contextual approach, as well as careful considerations in terms of timing, respect, and practical wisdom. Yet, in spite of these concerns, the literary and documentary dimensions of testimonies—even if their reception is delayed by protracted silences, as happened in the cases of Primo Levi, Roger Antelme, and Jean Améry and their accounts of the Holocaust—always leave open a demand for truth, regardless of whether the recognition of such truth is delayed. Their literary dimension keeps truth at the forefront while also leaving open and pending the call for an active response. Regardless of any delays or lags in its dissemination, writing is never a lapse of memory but a constant exercise of the truth of the experience that it represents.

GRIEF AFTER HARM: A DEMAND FOR JUSTICE

In experiences of harm, testimonies of the truth demand recognition. As I have argued, the demand in question is one that seeks a response not only from the actual or potential community in which an experience of harm takes place but also from the actual or potential community comprising the recipients of its representation. The demand for recognition of the truth is closely linked to the normative demand for justice: first, the demand is for justice to be done by acknowledging the truth, but it is also a call for harm to be addressed, repaired, and prevented. Thus, the third idealized moment in the elaboration of harm is one in which this type of normative demand is put forward. Representations of harm act in different ways as vehicles for those demands, which are also formulated in various ways and at multiple levels.

Ariel Dorfman puts forward precisely this sort of call to action in an immediate, direct, and almost militant fashion in his play *Death and the Maiden*. Set in the context of the Chilean democratic transition, the play tells the story of a torture victim's encounter with a man who may be her torturer. The victim's husband is, emblematically, a lawyer in the newly created truth commission. The task of finding out the truth about what has happened—is the antagonist really her torturer?—overlaps with the task of ensuring accountability. The task of discovery, however, is also affected by the suspicion that the forces of revenge and resentment bring further uncertainty about the perpetrator's identity. In the end, Dorfman turns the curtain into a mirror that requires an active judgment on the part of the audience.[5] The play thus brings to the fore the three idealized subject positions at issue in every experience of harm: the victim with her demands for truth and justice, the perpetrator with his reasons and excuses, and the judge (embodied by the husband but also, in the end, by the potential community formed by the audience) with doubts in the face of the former's demands and the latter's reasons.

However, as many of us may know from historical experiences of harm, the normative resolutions of the demands for justice can be much more complex and obscure. I would not say that normative demands in the face of an experience of harm ever disappear; rather, they may remain unresolved, or they may be articulated in less transparent, less linear ways than one might expect from the stylized and procedural workings of a court of law. In addition to the epistemic difficulties of the search for truth and the obstacles to accountability, the emotional resistance of the subjects involved in experiences of harm, as well as their attitudes toward the process that the demands for justice usually set in motion, also play an important role. As I pointed out with regard to the second moment, people find many reasons to choose silence and refuse to take part in that process, to act as a witness to the truth, and to denounce the wrongfulness of what has taken place. For example, a person may not want to relive the harms suffered or may wish to defend her dignity by exercising her right to silence. More fundamentally, some people doubt whether addressing in the public realm of justice a personal wound that can never be healed makes any sense at all. As noted earlier, Coetzee's novel *Disgrace* lays bare all of these obscurities in the context of South Africa's dismantlement of apartheid under the public motto and paradigm of acknowledging the truth in order to achieve political and even moral reconciliation in a fractured society. But

> in *Disgrace* the violence of the past informs the violence of the present. The right to remain silent is as important as the right to speak; speech is partial and occurs at unexpected times, in unexpected places. It will not appear on demand. There are no straightforward victims or perpetrators. Responsibility is repeatedly distorted.[6]

The harsh descriptions and representations of characters' motives in Coetzee's work truly reflect the reality of violence and of its perpetuation. Some critics have also pointed out that such violence is present in less explicit forms, either in terms of gender or of race, in the treatment of the violations addressed in the plot.[7] By representing the resistance to confession and the ambiguity of characters' feelings and resentments, and by restricting the ways in which a reader can identify or sympathize with them, the novel exposes the intricate web of difficulties pertaining to the grieving process. The tensions and hurdles of grief are made more evident by the impossibility or irrelevance of personal forgiveness than by public acts of atonement, which are always prone to distortion and falsehood. Still, the novel reflects the obscurity of the subjects involved in experiences of harm—those who inflict it, suffer it, and judge it, including the reader. The overall result is a denial of innocence.

Disgrace poses another deep problem, as the normative demands resulting from experiences of harm are not formulated or resolved in the same ways, nor do they follow the same logic in the private and public spheres. It is in the former, the novel proposes, where the process of grieving takes place or fails to do so. Moreover, an even greater tension exists insofar as the demands for justice in the public realm are transparent—partly given that they must accord to the language of law—while in the private sphere they are opaque, imprecise, incomplete, and always in a state of flux. Thus, in these forms of symbolic representation, experiences of harm expose their irresolvable and always unrealized character.

The representation in *Disgrace* of the obstacles to accountability might seem to paint justice as an impossible task. However, the novel is bringing to light the extent to which every reproach, accusation, denunciation, and act of atonement or forgiveness is always made under a veil of opacity, taking place between subjects who do not fully know each other or even themselves. As a result, any judgment is always similarly depicted as opaque. Readers are able to perceive and perhaps learn that justice processes are not linear not only in fiction but also in their lives as citizens. Literature thus emerges as a special medium, offering the best possible tools for describing the opacities and complexities of the human condition itself and as a warning about the uselessness of any attempt to reduce it to a single logic or dimension, including the public logic of justice. Literature depicts and exposes how the grieving process in the aftermath of an experience of harm—a process that only individual human beings can undergo, even if within the framework of public processes that allow and foster it, such as the South African Truth and Reconciliation Commission—is mediated by fear and impotence, despair and trust, acceptance and denial. Literature provides a subtle, precise, complex, and transparent grammar and lexicon of human experience that becomes indispensable for comprehending experiences of harm, not just within particular texts, but also beyond them. The conversion of a discovered, restated, or clarified subjectivity to the social subjectivity of the citizen through the act of reading is a transfer of meanings about what it is to be a subject, a person, or the difficulty of being so under conditions of social and political obscurity. Readers then perceive and learn that the normative demands pertaining to harm, which may require an active response on their part, are also formulated in terms of the fine grammar of moral life that literature has managed to capture.

Still, in addition to the normative demands arising from harm, this learning process can only be possible under certain conditions relating to the act of reading itself. The reader or spectator is responsible for responding to the text—or at least for responding as a citizen, beyond the text—to the experience of harm in question. In our assessment of the role that literature plays in relation to actual experiences of harm, we must also consider the fact that, under the aesthetic conditions of our increasingly reflexive modernity, every demand for justice—that is, the ethics of citizenship—is mediated by the demand for a response to its representation (in this case, the ethics of reading).[8]

If the ethics of representation and the ethics of action are to converge in capturing and facilitating the comprehension of experiences of negativity, the reader or the audience may have to be seen as being directly concerned by the experience of harm that is represented as well as in its representation. If the harm that is represented already concerns the reader as a citizen before doing so as a reader—something that depends on contextual and contingent conditions—that person is able to respond to the text by assessing and contrasting the work's viewpoint to her own; the reader can question the work while questioning herself through the work. If, by contrast, her personal experience does not correspond to the text, the reader can still consider whether the instruments that the text offers—for instance, in the case of Coetzee, the fine grammar of the forms of grief in a situation of social and personal obscurity—are in any way useful for interpreting her own world. But, even further, the reader can also reject her own involvement with what has been represented and with the way it has been expressed. That, too, constitutes a form of response, a stance in the face of the demand for involvement raised in the act of reading. Thus, just as authors assume responsibility for their descriptions and interpretations, for the aesthetic as well as the normative components of their writing, readers specify and define the responsibilities that may or ought to stem from their role.

The demands of the ethics of representation and of the ethics of the audience's response to it—in this case, the ethics of reading—are not identical.

Even admitting that the reader is responsible for her involvement in relation to an experience of harm and the ways in which it is elaborated, we cannot dictate the exact form of her participation. Neither literary works nor social and institutional processes designed to elaborate experiences of harm can do so, despite countless unsuccessful attempts to impose meanings and rules for reading and interpretation. Like everything that belongs to the symbolic realm, literature has an open texture and an open structure both for the writer and the reader, especially in relation to the normative demands that it raises. One of the positive implications of this openness is that every representation of harm can always be resignified and reinterpreted. Even works that were not originally intended in the past to represent a particular experience of harm can now be read as doing so.

MOURNING: THE WORK OF MEMORY

The representation of harm through language is always delayed in relation to the experience, as noted earlier, even when the temporal distance is almost nonexistent, as in the case of a synchronic, immediate testimony. This delay becomes greater when it takes the form of writing and even more so when it comes to its dissemination and reception. Insofar as the time and space of normative demands also tend to lengthen and widen, the elaboration of harm—its grieving process—is an exercise that unfolds in the place and time of memory. Justice and memory thus constitute the two pillars of elaborating an experience of harm. In some cases, their tasks converge; in others, they point in different directions.

The gap between the demands of justice emerging from experiences of harm and the forms they take in memory has been especially significant in societies in which the elaboration of harm remains pending. Whether the elaboration of harm is possible depends on social and historical conditions, particularly when addressing the demands for justice in terms of reparation, accountability, and institutional measures for nonrepetition. As the cases analyzed by scholars of transitional justice have made clear, the elaboration of harm also requires certain conditions of political freedom in order to be feasible. Even the identification of the obstacles to grief is not possible in the absence of such freedoms, reinforcing the common suspicion that historical contingencies and sociopolitical processes can delay the administration of justice. In those cases, symbolic, literary, or artistic elaborations of harm might be the only way to call attention to a society's failure to face its still unaddressed grief over the past. Akhmatova's *Requiem*, as well as works by Aleksandr

Solzhenitsyn, Joseph Brodsky, and others, provide testimonies of the obscurities of the gulag and Stalinism as well as attempts to find meaning in them, and the works serve as reminders of the unfinished tasks of recognition and reparation as relates to those experiences.

Such warnings may also be warranted as exercises in remembrance, even as a vindication of memory when it has been absent or as attempts to repair memory after it has been broken. Spain's democratic transition in the late 1970s following forty years of dictatorship can be seen as a relevant example of the constant convergence and divergence of the demands of justice and memory, and it has much in common with the experiences of dictatorship and oppression of Latin American countries such as Argentina, Chile, and Uruguay in the 1970s and 1980s. In the Spanish case, the silence forced upon part of the population after the civil war and the complicity of other segments with the dictatorship not only held back the task of reparations and justice but for several decades also restrained the open literary representation and interpretation of past harms by imposing exile or clandestineness upon them. In the aftermath of the transition to democracy, in the 1990s, when the country was forced to face its past and address its unsettled accounts in terms of recognizing past harms and repairing them, Spain also encountered a score of absent, fragmented, and silenced testimonies and memories. The novels *Literature or Life* and *Viviré con su nombre, morirá con el mío* (I will live with his name, he will die with mine)[9] by Jorge Semprún are examples of this literary reconstruction of pending historical and personal memories. Further, memory has also had to be recovered through fiction, as in Dulce Chacón's *La voz dormida* (The sleeping voice) or the aforementioned *Los girasoles ciegos (The Blind Sunflowers)* by Alberto Méndez. In these cases, the interpretive power of literature, especially fiction, not only complements or accompanies the grieving process following an experience of harm but also rearticulates or even acts as a vehicle for the exercise of memory.

Perhaps the need to remember and the process of recollection, even through fiction, are made necessary by the present reality of a society unable to reconcile with itself as long as some of the tasks of justice are still deemed incomplete or because previous attempts to face the past are viewed as insufficient or flawed. W. G. Sebald's writing and literary criticism were spurred by his belief—shared by a large segment of his generation—that his country, Germany, had not properly addressed its role in the Holocaust. In *Campo Santo*, Sebald analyzes the forms, blunders, and silences of German literature in the postwar period; in his novels (*Vertigo*, *The Emigrants*, *The Rings of Saturn*, and

Austerlitz) he depicts different forms of the exercise of and search for memory, unveiling that which had been hidden or distorted. At the same time, his fiction also exposes the difficulties of remembering. The exercise of memory in literature, just like the exercise of historical and personal memory outside of it, has been reflexively aware of its own obstacles, showing, as Sebald does, that remembering does not happen spontaneously but requires active work of remembrance. In this regard, the elaboration of grief in literary memory meets halfway the role of testimony in affirming the truth of an experience of harm against the tendency for forgetting, as discussed above in relation to the first moment of this process.

However, a number of problems pertaining to the memory of harm persist; literature cannot address them by itself, despite its particular methods. Unanswered questions remain in every grieving process: What are the demands and burdens associated with remembering? When is it necessary to remember, and when is it better to forget? The ultimate question is, why remember at all? The conflicting reasons behind all possible answers—that remembering is a moral imperative and remains a requirement as long as the wounds left by harm remain open or even as long as the scars remain visible; or, on the contrary, that the imperative to go on living trumps those and other exigencies—must be debated publicly and privately in the contexts where harm has taken place. In turn, such a debate defines to a great extent the moral and political caliber of the public sphere in which all of the different reasons and motives meet and collide. That debate belongs to the realm of societies' moral grammar, where other discourses and disciplines—ranging from historiography to law—also come into play. As we have seen, literature seems to play a special, perhaps even privileged role here. At a structural level, literature is always memory, for it operates in the space of the lag between itself and the experience that is being represented. Literature's instruments—its ability to name, to describe, to question, to expose the temporal structure of experience, to present an experience from the diverse viewpoints of all involved, and to make certain demands of readers and of their own experience in the act of reading—give it a special power to lay out the forms and limits of grief. More specifically, perhaps only literature can show the personal and public dimensions of harm and its generally multifaceted structure; perhaps only literature can visualize the obscurity of harm and frame it as something that concerns or affects the reader. As I have indicated, the reader can learn the forms of the fine grammar of harm and its elaboration, thanks to literature's representation of it through the instruments listed above. In contrast to objective documents and historical testimonies, literature can penetrate into the realm of motivations and emotions, capturing the demands and obstacles of judgments and expressing certainty and doubt.

In these and other ways, literature is a privileged medium for articulating the moral grammar of experience. By being represented, that grammar is expressed and codified. For this reason, literature constitutes a privileged learning site; for that same reason, literature is also an ideal medium for the exercise of memory in relation to harm and elaborating its grieving process. By describing it, narrating it, and exposing its complexities and obscurities, literature codifies the representational forms of the consciousness that experiences and elaborates harm.

CODA: READER AND CITIZEN, TRANSFERS AND TEACHINGS

I have put forward a stylized sequence of the moments involved in an experience of harm with the intention of explaining how literature configures and expresses the relevant meanings and interpretations of each one of those moments. They are relevant because they construct the central subject positions in experiences of harm; more specifically, they give voice to the victim and, from the victim's perspective, they performatively call for and bring about the emergence of a concerned audience. One could argue that this concerned audience, not just victims and perpetrators, is at the conceptual core of the perspective of a first person plural "us," a moral, political, and legal community that takes up the task of doing justice in reference to the harm at issue. That articulation of different perspectives—namely, those of victims to those of the communal "us"—assumes something that is worth considering further. The reader as the audience of a work perceives and learns about the demands that arise from that which is portrayed, described, explored, and interpreted, but how are those perceptions and teachings—the recognition of a victim's truth and demands for justice, and the construction of the perspective of the concerned "us"—transferred beyond the literary work from the reader as audience to the citizen?

Answering this question requires turning first to the question of how literary texts themselves channel the questions that a citizen brings to the act of reading. One can certainly come to literature with one's own demands for interpretation regarding one's own condition—often shrouded in obscurity and in need of illumination—in order to shed light on the unknowns that may affect an understanding of an experience of harm. In a certain sense, writing answers to the demands of its audience—just like the question the woman with frozen lips posed, asking whether the poet could describe her experience. But a risk lurks in this way of comprehending the relationship between a citizen who is looking for an articulation of the meanings of her experience and what a person can find as a reader. The risk consists in falling into a conception of literature that ties it excessively to its immediate responses, as if it were to provide a diagnostic and a guide for action. Some forms of militant literature, thanks to literary works' heuristic capabilities—for describing, specifying, giving voice to that which lacked it, remembering, and even fictionalizing such remembrances—certainly do have that immediacy. Those militant works are closely linked to their contexts of origin and reception, even if such linking does not necessarily bar the possibility of significantly reinterpreting the works in other contexts and through other interpretive practices.

The literature of modernity, however, has added the element of reflexivity to its relationship with context: it relates its descriptions, interpretations, and narratives not just to demands for interpretation but to its own aesthetic tradition, in the language and form of particular genres. Reflexivity is thus also intrinsic to the text. Even when describing reality—the reality of harm—the text no longer subscribes to a realist program in the same way that it may have done in the nineteenth century (as in the case of Zola, for instance). Literature relates to the world not in an immediate manner but is mediated by its own aesthetic reflexivity, which it enacts in every text. As I have indicated, that reflexivity is also incorporated in many ways in the act of reading. The distinct normative demands of writing and reading assign differentiated and specific responsibilities to the reader, requiring the exercise of the reader's own autonomy as such. In exercising her own autonomy, the reader constitutes herself reflexively in relation to the text from the beginning, and she does so in several ways: by learning from the voices that are present in it (and doing so in their own terms), at different levels of consciousness, in their own temporalities, and by attending to the particular ways in which the voices elaborate their own experiences of harm.

The question for this coda, then, is how does a reader who constitutes herself reflexively in the act of reading relate to her own subjectivity qua citizen? Conversely, what does a reflexive citizen—one who understands the forms and limits of social legitimation, the structures and processes pertaining to social forms of consciousness, and the normative demands of power configurations (as well as the ways in which they can be resolved), and who is aware of the demands that literature presents—look for in literature, and what can be found? Perhaps what a reader and a citizen can each find in the respective realms of representation and social action is a perception and an explanation of the specific exercise of those forms of reflexivity: an understanding of different behaviors within their own symbolic and interactive contexts, as well as the dynamics of obedience and resistance in relation to the formal and informal processes that govern those behaviors, starting with the right to everyday interaction. With regard to experiences of harm more specifically, what both a reader and a citizen require and are able to find is a means for elaborating such harm—for naming it, elaborating its grief, and laying out the conditions of its nonrepetition, even under conditions of obscurity. At this point, though, such obscurity is already recognized, assumed, and made explicit in a text and in life beyond it. These two subjects, then, can learn the exercise of the fine moral grammar of harm, which not only offers lessons to individuals as readers but also imposes certain expectations upon them as citizens.

The reflexive reader would demand the same level of reflexivity from the citizen, and vice versa, regardless of how differently literature (narrative, poetry, or theater) and social and political life exercise their respective reflexivities. A barrier exists between life in texts and life outside of them—a barrier that only Don Quixote was able candidly to cross. But also, at the same time, cognitive and emotional transferences and learning processes take place between what a reader learns from a text, on the one hand, and one's actions as a citizen, on the other—transfers and teachings of different forms of reflexivity. Transfers of expectations also occur from the citizen to the reader: what the former would like to find and what the latter does or does not find. Those cognitive, emotional, and expectation transfers operate at different levels at once: objective circumstances and processes, as well as the personal reactions they elicit, are contrasted with their narrative depiction. The motives of the characters involved in the experience of harm that is depicted are fleshed out so that they can be compared and contrasted with one's own. The emotions and beliefs involved in such experiences of harm are assessed, and their adequacy is judged. Citizens thus become critics of the symbolic representations they find in texts, but they can also become critics of their own experience.

What we look for and are able to find in literary works that address experiences of harm are illumination and obscurity, conviction and resistance to it, certainty as well as doubt. We can find instances of all of this, but what we always discover is a need for representation. Harm that cannot be narrated or represented through language, a type of harm that cannot be codified, would amount to invisible harm—no less painful, no less harmful, but certainly incapable of being elaborated and always prone to recur. Unrepresented harm could never be the object of the imperative of "¡*nunca más!*" (never again!).

NOTES

This chapter was translated into English by Juan Diego Prieto.

1 On the ways in which literature, far from illuminating, can also obfuscate the interpretation of experiences of harm, see W. G. Sebald, *Campo Santo* (New York: Random House, 2005).

2 Stanley Cavell, *Little Did I Know: Excerpts from Memory* (Stanford, CA: Stanford University Press, 2010), 204.

3 We may cite here, for example, the quasi-epic poetry of resistance contained in works such as Pablo Neruda's *Canto general* [General song], at least in the way it was read under Latin American and European dictatorships. Other, perhaps clearer examples are the epic and militant poems of the Spanish Civil War or of other revolutionary moments around the world. We may also include sarcastic testimonies of resistance such as Osip Mandelstam's "Stalin Epigram."

4 Anna Akhmatova, *The Word That Causes Death's Defeat: Poems of Memory* (New Haven, CT: Yale University Press, 2004), 135.

5 This ending contrasts with the film version directed by Roman Polanski.

6 Paul Gready, "Novel Truths: Literature and Truth Commissions," *Comparative Literature Studies* 46, no. 1 (2009): 156–76, 168. Gready analyzes several postapartheid novels and categorizes them according to their way of subscribing to or deconstructing the rubric of reconciliation.

7 For an analysis of some of the critical reactions to the novel, see the special issue of *Interventions: The Journal of Postcolonial Studies* 4, no. 3 (2002): 315–488, as well as D. Attridge, "Age of Bronze, State of Grace: Music and Dogs in Coetzee's *Disgrace*," *Novel: A Forum on Fiction* 34, no. 1 (Autumn 2000): 98–121.

8 Jacques Rancière declares, even more bluntly, that "Le réel doit être fictionné pour être pensé" [The real has to be fictionalized in order to be thought], *The Politics of Aesthetics* (London: Continuum, 2004), 38.

9 Translator's note: Originally published in French as *Le mort qu'il faut* [The missing dead one], the latter work has not been translated into English.

Contributors

Nidžara Ahmetašević is a journalist in Bosnia and Herzegovina currently working toward her PhD in Graz (Austria) on "media assistance in post-conflict countries as a tool of democratization and state building." Previously she was the regional justice editor at the Balkan Investigative Reporting Network (BIRN) Transitional Justice and Media Program. A journalist based in Sarajevo, since 2004 she has been working for the Institute for War and Peace Reporting, and later on for BIRN. In 2006 she joined BIRN BiH's Justice Report team as an editor, and from January 2010 she was the editor for its regional transitional justice program. She frequently appears as an analyst in local media, but also for Al Jazeera, BBC, and Radio Free Europe. She holds an MA in human rights from the Center for Interdisciplinary Studies Sarajevo and Bologna (2002) with her thesis about political propaganda and hate speech in broadcast media during wars in Bosnia, Croatia, and Serbia. In 2000 she was awarded the Ron Brown Fellowship, a US State Department award supporting young professionals from Central and Eastern Europe, and she spent one year as a media fellow with DeWalice Media Center at Duke University, Durham, North Carolina.

Stephanie A. Barbour is a lawyer specializing in post-conflict justice and rule of law reform. She is currently head of Amnesty International's office in The Hague. Previously, she worked as Amnesty's international justice coordinator, promoting access to justice, truth, and reparations for victims in domestic and hybrid justice mechanisms around the world and before the International Criminal Court. Stephanie served as a legal advisor for the Organization for Security and Cooperation in Europe (OSCE) Mission to Bosnia and Herzegovina in Sarajevo from 2008 to 2011, where she worked on a host of transitional justice issues in the region, including war crimes prosecutions, justice outreach, and witness protection and support. She worked in the Chambers of the International Criminal Tribunal for Rwanda in 2007, supported by a fellowship from the Center for Human Rights and Global Justice. Stephanie's legal studies at Trinity College Dublin and New York University

(NYU) School of Law focused on public international law, international human rights law, international criminal law, and transitional justice. Stephanie also lectures, publishes, and consults on a range of international criminal law and human rights topics.

Louis Bickford works at the Ford Foundation, where he manages the Global Human Rights program. Prior to joining the Ford Foundation in 2012, he served on the executive leadership team at the Robert F. Kennedy Center for Justice and Human Rights; before that, he was a founding staff member and director of the Policymakers and Civil Society unit at the International Center for Transitional Justice, where he developed the organization's memory and memorials programming, working in Bosnia, Cambodia, Liberia, and Morocco, among other places, on establishing memory sites. Bickford teaches regular graduate seminars on memory, human rights, and transitional justice at Columbia University, New York University, and the New School for Social Research. He received a PhD from McGill University and a master's degree from the New School, both in political science.

Carolyn Patty Blum is an independent human rights consultant to academic, philanthropic, and human rights organizations. She currently serves as the senior legal advisor to the Center for Justice and Accountability (CJA) on its El Salvador docket. Blum has worked with CJA since its founding on all its cases seeking justice and accountability for torture and extrajudicial killings during the Salvadoran state terror of the 1980s. Blum is a Clinical Professor of Law Emerita at the University of California, Berkeley; she founded and directed Berkeley's International Human Rights Law Clinic. She is a Visiting Clinical Professor of Law at Cardozo Law School, where she teaches transitional justice and accountability and supervises students in the Human Rights and Genocide Clinic. She also is a Visiting Fellow at Kellogg College, University of Oxford, and teaches and supervises the preparation of the dissertation in the Oxford Master's in International Human Rights Law Program.

Patrick Burgess is president of Asia Justice and Rights (AJAR), an organization specializing in sharing lessons from transitions from legacies of mass violations, particularly in Asia. Previous positions include Asia director for the International Center for Transitional Justice; director of human rights for the UNTAET and UNMISET missions in Timor Leste; principal legal counsel for the East Timor TRC (the CAVR); senior member of the Australian Refugee Review Tribunal; team leader of CARE International programs in the refugee camps in the Democratic Republic of Congo following the genocide in Rwanda; and team leader of humanitarian emergency programs in Uganda, Rwanda, Yemen, Burundi, Timor Leste, and Indonesia, including post-tsunami Aceh. He is an Australian barrister and trial counsel, having appeared in the senior Australian jurisdictions, including the High Court of Australia, and has advised governments and civil society on transitional justice and human rights issues in many countries in Africa, the Middle East, and Asia. He has been living full-time in Asia for the past sixteen years.

Catherine M. Cole is professor in the Department of Theater, Dance, and Performance Studies at the University of California, Berkeley. She is the author of *Performing South Africa's Truth Commission: Stages of Transition* (2010) as well as *Ghana's Concert Party Theatre* (2001). In addition to recently serving as the editor of *Theatre Survey*, Cole has coedited the book *Africa after Gender?* (2007), a special issue of *Theatre Survey* on "African and Afro-Caribbean Performance," and a forthcoming special issue of *TDR: The Drama Review* titled "Routes of Blackface." She curated the exhibit "Fiat Lux Redux: Ansel Adams and Clark Kerr" at the Bancroft Library in fall 2012 and created with Christopher Pilafian the dance theatre piece *Five Foot Feat*, which toured North America in 2002–5. Cole has published articles in *Africa, African Arts, Critical Inquiry, Disability Studies Quarterly, Research in African Literatures, Theatre, Theatre Journal*, and *TDR*, as well as numerous chapters in edited volumes.

Charlotte F. Cole is the senior vice president of global education at Sesame Workshop, where she oversees the global education department and leads the development of all curricula and research for the nonprofit company's international projects. Working with educators and production teams throughout the world, she has most recently been engaged in projects in Afghanistan, Bangladesh, Colombia, Egypt, India, Indonesia, Israel, Mexico, Nigeria, Northern Ireland, South Africa, and West Bank/Gaza. Dr. Cole received her doctorate in human development and psychology from the Harvard Graduate School of Education at Harvard University. She is a member of the editorial board of the *Journal of Children and Media* and served as the publication's first review and commentary editor. When not looking for lost luggage, she enjoys life with her family in New York City.

Camille Crittenden is the executive director of the Data and Democracy Initiative of the Center for Information Technology Research in the Interest of Society (CITRIS) at the University of California, Berkeley, a position she assumed in May 2012. Prior to this, she served as the executive director of the UC Berkeley Law School's Human Rights Center beginning in August 2006, where she was responsible for overall administration of the center, as well as fundraising, communications, and outreach. In May 2009 she helped to curate an international conference on human rights, technology, and new media. Before her appointment to this post, she served as assistant dean for development in the division of International and Area Studies and held previous positions in development and public relations at the University of California Press and the San Francisco Opera. She earned a PhD from Duke University in 1997.

Eduardo González Cueva is the director of the Truth and Memory program at the International Center for Transitional Justice, providing advice to countries on truth commissions, declassification of archives, memorialization activities, museums, and other instruments. He has provided technical and strategic support to truth-seeking initiatives in places as diverse as East Timor, Morocco, Liberia, Canada, and the Western Balkans. Before joining ICTJ, he helped organize and carry out the Peruvian Truth and Reconciliation Commission, where he worked as the director of public hearings and victim protection, and later as an editor of the commission's final report. Previously he worked as an advocate for the establishment of the International Criminal Court. A Peruvian sociologist with an MA degree from the New School for Social Research (New York) and from the Catholic University of Peru (Lima), he has published numerous book chapters and articles on human rights and truth commissions, and he teaches at the New School University. He is the author of a Spanish-language blog on politics and culture, *La Torre de Marfil* (The ivory tower).

Pablo de Greiff is the director of the Research Unit at the International Center for Transitional Justice. In 2012 he was appointed by the UN Human Rights Council to serve as the first special rapporteur on the promotion of truth, justice, reparation, and guarantees of nonrecurrence. He is a native of Colombia and has written extensively on transitions to democracy, democratic theory, and the relationship between morality, politics, and law; he is the editor of ten books on political theory and transitional justice. Before joining ICTJ he was associate professor in the Department of Philosophy at the State University of New York at Buffalo. From 2000 to 2001 he was the recipient of a fellowship from the National Endowment for the Humanities, and he was a Laurance S. Rockefeller Fellow at the Center for Human Values at Princeton University.

Wanda E. Hall was the founder and director of Interactive Radio for Justice (www.irfj.org), a community radio project that worked in communities in the Democratic Republic of Congo and the Central African Republic from 2005 through 2011. Wanda worked for twenty years, mostly through media projects, to promote civic society and foster rule of law through community-level projects, starting her overseas work in Moscow in the early 1990s with Search for Common Ground as director of their Russian initiative. Her first work in Africa was as project director in Rwanda and Tanzania for Internews Network, where she produced films on "Justice after Genocide," toured them throughout Rwanda, and managed a team of East African reporters covering the ICTR. She served as the outreach advisor to the Immediate Office of the Prosecutor at the International Criminal Court in 2003–4.

Hjalmar Jorge Joffre-Eichhorn is a German-Bolivian community-based theater practitioner who has worked extensively in different parts of the world, focusing on post-conflict countries. He was a theater consultant with the Afghanistan Program of the International Center for Transitional Justice and has worked closely with the members of the Afghanistan Human Rights and Democracy Organization, serving as a member of their Technical Advisory Board. He recently published a book about community-based theater work in Afghanistan (in German: *Das Theater der Unterdrueckten in Afghanistan*, Ibidem, 2011). Hjalmar holds master's degrees in peace and development studies and education management from the University Jaume I in Castellon, Spain, and the University of Western Australia in Perth, Australia, respectively.

Maya Karwande is a law clerk for the US District Court Central District of California. She received her JD from the University of California, Berkeley, School of Law in 2013 and a BA in political science and peace and justice studies from Tufts University in 2009. Her senior thesis, "Failure to Engage: Outreach at the Bosnian War Crimes Chamber," was informed by research in Bosnia and won the National Peace and Justice Studies Association Best Thesis of the Year Award in 2009. Maya has been involved with ICTJ, and specifically the outreach project, since working as an intern and later as a program assistant in the Research Unit. She has been a legal intern at the Extraordinary Chambers in the Courts of Cambodia, Altshuler Berzon, and the International Bar Association.

Virginie Ladisch leads the International Center for Transitional Justice's work on children and youth. From the time she joined ICTJ in 2006 until 2009,

Virginie worked as part of the reparations program, and with the Canada, Cyprus, and Turkey country programs. Prior to joining ICTJ, Virginie conducted research on reconciliation in Cyprus, was the project coordinator at the Crimes of War Education Project, and served as an election monitor in Guatemala. In 2000 Virginie was awarded a Thomas J. Watson Fellowship for independent research, during which she carried out extensive fieldwork on truth commissions and reconciliation in South Africa and Guatemala. The results of her research on the challenges of reconciliation in Cyprus have been published in the *Journal of Public and International Affairs* and the *Cyprus Review*. Virginie holds an MA in international affairs from the School of International and Public Affairs (SIPA) at Columbia University and a BA in political science from Haverford College.

June H. Lee is the assistant vice president of international research in the Department of Global Education at Sesame Workshop. She joined Sesame Workshop in 2005 and currently oversees the Workshop's international research agenda. She directs all of the summative evaluations that examine *Sesame Street*'s global impact and has managed over twenty-five studies (and counting!). She also oversees content development, research, and outreach activities for *Sesame Street* coproductions in China, Indonesia, and India. June graduated magna cum laude from Davidson College in North Carolina, where she majored in psychology and economics. In 2004 she received a doctorate in human development and family sciences from the University of Texas at Austin. At the university, she was involved in research on the impact and contexts of children's media use as part of the Center for Research on Interactive Technology, Television, and Children (CRITC) and the Children's Digital Media Center (CDMC). June lives with her husband in New York City, where they enjoy the sights, sounds, and food that the city has to offer.

M. Florencia Librizzi is a consultant at the International Center for Transitional Justice (ICTJ) and an intern at UN Global Compact. She graduated magna cum laude from Universidad Nacional de Cordoba (UNC) School of Law, Cordoba, Argentina. At NYU School of Law she graduated with a master of laws (LLM) in May 2012, where she was granted the Dean's Award and distinguished as a Transitional Justice Scholar. She has served as a research assistant for Dean Richard Revesz and a graduate editor for the *NYU Journal of International Law and Politics*. Florencia is a candidate for the PhD in 2014 at UNC, where she was granted the prestigious SECyT and CONICET fellowships. While in Argentina, Florencia taught several courses and seminars at

Universidad Empresarial Siglo 21 as well as at UNC, and was an active member of the UNC Institute for Environmental Law and Policy. She also participated in congresses where she presented research articles, many of which were published in various law journals. In 2009 she was granted first prize, "Best at Law, Legal Research," at Jornadas de Derecho Civil Necochea, Buenos Aires. Florencia has practiced law since 2006, as a sole practitioner as well as an associate attorney at Pizarro and Vallespinos, one of the most prestigious law firms in Cordoba.

Timothy Longman is associate professor of political science and director of the African Studies Center at Boston University. He has previously held research and teaching positions at Vassar College; the University of California, Berkeley; Columbia University; the National University of Rwanda; and the University of the Witwatersrand in Johannesburg, South Africa. He has served as a consultant for Human Rights Watch, the International Center for Transitional Justice, and USAID in Rwanda, Burundi, and the Democratic Republic of Congo. He is the author of *Christianity and Genocide in Rwanda* and *Memory and Justice in Post-Genocide Rwanda*, forthcoming from Cambridge University Press.

Tanja Matić is a journalist with SENSE news agency in The Hague, which specializes in court reporting from the International Tribunal for the former Yugoslavia. Currently she is covering the trials of Radovan Karadzic and Ratko Mladic, former political and military leaders of Bosnian Serbs. Previously, she was journalist and country coordinator for the Balkan Investigative Reporting Network (BIRN) in Kosovo and Serbia, producing analysis and investigative pieces covering political and social issues in these two countries. She also assisted in the production and implementation of BIRN's basic journalism training programs. Prior to that, she was the Kosovo correspondent for the Serbian-language section of Radio Deutsche Welle and Belgrade-based B92 Radio, covering the Kosovo riots in March 2003. She also served as the regional media coordinator and spokesperson for the regional human rights NGO Youth Initiative for Human Rights, whose work was focused on facing the recent past and raising awareness among the young people of the former Yugoslavia of the crimes committed during the wars.

Clara Ramírez-Barat is a senior associate for ICTJ's Research Unit and the Children and Youth Program, where she was previously a Fulbright Research

Fellow. Before joining ICTJ, she was a postdoctoral researcher at the Spanish High Council of Research (CSIC), where she collaborated on a study about the politics of memory in the European Union commissioned by the European Commission. She obtained a PhD in philosophy at the University Carlos III of Madrid in 2007 with a thesis on transitional justice. She holds a BA in humanities from the same university, an MA in philosophy from Columbia University, and a graduate degree in constitutional law and political sciences from the Center of Political and Constitutional Studies of Spain. She was the recipient of several grants during her graduate studies and did research and fieldwork at Oxford University and in Cape Town and New York. For the past ten years, her research has focused on different aspects of transitional justice, human rights, and democratic theory, and she has authored several publications on these topics.

Nadia Siddiqui is manager of grants development at the International Center for Transitional Justice, and prior to this worked with the Center's Afghanistan and International Policy Relations Programs. In this role, she served as the New York–based lead on arts-based programming and research as they relate to the Afghan context. She also organizes art and design events around New York City. She has a keen interest in research methodology, monitoring, and evaluation and worked in this capacity in a wide range of fields—from academic neuroscience to community-based substance abuse treatment—prior to joining ICTJ. She holds a BA in psychology from the University of Michigan and an MSc in evidence-based social interventions from the University of Oxford.

Carlos Thiebaut Luis-André is professor of philosophy at the University Carlos III of Madrid. After completing his PhD in 1977 at the University Complutense of Madrid, he held several teaching and research positions at the University Complutense of Madrid, the Autonomous University of Madrid, and the Institute of Philosophy of the Spanish High Council of Scientific Research. He has also been a visiting professor at the University of Frankfurt and Northwestern University and has delivered lectures at universities and research centers in Mexico, Peru, and Colombia. His research interests focus on contemporary moral and political theory—especially within critical theory and Anglo-Saxon philosophy—in the postanalytic and pragmatist traditions. For the past twenty years he has collaborated and led numerous research projects focusing on issues such as the relationship between philosophy and both literature and the social sciences, and more recently on the contemporary experiences of harm and trauma, with a particular interest in their social dimensions and conceptual characterizations. He is the author of several books, including *Cabe Aristóteles* (Close to Aristotle) (Madrid: Editorial Visor, 1988), *Historia del nombrar* (The history of naming) (Madrid: Visor, 1990), *Vindicación del ciudadano* (Vindication of the citizen) (Barcelona: Paidós, 1998), and *De la tolerancia* (On tolerance) (Madrid: Visor, 1999), and he has published more than 150 articles in journals and publications. He belongs to the editorial boards of several academic journals, including *Isegoría, Constellations, Philosophy and Social Criticism, Daimon, Azafea,* and *Revista de Libros.* His current research focuses on the contemporary relevance of Michel de Montaigne, and he is completing a manuscript titled, *El hueco de las palabras: Cuatro ensayos sobre melancolía, experiencia y escepticismo* (The space of words: Four essays on melancholy, experience and skepticism).

Galuh Wandita is a senior associate at the International Center for Transitional Justice. She was the deputy director of the Commission for Reception, Truth and Reconciliation (CAVR) in Timor-Leste and previously worked with civil society groups in Indonesia and Timor-Leste. She is a co-convener of the Coalition for Justice and Truth in Indonesia, a member of a citizens' assembly tasked to seek the truth on Indonesia's past crimes, and one of the founding members of Asia Justice and Rights (AJAR). She earned a BA in anthropology from Swarthmore College in 1988 and completed a master's in international human rights law from Oxford University in 2007.